DIVINE COMMITMENT AND
HUMAN OBLIGATION

Divine Commitment
and
Human Obligation

Selected Writings
of
David Noel Freedman

VOLUME ONE: HISTORY AND RELIGION

Edited by

John R. Huddlestun

WILLIAM B. EERDMANS PUBLISHING COMPANY
GRAND RAPIDS, MICHIGAN / CAMBRIDGE, U.K.

© 1997 Wm. B. Eerdmans Publishing Co.
255 Jefferson Ave. S.E., Grand Rapids, Michigan 49503 /
P.O. Box 163, Cambridge CB3 9PU U.K.

Printed in the United States of America

02 01 00 99 98 97   7 6 5 4 3 2 1

Library of Congress Cataloging-in-Publication Data

Freedman, David Noel, 1922-
Divine commitment and human obligation: selected writings of
David Noel Freedman / edited by John R. Huddleston.
p.   cm.
Includes bibliographical references.
Contents: v. 1. History and religion — v. 2. Poetry and orthography.
ISBN 0-8028-3815-4 (cloth: alk. paper)
1. Bible.   O.T. — Criticism, interpretation, etc.
I. Huddleston, John R.   II. Title.
BS1171.2.F67   1997
221.6 — dc20   96-6418
                                                      CIP

Contents

Editor's Introduction

To survey the writings of David Noel Freedman is tantamount to reviewing the history and development of nearly every facet of American biblical scholarship following the Second World War. From the confidence of the Biblical Theology Movement in the 1950s and 1960s, to the critical response to and subsequent rethinking of many of the assumptions associated with the Albrightian school's approach to ancient Israelite history in the 1970s and beyond, the emergence and rapid rise to popularity of literary approaches beginning especially in the 1970s, the proliferation of newer approaches to the re- (or de-)construction of ancient Israelite history in the late 1980s and 1990s with threatening cracks in — if not crumbling at some points of — the once seemingly invincible towering edifice known as the documentary hypothesis, and in general the uncontrollable bursting forth of countless alternative "criticisms" applied to the interpretation of the biblical text — through it all, as both author and editor, Noel has remained a vibrant and towering presence in the field. The creativity and originality of his many contributions are exceeded only by their prodigious number.

Given the rapidity with which the field has changed in just a few decades, one in Noel's position might be forgiven for being less than enthusiastic about every new development, but nothing could be further from the truth. In fact, through his legendary indefatigable labors as editor and unrelenting author, he has not simply kept up, as it were, but has often taken the lead, paving the way with creative new approaches and interpretations, and in turn challenging others to respond and follow. One thinks, for example, of his collaborative efforts with J. Arthur Baird, Dean Forbes, and Francis Andersen in establishing and promoting the use of computers and statistics in the study of the Bible.[1] While not computer friendly

---

1. Beginning with the *Computer-Generated Bible* (Lewiston, NY: Edwin Mellen, 1971-), now extending to more than thirty-seven volumes. See also F. I. Andersen and A. Dean Forbes, *Spelling in the Hebrew Bible.* Biblica et Orientalia 41 (Rome: Biblical Institute Press, 1986), and,

himself, Noel's uncanny facility for analyzing nearly anything numerical — from syllable counts to genealogical lists — allows him not only to ask the right questions, but to draw meaningful and relevant conclusions from the raw data.[2]

Noel's contributions to the field of biblical studies are immense, and one could not hope adequately to summarize them in a few short paragraphs. One thinks here particularly of his indelible mark as author and co-author in numerous studies relating to Hebrew poetry ("archaic" and otherwise), including especially verse structure and orthography, biblical history and chronology, the formation and canon of the Dead Sea Scrolls — all of which are represented in the writings collected in these two volumes. The importance of his pioneering work in early Hebrew poetry and orthography has been ably summarized elsewhere by Frank Cross in his preface to an earlier collection of Noel's writings, *Pottery, Poetry, and Prophecy*. Indeed, their earliest collaborative ventures — two joint doctoral dissertations written under William F. Albright (*Evolution of Early Hebrew Orthography*, submitted by Noel in 1948; *Studies in Ancient Yahwistic Poetry*, submitted by Cross in 1950) — remain to this day indispensable reading for any serious student of Hebrew poetry or language.[3] While their conclusions regarding the "archaic" character of particular poems may not command the consensus they once did,[4] none would dispute the seminal nature of these studies as a whole. It is fitting then that the present collection should acknowledge the contributions of this unique and legendary team with the inclusion of one of their early published articles (vol. 2, ch. 1),[5] and a later response (1972) to criticism of their work (vol. 2, ch. 8).

---

most recently, the essays of Noel and others in *Studies in Hebrew and Aramaic Orthography*, ed. D. N. Freedman, A. Dean Forbes, and Francis T. Andersen. Biblical and Judaic Studies from the University of California, San Diego, 2 (Winona Lake: Eisenbrauns, 1992).

2. Note, for example, his comments about the potential of computer-based study in 1980: "Perhaps the most important of these [techniques] will prove to be computer-based research of a mechanical and statistical nature, whereby more ancient and more recent theories can be tested, and material information supplied in unlimited quantity on short notice. Far from displacing original scholarship, computer technology will provide powerful weapons in the scientific assault on the biblical bastion with its unresolved questions and inaccessible secrets, but only for creative and courageous thinkers" (from the Preface to his *Pottery, Poetry, and Prophecy: Studies in Early Hebrew Poetry* [Winona Lake: Eisenbrauns, 1980], ix-x).

3. The latter volume, *Studies in Ancient Yahwistic Poetry*, was published in 1975 (SBL Dissertation Series 21 [Missoula: Scholars Press]) with a "Postscriptum" by the authors and has now been reprinted with new Prefaces by each author (Grand Rapids: Wm. B. Eerdmans, 1996). With respect to the earlier volume, *Early Hebrew Orthography*, see Noel's most recent synthesis, "The Evolution of Hebrew Orthography," in *Studies in Hebrew and Aramaic Orthography*, 3-15.

4. Contrast, for example, the following two studies: David A. Robertson, *Linguistic Evidence in Dating Early Hebrew Poetry*. SBL Dissertation Series 3 (Missoula: Scholars Press, 1972) and Martin L. Brenner, *The Song of the Sea: Ex 15:1-21*. BZAW 195 (Berlin: Walter de Gruyter, 1991).

5. Their first jointly authored article appeared in 1947 ("A Note on Deuteronomy 33:26," *BASOR* 108:6-7).

For Noel, the notion of the canon should be understood in its broadest possible sense to encompass the "process of composition, compilation, edition, and publication" of the writings that comprise the Hebrew Bible. His own work has focused particularly on Genesis through 2 Kings, the "Primary History," nomenclature that, as far as I am aware, was first proposed by him in his entry on the Pentateuch for *The Interpreter's Dictionary of the Bible* (Nashville: Abingdon, 1962; see below, vol. 1, ch. 12). His general thesis concerning the period of composition/compilation and general themes of the Primary History (or "First Bible") was further developed in various articles after 1962 (esp. vol. 1, chs. 14, 32, and 39) and thereafter supplemented and extended to account for the various additions to this initial collection (the "Second Bible"), and eventually the formation of the canon as we know it today (the "Third Bible"; see vol. 1, chs. 40, 42). His views on the development and structure of the canon receive their fullest exposition in his 1991 volume, *The Unity of the Hebrew Bible,*[6] which should be read in conjunction with his slightly later (1992) overview of the process (see vol. 1, ch. 42). Noel's use of symmetry as a defining element in the overall structure and organization of the books of the Hebrew Bible may in part stem naturally from his concern with such symmetry on a much smaller scale in Hebrew poetry, but his uncanny ability to view and play with the text as a whole, to isolate larger correlations between the structure, theme, and purpose — a kind of macro midrash, as it were — is unmatched among modern scholars and in certain respects finds its closest parallel in classic Rabbinic exegesis.[7] While some will inevitably disagree with Noel's analysis at various points, nevertheless, the attempt itself will no doubt generate further discussion and research, which is precisely what he himself would want.

It is perhaps first and foremost as editor of the various Anchor Bible projects that Noel is most widely recognized, and deservedly so given the seemingly inhuman pace at which he is able to edit and return a manuscript (provided he has a generous supply of chewing gum, a suitable classical music radio station, and an electric typewriter capable of withstanding his furious tempo). In the process, the unsuspecting author usually gets more than he or she bargained for in the form of a weighty parcel containing Noel's comments, single-spaced and straining the margins — comments that can sometimes equal (or in some cases even exceed) the length of the originally submitted manuscript. Bur oral tradition tells the story better than I. One need only ask the numerous authors, a veritable Who's Who in the field, who have benefited from his editorial expertise and wise counsel; or, better yet, glance at the acknowledgments to virtually any Anchor Bible volume published under his editorship. Given his enormous input and influence in the writing and development of many of the commentaries, were it

---

6. Published by the University of Michigan Press (Ann Arbor) as part of the University's Distinguished Senior Faculty Lecture Series.

7. See, for example, my comments on a Rabbinic parallel in *The Unity of the Hebrew Bible*.

not for his position as editor, Noel could easily qualify as co-author. But I suspect he is much more comfortable working behind the scenes where his creative and at times provocative comments and ideas may be offered uncensored, no doubt stimulating their recipients to rethink, reformulate, or even reject cherished positions or interpretations. As the foremost editor in biblical studies of this or probably any century — with the possible exception of Ezra himself — Noel has also done a great deal to promote and nurture the work of colleagues and students, providing encouragement and publishing opportunities for younger or emerging scholars, whether on their own or initially in collaboration with him (see, for example, vol. 2, chs. 5, 9, 12).

One area infrequently discussed (in print at least) in connection with Noel's contributions, but very much a motivating factor in his life and work from the beginning, is his magnanimous, almost obsessive at times, ecumenical spirit. His deep convictions in this area, even to the extent that he may remain silent on certain issues for fear of compromising his carefully guarded neutrality as editor, stem in large measure from his own history. Raised in a secular Jewish environment, it is somewhat ironic that interest in his own Jewish heritage was awakened through the study of Biblical Hebrew and the Hebrew Bible at Princeton Theological Seminary in the early 1940s. (For the record, his first Hebrew teacher was C. T. Fritsch.) At that point, as he himself once put it in conversation, he was hooked and knew where his future lay. A number of pieces illustrative of Noel's early ecumenical leanings, along with his mature forays into the subject, have been included in this collection in order better to give the reader a sense of this aspect of his career (vol. 1, chs. 5, 13, 16, 20, 21, 24). The continued existence and expansion of the Anchor Bible series, showcasing as it does the work of many of the world's foremost Jewish, Catholic, and Protestant scholars, is eloquent testimony to Noel's unparalleled talents in the ecumenical arena. The "credo" for the series, which appeared in 1963 under the joint authorship of Noel and William Albright, surveyed the then current state of biblical studies and the need for an up-to-date commentary series with world-class scholars as contributors. Particular stress was given to the ecumenical nature of the project and the diverse religious and geographical backgrounds of its authors. Although Albright was listed as co-author, Noel once confessed that he himself in fact was the sole author of the statement. Following Albright's death in 1971, Noel sought to solidify the ecumenical stance of the project through the creation of an editorial committee of three, consisting of Frank Cross, (the late) Jonas Greenfield, and Marvin Pope, a kind of "ecumenical triumvirate," as it were.[8] But, as one of the illustrious members of the short-lived committee has noted, "the contribution of the three of us [was]

8. I cannot take credit for the phrase (see the remarks of Frank Cross in "Reminiscences of David Noel Freedman . . . Presented to David Noel Freedman in Celebration of the 25th Anniversary of the Anchor Bible, November 1989," privately circulated pamphlet, Doubleday).

wholly symbolic at best, and Noel soon dropped us from the front matter in dispassionate recognition of our value to the series."

Having studied under Noel at the University of Michigan (his last doctoral student from that institution), I feel compelled to offer a few remarks on the experience of sitting at the feet of one of the great scholars of this century. Despite his massive erudition, Noel graciously — and with amazing patience — allowed and encouraged students to formulate and express freely their own interpretations of the Hebrew text, never insisting that his own views must take precedence over others published or offered in class. He was quick to praise a worthwhile seminar paper when he saw one and would not hesitate to offer assistance in getting it published. His seminars invariably focused on his greatest love, the Hebrew text. The unsuspecting student could dutifully prepare him- or herself by reading all the commentaries and other secondary literature, but once in class he/she soon realized that this was simply not enough — some original thought would be required. His incredibly creative mind never failed to come up with novel ways of looking at a verse or passage long dead, or at least dormant, from over-interpretation. Noel's proposals were frequently deceptively simple, effectively solving a textual dilemma in short order. The overwhelmed student soon realized that here was a scholar who puts the text first and that he would do well to imitate the master. I recall being relieved to discover that I was not the only one who thought Noel had the Hebrew text and its contents committed to memory.[9] In this day and age when it is too easy to become entangled or mired in the secondary literature — sometimes never to emerge — Noel always reminds one of the primacy of the Hebrew text: master the text, then worry about everything else.

Lastly, one cannot help but be struck by Noel's unbounded enthusiasm and love for the field and his great enjoyment of good scholarly debate, welcoming any opportunity to discuss and debate in any forum views contrary to his own. As Editor-in-Chief of the *Anchor Bible Dictionary* project, he on more than one occasion expressed to those on his editorial staff the desire to have ideally not one, but two or even three entries on each topic so as to present fully and fairly all sides of an issue for the benefit of the reader. One thinks, mutatis mutandis, of the words of another scholar of an earlier generation:

> Reasonable men may be allowed to differ, where no one can reasonably be
> positive. Opposite sentiments, even without any decision, afford an agreeable

---

9. In his most autobiographical writing to date, Noel explains his unparalleled knowledge of the text as due in part to the fact that in his early days of teaching he began the practice of never going anywhere without the Hebrew text, this being in imitation of his then colleague and teaching mentor, William F. Orr, who did the same with the New Testament. See "He Never Let Me Fall: A Reminiscence," in *He Came Here and Loved Us: A Festschrift in Honor of William F. Orr,* ed. R. C. Curry, T. J. Kelso, and C. S. Maue (Watsontown, PA: The William F. Orr Festschrift Foundation, 1990), 7-13, esp. 8-9.

amusement. And if the subject be curious and interesting, the book carries us, in a manner, into company, and unites the two greatest and purest pleasures of human life, study and society.[10]

It is this love of learning and scholarly debate, this willingness to reexamine the text with a student's curiosity as though reading it for the first time — Noel has always described himself as a student at heart — that endears him to so many colleagues and students alike. But alas, such legendary figures, such *gedolim,* are increasingly rare among us these days.

The genesis of these volumes dates to the summer of 1991, when Astrid Beck, Program Associate of the Program on Studies in Religion at the University of Michigan, approached me about the possibility of putting together a volume containing some of Noel's most influential articles. Noel himself had already drawn up a rather modest and provisional list of pieces. It soon became apparent, however, that one volume would not suffice. Indeed, given the size of his published output, excluding edited works, one could easily expand such a collection to four or more volumes. In the end, I more than doubled Noel's original list to include not only the most obvious choices, but also others illustrative of the early development of his career. The creation of two separate volumes, one on Israelite history and religion and the other dealing with poetry and orthography, provides a useful means of organization, but the division should not be pressed too far given that some articles could easily fit into either category. In addition, the present collection avoids duplication of earlier pieces reprinted in the author's *Pottery, Poetry, and Prophecy* (1980), as well as those contained in the more recent volume *Hebrew and Aramaic Orthography* (1992) from the University of California at San Diego.

An undertaking of this magnitude of necessity depends and draws upon the goodwill, support, and assistance of others. I am first and foremost indebted to David Noel Freedman, mentor, colleague, and friend, who honored me with the invitation to be a part of this publication. Any attempt to summarize a career as distinguished as his is a most humbling experience.

Throughout the long, and often interrupted, process of preparing the manuscripts, obtaining publisher permissions, and finding a suitable publisher, Astrid Beck provided all the assistance — logistical, financial, and otherwise — that any editor could possibly desire. It was only through her continuing support, advice, and encouragement that these volumes saw the light of day.

The reader will observe that some articles reprinted herein were written in collaboration with others (namely, Frank M. Cross, Chris Franke, and Austin Ritterspach). I sincerely thank the above named scholars for graciously allowing these

---

10. The quotation comes from the philosopher David Hume, in the prefatory remarks to his *Dialogues Concerning Natural Religion* (1779).

to be included in this collection. In addition, I thank those publishers — here in the United States, in Europe, and in Israel — who granted permission to reprint writings initially published by them.

Lastly, I am most grateful to Eerdmans Publishing Company, especially Senior Editor Allen Myers, for their willingness to take on the project, and the limitless patience they displayed with me in the face of repeated delays and deadline revisions. The tedious and painstaking process of editing, resetting, and proofreading previously published works of this nature is no easy task, and they have done a superb job. For the sake of consistency, minor editorial changes have been made in the text, for example in the use of abbreviations and the transliteration scheme. No attempt has been made by the author to revise the writings reprinted here; however, editorial additions and notes have been inserted at points in order to update the reader on works cited as forthcoming or ones that appeared elsewhere than indicated in the text. Additionally, I have on occasion also updated or supplemented bibliographic citations, but these generally have been kept to a minimum.

JOHN R. HUDDLESTUN
Charleston, S.C., October, 1996

Preface

In the pages of this and the companion volume *(Divine Commitment and Human Obligation: Poetry and Orthography)* are representative articles produced during a lifetime career devoted to the study of the Hebrew Bible. I began graduate studies at the Johns Hopkins University in the fall of 1945 under the tutelage of the famous Orientalist, W. F. Albright. Now, fifty years later, I am grateful to those who have assembled this collection of my minor works and have invited me to reflect briefly on my efforts and intentions during those years.

What have fifty years of activity in this field taught me about the Bible, or what have I learned from the energy and effort expended on the investigation of the text of the premier literary work of Western civilization? Chiefly, I have learned to be skeptical about claims (not least, but especially my own), large and small, which purport to resolve this problem or settle that question. In fact, the larger the claim the less likely it is to meet the requirements of evidence and argument. Even small claims rarely pass the tests of coherence and consistency, not to speak of plausibility. This initial reluctance to accept new hypotheses and ideas applies across the board, and not less to my own brilliant notions. So with built-in skepticism there also comes a generous dollop of humility. Progress in understanding the Bible is slow, even in grasping the dimensions of the problems and the depth of our ignorance, much less in being able to make advances or to assess their value when we make them.

These fifty years have seen a great deal of movement and activity, motion and commotion, but to paraphrase an apt political campaign question, How much better off are we now than then? Do we know more and understand better than our academic forefathers, and do we see further than they, even if we are standing upon their shoulders? Perhaps we would be better off if we applied to the Bible not only the standards and methods of scientific research, requiring objective data and logical demonstration — in short, rigorous historical criteria to times and places, persons and occurrences, which often remain elusively beyond our reach — but also the criteria and methods of the Arts. In that way, we might value more a variety of approaches and insights or interpretations and reconstructions, none of which might agree or be compatible with the others, but each or some of which could illuminate texts and contexts, circumstances and settings, in different ways, leading to multiple analyses and syntheses of the various assemblages of data.

Owing chiefly to my heavy and continuing duties as an editor of journals and books, I have pursued a highly eclectic course in my own scholarship, often reacting and responding to the authors of the manuscripts, mainly commentaries on biblical books, which I edited. In cases in which I remained unconvinced by the evidence and arguments offered and in regard to which I had a different opinion — and if persuasion failed as it most often did — I found an opportunity to develop alternate views, and published many of them. Under the circumstances, they deal with details of the text. It is said that the devil is in the details; so also with solutions. One detail can lead to another until a mosaic is formed, one or more patterns discerned, and a larger structure created or developed.

In fact, my first venture in scholarly print was a very brief Note that appeared in the *Bulletin of the American Schools of Oriental Research (BASOR)* in the fall of 1947, while Frank M. Cross, Jr., and I were graduate students at Johns Hopkins. In that issue of the *Bulletin,* which Albright had given us the responsibility of assembling and seeing through the press, we proposed a conjectural emendation of a passage in the Blessing of Moses, specifically Deut. 33:26. This poem was the major topic of the ongoing Seminar that Albright conducted for all graduate students, and the proposal was made jointly by us as our presentation during the term. Albright, who was always on the lookout for any spark of originality and creativity on the part of students, was quite taken with the proposal and gave it his highest accolade, namely, by affirming that it was publishable, and since he was the longtime editor of the *BASOR,* the words were meant literally. As he was about to leave on a trip, he urged us to prepare the Note and put it into the next number of the *Bulletin.* So, in a single transaction, I became both co-author and editor, roles that have persisted in my life and career ever since. Cross was already a published author (in the *Biblical Archaeologist* in the fall of 1947), and he would go on to a prolific career in both categories, but for me this was the true beginning of a life in the writing, editing, and publishing of biblical scholarship.

The experience was intoxicating, and the euphoria was augmented when the late great Semitics scholar H. L. Ginsberg put his approbation in a subsequent issue of the *Bulletin,* while using it as a springboard for a group of additional ingenious emendations to the text of Deut. 33:26-29. It was the end result, typical of Ginsberg's brilliant, slashing style, that also gave both of us our first qualms about this kind of progressive emendation, in which one small change leads to another, and ultimately there are so many of them that the link between the last stage and the first has almost vanished. Inevitably, we both were encouraged to carry on our endeavors to improve and emend difficult texts in subsequent years. Over the years and now certainly, I am less intoxicated than I was then both with the approach and with the application, although I would still contend that the proposed reading is possible and even plausible.

Fifty years later, I am still trying to read and make sense of biblical verses. The primary task of the student-scholar is to read the text closely and carefully and to grapple with problems in and of the text. I offer three specific textual problems and three solutions, reflecting my work as editor of recent manuscripts in the Anchor Bible Commentary series:

1) Ecclesiastes 10:7 in the Masoretic Text reads as follows:

rā'îtî 'ᵃbādîm 'al-sûsîm	I have seen slaves on horses
wᵉśārîm hōlᵉkîm ka'ᵃbādîm 'al-hā'āreṣ	and princes walking like slaves on the ground

The words are understandable and the sense is quite clear. The sage is offering an observation on the human scene, in which things are not as they should be, and a striking example is the reversal of roles between slaves at the bottom of the social scale and officials or princes, who are at the top. The image used to portray the reversal of roles is that of riding or sitting on horses in contrast with walking along the road. Princes should do the former and slaves the latter, but the roles have been reversed, a circumstance that the sage laments. So what is wrong with the text? We are informed that there are different readings in other Hebrew MSS, one which has the word *rōkᵉbîm* ("riders, those riding") inserted after the word *'ᵃbādîm,* while in another text the word is inserted before the same Hebrew word. In comparing the MT with these other texts, there are basically two possibilities: either the MT is an original and the word in question *rkbym* has been added by a scribe or editor in the other MSS to expand or clarify the message, or one or the other of the two MSS with the added word is original, and the MT reflects a defective text, in which the word *rkbym* has been lost through a well-known scribal error ("haplography").

After careful study and due deliberation, I would say that the latter is the correct interpretation, and that the word *rkbym* should be restored to the text to secure the original reading intended by the poet. The correct original reading would be:

ra'iti 'abadim rokebim 'al-susim "I have seen servants riding upon horses." The scribal error is called haplography induced by homoeoteleuton, in which succeeding words end in the same letters, in this case *-ym.* The supposition is that the scribe's eye (or that of the person doing the dictating) skipped from the letter *-ym* at the end of the first word *'ᵃbādîm* to the same letters at the end of *rōkᵉbîm,* thus eliminating the second word *rkbym.* The restoration would provide the proper word to balance the word *hōlᵉkîm* in the next colon (there can be no thought of applying the participle to the first colon, as a different verb is required for the sense). In addition, the added word would provide a better metrical balance between the cola: in MT the syllable counts would be: 9//13, whereas with the added word the totals would be: 12//13, a very close fit. For me, there is one more piece of evidence that tips the balance in favor of the expanded reading, and that is a parallel passage in an unlikely place, the Song of Deborah (Judg. 5:10), where we read:

rōkᵉbê ʾᵃtōnôt ṣᵉḥōrôt	You who ride (upon) tawny asses
yōšᵉbê ʿal-middîn	You who sit upon the judgment seat
wᵉhōlᵉkê ʿal-drek śîḥû	You who walk upon the road — Sing!

While most of the circumstances and details are different, the basic picture is much the same, namely a description of different classes and groups of people. The parallelism between *rkby* and *hlky* is inescapable. It is also noteworthy that the tradition extends over almost the whole sweep of biblical literature, because the Song of Deborah is one of the oldest preserved poems in the Bible, coming from the period of the Judges (12th-11th centuries), while Ecclesiastes must be one of the latest books of the Hebrew Bible, dating to the 5th-4th centuries, if not later. In view of the available data, I would judge that the original reading in Eccl. 10:7 included the word *rkbym* after the word *ʿbdym,* and that the word was lost in the course of scribal transmission by haplography owing to homoeoteleuton. At least one Hebrew MS retained the original reading, while another reflects a faulty effort to restore the word *rkbym* after it had been lost, but in the wrong place.

We turn now to a second textual emendation, of major proportions, but resulting from one of the simplest and most common errors in scribal transmission: Ezek. 36:23b-38. It has been observed that the oldest Greek witness to this text omits the entire passage as it is found in the MT. It begins with *nᵉʾūm ʾᵃdōnāy YHWH* (36:23bB), and it ends with *wᵉyādᵉᵉʿû kî-ʾᵃnî YHWH.* In a detailed study of this passage, Johan Lust ("Ezekiel 36–40 in the Oldest Greek Manuscript," *CBQ* 43 [1981]: 517-33) argues that the Hebrew *Vorlage* behind the Greek text is more original than the MT, and that the entire passage including 36:23b-38 is a secondary expansion of and addition to the original text. Moshe Greenberg, in his forthcoming commentary on Ezek. 21–37, correctly challenges this bold claim, and defends the originality of the MT. While the argument between the two scholars turns on matters of content, style, and tone, I think that the omission or addition in comparing the texts can be explained most easily on grounds of textual criticism and scribal transmission. I agree with Greenberg that the longer text of the MT is original, and that the shorter text is secondary. The explanation of the massive omission is simple haplography, owing to the repetition of the phrase at the beginning of v. 23b — *wᵉyādᵉʿû haggôyīm kî-ʾᵃnî YHWH* — at the end of v. 38 (with the omission of the word *haggoyim*): *wᵉyādᵉʿû kî-ʾᵃnî YHWH.* We posit that the scribe's eye jumped from the phrase *ky-ʾny YHWH* in v. 23b to the same phrase at the end of v. 38, thereby eliding or eliminating the entire section in between. It may seem surprising or even incredible that such a simple error could produce such a massive loss, but the same kind of error, including passages of lesser or greater length can be and has been documented in many major MSS of the Bible in both Hebrew and Greek and other languages. It should be remembered that losses go more easily undetected than repetitions, so haplography is a much more common occurrence than dittography, though both belong to the class of visual errors.

The third instance I wish to call attention to involves an emendation, but not in the text of the MT. Rather we propose a rectification in the way we look at a text, how we read and interpret it. This one comes from Mal. 2:7. Verse 7a reads as follows:

kî-śiptê kōhēn yišmᵉrû-daʿat	For the lips of a priest should guard knowledge
wᵉtôrâ yᵉbaqšû mippîhû	and men should seek instruction from his mouth.

I have taken the translation from the old RSV, but most modern translations reflect the same understanding of the text. On the face of it, both the text and the translation seem straightforward, and while one might prefer a synonym in English here or a different shading there, the text presumably has been written this way and understood this way, at least since the days of the Greek translation, which also says the same thing. So what is wrong? What is wrong is the sense of balance, the notion of symmetry, which pervades the Hebrew Bible, and especially its poetry. I suggest that we start with the second colon, the structure and syntax of which are quite clear. The verb has an otherwise unexpressed third masculine plural subject, and we must look backward to v. 6b or ahead to v. 8a for an expressed subject, namely *rabbîm* "the many." The rendering "men" is no longer appropriate in context, and "the many" serves better in any case. The rendering "they [i.e., "the many"] seek Torah from his mouth" is unexceptionable. Looking at the first colon now, it seems odd that a verb with the same form, namely third masculine plural subject, should have a different subject than the parallel verb in v. 7aB, especially when the assumed and presumed subject of *yišmᵉrû*, taken to be *śiptê* at the beginning of the verse, is actually a dual (or plural) feminine form. While on occasion such anomalies occur in the text, it is always more likely that the author observed grammatical niceties, and hence we should look to another third masculine plural form as the subject, namely the same *rabbîm* that serves as the subject of the balancing verb *yᵉbaqšû*. Following the established pattern of strict parallelism, we observe that the word which matches *tôrâ* in v. 7aB is *daʿat* in v. 7aA. These two words form a combination well known in Hebrew tradition, "the knowledge of Torah" being a major element in both prophetic and wisdom discourse, where the two traditions come together, in fact. That leaves us with the third pair in this bicolon, namely *mippihu* in v. 7aB and *śiptê kōhēn* in v. 7aA. The words "lips" and "mouth" form another pair, not synonymous but complementary. And the clue to the function of *śiptê kōhēn* in the first clause is to be found in the function of *mippîhû* in the second. The key is the preposition *min*, which is used to establish the relationship of the phrase "from his mouth" in the second clause, and we must interpret "the lips of the priest" in the same fashion. The poet has used a device, with which we are familiar, but which occasionally eludes us, especially when the gapping of a preposition occurs backward instead of the more common forward gapping, which occurs so frequently in English and other languages. But backward gapping has been documented enough times now to be accepted as a regular device in Hebrew writing, especially in poetry, and it applies here. We should render the bicolon therefore as follows:

> Indeed, [from] the lips of a priest they guard knowledge,
> and Torah they seek from his mouth.

Here the emendation is in the thinking of the reader and renderer.

If the study of the details is important for their own sake, it often is valuable as well for making connections and discerning patterns in larger units and ultimately the configuration of the whole Hebrew Bible itself. Moving to the other end of the scale or spectrum, I have spent much time and effort studying the macrostructure of the Hebrew Bible along with its major internal divisions. The keyword here is symmetry, or the balancing of matching parts. While unity and singularity are expressed and embodied in the number "one" (cf. the classic credo concerning the unity of God in Deut. 6:4), symmetry requires, at a minimum, the number "two," which is amply represented at all levels and in all parts of the Hebrew Bible. The ongoing recurrence of pairs beginning with the opening chapters of the book of Genesis is sufficient to illustrate if not establish this governing pattern. We will note later the even number of the acts of creation in Genesis 1 (eight in all), but here we call attention to the crowning act for creation, that of human beings, who are carefully designated as male and female, a complementary pair. Anticipating this bilateral pairing, God speaks in the first person plural (Gen. 1:26) for the only time in this entire series (but cf. Gen. 3:22 for another first person plural reference), anticipating the duality (and complementarity) of the human species by an allusion to the divine situation.

Just as the first human pair dominates the initial story in the Hebrew Bible, with the Serpent and God, another pair, in supporting roles in the drama, so a different pair is front and center in the second story. The story of rival brothers is an old and universal one, cropping up with different details in many cultures. It is even possible that Cain and Abel were twins, between whom the rivalry is often more intense than with brothers separated in age. The reason for this supposition is simply that the text (Gen. 4:1-2) specifies only one conception, followed by two births. Normally, except in the case of twins, the text specifies a conception before each birth. One is reminded of the fatal rivalry between the founding brothers Romulus and Remus in Roman tradition, or the bitter hostility between the un-doubted twins, Esau and Jacob, which began while the brothers were still in their mother's womb (cf. Gen. 25:21-26).

Sibling rivalry, often augmented by other pairings, is represented in each of the patriarchal generations, with considerable variation in the details: e.g., Ishmael and Isaac, the sons of Abraham, and behind them, the rival mothers, Hagar and Sarah. While Abraham and Lot are not brothers, although the word is used in connection with their relationship, they form another pair in the account of their migration and their subsequent separation. In a switch from the usual male-dominated patterns of the book of Genesis, Lot has two daughters, who cooperate with and complement each other, rather than engage in disputes. That leads to the complex multiple pairings of the central patriarch, Jacob = Israel. While the total number of mothers and children is much greater than the two, nevertheless the basic and parallel units are pairs. Thus Jacob ends up with two wives, who themselves are sisters, while the wives in turn have two personal slaves (one each), who also serve as surrogate mothers of the children that legally belong to Jacob and his wives. The sons themselves (the single daughter mentioned is an exception, no doubt deliberate to all the other pairs) are treated mostly in pairs, as the stories and lists show. Thus, in the account in Gen. 29–30, Leah bears the first four sons (twice two), but within that group the middle two, Simeon and Levi, form a pair, as in the Blessing of Jacob in Gen. 49:5-7. While Reuben and Judah are treated separately, they are linked in the Joseph story as each performs a parallel service and purpose in the account of Joseph's mistreatment at the hands of his brothers. The remaining eight brothers are all treated as pairs, with each of the four mothers bearing two sons. While the biological possibilities are wide open, some other factor is at work in the organization and arrangement of the persons/tribes, and the principle of balance and symmetry is simply realized.

The pattern continues into the next generation, with the birth of Joseph's two sons, who will be adopted as heirs of Jacob himself (cf. Gen. 48:17-22) on an equal basis with the other sons. We could also mention the twin sons of Judah, by his daughter-in-law, Tamar, the presumed harlot (Gen. 38).

We could go on tracing pairs in the Bible at some length, but perhaps this will suffice to show that pairing of different kinds is basic and essential to the biblical story-telling. From this point, we wish to go on to much larger structures in the Hebrew Bible, which illustrate the principle of symmetry embodied in the basic number "two," but which can be extended upward and in more complex combinations. The Hebrew Bible as a whole is traditionally divided into three parts — Torah, Prophets, and Writings, and while this would appear to be in conflict with the principle of symmetry ("three" is hardly a symmetrical number), a closer examination of the sections shows that in reality the symmetry is there, once we recognize the much larger middle section, the Prophets, not only divides into two equal parts, but the so-called Former Prophets ("Former" because these four books precede the four books of the "Latter" Prophets) are more closely connected to the Torah, of which it forms the direct literary and historical continuation, than with the Latter Prophets, which are separate books associated with individual prophetic personalities, such as Isaiah, Jeremiah, Ezekiel, and the twelve Minor Prophets. We do not deny the link between the two major parts of the Prophets, but the Latter Prophets serve as a supplement to the Primary History (Genesis through Kings), as does the remaining division, the Writings. In other words, the Hebrew Bible divides quite easily and conveniently into two major parts: the primary narrative which runs from Genesis through Kings, and the supplementary literature, including the many books that fill out many of the interstices in the primary narrative, and add supplementary materials carrying the story down to the time of Ezra and Nehemiah (i.e., the Chronicler's work, which parallels the latter part of the Primary History and then continues on into the postexilic period).

It may come as a shock to discover that when these two major groups are set off against each other, they turn out to be almost exactly the same length (in words), a fact that could only be confirmed in recent years when the Bible was computerized. If we exclude the book of Daniel, which is almost universally regarded as a Hellenistic work, then we can propound the position that sometime between the last writing in the Hebrew Bible (other than Daniel) and the inclusion of Daniel in the canon, i.e., between about 400 and 200 B.C.E., there was a Hebrew Bible in two major parts, each of which was also divided into two parts, of almost identical length — surely no accident. The difference is about $\frac{1}{10}$ of 1 percent (each part has almost exactly 150,000 Hebrew [and Aramaic] words), a precision that could hardly come about by simply collecting inspired books and adding them one at a time over an extended period. Here again the principle of symmetry and balance is realized almost to perfection.

Turning back to the large unit of the Prophets, we note that there are eight books, divided evenly between Former and Latter Prophets, four and four; and while individual books varying widely in length from about 10,000 words to over 25,000 words (in the Former Prophets) and from 14,000 to 23,000 (in the Latter Prophets), the totals for each group are very close to each other (70,000 for the Former Prophets and 72,000 for the Latter Prophets; in turn the Torah has 80,000 words, but the Writings without Daniel have 78,000, to produce the totals mentioned earlier).

This key number, "eight," has wide representation and ramifications in the rest of the Hebrew Bible as well. Thus in the story of creation in Genesis 1:1–2:4a, there are eight acts of Creation distributed among the six days in which God does his work. The division or allocation is symmetrical and bilateral: four acts in the first three days, and four more in the latter three days, in the pattern as follows:

DAY ONE:	1	DAY FOUR:	1
DAY TWO:	1	DAY FIVE:	1
DAY THREE:	2	DAY SIX:	2
	4	+	4 = 8

In turn, the acts of Creation can be connected with the eightfold pattern of the Great Psalm (No. 119), whose massive alphabetic acrostic consists of twenty-two stanzas (representing the letters of the Hebrew alphabet) each one having eight lines. The Psalm focuses on the Torah (the link with Genesis is apparent), which is the basic keyword of the whole Psalm, occurring more than any other content word in the poem, to which are added seven other keywords, each of which is spread throughout the poem. The Psalm may be described as a great wheel with eight spokes, each of which is the carrier of a keyword, and all of which are summed up in Torah, the verbal teaching of God. These eight words are divided symmetrically as well, with four of them being masculine and four of them feminine; four are predominantly singular and four are predominantly plural. The feminine singular word that pairs with Torah is *'mrah,* a relatively rare word, but based upon the very common root *'amar,* which is the central verb in the Creation Story in Gen. 1:1–2:4a. What the two passages are saying is that the oral word (root *'amar*), by which God created the universe and everything in it, is preserved in the written word, namely the Torah (including the whole Hebrew Bible), and together they form the matrix within which Israel is to live and have its being.

So the number "eight" is used by the biblical writers and compilers to represent and reflect the perfection and totality of God as creator and ruler of the world and of Israel specifically. And the Bible reflects the same perfection and totality, as well as the symmetry inherent in the creative and written word of God. The last leap I make in this series of the number eight is to the standard half-line or colon of Hebrew poetry, which has eight syllables on the average and in a large plurality of actual cases. The normal line of Hebrew poetry, as exemplified in large parts of the Psalter, Job, and Proverbs, the three designedly poetic books of the Hebrew Bible, is a bicolon of $8 + 8 = 16$ syllables (as Eusebius reports for the Great Psalm and the Song of Moses in Deut. 32). I rest my case.

A final example of textual preference or emendation is drawn from the New Testament. I do this with double trepidation, partly because I am better equipped by training and experience to deal with the Hebrew Scriptures and partly because of the early date and excellent quality of the best surviving manuscripts of the Greek New Testament, which make it difficult to defend marginal alternate readings, much less to offer conjectural emendations. Nevertheless, it seems to me that the overwhelming majority opinion in a striking and important case in the Epistle of James may be mistaken and that a minority reading is to be preferred as the more original and superior reading.

The text I wish to discuss is to be found in Jas. 4:4, and is restricted to the opening word of the text adopted by the *Greek New Testament* (ed. K. Aland, M. Black, B. M. Metzger, and A. Wikgren [American Bible Society, 1966]), which is *moichalides* "adulteresses." This reading is supported by the best and oldest uncial MSS, including Codex Sinaiticus, Vaticanus, Alexandrinus, and so on. An alternate, longer reading is found in the corrected text of Sinaiticus, and some later uncial and minuscule MSS, which runs as follows: *moichoi kai moichalides* "adulterers and adulteresses."

In the *Greek New Testament* (p. 786) the preferred shorter reading is given a rating of "A" on their scale of "A" to "D," from the most probable to the least. The general argument follows traditional established norms: the shorter and more difficult reading is to be preferred. There can be no argument with these claims, as the reading is both shorter and more difficult than the longer marginal reading. In fact, the shorter reading, as it stands, is extremely difficult to explain or even understand. The problem centers on the sudden intrusion of a feminine plural noun in the midst of a general statement to and concerning the whole community addressed in the epistle. It is as though the writer wished to isolate the women as guilty of violating this one of the Ten Commandments, while excluding the men from consideration. While in modern feminist English usage it is both possible and increasingly practicable to use the feminine form of nouns to represent the whole group (including masculine and feminine), in antiquity and particularly in the Bible it is unheard of. Such a gender selection would be very strange here, especially because the context shows that the author is addressing the whole community, and where a more particular audience is involved, and a gender distinction is to be made, there it is the men who would be singled out. Moreover, in the case of adultery, whether intended or understood here in a literal or figurative sense (as a symbol of apostasy or defection from the covenant relationship with God), persons of both sexes have to be included, which is why women are mentioned here explicitly. But mentioning only women here would exclude men, and in the case of adultery the consensual participation of two persons of opposite sex is required. To claim that the author is either excluding men from consideration here, or that men are subsumed under the feminine term for "adulteresses," is unjustified by usage or evidence.

The correct interpretation of the evidence, in my opinion, is to recognize that the longer reading is more original and to be preferred in this instance, even though such a conclusion seems to contradict conventional and prevailing wisdom about *lectio brevior* and *lectio difficilior preferendae sunt*. The point needs to be made and reiterated that in scribal transmission of handwritten MSS, mechanical errors are inevitable, and the most common among them or one of the most common is haplography, the omission of letters or words as a result of the eye of the scribe or the dictator skipping from one point to another and omitting what lies between the two points. Haplography, by definition, produces a shorter text than the original, and almost inevitably and invariably a more difficult, if not completely incomprehensible text. In every such case, the so-called shorter and more difficult text is wrong and should be corrected.

In the present instance, the preferred shorter and more difficult reading could easily have resulted from a simple haplography owing to homoeoarcton (the occurrence of the same letters at the beginning of two words on the same or different lines of the MS). In this passage, we propose that the scribe's eye jumped from the first four letters of the first word *moich . . .* to the first four letters of the third word *moich* . . . and that as a result of this error, the first two words of the text were elided and lost. Such errors arise when only one or two letters are identical, and in a case where four letters are the same, the chances of such an error are greatly enhanced.

Appeal to and argument from a mechanical error, such as haplography, are always better than appeal to and argument from a deliberate change in the text. We would contend therefore that the Corrector of Codex Sinaiticus was restoring the original text when he inserted the two words missing from the beginning verse. Whether he did so on the basis of an older and more original MS, or reconstructed the text on the basis of his general wisdom and experience in such matters, we may never know, but it is much more likely that the action he took was one of restoration, rather than the expansion and explication of an original that was intended to be mystifying.

The Bible: its text remains a great treasury of data, containing vital information about its structure as well as its story. Careful reading and close study are the watchwords, because out of them will come rich rewards, mostly unexpected and unpredictable.

DAVID NOEL FREEDMAN
14 February 1996

Acknowledgments

1. "The 'House of Absalom' in the Habakkuk Scroll." *BASOR* 114 (1949): 11-12.
2. "Notes on Genesis." *ZAW* 64 (1953): 190-94.
3. "The Book of Ezekiel." *Interpretation* 8 (1954): 446-71.
4. "The Babylonian Chronicle." *BA* 19 (1956): 50-60.
5. "The Unity of the Bible." *Western Watch* 7/4 (1956): 7-14.
6. "The Prayer of Nabonidus." *BASOR* 145 (1957): 31-32.
7. "The Slave of Yahweh." *Western Watch* 10/1 (1959): 1-19.
8. "History and Eschatology: The Nature of Biblical Religion and Prophetic Faith." *Interpretation* 14 (1960): 143-54.
9. "The Name of the God of Moses." *JBL* 79 (1960): 151-56.
10. "The Chronicler's Purpose." *CBQ* 23 (1961): 436-42.
11. Review of Yehezkel Kaufmann, *The Religion of Israel, from Its Beginnings to the Babylonian Exile. JBL* 81 (1962): 185-90.
12. "Pentateuch." *IDB* 3:711-27.
13. (with William F. Albright) "The Continuing Revolution in Biblical Research." *Journal of Bible and Religion* 31 (1963): 110-13.
14. "The Law and the Prophets." *VTS* 9 (1963): 250-63.
15. "On Method in Biblical Interpretation: The Old Testament." *Interpretation* 17 (1963): 308-18.
16. "Modern Scripture Research and Ecumenism." *Pittsburgh Perspective* 4/3 (1963): 15-22.
17. "Divine Commitment and Human Obligation: The Covenant Theme." *Interpretation* 18 (1964): 419-31.
18. "The Hebrew Old Testament and the Ministry Today: An Exegetical Study of Leviticus 19:18b." *Pittsburgh Perspective* 5/1 (1964): 9-14, 30.
19. "Archaeology and the Future of Biblical Studies: The Biblical Languages." *The Bible in Modern Scholarship,* ed. J. Philip Hyatt (Nashville: Abingdon, 1965), 294-312.
20. "Toward a Common Bible?" *Scripture and Ecumenism,* ed. L. J. Swidler (Pittsburgh: Duquesne University Press, 1965), 133-49.

21. "Religious Freedom and the Old Testament." *Religious Liberty: An End and a Beginning,* ed. J. C. Murray (New York: Macmillan, 1966), 83-94.

22. "The Biblical Idea of History." *Interpretation* 21 (1967): 32-49.

23. "The Old Testament at Qumran." *McCormick Quarterly* 21 (1968): 299-306.

24. "An Essay on Jewish Christianity." *Journal of Ecumenical Studies* 6 (1969): 81-86.

25. " 'Mistress Forever': A Note on Isaiah 47,7." *Biblica* 51 (1970): 538.

26. " 'Son of Man, Can These Bones Live?' — The Exile." *Interpretation* 29 (1975): 171-86.

27. "Canon of the OT." *IDB Supplement* (Nashville: Abingdon, 1976), 130-36.

28. "The Deuteronomic History." *IDB Supplement* (Nashville: Abingdon, 1976), 226-28.

29. "The Age of David and Solomon." *The World History of the Jewish People,* 1st ser.: *Ancient Times,* vol. 4: *The Age of the Monarchies,* pt. 1: *Political History,* ed. A. Malamat (Jerusalem: Massada, 1979), 101-25, 327-29.

30. "Problems of Textual Criticism in the Book of Hosea." *The Critical Study of Sacred Texts,* ed. W. D. O'Flaherty (Berkeley: Graduate Theological Union, 1979), 55-76.

31. "Temple without Hands." *Temples and High Places in Biblical Times,* ed. A. Biran, et al. (Jerusalem: Nelson Glueck School of Biblical Archaeology, 1981), 21-30.

32. "The Earliest Bible." *The Bible and Its Traditions.* Michigan Quarterly Review 22/3 (1983): 167-75.

33. "Discourse on Prophetic Discourse." *The Quest for the Kingdom of God,* ed. H. B. Huffmon, F. A. Spina, and A. R. W. Green (Winona Lake: Eisenbrauns, 1983), 141-58.

34. "Headings in the Books of the Eighth Century Prophets." *Festschrift in Honor of Leona Glidden Running,* ed. W. H. Shea. *Andrews University Seminary Studies* 25 (Berrien Springs: Andrews University Press, 1987), 9-26.

35. " 'Who Is Like Thee among the Gods?': The Religion of Early Israel." *Ancient Israelite Religion,* ed. P. D. Miller, Jr., P. D. Hanson, and S. D. McBride (Philadelphia: Fortress, 1987), 315-35.

36. "Yahweh of Samaria and His Asherah." *BA* 50 (1987): 241-49.

37. "When God Repents." *Amos* (with Francis I. Andersen). *Anchor Bible* 24A (New York: Bantam Doubleday Dell, 1989), 639-79.

38. "W. F. Albright as Historian." *The Scholarship of William Foxwell Albright,* ed. G. W. Van Beek. HSS 33 (Atlanta: Scholars Press, 1989), 33-43.

39. "The Nine Commandments: The Secret Progress of Israel's Sins." *Bible Review* 5/6 (1989): 28-37, 42.

40. "The Formation of the Canon of the Old Testament." *Religion and Law,* ed. E. B. Firmage, B. G. Weiss, and J. W. Welch (Winona Lake: Eisenbrauns, 1990), 315-33.

41. "Dinah and Shechem, Tamar and Amnon." *God's Steadfast Love. Austin Seminary Bulletin* 105/2 (1990), 55-63.

42. "The Symmetry of the Hebrew Bible." *Scandinavian Journal of Theology* 46 (1992): 83-108.

43. "Editing the Editors: Translation and Elucidation of the Text of the Bible." *Palimpsest: Editorial Theory in the Humanities,* ed. G. Bornstein and R. G. Williams (Ann Arbor: University of Michigan Press, 1993), 227-56.

Abbreviations

JAOS	*Journal of the American Oriental Society*
JBR	*Journal of Bible and Religion*
JBL	*Journal of Biblical Literature*
JNES	*Journal of Near Eastern Studies*
JSOT	*Journal for the Study of the Old Testament*
LXX	Septuagint
MT	Massoretic Text
OBO	Orbis biblicus et orientalis
OLZ	*Orientalistische Literaturzeitung*
OTL	Old Testament Library
PPP	D. N. Freedman, *Pottery, Poetry, and Prophecy*
RB	*Revue biblique*
RSV	Revised Standard Version
SBL	Society of Biblical Literature
SBT	Studies in Biblical Theology
TDOT	*Theological Dictionary of the Old Testament,* ed. G. J. Botterweck, H. Ringgren, and H.-J. Fabry
VT	*Vetus Testamentum*
VTS	*Supplements to Vetus Testamentum*
ZAW	*Zeitschrift für die Alttestamentliche Wissenschaft*

1

The "House of Absalom" in the Habakkuk Scroll

In the recently discovered Habakkuk scroll, ch. 1:13 and the commentary upon it read as follows:

> Why do ye countenance the treacherous and keep silence
> While the wicked doth swallow one more righteous than himself?

> Its meaning concerns the *house of Absalom* and the men of their counsel who were silent at the reproof of the Teacher of Righteousness and did not help him against the Man of the Lie, who had rejected the Law among all peoples.[1]

Brownlee interprets the phrase "house of Absalom" as "a cryptic reference . . . to a party which lived up to the name of Absalom who rebelled against his own father."[2] There is no basis in the text, however, for such an interpretation. The sin of the "house of Absalom" described in the *midrash* is not at all that of the rebellious son of David. The "house of Absalom" is accused, not of rebellion, but of indifference. This group was "silent" during a crisis in the career of the "righteous Teacher," and failed to support him in the struggle against the "Man of the Lie."

It is much more probable that we have here, not a symbolic allusion, but the actual name of a family which played an important role in the history of this sect.[3] The implication of the commentary on Hab. 1:13 is that the "house of Absalom"

---

1. Following the translation of W. H. Brownlee, "The Jerusalem Habakkuk Scroll," *BASOR* 112 (1948): 11 (italics mine).

2. *Ibid.,* 17, n. 36.

3. Prof. H. L. Ginsberg expresses the same opinion in a private communication: "I entirely agree with you that 'the House of Absalom' is not a figure of speech but designates an influential family or party contemporary with 'the Teacher of Righteousness.' "

was at the head of a party or group, at one time favorably disposed toward the "righteous Teacher," perhaps his followers or patrons. In the crisis, however, they found it expedient to disavow their connection with the "righteous Teacher." Although they were in a position to render substantial help to him when he was attacked by the "Man of the Lie," they preferred to remain neutral.

When the full story of the "righteous sect" has been unravelled, this reference to the "house of Absalom" may prove to be a significant clue to the precise chronology of the sect, and to the identity of its "righteous Teacher." At present, this historical detail offers only a temptation to speculate. Nevertheless, the possibility of establishing a point of contact in the extant literature ought not to be ruled out. Limiting ourselves to the Greek period,[4] investigation turns up a few scattered references which may have bearing upon the problem.[5] The "Absalom" mentioned in 1 Maccabees[6] is conceivably the father of the "house of Absalom" of the Habakkuk scroll. Another possibility is the son of John Hyrcanus I.[7]

4. The Greek period seems definitely established for the founding of the sect, and the appearance of the Teacher of Righteousness; cf. H. L. Ginsberg, "The Hebrew University Scrolls from the Sectarian Cache," *BASOR* 112 (1948): 19-23. By way of comparison, see the interesting comments of R. H. Charles in his treatment of the "Fragments of a Zadokite Work," *The Apocrypha and Pseudepigrapha of the Old Testament* (Oxford: Clarendon, 1913), 2:785-97.

5. It may be significant that so far as the extant sources are concerned, no Israelite living after the 10th century and before the 2nd century B.C.E. bore the name Absalom. Apparently it dropped out of use very early in the period of the Monarchy, and did not again become popular until the strongly archaizing Maccabean Age.

6. 1 Macc. 11:70; 13:11; presumably the same man is meant. Perhaps we meet him for a third time in 2 Macc. 11:17. Josephus repeats the first two references in the *Antiquities,* xiii.5:7; 6:4.

7. His name is given by Josephus, *Antiquities,* xiv.4:4; cf. also *Jewish War,* i.154. This was an important "house" which later achieved additional prominence through the marriage of Absalom's great-granddaughter Mariamne to Herod the Great. Since Absalom himself was still alive in 63 B.C.E., the apparent *terminus ad quem* for the sectarian documents, that would militate strongly against a possible identification of this Maccabean family with the "house of Absalom" of the Habakkuk scroll.

2

Notes on Genesis

1. Grammatical Points in Gen. 1:9, 11; 2:20; 3:17

a) On the syncope of intervocalic *he* in Gen. 1:11 and 9. The word *mîn* in the Old Testament always is preceded by the preposition l^e, and followed by the pronominal suffix. It occurs with the 3rd masc. sg. suffix in two forms: *l^emînēhû* (9 times) and *l^emînô* (4 times). Of these, *l^emînēhû* is quite regular. The connecting vowel is undoubtedly the old genitive case ending, preserved before the suffix. On the other hand, *l^emînô* is, strictly speaking, anomalous. Ostensibly derived from **l^emînāhû* > **l^emînāw* > *l^emînô,* it involves the preservation of an accusative case ending, which, after the preposition, is grammatically barbarous. Instead of *l^emînô,* read **l^emînēw,* contracted from the regular *l^emînēhû.* The contracted spelling reflects the ordinary or popular pronunciation of the word (following Sievers and Bergsträsser);[1] the longer *l^emînēhû* is formally correct, and reflects literary usage. Although the Massoretes did not recognize the form *-ēw* for the suffix, there is ample evidence in support of it: e.g., the word *rē'ēhû,* "his neighbor," occurs more than 100 times in the Old Testament, establishing this as the standard form. Once, in Jer. 6:21, it occurs without the *he, rē'ô.* The Massoretic pointing here, however, is in error, as the word was undoubtedly pronounced **rē'ēw,* contracted from *rē'ēhû.*

That the spelling *r'w* is not a scribal blunder in Jeremiah is demonstrated by the fact that the same word with the same spelling (*r'w*) appears repeatedly in the

---

1. E. Sievers, *Metrische Studien,* vol. 1: *Studien zur hebräischen Metrik* (Leipzig: B. G. Taubner, 1901), §222 and §231; G. Bergsträsser, *Hebräische Grammatik (Wilhelm Gesenius' hebräische Grammatik, 29. Auflage),* vol. 1: *Einleitung, Schrift- und Lautlehre* (Leipzig: Vogel, 1918), §16.

The substance of this paper was read at the 1951 meeting of the Society of Biblical Literature and Exegesis in New York City.

Siloam inscription (ll. 2.3.4). The short form in this Inscription reflects the common speech of Jerusalem, while the longer form in the Bible is a literary survival. Another example of contraction is to be found in certain anomalous verb forms.[2] In 1 Sam. 18:1, the Qere reads *way-ye'ehābēhû,* "and he loved him"; the Kethib, however, omits the *he* of the suffix, a clear indication of this process at work. Note also Hos. 8:3, where for MT *yird*epô,* we must read **yird*epēw < yird*epēhû.* Therefore in Gen. 1:11, read **l*emînēw* for MT *l*emînô.*

A related problem occurs in v. 9.[3] On the basis of the expression *miqwê hammáyim* in v. 10, and the reading of the LXX (συναγωγή, v. 9), *miqwê* for *māqōm* is commonly proposed (involving a single change in the consonantal text). From the viewpoint of sense and context, much may be said for this suggestion. It may also be assumed that the Greek translator interpreted the Hebrew word in front of him as coming from the root *qwy.*[4] At the same time there is no need to emend the consonantal text. We suggest, instead of *māqōm,* **miqwêm,* contracted from **miqwêhem* ("one gathering of them," i.e., waters).[5] The passage would then run: "Let the waters under the heavens be gathered into a single collection of them." The syncope of the *he* of the 3rd masc. pl. suffix would reflect the spoken language, as argued above.[6]

b) In Gen. 2:20, the verb *māṣā'.* Some commentators take the subject of the verb to be Yahweh, but this is forced and syntactically difficult. Others construe the verb impersonally: "one did not find," i.e., "there was not found." This is certainly to be preferred. Normally, however, a passive form, the niphal, is used to express this idea. We suggest here, therefore, a qal passive, **muṣa',* or the like; cf. also Num. 11:22. It may well be that some prefix forms of this verb, now pointed as niphal, are actually qal passive.

c) In Gen. 3:17, *tōkalennâ,* "thou shalt eat *it.*" As it stands the antecedent of the suffix is *'ªdāmâ,* which does not fit well with the root *'kl.* It is perhaps better to take this as the energic form of the verb *without* the suffix. A number of examples of this construction (common in Ugaritic) have already been located in early Hebrew poetry, and this one may be added to them.[7] The translation is simply: "In pain thou shalt eat all the days of thy life." In this connection, a note on *taṣmî*aḥ,* v. 18, may be in order. The hiphil of MT shows that the verb is construed with *'ªdāmâ* as subject; it seems preferable to take the verb with its logical subject, *qôṣ*

---

2. W. Gesenius-E. Kautzsch, *Gesenius' Hebrew Grammar* (Oxford: Clarendon, 1910), §60d, for references.

3. The note in BH[3] indicates the nature of the difficulty which centers on the word *māqōm.*

4. This implies that the word was spelled with the *waw, mqw(m); māqōm,* on the other hand, would have been spelled *mqm* in the early texts available to the translator.

5. In connection with the peculiar syntax of *'eḥād,* note the same usage in Gen. 42:19, *'ªḥîkem 'eḥād,* lit., "one brother of you." Cf. Gen. 42:33; Exod. 25:12; 37:3.

6. Cf. Sievers, §233, and Bergsträsser.

7. For instance, cf. F. M. Cross, Jr., and D. N. Freedman, "The Blessing of Moses," *JBL* 67 (1948): 203, n. 25, and the references there.

wᵉḏarḏaḏ Read then the qal 3rd fem. sg., *tiṣmaḥ* (cf. the text of the Samaritan Pentateuch), with a compound masculine collective as subject. This archaic construction has been identified in a number of places in Old Testament poetry.[8]

2. The Text of Gen. 4:22

The recovery of the original text of Gen. 4:22 is facilitated by the parallels in vv. 20 and 21. The rhyming names of the three men show that the sequence of phrases formed a single mnemonic ditty, each segment of which must have had the same structure. On the basis of vv. 20 and 21, it is clear that the name of the man was followed by the expression *hû' hāyâ 'ᵃḇî kol-* . . . Then came a participle with a double object. The inflexibility of the pattern is demonstrated by the relatively uneven sequence in v. 20: *yōšēḇ 'ōhel û-miqnê* (which, however, is unquestionably correct as it stands). V. 22 has a number of points in common with vv. 20 and 21 and the differences can be accounted for in the following manner. First, as is generally agreed, *qáyin* (i.e., the smith) is not part of Tubal's name, and also is not original in the passage. Instead there must have been: *tûḇal [ ] [hû' hāyâ 'ᵃḇî kol-*. The last four words fell out through a scribal lapse (haplography induced by homeoteleuton); note that the next word also begins with a *lamedh*. Third, the expression *kol-ḥōrēš* is an ancient variant, or doublet, which was added to the text, while the original part was still intact. The words *lōṭēš* (which is quite rare) and *ḥōrēš* are synonymous, both referring to one engaged in metalworking activity. The reconstructed form of the passage follows:

> *yāḇāl*   *hû'*   *hāyâ*   *'ᵃḇî [kol]-yōšēḇ 'ōhel û-miqnê*
> *yûḇāl*   *hû'*   *hāyâ*   *'ᵃḇî kol-tōpēś kinnōr wᵉ'ûḡāḇ*
>
> *tûḇal [ ] [hû' hāyâ 'ᵃḇî* $\begin{Bmatrix} kol]\text{-}lōṭēš \\ kol\text{-}ḥōrēš \end{Bmatrix}$ *nᵉḥōšeṯ û-ḇarzel*

3. The Poetic Material in Gen. 5:29; 12:1-2; 14:4; Etc.

a) In Gen. 5:29 we wish to call attention to the rhyming pattern, which is characteristic of some of the oldest Hebrew verse. It is not a particularly artistic feature, and is usually achieved by the repetition of the same pronominal suffix, as, e.g. in Gen. 4:23-25; 12:1-2; Judg. 16:23-24; etc. Thus we read:

---

8. Cf. W. F. Albright, "The Old Testament and Canaanite Language and Literature," *CBQ* 7 (1945): 23ff.

$$z\hat{e} \; y^e nah^a m\bar{e}n\hat{u} \qquad mim\text{-}ma^{\cdot a}\acute{s}\bar{e}n\hat{u}$$
$$\hat{u}\text{-}m\bar{e}\text{-}\cdot i\d{s}\d{s}^e \underline{b}\hat{o}n \; y\bar{a}\underline{d}\bar{e}n\hat{u}$$

Also to be noted is the metrical pattern, 2:2:3, which has recently been identified by Prof. Albright in Ps. 68[9] and Dr. Cross in Ps. 29.[10]

b) In Gen. 12:1-2, we note again the rhyming pattern in which the half-lines or cola regularly conclude with the 2nd masc. sg. suffix, *-kā*. The last phrase of v. 1 is to be read

$$\text{'}el \; h\bar{a}\text{'}\bar{a}r\d{s} \; [\;] \; \text{'}ar\text{'}ekk\bar{a}$$

(omitting *'ašer* which was not used in early Hebrew poetry). The translation is: "unto *that* land which I will show thee" (we take the article with its original demonstrative force). The last two words of v. 2, *wehyê b^erākâ*, present a difficulty. The Massoretic pointing of the verb as an imperative is commonly rejected; the emendation usually adopted is *w^ehāyâ* (without change in the consonantal text). The only objection to this is that it is pedestrian, and in effect makes prose out of poetry. The first part of the poem builds to a climax at the end of v. 2, and we expect here a culmination in the series of verbs in the first person beginning with *'ar'ekkā:* "I will show thee . . . I will make thee . . . I will bless thee . . . I will make thy name great. . . ." The conclusion ought to be "I will make it (i.e., the name) a blessing"; that is, a name famous for the blessing it bears, and through which others may gain this blessing for themselves. We suggest, therefore, that underlying the MT *whyh* was the form **wa'ahyēhû*, the hiphil prefix 1st sg. with the 3rd masc. sg. suffix: "and I will cause it to become a blessing." The existence of the hiphil stem of the verb *hyh* (from older **hwy*) is attested in the name Yahweh,[11] and also in various combinations.[12] This form would have appeared, in the early orthography, exactly as MT, except for the *aleph* (i.e., *w'hyh* as against MT *whyh*), which may have been lost in pronunciation, **wa'ahyēhû > *wāhyēhû*. The final *-û* of the suffix would not have been indicated in the spelling.

c) It is generally recognized that Gen. 14 is based upon an old poem, excerpts of which are still partly embedded in the prose text. Dr. W. L. Moran has pointed out the occurrence of enclitic *mem* in v. 6 (in the construct chain, *b^ehar^erê-m śē'îr*),

9. W. F. Albright, "A Catalogue of Early Hebrew Lyric Poems (Psalm LXVIII)," *HUCA* 23 (1950-51): 1-39.

10. F. M. Cross, Jr., "Notes on a Canaanite Psalm in the Old Testament," *BASOR* 117 (1950): 19-21.

11. W. F. Albright, "Contributions to Biblical Archaeology and Philology," *JBL* 43 (1924): 370-78; "Further Observations on the Name *Yahweh* and Its Modifications in Proper Names," *JBL* 44 (1926): 158-62, and other articles.

12. Most recently in connection with the expression *yahwê ṣ^ebā'ôt,* see W. F. Albright's review of B. N. Wambacq, *L'épithète divine Jahvé* S^ebā'ôt (Paris: Desclée, 1947), *JBL* 67 (1948): 377-81.

a feature of Hebrew *poetry,* not prose.[13] Another characteristic device of Hebrew (and Ugaritic) poetry is to be found in v. 4.[14] Translated literally, it reads: "Twelve years they served Chedor-Laomer, and thirteen years they rebelled." This is not a prose record, stating that they served the Elamite king for twelve years and rebelled *in the thirteenth* (as the versions and more recent translations have it), but rather imaginative poetry suggesting a state of rebellious subservience for a considerable period of time, or perhaps an unsettled situation fluctuating between the two extremes, as for example in the last years of the Kingdom of Judah. This enumerative pattern is quite common in Ugaritic (7/8, 60/70, 77/88, etc.)[15] and occurs in biblical poetry also, e.g. the 3/4 pattern in Amos 1–2, and Prov. 30.

We append with some diffidence a note on the blessing of Abram in Gen. 14:19b-20a. It is suggested that v. 20a was originally a direct parallel to v. 19b, but that this has become obscured through a common scribal lapse. From the context it is clear that Abram has been the recipient of the divine blessing, and this is what the priest asserts, first generically in the third person, and then directly to Abram, in the second person. Metrical considerations also suggest a revision of v. 20a to conform to the pattern of v. 19b (2:2:3). It is proposed that between the words *bārûk* and *'ēl* in v. 20a, the words *'attâ l*ᵉ have fallen out (haplography induced by homeoarcton; in the old consonantal orthography this would have been written: אל [ברך אתּ ל]). The result is the following couplet:

19b Blessed is Abram   of El Elyon
      Creator of heaven and earth

20a Blessed art [thou   of] El Elyon[16]
      Who has delivered thine enemies into thy hand.

(Completed July 6, 1952)

---

13. W. L. Moran, "The Putative Root *'tm* in Is 9:18," *CBQ* 12 (1950): 154.

14. The fourteenth year of v. 5 may be a continuation of the numerical pattern, though more likely it is the result of a misinterpretation of the poetical device in the previous verse.

15. C. H. Gordon, *Ugaritic Handbook. AnOr* 25 (1947), I, ch. XIII: "Syntax and Poetic Structure," has a number of examples.

16. For parallels to this construction, cf. 1 Sam. 15:13; 23:21; 2 Sam. 2:5; and Ruth 3:10. Note esp. Ps. 115:15, which has affinities with this passage.

3

The Book of Ezekiel

Introduction

In dealing with the books of the Bible, the basic presupposition of Christian scholarship is that it is the Word of God. As such it is the indispensable and unique source for the Christian religion, and its ultimate authority in matters of belief and practice. Thus there is imposed upon the believer, and even the inquirer, the inescapable obligation of studying and knowing the Book. There are of course inestimable values in the study of the Bible as great literature, significant history, and authoritative ethics, as well as for the understanding of the Hebrew-Christian tradition; but for the Christian it provides the absolute foundation of his faith. It is as an organic part of the Word of God that we will look at the book of Ezekiel.

Preliminary Propositions

The Bible is a record of divine activity in the world; this includes both words and deeds, which have a fundamental identity in Hebrew thinking, and are represented by the same term: $d^e\underline{b}\bar{a}r\hat{i}m$. It describes God's active relationship to mankind, especially to his people Israel, as seen through the eyes of his servants. These observations were reported, set down, collected, edited, and transmitted over a period of centuries. It is important to distinguish between the original action or message (given through a prophet), which had immediate relevance, and the record which was compiled and published by a later generation for the benefit of those far removed from the original scene.

The Bible is a message, as well as a record. The events of the past are made to speak to those who come after. The deed of God may have an influence long after the occasion of its occurrence; and his word may still be heard long after it

8

was first delivered. This after-effect is neither magical nor mechanical. Although many have tried to use the Bible (especially books like Ezekiel, Daniel, and Revelation) in this fashion as a guidebook to the course of subsequent history, it contains no secret code for unravelling the details of the future. Nor are there cryptic messages concealed in the material for the people of later ages. At the same time, there is little generalized wisdom or abstract instruction, characteristic of nonbiblical religion and easily adapted to modern use.

The striking thing about divine revelation in the Bible is its historical character. Events are fixed at the intersection of the lines of time and place; messages are delivered in the context of their circumstances. Even so apparently universal and timeless a pronouncement as the Ten Commandments is made in a specified setting to a limited audience, as part of a historical contract. This quality is at once the glory and burden of biblical religion: the emphasis on concrete occurrences in the framework of chronology and topography gives the Hebrew-Christian faith a vividness and actuality not shared by other religions. But it makes very difficult the problem of transference, of applying the words and deeds to the modern situation, of using the Bible here and now. The method of classic theology (that is, a systematic presentation of propositions and proofs) stripped away the local and temporal coloring, leaving, it was thought, the essential material of doctrine. It is true that the time gap was spanned in this fashion, but the effect was to substitute descriptive philosophy for historical narrative. Thus the colorful picture of God in the Bible as a living passionate person, whose very name is Zeal *(qannā')*, tends to become in theology a geometric pattern of absolutes, describing an abstract first cause or ultimate ground of being.

At the other extreme is the effort to remake the biblical scene in concrete detail, and then to apply the teachings of the Bible literally. This tendency is already present in the Bible itself (e.g., the Rechabites, Jer. 35), and has cropped up repeatedly in the history of the church. This method also is a denial of the historical factor, essential to the biblical story. The biblical writers acknowledge the validity of change, and the necessity to adapt principles, and modify practices. The prophets drew inspiration from Israel's experience in the wilderness, but they did not insist that the nation, with its large cities and complex commercial operations, must revert to a seminomadic existence. The monarchy was a comparatively late development in Israel's institutional history, yet the prophets, far from rejecting this innovation (however they may have regarded individual kings), recognized it as the instrument for the final establishment of the kingdom of God.

The Bible itself suggests the method by which the events of the past can be made meaningful to later generations without distorting or destroying their historical character. This may be described as the process of liturgical or dramatic reenactment. The great festivals of Israel's calendar, though agricultural in nature, have a strong historical emphasis: e.g., the Passover, which celebrates the deliverance from Egypt, and the Feast of Booths, which commemorates the wanderings in the wilderness. On these occasions, the central events were recited and enacted symbolically, so that those present became participants, dramatically, in the original events. There is strong evidence also for a covenant-renewal festival in early Israel (the original event is reflected in the story in Exod. 24; cf. Josh. 24 and Deut. 31:9-13). The Lord's Supper belongs essentially to the same category (that is, it is a covenant-renewal ceremony) with the participants accepting their obligations under the covenant by eating and drinking a sacred meal in the presence of the Lord, as did the disciples on the original occasion. The main object is to bring the reader or believer into the world of the Bible, and open to him a vital and direct experience of the decisive events of salvation history *(Heilsgeschichte)*.

The event of central significance for man is the direct personal encounter with God. For most people, this experience, its content and meaning, is mediated by the Bible. If we are to hear and see God at all, it will be through the eyes and ears of men like Abraham, Moses, and the prophets in the Old Testament, and the apostles in the New, with the most direct contact in the testimony of Jesus Christ. Imaginative entry into the world of the Bible, stimulated by diligent study and guided by the Holy Spirit, can bring these fateful encounters to life in our consciousness.

What has been said of the festivals and theophanies applies in varying measure to the whole Bible: the more we understand its background, contents, and meaning, the greater will be our participation in the life of the holy people, the more clearly will we hear and see the God who speaks and acts. There will remain the problem of modern relevance. We cannot live only in the world of the Bible, but must, at the same time, live in our own. In making the transfer, the reality of the encounter with God need not be lost, however, and our sense of his real presence, conditioned by the biblical experience, will be a true guide to the understanding of his purpose and activity today. Full appreciation of the biblical account will lead to a sensitive awareness of the same God today. In like manner, analogical reasoning can provide applications of biblical truth to different modern situations, though there is always a measure of risk in this procedure. In the end, only the church can pass on the validity of such interpretations, and often its judgment is long in being articulated.

In dealing with the book of Ezekiel, we shall endeavor to work from the basic presuppositions to the indicated goals: participation in the decisive events described in the book, identification with the prophet in his encounter with God, to make that experience ours, and the creative application of the contents of the book to the modern situation. Since this is not the place for a detailed study of the book, we will simply point out some of the main subjects for consideration, and some of the problems connected with them:

1. Approach to the book of Ezekiel; the importance of the original language
2. The setting of the book; the problem of integrity and authenticity
3. The key to the book: the vision of the glory of God and the temple
4. The chief contents of the book
5. Evaluation.

1. Approach to the Book of Ezekiel

The importance of being familiar with the contents of the book can hardly be emphasized enough. There is no adequate substitute for the direct study of the Scripture itself. The Bible is serious reading, and much of it bristles with difficulties. This is particularly true of the prophetic literature, and the book of Ezekiel is no exception. In addition to the usual textual and literary questions, there are peculiar problems not encountered elsewhere in the Bible.

Any serious study of a book of the Bible must begin with the original language. Every Christian ought to read and understand the Bible in the languages in which it was written; this is especially true of ministers and teachers of the church. While it is indispensably important to bring the Bible to the modern world and make it available to people in their own language, it is more valuable, though more difficult, to bring modern man into the world of the Bible, and to equip him to understand its message in its own language. Any translation is inevitably a form of modernization, and tends to defeat the initial objective of biblical study which is the participation of the reader in the recent biblical situation.

Biblical translations encounter numerous obstacles. For the Old Testament, Hebrew is strikingly unlike any modern European language; thus the quality or "feel" of the original is largely lost. It is almost impossible to render poetry from one language into another without sacrificing either the rhythmic and musical features, or literary quality, or both. In the Old Testament a large proportion of the most important material is poetic. More specifically, psychological and theological terms in Hebrew and in Greek have their own peculiar force and overtones, quite unlike the corresponding terms in English (e.g., terms like *ḥeseḏ,* "lovingkindness, steadfast love," and *agapē,* "love," for which there are no simple equivalents, and which require paragraphs of explanatory definition to convey their real meaning). Behind these terms lies the distinctive biblical approach to the nature of God and man, and their relationship. The substitution of familiar English expressions only conceals from the reader the important difference between our conceptions and theirs. So we continue to read the Bible through the spectacles of the 20th century, or what is worse the 17th, and never see the original at all.

2. The Setting of the Book

Having read the book a number of times (preferably in Hebrew) and being generally familiar with its contents, the reader may now block out the following areas for further inquiry: (a) the historical situation in which the action takes place; (b) the book as prophetic literature, and its place in the prophetic movement in Israel; (c) recent scholarly opinion and debate in connection with these matters.

A. *The historical background*

It is immediately clear that the contents of the book belong to the first half of the 6th century B.C.E. Effective understanding of the references and allusions to persons and nations and events will require a comprehensive knowledge of the history of the Near East in this period. The two foci of interest in the book of Ezekiel are Babylon and Jerusalem. In the foreground is Jerusalem and the tragedy of its fall. The circumstances and events leading up to it are under continuous discussion. The prophet uses obscure and symbolic figures in dealing with significant persons and events; clarification depends upon a detailed knowledge of the complex developments during the last years of the kingdom of Judah. Historical information is to be found chiefly in the books of Kings and Jeremiah, as well as background data for the tension and anxiety which permeated the kingdom: the desperate hopes and expectations, as well as the overwhelming fears and forebodings while the catastrophe approached. Archaeological excavations have revealed the terrible destruction of the invasions of 598 B.C.E. and 587 B.C.E., confirming in ash and rubble (and the famous Lachish letters) the vivid descriptions of the Bible. In the background of this tale of two cities is Babylon (where the prophet resides). While Jerusalem was falling, Babylon was rising. As the last kings of Judah were toppled from the throne of David, and perished ignominiously or were led away captive like animals in a cage, the new dynasty of Babylon became masters of the earth.

Ezekiel is not, of course, recounting history. He assumes that knowledge on the part of his hearers. His purpose is to interpret and explain the terrible paradox of events whereby the city of God becomes a heap of ruins, and the metropolis of idolatry becomes mistress of the nations. The prophet traces the history of his own people all the way back to the beginning in an effort to uncover the causes of the present calamity; at the same time he analyzes the rise of the Neo-Babylonian Empire and the assumption of power by Nebuchadrezzar. He draws the two lines of investigation together in a discussion of the present course of events. The resulting synthesis is a theology of history: the organization of historical data from the point of view of God and his purpose.

B. *The book as prophetic literature*

To grasp the book properly it is important to classify it (and its contents) according to its literary character, and to compare it with other materials of a similar type. The key word is "prophecy." Ezekiel was a prophet, and his book belongs to the genre of "prophetic literature." The prophetic movement has a long and distinctive history in Israel, and provides important background for an understanding of Ezekiel and his message. At first (or any) reading, Ezekiel appears to be an exceedingly odd individual. When compared with the whole group of prophets, however, most of his peculiarities fall into a recognizable pattern. Sense can be made of his strange visions and unusual behavior. Even the obscure symbolism of his speech corresponds to general prophetic usage, though details vary markedly from prophet to prophet.

Essentially, a prophet is one called by God and commissioned by him with a message for his people. Historically, the prophetic movement begins with Samuel. The prophets appear as religious reformers, not innovators in Israel. Their fundamental views derive from the revelation at Mt. Sinai and the norms of life established during the desert wanderings. Their message is basically an application of these principles to the current situation. The chief charge against Israel is rebellion against God through violation of the terms of the covenant ratified at Sinai, and since renewed regularly in the Holy Land. For this breach of law, the penalty is death; history is the arena in which judgment will be executed. Persistence in sin will certainly bring disaster. However, God may spare his people if they repent and continue loyal to the terms of the covenant.

By the time of the great 8th-century prophets, time was running out, and the possibility of escaping the threatened doom was practically gone. Only a tiny fragment of the southern kingdom (including Jerusalem) managed to survive a series of Assyrian invasions, and that at the cost of independence. Nevertheless, according to the prophets, even this emphatic instruction did not teach the people their lesson. In the preaching of Jeremiah and Ezekiel judgment is certain, and historically determined. Sinfulness has eaten away the character of the people, with the result that repentance, the necessary precondition of forgiveness, is no longer possible. This time the punishment is final. The nation, the city, and the temple will all be destroyed. And they are.

The people of God, however, cannot be destroyed. This paradox occupies a prominent place in the teaching of the prophets, especially Jeremiah and Ezekiel. Its resolution lies in the nature of the covenant commitment, whereby God remains bound by his oath to Abraham, even though Israel has broken the contract made through Moses. Both prophets make it clear that the survival of a remnant in exile is due to God's grace and self-binding promise to the fathers. Beyond survival there is also the prospect of a return.

It is sufficiently clear that Ezekiel, both man and book, fits into the prophetic movement; as we should expect, the closest affinities are with Jeremiah, who was his older contemporary. In fact Ezekiel can be pinned down with somewhat greater precision. Chronologically, Ezekiel comes between Jeremiah and 2 Isaiah; his message is in many ways the connecting link between the two. The chief emphasis in Jeremiah's career and message is the fall of Jerusalem and the captivity of the people; the hope for the future is touched on, but it is comparatively far off. This however is the main concern of 2 Isaiah, for whom judgment is over and done with. Return and restoration are his battle cry. Ezekiel's career on the other hand, straddles the fall of Jerusalem. The first part

13

of the book contains judgments against the city, and is much like Jeremiah. The latter part deals with the hope of the exiles; the prophet is concerned to prepare his people for return to the Holy Land. A few years later, that day is announced by 2 Isaiah.

The book exhibits many of the characteristic features of prophetic literature. It begins with the authentication of the prophet: his call (Ezek. 1–3). Though quite different in detail, it compares in principal elements with similar accounts in Isa. 6; Jer. 1; etc. As in the case of Jeremiah and Isaiah, the rest of the book is divided between oracles and narratives. In the case of the earlier prophets, their preserved utterances are poetic in form. With regard to Jeremiah and Ezekiel, prose discourses also are recorded. Ezekiel makes extensive use of parables; examples of these are found in other prophets also.

In Ezekiel the narratives are all autobiographical, unlike the stories in Jeremiah which are chiefly in the third person. The character of Ezekiel's narratives differs correspondingly, however. Though told in story form, Ezekiel's account is more a spiritual diary of personal experience of God and his inner reaction to it than a record of objective occurrences. For the most part Ezekiel lives in a separate world. Other people drift in and out of the book, but there is little direct contact. Jeremiah, on the other hand, lives in a world of men; his book is full of the noise and excitement of life. Occasionally he withdraws for personal dealings with God, but only to plunge back into the battle with kings, priests, false prophets, and princes.

C. The problems of critical scholarship

Thus far we have accepted the information in the book of Ezekiel substantially at face value. Our study of the historical and prophetic background of the book is based on the recognition of the essential authenticity and integrity of the book. Should this view prove wrong, an entirely different approach would be necessary. Before we go further, it will be wise to consider the opposing views of critical scholars, which have been expressed with increasing strength during the last forty years. The critics have exhibited great ingenuity and imagination in producing a bewildering variety of attacks on the traditional view of the book of Ezekiel. The result has been scholarly chaos, with no substantial agreement among the critics, and little prospect of an orderly resolution of the points in conflict. The chief issues are the reliability and unity of the book, i.e., that this is an authentic record of the career of the exilic prophet Ezekiel, and that the contents of the book are attributable to him. Generally, both are questioned. A number of scholars deny the validity of the picture of the exilic community in Babylonia as it is presented in Ezekiel, and go on from this to question the whole Babylonian setting of the prophecy. An extreme position is adopted by C. C. Torrey, who regards the entire book as a pseudepigraph of the 3rd century B.C.E.[1] Other scholars have attacked the unity of the book, denying smaller or larger sections to the prophet. Practically all scholars recognize the presence of doublets and glosses in the text; we are concerned here with more extensive parts of the book. Most widespread doubt is expressed with regard to Ezek. 40–48, the description of the new temple and the new Palestine; much the same holds for chs. 38–39, the apocalyptic story of Gog of the land of Magog. More radical treatments of the book, by men like Hölscher and Irwin, eliminate other extensive sections, leaving to the prophet only a small percentage of the total.[2] A third point of interest has to do with the location of the prophet during his prophetic career. Three positions are held: (1) the apparent point of view of the book itself, which is that the prophet was in Babylonia during the entire period of his ministry. This raises the problem of clairvoyant powers and parapsychic experiences on the part of the prophet, and many scholars prefer to find a different solution to the question; (2) the prophet began his career in Jerusalem, and at some later time removed to Babylon (perhaps with the second group of exiles). Several variations of this view are possible, including a number of trips back and forth between Babylon and Jerusalem. (3) This is simply the reverse of the first: that Ezekiel was in Jerusalem all the time.

We do not mean to brush aside the fundamental importance of critical scholarship, nor even to minimize the value of this study of the book of Ezekiel. Scholarship needs no defense. The results in this case, however, have been largely negative. It is clear enough that we cannot return to an older uncritical acceptance of the book as though we had it directly from the hand of the prophet himself. The book bears the marks of a relatively long history of compilation and edition. It also has a full quota of scribal variations and mistakes acquired through centuries of transmission (comparison with the old Greek translation, the Septuagint, bears this out). With regard to the positive assertions, however, not one of the critical conclusions will stand examination. Whatever outside evidence we have tends to confirm the traditional position concerning the book of Ezekiel. The results reached by H. H. Rowley, in a recent article, seem inescapable: "The ministry of Ezekiel I would place wholly in Babylonia in the period immediately before and after the fall of Jerusalem."[3] The contents of the book all go back to the prophet, though the book itself may have been compiled at a later date.

Difficulties remain, but they will not be solved by cutting the book into fragments, or by eliminating the historical framework, or adjusting the details to

---

1. C. C. Torrey, *Pseudo-Ezekiel and the Original Prophecy* (New Haven: Yale University Press, 1930).

2. G. Hölscher, *Hesekiel, der Dichter und das Buch.* BZAW 39 (Giessen: A. Topelmann, 1924); W. A. Irwin, *The Problem of Ezekiel* (Chicago: University of Chicago Press, 1943).

3. H. H. Rowley, "The Book of Ezekiel in Modern Study," *BJRL* 36 (1953): 146-90. The quotation is to be found on p. 190.

fit some more rational scheme. They arise rather from the inadequacy of words and language to convey the spectacular experiences of a remarkable man under extraordinary circumstances. Clarification will come perhaps as we probe more deeply into the religious psychology of Israel, and study more closely the prophets' experience of God and their relationship to the supernatural. The book of Ezekiel swarms with clues as to the real nature of the prophet and his experiences. But a mystic perhaps will be better equipped than a scholar to unravel the mystery.

3. The Key to Ezekiel

In many ways the book of Ezekiel resembles a modern detective story. On the surface, it seems straightforward enough. The prophet speaks of the fall of Jerusalem, explains the significance of the exile, and gives assurance of an ultimate return. But beneath it is full of oddities. We find ourselves in a strange world of mysterious visions, portentous but mystifying oracles; with a prophet who performs weird actions and suffers from peculiar disorders; who seems to pursue a twofold existence in Babylon and Jerusalem; who journeys in the spirit to far countries, yet never leaves his own house. What lies behind all these phenomena? If we are to seize the full meaning of the book, we must try to share the strange experience of the prophet, and understand what was happening to him.

Before looking at some of the clues to the mystery, two points are to be made. First we must reckon with the unusual personality of the prophet. Prophets were far from being average men, and Ezekiel was perhaps the least average of the lot. He was a highly sensitive person, living under great tension through Israel's most terrible crisis. Further, he had a direct personal encounter with God, the like of which is granted to few men. The possibility of parapsychic experiences ought not to be ruled out in the case of an extraordinary man like this. The second point is the overwhelming significance of the temple in the thought of the prophet. The theme of the temple runs through the entire book, and is the key to its unity. In a sentence, it is the story of the departure of the glory of God from the temple and its return. If we start with the extraordinary personality of the prophet, and couple that with his concentration upon the temple, then we should not be surprised at what we find in the book of Ezekiel.

The Clues to the Book of Ezekiel

1. Ezekiel is a priest (1:2). This is a significant clue, because much that otherwise would seem peculiar in a prophet can be explained from this fact. Many other details help to confirm the conclusion that Ezekiel was deeply imbued with the attitudes and perspectives of the Jerusalem priesthood. The close affinities between the book of

Ezekiel and the Priestly materials in the Pentateuch are not accidental; this is not unrelated to his interest in the temple. His attachment to the temple is not simply a matter of group or institutional loyalty, though these factors enter the picture. An important theological attitude is involved. Ezekiel and the Priestly writers share a common viewpoint in this regard, which may be called "*kābôd* theology." The tabernacle and later the temple is the abode of the *glory* of God. God himself dwells in heaven, in a temple not made with hands, but he has set his glory (*kābôd* symbolizes his presence) in the temple at Zion to dwell there permanently. This conception represented a serious effort to convey the transcendence and immanence of God in a meaningful way. God was present in his glory with his people, but he was at the same time the transcendent ruler of the universe, not bound by time and place.

Priestly theology tended to regard this relationship as permanent and unchangeable. The divine glory would always dwell in the temple in the midst of Israel. Two facts supported this view: the unconditional covenants between God and (1) the house of David insuring the permanence of the dynasty and its authority in Jerusalem, and (2) the house of Aaron giving assurance that there would always be a high priest of this line to preside in the house of God. It was the prevailing view that God would always defend his kingdom and his temple for the sake of his servants David and Aaron. Up until the time of Jeremiah and Ezekiel, events seemed to bear out this contention. Even during the terrible invasions which resulted in the demise of the northern kingdom and the devastation of the southern, Jerusalem and the temple and the house of David were spared (701 B.C.E.).

Micah, Jeremiah, and other prophets had little sympathy with this point of view. Jeremiah acknowledged that a permanent relationship existed between God and his people (described by the term used in the Deuteronomic literature: *šēm* or name theology). The idea was much the same as in *kābôd* theology, i.e., that God had set his name (symbolizing his presence) in the temple to dwell with his people. But the theological background was strikingly different. The basis for the relationship between God and people was the Sinai-Horeb covenant, which was conditional in nature. If Israel rebelled, then Israel would be punished. God would smash down his temple, just as he had centuries before at Shiloh. If any one doubted this, let him go out and look at the ruins (Jer. 7). Jeremiah's theology was not anchored in any mystical attachment to the temple; but Ezekiel's was. To Jeremiah, the temple had become a den of thieves, and those who worshipped there were hypocrites. He was a rebel and iconoclast; Ezekiel was a conservative and traditionalist. He could hardly go along with his fiery contemporary. One day he would learn that Jeremiah was right, but in his own way.

2. The vision in the sky. The remarkable vision of the glory of God with which the book of Ezekiel opens (and which is repeated a number of times) is a second clue of importance. It has often been remarked that there are affinities between this vision and Isaiah's vision in the temple, of the Lord sitting upon his throne. If we pass over the colorful details in Ezekiel's description, we recognize

the close similarity. In essence both pictures are one: the glory of God seated upon his throne in the holy of holies. There is, however, one striking difference: the wheels. In Ezekiel's vision, the throne is on wheels; it is in short a chariot, a flying chariot at that. What does it mean? Why should the glory of God fly from the temple? The ominous note of foreboding is confirmed by the message of lamentation and woe which is given to the prophet. Something catastrophic is about to happen, and he is to be herald of the bad tidings.

3. The journey to Jerusalem (chs. 8–11). Much scholarly effort has been spent on these chapters in an attempt to determine what actually happened. Was Ezekiel actually in Jerusalem visiting the temple and seeing the things reported as going on there? If so, why the camouflage which places him at home in Tel Abib? Was he, then, sitting at home, while traveling on the wings of a vision revisiting his old haunts in the spirit? If so, how can we explain the story of the death of Pelatiah, described in ch. 11? Rationally, scholarship seems to hit a stone wall. We may, however, examine the evidence in the light of the criteria suggested above.

It would seem that in these chapters something of shattering significance has happened to the prophet. He saw something, he heard something which removed his last doubts, and convinced him that the temple would fall. He even saw the destruction of the temple and city with his mind's inner eyes. Twice during the visions, he cried out to stay the hand of God. But when he had seen the total corruption of the temple, he knew that the glory of God could no longer dwell there. We are witnesses to the inner struggle of a man's soul, where belief is opposed by fact. He believed that the glory of God would abide forever in his temple; but the facts are against it. The meaning of the wheels and the wings has become clear.

In the visions in chs. 8–11, there is a blending of realistic factual elements, with highly colorful imaginative features. Thus chs. 8 and 11 involve presumably historical scenes in the temple and living persons. Chs. 9-10, on the other hand, are a futuristic and symbolic description of the destruction of the city. In interpreting this material scholars are largely divided between the view that Ezekiel must have been in Jerusalem in order to observe the events described in chs. 8 and 11 and the view that he was in Babylon, and through the power of clairvoyance was able to observe the things going on in Jerusalem at the same time. Of the two, the second would seem to be more in keeping with the evidence and the unusual circumstances.

Nevertheless, it is possible to do justice to the story without relying too heavily on a theory of supernatural powers. We see the prophet in a highly agitated state, knowing that Jerusalem is doomed because of its sins, yet believing in the permanent presence of the glory of God in the temple. As he passes into a trance, under the power of the Spirit, his attention is riveted on the temple. The beginning of his vision consists of recollections of things seen and heard while he was still resident in Jerusalem before 598. The tour of the temple in ch. 8 is built out of reminiscence and report, but in the vision of the prophet it is all fresh and contemporary. The events have been re-created in his mind, and they constitute decisive evidence against the sanctity of the temple. The inevitable consequence is vividly described in chs. 9–10. Sentence is passed against the sinful city; destruction is decreed. Then the glory of God departs. But before he leaves the scene, the prophet fixes on a final relevant piece of evidence: the death of Pelatiah in the temple. This also is probably based upon recollection or report: under peculiar circumstances the man died in the temple. Now the event takes on new significance. It is the climax of the sequence which reveals the wrath of God against the whole people (11:13). The original episode is reenacted in the present, and the prophet is on the scene. He denounces the plotters who devise iniquity, and at the critical point of his speech, Pelatiah dies. It is clear from the story that neither Pelatiah nor any of the others is at all aware of the presence of the prophet. It is as though a screen separated them. On one side are God and the prophet observing and discussing; on the other the action takes place as it had in the past. Only now the scene is placed in the new context of the prophet's vision. It is the clinching argument that the temple is irremediably defiled. Next he sees the divine chariot abandon the land. The temple will be destroyed and the city will fall.

However we attempt to explain these occurrences, it is important to note that in no case is there the slightest recognition on the part of the people in Jerusalem that Ezekiel is in their midst. In order to establish this point, we need only compare the record of Ezekiel's shadowy appearances in Jerusalem with the stories of Jeremiah's adventures in the same city during the same years (e.g., the stories of the deed purchase, the scroll burning, the altercation with Hananiah, or explicitly the temple scene in Jer. 7 and 26). The contrast is so great as to make it practically impossible to explain the Ezekiel story on the basis of a real trip to Jerusalem and reworked later to give it a Babylonian setting.

4. The vision of the new temple. After 598 B.C.E. most of the people focused their hopes on the temple. As long as the temple stood they had visible proof of the devotion and concern of God, and they were confident of a speedy return and restoration of the kingdom. Both Jeremiah and Ezekiel condemned this superficial optimism. When their words were confirmed by the destruction of the temple, most people lost hope entirely. This was the end of the nation; God had abandoned them forever. The prophets, however, had a word of hope. Out of the wreckage God would build anew, but it would take time.

For Ezekiel, this new conviction also had its roots in the miraculous vision of the divine chariot. The primary purpose of the vision was to anticipate clearly the devastating course of events which culminated in the destruction of the state. What then was the value of warning and preparing people for the doom to come, if that indeed was to be the end? The presentation of the message of judgment and its confirmation by events was actually the basis for a more startling message which in turn would be confirmed by future events. Just as a vision of the chariot signified the departure of God and the end of one era; so another vision of the chariot would symbolize the return of God and the climax of a new era.

Along the way there was a striking vision of the resurrection of the nation (Ezek. 37); and fourteen years after the destruction of the temple (573 B.C.E.), the prophet had a vision of a new temple in a new Jerusalem (chs. 40ff.). Finally he sees the chariot of God return to the temple and receives assurance that his glory will dwell there forever (ch. 43). Thus the cycle ends. Land and people are united, and the glory of God is at home in the temple.

We have suggested that the key to the book of Ezekiel is the prophet's intense concern for the temple as the abode of the glory of God. The visions of its destruction and rebuilding are the main clues to the content of the book. They help to explain and are explained by the other aspects of the prophet's experience and thought. Thus we have the image of the divine chariot which bears the glory of God away from the doomed city and back to the redeemed city. Again there is the image of the nation perishing under sentence of death and being brought back to life by the power of the spirit of God. Another is the picture of the people carried away captive from their land and being restored to it by the decree of the Almighty.

4. The Chief Contents of the Book

Outlining the book of Ezekiel is a relatively easy process, chiefly because the editor or compiler followed a discernible pattern and rather clear organizing principles in his work. Two general guides appear: one is chronological, the other topical. A series of dates is scattered throughout the book, beginning in the first chapter. With few exceptions the dates are in chronological order (from the 5th to the 27th years of the exile, and a possible reference in 1:1 to the 30th) and offer a ready device for arranging the contents of the book. At the same time, it must be noted that the system is incomplete, and many stories and oracles are undated. There is also in the book of Ezekiel a marked tendency to group materials of similar literary form or subject matter. Thus, e.g., chs. 25–32 are a collection of prophecies concerning foreign nations; chs. 40–48 are devoted largely to technical details relating to the new temple, the new Jerusalem, and the new Palestine. Chs. 12–23 are for the most part a series of oracles dealing with the impending fall of Jerusalem. Other smaller groupings likewise occur (as in chs. 1–3, 4–5).

Closer examination of the book reveals different stages of compilation and edition.[4] Thus chs. 1–24 form a well-conceived unit covering the period from 593 B.C.E. to the fall of Jerusalem. This edition of the book probably closed with the words announcing the fall of the city (33:21-22, which are out of place and belong immediately after 24:26-27). Attached to it, apparently as an appendix, were the oracles on the

4. For an excellent discussion of this matter, see C. G. Howie, *The Date and Composition of Ezekiel* (Philadelphia: SBL, 1950).

foreign nations (chs. 25–32), all of which are connected in some fashion with the destruction of Judah. The enigmatic 30th year in 1:1 may well indicate the year (568 B.C.E.) in which the material was compiled or dictated by the prophet (cf. Jer. 36 for the account of a similar procedure). A later edition of the book included chs. 33–39. These are undated oracles, all later than the material in Ezek. 1–24, and perhaps later even than the 30th year. Chs. 34, 36, and 37 emphasize the restoration of the people in captivity and the reestablishment of the house of David in authority. They might be connected with the improved status accorded Jehoiachin by Awel-Marduk in 561 B.C.E. (2 Kgs. 25:27-29) and growing hopes for a return from exile. Ezek. 40–48, dating from the 25th year (573 B.C.E.), constitute a separate section, which may have circulated independently for a while before being incorporated into the final edition of the book.

Working Outline and Summary

I. Chs. 1–24. The Basic Book: Prophecies against Jerusalem

   A. Chs. 1–11. The Prophet and His Message

      1. The Call of the Prophet (chs. 1–3)

         A. Ch. 1. The vision of the glory of God, which the prophet saw while in exile. The fantastically elaborate picture of cherubim and throne is a composite, drawing basic elements from the Israelite past and details from pagan mythologic monsters. The significance of the vision has been discussed.

         B. Chs. 2–3. The call and commission. The nature of the message is defined at once. It is one of doom and woe, and it is for the house of Israel. At the same time the prophet is to be watchman to his people and warn them of judgment so that they may escape it. The seeming paradox lies in the fact that while Israel is divided and scattered, it remains a psychic unity. The message of judgment is against Jerusalem, but it affects the exiles as well as those in the city. In like manner, the warning to repent is aimed at the Israel which will survive the holocaust, primarily the exiles, but also those in the city who may escape after the fall.

      2. The Basic Message: Woe to the City (chs. 4–7)

         A. Chs. 4–5. The prophet is told to perform a series of symbolic actions, typifying the city of Jerusalem and its fate. Thus the message is dramatized for the exiles, so that they can share vicariously in the punishment of Judah.

B. Chs. 6–7. These oracles present the situation explicitly. The disaster which is about to befall the nation has a cause and a reason. It is the will of God, and it is due to the ineradicable sinfulness of his people. These chapters constitute an incisive example of the prophetic interpretation of history.

3. The Journey to Jerusalem (chs. 8–11)

A. Ch. 8. The problem and significance of these visions of the temple have already been discussed. The sinful practices mentioned reflect religious borrowings from Israel's neighbors and masters (e.g., women weeping for Tammuz). Mesopotamian and Canaanite sources supply descriptions of similar rites.

B. Ch. 9. Execution of judgment in the city. This is carried out by angelic ministers at the express command of God. Six of them carry weapons for slaying, the seventh a writing instrument to mark the heads of those who because of their righteousness are to be spared. The theological viewpoint is based upon the discussion in chs. 14 and 18 (cf. also Gen. 19 and Exod. 32), dealing with the application of retributive justice in human affairs. Ideas of a final judgment in later books like Daniel and those of the New Testament reflect a similar approach.

C. Ch. 10. The glory of God is about to depart from the temple. With departure comes the destruction of the city by fire.

D. Ch. 11. The death of Pelatiah and the final departure of the chariot from the land (see discussion above).

B. Chs. 12–24. The Formal Charges

1. Oracles on the Doom of Jerusalem (chs. 12–19)

A. Chs. 12–14, 18. Oracles

1) Ch. 12. Like the symbolic actions in chs. 4–5. The prophet portrays the fate of the exiles who survive the fall of the city.

2) Ch. 13. An oracle against the false prophets who predict that all will be well. Like Jeremiah, Ezekiel condemns those who say, "peace," when there will be no peace. Compare the conflict between Jeremiah and the false prophet, Hananiah (Jer. 28). The struggle, as indicated here between true and false prophet, was crucial and bitter. In point of fact, often only time could determine which was which; but decisions had to be made then and there.

3) Ch. 14. This chapter continues the discussion of divine justice and how it operates. Abraham had argued with God to spare Sodom and Gomorrah for the sake of the righteous people in the cities. Ezekiel denies that this is possible for the inhabitants of Jerusalem. He contends that even three of the most righteous people that ever lived — Noah, Daniel (a legendary Canaanite hero, not the principal figure of the book of Daniel), and Job — could save no one (not even their families) except themselves (cf. ch. 9).

4) Ch. 18. The doctrine of individual responsibility receives its most explicit presentation. The popular view held that sons might be punished for the sins of their fathers, and so on through several generations (cf. Exod. 2–3). Ezekiel emphatically repudiates this position: every man is responsible for himself.

B. Chs. 15–17, 19. Parables and Allegories

1) Ch. 15. The parable of the vine branch. Though scholars are in dispute as to the precise relationship between the image and the interpretation, the comparison seems to follow this line: The vine is useless to begin with, by contrast with other trees, being good only for fuel; after it has been burned, it is completely valueless. In the same way the people of Jerusalem are useless, being good only for fuel. And they are going to be burned up.

2) Ch. 16. The story of a harlot: Jerusalem. Under this symbol the prophet engages in a long analysis of his people's history and destiny. Comparison with Sodom and Samaria is made; the promise is given of ultimate restoration.

3) Ch. 17. This is a rather complex parable about eagles and the branches of a cedar tree, describing the international situation. The first eagle is Nebuchadrezzar, king of Babylon, and the topmost twig is Jehoiachin, the captive king of Judah. The seed of the land is Zedekiah, regent and uncle of the king, but not in the prophet's eyes, the legal monarch. The other great eagle is the pharaoh of Egypt, with whom Zedekiah negotiated as part of a plot of rebellion against Nebuchadrezzar. The prophet condemns Zedekiah for his breach of covenant (vv. 11-21).

4) Ch. 19. The parable of the lioness and her cubs. This also deals with the royal house of Judah. The lioness is Judah, or more precisely the queen mother, a dominant figure in ancient orien-

tal monarchies. The first whelp is Jehoahaz, who was carried away to Egypt after a reign of three months (609 B.C.E.). The second is probably Jehoiakim, his brother and successor. In the latter part of the chapter the image has been changed to that of vine and branch. This is more obscure, but the branch here apparently is Jehoiachin, the young son of Jehoiakim, who was carried off to Babylon at the age of eighteen (598 B.C.E.).

2. Further Oracles against Jerusalem (chs. 20–24)

A. Ch. 20. A group of elders come to inquire of the prophet. There follows an authoritative discourse on the doctrine of the name of God. According to the prophet, the ultimate standard for God's actions is his name; in other words, he does what he does for his own sake. Although it sounds rather forbidding, actually it is a statement of the doctrine of unmerited grace. From the beginning, the prophet points out, God has spared his people (for his name's sake, i.e., out of his own nature and being) even though they deserved punishment and execution. Even though he is going to punish them finally for their sins, he will act again (for his name's sake) to save them and bring them back from the lands of their captivity.

B. Ch. 21. The chapter consists of a series of brief oracles of judgment, followed by a historical commentary. The Babylonian army is on the march to suppress rebellion in the West. Nebuchadrezzar stands at the crossroads: shall he march against Judah or Ammon? By lot and divination, Jerusalem is chosen. Her fate is sealed, but Ammon's turn will come later.

C. Ch. 22. A summation of the charges against the leaders of Judah: princes, priests, and prophets. The basic accusation involves murder and idolatry, though many other sins are specified. The verdict is guilty, the sentence, death.

D. Ch. 23. This is a long allegory similar to the one in ch. 16. The principal figures are two sisters Oholah and Oholibah, representing respectively the kingdoms of Israel (Samaria) and Judah (Jerusalem). The sisters became the brides of God, but they committed adultery, and must therefore perish. This is the figure the prophet uses to describe the diplomatic machinations and political alliances made by Israel and Judah with the different nations. Israel abandoned her Lord to submit alternately to the authority of Egypt and Assyria; Judah did worse in adding Babylonia as a lover. As Israel paid with her life for her crime, so now Judah's turn has come.

E. Ch. 24. In a final oracle against Jerusalem, Ezekiel uses the symbol of a cauldron; no amount of cleansing can remove the rust. It is dated on the same day that Nebuchadrezzar laid siege to Jerusalem. A last symbol of the fate of Jerusalem is the death of the prophet's wife (apparently at the same time). Ezekiel is commanded not to weep or mourn the passing of his wife; just so, the people must make no outcry over the loss of the temple. What is to happen is what they deserve.

II. Chs. 25–48. Miscellaneous Additions

A. Chs. 25–32. Oracles on the Foreign Nations

1. Ch. 25. Against the Neighbors of Israel. These oracles are directed against the nations of Ammon, Moab, Edom, and Philistia, because they gloated over the fall of Judah and helped her enemies to overthrow it. They will not escape the judgment of God.

2. Chs. 26–28. Oracles on Tyre. This great seaport island had revolted against Babylonian rule, and was about to undergo a thirteen-year siege (585-573 B.C.E.) by Nebuchadrezzar. The fate of the city was of great concern to all; would Tyre survive when Jerusalem had fallen? The prophet's charge against Tyre is essentially the same as against the other nations mentioned: rejoicing over the fall of Jerusalem.

A. Ch. 26. An oracle describing the siege and expected destruction of Tyre.

B. Ch. 27. A dirge over Tyre, described as a great merchant vessel, sinking in the sea.

C. Ch. 28. Two speeches directed against the king of Tyre for arrogating to himself the prerogatives of divinity. These poems have many obscure allusions, based ultimately upon Canaanite mythology. There is a reference to the ancient Canaanite king, Daniel (cf. ch. 14), and others to Eden, the garden of God, and the anointed cherub standing guard. In addition there is a catalogue of twelve precious stones in the garden, which curiously are the same as those which adorn the breastplate of the high priest of Israel (representing the twelve tribes).

3. Chs. 29–32. Oracles against Egypt. The judgment of God will fall also on Egypt. This nation had an evil influence on Judah from the earliest times, both as an enemy and even more so as an ally. Just as Judah fell, so will Egypt. All the oracles date from 588-586 B.C.E., from just before to just after the fall of Jerusalem, a period during which promised

help from Egypt failed to materialize, as so often in the past. There is an insertion, 29:17-21, dated to 571 B.C.E., in which the prophet promises Nebuchadrezzar victory over Egypt in lieu of the king's failure to gain much reward from the siege of Tyre (29:18). The prophet uses a series of different figures to describe Egypt and its king; all the oracles lead to the same conclusion: death and destruction. The final picture (ch. 32) finds Pharaoh and his host laid out in Sheol (the underworld) with the mighty dead empires of the past: Assyria, Elam, etc.

B. Chs. 33–39. Later Oracles

1. Ch. 33. The Prophet as Watchman. This chapter is largely a duplicate, based on 3:16-21 and ch. 18. The biographical note in vv. 30-33 is of particular interest. We learn that the prophet was a sort of matinee idol among the exiles. They came in droves to hear him speak, but they didn't pay much attention to what he said.

2. Oracles of Judgment (chs. 34–35)

    A. Ch. 34. Against the rulers of Israel. The prophet attacks them as false shepherds who, instead of feeding the sheep, feed on them. God will judge them and rescue the sheep from their clutches. The picture of the true shepherd (vv. 11-16) finds many adaptations in subsequent biblical literature.

    B. Ch. 35. Oracle against Edom. This is a bitter denunciation of the land, with a promise that judgment will be swift and total.

3. Oracles of Restoration (chs. 36–37)

    A. Ch. 36. The prophet elaborates his theology of redemption. The basis of all action is God's concern for his name (cf. ch. 20). First, he will bring back the exiles from captivity. Second, he will cleanse them of their iniquity, giving them a new heart and a new spirit. Third, he will renew the covenant between them and bless the land to which he has brought them. Finally, they will take note of their former evil ways and confess their guilt. Thus the goodness and mercy of God, not his severity, will lead them to repentance.

    B. Ch. 37. The vision of the valley of dry bones. This famous passage requires no discussion. It is instructive, however, as the first clear description of the idea of resurrection in the Bible. Here the prophet has in mind the revival of the nation. A similar idea is embedded in Isa. 53, where the resurrection of the suffering servant is described (though it is perhaps impossible to determine whether the servant is a group or an individual). The third link in the chain is

Dan. 12:2-3, where the future resurrection of the saints is explicitly taught. Here the emphasis is no longer on the life of the group as such, but on the individuals in it. The chapter closes with an idyllic description of the reunion of the kingdoms of Israel and Judah under a king of the house of David.

4. Chs. 38–39. The story of Gog of the land of Magog. Here is related the final invasion of the Holy Land by the pagan forces of evil and their annihilation in battle by God. The apocalyptic character of the account is noteworthy. The identity of Gog cannot be determined, though the name is known from ancient sources. He symbolizes the "threat from the North," repeatedly mentioned by the prophets; as such he is the ultimate enemy of Israel and of God. Daniel and Revelation also deal with the theme of the final battle, in which the God of history will vindicate his name and his actions.

C. Chs. 40–48. The New Order

1. Chs. 40–43. The new temple. It is described in considerable detail by the prophet, who follows the pattern of the temple of Solomon closely. It seems clear that the writer must have been personally acquainted with the original. The account reaches a proper culmination with the return of the glory of God, enthroned above the cherubim, to the temple.

2. Chs. 44–46. Regulations and prescriptions for the temple. Comparison of these ordinances with the corresponding legislation in the Pentateuch provides an important area of study. While the precise interrelationship is not altogether plain, it would appear that Ezekiel was familiar with the so-called Holiness Code (chs. 17–26) of the book of Leviticus. On the other hand, it appears that the Priestly compilers of the Pentateuch were acquainted with Ezekiel's work on the subject. The contents of the different codes in the Pentateuch are, of course, much older, and reflect very early practice.

3. The Topography of the New Land (chs. 47–48)

   A. Ch. 47. This chapter forms the basis of John's description of the new Jerusalem in Rev. 21–22. The river flowing out of the temple has cosmic significance and is related to the primeval life-giving freshwater ocean (mentioned in Gen. 2:6).

   B. Ch. 48. The last chapter describes the geographic distribution of the twelve tribes. The book closes with the new title of the holy city: "The Lord is there."

5. Evaluation

When we read the book of Ezekiel, we enter the world of the 6th century B.C.E. The period of the prophet is deceptively peaceful. After a generation of turmoil and struggle, diplomatic intrigue and costly battles, victory had been won, and the ancient world passed under the dominion of a mighty man of valor, Nebuchadrezzar, the king of Babylon. Only minor insurrections interrupted the long universal peace. One of the centers of trouble was Jerusalem, which was twice conquered (598 and 587 B.C.E.), the second time, destroyed. For those who lived through these disasters, times were anything but peaceful. For them it was crisis upon crisis, catastrophe compounded with cataclysm. Faced with impossible choices at every turn — to pay tribute or to rebel, to submit to Babylon or join with Egypt, to support Jehoiachin or side with Zedekiah, to believe Jeremiah and Ezekiel or any number of false prophets — each move brought them nearer the edge of doom, and finally the nation fell.

The atmosphere of tension, the sense of imminent disaster are points of contact between that age and ours. We recognize the fear, doubt, uncertainty, and despair reflected in the faces of native and exile. We know that we are one with them under the burden of constant and unrelieved crisis. But we learn something more as we watch Jerusalem go up in flames and huddle with the exiles in fearful expectancy. On this journey to the past we have a guide: the prophet. Not only does he tell us what to look at, but he explains the meaning of what we see.

It is not the usual record of victory and defeat, of trial and suffering, which with variation in detail has been the story of man from the beginning. We have analysis and forecast, an authenticated insight into the human predicament. History, according to the prophet, is not merely a series of wrestling matches between opposing forces, with a sequence of champions and challengers. God is the sovereign of time and event; the moral law is the standard by which Israel and the nations are judged. Ezekiel undertakes a threefold task in this connection: (1) to analyze Israel's past according to the principle of divine sovereignty and judgment, in order (2) to demonstrate that Israel's present calamity is the inevitable consequence of what has preceded, and (3) to forecast the course of future events on the basis of the purpose of God and the anticipated response of the exiles.

Two main points stand out in the prophet's message, which he maintained against the vigorous opposition of the leaders and the multitude. He said that Jerusalem would be destroyed; he also said that the exiles would return and that the nation would be restored. His contemporaries for the most part accepted the idea of a return, but this was while the city still stood. When the city was destroyed, they agreed that it was all over and there was no hope. The prophet's position to them was simply unbelievable; but it was based upon a profound understanding of the nature and will of God, who would bring about both events. History vindicated Ezekiel, and those who had regarded him as a musical entertainer belatedly realized

28

that a prophet had been in their midst (33:33). Jerusalem fell, as he said, and later, after his death, the exiles returned, as he had predicted.

We ought not to minimize the extraordinary insight of the prophet into the historical situation and its relationship to the will of God, or the almost miraculous foresight, whereby a pattern of events was laid out, to be followed through long afterward. At the same time it is possible to regard this prophetic power in too mechanical a fashion, as though the prophet had simply copied out the events of history present and future from a book already written. Ezekiel himself is witness against that: after predicting the destruction of Tyre at the hands of Nebuchadrezzar (chs. 26–28), he freely acknowledges that this objective was not completely achieved (29:17-20). Also, the return of the exiles in the time of Cyrus is to be taken as the historical fulfillment of Ezekiel's expectation; but the details were quite different from what the prophet envisioned. We are not speaking of the wholesale geographic and botanical changes, but of his hopes for the restitution of the Davidic dynasty and the reunion of Judah and Israel, which were never realized.

We wish to emphasize here the dynamic character of the prophet's words. He speaks out of an awareness of the mind of God. It is God's purpose to bring his exiles back from captivity; but this action is not simply going to be imposed from above. It will result from the interplay of historical forces. Cyrus, king of Persia, must act. Even though he does not know it, he is the anointed servant of God to carry out God's purpose (cf. Isa. 44:28–45:1). The Persian policy of tolerance matched God's intention perfectly at this point. But the exiles must act too. What will create in them the necessary conviction and enthusiasm to go back and start all over? A chief factor will be the words of the prophet Ezekiel. His assurance that they will go back is at the same time an exhortation to make ready for the day of return.

The Jewish community could scarcely have survived the destruction of the nation, much less have returned to start again, if it had not been for the prophets, particularly Jeremiah, Ezekiel, and 2 Isaiah. Many nations suffered destruction, and their populations were carried off. We heard nothing of a survival and a return. The false prophets in Israel had been discredited by the fall of Jerusalem; Jeremiah and Ezekiel, previously labeled as false, were vindicated by it. Now the truth of their later words on restoration could be accepted. At least there were many who believed. They built on this conviction: they held themselves together as a community under the mild policy of the Babylonians, and they waited patiently (as instructed) until the sign should come. When it came (in the form of a rescript by Cyrus), they went back. This is ample testimony to the creative power of the prophetic word.

It is not necessary to point out that the actual historical fulfillment was never quite the same as the prediction, and as a rule fell far short of the hoped-for result. This fact suggests a second aspect of the prophet's word. Its meaning is not completely exhausted by historical events. The word is not just prediction. It is also and always challenge. The return of the exiles was an extraordinary response to the words of the prophet. The rebuilding of the temple and the city illustrates the persistent power of that message. But these things were not enough. There was in the words a picture of a community better and beyond what was attained. The words acted continually as a goad and irritant. The prophets created in Israel a spiritual restlessness and dissatisfaction, a constant striving after unattainable goals, and a hopeful expectancy that God would by decisive acts fulfill his intentions for his people and the world. Thus the way was prepared for the Messiah, who would inaugurate in fact and in history the long-anticipated kingdom. Many would respond to the challenge of the king and the standards and principles of his kingdom, because they had been stirred by the prophets' message of their coming.

Is not this, after all, the purpose of this book and of the Bible: to bring us to Christ and his kingdom?

A Note on Other Literature

Since the principal object of this paper is to encourage the direct reading and study of the book of Ezekiel, rather than the investigation of the scholarly literature about it, there is no point in appending an extensive bibliography. A convenient listing of most of the significant literature is to be found in G. Fohrer, *Die Hauptprobleme des Buches Ezechiel* (Berlin: A. Topelmann, 1952), 266-82. Additional items are given in H. H. Rowley, "The Book of Ezekiel in Modern Study," *BJRL* 36 (1953): 146-90. This, the most recent article on the subject, is a splendid survey of current problems and opinions. C. G. Howie, *The Date and Composition of Ezekiel* (Philadelphia: SBL, 1950), is a product of the Baltimore School, emphasizing archaeological and linguistic evidence. An interesting discussion of the present status of the book of Ezekiel is to be found in O. Eissfeldt's chapter on "The Prophetic Literature," in *The Old Testament and Modern Study,* ed. H. H. Rowley (Oxford: Clarendon, 1951), 115-61. The most detailed commentary in English is by G. A. Cooke, *The Book of Ezekiel,* in the *International Critical Commentary,* 2 vols. (New York: Scribner's, 1937). [See now Walther Zimmerli, *Ezekiel,* 2 vols., Hermeneia series (Philadelphia: Fortress, 1979-83) and Moshe Greenberg, *Ezekiel 1–20.* AB 22 (New York: Doubleday, 1983) and *Ezekiel 21–37.* AB 22A (New York: Doubleday, 1977).] The commentary on Ezekiel in the *Interpreter's Bible,* written by H. G. May, will appear shortly. For the theological values of the book of Ezekiel, it is best to consult the older commentators, beginning with Calvin. Of particular worth are the books by A. B. Davidson (*The Book of the Prophet Ezekiel,* 2nd ed., Cambridge Bible [Cambridge: Cambridge University Press, 1916]), and J. Skinner ("The Book of Ezekiel," *Expositor's Bible* [Grand Rapids: Wm. B. Eerdmans, 1956], 4:213-350).

4

The Babylonian Chronicle

On the 2nd of Adar, in the 7th year of his reign, Nebuchadrezzar, king of Babylon, captured Jerusalem. The precise date, March 16, 597 B.C.E.,[1] which has been the subject of much debate among scholars, has now been supplied in a newly published tablet of the Babylonian Chronicle,[2] along with other fascinating details of the international power struggle in which the kingdom of Judah was caught and perished. D. J. Wiseman, Assistant Keeper in the Department of Egyptian and Assyrian Antiquities, is to be congratulated upon a splendid achievement. The Trustees of the British Museum are to be commended for bringing to completion the publication of the tablets of the Babylonian Chronicle in their possession: a process which began in 1907 with the appearance of L. W. King's *Chronicles concerning Early Babylonian Kings*.

The present volume contains all the extant tablets of the Babylonian Chronicle for the years 626-556 B.C.E., including four hitherto unpublished texts and one that had appeared previously, but is now out of print.[3] Together with the Nabonidus Chronicle, published by Sidney Smith,[4] these constitute the surviving formal record of the Neo-Babylonian Empire (626-539 B.C.E.). As such, and in spite of several sizable gaps, they are of great interest and importance.[5]

The tablets presumably were copied during the Persian period from older documents, which were compiled from the official annals (i.e., detailed yearly

1. The Babylonian like the biblical "day" extended from sundown to sundown, thus overlapping two of our days. In transferring dates to the Julian calendar, it would be more accurate to give two successive days: thus, 2 Adar 7 Nebuchadrezzar = 15/16 March 597 B.C.E.

2. D. J. Wiseman, *Chronicles of Chaldaean Kings (626-566 B.C.) in the British Museum* (London: British Museum, 1956), xii, 100, and XXI plates. [See now A. K. Grayson, *Assyrian and Babylonian Chronicles* (Locust Valley, N.Y.: J. J. Augustin, 1975), Chronicles 2-6.]

3. C. J. Gadd, *The Fall of Nineveh* (London: British Museum, 1923).

4. *Babylonian Historical Texts* (London: Methuen, 1924).

5. The gaps are for the years 622-617, 594-557, and 556-555.

records) of the Babylonian kings. They constitute a summary but most trustworthy source for the reconstruction of the historical era which they describe.[6]

B.M. 25127

The first tablet of the Chronicle covers the years 626-623 B.C.E. and describes the beginnings of the new Babylonian kingdom. As the text opens, Nabopolassar, the leader of the insurgent Babylonian forces, has defeated the Assyrian army outside the gates of Babylon. To celebrate their independence, the Babylonians enthroned Nabopolassar as their king on 23 November 626 (a new fixed date in Babylonian history). While the Assyrian Empire was disintegrating in the east, there were dangerous stirrings in the west also. Egypt, long since free of Assyrian suzerainty, was scheming to recover its long-lost Asiatic provinces.[7] Even Judah, doubtless spurred by reports of Assyrian confusion and defeat, was preparing for its day of freedom. Already Josiah had moved into effective control of the northern provinces, though still nominally a vassal of Assyria.[8]

During the following years, the Assyrians made unsuccessful attempts to regain control of Babylonia. Nabopolassar, on the other hand, was not yet strong enough to go on the offensive. The Chronicle for the years 622-617 is missing.

B.M. 21901

This tablet, already published by C. J. Gadd in 1923, now reedited by Wiseman, deals with the events of 616-608. The Medes have now made their appearance as leaders of the anti-Assyrian coalition; the Egyptians, on the other hand, have joined forces with the weakened Assyrians, to offset the overwhelming threat of the Medo-Babylonian alliance. In 614, the Medes under Kyaxares their king, captured

6. There is an interesting parallel between the Babylonian Chronicle and the two "Israelite Chronicles": the so-called Deuteronomic History comprising the books from Deuteronomy through 2 Kings, was compiled at the end of Judah's independent existence from a number of sources including the Annals of the Kings of Israel and Judah; the Chronicler's History (1 & 2 Chronicles, Ezra, Nehemiah) is a similar compilation made about two hundred years later from a variety of records including the Deuteronomic History.

7. Paradoxically the Egyptians were to fight as allies of the Assyrians, their age-old enemies, against the greater threat of the Medo-Babylonian alliance.

8. Extensive operations occurred in Josiah's 12th year (*ca.* 628/27), in anticipation of the final break with Assyrian authority in the 18th year (622): cf. 2 Chr. 34:3-7. F. M. Cross, Jr., and David Noel Freedman, "Josiah's Revolt against Assyria," *JNES* 12 (1953): 56-58.

the ancient Assyrian capital, Assur; Nabopolassar arrived with his forces after the fall of the city. There the two kings met, concluded a treaty of mutual assistance, and departed. With the Medes leading the way, the allies attacked Nineveh in 612. After three months of siege, the city was captured and destroyed. The masters of siege operations had been mastered.[9] While Medes and Babylonians divided the spoils, fragments of the Assyrian army and bureaucracy fled to Harran, where under Assur-uballit II an attempt was made to reconstitute the kingdom. In spite of extensive Egyptian help, the attempt proved unavailing. Assur-uballit had to abandon Harran in 610; a combined attack on the Babylonian garrison there in 609 failed. To what extent Josiah's interposition at Megiddo in 609 delayed or diverted the main forces of Pharaoh Neco from their rendezvous with the Assyrian army in that year at the Euphrates is difficult to determine. But it may be that the suicidal Judahite action contributed materially to the triumph of Medo-Babylonian arms.[10] In any case, the Assyrians disappeared from the picture, their position in North Syria being taken by the Egyptians.

B.M. 22047

The events leading up to the historic battle of Carchemish (605) are described in the next tablet, newly published B.M. 22047. During this period, the Babylonian armies — Nabopolassar and Nebuchadrezzar the crown prince had separate commands — campaigned against the mountain people on the Urartian border, to prevent raids on the former Assyrian provinces. They also reconnoitered against the Egyptians, who were firmly entrenched at Carchemish on the Euphrates. Efforts to contain the Egyptian army by garrisoning towns below Carchemish in the years 607-606 were frustrated by strong Egyptian thrusts at Kimukhu and Quramati, both of which were captured. Nabopolassar returned to Babylon at the end of the year 606/5 (= January-February 605); he did not again leave the capital, until his death in August.

9. A vivid description of the anticipated fall of the city which had dominated the world for centuries is found in the book of Nahum. The end of the ancient oppressor was greeted with universal rejoicing; cf. Nah. 3:7, 19.

10. The biblical accounts of the affair at Megiddo (2 Kgs. 23:29-30; 2 Chr. 35:20-24) make it clear that Pharaoh Neco had urgent business with the Assyrians at the Euphrates and did not wish to be delayed by the Judahites. Although the Kings account implies that Neco's intentions were hostile toward the Assyrian king, we know from the Babylonian Chronicle that Neco was coming as an ally. It is reasonable to conclude that Josiah was an ally (or vassal) of the Babylonians and that his action at Megiddo was part of a concerted plan to pin down the Egyptian forces while the Medo-Babylonian army disposed of the Assyrians. There was a long-standing tradition of friendship between Babylonians and Judahites, going back at least to the days of Merodach-Baladan and Hezekiah, who schemed together against Assyria (cf. 2 Kgs. 20:12ff.) just as their successors were to do a hundred years later.

B.M. 21946

The next tablet in the series covers the important years 605-594. It opens with the battle of Carchemish. Nebuchadrezzar, now in sole command of the Babylonian army, marched swiftly to Carchemish where he engaged the Egyptian forces directly. The Chronicle goes on to say: "He (Nebuchadrezzar) accomplished their defeat and to nonexistence [beat?] them. As for the rest of the Egyptian army, which had escaped from the defeat (so quickly that) no weapon had reached them, in the district of Hamath the Babylonian troops overtook and defeated them so that not a single man escaped to his own country. At that time Nebuchadrezzar conquered the whole area of the Hatti-country (i.e., Syria-Palestine)."[11]

Important for determining synchronisms between Babylonian and Judahite history and establishing the absolute chronology of this period is the date of the battle of Carchemish. While the precise date is not given, the battle must have taken place after April (= Nisan, the beginning of the regnal year) and before August (= Ab), when Nabopolassar died and Nebuchadrezzar had to return to Babylon. According to Wiseman's calculations, May-June 605 is the most probable date for the battle.[12] Jer. 46:2 provides a synchronism with Judahite history, dating the battle of Carchemish to the 4th year of Jehoiakim. This in turn fixes the year 609/8 for the commencement of Jehoiakim's reign, as well as for the death of Josiah, and the three-month rule of Jehoahaz (cf. 2 Kgs. 23:31-34).[13] Having been placed on the throne by Pharaoh Neco, Jehoiakim served him as vassal for four years. As a result of Nebuchadrezzar's victory over Neco, Jehoiakim transferred his allegiance (cf. 2 Kgs. 24:1).[14]

11. B.M. 21946 obv., ll. 5-8, following Wiseman's translation, 66-69. Both the Bible and Josephus refer to the battle and its important consequences for the history of the Near East; cf. Jer. 46:2ff. and *Antiquities,* x.6. Noteworthy is the striking agreement between Josephus and the Babylonian Chronicle (cf. Wiseman, 24f.).

12. Wiseman, 25.

13. It is most probable that regnal years were reckoned in Judah at this time in accordance with the Assyro-Babylonian "post-dating" system. According to this method the period between the king's actual accession and the beginning of the next calendar year (in April) was called the "accession year." The first "regnal year" began with the New Year's Festival. Thus Nebuchadrezzar was enthroned on 6 Sept. 605. His "accession year" extended until April 604, when his "first year" began. So also Jehoiakim's *4th* year commenced in April 605, the year of Carchemish. His first regnal year began in April 608, and his "accession year" from his actual enthronement in 609/8 until April 608. Josiah's last year began in April 609; he was killed at Megiddo, probably during the summer months. To this we must add the three months of Jehoahaz, and arrive at a date late in 609, or possibly early in 608, for the actual accession of Jehoiakim.

14. The occasion of Jehoiakim's submission to Nebuchadrezzar was probably the triumphal sweep through Hatti-land in 604/3: "In the first year of Nebuchadrezzar in the month of Sivan he mustered his army and went to the Hatti-territory; he marched about in the Hatti-territory until the month of Kislev. All the kings of the Hatti-land came before him and he received their heavy tribute" (B.M. 21946 obv., ll. 15-17; Wiseman, 69).

Nabopolassar died on 16 August 605. On receiving the news, Nebuchadrezzar hurried back to Babylon to be crowned king on 7 September 605. From then until the following April is designated his "accession year." Then in April 604, during the *akitu* or New Year's Festival, the official "first year" of his reign began.[15] During the early years of his reign, Nebuchadrezzar's chief military activity, according to the Chronicle, was to pacify the newly acquired western territories. Most of the time it was sufficient to parade the Babylonian army through Hatti-land in order to collect the annual tribute. Occasionally punitive action was required, as in the case of a city, probably Ashkelon, toward the end of 604.[16] Then in December 601, Nebuchadrezzar marched against Egypt. A fierce battle ensued, with heavy casualties on both sides. Neither place nor date is given, but the battle must have occurred near the Egyptian border between December 601 and April 600, the beginning of Nebuchadrezzar's fifth regnal year. Jehoiakim's rebellion against Babylon is related to this event, since the three-year period of submission ended in 601/600 (cf. 2 Kgs. 24:1). In all likelihood the act of rebellion was an independent move following the Babylonian defeat (though there is always the possibility of Egyptian encouragement).[17]

The Babylonian army suffered such serious losses that Nebuchadrezzar returned home immediately and spent the whole of the following year in reorganizing his military forces. Not until December 599 did he set forth to the west again. The Egyptians must have suffered badly also, because they made no overt move to establish themselves in Syria-Palestine. While the great powers were licking their wounds, Jehoiakim and Judah enjoyed freedom briefly. Nebuchadrezzar, however, countered the rebellion by enlisting the help of Judah's neighbors.[18] These measures proved insufficient, so Nebuchadrezzar led the main Babylonian force against Judah in December 598.

---

15. Cf. n. 13.

16. An Aramaic letter dating from this period contains a plea to the pharaoh for help against the Babylonians; it may reflect the same situation described in the Chronicle. For a brief account of this letter, cf. John Bright, *BA* 12 (1949): 46-52.

17. Jehoiakim, whatever intrigues with Egypt may have been under way, would have made no overt action until after the defeat of Nebuchadrezzar. Nebuchadrezzar would not have undertaken an invasion of Egypt unless the Judahite flank were secure. If Jehoiakim had been in open rebellion, Nebuchadrezzar would first have crushed resistance in Judah before attacking Egypt.

18. 2 Kgs. 24:2. Arameans, Moabites, Ammonites are mentioned along with Chaldean garrisons as the attackers. If this took place in 600/599, it would fit well with the Chronicle's statement that Nebuchadrezzar remained in Babylon with the main army during his 5th year. On the other hand, the guerilla action may have followed the campaign of 599/8 in which Nebuchadrezzar subjugated the Arab tribes of the west. On his return to Babylon in March 598 he may have left Babylonian garrisons behind to cope with the Judahite rebellion, aided by such native levies as could be mustered.

The Capture of Jerusalem

The siege and capture of Jerusalem are described as follows: "In the seventh year, the month of Kislev, the king of Akkad mustered his troops, marched to the Hatti-land, and encamped against the city of Judah and on the second day of the month of Adar he seized the city and captured the king. He appointed there a king of his own choice (lit. heart), received its heavy tribute and sent (them) to Baby-lon."[19] There can be no doubt that the captured king was Jehoiachin, while the appointed one was Zedekiah. We thus have a fixed date not only for the capture of Jerusalem, but also for the chronology of the last kings of Judah: 2 Adar 7 Nebuchadrezzar = 15/16 March 597 B.C.E.[20] Jehoiachin's brief reign of three months ended on 16 March 597.[21] His accession is to be dated in December 598, which also marks the death of Jehoiakim.[22] The latter's official regnal years include 608-598, with his accession in the year 609/8.[23]

Computing in the other direction, the end of Jehoiachin's reign also marks the beginning of Zedekiah's rule.[24] Zedekiah's first regnal year began the following month, April 597. His eleventh and final year began therefore in April 587; his reign terminated with his capture just before the destruction of Jerusalem, in July of the same year.[25] The new chronological information may be conveniently incor-porated into a table of the last kings of Judah:

---

19. B.M. 21946 rev., ll. 11-13, following Wiseman's translation, 73.

20. A long-standing debate among scholars concerning the chronology of the last years of Judah may now be settled. Many have favored the sequence 597 for the capture of Jerusalem and 586 for its destruction; others, 598 for the capture and 587 for the destruction. It is to be remembered that these figures are only approximate, since the Babylonian (and Judahite) year extends from April to April, thus overlapping two of the modern (Julian) years. Properly speaking, the patterns mentioned should be set down as 597/6 (8th of Nebuchadrezzar) and 586/5 (19th of Nebuchadrezzar), or 598/7 (7th of Nebuchadrezzar) and 587/6 (18th of Nebuchadrezzar). The Chronicle now establishes the first date (March 597) in the 7th of Nebuchadrezzar: therefore the second date is in the 18th of Nebuchadrezzar (July-August 587). The first sequence proposed is wrong, while the second is confirmed.

21. 2 Kgs. 24:8. 2 Chr. 36:9 gives three months and ten days, which may be a more accurate figure.

22. He died in the same month that the Babylonian army set out against Judah (see above). The exact manner of Jehoiakim's death remains a mystery. It is difficult to reconcile the accounts in Kings, Chronicles, Josephus (cf. Jer. 22:18-19). The Chronicle shows that he died before the siege began, supporting the statement in 2 Kgs. 24:6 (cf. vv. 10ff.).

23. Cf. n. 13. Jehoiakim reigned 11 years (2 Kgs. 23:36). His first regnal year began in April 608, his 11th and last in April 598.

24. Zedekiah's accession must have taken place in the same month, March 597 (the last of the year), since the Babylonian Chronicle records the event in the 7th year of Nebuchadrezzar.

25. 2 Kgs. 25:2-7 = Jer. 52:5-11.

King	Length of Reign[26]	Accession[27]	Regnal Years[28]	End of Reign
Josiah	31	640/39	639-609	609
Jehoahaz	3 months	609	—	609/8
Jehoiakim	11	609/8	608-598	Dec. 598
Jehoiachin	3 months	Dec. 598	—	March 597
Zedekiah	11	March 597	597-587	July 587

The following synchronisms between the kings of Babylon and Judah can also be established:

> Battle of Carchemish (May-June 605): 4th of Jehoiakim = 21st of Nabopolassar.
> Capture of Jerusalem (March 597): 11th of Jehoiakim = 7th of Nebuchadrezzar.
> Fall of Judah (July 587): 11th of Zedekiah = 18th of Nebuchadrezzar.

The synchronisms with the 7th and 18th years of Nebuchadrezzar agree with certain biblical references, but disagree with others. It is difficult to explain the discrepancy. On the one hand, Jer. 52:28-29 dates the first captivity in the 7th year of Nebuchadrezzar and the second in the 18th year.[29] On the other hand, 2 Kgs. 24:12 places the first captivity in the *8th* year of Nebuchadrezzar; and 2 Kgs. 25:8 dates the second in the *19th* year.[30]

Various suggestions have been made with regard to the discrepancies. In view of the statement in 2 Chr. 36:10 that Jehoiachin was brought to Babylon at "the turn of the year," Wiseman infers that there was some delay in rounding up the

26. In calculating the reign of a king, the biblical historian added the number of regnal years (i.e., full years beginning with the first of the new calendar year, plus the final partial year; the accession year was considered part of the previous king's reign in the numerical computation). Different procedures were followed at earlier periods in Israel's history.

27. The "accession year" includes the portion of the year remaining after the death of the reigning king and before the beginning of the next year in April. Thus Josiah's 31st year began in April 609; on his death, Jehoahaz succeeded to the throne. The latter's accession year is therefore the remaining months of 609/8 until the beginning of the new year in April 608. Jehoahaz, however, failed to finish his accession year, being deposed after three months. The remaining months to April 608 then constitute Jehoiakim's accession year; his first regnal year commences in April 608.

28. Regnal years are calculated from the beginning of the year following the accession of the king. Since neither Jehoahaz nor Jehoiachin reigned long enough to reach April of the year following their accession, they are not credited with any regnal years. Zedekiah, on the other hand, whose actual reign can be fixed at ten years and four months, is credited with eleven regnal years, the final partial year being added to his total.

29. We may infer from the documentary character of this excerpt (contrast the precise figures for the number of captives with the round numbers of the account in Kings) that it was copied from an official record kept in Babylon and which therefore followed Babylonian chronology accurately. A third captivity five years later is presumably to be connected with the punitive expedition sent to Judah after the assassination of Gedaliah (cf. 2 Kgs. 25:22-26 and Jer. 40–41).

30. Also Jer. 52:12; other references in Jeremiah follow the same chronology.

captives so that the exile did not actually begin until after the end of the 7th year and the start of the 8th year of Nebuchadrezzar. Thus the capture of Jerusalem is to be dated in the 7th year, but the captivity in the 8th.[31] This procedure, however, only accentuates the discrepancy, since Jer. 52:28-29 dates the *captivity* in the *7th* year, while 2 Kgs. 24:12 dates the *capture of Jerusalem* in the *8th* year. While it may be granted that the larger number of exiles did not arrive in Babylon until the 8th year, it is altogether probable that Nebuchadrezzar and the chief captives reached Babylon in time for the New Year's Festival.[32] Since the events described took place at the turn of the year, they might with some propriety be assigned to the 8th year, though strictly speaking 7th is correct. The difference is not great, only a month in fact, and may explain how this discrepancy arose. In the case of the second captivity, however, the Bible specifies a month in the middle of the year; so the discrepancy here is a full year (i.e., July-August 587 or 586).

A second suggestion explains the discrepancy as the result of a difference in methods of reckoning. The two principal methods used for calculating reigns were the post-dating (which has already been explained), and the ante-dating. According to the post-dating method used in Babylon, Nebuchadrezzar's first regnal year began in April 604, on the completion of his accession year. His 7th year began in April 598 and ended in March 597. According to the ante-dating system, however, the accession year was reckoned as the first regnal year, so that each succeeding year of the reign is assigned a number one higher than is accorded it by the post-dating method. Thus Nebuchadrezzar's first regnal year (official post-dating system) is equivalent to the second year (ante-dating system) though the calendar year is the same, 604/3. The year 598/7 is Nebuchadrezzar's 7th (post-dating) or 8th (ante-dating); his 18th (post-dating) is equivalent to the 19th (ante-dating), but in either case it is April 587–March 586. In short, there is no discrepancy in the biblical figures; the difference is simply due to variant methods of calculation. If there were any positive evidence that the ante-dating method was in use in Palestine at this time, the proposal would make the most satisfactory solution. We know, however, that the post-dating method was official in Babylon, and it appears certain that the same method was used in Judah for reckoning regnal years. It would therefore be quite strange if the regnal years of a king of Babylon were recorded by a Judahite historian according to the *ante-dating* system.

A third suggestion follows the main lines of the second in equating the two patterns of dates. However, the assumption of an ante-dating system is rejected as improbable, and a different explanation for the pattern 8th and 19th of Nebucha-

31. Cf. Wiseman, 34.

32. It was the regular practice of the Babylonian king to return to his own land before the end of the year, as repeated entries in the Chronicle show. Note the references for the early years of Nebuchadrezzar: for the years 1, 3, 4, 6, and 8 his return to Babylon, generally in the last months, is specified; in 2 the lines are missing, and in 5 he remained in Babylon all year.

drezzar is sought.[33] It is possible that the Palestinian historian, without using an ante-dating system, nevertheless reckoned Nebuchadrezzar's reign from the year 605 rather than the official 604. By 605, Nabopolassar was no longer active in the field. At the Battle of Carchemish, Nebuchadrezzar was in sole command of the Babylonian army, and may well have been recognized in the west as *de facto* king.[34] For the Judahite historian then, Nebuchadrezzar's first regnal year would have been 605/4, equivalent to the accession year of the official chronicle. The other equations would follow as in the previous hypothesis.[35]

The merit of suggestions two and three is that they deal not only with the negligible difference of a month with respect to the first captivity, but with the more serious disagreement of a full year in connection with the second. They also take into account all of the relevant data, biblical and nonbiblical. It is not always possible to reconcile divergent biblical data; at the same time a discrepancy of a single year in the chronology of events which occurred more than two-and-a-half millennia ago is rather a tribute to the accuracy of the biblical editors and scribes. It is to the credit of modern biblical and Near Eastern scholars that they are able to pin down chronological data of such antiquity with precision, and that a slight discrepancy can be the subject of serious debate.

The Last Years of Judah

After the account of the 7th year, the remaining entries on this tablet are brief and fragmentary. Of interest is the notice of the 10th year (595/4), when Nebuchadrezzar remained in Babylon to deal with a local rebellion. It was quickly suppressed, and all was apparently peaceful when the king set out on his annual tribute-collecting journey to the west. Nevertheless, news of the insurrection must have traveled quickly; in spite of the revolt's failure, it must have added to the false hopes for an early collapse of the Babylonian kingdom. Within the year, Hananiah the prophet openly announced that God had broken the yoke of the king of Babylon, and that

33. This suggestion comes from Professor W. F. Albright. I am grateful to him also for many valuable comments on the Wiseman publication.

34. Jer. 46:2 may reflect this point of view: ". . . Concerning the army of Pharaoh Neco, king of Egypt, which was by the river Euphrates at Carchemish, which Nebuchadrezzar, *king of Babylon,* defeated in the fourth year of Jehoiakim. . . ." Styling Nebuchadrezzar as king of Babylon may not be merely a minor anachronism.

35. We must also reckon with the possibility of a numerical error in the calculations of the Deuteronomic editor. As previously suggested, the source of the error may lie in the fact that the first capture of Jerusalem took place at the *end* of the 7th year. Then the second figure was erroneously calculated from the 8th year, instead of the 7th, and the 19th was arrived at, whereas 18th was correct.

within two more years the exiles would return and Jehoiachin be restored as king of the land.[36] With patriotic zeal whipped up by the false prophets both in Judah and in exile, there was also a good deal of undercover activity on the part of the Jews. Diplomatic intrigue with Egypt and the smaller nations of the west was the order of the day in Judah;[37] the Jews in Bablyon undoubtedly provided information about Nebuchadrezzar's difficulties at home, and may even have had direct connection with the Babylonian plotters against the king. By putting together various data — the unavailing struggle of prophets like Jeremiah and Ezekiel to keep their people from revolting against the authority of Babylon; the continuing power and influence of Egypt in Asiatic affairs, even after the defeat at Carchemish; the Babylonian insurrection against Nebuchadrezzar — we can better appreciate the extent and depth of anti-Babylonian activity throughout the empire and the rather substantial basis for the hopes of independence and restoration which appear repeatedly in the biblical record of this period. We may also understand more fully the formidable odds against which the prophets Jeremiah and Ezekiel had to contend in trying to persuade their people to be submissive to Nebuchadrezzar.[38] In the long run the prophets failed; Judah rebelled. But in its overwhelming defeat the prophets and their message were vindicated.

B.M. 25124

After tablet 21946, which ends with a notice of the 11th year of Nebuchadrezzar, there is a large gap in the series, extending from 594/3 down to the third year of Neriglissar (557/6). The events of this year are described in a new tablet, B.M. 25124. It records Neriglissar's campaign against Appuashu, king of Pirundu (West Cilicia), who had invaded Hume (East Cilicia), territory under the protection of the Babylonians. The campaign was successful, and is described at greater length than is usual in the Babylonian Chronicle. The tablet, however, does not have the dramatic contact with biblical events which is the case with

36. Hananiah's speech (Jer. 28:1ff.) is dated in the 4th year of Zedekiah (594/3).

37. The roster in Jer. 27:2ff. shows that most of the western vassals were involved in negotiations with the Judahite king. Contacts with Egypt are frequently mentioned. An Egyptian army did come to the aid of Judah during the final siege of Jerusalem (cf. Jer. 37:11; 34:21).

38. It is noteworthy that the prophets emphasize moral obligations in urging the king of Judah to keep his covenant with the king of Babylon, rather than realistic military and political considerations. It appears now that these latter may have favored the rebels. The picture is no longer that of a tiny, decimated group in isolated revolt against a monolithic, all-powerful empire. Rather, the empire seems less than solid; Judah is in league with many dissident groups within the empire; and there is a strong enemy without, Egypt, ready to mix in at any time. Choosing between true and false prophets was not an easy task.

the previous ones in the series. There is no reference to the people of Judah either in Palestine or Babylon.

Conclusion

The four new tablets of the British Museum, together with others previously published, provide a fairly continuous account of the Neo-Babylonian Empire from its inception in 626 B.C.E. to the 11th year of Nebuchadrezzar (594/3). After a gap of thirty-seven years, the final phase from the 3rd of Neriglissar to the fall of Babylon (539) is also available on tablets.[39] A number of new facts are presented, as well as more precise chronological data for the history of this epoch. While we could wish for more details and background information in the chronicler's terse reports — and the gaps, large and small, are especially frustrating[40] — nevertheless we have vivid glimpses of the empire, and general impressions of its structure and strength. It displaced Assyria as the imperial power in the Near East. Since its northeastern flank was protected by treaty with the powerful Medes, Nabopolassar and Nebuchadrezzar were able to devote their chief attention to the western regions and the ancient foe, Egypt. While Carchemish was a decisive victory, and the Egyptians were driven out of Asia for good, it was not conclusive. Behind their own borders, the Egyptians remained dangerous; and they could stir up trouble in Palestine and Syria. They were able to inflict grievous damage on the Babylonians (601; a hitherto unreported battle). During the early years of Nebuchadrezzar's reign, an uneasy balance between the rival kingdoms was maintained: Babylon ascendant, but Egypt strong and active. The critical predicament of Judah, caught between them, is more easily appreciated in the light of the new material. Political realism and the false prophets might advocate alliance with the closer power, Egypt, especially after the success in 601 against Nebuchadrezzar, but the true prophets were not primarily concerned with military prowess. They saw in Nebuchadrezzar the chosen servant of God, through whom the divine purpose for Israel and the world was to be accomplished. They held fast to their position regardless of the setbacks which the Babylonians experienced.

The tablets also reveal that all was not peace and quiet within the Babylonian Empire. Nebuchadrezzar had the usual troubles with vassal states, i.e., tribute was not always delivered in full or on time. So he had to parade his army regularly through the Hatti-land to intimidate the subject peoples; and on some occasions he

39. Cf. the Nabonidus Chronicle for the years 555-539, B.M. 35382 published in Smith, 98-123 [= Grayson, *Assyrian and Babylonian Chronicles,* Chronicle 7, 104ff.].

40. E.g., an account of the destruction of Jerusalem and the second captivity would be especially desirable.

had to resort to force. There was also difficulty at home: e.g., the hasty trip back to Babylon to claim the throne upon the death of his father, and the reported rebellion of the 10th year.

The historical information in the tablets fills out the picture of Judah's last years. The chronological data are of immediate value for fixing specific dates in biblical history. The two key dates are the Battle of Carchemish (May-June 605) and the Capture of Jerusalem (16 March 597). From these the regnal years of the last kings of Judah and the date of the destruction of Jerusalem can be calculated with a high degree of probability.[41]

41. See the chronological table above.

5

The Unity of the Bible

The unity of the Bible is one of the most important and most significant issues confronting the Christian Church today. It is more than the academic problem of simply setting the Old and New Testaments side by side and applying certain tests, literary, historical, or theological, to see whether or not they are made of the same stuff.

The unity of the Bible, together with the authority of the Bible, is one of the two cardinal axioms from which the main propositions of the Christian religion are drawn, and from which its chief proclamation goes forth. Without these axioms, there is no Christian faith, at least not in its full classical sense.

The Church did not write the Bible, nor does it confer authority upon it, but it does acknowledge the indissoluble unity of the Old and New Testaments. In this sense, the Church created the Bible, the Bible of Old and New Testaments.

Perhaps we should put it more realistically and historically: the Church has maintained that the events and the persons described in the New Testament belong organically and dynamically with the Old Testament record.

The Church has accepted the Old Testament as given — the legacy of Moses and the prophets, the common heritage of Jews and Christians. Then, beginning with the New Testament itself, the Church has tried to show that Jesus and the apostles are the successors of Moses and the prophets, and that the New Testament so fulfills the Old that the Church can rightly claim for the New Testament the same divine authority which it accords the Old.

Judaism has consistently denied this affirmation; and from the very first the position of the Church has been to present, explain, and defend its view of the unity of the Bible: its YES in opposition to the Synagogue's NO.

At the same time, early in its history the Church rejected the view of some of its own adherents who accepted the New Testament as authoritative but ignored the Old Testament and denied its authority. Marcion, for example, the arch-heretic of the 2nd century, dispensed with the Old Testament entirely. He asserted that the

43

God who was the father of our Lord Jesus Christ could not possibly be the vengeful tribal deity of the Old Testament.

A similar attitude, sometimes more politely expressed, has characterized Christian thinking about the Bible in different eras and places. What is involved is an attempt to repudiate the Old Testament and supplant it by the New.

The Church has never officially accepted this position because it could never officially accept it. The New Testament is built upon the Old, and presupposes and requires the Old. Moreover, the New Testament quotes or alludes to the Old on every page, so that to drop the Old Testament entirely would mean cutting out large sections of the New.

Hence the Christian is caught inescapably in the web of both Testaments and must defend their unity as a specifically Christian idea enshrined in the millions of Bibles that exist in the world.

What do we mean when we speak of the unity of the Bible? And how do we approach the subject?

There are three qualities or aspects to be discussed in defining the unity of the Bible. The first is *continuity,* dynamic continuity. There must be some organic relationship between what follows and what precedes. Only that literature which carries on the revelation of God in the Old Testament can claim unity with it. The New Testament not only makes this claim, but also provides much evidence to substantiate it.

Continuity alone, however, is not enough. There must be *newness,* an element of originality and change. Without this, the addition would be unnecessary. It would not be part of the divine Word unless it were different from the Word already spoken.

The Old Testament itself exhibits such a pattern of continuity and change. The initial actions of God and his revelation in history form the basis for later prophetic reflection and evaluation that become part of a new revelation that in turn affects the history of the holy community. Out of all of these events arises a new situation in which a further action of God takes place. Continuity and change thus unite the two Testaments.

Third, there must be *finality.* Unity implies totality, wholeness. With the New Testament the story of the Old Testament ends. Thus biblical unity involves not only continuity and change but completion. The New Testament is the fulfilling factor making the Bible a unity and a totality. For the Church in spite of many serious efforts has never been able to add to or subtract from this Scripture.

These, then, are the factors in the case presented by the New Testament for organic unity with the Old.

Now let us describe the framework in which the unity of the Bible, which is the unity of the Old and New Testaments, appears.

44

The focal point around which both Testaments revolve is the *God of the Bible,* and a God uniquely different from all other gods, known only in a decisive way through his revelation recorded in the Bible. There is unity between the Testaments in this God because the God of the Old Testament is the God of the New.

The Old Testament attributes to God those same qualities of justice and mercy, love and kindness, devotion and forgiveness, that are attributed to God by the New Testament (cf. Exod. 34:6, 7).

Moreover, the purpose of God to establish his Kingdom on earth is the common message of both Testaments. That God has created the world good, and placed men in it so that men might fulfill the potentialities of their lives and live in harmony on the face of the earth, and further, that God has dedicated himself with all his power and all his love to the realization of this objective — these are essential parts of the message of the whole Bible.

There are differences, nevertheless, between the Testaments. Perhaps the most significant is to be found in the statement that the God who revealed himself to the patriarchs, to Moses, to the prophets has revealed himself in the person of Jesus Christ: i.e., the Word which *came to* the prophets *became* Jesus Christ. The distinctive Christian view is expressed in the doctrine of the Incarnation, or of the Trinity.

Still, there are antecedents in the Old Testament for a trinitarian position, and also for a type of incarnation. The Father, Son, and Holy Spirit of New Testament teaching correspond to the Old Testament's God, his Word, and his Spirit, the essential difference being that in the New Testament the Word of God has been sent into the world to become a man. But even in the Old Testament the Word has personal qualities and serves as the creative, active agent of God (cf. Isa. 55:10, 11). It is an important but not inconsistent step to the personality of the Word in the New.

The Christian conviction that God became man in Christ likewise has its background in the Old Testament stories of God's self-revelation to men. When God appears to Abraham, or wrestles with Jacob, or speaks with Moses, it is as man to men (cf. Gen. 18:16-33; 32:22-30; Exod. 33:7-11). He manifests himself as his Angel, in human form. God also is bound in personal union with his servants, Moses and the prophets. Through his Word and Spirit, he speaks and acts in their lives so that these men are, in a sense, extensions of his divine personality.

In the New Testament story of the life and death of Christ the identification of God with men and his involvement in human experience are shown to be completed. There is no agony of suffering or humiliation which God is spared, not even death upon a cross. For this amazing ordeal we find no adequate parallel in the Old Testament; there are only hints in the ritual of the scapegoat (Lev. 16) and the account of the Suffering Servant (Isa. 53). In Old and New Testaments there is the difference between partial and temporary, and total and permanent identification of God with humankind.

Belonging also to the framework of Old and New Testaments is the idea of *community,* the community of faith. In the Old Testament the community is called Israel — the descendants of Abraham; in the New Testament it is called the Church, and also Israel — the children of Abraham. It is the same community in organic continuity. Paul describes that continuity in terms of the grafting of a wild branch, the Church, to the trunk of the old tree, Israel.

Usually, the distinction is made between old Israel as an essentially racial or ethnic community limited to the territory of Palestine and the Church as neither racial nor ethnic in character but extensive throughout the world. Israel, it is said, was a nation, a political commonwealth, while the Church is a spiritual kingdom.

No one would deny that there are differences between Israel and the Church. Organic unity involves change. But major items of continuity and identity ought not to be overlooked.

The fact is that from the first Israel is a community of faith not restricted to one racial group. It is an elect community whose members are chosen and invited by God, and who enter it when they respond in faith. Abraham, the great example of faith, was the founder of this community; and they are properly his children and members of the community who make the same commitment to God.

In the exodus and wilderness wanderings the community of faith consisted of those who obeyed the summons of God. Around the nucleus of the children of Jacob and Abraham many other groups gathered: Kenites, Kenizzites, Egyptians, Nubians, and others. The Bible itself calls the desert wanderers a mixed multitude and a congeries of peoples. In the light of the heterogeneous origins of Israel, any notion that the holy community was ethnically or racially pure is absurd!

Throughout its history, this community of faith has been open to those of any nation who were willing to profess the faith of Abraham, commit themselves to the God of Israel, and assume the burdens of covenant obligation. The stories of pagan converts like Ruth, Naaman, and others are sufficient to establish this truth for the Old Testament.

Inevitably the exigencies of national life prevented any large-scale extension of the holy community beyond the borders of Israel. But potentially, and in ultimate expectation, the community of God embraced all the peoples of the world. The only difference between the Old and New Testaments is that what was anticipated in the Old became actual in the New.

We may conclude the discussion of the framework of biblical unity with the *Covenant,* the bond between God and his community.

The titles of the two major divisions of the Bible ought to be rendered "Old Covenant" and "New Covenant," instead of Old and New Testaments, for both describe an agreement between God and his people. "Covenant" is the common word expressing the element of continuity between them, while *Old* and *New* express the difference.

46

The difference is not as sharp as the words *Old* and *New* imply. The words arise out of the disastrous consequences of Israel's violation of its obligations to God whereby the covenant made at Sinai was abrogated: the restoration of harmonious relations between God and his people required the ratification of a new covenant. We might better speak, therefore, of "original" and "restored" covenant, or "first" and "renewed" covenant.

Nor must the distinction commonly made between the Old Covenant as a "covenant of works" and the New as a "covenant of grace" be pressed too far.

The Old Covenant of works is described as a conditional arrangement. If the people obeyed, then all would be well; the covenant would remain in force, and material rewards would be heaped upon an obedient people. If the people failed to keep the terms of the covenant, then swift judgment would come upon them.

The New Covenant of grace, on the other hand, is described as a commitment on God's part based solely on his loyalty and love. Such a covenant involves no obligations, threatens no punishment. It is a gift to be received, not a reward to be earned.

While there is an important element of truth in equating the Old Testament with the covenant of works and the New Testament with the covenant of grace, it has had an unfortunate effect. It has made God in the Old Testament look as though he were motivated solely by considerations of strict retributive justice and dealt out rewards and punishments according to the behavior of his people, whereas in the New Testament he scraps the principles of justice in the interests of a compassionate affection for all, indifferent to moral demands.

Neither of these views, however, does justice to the profound understanding of divine-human relationships in both Old and New Testaments. The essential elements in the covenants of works and grace are present in both parts of the Bible. Love and justice are inseparable terms in describing the bond between God and his people.

Investigations in the business documents and diplomatic treaties of the ancient Near East have produced a mass of information which sheds light upon the contemporary biblical contracts. Since society in the ancient Near East was closely stratified for the most part, the typical relationship requiring legal definition or confirmation involved parties of unequal status, i.e., suzerain and vassal.

The common form of covenant reflects this inequality of status in its characteristic features. Thus the contract must be initiated by the superior. Customarily the stipulations are binding only upon the inferior, since his performance can be compelled, or his non-compliance punished. What the suzerain does is out of good will; what he gives is of grace.

Any formal agreement to which God and man are parties will necessarily be of the suzerainty type, for man is the creature, child, and servant of God. It is God who specifies the terms of the agreement, who writes in the penalties for disobedience, and who is alone able to enforce his will. It is man who must bind himself by solemn oath to obey before the contract becomes effective; and it will be his failure that breaches the contract and exposes him to dire punishment.

The covenant between God and Israel was drawn up and ratified at Mt. Sinai (cf. Exod. 19–24). Through the mediation of Moses, God offered to Israel the covenant that would establish Israel as the people of God and Yahweh as the God of Israel.

In order to enjoy this special status Israel must, however, bind itself by oath to the exclusive worship and service of God. Beyond this each Israelite is obligated to live according to fundamental rules of justice and decency with his neighbor — the Ten Commandments. The community is obligated to enforce these rules, and to punish those who disregard them. Israel swears its allegiance to the covenant in a solemn ceremony. Disobedience is punishable by death.

Israel's subsequent history is governed by the terms of the covenant. The message of the prophets is the indictment of a disobedient people. And the fall of the nation, with the destruction of Jerusalem, is the penalty for their disobedience. The covenant has been broken; the divine power sustaining national life is removed; and the nation collapses. This is the story of the Sinai covenant.

But there is another covenant of equal importance, and in fact of greater duration. It antedates the Sinai contract by several hundred years: it was not superseded by the Mosiac contract but operated with it side by side. When the Sinai covenant was abrogated, this one remained in force. It is still in force today. It is the foundation of the Christian faith.

This is the covenant between God and Abraham described in the 15th chapter of Genesis. In a strange and solemn ritual Abraham prepares the scene for contract negotiations. According to established procedure three animals are divided in the middle. In the ratification of the contract between superior and inferior it was obligatory for the inferior to stand between the severed animals. There he would take an oath of obedience, calling upon God to do to him as he had done to the animals, and even worse, should he fail to keep its terms.

At the crucial instant, however, a ball of fire passed between the pieces of the animals Abraham had severed, symbolic of the awesome truth that God had taken upon himself the obligations of the inferior, making himself the servant of Abraham his servant. Thus while God initiated the covenant with Abraham, he also obligated himself by its terms. Only God was bound by oath, not Abraham.

God's commitment to Abraham was also to his descendants, without limitations or conditions. This covenant cannot be broken, because God will not break it. Neither Abraham nor his descendants, neither Israel nor the church, can void the commitment made by God in love.

Therefore, although Israel violated the Sinai covenant and was overtaken by disaster, God's commitment remained. While the prophets could threaten punishment under the terms of the Sinai covenant, they could also promise restoration because of the unalterable word of God. However tragic the consequences of human sin, transcending all is the oath to Abraham, the permanent commitment of God to deliver his children.

There are two covenants: the covenant of grace, or self-imposed divine obligation; and the covenant of works, or man's acknowledgment of obligation to God. They are interrelated, but separate; they concern the same parties and interact, but they exist independently, each with its own terms and history. Both originate in the Old Testament. And both have their place in the New.

While the Sinai covenant was broken, the pattern of human obligation was not. The covenant between Jesus and his followers lays a heavy burden of duty upon those followers so that the obligations of the new covenant upon Christians are strongly reminiscent of the old covenant at Sinai. The two great commandments of Jesus are quotations from the law of Moses, a summary of the Ten. And the charter of Christian duty, the Sermon on the Mount, includes a penetrating commentary on several of the Ten Commandments.

The new covenant, ratified at the Last Supper, also involves God's ancient commitment to Abraham. The full cost of the divine commitment is revealed in the words of institution of the Lord's Supper. To fulfill his obligations God must surrender his own son and offer him up for the salvation of men.

As Paul tells it, Jesus Christ gave up his status of equality with God and emptied himself, becoming a human being, a slave of men, enduring suffering and death, thus giving ultimate meaning to the self-imposed obligation of God assumed two thousand years before in the presence of Abraham.

It is therefore to be seen that in both Old and New Testaments both types of covenant play their important parts in a complementary arrangement of divine commitment and human obligation. Israel was the beneficiary of God's commitment to Abraham in the deliverance from Egypt and the occupation of the Holy Land; but also Israel was obligated by the Sinai terms. The Christian Church is the beneficiary of God's commitment fulfilled in the death of Jesus Christ; but the Church is obligated by the terms of the new covenant.

From an understanding of the unity of the Bible comes an appreciation of biblical religion. Biblical religion is a religion of experiences in which we have a participating role rather than a set of doctrines or a list of rules to which we must adhere.

Just as it was with ancient Israel, so the new Israel, the Church, is the community of God bound by double covenant with him. Consequently, by entering into that holy community, the Church, we become the heirs and legatees of the covenant given to Israel. We are thus able to participate in the divine drama; and the presence and action of God become real to us.

This experience of God belongs to the unity of the Bible, an experience whereby we share in the adventure of Abraham and Israel, Jesus and the Church.

6

The Prayer of Nabonidus

Publication of the "Prayer of Nabonidus" fragments from Qumran Cave 4 offers the prospect of an early solution, or at least clarification, of several problems connected with the composition of the book of Daniel, on the one hand, and the background and history of the people of Qumran, on the other.[1] While detailed study of the fragments will be required for definitive judgments, some of the possibilities may be outlined here on the basis of what has appeared.

1. It would appear certain that the original story which underlies the present text of Dan. 4 concerned Nabonidus rather than Nebuchadnezzar.[2] The relationship of the text of Daniel to the 4Q fragments is more complex, and we cannot speak of direct literary dependence.[3] Comparison of the two accounts shows, however, that in the basic matter of the identity of the afflicted king, the Qumran material preserves the more original tradition. Since Nabonidus does not appear in the biblical record, we may argue that the Essenes had access to authentic Babylonian traditions. This in turn would support the view that the people of Qumran included later migrants from Babylonia than the principal groups of exiled Jews reported in the Bible, and that they had returned to Palestine at a comparatively recent date.[4]

2. The book of Daniel in its present form is clearly the work of a Palestinian author of *ca.* 165 B.C.E. At the same time, the case for the composite character of the book and the Babylonian origin of chs. 1–6 is strengthened by the new evi-

---

1. J.-T. Milik, " 'Prière de Nabonide' et autres écrits d'un cycle de Daniel," *RB* 63 (1956): 407-15. [For translation and discussion, see further F. M. Cross, "Fragments of the Prayer of Nabonidus," *IEJ* 34 (1984): 260-64; and G. Vermes, *The Dead Sea Scrolls in English,* 3d ed. (London: Penguin Books, 1987), 274.]

2. See already Sidney Smith, *Babylonian Historical Texts* (London: Methuen, 1924), 36, 46, 50, 78.

3. Milik, 410-11.

4. W. F. Albright, "New Light on Early Recensions of the Hebrew Bible," *BASOR* 140 (1955): 30 and n. 14.

dence.[5] Behind Dan. 4 there is a story of the 3rd (or an earlier) century, originating in Babylon. The substitution of "Nebuchadnezzar" for "Nabonidus" most likely took place after the story was brought to Palestine, since the more accurate tradition presumably persisted in Babylonian circles, where information about Nabonidus was available. There is no reason to suppose that the Palestinian author of the present book of Daniel was responsible for this shift. By his time apparently all memory of Nabonidus had been lost in Palestine, and he simply transmitted the tradition as it had come down to him.

3. If we are correct in holding that 1 Daniel (i.e., chs. 1–6) consists essentially of Babylonian traditions, we may argue further that the materials in chs. 3–5, at least, had already assumed substantially their present form in the pre-Palestinian period, and were incorporated as a unit by the author of Daniel (though with necessary changes). The case may be put as follows:

Ch. 5 contains the familiar but enigmatic story of the handwriting on the wall. It is generally conceded that behind the "etymological" explanation of the terms given by Daniel (is this perhaps a contribution of the author?) lies an older interpretation according to which the key terms signify different weights, each with its appropriate monetary value.[6] These in turn are held to represent various kings of the Neo-Babylonian Empire.[7] Of recent expositions, that of H. L. Ginsberg is the most ingenious.[8] He maintains that there were originally only three figures, represented by three weights: the *mina,* the *shekel,* and the *half-mina* or *peres.*[9] He concludes that the kings in question are Nebuchadnezzar, Evil-Merodach, and Belshazzar.[10]

The only difficulty with this solution is the presence of Evil-Merodach, who does not figure in the book of Daniel at all, and who plays so inconspicuous a role in history and the Bible that we may question whether he deserves even a shekel's worth of recognition. The discovery of the 4Q fragments makes it possible to suggest an improvement on Ginsberg's interpretation. In the earlier Babylonian recension of the complex Dan. 3–5, there were stories about *three* different kings. It is clear that the missing king between Nebuchadnezzar (ch. 3) and Belshazzar (ch. 5) was not Evil-Merodach, but Nabonidus (ch. 4). These three then are respectively the *mina,* the *shekel,* and the *half-mina* of Dan. 5:26-28.

It may be noted also that the awkward references to Nebuchadnezzar as Belshazzar's father (5:2, 11, 13, 18ff.) would naturally have specified or implied Nabonidus in the pre-Palestinian account, especially in vv. 18-23, which refer to

5. Cf. J. A. Montgomery, *A Critical and Exegetical Commentary on the Book of Daniel.* ICC (New York: Scribner's, 1927), 89-90, 96.

6. Cf. E. G. Kraeling, "The Handwriting on the Wall," *JBL* 63 (1944): 11-18.

7. For different views see Kraeling; and Arthur Jeffrey, "The Book of Daniel: Introduction and Exegesis," *IB,* 6:431-32.

8. *Studies in Daniel* (New York: Jewish Theological Seminary, 1948), 24-26.

9. *Ibid.,* 24; for analysis of the original text, cf. Montgomery, 261ff.

10. Ginsberg, 25. Evil-Merodach (562-560 B.C.E.) is mentioned in 2 Kgs. 25:27ff.

the episode in ch. 4. When the change to Nebuchadnezzar was made in ch. 4, it was carried through ch. 5 as well. Thus Nabonidus was permanently removed from the record. The only surviving trace of him would seem to be the single word *teqel,* written on the wall.

7

The Slave of Yahweh

In its modern form, biblical theology has to a considerable extent become a branch of the science of linguistics: the branch, increasingly represented in the published literature, which we call, for want of a more dignified title, word study. Not word study in the narrow etymological sense, nor even in the comparatively simple combinatory patterns of earlier investigation, but rather as a gathering point for data derived from the whole context of the Bible and the life and culture of the ancient Near East, emphasizing historical-critical method, and using a wide variety of ancillary disciplines. At the same time, word study itself gives way to the broader investigation of areas of meaning, including related terms and expressions. As Johannes Pedersen's monumental volumes (*Israel, Its Life and Culture,* I-IV [London: Oxford University Press, 1926-1940]) show, the significant theological and sociological terms of the Old Testament are so interwoven and enmeshed that none can properly be understood in isolation from the others. It is only through such a broad-gauge approach that the shortcomings of the "word study" can be overcome, and the justified charges against its haphazard and artificial character can be met.

Nevertheless, because of the continuing need to classify and organize data, and the inevitable limitations of time and space, the individual word study is still useful as a contribution to the unending task of reconstructing the religion of the Bible. In the present case, which is a study of the expression *ʿebed yahweh,* the primary material is still so extensive that a further narrowing is required. We intend to deal with "Yahweh's slave" as the expression appears in the oracles of Second Isaiah, with particular emphasis on the so-called Servant Songs, and merely to sketch in the background of Old Testament usage in the other books and the context of Near Eastern legal, social, and religious practice. Apart from the need to limit the presentation for publication, there are three reasons for this selection: (1) The oracles of Second Isaiah (by which I mean primarily chs. 40–55 of the book of Isaiah, with probable additions from chs. 34–35 and 56–66, e.g., 60–61) stand at the climax or denouement of Old Testament history, and constitute the culmination of Old Testament theological thought. This is true particularly of the ʿeḇeḏ yahweh, as Second Isaiah strikingly sums up earlier sources for this expression. (2) The picture of the Servant in Second Isaiah provides a direct and deliberate linkage with the New Testament. Of all the patterns or types of Christ found in the Old Testament, the figure of the Servant was not only present from the beginning, but has proved most durable, surviving even the critical attacks of the last sixty years, which demolished most of the others. While Jesus did not explicitly identify himself as the servant, both he and the New Testament writers relied on the pattern fixed in these chapters of Isaiah, especially ch. 53, as providing the essential clue to his ministry, and more specifically to his atoning death and glorious resurrection. (3) The problem of the Servant in Second Isaiah is still unresolved in scholarly circles, and would-be scholars can hardly resist such a challenge. It has taken more than one large volume simply to list and briefly summarize the scholarly excursions on this subject; so one more attempt to probe the mind of the prophet and solve the mystery of the Servant is not likely to be harmful. It is also not likely to resolve the difficulties, at least those in the minds of other scholars with other solutions.

A long and varied usage lies behind the appearance of the expression ʿeḇeḏ yahweh in Second Isaiah. A few preliminary observations about the meaning of the term in the total context of the Old Testament and the Near East may be in order. We have rendered provisionally, "Yahweh's slave," but do not mean to suggest that we have thereby gained some insight into its real significance. A word-for-word translation is at best only a superficial interpretation, while the connotations and associations of the English expression are almost always irrelevant if not misleading. It is only out of the variety of context and usage that the true meaning emerges. Intimately related to the word ʿeḇeḏ are the Hebrew word ʿaḇōḏâ, usually rendered "service," and the verb ʿāḇaḏ, "to work, labor." While in English we tend to distinguish more or less sharply between expressions like "slave," "service," and "labor," or "work," such distinctions do not exist in the biblical terminology. The three words, ʿāḇaḏ, ʿeḇeḏ, and ʿaḇōḏâ, are united at the base, i.e., they derive from the same root, which in its broadest sense means "to work"; but this root operates largely within the disagreeable context of compulsion. There are exceptions in the use of ʿāḇaḏ and ʿaḇōḏâ, and in one case, but only one, God is said to "work a work," or "perform a service": Isa. 28:21, "To do his doing, strange is his deed; to work his work, alien is his work." The expressions here are parallel to the words ʿāśâ and maʿaśeh, which are the customary terms referring to the activity of God. Poetic usage, such as here, is not to be regarded as normative, and it is not unusual for poets to take liberties not permitted in prose contexts. The unique usage here only serves to underline the distinction between human labor of the ʿāḇaḏ kind and the work of God. The term can hardly be separated from man's status as creature and dependent; it also stresses the obligatory character of man's labor. From the beginning work is imposed upon man as an inescapable obligation; and the term

ʿābad is quite properly used to describe it: "And Yahweh God took the man, and placed him in the Garden of Eden to work it *(leʿobdāh)* and to guard it" (Gen. 2:15; cf. also 2:5). It is to be noted that this obligation to perform assigned work belongs to the so-called orders of creation, i.e., it precedes the fall. Thus the obligation of assigned tasks belongs to the nature of man, and is not a consequence of his disobedience; or put in other terms, it reflects the basic relationship of creator and creature, of master and servant. The curse uttered in ch. 3 only aggravates the situation by making it more difficult for man to discharge his responsibility, in changing the locale and circumstances of his labor, but does not change the fundamental condition (vv. 17-19; cf. v. 23, where the same obligation to work the land as in 2:15 is affirmed).

It will be noted that the word *ʿebed* is functional in character, emphasizing the slave's obligation to work, rather than his status, which we may regard as primary in the corresponding English word. In this basic sense then all men are *ʿabādîm* or slaves, whatever their technical status may be. That man was made for work, and further that the pattern of labor is imposed from above, may simply be a pessimistic reflection on the conditions of life, where few are spared the necessity of work; but it may also include the theological recognition of man's subordinate position before God. For man therefore there is only a choice among different kinds of slavery. The wise man chooses the bondage of God; he becomes *ʿebed yahweh.* This theme is amply illustrated by the exodus account: God's intent in delivering Israel from slavery in Egypt is to claim the people for service to him. In order to fulfill their role as slaves of God, they must be free from human bondage. A verse in Leviticus, 25:42, brings out this point: "For they are my slaves whom I brought out from the land of Egypt; they may not be sold as slaves" (cf. v. 55).

If the etymology of the word *ʿebed* points to function, i.e., work as the primary feature of the slave, the term is also basically relational and requires the juxtaposition of slave and master. It is not only obvious in the construct chain, *ʿebed yahweh* (or any of the many other combinations which occur, e.g., *ʿebed hammelek,* etc.), but is also implied in the obligatory nature of *ʿabōdâ,* or the *ʿābad* type of work. Thus relationship stands next to function, is inseparable from it, and the two together define the actual significance of the term; Walther Zimmerli may be right (in his *The Servant of God* [SBT 20 (London: SCM, 1957)]) in stressing the personal relationship as paramount in the biblical concept of the slave. Status in the formal or juridical sense, while always present in the background, is not so important in determining the use of understanding of the term when used figuratively or in a theological sense.

Both in ancient and modern times, there was considerable variation between the official and actual status of slaves. Legally the slave in the ancient Near East (as in antebellum America) was a chattel, i.e., he was regarded as a piece of property, not as a human being. In practice, however, it was difficult to deny that he was human, and even the law was adjusted to recognize an occasional claim. Furthermore there was a good deal of fluidity in status: a free man might become a slave overnight, and while it was a more difficult feat, slaves could become free men. Relations between master and slave might often be on a personal basis rather than as legally defined, simply a case of property ownership. The personal relationship is emphasized in the Bible, and the humanity of the slave is both recognized and protected at least to some degree. Thus in evaluating the significance of the term *'ebed yahweh,* we must not restrict ourselves to the formal juridical position, but reckon with the personal relationship which transcends the legal prescriptions; even in the law the slave is not only chattel but man.

The two main classes of slaves in Israel and the ancient Near East were the domestic or privately owned and the publicly owned or institutional slaves. We find the first class attested in the Bible from patriarchal times on, and continuously through the history of Israel; a further subdivision is made between native Israelite slaves and foreign slaves, with this difference in treatment, that the native-born must not be held in slavery permanently, while the foreign-born may be. The second class is also to be divided between state slaves and temple slaves. These become a prominent feature of Israelite life only with the establishment of the Davidic monarchy and the erection of the temple by Solomon. Since prisoners of war were the chief source of supply, it was not until the time of David that any number were actually taken and pressed into service. Before then, in accordance with the rules of Israelite holy war, no prisoners were taken, and the entire enemy population was supposed to be annihilated. With the exception of the Gibeonites whom Joshua enslaved and dedicated to service in the tabernacle, and other possible instances, large-scale state and temple slavery were unknown in early Israel.

The great public works and extensive mining operations of David and more particularly Solomon required large numbers of slaves to fill the labor gangs, thus making mass slavery feasible; and the wars of conquest had in fact brought in the necessary manpower. The corvee, i.e., public service, was imposed upon Israelites, while the foreign slaves were used in the copper mines of Ezion-geber. The concentration of power in the hands of the king and his steady encroachment on the prerogatives of the tribal governments brought about the growth of a vast royal bureaucracy. These civil servants were called *'abdê hammelek,* "slaves of the king." In official political theory they were his personal slaves, who derived their duties and powers entirely from him; in practice they constituted the government of the nation, and the term thus gains an impersonal quality, and incidentally loses its disagreeable overtones. The most powerful men in the kingdom next to the king, and sometimes in his place, were called "slaves." Nevertheless the term pointed to the source of all civil authority, the king, and the precariousness of the rank and status of the *'abdê hammelek,* no matter how exalted they might be. It could not be entirely forgotten that strictly speaking they were slaves of the king: they were obligated to carry out his commands, and in relation to him they had no rights whatever.

Temple slavery was likewise common to both Israel and the Near East. The temples were the centers of great power and wealth, and the priests were masters of great hordes of slaves. For the most part these slaves worked on temple lands, or as domestic servants in the house of the god, performing menial duties. In the Bible temple slaves included both Israelites and foreigners; they are called *'abdê yahweh,* our first concrete evidence of the use of this term in a known cult situation. It is curious that in the Old Testament the priests are not described as *'abdê yahweh,* but only other temple personnel. This avoidance may derive from the original usage of the term which included the temple slaves as distinguished from the priests who were the actual masters. The term is used of some high officials like Eliakim (cf. Isa. 22:20); just recently I learned of an Israelite seal bearing the name of a man whose title was *'ebed yahweh.* It dates from the period of the monarchy and doubtless signifies that the man was a temple official, one of those in charge of the building itself, e.g., custodian, treasurer, etc. The term thus could be construed literally of a temple slave or of a relatively important official. In these uses the impersonal aspect of the term is emphasized as in the parallel *'ebed hammelek.* Much more significant in our investigation of the meaning of *'ebed yahweh* is the highly personal relationship embedded in the construct chain, and attested by the long list of individuals designated *'ebed yahweh,* whose distinction is not their association with the temple or other cultic installation but rather their personal contact and experience of Yahweh. It is on the basis of these and the total experience of Israel in its perennial service of the Lord that the real foundation of 2 Isaiah's "servant" concept is to be found, and the proper understanding of his picture of the *'ebed yahweh.* Behind the technical term *'ebed yahweh* and its association with the temple cult there is the broad and more meaningful area of God's personal dealings with men. And alongside the technical liturgical service *('abōdâ)* rendered in the temple by the Nethinim and other *'abdê yahweh* ("servants of Yahweh"), there is the more significant duty performed outside the sanctuary by other less technical *'abdê yahweh.*

The importance of the *'ebed* concept in the Old Testament may be gauged by the dimensions of this figure in the oracles of Second Isaiah. The prophet's presentation of the servant is both subtle and complex, and has baffled inquirers since the days of the Ethiopian eunuch, if not before; and has challenged the sharpest scholarly minds ever since. If even a small part of the exegetical interpretations drawn from these chapters of the book of Isaiah actually reflect the thought of the prophet, then he must be regarded as one of the most versatile and imaginative poets in the history of our religion. And in fact he is.

Nor is this entirely surprising. Second Isaiah stands at the pinnacle of Old Testament history and thought. He was the heir of Moses and the prophets; he had the whole rich history of the people of God to draw upon in presenting his summation. The figure of Jeremiah towered over his century and his people, leaving an indelible mark upon the sacred story. Ezekiel was his immediate predecessor, and perhaps his mentor. The major theological issues were debated by the best theological minds in the same era, while God through the violent actions of history wrote his own conclusions to the deliberations. Along with an unsurpassed insight into the meaning of Israel's past history, Second Isaiah had a unique vision of its future. He spoke at the turning point of human history. The end of the old order had already come, and God was even now preparing his final mighty deed of redemption. The great king of the East had made his appearance, and would shortly execute the judgment of God against the evil city: Babylon. Then the captives would be released, and God himself would lead the remnant of his people through the wilderness in a new and triumphant exodus back to their holy land. Along with the establishment of Israel would come the salvation of the whole world. The details are not always clear, for the process is described in the incandescent language of a prophet-poet. But all would take place now; even while he spoke, the course of events took shape, and history blended into eschatology. The fall of Babylon and the rise of Cyrus were not only historical markers but the final moments of the old age. With the departure of the exiles, the new age had begun; and the sequence of events was inexorably fixed by the determined will of God, who by his own word would bring the new world to pass.

It is only in the light of Second Isaiah's total message and outlook that a proper estimate of the Servant is possible. For Second Isaiah, the Servant is the chief human agent of the eschaton, the one through whom the new age is inaugurated and consummated, and beside whom the other actors, like Cyrus, are mere scene-shifters . . . and this I believe includes the prophet himself, who is the herald, but not the agent of the end time. (We will call the Servant "he" without attempting now to decide the difficult question of his identity, i.e., whether an individual or the community.) We are accustomed to seeing the prophet approximately at the center of biblical history chronologically speaking, about as many centuries before Christ as after Moses, and it may be difficult for us to apprehend the eschatological character of his message. But he saw himself at the end of history in the ordinary sense and standing on the threshold of an entirely new age. That he may have been mistaken on this point need not detain us now; the matter of orientation is essential to an understanding of his presentation of the Servant. For the new order is totally unlike the old; there is no continuity with historical figures or institutions, but a complete renovation. Thus contrary to the earlier prophets (but similar to the doctrine of the new covenant in Jer. 31) there is little place for monarchy or priesthood in the new order. Some modification may be necessary since the prophet foresees the rebuilding of the temple, but there is no specific reference to the restoration of the priesthood; his view may be compared with that picture of universal worship at Zion in Isa. 2 (Mic. 4), or the similar view in Isa. 56 (which may be by Second Isaiah), in which the emphasis is upon the gathering of the peoples rather than upon special priestly orders or prerogatives. Thus the office of

Yahweh's anointed can be filled by the Gentile Cyrus since he is the only royal participant in the eschatological drama; but his role while important is nonetheless secondary. Likewise there is no mention of prophets in the new age because there will be none: Second Isaiah himself, if we may make the suggestion, is the eschatological prophet, his is the last message before the consummation. Combining the functions and prerogatives of prophets, priests, and kings, and transcending them is the Servant who alone has place in the new order.

Contrary to the opinion of those scholars who have attempted to see in the Servant a kingly or prophetic figure, it is to be asserted that both prophetic and royal features are present, but that the servant is more than either and displaces both. A similar comment applies to those who see the Servant prefigured in one or more of the mighty heroes of the past, themselves notable servants of the Lord. Of all those designated servants of Yahweh, Moses and David are the individuals cited most often, while the prophets as a group are characteristically described as "his servants, the prophets." The very fact that features from different individuals and groups are all identifiable in the figure of the Servant momentarily strengthens and then demolishes the case for any particular identification with some individual or group (like the prophets) of the past. At the same time the outlook of the prophet makes it clear that he is not looking forward to some distant figure in the future. The Servant is already on the scene, already fulfilling his decisive role in the culmination of the age. And yet he is a new figure, unlike any servant of the past, and yet like them all. But this in itself is not surprising, because the prophet in constructing his image of the servant has drawn upon all the servants of the past, and Israel's whole history of service. But the servant is not merely a composite picture of the past; he is set in the new context of fulfillment and consummation, and this gives him his unique identity.

The basic pattern of Old Testament history and thought is fixed by the mighty deed of God in the exodus from Egypt: the cycle of deliverance, wandering, and settlement is normative for biblical religion, and it turns up repeatedly in the message of the prophets, as well as forming the backdrop of the New Testament kerygma. For Second Isaiah the exodus serves not only as a general pattern, but fits in detail into the historical situation in the latter half of the 6th century B.C.E. As already indicated, the prophet sees the climactic event as a New Exodus and new settlement in the Promised Land. Instead of the Second Moses (foreseen, e.g., in Deut. 18:18), God himself will lead this march across the desert. Aside from minor changes, the essential pattern remains the same. Israel suffered for forty years in the wilderness until the wicked generation of those rebellious to the will of God had perished. Ezekiel's thought about the Babylonian captivity is much the same (cf. 4:4ff.): forty years of punishment in exile will exhaust the sinful generation; a new generation will be raised up to return to the Holy Land. This rising from the dead, prefigured in the wilderness wanderings, is explicitly affirmed by Ezekiel, and forms the basis of Second Isaiah's thought. For the latter the period of trial and suffering is now ending, and like the second generation in the wilderness, so the second generation of the exiles will return to the Promised Land. A central theme of the Exodus is the transfer of authority over Israel from Pharaoh to Yahweh: Israel the unwilling bondslave of Egypt is set free in order to render service to Yahweh. So emphatically in the summons to Moses, Exod. 3:12, "When you bring the people out of Egypt you shall serve *(ta'aḇḏûn)* God upon this mountain" (and elsewhere, Exod. 4:23; 7:16, 26; etc.). The purpose of the deliverance is that Israel may render Yahweh service. In similar though not identical fashion, service and divine deliverance are interrelated in Second Isaiah. In the case of the latter, the service of the servant is combined with the action of God to produce eschatological fulfillment. And in both cases the servant is Israel.

In the light of the general discussion we may now approach the specific passages dealing with the Servant in Second Isaiah:

1. Isa. 41:8-9

> And thou, Israel my servant, Jacob — I have chosen thee
>> Descendant of Abraham who loved me
> I have grasped thee from the ends of the earth
>> And from its borders I have summoned thee
> And I said to thee, My servant art thou
>> I have chosen thee and have not rejected thee.
> Do not be afraid, for I am with thee
>> Do not be alarmed for I am thy God
> I have strengthened thee, also I have helped thee
>> Indeed, I have sustained thee with my vindicating (righteous) right hand.

In this passage the identification of the Servant with Israel (Jacob) is made explicitly. On the basis of the association with the exodus pattern, and then the general theme of Israel's obligation of service to her lord and master, we would expect this equation Israel = Servant to be a commonplace of Old Testament literature. But such is not the case. If Second Isaiah is not the creator of this equation, he is certainly the first to give it central importance in his theology. The same equation is to be found in Jer. 30:10, and repeated in fuller form in Jer. 46:27-28.

> And thou, do not be afraid, my servant Jacob
>> And do not be dismayed, Israel
> For behold, I am your savior from afar off

> And of your progeny from the land of their captivity.
> And Jacob will return and be at peace
> > And will be secure, with none to frighten him.
> Thou, fear not, my servant Jacob — oracle of Yahweh —
> > For I am with thee
> For I will make a full end of all the nations
> > Whither I have driven thee
> But I will not make a full end of thee
> > I will punish thee with judgment
> > And I will not declare thee innocent.

In part, especially the latter part, this contains characteristic Jeremiah material, but the servant expressions are unusual in Jeremiah, and sound much more like the phrases of Second Isaiah. They are usually regarded as secondary additions to Jeremiah, and there is weight in this contention. However it is of no great moment since we are not concerned to establish the absolute originality of the concept in Second Isaiah, and it is altogether possible that he borrowed the formula itself from another, perhaps Jeremiah. What is important is the use to which he put the idea, making it the basic theme of his teaching. The passage itself, 41:8-10, is in accord with the initial oracle announcing the imminent salvation to be effected by God, with the deliverance and establishment of Israel in its homeland the primary objectives. Here Israel is identified as the servant, the object of divine election. The formula of adoption as servant, or the transaction by which this status is conferred, is quoted to establish its legal, formal character.

While the choice as servant implies obligation, here it is not the work to be performed by the servant that is emphasized, but rather the responsibility of the owner or master. The relationship between master and slave involves not only the obligation of the slave as an unlimited commitment to work at the behest of the master, but also the unconditional responsibility of the master for the slave. Here it is spelled out in the verbs: grasp and summon, strengthen, help, support, and above all, reassure by his constant presence. The whole passage points to the future when God will accomplish these things in behalf of his servant. Apparently the master here goes far beyond any requirement or expectation that might apply to the ordinary master-slave relationship; it is for this reason that we must emphasize the personal character of the relationship, and interpret the expression accordingly. The divine attitude toward a slave, his slave, can be understood in the light of the exodus narrative, and also on the basis of God's relationship to individual servants of the past. Thus Abraham here is specified as the lover of God; elsewhere he is called servant, but it is to him that God made an irrevocable commitment, and repeated demonstration of his concern and favor. What service is required of the Servant is not indicated here, and while the relationship necessarily implies continued trust and loyalty, it might appear that the principal service of the servant has already been rendered, or at least that the present situation does not require special work on his part. The moment for divine action has arrived, and the servant need only accept God's intervention in his behalf.

While the identification of Israel and the servant fits in with the general scheme of biblical history, the specific equation does not occur outside of exilic literature, and this in itself is both an oddity and relevant to our inquiry. It is at least suggestive that at a time when the community was in danger of total dissolution, and its visible identity had largely disappeared, such a figure of social solidarity should make itself felt so forcibly. The similar figure in Lam. 3, also representative of the whole community, points to the deep feeling for the continuity and unity of Israel in spite of growing emphasis on the individual and the disruption of the political entity. It would appear also that the prophet, by the use of this collective image, has moved away from the literal or technical figure of the slave to a more symbolic picture in which the essential inter-involvement of God and his people is portrayed. This brings the symbol into the same level of intensity as that of husband and wife, or parent and child, thus emphasizing the closeness of the bond and the intimate and unique quality of the relationship. The personal and domestic character of the relationship is emphasized as over against the formal and impersonal side which the term itself, *'ebed yahweh,* could as easily convey.

2. Isa. 42:1-4

Behold my servant (Jacob), whom I uphold
  My chosen (Israel) in whom my soul takes pleasure
I have put my spirit upon him
  Judgment to the nations he will bring forth
He will not cry out, not raise (his voice)
  And he will not shout in the street
A bruised reed he will not break
  And dimly-burning flax he will not snuff out
Faithfully he will bring forth justice
  He will not fail or be crushed
Until he has established justice in the earth
  And for his Torah the coastlands wait.

The LXX here specifies the servant as Jacob/Israel in accord with the previous passage where the same terms, servant and chosen one, are also used. If the LXX is not original here it indicates strongly that the identification of the servant with Israel was accepted in some Jewish circles, and further that this identification had already crept into an authorized Hebrew text. It is most unlikely that these words were added to the Greek text when the translation was made. Whatever may have been the original text, there is no reason to doubt the identification of the servant with Israel here. In this passage the return to Palestine is presupposed, and the further work of the servant is spelled out. His primary obligation is in relation of the nations; he is to bring forth to them *mishpat* and *torah*. He is to act therefore in the traditional roles of Judge (later King) and Priest (the official in charge of *toroth* or religious instruction). More specifically *mishpat* reflects the dispensation of justice which is the responsibility of the state, while *torah* is the responsibility of the church: the specific figures, servant figures in the mind of the prophet, may be David and Moses.

In any case the servant is to fulfill in combination the principal roles of the leaders of the people — not however in relation to Israel, but rather with respect to the nations. The sequence indicates that the restoration of Israel precedes the executive and educational work of the servant. The gift of the spirit could apply equally to the royal and prophetic figures, and is in keeping with the intention of the prophet: the servant combines and transcends the individual figures of the past.

3. Isa. 42:19-20

Who is blind but my servant
 Or deaf like the messenger whom I send
Who is blind like the dedicated one
 Or blind like the servant of Yahweh
You see many things but do not grasp them
 He opens his ears, but he doesn't comprehend.

This passage is highly critical of the slave, and to many scholars does not seem compatible with Isa. 42:1-4. Widespread is the scholarly view that the servant described in the four so-called Servant Songs is not the same as in the other passages of Second Isaiah where he is either explicitly or impliedly identified with Israel. Some scholars hold that these poems are intrusive in Second Isaiah and are by a different poet. That view, which has lost ground in recent years, at least avoids the difficulty inherent in supposing that Second Isaiah is the author of all the songs as well as the rest of the oracles in chs. 40–55, and that he uses the term *'ebed yahweh* in two different ways, identifying it with two different subjects. Once it is recognized that the identification with Israel is itself principally the work of Second Isaiah, it is difficult to suppose that he has gone on from there to another and more mysterious equation. The view which seems most reasonable to me accepts the essential unity of Isa. 40–55 (as a minimum), and the explicit identification of the servant as Israel as applicable to all other cases, where the identification is not explicit. This position ought not be abandoned except in the face of overpowering evidence to the contrary. So far at least, it would appear that such evidence has not been presented. An ambivalent estimate of the servant on the part of the prophet is not really surprising. Israel the servant, the agent of a crucial divine mission, is nevertheless Israel; while summoned to great things, he is not always prepared.

4. Isa. 43:10

You are my witnesses, oracle of Yahweh
And my servant whom I have chosen
That you may know and believe me
And understand that I am he
Before me no god was formed
And after me there shall be none.

Again we have the combination of servant and election. Here the choice relates to another specific service to be performed: the witness to God, as the only true deity, the creator, the savior, the one beside whom there is no other. Along with the other obligations already specified, the duty of witnessing, of testifying to what they have witnessed (in the legal sense) is affirmed.

5. Isa. 44:1-2

And now listen Jacob my slave
And Israel whom I have chosen
Thus has said Yahweh your maker
And your creator from the womb, who helps you
Do not be afraid my servant Jacob
And Jeshurun whom I have chosen.

Once more the identification of Israel with the chosen is parallel to Jacob the servant. This tends to reinforce the combination of the four elements as fairly fixed in Second Isaiah: election and service are inseparable, but so also is the identification with Jacob-Israel. The following verse repeats the gift of the spirit, as in previous passages already discussed. The gift of the spirit ties in with the passage 42:1-4 and likewise places the servant as the principal participant in the eschatological age. The spirit provides him with the power to achieve his tasks and makes him the central figure in the fulfillment of the divine purpose.

6. Isa. 44:21-22

Remember these things Jacob
    And Israel for you are my slave
I formed you to be my slave
    And Israel you will not be forgotten by me (?)
I wipe away as a cloud your transgressions
    And like a rain-cloud your sins
    Return to me for I have redeemed you.

The reference here again would seem to be to the past rather than the future. The sins and transgressions lie in the past, and the past has been erased. The time for united action has arrived. The final clause refers not so much to repentance as to reunion, the joining of forces; now that the cause of alienation has been removed, and the captivity is at an end, the purpose of God and the function of Israel can be fulfilled.

7. Isa. 45:4

For the sake of my slave Jacob
    and Israel my chosen,
I will give you a name
    I bestowed a title on you though you did not know me.

The reference here is to Cyrus, who is dealt with in the context. The selection of Cyrus as the Lord's Anointed and his commission to overrun the earth — his elevation and enthronement over the world — are part of the purpose of God. This is done for the sake of his servant, Jacob, specifically so that Cyrus will restore the captives to their home land. The royal anointed is subordinate to the servant. Once again the combination of slave, chosen, and Jacob/Israel is to be noted. And as the servant is the beneficiary of the action of Cyrus, so the world will be saved by the work of the servant.

8. Isa. 48:20

Depart from Babylon
Fly from the Chaldeans
    With the sound of a shout make known
    Cause this to be heard

Bring it forth to the ends of the earth
Say Yahweh has redeemed his slave Jacob.

The first act of the drama is concluded: the redemption of Israel through the intervention of Cyrus the anointed of the Lord. Thus the stage is set for the next phase of the drama, in which the servant occupies the center of the stage. The deliverance of the servant is preparation for the work of the servant itself; this in turn will result in the deliverance of the world.

9. Isa. 49:1-6

Listen O coastlands to me
    And pay attention O peoples from afar
Yahweh from the womb summoned me
    From the entrails of my mother he mentioned my name
He made my mouth like a sharp sword
    In the shadow of his hand he hid me
He made me a polished arrow
    In his quiver he concealed me
And he said to me, (Jacob) my slave art thou
    Israel, in thee I will be glorified
As for me, I said I have labored in vain
    For emptiness and waste breath I have spent my strength
Yet my right is with Yahweh
    And my recompense with my God.
But now, said the Lord, Who formed me from the womb to be his servant
    (To restore Jacob to him, and that Israel should be gathered to him)
And that I should be glorified in the eyes of Yahweh,
    And my God has become my refuge
Then he said, It is too light a thing for your being my slave
    To raise up the tribes of Jacob
    And to bring back the captives of Israel
So I will make you a light to the nations
    That my salvation may reach to the ends of the earth.

This is perhaps the most difficult of all the servant passages in Second Isaiah, as there is confusion if not contradiction between the identification of the servant as Israel in v. 3 (Jacob also seems to have fallen out in the first half of the line), and the mission of the servant to Israel in vv. 5 and 6. While it would appear that the restoration of Israel is not necessarily part of the work of the servant, that task being consistently assigned to Yahweh in Second Isaiah, there nevertheless seems to be a distinction between the servant on the one hand and Israel/Jacob on the other. The shift between the first person used of the servant in vv. 5 and 6 and the third person applied to Israel and the distinction made between the servant who is to be a light to the nations and Israel which is to be restored seem fairly decisive.

The general pattern remains the same: first the restoration of Israel and then the mission to the peoples. The mission rests upon the servant, and the restoration of Israel is God's doing. But if the statement that the restoration of Israel was on account of the servant, as both vv. 5 and 6 imply, then the prophet has used a peculiar mode of expression if he meant also to equate the servant and Israel. There is no suggestion here that the servant had or has a mission to Israel, but only that the restored Israel and the servant are not quite the same. Since this contradicts all the other passages so far discussed, it is perhaps best to suspend judgment about its meaning. The clear parts are in conformity with the pattern already established, but the rest is obscure if not contradictory. If as we suppose the prophet identifies the servant specifically with the exiles, then the distinction between the servant and the fully restored Israel is understandable.

The information about the servant's hidden life with God is original and not found in the other passages. His complaints about his suffering and vexation refer to his prior period of service, for which the reward was the deliverance from captivity. In the future lies the mission to the nations.

10. Isa. 50:10 (cf. 4-11)

Who among you is a fearer of Yahweh
Who obeys the voice of his slave
Who has walked in darkness, with no light for him
He trusts in the name of Yahweh
And leans upon his God.

This passage describes the suffering of the servant as he tries to carry out the duties assigned to him by Yahweh. Exactly who his enemies are and what his vindication will be are not at all clear. The identity of the servant here remains something of a mystery, though it cannot be said that the passage contradicts the others in which the identification with Israel is plain. The chronology of the passage in relation to previous chapters and subsequent ones is also not clear. Does this describe the experience of the servant after the restoration of Israel, and during his mission to the nations? Or does it look back to the previous period of suffering before the deliverance from bondage? There is insufficient evidence to pin down these points. The main theme of the chapter is the suffering of the servant as a consequence of his loyalty to Yahweh, and the disastrous effects of his attempt to complete his mission. Suffering is one of the hazards of the servant role, and will be resolved in ultimate vindication.

11. Isa. 52:13 and 53:11 (cf. 52:13–53:12)

Behold my servant will prosper
  He will be high, and elevated and exalted very much

From the travail of his soul he will see (light)
  He will be satisfied with his knowledge
My servant will make the many righteous
  As he bears upon himself their iniquities.

Unfortunately this is not the place for a detailed examination of the most important of the servant songs. A few points can be made however. The identity of the servant is once again unclear, though it is difficult to avoid the collective interpretation since evidence in the other direction is by no means convincing. The poem itself is not to be regarded as a sequel to the other servant poems and references but rather as a survey of his entire career. The summary offered in 52:13-15 suggests that the pattern of the servant's experience stretches between the extremes of humiliation and exaltation, from death to resurrection, from condemnation as a criminal to acknowledgment as the lord of men. The principal obligation of the servant here is to suffer; this is his work for his master; in this manner his mission to the nations is accomplished, and the purpose of God through the servant is fulfilled. This program differs in detail from that offered in other servant passages, though the main points are not seriously affected. There the restoration of the servant follows upon his suffering, and the salvation of the peoples is a consequence of his restoration. But here the suffering precedes the restoration, and the mission to the nations seems to belong to the period of suffering, though the results are not garnered until after the servant's resurrection.

The story of the servant may be briefly outlined as follows. The servant was a typical, shabby, unattractive person suffering from a loathsome disease, from which he died. He is also presented as a criminal condemned and executed for a crime, which however he did not commit. The episode was not worthy of the attention of the onlookers, who are the kings of the different nations, thus representative of the world. Then several startling truths are made known. According to the prophet this is original teaching and interrelationship of cause and effect not hitherto suspected. When the kings considered the fate of the servant, they reasoned back from his horrible death to the conviction that he had been punished by God. This proved to be fallacious reasoning. The servant was innocent; though his death was part of his service to God, and in an ultimate sense part of the divine purpose, it was nevertheless due to the sinfulness of men, not only of those who had a hand in his execution, but also of the kings themselves, as representatives of all humanity. It was the burden of their sins, the malignancy of their diseases, which destroyed the servant. Not only was he innocent and they guilty, but their guilt was responsible for his death, whether it is described in terms of disease and death, or crime and punishment. His death brought home to them their guilt and involvement in his death, but also in a more mysterious fashion had power to effect their forgiveness and salvation. The final act in the drama was the resurrection of the servant to life and his elevation to kingly authority; as the spoils of his victory, i.e., his completion of his service to God, he claims and receives a redeemed humanity.

Here is the final portrait of the servant in Second Isaiah; it gathers the details previously offered into a coherent pattern, and establishes the role and obligation of the true servant, the human agent of the divine purpose. The highest level of this service is suffering, innocent suffering for the sake of the guilty. The vicarious character of this suffering has affinities with the theory and understanding of sacrifice (which is always substitutionary or vicarious in character), especially the scapegoat in the Day of Atonement observance. But the suffering of the servant and his sacrifice transcend in meaning and import any merely mechanical view of sacrifice or atonement, and the symbol of the sacrificial animal can be used only with the greatest caution in depicting the work of the servant, if indeed it can be used at all.

In attempting to fit the story of the servant into the structure of Second Isaiah's message as previously outlined, the following observations seem appropriate. The story of the servant comes out of the contemporary experience of Israel and covers the period from the immediate past to the imminent future. In the past lie the suffering, the humiliation, and death of the servant. At hand or already in process is the resurrection of the servant, while his exaltation lies in the future. The theme of death and resurrection has already been anticipated in the oracles of Ezekiel, and there is no reason to doubt that Second Isaiah's conception is essentially the same though his portrayal is quite different in detail. Behind both lies the story of Israel's experience in the wilderness when one generation had to perish before the next could take its place and march into the Promised Land; here potentially at least was a kind of death and resurrection in the experience of early Israel. Ezekiel makes this explicit in his story of the valley of dry bones. Israel has perished, but God in his power and goodness will restore the dead bodies; so Israel will be restored and brought back to its land. The exile has been the death of the people; and after a generation has passed, the new generation will be brought back to the land, and the people will come back to life. So for Second Isaiah the servant has died in exile innocently (cf. Isa. 40:2; they have paid double for all their sins), and for the sake of the guilty nations. Israel will be raised from the death of exile, and restored to life on the land from which its people were taken. The nations responsible for the disaster will awaken to the realities of the case, acknowledge that the servant by suffering and dying has in fact interceded with God

69

for them, and won them forgiveness. In this way the goal of universal order and harmony is achieved.

It is in his analysis of the meaning of the exile and the suffering of Israel that Second Isaiah has produced a solution to the burning theological issue of the day, and incidentally justified his eschatological hope. The earlier prophets and the historians had acknowledged that Israel's destruction was the punishment of God for her sin. Nevertheless questions were raised about the justice and mercy of God in taking this action against his people. Habakkuk asked about the relative righteousness of Israel and her oppressor the Chaldeans, while Job undermined the whole structure of orthodox theology and its delicate balancing of rewards and punishments; and Lamentations wept at the enormity of the punishment, not more than was deserved, but more than could be borne. Second Isaiah affirmed that the suffering had been excessive, more than what was deserved, but not more than what was necessary. The necessity here was the purpose of God which was not just the restoration of Israel but the redemption of the whole world. Only an excess of suffering could accomplish the miracle of atonement, and this was provided by the servant in the humiliation and death of exile. Thus the way was cleared for the eschatological fulfillment of the kingdom of God.

The figure of the slave of Yahweh is vitally important in biblical theology. Rooted in the complex pattern of slavery in the ancient Near East, and more specifically in the practice of Israel, the function and relationship of the servant of Yahweh have distinctive aspects requiring special attention. The fullest presentation of the servant is to found in the oracles of Second Isaiah, which are the climax and culmination of Old Testament thought. This figure is built out of the many and varied traditions of divine service in Israel, including the account of the individual servants who gave to the concept vitality and content stemming from their own experience and direct contacts with God; and also the more formal associations of temple servants, the prophets as a group, and others. Out of all that had gone before emerges the servant of Yahweh, the embodiment of Israel, who shares in the qualities of the ancient worthies like Moses and David, but transcends them all in his function as the agent of the new order of God. In the course of his ministry he takes on at different times the responsibilities and prerogatives of prophet and king, but he also suffers the humiliation of attack and rejection. His ultimate triumph is bound up with his death by suffering; in this he attains to the full stature of Yahweh's servant: as the prophet describes it:

> Therefore I will apportion to him the multitude
>> And he will take the many as his spoils of war
> Because he was willing to suffer death
>> And be counted among the covenant-breakers
> For he bore the sin of the many
>> And for the covenant-breakers he made supplication.

Postscript: The Lord as Servant

As we should expect, the word *'ebed* is never used of God, and the verb *'ābad* and other noun *'abōdâ* are used only once. Strictly speaking God is not and cannot be the servant or slave of anyone. Nevertheless there is a suggestion here and there in the Bible that God does and has assumed the role of servant to his own servants in his relationship with his people, and in order to fulfill his purpose for Israel and mankind.

The most striking example is the ceremony described in Gen. 15, in which God assumes the role of the inferior, or vassal, binding himself by solemn oath to the performance of certain obligations to Abraham. In this covenant, God is bound by his own oath, but Abraham is not. The divine commitment is thus unconditional, and this obligation or service is comparable in all respects with the obligation of the slave to his master. The difference is that the obligation is limited to the oath, and the obligation was self-imposed. Nevertheless it is unconditional, and irrevocable, and it was sealed by oath, all of which constitute an interesting insight into the purpose and character of God. This may also offer a line of approach in evaluating the role of Jesus as the *'ebed yahweh*.

8

History and Eschatology:
The Nature of Biblical Religion
and Prophetic Faith

The God of the Bible is identified by his participation in human history. Biblical religion is concerned with names, places, events. Primary emphasis is on the historical, as against the cosmic or cyclical character of nature religion. Significant events are actions of God, vehicles or channels of revelation.

In the biblical tradition the "mighty deeds" are the crucial or decisive events. For the Old Testament they are: exodus, wanderings, conquest — at one and the same time visible, observable, determinable occurrences, with dates and places, and actions of the hidden God. At this point a distinction must be made between the biblical record and the actual historic occurrence. The mighty deed in the nature of the case must be what God did. To the extent that the tradition and the facts coincide there is no serious problem. Should they diverge a choice is obligatory. This is a relatively new problem, the product of the age of criticism — historical, exegetical, archaeological. We now have concrete historical data with which to check biblical record. Determination of facts in the case is our primary obligation: that is, the reconstruction of the actual history of Israel and of the so-called mighty deeds. This picture changes from generation to generation. There is a general correspondence with biblical picture, but it is always subject to revision. We cannot equate the two without questioning; this constitutes a permanent and embarrassing factor in organizing our belief. There is an element of contingency which cannot be eliminated without fundamentally changing the nature of biblical religion. It was not a significant factor until the 18th and 19th centuries, but it is now inerad-icable. And it must be faced. We cannot surrender either to the fundamentalist presumption that the facts and the tradition are identical, in the face of overwhelming evidence that this absoluteness cannot be maintained, or to the view that the tradition supersedes the facts, and that our belief centers on the fixed tradition of the Bible, regardless of new evidence, which is to make myth of the mighty deeds, and contravene the essential contention of the biblical writers that what God had done occurred to Israel and before the eyes of the world.

Thus we are not only justified but obligated to recover all the relevant data bearing on biblical history and to reconstruct the actual history of Israel. Theological significance can attach only to what, in fact, occurred, though the growth of tradition and its divergence from the original sequence of events are factors in the reconstruction of the history of the holy commonwealth. At present the historical picture is substantially the same as the biblical picture, though the further back we go the less certain we can be. There remains and will remain for some time a broad area of possible reconstruction within the limits set by confirmed historical evidence. Here the predilections of the scholar appear. Thus M. Noth takes the most minimal view possible of the data pertaining to the age of Moses and the patriarchs, regarding the traditional picture as in no way substantiated by the data now available. At the opposite extreme of competent scholarship, W. F. Albright regards the biblical picture as substantially confirmed in its general pattern by the archaeological data, but he does not attempt to defend the exact details or sequence of events as they are recorded. The situation is likely to shift somewhat in coming years, but we maintain that underlying the biblical tradition there is authentic historical experience, quite apart from the question of specific people and private occurrences, as well as the miraculous or unrepeatable type of event, which are almost impossible for an archaeologist to recover in any form, or for a historian to control. These latter belong rather to the area of decision and commitment.

The Divine Action

The mighty deed is not only an event observable in the context of history; it is also the result of divine action. The question of divine participation must also be answered, but obviously cannot be by the same methods as the historical question. A naive but useful test is suggested by the biblical writers — the sign of divine intervention is the unique and remarkable character of the event (called "signs and wonders"), as well as the fact that it was predicted. This approach poses some knotty problems of its own, and one may wonder whether the miraculous is more a hindrance than a help in establishing the event and its meaning theologically. Or it may be put this way: for the Bible, the miracle combines the historical and the theological, and the more wonderful the event the more closely are these cemented together. In a modern setting, these factors tend to nullify each other — the more miraculous the less historical an event appears, and vice versa. Is it possible, as we rigorously pursue a historical reconstruction of Israel's experience, to leave any room for the commitment of faith?

If so, it does not appear likely that it will be by way of the objectively miraculous. It may be suggested that the divine action is completely clothed or disguised in the human history, that from the observable data the experience of Israel can be regarded as entirely human, and in fact inconsequential, by contrast with the record of achievement of other, greater nations. Whereas in the past the spectacular events described in the Bible were taken to be evidence of divine intervention, we must perhaps recognize that there are two sides to the miraculous. The spectacular feature is not necessarily central, and what remains after careful historical analysis is a determinable series of events, unusual in their total impact, but plausible and reasonable, as the pieces are fitted together. The divine aspect is to be found, not so much in the observable phenomena, but in the underlying meaning and motif, to be discerned in short by the eyes of faith, hidden as it is within the mundane sequence of events. We cannot seize upon a particular occurrence, or group of occurrences, verify them scientifically, and then claim that here is proof positive of the divine intervention. We cannot do this for two reasons: first, because the process of verification strips the miraculous element almost entirely, and what remains is a mystery; and second, because the most amazing occurrences are not necessarily proof of anything except that they are amazing.

This is not to deny the biblical importance of the miraculous, since finally we cannot evade it (e.g., the Resurrection), but rather to suggest that modern developments in critical study tend to make this approach self-defeating, or at least impossible of rational resolution. If the whole purpose of archaeological and literary investigation is to elaborate the meaning and interrelationships of the biblical materials with those of the ancient Near East, then its success will consist in the reasonableness and plausibility of the picture which research reconstructs; but the miraculous becomes less and less compatible with such a synthesis. The uniqueness and distinction of the biblical story will lie in the end results, and in the total configuration attained, rather than in the strange and wonderful devices employed by the Almighty. The demonstration of divine participation will lie in the consequences of that impact in the life and habits, thoughts and practices of Israel, rather than in one or the other of the accompaniments of that story, or in the whole sequence of such extraordinary accompaniments. Thus research may well be able to validate, at least in general, the story of exodus and conquest, though perhaps not in detail. But it can hardly be expected to deal successfully with the crossing of the Red Sea, or the manna, except perhaps to reduce them to observable phenomena.

But beyond the "wonder" is the question of the hand of God. Even a wonder is not necessarily divine. And something quite ordinary in appearance to the outsider may, in fact, be an action of God, an expression of his particular purpose. In dealing with this subject the first question is one of revelation, which we take to be the communication of God with man. Temporally prior to and logically basic to the mighty deed is the *word* of God.

While historical data are indispensable to biblical religion, and while it cannot survive without them, absolutely central to biblical faith is the contact between God and man. The connection of God with the events described in the tradition — whether we find it in the spare language of the critical historian, or in the original richness, even hyperbole, of the biblical narrator — does not depend upon the verdict of research (except to the possible degree with which research can dissolve the event entirely), but on the testimony of the men who serve as links between God and the observable events, the crucial bearers of the Word which becomes Deed (cf. Heb. *dābār*).

Here is the foundation of biblical religion: the record of the person-to-person meetings between God and chosen individuals and the content of their conversation. This sort of tradition is the least likely to be verified by known historical methods. Moses and the prophets can be validated as authentic human beings, as can something of their experience, and their message, but hardly can the contact with God itself be so validated. The acceptance of a report of contact with God requires an act of faith, or commitment. Belief in the reality of a divine-human confrontation — not in some universalized existential sense, but in the concrete and even scandalous particularity of names, dates, and places (e.g., the God of Abraham, Isaac, and Jacob, who revealed himself at Bethel, at Beer-sheba, etc.) — can hardly be compelled, not even in the sense that some agreement can be reached on the historical reconstructions. That does not mean that such belief is completely out of reason or is in contradiction to the most rigorous application of critical method. On the basis of the data we can check, we know we are dealing with men who shared the world view of their contemporaries in many respects, though differing sharply in others; we know that they were empirical, if not pragmatic, in their approach to life, social and individual; and we know that while not critical in the scientific sense of evaluating data, and discriminating between fact and legend, they were, nevertheless, practical in their outlook, and for the most part exercised sound judgment. Whereas for their contemporaries, equally pragmatic in their ordinary living, religion belonged to the realm of poetry and the free run of imagination, so that fantasy and contradiction dominate the mass of heterogeneous myths which developed in polytheistic society, the Israelite approach was also empirical in the realm of theology. The reports of divine-human contacts ought not to be classed with the pagan myths as mere fantasy, but rather as the honest and sober effort to communicate an extraordinary but nevertheless actual human experience. What was the nature of it? It is precisely because it lies outside of ordinary human experience that definition or description by analogy (working from the known to the unknown) is unsuccessful; such experience is *sui generis*. There is very little to compare with or check by except other biblical experiences of a similar kind, and these do not bring us closer to the heart of the question. It must be a matter of the total witness afforded by the men in question — the fathers, Moses, and the prophets — and whether in the light of such witness we can accept the

75

primary claim of direct discourse between God and man, or specifically, between God and these men.

We can pass by the matter of anthropomorphic language, since human beings can hardly communicate in any other language; and it does not finally help the case to substitute complex abstractions or logically purified terminology for the supposed crudities of biblical speech. We cannot fool ourselves into supposing we have solved the problem of direct contact by substituting less disturbing vocabulary for the plain words of the biblical text. Moses' conversations with God are so intimate, direct, and "face to face" that no one can possibly mistake the meaning of the Bible on this score, or avoid the scandalous situation we confront in making a decision. In brief the problem is this: did the communication come directly from God to man, as the text states, or is this phenomenon explicable as an entirely human experience? We do not deny at all the large, even dominant, human element in the report of such conversation. Not only has God condescended in some mysterious fashion to comport himself in humanly discernible and understandable ways, but the report itself is delivered by the human participant, and has even been filtered through his consciousness, his pattern of thinking and speaking. One can never suppose that it is possible to secure the pure uncontaminated word of God. The human, fallible, corruptible channel is our only device, at least so far as the Old Testament is concerned.

The Prophet as Mediator

The human figure, who in effect mediates the word, who announces the divine action which is to take place, who himself may be, and in some sense usually is, the instrument of that action, and who interprets the action theologically (i.e., its relation to the purpose of God) — him we may term the prophet. This is to a very large degree an artificial designation, since it does not fit the historical picture of the prophet, or of the prophetic movement, nor does it distinguish the prophet from other charismatic heroes, like the patriarch, or the judge. The use of the term emphasizes, however, the verbal side of the contact with God. While Moses was not a prophet in a correct historical usage of the term, nevertheless in the eyes of later Israel he was the prophet par excellence. He is so designated by the writer of the book of Deuteronomy, which is basically an attempt to reinterpret Moses and his work, and the events of the crucial and creative period of Israel's history in the light of later circumstances, particularly the situation in which Israel found itself in the 7th century B.C.E. And the biblical understanding of the prophetic movement was conditioned by this reconstructed figure of Moses as first and chief of prophets. It can hardly be accidental that the message of Moses in Deuteronomy, i.e., the prophetic sermons of this book, have the same basic contents and structure and deal with the same crisis (the threat of national destruction and exile, followed by the hope of restorartion) as the prophetic utterances of the principal prophets, beginning with the 8th-century foursome, Amos, Hosea, Micah, and Isaiah; but especially striking is the close similarity between the Moses of Deuteronomy and the three prophets contemporary with the Deuteronomist (or roughly so) — Jeremiah, Ezekiel, and 2 Isaiah.

The *prophet,* using the term in the broadest possible sense, thus stands between God and his people, between God and history, between God and religious commitment and faith. For the ordinary citizen, even of the community of faith, it was necessary to come first to grips and then to terms with the prophet, for he was the way to the Most High, and no man could come to the Father except by him. Biblical religion is mediated religion, as both Old and New Testaments make clear. We are accustomed to this in dealing with the New Testament, but perhaps we overlook the fact that the pattern of mediation is firmly planted in the Old, and that this pattern has been adopted in the New, and is essentially derived from the prophetic movement. For the biblical writers the pattern was initiated by Moses who was the mediator of the Covenant, and the model for all subsequent mediators. This role was practically forced upon Moses at Mt. Sinai when the people begged him to stand between them and God. Though they were offered the option of direct dealings with the Lord, they preferred the method of mediation, which then was permanently fixed in biblical religion, with the proviso that at the end, in the eschatological age, mediation would be done away with (so, e.g., Joel 3:1ff. with regard to the pouring out of the Spirit; cf. Acts 2:16ff.). In the New Testament, Jesus is the absolutely indispensable mediator between God and man, but even his mediatorial activity will end, as e.g. in 1 Cor. 15:24-28, where God will assume direct rule at the conclusion of all things.

The question of biblical religion hinges, therefore, on the validity of the prophet's experience and the authority of his message. He constitutes the link between the history of the people and God. Without the prophet and his person-to-person contact, it would be difficult, if not impossible, to establish such a connection; not that the prophet can solve the problem of faith, but without him the problem cannot even be stated. With him there can be affirmation of the connection, and the challenge to believe; without him we have only the egotism of the national spirit affirming its divinity. This happens also to be the manner in which the Bible affirms or rather assumes the basic theological question of the existence of God, although in the historical context of pagan polytheism this was not so much the question as was that of his authority as God against gods. His status and power were vindicated by the mighty deeds, duly authenticated by the prophet, who also delineated his name and personality and who identified him through personal contact and conversation.

The tradition consists of the combination of revelation and event, when the historical moment has come and gone. It is the memory of the event, framed by the prior announcement, and the subsequent interpretation and evaluation. Or in other words, the theophany to the prophet, the mighty deed, and its meaning, all wrapped together in the collective and authoritative memory of the community, constitute the tradition.

The Tradition Maintained

The principal technique used for maintaining the tradition, apart from recording it (and this must be a relatively later development) was the liturgy, i.e., the dramatic reenactment of the event as a cultic exercise. In this way later generations could participate in the mighty deed and share the experience of the ancestors. Thus the greatest of all mighty deeds — the exodus, the wanderings, the conquest, centering around the Sinai covenant — was enshrined in the great festivals. Passover, Pentecost, and Tabernacles involved the reenactment of the deliverance, the giving of the law, and the wanderings, along with or including some sort of covenant renewal; and other celebrations like the New Year and the Day of Atonement were designed essentially to re-create the decisive events of the history which linked God and Israel. In this way, a notable attempt was made to recapture the spirit and excitement, and the inner reality of the original occurrence, though it must be recognized that the original event could only be imitated in dramatic form. The historical particularity of biblical religion does not lend itself easily to liturgical transformation. Such technique owes much to the liturgical practice of pagan religion, to which it is much more amenable. The biblical cultic celebration is distinguished by an emphasis on the historical event as over against the nonhistorical, nature- or fertility-cycle pattern, with its recurring seasonal phenomena. Because of its historicity, the biblical festival emphasizes the aspect of memory, and the memorial character of the celebration divorces it from the original occurrence. On the other hand the pagan festival renews itself in actuality every year, and is not a mere dramatic reconstruction of a decisive event which once happened. The once-for-all, unrepeatable event in biblical religion militates against the effective use of the festival to create its own religious reality. The cult rite is always secondary in Israel, and is derivative rather than primary, despite serious efforts to elevate the cult to the prime place. The essential conflict between a religion of historically distinct and unique events and a cultic religion of nature and its renewal is attested in the biblical record. The success of the cult reflected the decline in the religion of event; here at bottom is the antithesis between priest and prophet.

A second technique for maintaining the tradition was didactic in principle. In practice the dramatic and didactic were united, e.g., in the Covenant renewal ceremony as well as in the other festivals, where the cultic pattern was used to inculcate and educate. It is quite understandable that priestly responsibility extended to both areas. They were responsible for instruction in Torah, as well as for the celebration of the feast; the Feast was Torah acted out, and Torah was the record of the event celebrated in the Feast, with its meaning, its implications, its obligations spelled out. In Torah the attempt was made to distill from the tradition, from revelation and event, a permanent deposit of the impact of God upon people, and to sum up the divine purpose and requirements in formulas which could be learned and obeyed by subsequent generations. Very early in Israel's history the attempt was made to consolidate experience, to universalize and generalize from the particular experiences, to etch the personality and purpose of God, his nature, and being, and to describe his will and demands in terms which would be permanently applicable. Such a formula, perhaps the oldest of its kind in the Old Testament, is to be found in Exod. 34:6-7, a statement of the nature of the God of the mighty deeds, divorced from the specific event and place, but in words applicable to all events and places, emphasizing the specific features or attributes revealed in the mighty deeds. Likewise there were evolved from the basic Covenant demands (e.g., the Ten Commandments) detailed rules to govern the whole operation of life in the Covenant community, to protect the community from violation, and as well general principles of ethical practice, defining the motivation behind the detailed rules. The end result of the former was the detailed codes of rabbinic jurisprudence, of the latter the practical advice of the wise men, enshrined in books like Proverbs. In this way, the limitations of the once-for-all historical event of biblical tradition were transcended, and something significant and usable could be attained for later generations. But something of the dynamic character of biblical religion, the thing which made it distinctive, was lost. Dramatic and didactic values are a poor substitute finally for the epic events of historical particularity and uniqueness. So long as history endured and events followed in chronological sequence, the possibility of renewing the historical character of biblical religion remained. There remained the possibility that there would be new events with distinctive and unique meaning, to attach to the older tradition, that God might act again in relation to his people in the sequence of announcement, deed, and interpretation; all this remained as the other side of a religion increasingly static and repetitive, living by exegesis rather than by revelation. So besides the tradition, which was essentially the prerogative of the priests, was the prophetic responsibility for announcement and interpretation of new event, the cutting edge of historical religion. Here was new tradition in the making.

The Continuing Prophetic Activity

The prophet participates in the historical present. He is part of the community with its tradition, its dramatic and didactic continuity with the past, confirming the all-important character of divine deeds and their permanent significance. But the prophet likewise constitutes the expectation of a new word and a new action. He represents the possibility, for without him the word is not heard, and the action cannot be understood (cf. the ironic statement of Isaiah that his purpose as a prophet was to do just the opposite: to close the ears and blind the eyes, indicating that the normal purpose was to reveal and interpret). Without him the word is not spoken, and the action is not accomplished. Thus the prophet, by virtue of direct contact with God, speaks the divine word directly to the community, not by exegesis or inference, though these have their role. Thus the word of Jeremiah to the people of Judah was to surrender to Nebuchadrezzar and make no defense of city or temple — a word of treason, according to the holders and interpreters of the tradition, whose exegesis and inference from the tradition was sound enough (for where in the tradition was there any word of surrender to the pagans?), but who could not receive or endure the new word spoken by God in their own day. We may note two points about the continuing prophetic activity:

1) It is the word for today, the day when it is spoken. It constitutes revelation antecedent to action (so Amos in ch. 3 describes the prophet as one who bears the decision made in the divine council before the sentence is executed). It is an essential feature of biblical religion, a mark of the continuing contact between God and people, and of his participation in human affairs. Once the moment of the contact is past, the combination and event becomes part of the tradition with its own contribution to the liturgy (though of a secondary nature) and teaching. But as time makes tradition out of revelation and event, new revelation and event displace the tradition, appropriating, modifying, and applying its meaning, thus pointing to the common source and unity of all revelation in God, but also reflecting the dynamic relationship of two living parties.

2) The continuity of history, conceived as revelation and occurrence (or word and deed) might itself seem endless and aimless, as human history with its notorious backing and filling and circular drifting very often appears to be. But notable in the prophetic message is the sense of objective or goal. Revelation always anticipates the mighty deed to come, and the mighty deed invariably had the note of finality about it. For the Bible, history and eschatology are essentially one; eschatology is the conclusion of history but it proceeds from historical occurrences, and history is the setting for the eschaton. In the sense that the acts of God are decisive, they are at the same time final. But the finality is itself historical; it occurs in time and place. The deed is part of the fulfilment of the divine goal — not total fulfillment, but partial. Fulfillment nevertheless belongs to the eschaton. From the time of Moses on, history has an eschatological element, involved in the very notion of fulfillment. Every act of God aims at an ultimate fulfillment. So long as history continues, the final fulfillment has not taken place, but history itself is eschatological to the degree that any fulfillment at all takes place. The eschatological note is particularly strong in the later prophets, e.g., in their representation of the remaking

of nature, the new heavens and a new earth, and the figures and symbols of total destruction and renewal, which go beyond historical reality; but this element is already present in the earlier prophets. Without debating S. Mowinckel's subtle distinction between future hope and eschatological expectation, we may point to this feature of the prophetic message as giving the whole pattern of revelation and event its meaning. The prophet is the mediator between God and the world and Israel and man. His purpose is to announce, and thus initiate, the action of God which will advance the eschaton, which will accomplish a part of the ultimate purpose; through all the prophets and their works will come the final fulfillment of the Kingdom, and with it the end of prophecy and of history. The prophet, therefore, is the key to the historical moment when decisive action takes place, predicated upon revelation. Once past it constitutes tradition. The prophet stands upon the platform of tradition, forming the link between heaven and earth; his word is the present divine reality in human affairs, but not merely as the accompaniment of an eternal historical process (i.e., as a kind of exalted commentary). The prophetic utterance is not subordinate to and victimized by the historical process; it rather controls and directs the future through the power of the divine, which is itself the deed announced and guaranteed, the event being the word enacted. Each word of revelation speaks not only of the immediate action to take place, but at the same time of the ultimate fulfillments. One might say that the word describes an ideal action, which is eschatological, and is related historically to a temporal action. What happens is related to, but not precisely the same as, what has been said. The word functions here and now, producing its event, but it speaks also to a final resolution, which lies at the end. This is not to say that the prophet made such a distinction or was conscious of it. For him history and eschatology were one; and the responsibility for the distinction lies with us who make it, and more specifically with the God who is source of both word and action. It can hardly be that all the prophets were equally mistaken about the end; the source of this difficulty must be found in the urgency of the word, and the desire of God himself to achieve his purpose. The partial failure or partial fulfillment must be the result of other causes operating upon God or within him, to postpone the end already announced.

9

The Name of the God of Moses

An important biblical tradition associates the revelation of the personal name of God, the Tetragrammaton, with Moses. This is explicitly affirmed in Exod. 6:2-3 (commonly attributed to the Priestly stratum of the Pentateuch): "And God said to Moses . . . 'I am Yahweh. And I appeared to Abraham, to Isaac, and to Jacob as El Shaddai; but (by) my name Yahweh I was not known to them.'" Exod. 3:13-15 (usually regarded as E) supports this view with an account of the revelation of the name of God, which had not previously been known. Even in the J stratum, the name which otherwise is traced back to the earliest times, is given special emphasis in the divine communications to Moses (cf. Exod. 34:5-6 and 14). At the very least, in the biblical record, a new and extraordinary significance is attached to the name of God in the Mosaic era.[1]

In the light of the tradition, we may pose three questions, and then attempt to answer them: (1) What was the name of the God of Moses? (2) What is the meaning of the name? (3) What is its significance in the context of the book of Exodus?

The simplest form of the name is provided by the Priestly writer(s) in Exod. 6:2-3: the Tetragrammaton alone, YHWH. Admittedly there is no scholarly consensus

---

1. The general validity of this tradition of the name of God is further attested by the close association of the revelation of the name with the Sinai-Horeb events. YHWH is peculiarly the name of the God of the Sinai covenant; the inescapable association of the latter with Moses supports the view that the revelation of the name forms part of the covenant-making process. The preamble to the Decalogue (Exod. 20:2) opens with the same words: "I am Yahweh . . ." as does the P account of the revelation of the name (Exod. 6:2, with the alternative first person pronoun). The third commandment deals explicitly with the profanation of the (newly revealed) name. And in Exod. 34, the proclamation of the name precedes directly the (re)making of the covenant. The interrelationship of name and covenant is best preserved in the J stratum of Exod. 34, which in other respects as well retains a more archaic tradition: e.g., the form of the first commandment in 34:14, כי לא תשתחוה לאל אחר, is clearly more original than the prosaic אלהים אחרים על־פני, לא יהיה לך, with its necessary addition, לא־תשתחוה להם ולא תעבדם (Exod. 20:3 and 5).

82

about the form or meaning of this word. And the question of its ultimate origin has not been resolved to the satisfaction of all. The position advanced in this paper is based upon the following points, which appear to the writer to be most in accord with the available data: (1) that the Tetragrammaton was pronounced *Yahweh;* (2) that it is a verb derived from the root **hwy > *hwh,* which in accordance with recognized linguistic laws appears in biblical Hebrew as *hyh;*[2] (3) that it is a hiphil imperfect 3rd masculine singular form of the verb; and (4) that it is to be translated, "He causes to be, he brings into existence; he brings to pass, he creates."[3]

Elsewhere in the book of Exodus the name of God is given in a variety of expanded forms (cf. 3:13-15; 34:6-7, 14), while in 1 and 2 Samuel a different expansion is presented as the name inscribed upon the ark of the covenant. In attempting to determine which is the more original form, the simple Tetragrammaton, or one or more of the expanded formulas, two observations are in order: (1) the term "name" itself is not a decisive criterion, since it is applied equally to names as we understand them, and to titles or descriptive formulas. (2) If, as we contend, *yahweh* is a verb form, then it must have formed part of a longer expression. The evidence of the onomastica of the Near East in the 2nd millennium B.C.E. points unmistakably in this direction.[4] The conclusion, already suggested by W. F. Albright, is that these names are derived from a formulary or litany describing the covenant God in a series of affirmations beginning with the word *yahweh.*[5] As both the first and common element in the series, *yahweh* was the logical and inevitable abbreviation, and thus emerged as the "name" of God.

We may now turn to the Mosaic formulas in the book of Exodus. The *locus classicus* is Exod. 3:14: *'ehyeh 'ᵃšer 'ehyeh.* The interpretation remains problematical in spite of the concentrated efforts of scholars. The form *'ehyeh* is to be understood as the first person equivalent of the Tetragrammaton (as the writer clearly intends; cf. *'ehyeh šᵉlāḥanî* in v. 14). While it is now vocalized as a qal form in MT (based

2. This is in accord with the view of the biblical writer in Exod. 3:13-15, who directly associates the Tetragrammaton with the root *hyh,* though in MT the form is vocalized as a qal instead of a hiphil.

3. The chief contemporary exponent of this view, which has a long scholarly prehistory, is W. F. Albright, following the lead of P. Haupt: cf. "Contributions to Biblical Archaeology and Philology, 2: The Name *Yahweh,*" *JBL* 43 (1924): 370-78, with a variety of additional material since then, most recently in the Introduction to the Anchor edition of *From the Stone Age to Christianity* (Garden City: Doubleday, 1957), 15-16. There is no need to repeat the case presented by Albright, which is entirely convincing to the writer for the analysis of the form *yahweh;* see e.g., his explanation of the expression יהוה צבאות in his review of B. N. Wambacq, *L'épithète divine Jahvé* Sᵉba'ôt, *JBL* 67 (1948): 377-81. [Further discussion in *CMHE,* 60-75, and W. H. Brownlee, "The Ineffable Name of God," *BASOR* 226 (1977): 39-46.]

4. Cf. Albright's discussion of hypocoristica in *JBL* 43 (1924): 371-72; there can be no doubt that *yahweh* belongs to this class of name. For other examples, see *From the Stone Age to Christianity,* 260-61.

5. *From the Stone Age to Christianity,* 16 and 260.

upon a tradition that lies behind the LXX, and may be even older), this must be regarded as a secondary development.[6] The original form was hiphil, and the meaning is "I bring into being." In dealing with the whole expression, P. Haupt emended the second *'ehyeh* and read: *'ahyeh 'ašer yihyeh,* "I cause to be what comes into existence."[7] Though this is an eminently satisfactory solution to the problem of Exod. 3:14, it is possible to improve upon it by avoiding even the relatively slight textual emendation, and also by relating the "name" more significantly to the context of the book of Exodus. While the Creator God figures prominently in biblical as well as Near Eastern religion from patriarchal times on, and is, of course, not out of place in the Mosaic age, nevertheless the principal emphases in the book of Exodus are upon the merciful intervention and the saving action of the God of the Fathers in behalf of his oppressed people.

Unemended, the formula in Exod. 3:14 falls into the category of *idem per idem* constructions, which are common to both Hebrew and Arabic. S. R. Driver (basing himself on the prior work of P. A. de Lagarde) discusses this construction in his *Notes on the Hebrew Text and Topography of the Books of Samuel,*[8] and his commentary on *The Book of Exodus* in the Cambridge Bible.[9] He connects, rightly in our judgment, Exod. 3:14 with 33:19, where the *idem per idem* construction also occurs, and affirms that this idiomatic repetition is "employed where the means or desire to be more explicit does not exist."[10] The second verb serves as a predicate, and thus, like a cognate accusative, emphasizes the verbal action: e.g., Exod. 16:23, את אשר־תאפו אפו, "What you bake, bake"; and את אשר־תבשלו בשלו, "What you boil, boil."[11]

Exod. 33:19 is related to Exod. 3:14 not only in grammatical construction, but also with regard to the revelation of the name of God: "And He said, 'I will make all my goodness pass before you, and I will pronounce the name, YHWH, before you. . . .' "[12] What follows is a first person utterance by God to Moses, in

---

6. Since the original meaning of *yahweh* had long since been forgotten, this interpretation as a qal form was the only one possible within the structure of the language as it was constituted in postexilic times.

7. P. Haupt, "Der Name Jahwe," *OLZ* 12 (1909): 211-14, quoted and discussed by Albright, *JBL* 43 (1924): 375-76. Albright adduces Egyptian parallels to this formula (377-78).

8. 2nd ed. (Oxford: Clarendon, 1913), 185-86.

9. (Cambridge: Cambridge University Press, 1911), 362-63, etc.

10. *Ibid.,* 363.

11. Other passages with the same construction are Exod. 4:13; 1 Sam. 23:13; 2 Sam. 15:20; 2 Kgs. 8:1; and Ezek. 12:25. Each needs to be examined separately, but in every case the emphasis is on the verbal idea; the element of arbitrary choice, or wilfulness, which crops up in the English translations, is not inherent in the Hebrew expression. See below.

12. The material in Exod. 33:12-23 is usually attributed to J, but the analysis is by no means certain. Scholars resort to desperate measures to secure continuity. It is much more likely that a mixture of J and E strands is involved here. For the purpose of this paper it is not directly significant, except that the first person expressions which follow in v. 19 logically connect with 3:14, and may therefore come from the E source.

the *idem per idem* construction, precisely parallel to Exod. 3:14:ואחנתי את־אשר,
אחן ורחמתי את־אשר ארחם, "And I will be gracious to whom I will be gracious;
and I will show mercy on whom I will show mercy." The stress in this passage is
upon the verbal action: showing grace and mercy. There appears to be no suggestion
of wilfulness or arbitrary free choice in the Hebrew, in spite of the theological
deductions commonly drawn by commentators. To quote Driver once more: "All
that is said here is that God is gracious to those to whom he is gracious." And
further on, "The second 'will' in each sentence is a simple future: it must not be
emphasized as though it meant 'wish to'. . . ."[13] We are now in a position to render
the enigmatic expression in Exod. 3:14: "I create what I create," or more simply,
"I am the creator." Similarly in 33:19: "I am the gracious one; I am the compassionate one."

A related name formula is found in Exod. 34:6-7 (J), which is a continuation
of the Exod. 33 passage just discussed. It begins with a repetition of the Tetragrammaton (YHWH YHWH), itself remarkable, and so far as I can determine, unique
in the OT. It is strikingly parallel to the first person repetition in Exod. 3:14 (with
the exception of אשר, which belongs rather to the prose adaptation of the original
poetic formula). There follows in 34:6 the expression אל רחום וחנון, "God compassionate and gracious," which in turn is parallel to the material in Exod. 33:19,
where the same verbal roots are used. On the basis of these three "name" passages
we are now in a position to reconstruct the parallel first and third person forms of
the name of the God of Moses. The name itself, properly speaking, is to be found
in the third person formula in 34:6: "The compassionate and gracious God creates
what he creates." The parallel first person formula adapted for divine utterance
comes from 3:14 and 33:19: "I create what I create, and I am gracious to whom I
am gracious, and I show mercy to whom I show mercy." In both forms the creative
action of the gracious and merciful God is stressed.

The formula in 34:6-7 continues at some length, with a series of adjectival
modifiers describing in greater detail the nature of the Mosaic God. It is difficult
to say how much of this material belonged originally to the "name," though it
doubtless derives from various litanic formulations of the earliest period.[14]

Still another name formula is found in Exod. 34:14: אל קנא, "the zealous
or passionate God." It occurs also in the Decalogue in the comment on the second
commandment, where it is associated with the visitation of punishment upon the
third and fourth generations, an element in turn in the name formula of Exod.

13. Driver, *The Book of Exodus* [Cambridge, 1911], 363. That God is free to bestow or
withhold favor follows from the biblical view of his authority as creator and judge. Mercy and
grace are consistently emphasized as paramount qualities of his nature, however, and in this
passage it is specifically asserted that the name formula reveals God's "goodness *(ṭūb)*."

14. Cf. D. N. Freedman, "God Compassionate and Gracious," *Western Watch* 6 (1955):
6-24. Some of these formulas go back to patriarchal times, but much is distinctively Mosaic, as
the biblical tradition itself makes clear.

34:7.[15] The expression in 34:14 is difficult to render. MT reads: שמו אל קנא הוא
כי יהוה קנא, which is commonly translated, "For Yahweh, whose name is Jealous,
is the Jealous God." This is awkward, however, and in view of the previous
discussion, the "name" here must be *yahweh qannā'*, "the Zealous One Creates."
LXX offers a variant reading, with the addition of *'ēl* (ὁ θεός) after the Tetragrammaton; this plus is not unexpected since *qannā'* (or *qannō'*) occurs elsewhere in
the Old Testament only in combination with *'ēl*.[16] It is not necessary to emend MT,
however. The omission of *'ēl* before the qualifying noun is attested in a series of
similar name formulas: e.g., El Shaddai and Shaddai, El Elyon and Elyon, and
probably El Olam and Olam (Deut. 33:27).[17] Another possibility is to read *qin'â*
for the first *qannā'* in MT; we may render the expression: "For 'He Creates Zeal'
is his name." The formula would be parallel in structure to several others in the
early sources, in particular *yahweh yir'â* (Gen 22:14), "He creates reverence," as
reconstructed by Albright.[18]

We can sketch our conclusions regarding the name formulas in the book of
Exodus: (1) The initial and common element is the word *yahweh,* which describes
the activity of the Creator God, a concept common to the high religions of the
ancient Near East, basic to all the strata of the Bible, and certainly reaching back
to the patriarchs. The term itself, as the J source affirms, is doubtless pre-Mosaic.
(2) What emerge as distinctively Mosaic in the name formulas are the qualities and
attributes of the Creator God of the Fathers revealed in the unique historical setting
of the Sinai covenant, between the past event of the exodus, and the future prospect
of the conquest. These are grace and mercy, patience, great kindness and devotion,
all of which mark the action by which he delivers his afflicted people, creates a
new community — and not least the passionate zeal by which he binds Israel to
himself in an exclusive relationship of privilege and obligation, of promise and
threat, of judgment and mercy.

We append two notes, which follow upon the main argument:

1. An important early name formula is יהוה צבאות, which in various forms
was inscribed upon the ark of the covenant.[19] The original verbal force of *yahweh*

---

15. *Ibid.,* 14ff. The essential meaning of *qn'* is "ardor, passion," which finds expression
either in judgment or kindness (cf. Exod. 20:5-6); it is parallel to "love" in Cant. 8:6, and perhaps
is best translated, "zeal, zealous." Because of its modern connotations, "jealousy" is a misleading
translation, especially when the term is used of God.

16. The form *'elōhîm,* as suggested by BH³, is thus mistaken. The interpretation of the
passage would be the same: "For 'El Qanna (the Zealous God) Creates' is his name."

17. The term *qannā'* and what it signifies regarding the exclusive relationship between
Yahweh and Israel seem to the writer uniquely and distinctively Mosaic. The persistence of the
poetic form *'ēl* in connection with it even in later prose contexts (e.g., Deut. 4:24; 6:15) is sufficient
evidence of its antiquity.

18. *From the Stone Age to Christianity,* 16.

19. Albright, *JBL* 67 (1948): 377-81.

is strikingly evident here: "The One Enthroned upon the Cherubim creates the hosts (of Israel)." According to the biblical tradition, however, this formula comes from the period of the judges, and is not to be found in the Mosaic material. Since the ark served as the sacred emblem of the cult center, its "name" doubtless served as the amphictyonic motto, and in this period was the name of God par excellence. In spite of the fact that the ark itself is traced back to the wilderness wanderings, and even the cherubim are read back into Mosaic times by the Priestly writer(s), the formula itself is lacking in the Pentateuch. Priority would appear to belong to the Exodus formulas.

2. From Exod. 34:6 and 14, it is clear that the proper subject of the verb *yahweh* is *'ēl*. Thus the name is structurally identical with the numerous *'ēl* names of the 2nd millennium, which often appear as hypocoristica like *yahweh* itself.[20] The continued use of the designation El throughout the Bible (though limited largely to poetry), despite its obvious Canaanite associations, shows that the name was deeply rooted in Israelite tradition. The patriarchal names for their deity are built around this element: e.g., El Shaddai, El Elyon (specifically the Creator God, Gen. 14:19), El Olam; comparable in form therefore are the El Qanna and the El Raḥum wᵉHannun of the Mosaic age. The anomalous combination *yahweh 'elōhīm,* usually regarded as the result of a mixture of sources, or an artificial construction, may simply be the survival in occasional passages of the prose equivalent of the poetic or formulaic *yahweh 'ēl,* etc., under discussion, with the same original meaning, "God creates." It survives merely as a title in the passages in which it occurs.

20. Cf. Exod. 34:6 and 14; once it is recognized that the use of the term *yahweh* goes back to patriarchal times, the *'ēl* element becomes virtually certain. For a comprehensive study of the relationship of *yahweh* to the God of the Fathers, see the paper by F. M. Cross, Jr., which was read at the Oxford Congress of the International Organization for the Study of the OT (1959), and will appear in the forthcoming Congress Volume. [See *CMHE*, 3-75.]

10

The Chronicler's Purpose

The present state of studies in the Chronicler's work may fairly be said to border on chaos. The scope, purpose, date, and historical value of this work are all subject to violent debate on the part of scholars who affirm exactly opposite conclusions in the strongest possible language. Between extremes — represented for example by Torrey and Welch — there are numerous mediating positions, which nevertheless differ sharply among themselves. Because of the pivotal nature of Chronicles (along with Ezra-Nehemiah), it is nevertheless important to persist in the struggle toward a scholarly consensus. If satisfactory answers could be secured to the basic critical questions, these in turn would bear significantly on the study of the biblical works to which the Chronicler's history is directly or indirectly related: e.g., Samuel-Kings upon a version of which Chronicles is directly dependent, the Pentateuch (in whole or in part: the interrelationships with D and P are still much in dispute), the later prophets, and the Psalms. In this preliminary presentation, we intend to skirt the chief centers of controversy, and begin with a reexamination of the Chronicler's purpose, indicating the necessary assumptions or opinions which bear upon the matter as we proceed.

It is not easy to answer the basic question: What was the underlying intention or primary objective of the Chronicler in compiling his work? At the same time it is not difficult to isolate the major themes which run through the history: the author is above all a legitimist, and he is concerned with the divinely appointed institutions and duly authorized personnel which administer them in behalf of the people of Israel. Thus, his interest focuses on the kingdom of Judah, its capital city Jerusalem, and at the very center the temple; with respect to personnel, on the monarchy and the priesthood, or more particularly David and his dynasty, the high priest Zadok, his descendants, and ultimately all those belonging to Aaron and Levi. But to determine the principal objective requires a judgment as to the scope of the work, and at least a plausible suggestion as to the reason and occasion for writing it. Problems immediately arise in the attempt to settle the limits of the Chronicler's history, i.e., where it begins and ends. With respect to the conclusion, the present division into books (Chronicles-Ezra-Nehemiah) poses the question of the relationship of the former to the latter. The very fact that the books overlap (2 Chr. 36:22-23 = Ezra 1:1-3a) would seem to settle the point: Ezra is the immediate sequel to Chronicles, and together they form part of the same original work. Nevertheless eminent scholars have interpreted this datum in the opposite fashion: i.e., the verses are repeated to bind together two originally separate works. It seems to me that the repetition of the verses is a late phenomenon, and the result of the division and ordering of the books in the Massoretic text, and has no immediate bearing on the question. But the internal problems of Ezra-Nehemiah persist: the proper arrangement of the parts and their interrelationship remain unsolved. The chronological sequence of the two principal figures, Ezra and Nehemiah, is still an open question, and leaves unsettled the matter of the ending of the Chronicler's work, if in any case we can find a conclusion in Ezra-Nehemiah.

When we turn to the beginning of the Chronicler's history we are confronted with the problem of the opening nine chapters of genealogies. Whether they form part of the original work is a matter of controversy, and need not be decided at this point. We freely grant that genealogical considerations loom large in the thinking of the Chronicler, as they do in the P material in the Pentateuch, and for similar reasons: the concern for legitimacy is fundamental in both. At the same time, the lists in themselves tell us little about the author's purpose; for this we must turn to the narrative which begins in the tenth chapter. It is here that we find a fundamental clue to the Chronicler's intention. It is instructive that he does not begin his story with the fathers, or with Moses and the exodus (aside from stereotyped references to the law of Moses, these traditions play no significant part in the narrative), but with the death of Saul and the enthronement of David. The concern for the house of David as the sole legitimate possessor of royal authority in Israel is apparent throughout the Chronicler's history. The related interests — the city of Jerusalem, the temple, the priesthood, and the ordinances for worship in song and sacrifice — all nevertheless center in the person of David, and his descendants, beginning with Solomon and continuing down through the centuries to the end of the kingdom and beyond. It seems clear therefore that the principal objective of the Chronicler was to write a history of the dynasty of David, not primarily in terms of its historical and political achievements (though these form the framework, appropriated from Samuel-Kings), but its accomplishments in the religious and specifically cultic areas. To summarize, the Chronicler establishes through his narrative of the reigns of David and Solomon the proper, legitimate pattern of institutions and their personnel for the people of God; and they are the monarchy represented by David and his house, the priesthood, by Zadok and his descendants, the city and the temple in the Promised Land. City and ruler, temple and priest — these appear to be the fixed points around which the Chronicler constructs his history and his theology. There is no reason to suppose that the Chronicler ever abandoned or changed his convictions about them.

Of the legitimacy and permanence of the institutions mentioned no question can be raised so far as the mind of the Chronicler is concerned, except perhaps with respect to the dynasty of David. This is in itself curious, since David and Solomon are clearly the central figures in his story, outranking all other personages, and under the guidance of God the builders of both city and temple. The problem centers in the ambiguous statements of the Chronicler (taken over almost verbatim, however, from the Deuteronomic history) concerning the status of the Davidic dynasty. In the report of the word of Yahweh through Nathan (2 Sam. 7 = 1 Chr. 17), the divine commitment to the house of David is stated in absolute and irrevocable terms: "He shall build a house for my name, and I will establish his royal throne for ever. I will be a father to him, and he will be a son to me. If he should be guilty of wrongdoing, I will chastise him with the rod of men, and with the blows of human agents; but I will not take my devotion from him, as I took it from Saul. . . . And your royal dynasty shall be secured forever before me; your throne shall be established forever" (2 Sam. 7:13-16; 1 Chr. 17:12-14 omits the reference to punishment, and rewords the last statement: "But I will confirm him in my royal house forever, and his throne shall be established forever"). Elsewhere in the Deuteronomic history as also in Chronicles, the commitment is made conditional upon the faithfulness and obedience of the reigning king of the dynasty: e.g., 3 Kgs. 2:4 and especially 9:4-7 = 2 Chr. 7:17-20 — "And as for you, if you will walk before me, as David your father walked, with integrity of purpose and with uprightness, doing everything that I have commanded you, and if you abide by my statutes and my decisions, then I will establish your dynastic throne over Israel forever, as I affirmed to David your father: You shall never be deprived of a descendant upon the throne of Israel. But if you or your sons persistently turn back from me, and do not observe my stipulated requirements, which I have set before you, but proceed to serve other gods and worship them, then I will banish Israel from the land which I have given them; and Israel will become an object-lesson and a byword among all peoples." (Cf. also 4 Kgs. 21:10-15; 22:16-20; 24:3-5.)

The conclusion to be drawn is that both historians acknowledged the undoubted frailty of reigning kings and the disastrous consequences of dereliction of duty toward God both to the royal house and the nation; at the same time they must have retained confidence in the overruling grace of God and the ultimate fulfillment of his words, that the day would come when the kingdom would be restored with a descendant of David upon the throne. Such indeed was the view of the prophets who expressed themselves on the subject (e.g., Hosea, Isaiah, Micah, and even Jeremiah and Ezekiel at the time of the collapse of the state and the removal of the Davidic king). The paradox of present judgment and future hope with regard to the house of David is clearly visible in Jeremiah, who was thoroughly disillusioned about the last kings of Judah (not only Jehoiakim and Zedekiah, but also Jehoiachin; cf. Jer. 22:24-30), yet expressed his hopes for the future in terms of a restored kingdom under the rule of a son of David (23:5-6; 33:15-17). Ezekiel likewise assigned a place in the restoration to the king of the line of David (Ezek. 34:23-24 and 37:15-28, esp. 24-25; he is referred to both as prince and king). Second Isaiah alone may have abandoned or transferred the traditional view regarding the house of David (cf. Isa. 55:3ff.).

The hope for and confidence in the Davidic line continued, as we have seen, after the destruction of the kingdom, through the exile and on into the postexilic period. This view is confirmed both by the historical records preserved in Ezra, and the prophetic utterances of the early postexilic prophets, Haggai and Zechariah. As for the legitimist Jews returning from exile, their hopes included restoration of the land, the city, the temple, under the leadership of the proper representatives of the house of David and of Zadok. Thus, Sheshbazzar is characterized as "prince of Judah," and while there are some difficulties with the name, it is reasonable to suppose that he was one of the sons of Jehoiachin (presumably Shenazzar; both names are apparently corruptions of an original Sin-ab-usur). About his successor Zerubbabel, a grandson of Jehoiachin, there is no doubt whatever. Similarly, Joshua is formally acknowledged to be the legitimate high priest. The traditional prophetic expectations concerning the restoration of the community of God in terms of city and ruler, temple and priest are voiced by the prophets Haggai and Zechariah, and specifically applied to these men. Without pressing the details, which are not entirely clear, we can affirm that the prophets anticipated the restoration of the state under the dual authority of the civil and ecclesiastical leaders, the duly anointed scions of David and Zadok respectively, whose immediate task was the rebuilding of the temple.

From the beginning of the story to this point at least, the unity in theme and purpose in the Chronicler's work is apparent. The continuity of the narrative is equally impressive. The parallel between the first building of the temple under the direction of David (and Solomon) and the second building under Zerubbabel is too striking to be accidental, and must have formed part of the original structure of the work. Thus far, we can see the Chronicler's intent and hand clearly in the work; but beyond the story of Zerubbabel and Joshua and the rebuilding of the temple there is considerable confusion. In the first place there is a serious gap in the records; not only does the story of the work of Zerubbabel and Joshua end abruptly, but a period of sixty or more years passes with only a single incidental reference. Hard on the heels of the narrative of the rebuilding of the temple come the accounts of Ezra and Nehemiah, and their strenuous efforts to confirm the struggling Jewish community in the midst of its enemies. Not only is there a break in the narrative, but the chief concerns of the story are quite different. While the familiar interest in legitimacy is present and the authority of David and Solomon is claimed for the reestablishment of the cult (Neh. 12:45f.), an important shift is noticeable: there is no present concern for the house of David as a constitutive factor in the restored community (note the passing reference to Zerubbabel in Neh. 12:47). It is instructive that in the historical reminiscences contained in the long prayer of Ezra (Neh. 9:6-37), chief emphasis is placed on the mighty deeds of old: the exodus and wanderings and conquest, while there is no mention of David or his house — this constitutes a complete reversal of the Chronicler's treatment of the tradition. A further point to be made concerns the role of prophecy. For the Chronicler monarchy and prophecy go hand in hand; his emphasis on the function of the prophet as adviser to the king is distinctive of his work. Throughout, the kings are confronted, warned, and advised by a line of prophets: from Samuel and Nathan, who were messengers of God to David, down to Haggai and Zechariah, who filled this role in the time of Zerubbabel. But in the memoirs of Ezra and Nehemiah, prophets have disappeared along with the house of David; notice how Nehemiah dismisses as a vicious rumor the charge that he is in league with prophets so as to designate himself a king (cf. Neh. 6:6-8). In view of the break in continuity, the shift in emphasis, and the disturbed condition of the present arrangement of the materials in Ezra-Nehemiah, we suggest that they were derived from originally independent memoirs of Ezra and Nehemiah, and were attached, not long after their composition, to the work of the Chronicler.

The principal point we wish to emphasize is that the Chronicler, the composer of the original work, structured his history around the figure of David and his dynasty, focusing attention on the religious activity of the monarch and his successors. The following additional inferences may likewise be drawn:

1. That the purpose of the writing was to establish and defend the legitimate claims of the house of David to preeminence in Israel, and in particular its authoritative relationship to the temple and its cult.

2. That the occasion and inspiration for the work was the return from exile and the rebuilding of the temple under the supervision of Zerubbabel, leader of the Jewish community, and himself a direct descendant of David and head of his house.

3. That the Chronicler was influenced by or collaborated with the prophets Haggai and Zechariah, who designated Zerubbabel as the scion of the house of David, and legitimate heir of the divine promise to the Davidic dynasty. Haggai identified him as the reclaimed "signet ring" of Yahweh, in contrast with the discarded Jehoiachin (cf. Hag. 2:23; Jer. 22:24), while Zechariah names him the "branch," the term used by Jeremiah to describe the future Davidic king (Zech. 6:9-14, based on a commonly accepted reconstruction of the text restoring Zerubbabel to the account; and Jer. 23:5-6). Whether these men and the Chronicler thought of Zerubbabel as anything more than the governor of the Persian province, or possibly in the status of a puppet king, is a matter for speculation and does not greatly matter (though it is possible that they or others entertained a bolder expectation). There is no suggestion of a revolt or of its suppression; there is in fact no word about the fate of Zerubbabel or his successors or descendants. We hear nothing further about the house of David, except in the mute genealogy of 1 Chr. 3.

4. That the Chronicler composed his work shortly after the completion of the temple, *ca.* 515 B.C.E., and that this date provides an explanation for the failure to deal further with the fortunes of Zerubbabel and the house of David. The ending of the original work is no longer determinable; the narrative of Zerubbabel and the temple has been supplanted by an Aramaic record which is included in the present work (Ezra 4:6–6:18).

5. That the memoirs of Ezra and Nehemiah, who were roughly contemporaneous, and who together reconstituted the Jewish community in the latter half of the 5th century B.C.E., were attached, in a somewhat haphazard fashion, shortly after their time. At about the same time the genealogies of chs. 1–9 of 1 Chronicles were attached in their present form (though a substantial section of the material may have been part of the original work). We may suggest that the reason for the addition of the records of Ezra and Nehemiah to the Chronicler's work was twofold: to bring the earlier work up to date, and to adapt it to the changed circumstances of the 5th-century community. Ezra and Nehemiah oriented the community in accordance with the presumed pattern established by Moses in the wilderness, as over against the Chronicler whose model was derived from the monarchy established by David in the promised land. Both political and religious factors were involved, and the concern for legitimacy was paramount, but the differences in presuppositions, in method, and objectives between the original Chronicler and his successor are significant. Above all, the Chronicler was a monarchist, while the other was a clericalist, i.e., a scribe.

11

Kaufmann's *The Religion of Israel*

The Religion of Israel is a highly original and important contribution to OT scholarship. The English-reading community is particularly indebted to Moshe Greenberg for his lucid translation and skillful abridgment of Y. Kaufmann's multivolumed classic in Modern Hebrew. Selections from the first seven volumes of האמונה הישראלית תולדות have been organized in a cohesive presentation of the principal themes and supporting arguments of the gifted and controversial Israeli scholar. As the subtitle indicates, the present work is limited to the period ending with the exile, omitting entirely Kaufmann's eighth volume on the postexilic era. While the limitation may be justified on the basis of the author's own emphasis on the earlier period as the truly creative age of Israelite religion, and the one in which the great bulk of OT literature was composed, nevertheless it is regrettable that the volume ends where it does. It is important to have the whole picture of Kaufmann's reconstruction of Israelite religion and literature; and we may hope that a supplementary volume in English containing this material will be made available, or that it will be incorporated in subsequent editions of the present volume. [See Y. Kaufmann, *History of the Religion of Israel, Volume IV, Chapters 1, 2: The Babylonian Captivity and Deutero-Isaiah,* trans. C. W. Efroymson (New York: Union of American Hebrew Congregations, 1970).]

Kaufmann's assignment of most of the OT to the preexilic period is in striking contrast with the dominant critical scholarship of Europe and America, though the divergence is greater with respect to the more radical scholars of the late 19th and early 20th century than with more recent scholars, who have tended in a generally conservative direction. Kaufmann's debate is primarily with the older Wellhausenist scholarship, though it is not less interesting and pertinent on that account. To illustrate the nature of the conflict, we may summarize Kaufmann's views on the unity and date of the books of the Old Testament: (1) The whole of the Torah literature (the Pentateuch

---

Review of Yehezkel Kaufmann, *The Religion of Israel, from Its Beginnings to the Babylonian Exile;* trans. and abridged by Moshe Greenberg (Chicago: University of Chicago Press, 1960).

and Former Prophets) is preexilic; (2) the Latter Prophets were completed by the middle of the 5th century B.C.E.; (3) many of the Writings are also preexilic, including Job, Proverbs, and Psalms. Perhaps the most extreme contrast with prevailing opinion is to be found in the statement on the date of the Psalms: "There is no Psalm whose plain sense . . . requires a dating later than the exilic Psalm 137" (311). Lest there be any misunderstanding, Kaufmann's work is in no sense an uncritical return to traditional or orthodox views. He accepts the basic principles and methods of scientific scholarship, but uses them to arrive at radically different conclusions.

Kaufmann is essentially concerned with the history of Israelite religion, the development of its principal ideas and ideological patterns. This quest is inevitably linked with source analysis and the reconstruction of OT literature. Thus Kaufmann finds himself in the company of the great biblical critics of the 19th century, especially Wellhausen with whom he is primarily engaged in conversation and controversy. There is an archaic quality about Kaufmann's work, which may be partly attributed to the fact that the original began to appear twenty-five years ago (vols. 1-7 were published in 1937-1948), but more to the character of the discussion which is limited largely to literary criticism and the evolution of religious ideas, as it was in Wellhausen's day. The more recent subjects of scholarly debate — form criticism, tradition-history, oral tradition, etiology, *Sitz im Leben,* etc. — are not discussed (though this may be due in part to the nature of the abridgment). Even more conspicuous is Kaufmann's bland dismissal of archeological data (cf. 3).

It would be a mistake, nevertheless, to treat the book as an anachronism. Kaufmann is too forceful and independent a thinker to be ignored. It may be of special importance to us that he has refocused attention on the earlier results of critical scholarship. Whatever the developments and refinements in recent years, the foundations of modern biblical scholarship were erected by Wellhausen and his associates (based on the work of precursors). While Wellhausen's reconstruction of the history of Israelite religion has proved untenable, his evolutionary approach has survived. While there has been widespread dissatisfaction with the details of the documentary hypothesis, the classic pattern, JEDP, for the sources of the Pentateuch is still widely accepted. Kaufmann has challenged frontally the whole Wellhausenist structure, and proposed an independent synthesis of Israel's religion and literature. Kaufmann accepts the basic source analysis of the Pentateuch, but reverses the order of D and P. He argues persuasively and in detail that P is preexilic throughout its contents, does not presuppose the doctrine of the single central sanctuary promulgated in D, but clearly antedates the latter. There are many implications in such a radical shift, and it will be necessary to restudy all the evidence before a verdict can be reached, if one is possible. In view of the complexity of the material in each source, and the apparent incorporation of older and newer elements, a clear decision as to priority may never be reached. It is the present view of the reviewer that D and P are roughly parallel and contemporary sources, and that direct dependence of either upon the other cannot be demonstrated.

Kaufmann likewise denies the evolutionary approach to Israelite religion, and specifically the Wellhausenist view that ethical monotheism developed from more primitive stages of Israelite faith. He affirms Mosaic monotheism as a revolutionary emergent, and interprets the devolution of Israelite religion in the light of this traditional but novel view. Israelite religion is thus radically different from all forms of paganism. Kaufmann defines the distinction in terms of basic or ruling ideas: that of paganism is the recognition of an eternal meta-divine realm which ultimately controls the destiny of gods and men, while that of Israel is the acknowledgment of one supreme personal being who is the source of all existence, the creator and controller of everything. Kaufmann's presentation is a brilliant tour de force, a modern scholarly statement of the classic Judeo-Christian apologetic for biblical religion. It may be asked, however, whether such an analysis does full justice to either pagan or biblical religion. To classify all varieties of paganism under a single overarching generalization is an intellectual triumph over a heterogeneous mass of intractable data, but we seriously doubt that this was the ruling idea in any of the Near Eastern religions; in any case the more vivid aspects of these religions have been minimized or ignored. On the other hand, the biblical account stresses the themes of election, covenant, divine action in history — in short the personal involvement of God in the affairs of men. What seems to have been central to the religions of the Near East was direct contact with deity. For the pagan this was achieved through cultic participation in the life of the divine, i.e., in the ultimate processes of nature; for Israel it was found in dialogic confrontation between God and man, and their mutual participation in historical events. From the Israelite point of view, the issue between them was one of reality: Israel claimed a true experience of the living God, and denied the validity of the pagan's claim. Kaufmann points out that the Bible misrepresents pagan religion as the worship of idols, gods of wood and stone, ignoring its profounder aspects and meaning. This Kaufmann attributes to the Israelite inability to understand the nature of paganism. Thus Israel equated the complex beliefs and practices of the "higher" pagan religions with the "fetishism" of the Israelite people, and identified both as the worship of gods of wood and stone. Kaufmann argues the case brilliantly but is less convincing on the score of Israelite ignorance. Even if true pagan worship and practice were limited to royal circles and a few others, knowledge of these was always available, and understandable. It is difficult to deny some awareness of the character of pagan religion, since mythological motifs are reflected in a number of Old Testament passages; but Israel rejected the reality of the pagan experience of religion, and specifically of its gods. The only aspect of reality left to these no-gods was the material objectivity of the images, which could be and was affirmed with mounting sarcasm. Is this ignorance or studied insult? It may be suggested that "fetishism" or the superstitious attachment to such objects is the common denominator of all religions, or the lowest level to which they tend to deteriorate. Therefore the biblical writers correctly equate it with apostasy, the abandonment of true religion for false, of Yahweh for other gods.

In the course of the volume, Kaufmann pronounces with characteristic vigor and self-assurance on innumerable major and minor issues. We do not have space to deal with these as they deserve, nor to do more than mention a few of them. Kaufmann notes the fact that in the Torah literature the canonical literary prophets are practically ignored (Isaiah is mentioned, but in a mantic capacity). He draws the conclusion that the Torah literature is preprophetic in its outlook, and that its contents were unaffected by the great ideas and ethical insights of the classical prophets. The latter, according to Kaufmann, are responsible for isolating the ethical principle, and elevating it to a supreme place in Israelite religion, while subordinating the cultic and ritual. Once again, Kaufmann has reversed the conventional order, in which the Torah literature was regarded as being produced under prophetic influence, a compromise among popular, priestly, and prophetic viewpoints. But the reverse order may be just as questionable. Is any particular chronological sequence a necessary conclusion from an examination of the data? Since the Deuteronomic historian has ignored these prophets though he lived long after several of them, the same could be true of other contributors to the Torah literature. The isolation of the prophetic literature from earlier prophetic traditions and the identification of the supremacy of the ethical principle as a new prophetic insight seem exaggerated. The difference is one of emphasis rather than of essence. And the origin of both blocks of literature lies in the Mosaic covenant, which clearly emphasized the supremacy of the ethical principle, while being embedded in a ritual context. Both Torah literature and prophets represent adaptations of the covenant idea, not in contradiction, or in chronological sequence, but supplemental, as they were regarded by the postexilic compilers of the canon.

With respect to the later prophets, Kaufmann's views are particularly controversial. He holds that Jeremiah and Ezekiel especially, in order to vindicate the righteousness of God in condemning his people to destruction, grossly exaggerated and even invented the sinfulness of the nation. Thus in the interests of a certain theological interpretation of history, they falsified the moral situation in Judah, and permanently stigmatized a whole people. Kaufmann maintains that theological and moral factors are irrelevant in discussing the fall of Judah, which was attributable to geopolitical factors, i.e., the superior force of the Babylonian armies. Thus the moral/theological indictment of the nation by the prophets is without merit. It would appear that Kaufmann, like most of the citizens of Judah and Jerusalem of the time, rejects the notion that God could actually judge his own people, though of course his point of view and line of reasoning are quite different. But it is one thing to deny the theistic interpretation of history on philosophic or sociological grounds, but quite another to question the validity of the prophetic charges against the people of Judah. That Jeremiah would have fabricated the case against his people in defense of divine justice is highly improbable on the face of it, but especially in view of his resistance to the prophetic role and to the message of doom which he was commissioned to bring. His bitter excoriations of God, his pleas for his people, his exhortations to repentance and advocacy of a policy of surrender (personally distasteful to him as a loyal citizen), so that city and people could escape the threat of disaster, do not comport well with his supposed zeal to vindicate God's impending judgment. We may concede that Ezekiel seems to be more doctrinaire in his presentation, but his case in defense of divine justice is based upon evidence, not the other way around.

Additional points made by Kaufmann include: (1) two Hoseas: chs. 1–3 are from the 9th century and reflect a denunciation of the house of Ahab and the institution of Baal worship in the northern kingdom. The remaining chapters are from the more familiar prophet of the 8th century. While the case is argued ingeniously, and merits serious consideration, the conclusions rest in part on Kaufmann's reconstruction of the religious history of Israel. An 8th-century date for chs. 1–3 would prove an embarrassment. (2) a date in the 8th century for the book of Jonah. This is hard to swallow. Kaufmann manages to twist the "historical" argument around so as to support the early rather than the usual late date. The net effect is to show how little evidence there is for dating this work. (3) the unity of First Isaiah. Kaufmann argues that Isa. 1–33 is a literary unit dating from the 8th century. This is an admirable corrective to the vivisectionist tendencies in recent scholarly treatments of the book, but goes too far in the opposite direction. The defense of Isa. 13–14 is more ingenious than convincing.

A couple of minor slips may be noted: On p. 78, "Isaiah" should be "Second Isaiah" since the reference is to Isa. 47:9, 12 (the citation in the Index is correct however, p. 477). On p. 224, "jeaous" should be "jealous."

In sum, this book is indispensable reading. Kaufmann has reopened questions long since considered closed, and has done so in a way to command attention and respect. Of the many provocative suggestions and accompanying arguments, a number are convincing to this reader, others are entirely reasonable, while a few seem merely bizarre. But all are worthy of consideration and study. OT scholarship can only profit from a thorough reexamination of its principles, methods, and conclusions, especially in connection with the history of Israelite religion and literature. [For two recent volumes dealing with Kaufmann's life and work, see Thomas M. Krapf, *Yehezkel Kaufmann: Ein Lebens- und Erkenntnisweg zur Theologie der Hebräischen Bibel* (Berlin: Institut Kirche und Judentum, 1990), and idem, *Die Priesterschrift und die vorexilische Zeit: Yehezkel Kaufmanns vernachlässigter Beitrag zur Geschichte der biblischen Religion.* OBO 119 (Freiburg: Universitätsverlag and Göttingen: Vandenhoeck and Ruprecht, 1992). See also M. Greenberg, "Kaufmann on the Bible: An Appreciation," *Judaism* 13, no. 1 (Winter 1964).]

12

Pentateuch

The Pentateuch, or Five Books of Moses, constitutes the first and most important division of the Hebrew Bible (Old Testament). It holds pride of place in the Jewish canon, and was regarded as having the highest authority, higher even than the Prophets and the Writings, since it was traditionally thought to be the work of Moses, who alone of the biblical heroes spoke with God face to face (cf. Exod. 33:11; Deut. 34:10-12).

A. Composition
  1. The primary history
  2. G (the underlying source)
  3. J and E
     a. J
     b. E
     c. JE
  4. D and DH
     a. The Deuteronomic Code
     b. The Deuteronomic history
  5. P
B. Form and contents
  1. The beginnings (Genesis)
     a. The primeval story (chs. 1–11)
     b. The patriarchal narratives (chs. 12–50)
  2. The Exodus (Exod. 1–18)
  3. Sinai (Exod. 19:1–Num. 10:10)
  4. The wilderness wanderings (Num. 10:11–36:13)
  5. The epilogue (Deuteronomy)
C. History of Pentateuchal criticism
  1. Documentary hypotheses

2. Form-critical analysis
3. Traditio-historical criticism
4. Synthesis and summary

Bibliography

A. Composition

The Pentateuch itself is the first part of a larger literary complex, which we may designate the "primary history." This comprises the books from Genesis through 2 Kings, but omits Ruth (which in the Hebrew Bible is to be found among the Writings). The primary history recounts the story of Israel in the context of the total human experience from the beginning (i.e., creation) to the collapse of the kingdom of Judah and the Babylonian exile. It is to be distinguished from the Chronicler's history (1 and 2 Chronicles-Ezra-Nehemiah), which, while covering the same general subject matter, omits most of the earlier narratives and focuses attention on the kingdom of David and Solomon and their successors. It continues down to the Persian period and the reconstitution of the Jewish community under the leadership of Ezra and Nehemiah. It is apparent from an examination of the two histories that not only do they reflect drastically different points of view, but they are also the products of vastly different periods in Israel's history. The inconclusive endings point toward a date of composition shortly after the events with which the story closes (i.e., before the next significant occurrence). Thus with regard to the primary history it is difficult to suppose that the return from Babylon would not have been mentioned had the primary history been completed subsequent to that momentous event. By contrast the Chronicler's account includes this datum, and brings the narrative down to the reforms of Ezra and Nehemiah (late 5th century B.C.E.). His story ends at this point somewhat inconclusively, and it is a reasonable inference that the Chronicler's history was compiled about this time, or in any case not later than the early 4th century.

1. The primary history

The date of composition of the primary history may be fixed by the final entry in 2 Kings, itself a footnote to the story of the fall of Jerusalem and the exile. This note refers to the favor shown the shadow-king Jehoiachin by Evil-Merodach the Babylonian emperor, in the year 561 B.C.E. Since the death of Jehoiachin is hinted at in these verses (2 Kgs. 25:29-30), we may date the work of the editor (R_{PH}) in the decade following. By 550 the primary history in substantially its present form was completed.

The compilation of this sacred history was itself a remarkable achievement. It reflected the determination of the exilic community to remain alive and to retain its identity as the people of God, in spite of a series of catastrophic blows culminating in the loss of king and land, temple and priesthood. Nor could they minimize the significance of the disaster by attributing it to a hostile fate or the changing fortunes of war, or the superiority of alien gods or peoples; rather, it was the deliberate act of judgment by their own God, the covenant God of Israel, who was Lord of heaven and earth and the disposer of the affairs of men. Soberly the exiles reviewed their history in order to discern the meaning of their fate: What had happened between God and his people in the past, from the start? How had they come to their present unhappy state, and what, if anything, might the future hold for them? They could delineate throughout the course of history a consistent pattern of divine grace and favor toward men: a special commitment by God to Abraham and his descendants, fulfilled in the mighty deeds of exodus and conquest surrounding the covenant-making mystery of Sinai, wherein God had declared Israel to be his people and they had claimed him as their God. Successive generations saw the unfolding of this relationship of promise and demand, of grace and obligation, of hope and threat, through the tumultuous period of the judges until it reached fruition in the kingdom of David and Solomon. At the same time the unity and cohesion of the nation were flawed by disobedience to the terms of the covenant and defiance of the will of God, so that the state divided under pressure from within, and finally collapsed in ruins from the attacks of foreigners. Thus had a singularly blessed, but persistently sinful, people reaped an inevitable judgment. Nevertheless, the end was not the end. Before and beyond the law of sin and death, there was an unconditional commitment and an eternal relationship of love (cf. Jer. 31:3). The God who had summoned Abraham from the East would call his seed to a new pilgrimage westward. And the God who had saved his people from Pharaoh would deliver them again from bondage. Out of the momentous past, and in view of the present agony, the serious student could read sobering lessons for himself and his people. This history was not only a record of what had happened, but words of life and hope for today and tomorrow.

Here was Israel's legacy to Israel: the remains of the old age and a foundation for the new. Old Israel perished in the furnace of exile, but a new Israel was to emerge. The authoritative guide of postexilic Judaism was the Pentateuch. The division of the primary history into Pentateuch and Former Prophets (Joshua-2 Kings) was occasioned by the needs and insights of the postexilic community: the law of Moses and the social and cultic pattern of the wilderness society were to be normative for the Persian province of Judea. It may well have been Ezra who permanently fixed the authority of the Pentateuch in the Jewish community, although the books themselves had long since been written. There can be little doubt of the relative antiquity of the text of the Pentateuch (and the Former Prophets) as compared with the other books of the Old Testament. Not only do we have distinct

101

recensions — e.g., the MT, the LXX, the Samaritan — but also a long, traceable history of textual transmission. The *Vorlage* of the LXX text goes back at least to the 3rd century B.C.E., and almost certainly to the 4th, while the Samaritan is almost as old. The MT, on the other hand, may be even older. All three are represented in ancient manuscripts from Qumran.

If the Pentateuch was a finished product by the 5th century B.C.E. (probably it was already complete in the 6th century B.C.E., as part of the primary history), is it possible to trace the earlier history of this great work and the sources which contributed to its compilation? Such questions have exercised the minds of biblical scholars for hundreds of years, and the results of their inquiries have varied considerably. While there is as yet no consensus, and the "assured results" of critical analysis are no longer so sure, certain conclusions may be regarded as highly probable, and others as likely. The documentary hypothesis, commonly associated with the name of Julius Wellhausen, but actually the product of the labor of many eminent Old Testament scholars of the past two hundred years, remains the point of departure for the scientific study of the Pentateuch. The minute source analysis, which was one of the crowning achievements of 19th-century biblical criticism, grew out of repeated efforts to deal with the difficulties apparent in the received text. Inconsistencies in content, duplicate or parallel narratives, and significant variations in diction and style militated against the traditional view of the unity of authorship. Obvious anachronisms, and shifts in the historical and geographical perspective, likewise indicated that a Mosaic date for the composition of the Pentateuch was untenable.

In its standard form the documentary hypothesis rested upon arguments of two kinds: those based upon literary and linguistic evidence, which resulted in the division of the Pentateuchal material into various written sources; and those based upon historical evidence for the evolution of religious institutions and ideas in Israel, which produced an analytical description of the interrelationships among the documents, and a chronological arrangement to account for them.

Literary investigation isolated four primary written sources: J, E, D, and P. D was the simplest to identify, since it stands out as a literary unit (i.e., the bulk of the book of Deuteronomy — hence the designation D), with a distinctive style and viewpoint. The separation of P (for "Priestly document") from the remaining narrative material was also a comparatively routine undertaking, and practical unanimity has been achieved by scholars in defining the contents of this work. It consists chiefly of archival and institutional data spread out on an elaborate genealogical framework. What remains is the general narrative, itself manifestly composite. Thus the separation of the two creation stories in Genesis (1–2:4a; 2:4b–3), and the assignment of the former, with its schematized and formulaic pattern, to P, and the latter to the narrative source (in this case J), is easily seen. On the other hand, the disentanglement of the narrative strands has proved much more difficult. The Joseph story (Gen. 37; 39–50) is clearly composite. In the episode describing the brothers' treachery against Joseph

(37:12-36), there are two accounts of what happened, which have been blended into confusion. In one, Joseph was thrown into a pit and left there to die. He was found by Midianites, brought to Egypt, and sold there (vv. 22-24, 28a [to "pit"], 28c-30, 36; the source is E). In the other, he was sold to a passing band of Ishmaelites (vv. 25-27, 28b [to "silver"], 31-35; the source is J). Reuben figures as the intercessor for Joseph in one (E), Judah in the other (J). Only such a separation offers an intelligible account of the episode.

Two principal narrative sources were identified: J (so-called because of its standard use of the name Jehovah [YHWH] for God; it has also been associated with the southern kingdom, Judah), and E (because of its use of Elohim for God, though with less consistency beyond the book of Genesis; it has been connected with the northern kingdom, Ephraim). The details of the division are not nearly so certain as in the case of D and P; in many passages where J and E have been fused, the analysis is disputed (e.g., Exod. 32–34).

D was the starting point in the determination of the chronological relationships of the sources among themselves and with respect to the history of Israel. D was identified with the law code discovered in the Jerusalem temple in the 18th year of Josiah (622 B.C.E.); its composition has generally been dated in the 7th century. Careful comparison of D with JE, on the one side, and with P, on the other, showed that D was the middle term chronologically. With regard both to narrative and to legal material, D proved to be later than and dependent upon JE; but independent of and prior to P. JE therefore belonged to the monarchic period (10th to 8th centuries), while P was exilic or later. More precise examination of JE established the priority of J (10th-9th century perhaps) over E (9th-8th century). This decision was based in part on the opinion that J was more primitive in his theology (i.e., grossly anthropomorphic), more exuberant and naive in his storytelling. E, on the other hand, was more subtle and sophisticated, and therefore of a later date.

The major conclusions of the documentary hypothesis with regard to source analysis and the relative dating of the documents stand fairly firm. Some of the premises are less certain, particularly the theory of a simple evolutionary development of Israel's religious institutions and ideas. And the details of the analysis are open to question in a number of instances. In addition, important new areas of interest have been opened up in the continuing quest for knowledge about the Pentateuch. (See bibliography.)

A synthesis of what appear to be the soundest insights of scholars who have worked and are now working in the field follows:

2. G (the underlying source)

In the beginning was G. This symbol represents the original narrative source *(Grundlage)*, which dealt in connected fashion with the principal themes of Israel's early history and prehistory: including the primeval history, patriarchal sagas, the exodus and wanderings, and presumably the settlement in the Promised Land. G is no longer extant, but what remains of its contents is scattered through the books from Genesis to Joshua. Its outline is still to be found in the Israelite credos (to use the happy expression of G. von Rad) — e.g., Deut. 26:5-10 (cf. Exod. 13:14-16). Josh. 24 preserves a much more detailed account based on the same pattern. G thus constituted the official tradition of "all Israel." It traced the beginnings of the people back to the fathers and their wanderings, and brought the story of hardship and deliverance, wandering and conquest, down to the present circumstance: the confederation of tribes settled in the land chosen and promised to the fathers.

The precise character of G can hardly be determined now; it was composed of older poetic materials, perhaps a sequence of patriarchal sagas, and a continuity dealing with the exodus-conquest cycle. Behind these are the individual stories, legends, etiological tales, cult narratives, the original data which formed the oldest traditions of Israel. G may have been a connected poem or series of poems orally transmitted and recited in whole or in part at the sacred festivals of "all Israel." Or it may have been a prose document derived from such an oral poetic collection. The former would seem more likely for the period of the judges. We conclude that G was a poetic composition, orally transmitted, relating the official story of Israel and its forebears. It is to be dated in the 12th-11th centuries B.C.E. and finds its cultic locus in the amphictyonic festivals.

3. J and E

J and E, the familiar narrative sources of classic Pentateuchal analysis, are prose compositions derived from G. In the Tetrateuch at least, J and E follow the same basic pattern and order of events, thus presuppose a common source. At the same time they are distinct compositions, with diverging concerns and attitudes, and differ strikingly in numerous details. On the basis of a minute analysis of these sources, so far as they can be extricated from the Hexateuch, scholars have concluded that J has a southern orientation, as against E, which is northern; that J is concerned with David as king and with his dynasty, while E has marked affinities with and interest in the prophetic movement, especially as it was related to political developments in the north. In general, J has been regarded as a product of the United Monarchy (*ca.* 10th century), E of the northern kingdom (*ca.* 9th-8th centuries). Subsequent editions (e.g., J_2, E_2, etc.) would be dated still later.

The distinctive historical character of Israel's religion made it inevitable that the story would be rewritten repeatedly so as to include the most recent events which were the result of Yahweh's dealings with his people. Unlike pagan myth, which was timeless and self-completing, and which required only to be rehearsed and reenacted in the cult, Israelite traditions could not finally be contained in this fashion; and reenactment did not exhaust the historical significance or future possibilities of the tradition. In like manner the pagan epic was a self-enclosed entity describing a distinct era of the past: the age of the heroes and their great deeds. But Israel, even with the "epic" tradition reflected in G, could not simply look back to the glorious past, but was concerned with the continuing actions of God. Even G may have been expanded and revised during the period of the amphictyony.

a. J

While scholarly agreement on the scope of J and E has never been reached, and end points for both have been fixed all the way from the end of Numbers on into Samuel and Kings, it is likely that the end point is determined roughly by the date of the writer. The interpretation herein adheres to the common, if somewhat conservative, view that J dates from the United Monarchy (i.e., 10th century), and that E is northern and is to be dated in the late 9th or early 8th century. This means that both J and E are not simply prose abstracts of G, but rather separate historical accounts based upon G, carrying the story beyond G to their own time. Thus J finds the complete fulfillment of G's promise to the fathers, not in the original settlement under Joshua, but in the conquests and kingdom of David. Without attempting to pin down precisely the J material in Judges and Samuel, one may nevertheless point to the two sources of 1 Samuel and identify the earlier, pro-monarchy source with J. The transference of the Abrahamic covenant (Gen. 15 — originally G) to David and his house (2 Sam. 7) is also to be attributed to J. Whether J extends beyond this point is debatable (the so-called court history — 2 Sam. 9–20; 1 Kgs. 1–2 — is a separate source); other possibilities for the reign of Solomon are 1 Kgs. 4:20-21 (Heb. 4:20–5:1): "Judah and Israel were as many as the sand by the sea; they ate and drank and were happy. Solomon ruled over all the kingdoms from the Euphrates to the land of the Philistines and to the border of Egypt; they brought tribute and served Solomon all the days of his life." Subsequent editions of J may well have carried further the story of the fortunes of the house of David and the kingdom of Judah.

b. E

E is more difficult to fix as to date and extent. On the basis of a northern provenience and demonstrable interest in the prophetic movement, E may be regarded as a product of the religious enthusiasm stimulated by Elijah and Elisha, and his work may be placed in the age of Jehu and his successors (*ca.* 842-745 B.C.E.). A clue to the character of E may be found in the evaluation of Jehu's revolution in 2 Kgs.

105

10:28, 30: "Thus Jehu wiped out Baal from Israel. . . . And the Lord said to Jehu, 'Because you have done well in carrying out what is right in my eyes, and have done to the house of Ahab according to all that was in my heart, your sons of the fourth generation shall sit on the throne of Israel.' " This material is embedded in a typically hostile Deuteronomic estimate of the same king (vv. 29, 31) and must therefore derive from a different, and sympathetic, northern source. The reference to the descendants of Jehu to the fourth generation would bring us down to Jeroboam II, whose dominion might be regarded more suitably as a fulfillment both of promise and of prophecy. The assertion that Jeroboam's victories were achieved as fulfillment of the word of the prophet (Jonah son of Amittai) is particularly instructive: "He restored the border of Israel from the entrance of Hamath as far as the Sea of the Arabah, according to the word of the Lord, the God of Israel, which he spoke by his servant Jonah the son of Amittai, the prophet" (2 Kgs. 14:25). E reconstructed the story of Israel in the light of the prophetic movement, beginning with Abraham, anachronistically described (by E) as a prophet and similarly identifying Miriam, Deborah(?), Samuel, and other ancient figures by the same term. If we remove the Deuteronomic framework and commentary, what remains of Kings (through 2 Kgs. 14, essentially E) is predominantly the story of the prophets and their impact on the history of the northern kingdom; for it was the prophets who were the successors to the judges, and the northern kingdom that inherited the traditions of the amphictyony and its cult center. Thus E was the defender of the older tradition against the claims of the Davidic dynasty. It may be concluded that E was composed in the 8th century B.C.E., in the north, and represented an attempt, in the prophetic tradition, to relate the ancient pattern of G to the history of the northern kingdom, and to establish the latter's claim to be the true successor and heir of "all Israel."

c. JE

JE is the product of a literary merger. At some time after the completion of J and E as separate entities, they were blended into a continuous narrative by an editor or redactor, R_{JE}. Analysis of the surviving material in the Pentateuch (or Tetrateuch, since J and E are practically nonexistent in Deuteronomy) indicates that the editor used a variety of methods in weaving the narratives together. First, it is clear that the dominant strand is J, which, in fact, formed the basic narrative. E has actually been broken up and inserted piecemeal into the overall structure of J. On occasion there are parallel accounts (J and E) of the same episode; on occasion one version has been suppressed in favor of the other (where apparently they were practically identical); elsewhere they have been woven together into a single narrative. On the face of it, JE is the work of a southern (Judahite or Jerusalemite) editor whose object was to preserve the traditions of the north and to harmonize them with the J narrative to form a single composite history of the people of God. The logical occasion for this work would have been the destruction of Samaria and the collapse of the northern kingdom (722-721 B.C.E.). Its purpose was to win the surviving population of Ephraim to allegiance to the temple in Jerusalem and the Davidic king of Judah. Since this was the announced policy of Hezekiah, according to the account in 2 Chr. 30:1–31:1, in which a determined effort was made to establish Jerusalem as the center of worship for northerners as well as southerners, we may plausibly connect the compilation of JE with the movement toward religious re-union initiated by Hezekiah. We may date R_{JE} in the early 7th century B.C.E., and hold that his work included the major part of J, selected material from E, and closed with the reformation of Hezekiah and the attempt to unite "all Israel" in the worship at Jerusalem.

4. D and DH

a. The Deuteronomic Code

The next major subdivision in the classic analysis of the Pentateuch is D, identified with the document found in the temple in the 18th year of Josiah (622 B.C.E.) and corresponding roughly to the present book of Deuteronomy (perhaps chs. 5–26; 28). Scholars have been divided on the questions of the date of composition and provenience of this document, though there is increasing agreement that D, like E, has northern affinities, and that it was composed during the century preceding its discovery. Its nucleus is a legal corpus, preserving many ancient laws and customs derived from the days of the confederation (e.g., the law of holy war), and reflecting the traditions of the cult center at Shechem and its priesthood. In their present form, chs. 5–26; 28 constitute a series of warnings and exhortations uttered by Moses just before his death. A date of composition in the reign of Hezekiah or later is practically required by the emphasis upon centralization of worship in a single sanctuary, presumably the temple at Jerusalem. The tradition of the central sanc-tuary is very old, going back to the days of the amphictyony, if not to the wilderness wanderings. But the principle of exclusiveness — i.e., the single, central sanctuary — is new. It reflects the circumstances of Hezekiah's time: the fall of the northern kingdom and the emergence of the Jerusalem temple as the only "independent" cult center. The temple at Bethel apparently survived, but was under constant attack from the south as heterodox, and had suffered considerable loss of prestige with the fall of Samaria. It was finally wrecked by Josiah (cf. 2 Kgs. 23:15ff.). Further-more, the sermonic addresses anticipate or more probably presuppose the destruc-tion of the northern kingdom and the captivity of its inhabitants, thus pointing likewise to a date *ca.* 700. A date in the reign of Manasseh is also possible but less likely, while the idea that D was composed in the reign of Josiah and deliberately planted in the temple in order to be discovered there, may be dismissed as a fantasy.

The principal concern of D is the Horeb (Sinai) covenant, and its significance for the life of Israel. The covenant is a guarantee of life to those who obey its stipulations (the Ten Commandments and subsequent legislation), but for those who forget, ignore, or defy its demands, there is certain disaster. Placed in the mouth of Moses, these sermons are not only a reminder of the solemn bond between God and Israel; an explanation of the requirements of the covenant, with its promise of security and threat of destruction; but also a prophetic anticipation of the culmination of Israel's history. For D, Moses is the true prophet (18:15ff.; cf. 34:9-10, which is secondary), who, long before the great prophets of more recent times, foresaw the threatened catastrophe of military invasion and conquest, intensified by that peculiarly inhuman practice of mass deportation. The only hope of Israel, or what survived of it, lay in strict adherence to the covenant obligations beginning with the first commandment, which requires the exclusive worship of Yahweh, and which, on the Deuteronomist's reasoning, restricts worship to the one place which he has chosen for his name.

b. The Deuteronomic history

The effect upon Josiah and Judah of the discovery of D in the temple is familiar to all. The great reformation of the national life and religion is described in detail in 2 Kgs. 22:3–23:25 (cf. 2 Chr. 34:8–35:19). The so-called Deuteronomic history (DH) probably owes its inspiration and composition to the reformation stimulated by the discovery of D. In a major contribution to the higher criticism of the OT, Martin Noth has identified and isolated the Deuteronomic history as a single work including the books from Deuteronomy through 2 Kings. Beginning with the Mosaic sermons (to which he has prefixed an introduction, Deut. 1–4), the Deuteronomic historian has traced the Horeb covenant through the history of Israel, interpreting it in the light of the covenant requirements, and evaluating kings and people according to their adherence or defiance of them. He has incorporated much older material practically untouched — e.g., the court history of David (2 Sam. 9–20; 1 Kgs. 1–2) — while providing for the whole a chronological and theological framework. Thus in the book of Judges he has organized chronologically and classified theologically a heterogeneous group of ancient heroes and the folk tales handed down about them. In the books of Kings he has inserted from the official court records the necessary chronological data of accessions, reigns, deaths, and successions; he has also interspersed a theological commentary grading each king in relation to his good or evil deeds.

According to Noth, the Deuteronomic history was compiled during the exile (i.e., after the last date in 2 Kings), but it has been cogently argued by others that the first edition of this work was issued earlier, during the reign of Josiah. It is clear that the description of the Josianic reform in 2 Kgs. 22–23 is the climax of this history, while what follows is a melancholy epilogue. Note especially the fulfillment of the prophecy concerning Bethel (from 1 Kgs. 13:1-3) in 2 Kgs. 23:15-18, with particular reference to the name of Josiah (which is anticipated in the prophecy), and the conclusion in v. 25: "Before him there was no king like him, who turned to the Lord with all his heart and with all his soul and with all his might, according to all the law of Moses; nor did any like him arise after him." This, together with the formal summary of his reign in v. 28, looks like the original ending of the historical work. It is interesting that the notice of his defeat and death at Megiddo follows the summary.

The Deuteronomic historian was inspired by the conviction that Josiah was the long-awaited scion of David who in his work and life would fulfil the ideals of kingship, restore the empire of his illustrious ancestor, and also lead his people to renewal of life in obedience to the terms of the ancient Mosaic covenant. The entire history aims at this conclusion, the happy climax of the biblical story. At the same time the Deuteronomic discourses of Moses and the disastrous experience of the northern kingdom served as a warning of another denouement, so that the catastrophe which actually ensued was not entirely unprepared. All along there had been two possibilities. With the tragic death of Josiah, it became clearer which alternative was the more likely. It is probable that the Deuteronomic history originally ended with the successful reformation of Josiah, and was subsequently revised to accord with the somber facts of history (cf. the pathetic attempt at reinterpretation, 2 Kgs. 23:26: "Still the Lord did not turn from the fierceness of his great wrath, by which his anger was kindled against Judah, because of all the provocations with which Manasseh had provoked him").

Concerning the scope of DH, the question must be raised whether Deut. 1 actually constitutes the beginning. In other words, does Deut. 1–4 serve simply as an introduction to DH, or is it rather a bridge between the narrative of the Tetrateuch (JE) and DH? When it is remembered that D is explicitly attributed to Moses, then the necessity for placing these addresses in the context of the JE narrative becomes clear. Unless JE (and G) is to be cut off at the end of Numbers plus a few verses on the death of Moses, it is not possible to argue that DH is an entirely independent work. Not only does such a view leave JE in the Tetrateuch a hopeless torso, but it offers no explanation for the beginning of DH in the 40th year of the wanderings. If in the course of D, Moses actually reviewed the previous sequence of mighty deeds, then we could recognize here an imitation of epic style. But there is specific recapitulation only as far back as the Horeb (Sinai) experience, while the antecedent history is dealt with in the vaguest possible way. In short, JE is assumed, because it was attached. If J and E actually carried the story down into the period of the monarchy, then DH must have used them, as he used the court history, D, and other sources. And if he made use of JE for the post-Mosaic period, he could hardly have dismissed or ignored it in the pre-Mosaic and Mosaic eras.

It is likely, therefore, that DH compiled his history along the same lines as J and E (or JE, which is presumably all that was available to him) — i.e., he began with Genesis and carried the story down to the reign and reformation of Josiah. However, the fulcrum of his account was the major prophetic exhortations of Moses, the new document, D, found in the temple. DH had little or nothing to add to the JE narrative in the Tetrateuch, though there may be traces of his work (so-called D$_2$, which need not be categorically dismissed). His creative enterprise begins with Deut. 1–4, which constitutes an introduction to the history which follows but also serves as a bridge connecting it with what has gone before. It is clear that DH did not think that Israelite history began with Moses, whatever may be the opinion of scholars since Wellhausen.

We conclude that the Deuteronomic history was originally composed before the fall of Jerusalem, and that it consisted of JE and D, plus other materials of a narrative and archival nature, covering the period from the creation down to the reign and reformation of Josiah.

5. P

It remains to deal with P, the last of the sources identified in the classic Pentateuchal analysis. It is generally agreed that P was compiled, chiefly from older sources, during the exile, if not in postexilic times. P consists mainly of archival data of different kinds: genealogical tables, tribal lists, including a pair of census tabulations, and priestly data and regulations — concerning, e.g., the tabernacle, the priesthood, sacrifices, questions of clean and unclean. Embedded in P, there are also legal prescriptions which form part of the complex legal corpus of the Pentateuch (e.g., the Book of the Covenant and Exod. 34, usually associated with JE; the law code in D; and H, the so-called Holiness Code of Lev. 17–26). The principal questions concerning P are: (a) Is P an independent source, or is it merely supplemental to JE in the Hexateuch (or Tetrateuch)? Put another way, is P himself the compiler of the Pentateuch incorporating into the narrative such archival data as seemed desirable? (b) What is the extent of P? It is generally agreed that P is to be found in the books through Numbers, and not in Deuteronomy (except for a couple of verses). But what about Joshua?

The two questions are linked, and the answer given to one will influence one's view of the other. It would seem that the meticulous analysis of earlier scholars and their conclusions concerning the nature of P have not been overthrown by more recent advocates. It still appears that the case for P as an independent source is stronger than the case against it. If P was a self-contained entity, what was its character and scope? That P in Exodus–Numbers is primarily concerned to fix in detail the cultic practice of the wilderness encampment and to establish it as a permanent norm for Israel through the unquestioned authority of Moses is clear. Here there is essentially a static treatment of ancient materials, with a concern, not, as in the older sources, for the movement of God in history, but for the original pattern of worship, which is binding forever. The particular historical event has partly given way to the timeless and unchangeable pattern of heavenly things. If P were limited to Exodus-Numbers, then the question of its independent status would not figure seriously, and its incorporation into the narrative as essentially supplementary data would be understandable. But the presence of P in Genesis, where it provides the chronological framework and some narrative details, suggests a broader, at least partly historical, concern. If this is true, and it can hardly be doubted, then we must recognize in P the old *heilsgeschichtliche* pattern of Israelite religion already observable in G, present in the other historical works, and preserved in the festivals which are a principal interest of P. P's interest in the patriarchs, however, requires a corresponding concern with the settlement in the Promised Land. While Moses and the pattern of life and worship in the wilderness are central to P, the prelude in Genesis can only be balanced by the fulfillment in Numbers and Joshua; but it is only in Joshua that the specific expectations of P in the patriarchal narratives are fulfilled. In no way can Moses and the wanderings or even Sinai be regarded as the resolution of patriarchal anticipation. The divine promise can only be realized in the occupation of the land (which is explicitly not Transjordan, and for P does not even include it). Therefore, if P is an independent source, and is found in Genesis, as well as in Exodus-Numbers, then we should expect to find it in Joshua also.

It is probable that P was compiled early in the exile and was incorporated by the final redactor into the so-called Deuteronomic history (including JE, as already pointed out) shortly after. Apparently R_{PH} added the final reference to Jehoiachin, and this points to the completion of the work in the decade 560-550 B.C.E. Thus by the middle of the 6th century, the primary history was complete, and has been preserved substantially without change. Subsequent to the completion of this work the Pentateuch was abstracted, and not later than the time of Ezra it was firmly established as the Holy Scripture of Israel.

B. Form and Contents

The separation of the Pentateuch from the primary history, and its assignment to a unique place of honor and authority in Israel, was a development of the greatest importance. The factors responsible for the division between Deuteronomy and Joshua were neither literary nor historical, but primarily theological; they arose out of the concerns and needs of the exilic community. As we have seen, classic critical scholarship identified the Hexateuch as the basic literary compilation, recognizing the close connection between the occupation of the land described in Joshua and the preceding stories of the Pentateuch. More recent scholarship has identified the Deuteronomic history as a single literary work, thus dividing the primary history at the end of the book of Numbers and connecting Deuteronomy with the following books. It will be seen that neither approach allows for a normal break at the end of Deuteronomy. At the same time, the ultimate sources, oral and documentary, cut across the same dividing line. The conclusion seems inescapable that the isolation of the Pentateuch from the primary history was the last stage in the process, and that it was occasioned by the special interest of the exilic community in the person of Moses and the experience of Israel in the wilderness. A subtle shift in emphasis from the historical pattern of the older sources (e.g., the *heilsgeschichtliche* promise and fulfillment of G, elaborated in J and E, and the theme of covenant and consequence in D and DH) to the more static pattern of P is discernible in the new arrangement. Where the primary history is essentially the record of God's dealings with his people, and their experience together through more than twelve hundred years, the Pentateuch, while retaining a chronological framework and, of course, sharing the same narrative for the first half of this era, nevertheless has its central interest, not in the mighty deeds of God nor in the historical vicissitudes of Israel, but rather in the description of an eternal, perfect, and unchangeable pattern of community life, first and fully revealed at Sinai and successfully achieved by Israel in the wilderness. For the Pentateuch, the desert encampment governed by all the laws, civil and criminal, cultic and dietary, was the first true realization of the anticipations outlined in Genesis, and the embodiment of the kingdom of God. The pattern of the desert constituted the authoritative example and model for the postexilic community. History has been subordinated to revelation, and mighty deeds to eternal words. Essentially what was required of Israel was conformity to the Sinai pattern; in this would be found the guarantee of its survival and the promise of its security. To a considerable extent, the Pentateuch defined and also restricted the future hope of the postexilic community. While Pentateuchal passages could be pressed into service for messianic purposes, such expectations were more at home in the prophetic literature. The themes of a second Moses, a second exodus, and the perfect realization of the Sinai pattern reflect the shadow cast by the Pentateuch upon all hopes and speculations about the future. Alongside the controlling pattern of community life is the figure of Moses, which dominates the Pentateuch. His life constitutes the frame and thread of the story from the beginning of Exodus to the end of Deuteronomy (to which may be added the traditional view that he was the author of all five books). Not only is he the charismatic hero of the JE narrative, but he is also the prophet "nonpareil" of D, and Israel's sole lawgiver of P. Thus all the sources and strands of the four latter books of the Pentateuch are drawn together around the superhuman figure of Moses (cf. Exod. 34:29-35), while Genesis serves as prologue to the great drama. The chief emphases of the Pentateuch are upon the intricate but ultimate pattern of laws governing the life of the people of God, and the mediator of these laws, Moses, who at the same time receives a full biographical treatment.

1. The beginnings (Genesis)

a. The primeval story (chs. 1–11)

Here is provided the universal setting of the *Heilsgeschichte,* which follows. The Mesopotamian orientation of the familiar legends and folk tales is striking, confirming the traditions associating the patriarchs with that region (i.e., Ur, and more particularly Harran). The selection and arrangement of the materials serve to stress certain points essential to the whole narrative. Thus creation is not only the proper starting point for world and faith history, but stands out starkly as the uniquely divine achievement of the sole God. Both absolute power and ultimate goodness are revealed in the mounting sequence of creative acts, while corollary to divine authority are human dignity and responsibility. Man is not only obliged to obey, but is also answerable for his deeds, from which flow irreversible consequences, as the tragic stories of Adam and Eve, Cain and Abel show. Alongside the power and authority of the Creator are revealed his righteousness and wrath; but these latter are punctuated by mercy. The flood story, ultimately derived from a widespread myth of great antiquity, is nevertheless the vehicle of profound insight into the nature of God and his ways with men. An angry judgment overwhelms a sinful world; the righteous Noah is spared, and the operation of moral law is confirmed. The aftermath, however, involves the revocation of the divine curse upon the earth (compare 8:21 with 3:18), and the unilateral commitment to preserve the world from natural catastrophe in spite of, or rather in view of, man's sinfulness. The covenant with Noah, sealed by the sign of the heavenly bow, establishes the basis for the future action of God described in the Bible — an action essentially gracious and kindly, in full recognition of man's failure to discharge his responsibilities and his inability to rectify either his attitudes or his behavior. Already in the primeval history, the basic features of the biblical narrative are present: the power and authority, the righteousness and mercy of God; man's dignity and inferiority — his responsibility and his defiance; God's commitment in grace to man and man's obligation in love to God.

b. The patriarchal narratives

In the tradition, both literary and liturgical, the patriarchal figures are Abraham, Isaac, and Jacob, but in the Genesis narratives Isaac plays a minor role, while Jacob's son Joseph is the hero of the longest sustained narrative in the book (chs. 37; 39–50). Doubtless in this case the tradition is more conservative, while the Genesis narratives are the end product of a lengthy process of sifting and selection. The material falls conveniently into three sections of approximately equal length: (a) Abraham, chs. 12–25; (b) Jacob, chs. 25–36; (c) Joseph and his brothers, chs. 37–50.

Without analyzing the stories in detail, one may sketch the principal themes. From the biblical point of view, the history of Israel properly begins with the patriarch Abraham, since he was the ancestor from whom Israel traced its origin. At the same time, it is with the appearance of the fathers that we can speak of general historical reliability, though not of history in the proper sense. However the chronological sequence and factuality of the events are to be reconstructed, there can be no doubt of the substantial validity of the account of the fathers in the Middle Bronze Age, and their movements from Harran through Canaan to the Nile Delta.

The main theme of Genesis is the promise to the fathers. This promise is first made to Abraham, when he is summoned to embark on a new adventure: "Go from your country and your kindred and your father's house to the land that I will show you. And I will make of you a great nation, and I will bless you, and make your name great, so that you will be a blessing. I will bless those who bless you, and him who curses you I will curse; and by you all the families of the earth will bless themselves" (Gen. 12:1-3). It is repeated frequently throughout the book, in almost identical language, both to him and to his descendants. This promise, which is solemnized by oath in a covenant ceremony (cf. Gen. 15:17ff. and the repeated expression: "The land which I swore to give to your fathers," in later sources), represents the unilateral, unconditional commitment of God. It consists of three major points: (a) the assurance of a posterity, which has particular relevance to Abraham's childlessness at an advanced age; but it also refers to the innumerable population of the patriarchs' descendants; (b) from the uncounted progeny a great nation will emerge in the future; and (c) they will possess the Promised Land — i.e., Canaan, specifically as surveyed by Abraham after his separation from Lot (ch. 13).

Posterity, nationhood, and the gift of the land are the different facets of the divine promise; and to these are attached the rather heterogeneous narratives of Genesis. Alongside the divine commitment and corresponding actions are human obligation and response, reflected in the behavior of the patriarchs. These are intertwined in a series of dramatic episodes, which maintain interest, even suspense, though overall plot development and story movement in the book of Genesis are more illusion than fact. Thus the theme of progeny is stressed in connection with the birth of Isaac (and repeated in connection with Rebekah and Rachel), which requires miraculous intervention by God. Once born, Isaac is the sole heir of the promise; consequently the hope of progeny remains in jeopardy with each threat to the child's life. The masterful story of the sacrifice of Isaac (ch. 22) weaves this theme into the testing of Abraham, by portraying God as the instigator and Abraham as the reluctant instrument of the plot to destroy the child and wreck the promise altogether. When the angel intervenes at the last moment, it is more than Isaac that is saved. On a broader scale, the theme involves the survival of the patriarchs and their families, constantly threatened by the violence of nature and man. In addition there is the delicate problem of maintaining identity in the midst of an alien population whose friendship poses a graver danger (of submersion) than its hostility, which is bad enough. Just to secure and maintain a foothold in Canaan proves beyond their power. In fact, they are almost as far from the Promised Land at the end of Genesis as they were at the beginning — i.e., in Egypt instead of Mesopotamia. Nevertheless, a certain symbolic success was achieved: Abraham, though paying an exorbitant price (cf. ch. 23), was able to secure outright a small plot of ground as a graveyard for his family and himself. So the book closes symbolically with the children of Israel making a pilgrimage to this graveyard in Canaan in order to bury their father, Jacob, who had died in Egypt.

According to the tradition a long interval (400 years) separated the patriarchs from the exodus and the age of Moses. While the accuracy of the number may be questioned, the efforts of certain scholars to close the gap entirely and bring the patriarchs, and Joseph in particular, down to the Late Bronze Age have not been successful. The patriarchal stories reflect a Middle Bronze (*ca.* 2100-1500 B.C.E.) orientation and background, while Moses belongs to the end of the Late Bronze Age, specifically the 13th century. The sharp break in narrative sequence confirms the validity of the tradition: a new era has begun with the book of Exodus. The life of Moses, 120 years according to the biblical record, spans the remaining books of the Pentateuch. There is a convenient division into three generations of 40 years each: from birth to banishment; the shepherd in the desert; the deliverer and lawgiver. The Bible, however, passes briefly over the first two phases of Moses' life (chs. 1–2 of Exodus) and concentrates attention upon the third (from ch. 3 on). The biblical materials fall into the following convenient pattern: (a) the events surrounding the exodus from Egypt; (b) the experience of Israel at Mt. Sinai; (c) the wanderings in the wilderness and the conquest of Transjordan; (d) Moses' farewell discourses.

2. The Exodus (Exod. 1–18)

On the basis of the close association of the exodus tradition with the Passover festival, it has been argued that the narrative (chs. 1–15) actually constituted the liturgy of the Passover. Though the case can hardly be proved for the chapters in their present form, the idea has nevertheless proved fruitful. The story is related in such a way as to emphasize both its unrepeatable historicity and its dramatic character, designed for liturgical reenactment. It is at once the unique adventure of the generation of slaves in Egypt, and the common experience of all the generations of Israel. The artificial pattern of the material suggests both a long period of transmission and a liturgical setting for its preservation. Whatever relation to a sequence of natural phenomena the plagues may originally have had, they are now immobilized and isolated by stereotyped formulas, and arranged like tenpins or wooden soldiers in the conflict between Moses and Pharaoh for the release of the slaves. In the present form of the narrative, even protagonist and antagonist are puppets acting out the parts already prepared for them. The only independent participant is God himself, and the whole order of events is designed as a pyrotechnic display of divine power and majesty: to show, in short, that God is God, and that Moses and Pharaoh are both his servants, but in different ways. Through the agency of Moses and the obstinacy of Pharaoh, miracle is piled upon miracle until the triumphal climax is reached. In order to achieve this cumulative effect, God finds it necessary not only to encourage Moses and the Israelites, but also to stiffen Pharaoh's resistance, lest he falter and release the slaves too soon.

While the actual course of events is obscured, and the interplay of human factors is distorted by the one-sided presentation of the mighty deeds of God, nevertheless the theological emphasis is valid. Except for the powerful intervention of the almighty God, deliverance of a rabble of slaves from Egypt, the greatest empire in the world, was both impossible and unthinkable. Let no one, Israelite or Egyptian, or anyone else, whether of that time or of any future time, delude himself with the notion that what happened was natural, or explicable in human terms. The decisive, and only truly significant, factor was the hand of God. If not for that, the bravery of a Moses and the loyalty of his followers would have gone for nought. As it is, Moses is characterized more by reluctance than by enthusiasm for the cause, and the people by cowardice rather than by courage. But it is all one. God acts in a series of shattering blows, which reach a climax in the slaying of the firstborn and the hasty departure of the Israelites. These two events constitute the occasion of the Passover, and doubtless formed the nucleus of the liturgy. The famous crossing of the Reed Sea caps even this climax, and constitutes the mightiest deed of all. This event is described in a prose account in ch. 14, which is divided, according to most scholars, among J, E, and P. It is also celebrated in the victory song of ch. 15, which may have served Israel as its national anthem and the culmination of the Passover observance. The crossing of the sea marks not only the end of bondage and the beginning of freedom, but also the separation of Israel from the world, and the commencement of its history as the peculiar and distinctive people of God. In the course of the wandering, the process of separation gains sharpness and clarity. Already in the later plagues this tendency was apparent; the plagues afflict only the Egyptians, while the Israelites are spared. In the wilderness the special marks of favor and protection are likewise present: the pillar of cloud and fire, the angel, the miraculous gifts of quail and manna, all identify Israel as uniquely different. The distinguishing characteristic is the relationship with God. It is precisely in the fact that God was with them that their separateness is to be seen (cf. Exod. 33:16). Both people and era were thus marked off by special signs of divine protection. Only the wilderness generation enjoyed the miracles of manna and quail; the pillar and the angel; and, above all, the man Moses, whose shining face reflected the glory of God. While this was a period of testing for all and punishment for many, it was also the uniquely creative and normative experience of Israel, determinative for its whole future history.

3. Sinai (Exod. 19:1–Num. 10:10)

The Sinai revelation and the Covenant of the Ten Words are justly regarded as the crucial event in Israel's religious experience. The compiler of the Pentateuch has underlined the importance of Sinai by making it the scene, and Moses the agent, for the ordering of the whole life of Israel. Practically the whole legislation of Israel, including the prescriptions for the tabernacle, priesthood, feasts, sacrifices, and services, as well as the rules of community life, is assigned to the Sinai sojourn. The demands or obligations of the covenant are the principal word of God to Israel, while for Israel the ultimate goal was to achieve in word and deed the pattern of holiness established for it at the beginning of nationhood, and to fulfill by enthusiastic obedience and detailed observance the requirement of the summons of God to be a "kingdom of priests and a holy nation" (Exod. 19:6). It is therefore no accident that the chief efforts of the postexilic community were bent toward reconstituting the Mosaic commonwealth. From the exile on, community life was governed by the prescriptions of the Pentateuch, as elaborated and interpreted by priest, Levite, and scribe — and later, rabbi — in the extensive body of legal opinion and decision which accumulated over the centuries, and were gathered in the tractates of the Mishna and the Gemara. There has been, therefore, a legal tradition in Israel going back to patriarchal times and continuing down through biblical and postbiblical times to the present. The tenacious conservatism as well as flexible adaptability of biblical law can be illustrated amply by comparison between legal procedures recorded in early Mesopotamian codes to which patriarchal legal customs are related, and those described in the Talmud 2,500 years later. The biblical datum constitutes the middle term in the long process of legal transmission and development. Thus in the division of the inheritance among the heirs, the old Mesopotamian practice of assigning a "double portion" to the oldest son is reflected in the patriarchal stories. The same practice is attested in Pentateuchal law, and explained and confirmed in detail by the Talmud.

In this long process the period of the monarchy may be regarded as a legally insignificant interlude. The Pentateuchal legislation, with roots in the patriarchal customs, and its substance derived from the decisions and precedents of the age of the judges, shows little influence of or interest in the monarchy (cf. Deut. 17:14-20, which is the only specific reference to the king in all the legal codes of the Pentateuch, and hardly to be regarded as codified law). That the monarchy powerfully influenced judicial procedure and legal practice may be seen from the frequent allusions in the historical books: e.g., the different judicial reforms instituted by various kings, and the combination of royal decrees affecting the population or some part of it, and royal decisions made in a variety of cases creating precedents with binding force. But of all this, little or nothing has survived in the law. The cultus was doubtless an exception, since the monarchy was the period of the great elaboration of public worship at the temple; such, at least, is the tradition preserved in the Chronicler's history. Even here, however, the sacred customs of the pre-monarchic age were preserved, embedded in the later ritual of the temple. Furthermore, the repeated purges and reforms of Israel's worship tended to restore the older practice and remove later accretions. Thus the Pentateuchal legislation was the result of a deliberate effort to compile the ancient laws and customs of Israel, even to recover the original pattern given at Sinai and publish it as the work of the architect of the nation, Moses. While the claim is somewhat greater than the fact, we have nevertheless an archaic collection of legal and cultic material reflecting the earliest period of the nation, between Moses and the monarchy. The differences in the legal formulations of the codes of the Pentateuch do not, as a rule, indicate evolution in the pattern of law, but local variation and development. The codes embody the traditions of different shrines.

The events of Sinai were associated in later Judaism with one of the three great religious feasts of early Israel — the Feast of Weeks (Pentecost) or First Fruits. The other phases of the Exodus-Deuteronomy complex are likewise associated with the major festivals: the exodus with Passover (or Unleavened Bread), and the wanderings with the Feast of Tabernacles (or Ingathering). Thus the three annual celebrations together reproduced the cycle of exodus-Sinai-wanderings, which are the very substance of the Pentateuch. Each year Israel relived the most important days of its existence: once again delivered from bondage, created the people of God by covenant rite, and tried and purified by the rigors of the desert sojourn to be fit for the life of the Holy Land promised to the fathers.

Sinai and its covenant are the central theme of the Pentateuch in its present form. For the compiler, Sinai is the main objective of the exodus, the creation of the covenant community the purpose of the divine deliverance (cf. Exod. 3:12: "When you have brought forth the people out of Egypt, you shall serve God upon this mountain"). It has long been recognized, however, that the Sinai events are intrusive in the pattern of promise and fulfillment of the older narratives, in which the possession of the land is the goal. Thus one would expect the story to proceed from the initial experience of the patriarchs to the oppression in Egypt, the deliverance from bondage, the movement through the wilderness, and the invasion and conquest of the Holy Land (as, in fact, we find it in the confession of faith, Deut. 26:5-9). At this point, the formal establishment of the new state should take place with the ratification of a solemn agreement between God and his people. Such an event is actually recorded in Josh. 24, the historical significance of which has increasingly been recognized. With the reconstruction of this logically cohesive sequence of events, matters ought to rest. But the Shechem celebration is treated as the occasion for renewing and not initiating the covenant. Sinai has entirely

118

replaced it in the latter role, so far as the tradition is concerned. Sinai may come embarrassingly in the middle of the story, but it is no late invention capriciously inserted where it would do the most damage. It is too ancient and important a tradition (in both J and E, and therefore G) to be set aside. While the Sinai events might fit better in a different locale or a different time, the awkwardness of their present position may help to validate the tradition.

The difficulty with Sinai, however, concerns not only questions of geography and history. There is also a conflict in motivation between the basic story of promise and fulfillment and the Sinai covenant. In the former we have the divine commitment to the fathers, which finds its realization in the mighty deeds of deliverance and conquest. These constitute the gracious action of the deity, to be duly acknowledged by a grateful people. But Sinai, with its demands and threats, comes in the middle of this story: after the exodus, which is the down payment on the original promissory note, but before the obligation is fully discharged through the conquest. At Sinai the movement of the story is temporarily halted, for the storyteller wishes to reexamine and specify in more formal terms the meaning of the relationship between God and his people. Already in the patriarchal narratives the significance of the divine promise and protection had been assessed in terms of obligation. Gratitude itself is the heaviest of obligations; and the unsolicited gift evokes the most elaborate response. An unconditional commitment actually imposes an unlimited obligation: the stories of Abraham in Gen. 15 (of unilateral divine promise); 22 (of unlimited human obligation) illustrate this inescapable interrelationship. Less dramatically, Jacob likewise recognizes both the privileges and the responsibilities of a junior partnership with El Shaddai (cf. Gen. 28:10-22).

Such stories, however, reflected the indeterminate scope and depth of a personal relationship, and could not define the formal status of a people. Only after definite assurance had been given of God's powerful good will, and independently of the course of predetermined grace, the Sinai interlude occurred, to establish a responsible community and to specify the nature and extent of its obligation to its suzerain. Just as God had previously announced his responsibility for and involvement in the destiny of Israel, so now the cost to Israel of its own responsibility and involvement is revealed. The formulation of the terms is put in negative form to indicate the limits within which the community of God is to conduct its affairs and beyond which it may not go. The commands are binding upon each member of the covenant community, but society as a whole is responsible for their enforcement. Essentially, what is required of Israel is obedience, formally in the sense of subscription to the divine demands, but more than this, conformity to the character and purpose of God. The distinction of Israel is the presence of God in its midst, at once its source and hope of glory and the chief threat to its existence. To ensure that blessing and honor, peace and security, rather than judgment and destruction, are the accompaniments of this intimate relationship is the purpose of the covenant codes. The object is to attain to the

119

holiness of God: "You shall be holy; for I the Lord your God am holy" (Lev. 19:2; cf 11:44; 20:7; Exod. 19:6; etc.).

That the whole of Israelite life was involved in covenant regulation was recognized from the start. The original stipulations are summed up in the Ten Words, as tradition attests. But case and cult law, moral and ethical behavior, social and economic practice, religious observance and festival are subsumed under the covenant terms, so that the major part of Pentateuchal legislation was regarded as an extension of the Sinai agreement. The Book of the Covenant and its incomplete parallel in Exod. 34 (cf. also the Holiness Code [Lev. 17–26]) represent historically the penetration of the Sinai covenant into the life of the community after the settlement in Canaan. The process of expansion and proliferation is carried on through Leviticus and Numbers, while Deuteronomy is a recapitulation of this process, stemming from a separate (northern Israelite) source. The elaboration of the covenant in the detailed regulations associated with the Sinai encampment reflects in an artificial and static way what was nevertheless true in a historical sense. The Pentateuchal legislation grew out of the Sinai covenant. The compiler sees it as a perfect whole originating in a single revelatory event.

While the law unfolds in glacial fashion, emphasizing permanence and immutability, the narrative pursues a different tack. Here the covenant is broken almost as soon as it is made. After suitable protestations and ceremonies, the covenant is ratified through a common meal eaten by the elders in the presence of God (Exod. 24:9-11). Within forty days, the people have rebelled, violated the principal terms of the covenant, and incurred the wrath of the suzerain. The penalties implicit in the covenant are threatened, but disaster is narrowly averted by the intervention of Moses. A second covenant is made, with new tablets to replace the broken ones.

The essential conflict between the two covenant ideas — the one of divine commitment to Israel through the fathers, which is irrevocable, and the other, of demand with the threat of annihilation through Moses — is brought out clearly in the episode of the golden calf. The result is that the promise to the fathers remains unbroken — i.e., Israel survives — but this by no means guarantees blanket protection or exemption from the consequences of the Sinai covenant. At the same time, although the penalties for violation of the Sinai covenant are inescapable and devastating, they nevertheless are subject to the prior and unbreakable divine commitment. So divine and human obligation are intermeshed, but without contingency or dependence upon each other. Each pursues remorselessly the logic of its own character, and together they determine the course and consummation of Israel's history. Israel's defection at Sinai is grievously paid for, but the divine commitment is fulfilled in a renewal of the covenant. A second and a third defection are similarly disastrous for Israel; in fact, the whole generation must perish in the wilderness, but the oath to the fathers is maintained when the next generation makes successful entry into the Promised Land.

The chief practical consequence of the sojourn at Sinai and the solemnizing of the covenant was the construction and dedication of the tabernacle. The detailed instructions concerning the tabernacle and its furnishings, and the priesthood who serve in it, were given to Moses by God himself (Exod. 25–31). These are repeated *in extenso* (Exod. 35–40), when the work was actually carried out, perhaps to emphasize the meticulous care with which each detail was accomplished in conformity with the original pattern. While the aniconic character of Israel's religion (i.e., the absence of an image of the deity) militated against a complete identification of the tabernacle with the heavenly abode as in pagan religion, nevertheless the presence of God was localized in the tabernacle (for P in the expression כבוד יהוה, "the glory of the Lord"; for D in the expression שם יהוה, "the name of the Lord"). The tabernacle was designed to serve a twofold function: to protect the holiness of God from contamination by the people (note the regulations restricting the approach to Mt. Sinai and the reasons for them, in Exod. 19); and, on the other hand, to protect the people from an outburst of divine wrath. The priests also perform a double function: to serve the Lord of the tabernacle, according to his needs and wishes; and to mediate his presence to the people, including instruction in, and interpretation of, the divine will. Appropriately in the book of Leviticus, the service of the tabernacle is described in detail: the types and purpose of the sacrifices which are central to worship (chs. 1–8), and the responsibilities and prerogatives of the priesthood (chs. 9–15) culminating in the liturgy of the Day of Atonement, later Israel's most solemn observance (ch. 16). Here the high priest, who alone may enter the holy of holies, mediates the mercy of God to his people through the scapegoat ritual. In this fashion the accumulated sins and iniquities of the previous year are removed, and the reconciliation between God and people achieved.

The so-called Holiness Code (Lev. 17–26) is a summary catchall of legal prescriptions, cultic regulations, and moral exhortation, which may well have served as a catechism for some sanctuary school, or as a guide for priests and Levites in their work as teachers of the people.

Numbers begins with the final action at Sinai: the dedication of the tabernacle. Only when this elaborate and prolonged ceremony was completed, the last animal sacrificed and the last gift offered, was Israel ready to march.

In its present form the Sinai tradition centers upon the elaboration of covenant obligation, in close association with the construction and dedication of the tabernacle. The tabernacle symbolized the presence of the holy God in the midst of his people, while the covenant legislation defined the character and duties of a not-yet-holy people. Behind the tabernacle of P, as also behind the different codifications of law, lay a simpler and perhaps historically more valid tradition of the Sinai covenant, and the tent of meeting. This tent was no replica of the heavenly house, but rather the place where God and man met to settle their pertinent business. Central to its function was the ark of the covenant, symbol of the legally binding nature of the relationship between God and Israel. The association of ark and tent made legal righteousness rather than cultic holiness the principal concern of the worshipping community. To render just decisions and carry them out in conformity with covenant regulations was the chief obligation of the community gathered at the ark.

From ark and tent developed the elaborate scheme now preserved in the Pentateuch, but the essential emphases are still discernible: a holy God joined to a holy people, but holiness defined in terms of moral and legal obligation, as well as of cultic and ritual purity.

4. The wilderness wanderings (Num. 10:10–36:13)

This section consists of a patchwork of narrative material intermingled with priestly data, which have some apparent or superficial connection with the stories or their personnel. Its purpose is to explain how it happened that Israel, which set out from Sinai for Canaan at the start of the second year after the exodus (Num. 10:11), managed to end up thirty-eight years later far off course in Transjordan, still trying to make entry into the Promised Land. This state of affairs posed serious problems to the compiler, who made little effort to relate a continuous narrative — e.g., thirty-eight years are passed over in silence. While granting that there are numerous gaps in the story, which is itself strange and improbable, these facts alone suggest that an authentic nucleus of tradition is at the bottom of it. Invention would have produced a smoother account, and would hardly have led Israel by the bizarre route described, to the wrong country.

The gap in the chronology is largely a blank, so the narrative is artificially divided between the events of the second year and those of the fortieth (after 20:1). This awkwardness clearly reflects a firm tradition that the generation which came out of Egypt did not reach the Promised Land, but perished in the wilderness — including specifically the leaders, Moses, Aaron, and Miriam. This contretemps, which seems factual on the face of it, is explained rather elaborately as the result of the mishandling of the report of the spies (chs. 13–14). The mixture of *Realpolitik* and theology may not be convincing, but it doubtless preserves the important truth that an attempted invasion of Canaan from the south failed. It failed so badly, in fact, that a generation passed before Israel could build up strength for another effort, and even then it had to be made from another direction. The avoidance of war with Edom and Moab (here a kind of reciprocal evasion was practiced) tends to confirm the impression of military diffidence, though doubtless other factors, not excluding kinship, played a role. At the same time, the rather aimless wanderings of Israel, during the whole period from the exodus on, may suggest that the Promised Land was not so fixed an objective as our present sources indicate. It may be that they drifted about until they found a weakness in the settled areas. The conquest of

Transjordan was not part of the original plan; according to the biblical account, it resulted from the obstinacy of Og and Sihon, who refused the Israelites passage through their territories.

The impression made by the stories is that of growing strength and consolidation of forces until the Israelites were able to meet the enemy in the field and defeat him. Internal difficulties continued: the aftermath of the spies episode is disastrous, and the revolt of Korah (P) and Dathan and Abiram (JE) threatens the very existence of the community. On the other hand, the Balaam narrative shows Israel in a most favorable light, as this international diviner is unable to resist the persuasive pressure of the God of Israel and prophesies the splendor and power of the new nation to the dismay of his patron and the serious detriment of his own fortune. The oracles of Balaam, like the Song of the Reed Sea, are a potent example of early Hebrew poetry, authentically portraying the Israel of the wilderness wanderings.

With the defeat of Og and Sihon, Israel at last was able to claim possession of a suitable territory. While the settlement in Transjordan was provisional and preliminary, it is on this note that the Tetrateuch closes. The wanderings have come to an end, and Israel is poised for the final adventure.

5. The epilogue (Deuteronomy)

Before the invasion of Canaan, there was an interlude: Moses' farewell sermons in the Plains of Moab in the last year of the wanderings, and shortly before his death. It is this break in the narrative sequence which focuses attention on the special significance of the wilderness experience. For in these addresses Moses recapitulates the desert experience beginning with the revelation at Horeb (Sinai). Particular emphasis is placed upon the covenant and its stipulations. The Ten Words are repeated (in ch. 5); then the sense of the first commandment is explained and elaborated for six additional chapters (6–11), beginning with a restatement of the main theme of the covenant in positive terms: "You shall love the Lord your God with all your heart, and with all your soul, and with all your might" (6:4). There follows (chs. 12–26) a body of legal material similar to the collections in the earlier books of the Pentateuch, but worked out in a special hortatory style. Additional and presumably original features of the covenant pattern are preserved in ch. 27 (blessings and curses); the covenant-renewal ceremony is connected with Mounts Ebal and Gerizim, in the vicinity of Shechem (cf. Josh. 24).

Two old poems (Deut. 32–33, both probably dating from the period of the amphictyony or early monarchy) are attached to the book, which closes with the death of Moses. For the Deuteronomist, Moses was a prophet, but more than a prophet: "There has not arisen a prophet since in Israel like Moses, whom the Lord knew face to face" (34:10).

The Pentateuch is a composite presentation of the beginnings of Israel. Genesis, including the creation and primeval history, even the patriarchal narratives, is preamble. The center of interest is the formation of Israel: exodus, Sinai, wanderings, and Transjordan are the key words. The story is bounded by the life of Moses, who is the master agent of God's will and the chief architect of Israel. The mighty deeds of God constitute the basic narrative, set in sharp relief by the stupidity and wickedness of Israel. Tabernacle and covenant describe the presence of the holy God in the midst of his chosen people, while the interaction of divine commitment and human obligation defines the area of Israel's experience. The special emphasis of the Deuteronomic sermons, with which the Pentateuch closes, is on the covenant responsibilities of Israel: to obey means life, to disobey death, in the simplest possible terms (cf. Deut. 30:15 in the context of this speech). These words were aimed at a community on the verge of disaster (cf. also Jer. 38:2ff.). The Sinai-Horeb covenant, with its sanctions and penalties, could not be set aside in favor of some more palatable doctrine of election privilege. But the last word even of the Deuteronomist was one of hope. The commitment to Abraham was eternal and irreversible: "For the Lord your God is a merciful God; he will not fail you or destroy you or forget the covenant with your fathers which he swore to them" (Deut. 4:31).

C. History of Pentateuchal Criticism

The systematic, critical investigation of the Pentateuch has been carried on for the past two hundred years. Practically every Old Testament scholar of note has written extensively on the subject, with the result that the pertinent literature is so vast as to defy satisfactory compilation, much less adequate review and evaluation. We must be content with a hasty sketch of the subject.

Scientific Pentateuchal criticism is commonly said to have begun with Jean Astruc, a French Catholic physician, who published his *Conjectures sur les mémoires dont il paroît que Moyse s'est servi, pour composer le livre de la Genèse,* in 1753. Nevertheless, he had precursors, and some of his conclusions about the diversity of sources in Genesis had been anticipated but forgotten. During the hundred years following, the main issues of the literary analysis of the Pentateuch were worked out by a succession of brilliant Continental scholars until the proponents of the "new documentary theory" emerged triumphant. By the last quarter of the 19th century, the Reuss-Graf-Kuenen-Wellhausen hypothesis had swept the field, and was widely accepted as the definitive solution to the literary problems of the Pentateuch. In particular, the writings of Julius Wellhausen summed up the scholarly contributions of previous generations and presented the assured results of literary criticism in a compact and decisive fashion, briefly symbolized by the scholarly tetragrammaton JEDP. J and E were narrative sources, dating in the 9th and 8th centuries respectively, while the compilation JE was achieved in the 7th. D was composed in the 7th century, while P was postexilic. The final editing of the Pentateuch took place *ca.* 400 B.C.E.

Many new developments have occurred since the time of Wellhausen, though it is fair to say that the documentary hypothesis remains the landmark of Pentateuchal criticism, and the foundation for all further research. These developments may be grouped under three classifications: literary analysis, form-critical investigation, and tradition history. While these overlap, and scholars work across the lines of division, they are helpful in indicating the direction of interest and investigation.

1. Documentary hypotheses

Since the Pentateuch is literature and behind its present compilation there are sources (whether clearly defined documents or oral traditions), literary analysis will remain a basic task in Pentateuchal criticism, though other disciplines may be useful and necessary. For many years scholars have been engaged in refining the documentary analysis. It has generally been conceded that none of the major sources is itself a unity.

On the one hand, secondary and supplementary data have been separated from primary source material (thus, e.g., D_S is the Deuteronomic redaction of D, the code found in the temple); on the other, independent sources have been identified within the larger groupings of older analysis. Just as P and E were separated out of the original E source, so J_1 and J_2 were isolated, P_A and P_B, and so on. Because the sigla used to identify separate sources and secondary additions tended to be confused, new letters have appeared in the documentary formulation: L (for J_1, Otto Eissfeldt); K (Julian Morgenstern); and S (Robert Pfeiffer). As part of the same process of reexamination, two of the older sources have been challenged, E and P. Are these independent documents or supplements and insertions into the basic J narrative?

The net effect of the close investigation of the sources has been to blur the clear lines of the documentary hypothesis. Looked at from one point of view, there are too many documents; thus the fragmentary hypothesis revives. From the opposite viewpoint, there are too few or none at all. As a result, the documents appear to be compilations themselves rather than original compositions, and to reflect a process covering hundreds of years and reaching back into the period of oral tradition with its discrete entities. The increasingly unsatisfactory results of literary analysis (for no new scheme has commanded anything like the support given to the older documentary alignment) have led scholars behind the literary sources into the preliterary origins of the contents of the Pentateuch, and also to a new investigation of the process by which the sources were gathered and preserved, and the Pentateuch compiled.

2. Form-critical analysis

The form-critical analysis of the Pentateuch is associated primarily with the name of Hermann Gunkel, whose monumental commentary on Genesis (HKAT [Göttingen: Vandenhoeck & Ruprecht, 1902; 3rd ed., 1910]) marked an epoch in Old Testament scholarship (cf. also *Die Urgeschichte und die Patriarchen* [2nd ed. (Göttingen: Vandenhoeck & Ruprecht, 1921)], and Hugo Gressmann's *Die Anfänge Israels* [2nd ed. (Göttingen: Vandenhoeck & Ruprecht, 1922)]). Gunkel was mainly concerned with two matters: to classify the biblical materials according to formal characteristics (i.e., the structure or pattern of the unit, rather than its content), and also to determine the *Sitz im Leben* (life situation) reflected by the particular item, out of which it arose, or in which it found its function and place. By close examination of the biblical materials, and comparison with similar literature of the other peoples of the Near East, it was possible to deal with both questions in a highly satisfactory and stimulating way. Some authentic idea of the prehistory of the literature of the Pentateuch could be gained, as well as helpful insights into the nature of Israelite and pre-Israelite patriarchal life. The danger of circular or self-validating reasoning was always present — i.e., to reconstruct a *Sitz im Leben* from the contents of a given piece, and then to interpret the piece on the basis of the supposed *Sitz im Leben*. In addition, while the purely scientific and objective discipline of form-classification has proved extremely useful, inferences concerning historicity and accuracy have been drawn on the basis of such classifications, which are often given tendentious titles — e.g., legend, myth, etc. With the aid of archaeological research, and in the light of the enormous quantities of inscriptional and other data bearing on the life of man in the ancient Near East, it was possible to put Pentateuchal criticism on a much sounder historical foundation than ever before. While the literary interrelationships of the Pentateuchal sources could be dealt with by the tools of literary analysis, and the relative chronology of the sources worked out, the question of the antiquity of the P material, e.g., could only be guessed at, or treated inadequately by the hazardous comparison of the Pentateuch with the historical books. Now it was possible to evaluate the traditions, customs, and nomenclature of the Pentateuch on the basis of contemporary data from the Near East and to show that the date of compilation of a Pentateuchal source did not necessarily bear upon either the antiquity or the accuracy of its contents. As a result of the archaeological revolution there has been a wholesale reevaluation and redistribution of the Pentateuchal materials, especially those assigned to P. While this does not signify a return to the traditional view of Mosaic authorship or date, it has meant the rehabilitation in appropriate settings of the large mass of data hitherto regarded as mere priestly invention. Used cautiously, the Pentateuch is an invaluable source, not merely for the point of view of its compilers, but for the actual early history of Israel.

Albrecht Alt, following the labors of Anton Jirku (*Das weltliche Recht im AT* [1927]), and Alfred Jepsen (*Untersuchungen zum Bundesbuch*. BWANT 3/5 [Stuttgart: Kohlhammer, 1927]), established a landmark in the application of the form-critical method to the laws of the Pentateuch in his *Die Ursprünge des Israelitischen Rechts* (*BZAW* 86/1 [1934]; now available in Alt's *Kleine Schriften zur Geschichte des Volkes Israel* [Munich: Beck, 1953], 1:278-332; Eng. trans., *Essays on Old Testament History and Religion* [Garden City: Doubleday, 1968], 101-71). Alt distinguished formally between casuistic and apodictic laws, the former being characteristic of the jurisprudence of the ancient Near East, while the latter (with the form "Thou shalt not . . .") were peculiarly Israelite in their formulation and belonged to the sphere of sacral usage. Subsequent investigation has followed the lines laid down by Alt, though some of his conclusions have been questioned or modified. It does not seem likely that Israelite case law developed directly from contemporary Canaanite practice, but rather that it evolved indigenously in Israel from older, pre-Israelite patriarchal custom, going back ultimately to Mesopotamian sources. On the other hand, George E. Mendenhall in *Law and Covenant in Israel and the Ancient Near East* (Pittsburgh: Biblical Colloquium, 1955) has suggested that the suzerainty treaty of the 2nd millennium provides an appropriate setting for categorical stipulations such as we have in the apodictic laws in the Pentateuch. Just as the suzerain imposes obligations upon his vassal, so the God of Israel requires obedience to the terms of the covenant (Exod. 19–24). The possible cultic *Sitz im Leben* for the presentation of the Decalogue — i.e., the covenant-renewal festival — had already been described by Sigmund Mowinckel in *Le décalogue* (Paris: Alcan, 1927).

Another development of the form-critical approach is to be seen in the works of Gerhard von Rad and Martin Noth. Von Rad retains the traditional JEDP pattern but regards the sources as aggregates of tradition accumulated or compiled over centuries. The basic pattern of the Hexateuch is defined by the credo (e.g., Deut. 26:5-9), while it is out of the cult that the Pentateuchal sources and the Pentateuch itself emerge. The sources, beginning with J, reflect the same historical (i.e., *geschichtliche*, or really *heilsgeschichtliche*) pattern, because it antedates them, having already been shaped by the confession of the worshipping community at the (central) sanctuary.

Noth deals similarly with the process of oral tradition which lies behind the documentary sources of the Pentateuch. He identifies a number of major themes, like the promise to the fathers, the deliverance from bondage, the Sinai experience. Around each of these cluster the etiological tales, cult legends, etc., which constitute the original oral materials. In his analysis of the documents, Noth separates Deuteronomy from the rest of the Pentateuch and attaches it to the Deuteronomic history. The other sources, J, E, and P, do not extend beyond Numbers, with the exception of some material at the end of Deuteronomy. On the other hand, there are no traces of the Deuteronomist in the Tetrateuch. Behind J and E, he recognizes a common source G *(Grundlage)*. Some of the implications, and difficulties, of Noth's position have been considered above. Whether the Deuteronomic history will succeed the Hexateuch as the basic literary unit of the primary history remains to be seen. It is clear that both cannot survive.

Counterbalancing Noth's restriction of JE to the Tetrateuch is Gustav Hölscher's extension of these sources throughout the primary history. For him, J comes down to the division of the monarchy (1 Kgs. 12), while E includes the whole history from Genesis to the end of 2 Kings. His views have not met with general acceptance. The contrast with Noth is so striking as to provoke the question of the nature of Israelite history writing, and the proper approach to the materials at hand. Eissfeldt has treated both presentations in a short but penetrating critique (*Geschichtsschreibung im Alten Testament* [Berlin: Evangelische Verlagsanstalt, 1948]).

3. Traditio-historical criticism

The most radical resistance to the Wellhausen hypothesis has come from the so-called Uppsala school. Its chief representative is Ivan Engnell, who has proposed a new analysis of the Pentateuch, based upon the view that oral tradition played a much larger and longer role in the formation of the Pentateuch than is usually assigned to it. While much of the technical and legal material in the Pentateuch was written down, the narrative traditions were transmitted orally. It is useless, therefore, to try to isolate documentary sources, since these did not exist, and what sources there were had already been fused with one another and the P narrative framework in the preliterary stage. Engnell distinguishes two principal collections of material: the "P work," which corresponds to the Tetrateuch, and the "D work," which corresponds to Noth's Deuteronomic history. These works developed independently of each other, and were ultimately written down separately in postexilic times (5th century). Later they were joined, since the D work begins approximately where the P work leaves off. The P work centers upon the exodus tradition (Exod. 1–15), which reflects the cultic celebration of the deliverance from Egypt. (Here Engnell follows the lead of Johannes Pedersen, whose own views of the Pentateuch are highly original and anti-Wellhausenian.) It is around this nucleus that the rest of the material has accumulated in P circles. By the time the traditions were reduced to writing, they were verbally fixed, so that the MT reflects faithfully the original. This conservative approach to the MT is a welcome shift from the days of free emendation. At the same time, however, the well-known Uppsala disregard for the LXX is less defensible, especially since the Qumran discoveries. A number of Hebrew manuscripts have been found which preserve a LXX-type text, thus confirming the fact that in the Pentateuch and historical books the LXX was a faithful, almost literal rendering of its *Vorlage*. The existence of distinct scribal recensions of the Pentateuch can only be damaging to the Scandinavian view of the very late compilation of the text.

There can be little doubt that Engnell's general emphasis upon the importance, the tenacity, and the reliability of oral tradition is warranted and commendable. His contention that much ancient material has been preserved faithfully in the text of the Pentateuch is likewise valid, and the idea of continuing circles of "P" and "D" may offer a solution to the problem of the accumulation of traditions. Nevertheless, the sharp distinction between oral and written transmission tends to break down, the more the tenacity and reliability of oral tradition are maintained. There is no reason to doubt that the art of writing, even of narrative and poetic material, was practiced in early Israel, especially after the rise of the monarchy. It is very difficult to suppose that the court history of David was not written down within a comparatively few years of the events described, and so with other narrative materials, particularly those in prose. Moreover, the problems of the Pentateuch are literary, at least to a considerable extent; and one cannot banish them by transferring them from a written to an oral setting. In the future we shall have to reckon more with the oral traditions and their transmission, but hardly less with the written materials and their transmission.

4. Synthesis and summary

Artur Weiser in his *Einleitung in das Alte Testament* (2nd ed. [Göttingen: Vandenhoeck & Ruprecht, 1949]; Eng. trans., *The Old Testament* [New York: Association, 1961]) attempts a synthesis of the different approaches and methods of dealing with the Pentateuch. Instead of choosing one over another, use can be made of all, since the Pentateuch is more than a collection of traditions, more than a mixture of literary sources. It is closely bound to the cult and faithfully reflects the religious life and experience of the people. Its basic structure and unity come out of the cultic confession, which itself is the affirmation of Israel's historical experience. So Israel's authentic history, focused in the cult, finds expression in the Pentateuch, which is the precipitate of accumulated cultic traditions.

Christopher R. North [1951], after surveying recent developments in Pentateuchal criticism, summarizes as follows: (a) It must now be recognized that the Pentateuch consists of traditions concerning the history of Israel down to the death of Moses, and that they do not have the values of scientific history. This is *Heilsgeschichte* — Israel's confession, its affirmation of what God has done for and to Israel in the world. That it is based upon some nucleus of fact may be granted, but this is not the most important fact about this type of literature. It has its *Sitz im Leben* in the cult; it is first of all a religious document. (b) Can the development of Israel's religious ideas be traced in the familiar JEDP arrangement, or are the evolutionist assumptions of the Wellhausen school no longer acceptable now that the simple chronological scheme of documents can no longer be sustained? North believes that some defense can be made both of the documents and the "evolution" of Israelite religion, though hardly with the assurance of the earlier scholars. North's view is judicious, and reflects the evolution of Old Testament scholarship in its grasp of the nature and complexity of the Pentateuchal traditions. Nevertheless, we suggest that the distinction between *geschichtlich* and *historisch* should not be pressed too far in dealing with the Pentateuch. A religion that affirms the mighty deeds of God and attempts to place them in a historical context cannot afford to make nice distinctions between the fact and the affirmation of it. Admittedly what is central is the interpretation of the event, which itself is the confession of faith. But the event is or must be historical. Beneath the layers of tradition there was an event, which may not now be recoverable, though pessimism about the possibility of such recovery is excessive. It is that event (i.e., what actually happened, but theologically interpreted) which faith must affirm, not some imaginative tradition about it.

With regard to the second point, the question of evolution in Israelite religion can be separated from the chronological interrelationship of the sources. One may accept the scholarly dating of the sources without accepting also some evolutionary scheme concerning the religion of Israel: e.g., from polytheism to henotheism to monotheism; or from a tribal to a national to a universal God; or in ethical and moral principles. The arrangement and dating of the contents of the Pentateuch (as distinguished from the documents) will depend, not upon the inner criticism of the sources, but on comparison with objective nonbiblical data from the contemporary Near East.

The Pentateuch is the end product of an incredibly long process of accumulation, transmission, and redaction. Its original traditions go back to dim antiquity (e.g., the traditions behind the flood story must be many thousands of years old), and were transmitted orally for hundreds of years: folk tales, cult legends, etiological stories, and the like, each with its characteristic form, shaped and polished through repeated telling. These were linked into more complex collections, until a connected narrative emerged, built out of the basic pattern of the credo, or confession of faith. These poetic materials were consolidated into the official tradition of the confederation around its sanctuary during the period of the judges (G). Likewise going back to patriarchal times was a legal tradition, around which gathered customs and precedents, and from which emerged the various bodies of law preserved in the Pentateuch. With few exceptions, the mass of the material is premonarchic. Cultic practice is also of great antiquity; and in various collections, the Pentateuch preserves the sacral customs of early Israel. Because of the tenacity and conservatism of religious observance, it is almost impossible to trace development, but in general the Pentateuchal cult legislation reflects the practice of the early monarchy.

Formal classification, oral tradition, cultic setting, and function are important new tools in the struggle to understand the Pentateuch. Even more significant is the mass of archaeological data, which increasingly provides an external, histori- cally reliable check upon the theories imposed upon the Pentateuchal material, and the reconstructions made of them. The Pentateuch apparently consists of essentially authentic data concerning the history of Israel from the time of the patriarchs down to the death of Moses, but including cultic, legal, and other technical data, which in their present form derive from later periods, particularly the amphictyony and the early monarchy. The documents themselves were composed at various times, beginning in the 10th century B.C.E. and ending in the middle of the 6th, when the whole of the primary history was completed. During the next century the Pentateuch was separated, and officially promulgated as the authoritative word of God for Israel, the only infallible rule of faith and practice.

Bibliography

The most recent presentation of the general subject of Pentateuchal criticism is to be found in O. Eissfeldt, *Einleitung in das Alte Testament,* 2nd ed. (Tübingen: Mohr, 1956), which has an extensive bibliography [*The Old Testament: An Intro- duction,* trans. P. R. Ackroyd (New York: Harper & Row, 1965)] . Very worthwhile are: C. R. North, "Pentateuchal Criticism," *The Old Testament and Modern Study,* ed. H. H. Rowley (Oxford: Clarendon, 1951), 48-83, which also includes a useful bibliography; and H. F. Hahn, *The Old Testament in Modern Research* (Philadel- phia: Muhlenberg, 1954).

General treatments in English: A. Bentzen, *Introduction to the Old Testament,* 2nd ed. (Copenhagen: Gad, 1952). R. H. Pfeiffer, *Introduction to the Old Testament,* 2nd ed. (London: Black, 1953). The old classic is S. R. Driver, *Introduction to the Literature of the Old Testament,* 9th ed. (Edinburgh: T. & T. Clark, 1913). The most comprehensive publication of the Wellhausen hypothesis, along with a complete history of criticism to that time, is to be found in J. E. Carpenter and G. Harford- Battersby, *The Hexateuch According to the Revised Version,* 2 vols. (London: Longmans, Green, 1900).

Relevant books and articles in other languages: J. Wellhausen, *Prolegomena to the History of Ancient Israel,* trans. J. S. Black and A. Menzies (Edinburgh: Black, 1885); *Die Composition des Hexateuchs und der historischen Bücher des Altes Testaments,* 3rd ed. (Berlin, 1899). J. Pedersen, "Die Auffassung vom Alten Testament," *ZAW* 49 (1931): 161-81. P. Volz and W. Rudolph, *Der Elohist als Erzähler: Ein Irrweg der Pentateuchkritik?* BZAW 63 (1933). G. von Rad, *Die Priesterschrift im Hexateuch.* BWANT 13 (Stuttgart: Kohlhammer, 1934); *Das formgeschichtliche Problem des Hexateuchs.* BWANT 26[78] (Stuttgart: Kohlham- mer, 1938) ["The Form-Critical Problem of the Hexateuch," *The Problem of the Hexateuch* (London: SCM, 1984), 1-78]. W. Rudolph, *Der "Elohist" von Exodus bis Josua.* BZAW 68 (Berlin: A. Topelmann, 1938); J. Pedersen, *Israel, Its Life and Culture,* 2 vols. (London: Oxford University Press, 1926-1940). G. Hölscher, *Die Anfänge der hebräischen Geschichtsschreibung* (Heidelberg: Winter, 1942). M. Noth, *Überlieferungsgeschichtliche Studien,* vol. 1 (Halle, 1943); *Überlieferungsgeschichte des Pentateuch* (Stuttgart: Kohlhammer, 1948). G. Hölscher, *Geschichtsschreibung in Israel* (Lund: Gleerup, 1952). G. von Rad, *Studies in Deuteronomy,* trans. D. M. G. Stalker. SBT 9 (London: SCM, 1953); *Das erste Buch Mose: Genesis.* ATD 2/4 (Göttingen: Vandenhoeck & Ruprecht, 1953). Y. Kaufmann, *The Religion of Israel, from Its Beginnings to the Babylonian Exile* (Chicago: University of Chicago Press, 1960).

For an extended and authoritative presentation of the documentary hypothesis, see: S. R. Driver, *Introduction to the Literature of the Old Testament,* 1-159. Cf. also J. E. Carpenter and G. Harford-Battersby, *The Hexateuch According to the Revised Version,* 1:1-179. R. H. Pfeiffer, *Introduction to the Old Testament,* 129-289. [For more recent surveys of Pentateuchal scholarship, see, among many, J. H. Hayes, *An Introduction to Old Testament Study* (Nashville: Abingdon, 1979), 156-237; *The Hebrew Bible and Its Modern Interpreters,* ed. D. A. Knight and G. M. Tucker (Chico, CA: Scholars Press, 1985), 263-305; and R. N. Whybray, *The Making of the Pentateuch. A Methodological Study.* JSOT Suppl. 53 (Sheffield: Sheffield Academic Press, 1987), 17-219.]

13

The Continuing Revolution
in Biblical Research

There is at present a steadily increasing lag between the quality of current Bible translations and commentaries, and the actual state of knowledge. This statement applies to virtually all books now in print. Bible dictionaries are in a somewhat better state, thanks especially to the new four-volume *Interpreter's Dictionary of the Bible* [1962] and the one-volume *New Bible Dictionary* of the Tyndale Fellowship [1st ed., 1962], but these works suffer greatly from the inescapable defects of multiple authorship within restricted areas.

In 1956 the authors of this article accepted an invitation from Doubleday Anchor Books to edit a series of paperbacks dealing with the books of the Bible in the light of recent discovery and research. Plans were fully discussed and negotiations with prospective authors were undertaken. After the usual delays and not infrequent disappointments, the series is now well along, and the first five volumes are scheduled to appear in early 1964.

I

Biblical research is being revolutionized by archaeological and linguistic discoveries of every conceivable kind. We can provide here only a very few illustrations from the great mass of archaeological discoveries and interpretations of material found by archaeologists. One of these involves the excavations at Ugarit, which have continued since 1929 with a whole series of sensational finds. Even as recently as the autumn of 1960, after more than a score of campaigns, quantities of inscribed tablets were still being found. In that campaign the French excavators discovered a whole new archive in the southern part of the site, which yielded thirty boxes of additional tablets, divided between Babylonian and Canaanite alphabetic texts. Material for reconstructing the Ugaritic epics continues to be discovered; all of it has prime value for restoring the early history of Hebrew poetic style.

These texts, most of which date from the 14th century B.C.E., were copied down for the first time not long before that period, but they had all been composed orally about the first half of the 2nd millennium B.C.E. While it is true that their Northwest Semitic verse style was beginning to be modified in the latter part of the pre-Israelite period, there is still much close resemblance between Hebrew poetry, especially between the earliest preserved Hebrew verse — most of which we should date between the 13th and 11th centuries B.C.E. — and Ugaritic verse. We can now, e.g., understand a great many hitherto obscure passages in the earlier Psalms, with reference to which scarcely a week passes without some new discovery being made.

We may list, in addition, the Northwest Semitic inscriptions in our own ancestral alphabet, which begin about the 17th century B.C.E. At present, every century after the 18th seems to be represented by texts in the linear script, usually very short. When we reach the 10th century B.C.E., these become numerous. The inscriptions are exceedingly valuable for details of script, spelling, and language, and they permit independent dating of biblical texts. In their study of the history of Hebrew orthography, Frank M. Cross, Jr., and one of the present writers (D. N. Freedman) have been able to contribute many new observations as a result of intensive study of these inscriptions, which can now be dated as a rule within a century and often within a few years.

The Sefire treaties from the middle of the 8th century B.C.E. are the longest inscriptions which have survived in a Northwest Semitic alphabet and dialect from the early 1st millennium B.C.E. They are particularly important for our purpose because they throw light on a very significant source of misinterpretation of the Bible through wrong word division. These treaties have no dots between words as is the practice in most shorter Hebrew inscriptions. In general, one can rely on the word division of our Hebrew text, but there are many passages — apparently many more than we had suspected — where the original text must have run together, just as in cuneiform texts or, for that matter, in medieval Greek and Latin script. Wrong word division of a string of consonants was often inevitable.

We have a wealth of early Aramaic texts. The development of Aramaic language and vocabulary can be followed from the 9th century on down. The Persian period has yielded a great deal of such material, much of which is still unpublished. These finds have completely revolutionized our understanding of the development of Biblical Aramaic from the time of Ezra and Nehemiah to that of Daniel. The Dead Sea Scrolls preserve many Aramaic texts, sometimes of the standard classical Aramaic type which we find in the Persian period and sometimes in later forms of Jewish Aramaic.

The Dead Sea Scrolls are the most important of all manuscript discoveries. It is surely no longer necessary to defend their antiquity or authenticity. Recently, however, a number of voices have been raised again to claim that the Scrolls actually have very little significance for biblical studies. As an illustration, G. R. Driver of Oxford, editor-in-chief of the forthcoming British translation of the Old Testament [*The New English Bible,* Old Testament 1970], declared in the *London Times* (19 August 1962) that the Scrolls "have been of much less value than was expected when they were first discovered." This statement is simply not in agreement with the actual expectations of most other scholars in the field, after a few descriptions and photographs of the Dead Sea Isaiah had been published within months of the first announcement of the discovery in 1948. The real value of the Scrolls for biblical studies was not realized for some seven years; it resides not in the text of Isaiah nor even in the much more striking divergences in other books, but in our new understanding of the textual character of the Hebrew Bible and its relation to the Greek translation of the Seventy.

To take the books of Samuel as an example, Frank Cross has published samples from a rather extensive collection of fragments belonging to a single manuscript of archaic textual character, copied during the 1st century B.C.E. In this manuscript we find a recension which differs from both the Greek and the Massoretic Hebrew Bible. Since it preserves a good deal of material which is lacking in one or even both of our two previous recensions (the Hebrew and the Greek), this new recension is of unusual interest for our purpose. As a result of Cross's publications, it is perfectly clear that the prototype of the various recensions that have survived — including an even more archaic text from the 3rd century B.C.E. — was considerably longer than any previously known recension. Both Hebrew and Greek recensions often dropped words, phrases, and whole passages, especially when they were duplicates. We already knew that in ancient Near Eastern literature it was extremely common to repeat a prospective text in narrative form. In other words, first came the announcement of what was to be done or said, and then the narrative (what was done or said), usually couched in identical language. In the Keret epic of Ugarit, for instance, we find many such omissions, sometimes in the prospective text and sometimes in the narrative text. These gaps can often be filled by use of a complete text in one of the duplicate passages. The same is true of Samuel; future translations will have to expand the text substantially — including many passages which dropped out of all previously known recensions and translations, some of great importance for their content.

In the Pentateuch, judging from scattered examples which have been published, especially in Exodus and Deuteronomy, there was also a good deal of recensional difference between the Hebrew and the Greek texts. For instance, in the so-called Song of Moses in Deut. 32, we note much variation, which again suggests that the original text was longer than either of the two previously known recensions. From previous study of the Septuagint in Joshua, where first-class work was done by Max Margolis [see his *The Book of Joshua in Greek,* 4 vols. (Paris:

Geuthner, 1931-38)], it has become clear that the divergences of the Greek text may very often be traced back to divergences in the lost Hebrew recension which underlay the Greek translation. It now appears also that the situation with respect to Judges and Kings was even more complex than in the books of Samuel.

We can interpret the differences between the recensions in Judges along similar lines. Originally, there was a text of Judges which was a good deal longer than any of the three most important extant recensions (Massoretic Hebrew and Greek A and B), and this text can be in part restored by a careful comparison of Hebrew and Greek, just as was done by Max Margolis for Joshua. The so-called A recension is in some respects older and better than the B recension, as already recognized by Alfred Rahlfs in his edition of the Septuagint. Here, too, we find many cases in which the Greek is superior to the Hebrew. In other words, the Greek goes back to a Hebrew text much older than our current Hebrew and preserves many passages which have been lost in Hebrew.

It is clear that in Kings and Chronicles the divergences between the two books in their Hebrew recensions may often be explained in the same way. The original text often differed from both. At least one such recension has been identified among the Qumran fragments. A similar state of affairs may be found in Jeremiah and other books. In short, there can no longer be any reasonable doubt that we must deal with the Hebrew and Greek Bibles just as we would with different recensions of any other ancient work. Some of the differences are the result of inner Greek or later Hebrew development, but a high proportion of them go back to recensional differences antedating the translation of the Greek Bible in the 3rd and 2nd centuries B.C.E. Under such conditions it is idle to deny the importance of the Dead Sea Scrolls for our understanding of the Old Testament. In fact, from now on we will have to estimate the probable value of most study of the text and exegesis of the Old Testament according to its relation to the progress of studies in the Scrolls.

Our Hebrew text has suffered much more from losses than it has from glosses. These losses are mostly scribal, as we have seen, though some of them may probably be attributed to oral transmission. For example, a scholar might find himself in a new city and without manuscripts. He would often know several biblical books by heart, and could dictate these from memory; or if he was a scribe as well, he could simply write down the text.

When we turn to the New Testament we find a very anomalous situation. There is still a partial boycott of the Dead Sea Scrolls on the part of New Testament scholars, despite the fact that in the Scrolls we have for the first time a direct Jewish background of the New Testament. Hitherto we have been partly dependent upon intertestamental literature (Apocrypha and Pseudepigrapha) and partly upon early rabbinic literature, which is, unfortunately, a century or two later than the deeds and words of Christ and the apostles. Thanks to the Dead Sea Scrolls, we now have direct evidence that is of the greatest significance and which bears on all our New Testament books.

We are now provided with a rapidly increasing mass of parallels relating to both the Synoptic and the Johannine traditions about John the Baptist and Jesus. We have also an impressive body of material illustrating obscure points in the epistles of Paul, including Ephesians and the Pastoral Epistles. Hebrews, the Catholic Epistles, and Revelation are also brightly illuminated. Our literary understanding of the Apocalypse is particularly enhanced; the new data partly confirm the views of R. H. Charles and partly support the ideas of C. C. Torrey. New Testament scholars have scarcely begun to take this material into consideration. It is, however, already possible to form some idea of what is coming. We refer in this connection particularly to the work of William H. Brownlee and Jean Daniélou, S.J., on John the Baptist; of Krister Stendahl and Kurt Schubert on the Synoptic Gospels; of K. G. Kuhn, Raymond E. Brown, S.S., and others on the Gospel of John; and of Sherman Johnson, begun quite a number of years ago and continued by Daniélou and others, on the book of Acts and the organization of the earliest church. Such men as K. G. Kuhn, W. D. Davies, and David Flusser are amassing data to illustrate and often to explain Pauline ideas.

II

Collaboration with a secular press such as Doubleday Anchor Books has one great advantage among others. There is no need to limit contributors to men belonging to specific institutions, churches or countries, with the lack of sufficient control upon competence that this entails. The chief criterion for selection has been expert front-line knowledge of the tremendous new world recovered by archaeological and philological research during the past century, and especially during the past two or three decades. This world underlies and undergirds the Bible. To understand it one must have sound training in philology and complete freedom from such dogmatic trammels of the past as Scholastic and Reformation exegesis, 19th-century conservatism, the Fundamentalism of early 20th-century America, and such equally dogmatic trammels as the analysis of Wellhausen and its offshoots, as well as the constructions of the Bultmann school — or of any scholarly circle which bases itself on modern philosophies or ideologies, such as Marxism.

Flexibility and willingness to change one's own ideas are both absolutely essential. We do not attempt to dictate what our collaborators are to write or the views they are to hold. If we have new information or ideas that we think should be taken into consideration, we mention them, but we do not attempt to hold contributors to any particular line. Thus there are Catholics, Jews, and Protestants from America, Europe, and Israel, of varying backgrounds, all of them professors in universities or theological seminaries. The largest single group consists of American Protestants. Where feasible we have asked members of the so-called Baltimore

School to collaborate, since the editors belong to it, but members of this School remain in the minority. Of the six manuscripts now going through the press, only two have been prepared by members of the Baltimore School — on Jeremiah by John Bright (Union Theological Seminary, Richmond) and Chronicles by Jacob M. Myers (Lutheran Theological Seminary, Gettysburg). Others who have finished their assignments are Marvin Pope (Yale) on Job, Bo Reicke (Basel) on the Catholic Epistles, E. A. Speiser (Pennsylvania) on Genesis, and R. B. Y. Scott (Princeton) on Proverbs and Ecclesiastes. All of these men are entirely independent scholars. The second group of volumes, scheduled for release in 1964-65, will include contributions by Mitchell Dahood, S.J. (Pontifical Biblical Institute) on the Psalms, H. L. Ginsberg (Jewish Theological Seminary) on Isaiah, Louis Hartmann, C.S.S.P. (Catholic University of America) on Daniel, and George E. Mendenhall (Michigan) on the Early Laws of the Pentateuch. It is hoped that similar installments will appear annually until the series is completed by about 1968.

We are certainly not under the impression that the new series is in any way "definitive." But we have tried to get only trained scholars who are not opposed either to new ideas or to full utilization of new discoveries. This is essential, for biblical scholarship, in order to be productive, must be fully informed as well as staunchly independent.

14

The Law and the Prophets

The expression, "The Law and the Prophets," familiar to us from the New Testament,[1] refers to the first two major sections of the Hebrew Bible. Most Jews, including Pharisees and Essenes, and the followers of John and Jesus, accepted the authority of the Torah and the Nebi'im, and recognized their essential unity. These were the central core of Scripture, to which the Writings were subordinate, and upon which they were dependent. It will not be amiss in this assemblage, and especially at this time and place, to remind ourselves that Christianity and Judaism, in all their varied forms, are built upon the twin foundations of Law and Prophecy. Of their ultimate religious significance Jesus Christ is himself the chief witness: "Think not that I have come to abolish the law and the prophets; I have not come to abolish them, but to fulfil them. For truly I say to you, till heaven and earth pass away, not even the tittle on the *yodh* will pass from the law until all is accomplished" (Matt. 5:17-18).

In a similar fashion the story of the Transfiguration (Mark 9:2-10 and parallels) emphasizes the close interrelationship between Law and Prophecy, symbolized by Moses and Elijah. These passages in turn may be connected with the closing verses of Malachi (Heb. 3:22-23): "Remember the law of my servant Moses, the statutes and ordinances that I commanded him at Horeb for all Israel. Behold I will send you Elijah the prophet before the great and terrible day of the Lord comes."[2]

In this paper, our concern is with the literary history of the Law and the Prophets: the process of composition, compilation, edition, and publication. According to the common scholarly opinion, the literary process runs parallel to the cultural history of Israel. Thus a span of more than a thousand years is involved from the

---

1. Cf. Matt. 5:17; 7:12; 11:13; 22:40; Luke 16:16; Acts 13:15; 24:14; 28:23; Rom. 3:21b.
2. Prof. David Flusser of Hebrew University has suggested that these verses constitute a poetic summation of the whole of the preceding portions of the Old Testament, the Law and the Prophets.

139

earliest oral sources until the final appearance of the Torah and Nebi'im as we have them. The long complicated story of the development and interrelations of the sources, their adaptation, amalgamation, and editing into a single composition has been the subject of intensive study by scholars for more than two hundred years, and it is not our intention to recapitulate their investigations at this point.[3] There is widespread agreement that the Pentateuch was formally published around 400 B.C.E., and that the Prophets received a similar imprimatur about two hundred years later.

In our judgment, both dates are too low, whether they are taken to refer to the completion of the literary process of compilation and edition, or to the recognition of the authority of this literature in matters of faith and practice. The thesis which we advance here is that the literary process, strictly conceived, came to its conclusion at a much earlier date for both the Law and the Prophets, and that the question of authority is inseparable from that of formal publication. We hold that the Law and the Former Prophets (which we designate the primary history, i.e., the books from Genesis through 2 Kings in the Hebrew Bible) comprise a literary unit which was compiled and published in its entirety by the middle of the 6th century B.C.E.,[4] and that the Latter Prophets (i.e., the books of Isaiah, Jeremiah, Ezekiel, and the twelve minor prophets) appeared in finished form toward the end of the 6th or in the early part of the 5th century B.C.E. We hold further that these were public documents, for which the highest religious authority was claimed, promulgated by an official ecclesiastical group in the Jewish community.[5] In short, these

3. See the standard Introductions by O. Eissfeldt, A. Weiser, R. H. Pfeiffer and A. Bentzen. For a survey of the literature and scholarly contributions toward a solution of Pentateuchal problems, see our article on the Pentateuch in *IDB* (Nashville: Abingdon, 1962), 3:711-27 [see above, Chapter 12].

4. We wish to acknowledge the influence of Y. Kaufmann's views and arguments in dating the Torah literature, especially with respect to his case against a postexilic date for the P source. At the same time we do not accept his reversal of the order of D and P, or his reconstruction of the preexilic history of the sources. Cf. his *Religion of Israel,* trans. Moshe Greenberg (Chicago: University of Chicago Press, 1960), esp. ch. 5 [see review in Chapter 11 above].

5. At the Congress, Prof. J. Hempel raised the question of the place of publication of such a monumental work, and the nature of the group which could exercise the necessary authority to promulgate it. In our opinion the logical place to look for the publication of this work is Babylonia rather than Palestine. While the great concern for the Holy Land as the only suitable place to settle and worship in the one authorized temple might indicate a Palestinian location, even greater emphasis is placed upon the twin themes of exile and return. It is repeatedly affirmed that the people will be taken from this Holy Land, and will be forced into captivity in foreign territories, where they must stay until God in his mercy restores them to their proper home. We would expect Palestinian Jews to emphasize rather the theme of continuous occupation of the land, even after the destruction of the temple. If a postexilic date of publication were posited for the primary history, then a Palestinian location would be perfectly in order. Such a line of reasoning would apply specifically to the Chronicler's history, which reflects the orientation of the Babylonian exiles, but was composed in Palestine (cf. our article, "The Chronicler's Purpose," *CBQ* 23 [1961]: 436-42 [see above, Chapter 10]).

works constituted the authorized history of the people of God, along with relevant prophetic commentary, interpretation, and proclamation. The special status of the Torah was doubtless recognized from the beginning, but it was only later that the five books of Moses were set apart from the larger literary entity, resulting in the tripartite division we now have: Torah, Former, and Latter Prophets.

In dealing with these portions of the Bible, we distinguish between their literary and textual history. The former is concerned primarily with the creative literary activity by which earlier oral traditions were shaped into a continuous record, the extensive editorial redaction of the different written sources, and the final compilation of available materials resulting in the appearance of the completed work. The latter is concerned with the transmission of the text and the process by which it was finally fixed. Together they constitute an account of the literature from its beginnings to its final form. With the formal promulgation of the work, in which contents, scope, and order of the parts are fixed, without further significant change, literary history comes to an end, and textual history, properly speaking, begins. The transmission of the text, with the development of recensional patterns, manuscript families, and the emergence of distinctive text-types, represents a phase in the history of biblical literature quite different from the preceding literary phase. Comparison of all existing manuscripts and versions of the books of both the Old and New Testaments reveals a relatively narrow range of variation; most of the alterations are of minor significance and belong to categories characteristic of scribal activity. Many of these are accidental; others are the result of grammatical, orthographic, or lexical revision. But creative literary work and extensive editorial revision belong to an earlier period before formal authoritative promulgation. We can trace the textual history of the Law and Prophets back to manuscripts of the 3rd century B.C.E., and we can make reasonable projections into the 4th and even the 5th century, to which we can assign the archetypal manuscripts which underlie all subsequent texts and versions.[6] It is also our opinion that the changes during the 6th-5th centuries were of the scribal-textual kind, rather than of the literary-editorial variety. But in order to determine the critical period when literary history ends and textual history begins, i.e., the point at which the literature becomes fixed in permanent and at least quasi-official form, it is necessary to examine the relevant criteria, as well as the principles and methods by which they are isolated and evaluated. It is to these matters that we now turn.

6. See our article, "The Massoretic Text and the Qumran Scrolls: A Study in Orthography," *Textus* 2 (1962): 87-102 [see Volume II, Chapter 3]. Our conclusions agree substantially with those of F. Cross, *The Ancient Library of Qumran and Modern Biblical Studies,* rev. ed. (Garden City: Doubleday, 1961), 188-94. Cf. also W. F. Albright, "New Light on Early Recensions of the Hebrew Bible," *BASOR* 140 (1955): 27-33; and M. Greenberg, "The Stabilization of the Text of the Hebrew Bible," *JAOS* 76 (1956): 157-67.

In attempting to determine the date of publication of a literary work, it is immediately clear that a *terminus a quo* is provided by the latest specific historical reference found in it. Under any circumstances, the work cannot be earlier than the date of such material. It is, of course, quite possible that such an historical note has been added to a previously completed entity, which except for the addendum should then be dated according to its other historical data. This appears to be the case with the last paragraph in 2 Kings (25:27-30), which stands apart from the narrative, and is to be dated at least twenty years later than any other historical reference in the primary history. This possibility does not affect the principle involved, but points toward the determination of a *terminus a quo* for different parts of a composite work, using the same criterion.

In pursuing this line of inquiry it is important to distinguish between authentic predictive materials in the Old Testament, and the rare *vaticinium ex eventu,* which is to be classified with ordinary historical data. Specific information, giving names, dates, places, is to be treated historically. Thus the name "Josiah" in the well-known prophecy concerning the destruction of the temple at Bethel in 1 Kgs. 13:2 must be a retrojection from the time of Josiah or later, though there may have been an authentic original prophecy couched in more general terms. In its present form, however, the *terminus a quo* for that passage is the last part of the 7th century B.C.E. General predictions of the collapse of the nation, the exile and return, do not necessarily presuppose these events, however. On the contrary, their vagueness and notable divergence from the known course of history argue for their authenticity, and provide instead a *terminus ante quem* for the composition of this material.[7] The situation is well illustrated by the predictions in the books of Jeremiah and Ezekiel concerning the duration of the exile,[8] and the manner of its termination. Far from reflecting the actual events, they can only be regarded as previsions of a course of history which followed the main outlines, but differed markedly in detail; and which were left undisturbed by subsequent editors and scribes.

In general, historical information helps to determine the terminus a quo for the completion of a literary work, but the *terminus ante quem* is fixed by other

7. Kaufmann, 347-58, makes extensive and, in our judgment, generally effective use of this argument in connection with the prophetic writings.

8. Jeremiah's seventy years (25:11, 12) are to be dated from the 4th year of Jehoiakim, 605 B.C.E. The reference in 29:10 (which may be dated about ten years later) is to be interpreted in the light of the earlier passage. The starting point for the forty years of Ezekiel (4:6) is uncertain, but it must fall between the beginning of his ministry (593 B.C.E.) and the fall of Jerusalem (587 B.C.E.). The terminal dates for the fall of Babylon (Jeremiah) or the end of the exile (Ezekiel) differ somewhat, and neither coincides with the historical event (539 B.C.E.). It is to be noted that Ezekiel uses the same forty-year pattern in predicting the downfall of Egypt (29:10-16), and its subsequent restoration. Here the results did not match expectations, and the chronology is left dangling. But all this is clear evidence that the prophecies antedated the events, and were not subsequently altered. Cf. G. A. Cooke, *The Book of Ezekiel.* ICC (New York: Scribner's, 1937), 2:328-29.

criteria. Thus the primary history could have been finished at any time after, say, 550 B.C.E.; the lower limit, strictly considered, would be fixed by the date of the oldest manuscript containing the completed work, or adequate evidence for the date of such a manuscript. No one would doubt now, on the basis of existing fragments from Qumran, and our knowledge of the Septuagint and its history, that the primary history in substantially its present form existed in the 3rd century, or even the 4th century B.C.E. But it is possible to make further use of the historical references in the work in narrowing the range between termini. It is universally recognized that historical works reflect not only the period of the subject matter, but also the time of composition. We all remember Wellhausen's dictum that the stories of Genesis tell us about the period of their authors rather than about the era of the patriarchs.[9] Wellhausen was perhaps too skeptical concerning the preservation of authentic traditions and reminiscences, and too ingenious in interpreting veiled allusions to contemporary situations. Nevertheless the principle is an important one. It is almost impossible for an author or editor to conceal entirely either his point of view or his historical position; clues to these will be found here and there throughout the work. Especially in the case of historical works, significant recent or contemporary events will inevitably find their way into the narrative. In the biblical histories there were compelling reasons for bringing the narrative up to date. For the biblical writer, Israel's history was its experience with God.[10] Events were the signs of his presence and embodied his activity. History was theologically conceived as a continuous chronological process, beginning with election (or creation), following the complex course of past events, leading to the present circumstances and experiences, and pointing to an as yet unfulfilled future. While chronicles and narratives can be of limited scope, sacred history can only have an eschatological terminus. The provisional stopping place in the sequence of historical events is fixed by the horizon of the author or compiler. We maintain therefore that if the last historical reference in such literary works as the primary history is the *terminus a quo,* it also points to the date of composition within a few years of that event. The *terminus ante quem* is determined by the next significant historical event, known from other sources, which, so far as we can determine, would have figured in the historical account had the author or editor known of it. For the primary history, these decisive events would be the fall of Babylon and the consequent return of the exiles. The fact

9. Wellhausen's language is characteristically strong: "It is true, we attain to no historical knowledge of the patriarchs, but only of the time when the stories about them arose in the Israelite people; this later age is here unconsciously projected, in its inner and its outward features, into hoar antiquity, and is reflected there like a glorified mirage." *Prolegomena to the History of Israel* (Edinburgh: A. & C. Black, 1885; repr. Atlanta: Scholars Press, 1994), 318-19.

10. On the historical nature of biblical religion, see our article, "History and Eschatology," *Interpretation* 14 (1960): 3-15 [see above, Chapter 8]; and G. E. Wright, *God Who Acts.* SBT 8 (London: SCM, 1952); and his "Faith of Israel," *IB,* 1:349-89.

that the primary history comes to an end before these occurrences indicates that it was compiled and completed before that time.

More difficult to assess are obscure allusions and hidden references to current personalities and events. These abound in the late literature, especially of the Hellenistic era. The canonical book of Daniel and other apocalyptic books contain much material of this kind; the Qumran commentaries are especially rich in this respect. There is no doubt of the intent of the author to convey historical data, and it is only necessary to penetrate the disguise, which is frequently rendered more obscure by our lack of information about times, persons, and places. But there is little or none of this in the earlier biblical literature.[11]

Even more hazardous is the attempt to determine relative or absolute dating on the basis of a supposed evolution of ideas, institutions, or practices. Perhaps we do not sufficiently appreciate how much of Old Testament scholarship in the 19th and 20th centuries has been influenced by simple developmental formulas, or to what extent the modern reconstruction of Israelite literature, culture, and religion has been based upon such patterns. Thus the scholarly commonplace that the Priestly source of the Hexateuch (whatever ancient materials it may embody) deals with and reflects the postexilic situation in Palestine must be challenged on the grounds that verifying data have never been adduced.[12] While the theory has always been attractive, ingeniously argued, and embellished with numerous plausible connections between the P materials and postexilic practice or purpose, it remains only an intriguing possibility. What is required is to demonstrate that postexilic institutions and practices are antecedent to and reflected in P, and not influenced by or adapted from the material in P. It is not enough to show similarities, or even connections; it is necessary to demonstrate priority and the flow of influence, in short that P was produced by the postexilic community.

In applying these criteria to the question of the date of the primary history, we note that the last dated reference is in the closing verses of 2 Kings. The date

11. It is only with the Babylonian exile that an underground literature begins to emerge, in which some measure of concealment, both of author and subject, was necessary. Note, e.g., the use of *athbash* for Babylon and the Chaldeans in the prophecies of Jer. 51 (vv. 1, 41); and the veiled references in Ezek. 34, 38–39 and Zech. 9–14. Here our ignorance of the historical circumstances prevents us from making a reliable analysis of the material. We should be warned against the many ingenious connections suggested by scholars. At best they can only be possibilities, and what is required for the purpose of dating a composition is proof or high probability. In the nature of the case, allusive material can only offer tantalizing hints, and must be subject to the heavier weight of more objective and perspicuous data.

12. Cf. W. F. Albright, *From the Stone Age to Christianity,* 2nd ed. (Garden City: Doubleday, 1957), 345: "Since there is not a single passage in the whole Pentateuch which can be seriously considered as showing post-exilic influence either in form or in content, it is likely that the entire Pentateuch was compiled in substantially its present form before 522 B.C." See also E. A. Speiser, "Leviticus and the Critics," *Yehezkel Kaufmann Jubilee Volume* (Jerusalem: Magnes, 1960), 29-45, esp. 41-45.

given is 561/60 B.C.E., but the statement also mentions the remaining years of Jehoiachin's life.[13] Since at that time he was already fifty-five years old, an elderly man by ancient standards, we may assume that he did not long survive, but died within five or at most ten years. Since the event was of no great or lasting significance, it is likely that it was recorded within a short time. The next known events in the history of Israel, far more important than the pathetic notice of the king-in-exile, were the dramatic rise of Cyrus to world-suzerainty, his conquest of Babylon, and subsequent edict of release and return. It is difficult to imagine that the author or compiler would have closed his book so inconclusively and anticlimatically, had he known of the momentous events which took place in the succeeding decades, especially in view of the prophetic oracles about the end of the exile and return to the land. The argument would hold even more strongly if we suppose that the book originally ended with the report of the capture of Jerusalem and the exile to Babylon. If it is argued that the general predictions of exile and return which occur in Leviticus and Deuteronomy presuppose those events, then the omission of the historical fulfillment at the end of Kings is even more surprising.[14]

When we compare the primary history with the Chronicler's history, we find in the latter precisely what we should expect in an historical account written after the return. There is explicit reference to Cyrus, the edict, and the return as the fulfillment of prophetic expectation.[15] This is the way in which the narrative in Kings would have continued had it been written after those events. In fact, there is no allusion to any of them, explicit or veiled, in the entire corpus. We may go further and suggest that the reference to Jehoiachin in the last paragraph of 2 Kings is itself the postscript to an already completed work. Thus the history proper concludes with the story of the fall of Jerusalem, the exile, and aftermath ending with the death of Gedaliah and flight to Egypt.[16] They may be dated approximately 587-582 B.C.E. and the whole of the primary history, except for the postscript, may be dated shortly thereafter, in the early stages of the exile. The stereotyped references to the exile in the primary history do not reflect actual conditions and experiences, as do the stories, e.g., in the book of Ezekiel. We may conclude that the compiler finished his work shortly after the events described, and was not familiar with the subsequent experiences of the exiles.

---

13. Cf. 2 Kgs. 25:29, 30, where the expression "all the days of his life" occurs twice. Jer. 52:33, 34 retains the double reading, and adds in v. 34, "until the day of his death." Apparently the notice was added after the death of Jehoiachin.

14. The compiler would hardly have missed the opportunity to stress the fulfillment of earlier predictions by adding the necessary historical information at the end of his account.

15. The Chronicler omits the episode concerning Awel-Marduk and Jehoiachin, presumably because of its unimportance, especially by contrast with the momentous events which followed. It is also possible that he used a text of Kings which did not include this addendum.

16. The latter events are described in much greater detail in the book of Jeremiah, since the prophet played a central role in them.

The outlook and orientation of the compiler fit very well the period immediately following the collapse of Judah. Throughout, the work is in the form of a
theodicy, a vindication of the creator God who is at the same time the covenant
deity of Israel. The catastrophe that has befallen his people is not due to his
weakness, but rather to his power: the inevitable consequence of covenant violation
and rebellion against his holy will. While most of the material belongs to earlier
sources, and traces the long course of salvation history, the point of view of the
editor has permeated the whole, which serves as a paradigm for the current generation. His purpose is to explain how it happened that the God who chose the people
of Israel in the fathers, and saved them from bondage in Egypt through Moses,
who gave them the land through Joshua, and sovereignty through judges and kings,
could in these last days destroy their nation, cast them from their land, and surrender
them to the tyranny of a new cppressor, the king of Babylon. The threat of doom,
so strongly articulated in the Deuteronomic sermons, is not lacking elsewhere in
the primary history; prominent is the thread of tragedy, foreseen but unavoidable.[17]
Along with the mood of disaster is confidence in the future: the certainty of a return
and restoration, which is rooted in the mystery of election. The God who has
punished the sinful nation in accordance with the conditions of the Sinai covenant
is nevertheless committed irrevocably to his people, and out of his inexhaustible
grace will resettle the unworthy ones in the Promised Land, even as they were torn
from it for being unworthy. It is clear, however, that the restoration has not yet
taken place: there is hope, even assurance, but not the exultation in the fact which
we find in 2 Isaiah, or the explicit references to the event in Haggai, Zechariah,
and the Chronicler's history. The prevailing mood is somber, as befits a community
under judgment, enduring its days of punishment in exile.

The Latter Prophets present a more complex problem of dating, since we are
dealing with a collection of works in which the process of organization and uni-
fication is incomplete. Nevertheless, there is a certain continuity of theme and
treatment in the separate books; and it is of the collection as a whole that we wish
to make the following observations: (1) That the Latter Prophets as a whole are to
be dated toward the end of the 6th century, or roughly about 500 B.C.E.; and (2) that
the bulk of the materials belong to an earlier collection which is to be dated to the
middle of the 6th century, at about the same time as the final edition of the primary
history. (3) We hold further that the prophetic collection was organized as a supplement to the primary history, and that the chronological and editorial links are
deliberate. It has often been noted that the so-called literary prophets (i.e., those
whose names are attached to books in the prophetic canon) have been largely
ignored in the primary history (only Isaiah and Jonah are mentioned), though there
is great interest in prophecy in the primary history, and much space is devoted to
the earlier prophets like Samuel, Nathan, Elijah, Elisha, etc. We suggest that the

17. Cf. e.g., Lev. 26, esp. vv. 32ff.

existence of a prophetic corpus made unnecessary the kind of treatment accorded to the earlier prophets, for whom no extensive literary materials were available.

The bulk of the prophetic literature reflects the circumstances of the Babylonian exile, whatever may be the date of the original prophet and his oracles.[18] This is not only true of the 7th-6th century prophets like Jeremiah and Ezekiel, Habakkuk, and probably Obadiah, but also of the book, 1 Isaiah, which contains extensive materials from the Babylonian exile (e.g., chs. 13–14), and Micah, in which 8th-century Assyrian oracles have been mingled with 6th-century Babylonian material (chs. 4–5). The same may be true of Amos and Hosea, though the evidence is less certain. If we add Nahum and Zephaniah, which are preexilic, we have a sizable collection of oracles, dating from the 8th to the 6th centuries, and bearing the marks of exilic editing. At the same time, there is nothing in the literature mentioned which requires or implies a postexilic date. Cyrus and the Persian Empire, the actual capture of Babylon and return of the exiles, are all beyond their horizon.

In the case of Ezekiel, we hold that the book is essentially a unity, that it derives in its entirety from the inspiration of the prophet, and is a product of the Babylonian exile.[19] In spite of numerous scholarly efforts to show that the book contains allusions to and reflections of the Persian and Greek periods, the evidence is at best ambiguous and the arguments unconvincing. Thus the passing references to Persian soldiers in association with those of Lud and Put (27:10), or Cush and Put (38:5), are historically unexceptionable for that period, and far from reflecting the era of Persian supremacy, as Torrey among others supposed,[20] actually point to an earlier period.[21] Similarly the vision of the new Jerusalem in chs. 40–48 is an anticipation of the return and rebuilding of the temple, rather than a reflection of it.

The book of Jeremiah is likewise a product of the exilic period. Not everything in the book comes directly from the prophet or his biographer. There are substantial additions which are later than Jeremiah, and the book has undergone extensive editorial revision. But there is nothing here or elsewhere in the book that presupposes or reflects the historical return from exile, or the events connected

18. In this collection we would include Isa. 1–39 (with the possible exception of 34–35), the whole of Jeremiah and Ezekiel, and the minor prophets Amos, Hosea, Micah, Nahum, Zephaniah, Habakkuk, and Obadiah.

19. There has been a significant reaction to the radical criticism of earlier decades, though the problem of the unity and date of the book of Ezekiel has not been entirely resolved. The differences in point of view are reflected in recent commentaries, e.g., by H. G. May in *IB*, and G. Fohrer and K. Galling in the *Handbuch zum Alten Testament*.

20. Cf. C. C. Torrey, *Pseudo-Ezekiel and the Original Prophecy* (New Haven: Yale University Press, 1930), 84.

21. Similarly the reference to the Chaldeans as desert marauders, in Job 1:17, points to the period before the rise of the Neo-Babylonian Empire in the last quarter of the 7th century B.C.E.

with it. In fact the prophecies concerning the impending destruction of Babylon (chs. 50–51) differ so markedly from the actual and comparatively peaceful capture of the city by Cyrus that they must be assigned to the exilic period. A vaticinium ex eventu would have been more accurate in this respect. In 1 Isaiah the oracles on Babylon (e.g., chs. 13–14) must be assigned to the 6th century; but there is nothing of a later date in our opinion. The so-called apocalypse (24-27) is obscure, but that alone is no indication of date. Its affinities are chiefly with Ezekiel, and we believe that it belongs to the same general period.[22] The prevailing mood of the exilic collection is the same as that of the primary history: principal emphasis is upon the threat and judgment of God, spelled out in terms of military invasion, devastation of the land, and exile. It is this theme which unites the prophets of the 8th and 7th-6th centuries; very little editorializing was needed to make the 8th century speak to the 6th, or the northern prophets to the south. But the prophets also spoke with assurance of the ultimate future; hope and confidence in a return to the land, and the restoration of the nation, are equally a part of their message. Taken together, the collection reflects the situation after the destruction of Jerusalem, but before the return.

In its present form, however, the collection has been supplemented by a group of prophecies which belong to a later date, and which refer directly to the return from exile and the rebuilding of the temple. These are to be found in 2 Isaiah, Haggai, and Zechariah. Apart from the authentic oracles of Haggai and Zechariah (1–8), specific attributions are impossible, and much of the material is shrouded in historical obscurity (e.g., Zech. 9–14; Isa. 56–66). All the explicit historical references in this material belong to the latter half of the 6th century; there is no compelling reason to assign any part of it to a different period. If we could penetrate the obscurities of Zech. 9–14, we might be able to suggest a more definite date of composition, but perhaps the wisest procedure at present is to suspend judgment.[23] With respect to Malachi, we agree with most scholars in dating the book between the rebuilding of the temple and the period of Ezra-Nehemiah. The marriage problems under discussion in the different books are not precisely the same, though

22. Prof. G. W. Anderson read a paper at the Congress on Isa. 24–27, and made a convincing case for a 6th-century date of composition, roughly in the period of 2 Isaiah, Haggai, and Zechariah. While we lean toward a slightly earlier date toward the end of the exile, it is to be recognized that the whole book of Isaiah in its present form cannot be dated earlier than the last years of the 6th century. Such passages as Isa. 24–27 and 34–35 may have been composed and inserted into the text in postexilic times.

23. With regard to the date of Zech. 9–14, the reference to the Greeks in 9:13 does not reflect the period of Greek supremacy in the time of Alexander the Great and his successors, any more than does the reference in Joel 4:6. What is described here is a conflict between the people of Zion and those of Yavan, treated as approximately equal contestants. This would fit the 6th or early 5th centuries, but hardly any later period; in the present state of our knowledge it is hazardous to offer any date for this material.

they may be related;[24] otherwise the situation presupposed in Malachi more closely resembles that of Haggai and Zechariah. Joel may be dated with some confidence in the same general period, *ca.* 520 B.C.E.[25] For Jonah the data are too limited to fix a date of composition. A reasonable estimate would place it also in the early postexilic period, but more than this can hardly be claimed.

The last specific date we have in the Latter Prophets is the 4th year of Darius I, 518 B.C.E.[26] A better knowledge of the period between the rebuilding of the temple and the age of Ezra-Nehemiah, along with a more accurate understanding of the obscure historical allusions in the postexilic prophetic literature, would permit a more precise dating of the corpus, which we set provisionally around 500 B.C.E. At the same time, the scope and orientation, the tone and outlook of this supplemental collection of prophecies fit very well with what we know of the early postexilic community. The reason for the expanded collection is clear. In the sequence of events culminating in the return of the exiles, and the rebuilding of their community, former prophecies had been fulfilled; and new prophets had arisen to announce the purpose and promised actions of God to his people. Just as in the earlier period threat had been followed by judgment, so now promise was to be achieved in fulfillment. The principal theme of 2 Isaiah, Haggai, and Zechariah is the realization of prophecy and promise in the immediate historical situation. 2 Isaiah speaks of a recapitulation of salvation-history in terms of a second exodus and permanent settlement in the Holy Land. Haggai and Zechariah concentrate attention on the Second Temple, and the revival of the house of David and the Zadokite priesthood, the traditional institutions of the divinely established community, and the marks of its legitimacy. There is an intimate association of monarchy and prophecy but especially of the house of David with the whole line of prophets from Samuel to Haggai/Zechariah. Regardless of their attitude toward particular kings, and this was often hostile, the prophets never abandoned confidence that the house of David would have its place of dignity and authority in the restored kingdom of God. But the prophetic-Davidic association continued only to the end of the 6th century B.C.E.[27] in datable prophecies. Zerubbabel was the last of the line of David to figure significantly in the history of Judah; after his time we have only a list of his descendants. What happened to Zerubbabel and his successors of the line of

---

24. Malachi is concerned primarily with the problem of divorce, though he makes passing reference to mixed marriages (cf. 2:10-16). Ezra and Nehemiah are concerned with the problem of mixed marriages in the Jewish community, and carry through a rigorous policy of excluding these foreign wives.

25. This is the conclusion of J. M. Myers in a well-reasoned article, "Some Considerations Bearing on the Date of Joel," *ZAW* 74 (1962): 177-95.

26. Zech. 7:1, the 4th day of the 9th month, apparently December 8. Cf. R. A. Parker and W. H. Dubberstein, *Babylonian Chronology, 626 B.C.–A.D. 75* (Providence: Brown University Press, 1956), 30.

27. The messianic or Davidic references in Zech. 9 and 12–13 cannot be dated with any assurance. We see no reason to date them later than the close of the 6th century.

David we do not know, but by the time of Ezra and Nehemiah, power and prestige had passed to other hands. There were prophets after Haggai, Zechariah, and Malachi; some of them are mentioned in Nehemiah, and others were doubtless active in that and even later periods. Since the house of David also survived, a connection between them may have persisted into late times. But of this there is no clear-cut evidence.[28] The sequence of prophetic oracles on the glorification of the Davidic dynasty reached a climax, and we believe a conclusion, in the age of Zerubbabel, Haggai, and Zechariah. Afterwards it was a matter of preserving the ancient traditions, and renewing hope of their fulfillment. But it was many centuries before Davidic messianism made an authentic historical appearance in Palestine.

It may be asked why, if the prophetic collection which first appeared in the course of the exile was brought up to date with the addition of the oracles of 2 Isaiah, Haggai, Zechariah, etc., no similar effort was made in connection with the primary history. In its present form it ends rather inconsequentially; certainly the story of the return of the exiles and rebuilding of the temple would make a more fitting conclusion to the whole work. But this is precisely what has happened in the Chronicler's history, where the story of the return rounds out the narrative of the conquest of Judah and the captivity. At the same time, there was a drastic overhauling of the earlier history, especially in the account of David and Solomon. Whatever may have been the intention of the Chronicler with respect to the primary history, his account did not displace the older compilation, nor were the two amalgamated into a single literary work.[29] It was ultimately accepted as a sup-

---

28. The references in Nehemiah (6:7 and 14) to various unnamed prophets and the prophetess Noadiah are of interest. In the first instance, Nehemiah denounces as false the rumor spread by Sanballat that Nehemiah had employed prophets to proclaim him king in Judah. We may infer that "king-making" was still considered a possible prerogative of the prophets, in the manner of ancient heroes like Samuel, Nathan, Elijah, and Elisha. At the same time a true prophet presumably would restrict such activities to the house of David. In the second instance, Nehemiah complains about certain other prophets who along with the prophetess Noadiah tried to intimidate him. We may speculate that they objected to his exercise of temporal authority. Though legally authorized by the Persian king, Nehemiah may have been regarded as a usurper by the prophets, who would reserve such an office to the leader of the house of David. This would be in line with the tradition of Haggai and Zechariah in connection with Zerubbabel. In any case, Nehemiah dissociates himself entirely from the prophets, and their authority.

29. The Chronicler's history may have been intended as a supplement to the primary history, rather than as a competing version of the same period of history (i.e., the monarchy). The extensive materials on David and Solomon are largely additions, while the stories in Samuel and Kings about these monarchs have been severely cut. Perhaps the objective was not so much to erase a previous picture of these kings, as to balance the existing picture with data not previously incorporated. Does the omission of almost the entire account of the northern kingdom imply that the Chronicler had no use for either the kingdom or its story, or simply that he had nothing to add or alter in the existing account? That the Chronicler meant for his work to be taken seriously, and to be regarded as official and authoritative, is quite clear. But did he mean for it to replace the existing historical account (in Samuel and Kings), or to be regarded as a supplement of great if not equal value?

plementary account, and preserved in the Writings. Most important is the fact that the primary history escaped revision, even the slight addition which would have brought the story to a more satisfying conclusion. It would appear that the primary history was no longer subject to this sort of literary modification because it was already the official record of Israel's experience.

We may summarize our proposed synthesis of the Law and the Prophets as follows:

1. In the course of the Babylonian exile, roughly between 580 and 550 B.C.E., a great compilation of Israelite literature was made under appropriate authority and supervision. This collection included the whole of the primary history as we know it (all the books from Genesis through 2 Kings in the Hebrew Bible) and a large selection of prophetic materials, including the bulk of 1 Isaiah, Jeremiah, Ezekiel, and the major portion of the minor prophets: Amos, Hosea, Micah, Nahum, Zephaniah, Habakkuk, and Obadiah.

2. After the exile, and under the influence of new prophetic voices, who encouraged the return of the exiles and the rebuilding of the temple, a supplement to the prophetic collection was compiled, sometime between 518 and 450 B.C.E., perhaps around 500, including Isa. 40–66, Haggai, Zech. 1–8, and Malachi; possibly also Joel, Zech. 9–14, and Jonah, though these books are difficult to date and place, and we may wisely reserve judgment.

3. Thus we hold that the core of the Old Testament, the Law and the Prophets, emerged as a literary entity during a comparatively brief period in Israel's history, but a decisive one, during which the nation came to an end, and out of the trials of captivity a new community was born. The whole of the literature bears the stamp of this period, with its dramatic experience of death and resurrection.

15

On Method in Biblical Studies:
The Old Testament

Method is an essential element in the process of study and research, whether in relation to the Bible or to any other subject. In addition, it is clear that every scholar not only uses a variety of methods or techniques in the course of his work, but behind the methods is *the method,* the individual pattern of thought which controls his procedure. And to some extent, his method will determine the scope and nature and even the content of his conclusions. At the same time there is danger in considering method as a subject in its own right, as though the problem of method could be solved independently by rigorous mental activity, and the newly fashioned tool be applied to any given area of inquiry with guaranteed results. With method and subject so closely tied together, it is inevitable with subject matter as diverse and complex as the Bible that the principal characteristics of *effective* method will be flexibility and adaptability. With this disclaimer we may proceed to the presentation of elements in a methodology of biblical studies. It need not be pointed out that solid training, careful scholarship, meticulous research, and clear reasoning are requisite in this as in any other field; we are concerned here primarily with orientation and approach.

An Inductive Approach to Biblical Studies

I have been impressed by the example of research in the physical sciences, and believe that there is much to be gained by an inductive approach to biblical materials also. Since Bible scholars are involved in processes of organizing, classifying, and interpreting heterogeneous materials derived from a variety of sources and belonging to many different periods of history and culture, it is clear that objective extrabiblical controls are an important desideratum if we are not to be permanently locked inside the Bible itself, dependent upon private judgment and evaluation. Biblical criticism has suffered too much from the subjectivity of scholars, and the pages of our literature are filled with endless arguments between scholars who simply reiterate their prejudices. The science of archaeology, which has had an increasingly important relationship to biblical studies in recent decades, is an excellent example of successful scientific induction. The early days of archaeological investigation were marked by spectacular discoveries, some with the greatest importance for biblical studies. But the field of Bible study as a whole was in a state of confusion bordering on chaos because there was no reliable way of relating the various materials at a site in sequence. By means of pottery analysis and stratigraphy, the relative chronology of a site and its connections with other sites could be established with remarkable precision. The vast accumulation of data confirming the original results of sequence dating has fixed the archaeological pattern for the whole of the Near East, and Palestine in particular, with astonishing accuracy. It is significant that recent radio-carbon tests for the historical periods in the Near East have contributed little except confirmation of the chronological pattern already established by archaeologists.

Moving a little closer to biblical studies proper, we may mention the parallel sciences of epigraphy and orthography. Thanks to the unremitting labors of men like W. F. Albright and his student Frank M. Cross, the principal workers in the field (along with a handful of others), it is now possible to trace the evolution of alphabetic writing in Palestine from its earliest appearance down to postbiblical times. Nonbiblical inscriptions and documents have been successfully dated to within a generation. And more to the point, we now have an accurate sequence dating of biblical manuscripts from the middle of the 3rd century B.C.E. to about the middle of the 2nd century C.E. For the investigation of the text of the Old Testament, such information, objectively grounded, is invaluable. As for the development of orthography, it is now possible to trace the major features of Hebrew spelling from premonarchic times in Israel down to the end of the biblical period, though some serious gaps remain. Orthography thus provides, also, a tool for the analysis of biblical data; its application to the biblical text has offered clues concerning textual transmission and the dating and interpretating of particular passages.

Thus far we have dealt with procedures rooted in the technical examination of objective data. While particular scholarly conclusions may be challenged for competence, there can be no question of the value of the procedure or of the underlying methodology. A similar approach to the literature of the Old Testament can and has been attempted. On the one hand, it should be possible to trace the history of the Hebrew language from Mosaic times to the end of the biblical period and beyond, and to classify its characteristic features and changes from the earliest period. There are still many gaps in our knowledge, but considerable progress has already been made; and it is at least possible to distinguish classical Hebrew of the 10th and following centuries from that of Jeremiah and the Deuteronomic historian, e.g. — to say nothing of the postexilic Hebrew of Nehemiah and Chronicles. Archaic elements have likewise been identified; careful study of transcriptions of Canaanite and Hebrew elements in other languages has provided clues to developments in linguistic forms. Dialectal variation and the survival of archaic features hinder the effort to classify the literature of the Bible according to these linguistic patterns; it must be recognized that private judgment enters more largely into such matters as literature and language than in the fields previously mentioned.

If we move still further into the realm of concepts, we must be extremely cautious about positing evolutionary or developmental patterns in biblical thought or belief. This area of inquiry has been a fruitful source of error in the past: e.g., in the reconstruction of the history of Hebrew religion and institutions, or in the development of ethical ideals and political principles. While we may properly recognize such an evolutionary pattern in the full range of human history, the biblical period is too short and too complex to allow for so simple a classification of its history of ideas. A more exact tool of investigation will be required to unravel the tangled threads of biblical religion and sociology, and to elucidate its dominant motifs and patterns.

To illustrate the value and effectiveness of the inductive approach to biblical studies, we may consider the text of the Old Testament in the light of the Qumran discoveries. There is now available a wide sampling of manuscripts covering practically every book of the Old Testament, and spanning a period of approximately three hundred years, thus attesting to the state of the text during a particularly important period in its transmission. The effect of studies thus far has been to substantiate certain theories about transmission of the text of the Old Testament in pre-Christian centuries, and to undermine other conjectures, but it is now possible to write a reasonably accurate account of the transmission of the text during those centuries. The story is much like that of the New Testament, though with certain significant differences. There were at least three different text-types of the Pentateuch in circulation, and presumably two of the Former Prophets (and probably of others, like Jeremiah, as well). These were, properly speaking, recensions, pointing back to a common original of an earlier century. We may thus speak of textual transmission and scribal traditions covering the last four centuries of the millennium, and have a fairly clear picture of the state of the text during that period. The evidence shows, too, that the Septuagint was a faithful, literal rendering of an early Hebrew text (at least for the historical books), which differed materially from the proto-Massoretic text, also attested at an early date. The significance of these data for future textual studies can hardly be exaggerated. It is clear that much of the variation between recensions is due to mechanical reasons (i.e., scribal lapses), and that we must revise somewhat the traditional rules governing text criticism. Thus the most common error of all turns out to be haplography, so the shorter text is not necessarily the better. It is now possible to arrive at an eclectic text of some books of the Old Testament, which would be essentially that of the 3rd or 4th century B.C.E., before the emergence of clearly defined recensions, and distinctly superior to the present Massoretic Text. To this end we eagerly await further publication of the biblical manuscripts from Qumran.

Along with the statement concerning the possibilities of an inductive approach, a balancing statement should be made about the dangers of deduction in connection with biblical research. Here we are interested in the other side of the text history of the Old Testament: the period leading up to the official text from which the recensions and early manuscripts are derived. The literature of the Old Testament has been subject to a great deal of analytical study; we are all familiar with the monumental results of dedicated labors over the last centuries. One of the chief products of literary criticism is the justly famous documentary hypothesis, which still stands (perhaps on wobbly legs, but not likely to be replaced by anything better in the immediate future). One may comment similarly on the results of form criticism or *Gattungsforschung;* the analysis and classification of the literary types and elements is likewise a significant achievement of permanent value in the study of the Bible.

The contribution of tradition history is more difficult to evaluate, but we may at least acknowledge the legitimate emphasis placed upon oral tradition in the development of biblical literature, and the effect of this kind of transmission upon the ultimate text of the Old Testament. In all three methods of study we recognize the enormous value of the technical results, the refined methods of analysis and classification, the accumulation of interpretive data, and the numerous insights into the meaning of passages and relationship of segments to the whole. But now we must enter a caveat. Each of these — literary criticism, *Gattungsforschung,* and tradition history — ostensibly formed the scholarly basis for a reconstruction of the people of Israel: its religion and institutions, its beliefs and the pattern of its life. However, the reconstruction does not commend itself in the way that the technical analysis did because of the introduction of unexamined presuppositions and the danger of deductive consequences. Thus it is now clear that the Wellhausenist reconstruction of the religion of Israel and its cultic institutions is unsound; it does not conform to the facts as we now know them. Simple evolutionary principles do not apply. The chief weakness, however, is to be found in the naive assumption that the contents of the documentary sources reflected the age in which the documents were written, rather than their having been derived by way of a long and fixed tradition from the period to which the contents referred. Thus on the basis of a chronology of documents, Wellhausen and his followers arrived at a chronology of the ideas thought to be contained in them. At the time, it was universally convincing, and the world of scholarship has had a long struggle in freeing itself from this particular delusion about Israelite literature and religion.

Similarly, form-critical studies have provided the basis of a reconstruction of early Israelite traditions which has gained wide acceptance both in Europe and America. The point of contact and departure is the *Sitz im Leben* (usually cultic) out of which the story or other literary form emerges and which it reflects, and in which it finds its proper place. We may recognize the importance of the background and setting of the stories and traditions, and even the probability that the *Sitz im Leben* has been correctly identified or reconstructed — though in many cases it is a matter of inspired guesswork and details remain uncertain. There are several causes of dissatisfaction with the results. Two are methodological, and are inherent in the procedures. With respect to the classification of literary types, the labels are occasionally tendentious and imply something about the quality (i.e., credibility) of the material, rather than being limited to its character or nature. Thus terms like "legend," "myth," "fairy tale," "fable," and especially "etiology" tend to contain a value judgment instead of being titles of literary categories. Also, with respect to the *Sitz im Leben,* it is commonly reconstructed on the basis of the material which is said to reflect a certain kind of setting; then the reconstructed setting is used to interpret or reinterpret the contents or related materials. This process can be carried through any number of steps with additional refinements, but the reasoning remains circular. Perhaps the chief difficulty lies in what appears to be the arbitrary isolation of traditions and themes, and their assignment to individual local shrines and particular celebrations; thus are dissolved both the unity and continuity of the early traditions of Israel.

The deductive consequences of the methods of tradition history are not persuasive. For example, the elaborate reconstruction of the kingship cult and the intricate analysis of the growth of the prophetic literature seem remote from the biblical data.

A Respectful Approach to the Bible

The phrase "respectful approach" is not meant in a theological or cultic sense, but rather in a scholarly sense. There are two matters involved: first, a respect for the plain meaning of the text and for the intention of the author or speaker (a common justice rendered to every piece of literature, and equally owed to the Bible); and second, a respect for the biblical tradition, i.e., the pattern of Israelite religion and history which it contains. Let these be regarded as the attitudes which must be basic in the study of the Bible's contents. Admittedly, the whole of the Bible cannot be taken at historical face value, and we must resist efforts to revert to a precritical frame of mind. But there is a good deal of scholarly enterprise which seems to proceed from the assumption that the biblical pattern is automatically wrong and that the first principle of operation is to discard it for something else.

With regard to the meaning of the Bible, a word should be said in behalf of straightforward grammatical-historical exegesis of the text, passage by passage. It is clear that for some who work with the Bible such a procedure no longer holds much appeal. They are interested in more esoteric meanings to be derived from or read into the text, or drawn from themes, patterns, and unities which transcend the limits of exegesis and which are largely of their own creation. I believe that both of these popular pursuits are rooted in the supposed needs or desires of religious bodies (and their representatives) who think that the Bible must say the same thing everywhere and at all times. Thus in certain circles the Old Testament is interpreted esoterically to teach New Testament doctrines; and by a different technique the whole Bible is made to conform with certain ruling concepts or themes, while divergent or contradictory details are explained away or simply ignored.

With regard to esoteric meanings, such wresting of Scripture is already found in the Scripture, and is formalized as an exegetical tool as early as the Qumran commentaries. Thus in the book of Daniel, Jeremiah's 70-year prediction concerning the hegemony of Babylonia, or the length of the exile, has been adapted to the author's purpose. He has altered the 70 years to 70 weeks of years (that is, 490 years) in order to encompass the history of Israel to his own time. Such an alteration is quite understandable; but when it is indicated that the real meaning of Jeremiah's prediction is to be found in Daniel's adaptation, we are faced with a critical exegetical question. Even more clearly, the Habakkuk commentary affirms that while the prophet (Habakkuk) referred to the Chaldeans in his pronouncements, God actually had in mind the Kittites — a fact only revealed to the Righteous Teacher. It does not seem possible that scholars can accept this approach to an understanding of the Scriptures, and as men of faith and commitment to religious truth, we have no need to. Such a view arises from a misunderstanding of the nature of biblical literature and biblical religion. It is rooted in the notion that the Bible is the infallible body of all revealed truth, and that everything which happens later must have been anticipated in it — in short, that God is subject to the biblical record (instead of the other way around), and that history works out according to the predetermined plan already spelled out (if cryptically) in Scripture. The only way such a view could be maintained was by exempting the biblical content from the ordinary rules of interpretation. But such questionable reassurance about the divine character of the Bible is too dearly bought at the price of historical accuracy and scholarly relevance. In any case, it is not the province of the scholar to go beyond the meaning of the text and the presumed intention of the author. The most careful attention to linguistic detail, to grammatical form, and to lexical nuance will be well rewarded by a better understanding of what the passage meant when it was uttered. To accomplish this is to fulfill our obligation.

With respect to a more generalized interpretation of the Old Testament (specifically, the isolation and identification of common themes and patterns, as well as a definition of overall unity), we must recognize the value and importance of such endeavors. The attempt to generalize findings is a feature of every scientific inquiry, and could hardly have been avoided in the case of the Bible. It would, perhaps, be more useful to concentrate upon the detailed examination of individual books, sections, and passages, for it is only on the basis of an exhaustive exegetical study that any serious discussion of themes and patterns is possible. It is only as these emerge inescapably from the material and come under serious study that they will have any intrinsic value and usefulness as organizing principles. The unity of the Bible does not lie primarily in the areas where it is looked for (in the unity of theme and pattern, which belong rather to the area of human thought and reflection), but in the historical continuity of the community of Israel and its conviction concerning a continuing, active relationship with the one living God, Yahweh. Since there is considerable conflict in the Bible as to the nature of that relationship, and even some question (as in Job and Ecclesiastes) as to whether it exists at all, we should be skeptical of attempts to find the same truth everywhere in Scripture, or a general pattern under which all the different segments of the literature can be subsumed. If we read individual passages in the light of certain convictions about the general position of the Bible, or about certain common themes, we may easily ignore or misconstrue particular and divergent details which do not conform, or seem to conform, to the pattern.

With regard to the question of tradition, it is logical to begin with the biblical pattern, not uncritically but not unsympathetically, either. Before suggesting or adopting another hypothesis we must test the biblical hypothesis concerning the origins and development of the people of Israel, and then correct and adapt (and sometimes ultimately discard), as required by the total evidence. Without making extravagant claims — which may tempt us in moments of unguarded enthusiasm — it seems safe to say that the evidence generally confirms the biblical traditions, even those concerning the earliest periods of the patriarchs and Moses. While the details will, for the most part, never be recoverable in a strictly historical sense, and while the present form of the tradition is the construction of a later age, it nevertheless remains a good working hypothesis for the period of Israelite origins. The debate over the validity of the early traditions (from Abraham to the conquest) has been going on for some time without notable results, or even a successful joining of issues. The reason is that presuppositions hold the field in the absence of concrete evidence pro or con. For those who hold to the essential historicity of the traditions, the abundant extrabiblical evidence fits with and fills in the common background. In other words, there is an acceptable correspondence between the biblical materials and Near Eastern archaeological data, and this constitutes generic confirmation. For those who do not accept this thesis, it is equally clear that there is no decisive extrabiblical evidence to support the historicity of any particular person or event in the traditions.

At present I see no way out of the impasse; perhaps new evidence will be forthcoming which will tip the scales, but this may be too much to ask. The nature of the problem may be seen in the debate over the patriarchal period, i.e., where the patriarchs fit into the chronology of the ancient Near East. The range of scholarly opinion about these dates, from the 21st to the 14th century B.C.E., is discouraging;

and even the enormous life spans assigned to the fathers are inadequate to cover the divergence. The biblical tradition points (correctly, it would seem) to the Middle Bronze Age (first half of the 2nd millennium) for the patriarchs; but it cannot be relied on in detail because its specific chronology is notably at fault in the early period (e.g., 480 years from the exodus to the building of the temple, which is approximately 50 percent too long).

Another disturbing problem, in which divergent and opposing views do not even intersect but pass each other without contact, concerns the dating of the poetry found in the early books of the Old Testament. The importance of the question is considerable, because if a solution could be found, or even a method of testing different hypotheses, then a basis for interpreting and understanding the thought of Israel at a given stage in its history would be provided. Most scholars agree that the Song of Deborah (Judg. 5) is early — nearly contemporary with the event it describes. Thus it becomes an important source for the thought of premonarchic Israel. On the other hand, most scholars seem to be equally agreed that the Song of Moses/Miriam in Exod. 15 is late (except for the two-line refrain). On the basis of the published literature, it is very difficult to evaluate the reasons for these divergent opinions. There is a great deal of discussion of details such as the so-called Aramaisms which, in the case of Exod. 15, are regarded as signs of late postexilic authorship; in the case of the Song of Deborah, they are regarded as reflections of the early affinities between the northern dialect and Proto-Aramaic. Other features are regarded as archaic in Deborah and archaizing in Miriam. The point is that the arguments could be reversed, and with equal justice Deborah could be dated late and Miriam early. I suspect that at bottom it is really a matter of "feeling." Deborah somehow sounds primitive to scholars, while Miriam seems too sophisticated for early Israel. This is all rather sad, but it must be admitted that as yet there are no decisive criteria for settling the question of date for these poems, or others like them: Gen. 49; Num. 23–24; Deut. 32–33; 1 Sam. 2; and 2 Sam. 22–23. Nevertheless, a considerable accumulation of pertinent data dealing with literary form, grammatical and lexical features, orthographic details, and the like has been made through the efforts of Albright and his students. The results point uniformly in the direction of the biblical tradition. A discriminating respect for the tradition may thus be in order: while the specific attributions are questionable, the assignment of the poems to the early stages of Israel's history appears to be authentic.

A Synthetic Approach to the Bible

With one more comment we may conclude. Two scholarly processes in connection with the Bible go together. First, there is the accumulation of a body of data, and the refinement of techniques of investigation and interpretation: over the years an

159

impressive collection of useful information has been made, and there is every reason to expect that it will increase considerably in the future. In the long run this is the best hope and guarantee of eventual mastery of the material, and the attainment of true knowledge and understanding of the Bible. Second, along with the accumulation of useful data is the formulation of working hypotheses which serve to collate, organize, systematize the knowledge, to bridge the gaps, to develop a structure of thought, and to provide an overall view, essential to a proper perspective in biblical studies. Especially in a field where data are scarce, lacunae numerous, and problems both serious and unanswered, synthetic reconstructions are essential to progress. It is only important to remember that all hypotheses are working proposals until confirmed in detail, and that many must be discarded while others will require drastic overhauling in the face of new evidence. There is a grave temptation to hold on to a hypothesis that has served well in the past, and the more serious temptation to bend data to fit, or to dismiss what cannot be accommodated into the system. The commitment must always be to observable or discoverable data, and not to an hypothesis, which is always expendable. The interaction between the accumulation, analysis, and organization of data, and the development, refinement, revision, and alteration of hypotheses should accelerate the progress of biblical study. We may look forward to the day, although it must be still some distance off, when facts and theories will coincide, when the last working hypothesis will be confirmed by the final pieces of new evidence, when we shall really know what the Bible means and understand — as the most attentive contemporary hearer or reader understood — what the speaker or writer intended. When that day comes, Jeremiah tells us, the teachers will be permanently retired, and doubtless a good thing, too!

16

Modern Scripture Research and Ecumenism

Our subject is the remarkable revival of biblical studies across the ecumenical spectrum in recent years, not only in the Protestant and Catholic churches, but also in Jewish circles where interest in the subject is not so explicitly religious but is part of the general search for and recovery of national traditions. Their biblical scholarship is not less enthusiastic or effective for that reason.

The change in the general situation from as little as twenty years ago is astonishing. In the Protestant churches, one boom in biblical studies has been noteworthy; for ever since the discovery and publication of the Dead Sea Scrolls, biblical teachers have become the "glamor boys" of the profession. A symptom of it in our theological seminaries is the fact that the debate over the language requirements in the curriculum has been settled in favor of compulsory study of Hebrew and Greek. It is taken for granted that a properly trained minister will be skilled in the original languages of Scripture. In the Catholic Church there has been a long-term growth of scholarly interest in and study of the Bible — which was synthesized and brought to focus and felicitous expression in the famous encyclical, *De afflante Spiritu,* issued by Pius XII in 1943. Dealing with the interpretation and use of Scripture, it has in turn encouraged continuing scholarly investigation as a major responsibility of the Church through its teachers.

Perhaps my own experience in this respect will be of some help. I studied Old Testament, as part of a rigorous course in ancient Near Eastern literature and languages, at Johns Hopkins University, under Professor W. F. Albright, who was and is a Methodist layman. During my stay there, from 1945-48, there were two or three Catholic students in the group, Jesuits as it happens. In the course of the next fifteen years an evergrowing stream of Catholics, principally Jesuits but including representatives of other congregations and orders, came to Johns Hopkins and studied side by side with Protestants of many different kinds as well as Jewish students, both American and Israeli.

The important thing was that we learned the same methods and so far as the scientific study of the Bible was concerned had the same presuppositions and the same objectives. Now this created a common spirit, or atmosphere, or setting for the study of Scripture, which so far as I am aware had never existed in this country before. There has been something like this in Europe for a much longer period of time, especially in those countries which are peacefully divided between Catholics and Protestants. In many of the universities there are Protestant and Catholic theological faculties on good terms with each other, and a creative interchange of ideas and opinions is possible. But in this country, with respect to biblical studies, it is a brand-new phenomenon.

The question immediately arises as to what has stimulated the revival of biblical studies in both the Catholic and Protestant churches and at the same time has made possible bipartisanship and cooperation in this area. A primary factor in the recent developments has been a gentle disengagement of the Bible from explicitly dogmatic and ecclesiastical considerations. It is essential to the scholarly approach that the integrity of the Bible be respected, that it be allowed to speak in its own accents and tones to its audience and period first before it is adapted and adjusted to the needs of others. And it is the business of scholarship to discover as closely and accurately as possible what its original meaning and reference were. This is the basic scholarly objective, and to the extent that it has been faithfully pursued, a remarkable number of common findings has been achieved. The area of agreement is astonishing, at least to some men on both sides.

For example, a very good friend of mine, an ardent Protestant, recently reviewed a book by a prominent Catholic biblical scholar, a general introduction to or survey of Old Testament thought. The opening sentence of the book review was something like this: "Here is a book which could be recommended to any Protestant seminary for orienting students in the thought patterns of the Old Testament." When he wrote it, he told me that he was surprised to discover that such a point of view was possible in Catholic circles. It may reflect rather his ignorance of certain Catholic circles. At the same time I think that it is instructive that the results of independent study by Catholics and Protestants, on the basis of common scholarly presuppositions and methods, should be so much alike. It is therefore quite possible to achieve a common position on what the Bible says and means.

For this reason, the project of a common Bible to be produced by scholars of different faiths and to be used in the public schools, which has received support in Catholic circles, is an entirely feasible undertaking in the light of the present situation in biblical studies, however desirable it may be for other reasons. I am sure that very little consideration would have been given this proposal twenty years ago. Let us recall that during the past twenty years Protestants have been deeply involved in the production of the Revised Standard Version of the Bible, and

162

Catholics in this country have been equally engaged in the new Confraternity translation of the Scripture. At the same time, Jewish scholars are engaged in the preparation of a new translation of the Hebrew Bible, and a portion of this has already reached publication. In view of the enormous investment of scholarly time, effort, and money in the production of sectarian versions of the Bible, it is remarkable to find the movement toward a common Bible gaining momentum.

What has made such developments initially possible is the disengagement of the Bible from direct involvement in dogmatic and ecclesiastical concerns. In the Reformation churches, the official view has been that dogmatic and confessional statements simply embodied scriptural teaching and derived their authority from the Bible. In point of fact, the Scriptures have been subject to the confessional standards and interpreted in accordance with them. The Bible, in other words, was part of the armament with which the different Protestant churches confronted their immediate or more distant enemies. Similarly the Catholic Church has always maintained that its doctrine was consonant with Scripture, especially since interpretive authority rests with the Church. On both sides, the conformity of Scripture with Doctrine or Doctrine with Scripture was posited or imposed; and in extreme cases absolute identity was assumed. The necessity of incorporating the Bible into the dogmatic structure as the indispensable and unchallengeable teaching of the Church was acknowledged in both camps.

Although traditional views persist and retain the authority of age, there has been increasing recognition among students of Scripture and Dogma that there are significant differences in language and form between the biblical materials and the formulations of the Church and its Fathers and Teachers — and that it is no service to the Church or the Christian religion to force either into the mold of the other, but that each makes its most valuable contribution by being treated in accordance with its own background and character. The common sense view in no way denies the continuity or consistency of the teaching of Scripture with that of the Church, but recognizes the historical differences which inevitably develop in the long history of a living organism, the people of God. It was the recognition of the differences between Scripture and Dogma and the importance of studying Scripture for its own sake that opened the way to the free exercise of scientific scholarship. And the common pursuit and the common results, I think, indicate the measure of the objectivity which can be achieved. Absolute objectivity is doubtless impossible, but progress in scholarship depends upon the general acceptance of scientific methods and conclusions unaffected by personal bias.

Interfaith investigation, discussion, and criticism tend to eliminate private or sectarian axe-grinding. Agreement concerning essential questions of historical evidence, literary criticism, hermeneutics, and exegesis can and will be reached increasingly, provided the present atmosphere is maintained. Cooperative effort between Catholics and Protestants has only begun in this field, but it promises to be one of the most fruitful fields for common enterprise because the Bible, whatever the technical differences concerning it in Catholic and Protestant thought, is the sacred Scripture of both communions. Even the obvious disagreement over the extent of the canon of the Old and New Testaments is no hazard with respect to scholarship because Protestant interest in the Apocrypha of the Old Testament has increased tremendously as a result of the Scroll discoveries in the Dead Sea region and the renewed investigation into the intertestamental period. Catholic and Protestant scholars have happily joined hands and minds in the study of the Scrolls which have provided a vast amount of information about the Old Testament, contemporary Judaism, and many of the dominant motifs and the specialized theological vocabulary of the New Testament.

For Protestants, Catholics, and Jews there is an excellent prospect of cooperative efforts in the biblical field. It is difficult to predict what the future will bring, and we know how often in the past high hopes for joint enterprises have been dashed. Nevertheless, possibilities are brighter now than they have been in many years, and it will do us no harm to think positively, even optimistically at this time.

One very hopeful sign is a publishing venture (with which I have been connected for a number of years) involving scholars of the three major faiths in the production of a series of volumes on the Bible: an annotated rendering of the books of the Old and New Testaments, with lengthy introductions designed to acquaint the general reader with the latest and best guides to the understanding of the Scriptures. As a result of my experiences I would like to bear testimony to the good will and friendly response that I have always received in Catholic circles and correspondingly the growing sense of brotherhood in the pursuit of a better understanding of the Scriptures. This project was conceived from the first as a tribute to Professor Albright, who has been unquestionably the leading figure in biblical studies in our generation. One of the unique features of his career here has been the extraordinary influence he has exerted not only in Protestant circles, but among Catholic and Jewish scholars as well. His students have been numbered in the scores in the three major religious groups in our country. By rigorous concentration on scientific methodology in the study of languages, history, and archaeology, he effectively trained men of the most divergent beliefs and attitudes, so that those who studied under him came away strengthened in their convictions but at the same time much better scholars.

With Dr. Albright as editor-in-chief it had been our intention to enlist as many of his former students as possible in the production of the *Anchor Bible* series. While it was not originally so intended, the cosmopolitan diversity among Albright students made it inevitable that the project would become an interfaith enterprise. There was an immediate response on the part of numerous Protestant contributors, and several Jewish scholars were added without delay. It may be of interest to note that the book on the epistle to the Hebrews is being written by two Israeli scholars. These men are eminently qualified for the task, though it is unusual for Jewish scholars to write commentaries on New Testament books.

[This is another area of biblical research which holds rich promise for future cooperative scholarly labors. In Jewish circles both here and abroad there is keen and widespread interest in the New Testament as a movement of Jewish literature, quite apart from the religious questions involved. Especially in Israel, the concern for the recovery of the past has stimulated research into the whole history of Palestine from early times through all the periods of human occupation and culture — including the 1st century in all its aspects. Here also the Dead Sea Scrolls have played a significant role in stimulating interest and bringing scholars of different backgrounds and persuasions together in a common endeavor. The Scrolls too have illuminated the Jewish background of the New Testament in all its aspects. It has become increasingly clear that the investigation into Jewish backgrounds is all the more important, and that Jewish scholars have a major contribution to make to the Christian understanding of the New Testament. On the other hand, Christian scholars have made increasingly important contributions to the Jewish understanding of the Hebrew Bible.]

In the initial stages it was impossible to secure any Catholic scholars for work in the *Anchor Bible* series; and this was rather disheartening, especially because there was a sizable number of first-class men in both the Old and New Testament fields. The men seemed agreeable to the idea, but we were never able to bring the negotiations beyond the stage of general discussion or future possibility. There was some obstruction in the machinery, but where and why were never made explicit. It was understood that the matter should not be pressed because then the decision was likely to be negative. While we were disappointed, it seemed best to let matters stand for the time being.

The following summer I was in Jerusalem and happened to run into a fellow-graduate of the Oriental Seminary at Johns Hopkins, Father Mitchell Dahood. He teaches Scripture at the Pontifical Biblical Institute in Rome, and was then studying in the Holy Land. He is one of the leading authorities on the Wisdom Literature, and a specialist in Psalm studies, who has cleared up innumerable difficulties in the text of the canonical Psalms. One day we happened to be discussing Dr. Albright and the *Anchor Bible* series, and I asked him whether he would consider doing the books of Psalms for the series. He indicated that he might be willing to try his hand at it; since he had devoted a great deal of attention to the Psalms over the years, this would give him a chance to bring the material together in a single publication. Then I asked him about proper ecclesiastical authorization. He said there might be some difficulty, but that the best thing was for me to come to Rome and discuss the matter with the rector of the Pontifical Biblical Institute. If he approved, then there would be no further question. In the fall I was in Rome, and called at the Pontifical Institute. Father Dahood introduced me to the rector, who, in addition to being an outstanding scholar and editor of *Biblica* (which is the best bibliographical journal on the Bible in the world), is also a gracious gentleman. He inquired about the purpose of my visit, and I began to tell him about the series and our hopes for it. After a few minutes, he asked me, "Do you wish Father Dahood to participate in the project?" and I said, "Yes, we'd like nothing better," and proceeded to present all my arguments. But he interrupted me with a smile: "It will be an honor and a pleasure for us to do this," and that settled the matter. Since that time several other Catholic scholars have joined the enterprise. Work on the project has proceeded steadily, and we expect to publish the first set of volumes next year.

The present instance is only one illustration of the possibilities for cooperative efforts in the study of the Bible. Further projects may include dictionaries and other reference works, as well as the common Bible already mentioned. For the foreseeable future such cooperative projects can only be of benefit to all the participants. A more accurate knowledge of the facts and a better understanding of the contents of the Bible will help us all, and will help to bring us together as we study and reflect upon our common heritage and origins.

But what lies beyond? The progress in research and cooperation has been due in large measure to the freedom accorded biblical scholars. So far the effects of that research have not impinged seriously on doctrinal matters in the Catholic Church, though here and there theologians and ecclesiastics have voiced alarm as to the effect of unrestrained scholarship on the beliefs of the people. A similar situation obtains in the Protestant churches, though for different reasons. Given the predominant role of the Bible in the doctrine of the churches, the effect of scholarly reinterpretation of the Bible was explosive. The result of the battle, at the present time, has been to isolate biblical from theological studies so that the doctrinal debate remains aloof in large degree from the investigation of the Bible. The theological use of the Bible tends to diverge more and more from the currents of biblical scholarship, while the implications of biblical exegesis for theology and the inferences drawn by biblical investigators lead away from the conclusions of the dogmaticians. So long as the compartments remain sealed off from each other for one reason or another — and so long as the administrators of the Church in its activities do not feel that the stability of the community or the cherished beliefs of the faithful are threatened — then biblical scholars may continue to theorize and verify, analyze and synthesize at their pleasure. But let them suggest that the Bible may have a relevance for the life and thought of the Church which may be at variance with traditional modes, or that it stands in contrast to accepted norms of belief and practice, then there may be a reaction of the strongest kind. The dogmaticians may insist that the interpretation of Scriprure conform to patterns of the past regardless of new insights, and that doctrine be imposed as the norm of exegesis and hermeneutics. And the hierarchs may discipline the more daring investigation of the biblical message. Such a setback, like the many in the past, will be temporary; and sooner or later the spirit of free inquiry and the irrepressible search for new knowledge and verifiable truth will assert itself and further steps forward will be achieved. For it is in the pursuit and attainment of truth that true unity is to be won.

166

On the other hand, biblical exposition may win a respectful hearing among the dogmaticians and ecclesiastics. Its message may find a way into the areas of faith and practice. Just as the liturgy has been studied and revised in the light of ancient tradition, so doctrine itself can be scrutinized in the light of biblical truth. Adaptation and adjustment to the changing conditions of life have always marked the Church. Reformulation, even revision and reformation may be the ultimate consequence of renewed study of the Scriptures. Herein lies the great promise as well as the great risk of cooperative research into the meaning and message of the Scriptures. To be effective, research must be free — but in freedom there is danger to established patterns and institutions. For Catholics and Protestants alike, the future is rich with hope and fraught with danger. But we may have confidence in the God of the Church who is also Author of the Scriptures, and who has willed to make his truth known to all.

17

Divine Commitment and Human Obligation: The Covenant Theme

Of the central importance of the covenant theme in the Old Testament there can no longer be any doubt. When Walther Eichrodt published his *Theology of the Old Testament,*[1] which was constructed entirely around the covenant theme, there was widespread skepticism among scholars as to the validity of this approach. But a significant body of archaeological data illuminating the covenant-making procedures of the ancient world — and brilliantly interpreted in special studies by George E. Mendenhall[2] and Klaus Baltzer[3] — has demonstrated that Eichrodt's tour de force was not a falsification or even an exaggeration of the biblical situation. The new material has largely confirmed his position in principle while offering considerable refinement in detail.

It can therefore be affirmed that the covenant principle is intrinsic to the biblical material and that it defines the relationship of God to his people. Further, the term "covenant" itself was consciously applied by the Israelites to their relationship with Yahweh, from the earliest times.

The covenant theme, of course, is not a universal key to the Scriptures, for no single theme could be sufficiently comprehensive to encompass the great variety of the biblical materials. Because of the intractability of this mass of data, however, the

---

1. *Theologie des Alten Testaments* (Leipzig: J. C. Hinrichs, 1933-39), in three volumes. An English translation of vol. 1 [5th ed. of German] has appeared: *Theology of the Old Testament.* OTL (Philadelphia: Westminster, 1961) [vol. 2, 1967].

2. *Law and Covenant in Israel and the Ancient Near East* (Pittsburgh: Biblical Colloquium, 1955).

3. *Das Bundesformular* (Neukirchen: Neukirchener Verlag, 1960); Eng. trans., *The Covenant Formulary* (Philadelphia: Fortress, 1971). [See also *CMHE,* 13-43.]

search for an organizing principle or useful guide becomes necessary — and necessarily frustrating. A thematic approach commends itself for a number of reasons and is preferable to a more formal word-study. The latter tends to be limited by whatever term is chosen and by its actual occurrences in the Bible. The result may well be the inclusion of numerous items, for the sake of completeness, which are not germane to the central interest or which do not advance the discussion. On the other hand, much pertinent material may be slighted because different terms are used, even in cases where the framework of thought may be the same or closely related. A thematic treatment of biblical material is often more rewarding than a word-study because it can be free of mechanical computations and can also delineate a structural pattern more precisely. At the same time it requires more expert management and is exposed to greater danger of arbitrary selection and subjective arrangement.

In the Bible there appear to be two kinds of covenants describing the relationships between God and man. (The human subject of these covenants varies somewhat — from Noah, representing all mankind, to Phinehas, representing the Aaronic priesthood — but the principal group involved is Israel.) The general framework is the same throughout, in that the two parties to the agreement are not on equal footing: one is vastly superior to the other. This constant feature of the relationship of God to man gives a special character to the covenants of the Bible, though the details of the arrangement differ from case to case. In all, however, the initiative rests with the divine Lord. In one series, which corresponds generally to the pattern of the Hittite suzerainty or vassal treaties, the terms or stipulations are imposed upon the human party in what may be called a covenant of human obligation. In the other series the roles are partly reversed: God takes upon himself certain obligations. Since these agreements also proceed from the divine initiative, we cannot speak of the human imposition of terms upon God. Rather, we may call this type a covenant of divine commitment. So far as I am aware, the biblical series of covenants between God and man is unique. There are no convincing parallels in the pagan world, whether in the more typical case of God as suzerain binding Israel to serve him or in the more unusual position of God binding himself by oath to the service of his own servants.

The covenant of human obligation has its classical locus in the events at Mt. Sinai/Horeb, where Moses mediated the covenant between God and Israel (Exod. 19–24). Covenant renewals belonging to this series are scattered through the Pentateuch and historical books: e.g., in the plains of Moab (Deut. 29–31), at Shechem (Josh. 24), and in the days of Hezekiah, Josiah, and Ezra-Nehemiah.

The covenant of divine commitment finds its principal illustration in the story of God's promise to Abraham in Gen. 15. Essentially the same commitment is made to Isaac and Jacob, and there are frequent allusions to it in the later literature, as in the oath which God swore to the fathers. Others in this series include divine commitments to Noah and his descendants (mankind as a whole), to the high priest Phinehas and his line, and to the royal house of David.

169

Part of the objective of this study is to explore the connection between these covenant types and to examine the prophetic treatment of the covenant theme. It is well known that the term is used sparingly by the earlier prophets, but in view of the evidence there is no reason to suppose that the prophets were unaware of the covenant concept or did not subscribe to the general view expressed above, namely, that the relationship between God and Israel was definable as a compact. But this discussion focuses chiefly on the prophets of the 7th and 6th centuries B.C.E., who made use of the term covenant and developed specific ideas concerning the nature of the bond between God and his people. It will be argued that Jeremiah, Ezekiel, and Second Isaiah recognized the essential validity of both covenant types or traditions and that they attempted to resolve the dilemma inherent in their opposing tendencies (threat versus promise) through an eschatological fulfillment of their ultimate intention to produce a society well pleasing to God and embodying his purposes among men. Thus the prophets acknowledged that the destruction of the nation was the inescapable consequence of its defiance of the divine suzerain and of its deliberate and persistent violation of the terms of the covenant with God. Yet they were convinced that the divine promise to the fathers and their descendants had not been annulled; it remained in force and would be actualized in the return of the exiles and a restoration of the covenant community. Both covenant types would be fulfilled and transcended in the age of the new covenant. The new society would possess in perpetuity the land promised of old; it would no longer be subject to the threats and penalties of the Sinai covenant, since every man would be filled with the Spirit of God, and all would obey his will. The covenant relation would never be broken because it could never be broken.

I

The covenant of divine commitment is chiefly a concern of the Priestly document in the Pentateuch: e.g., the covenants with Noah (Gen. 9), with Phinehas (Num. 25), with Abraham (Gen. 17; and cf. Exod. 2:24; 6:4-5; 9:8). But it is not limited to P. (Note, among others, the divine promise to David in Ps. 89:4, 29, 34, 39; Jer. 33:21; and 2 Sam. = 1 Chr. 17.) The key passage dealing with the promise to the fathers belongs to the J source, or JE, while the tradition that Yahweh had sworn an oath (a central element in covenant-making) to the fathers is scattered through all the strands — JEDP — of the Pentateuch (Gen. 22:16ff. [JE]; Deut. 1:34ff. [D]; Num. 32:10ff. [P]; cf. Gen. 24:7 [J]; Exod. 13:5, 11 [J]; Deut. 7:8; 9:5, and others). In short, the tradition behind this covenant type, while systematized by the Priestly editor, is widespread in the sources and belongs to the primitive nucleus of biblical narrative.

Gen. 15 is usually assigned to J, but there is evidence of another hand, probably E. The chapter appears, furthermore, to be a composite of two stories, one dealing with the question of patriarchal progeny (vv. 1-6), the other with possession of the Promised Land (vv. 7-21). The approach to and treatment of the covenant theme are the same in each case, however, and it may be assumed that the linkage between related themes is an old one.

In the first case, God reassures Abraham, who is deeply concerned about the promised heir now so long delayed. God can only repeat his commitment, but this time he dissolves the patriarch's doubts by a vivid figure of speech offering visual confirmation of the word: "Count the stars in the sky, if you can count them; so many shall your progeny be!" (v. 5). Abraham need only lift his eyes to the sky to see the myriad symbols which guarantee his hope. Or, following another common image used elsewhere, he could look down at the sands on the seashore to see in them the tokens of the numberless descendants who should people the land in which he sojourned. Encouraged by such signs of divine favor, Abraham believed and, for that confidence, was reckoned among the righteous. Here, as elsewhere, a covenant of divine commitment is preceded by an act of faith or devotion. The divine promise to Noah, Phinehas, and David follows upon an act of obedience and faithfulness, beyond normal expectation, on the part of each of these men: Noah builds the ark, Phinehas slays the sinners who wantonly desecrated the sanctuary, while David, in addition to all his other services, had expressed the earnest desire to build a house in honor of God. Here it is Abraham's confidence in the word of God which forms the background for the divine affirmations which follow; at least that is the way in which the editor has connected the two stories. From the matter of progeny, God proceeds to the question of the land. In language which clearly echoes the prologue to the Ten Commandments, God solemnly affirms that as he has brought Abraham out of the land of the Chaldeans to this country (Canaan), he reasserts his intention to give the land to Abraham's descendants. Abraham enters a demurrer: perhaps; but how can Abraham know this? What assurance can he have now? This promised wonder cannot come to pass until the previous promises concerning his progeny have been fulfilled and his descendants have become sufficiently numerous to occupy the land — surely a matter of centuries, at the least. Abraham will have been long in his grave before the land belongs to his descendants.

In this case, God provides the needed assurance in a somewhat different fashion. It is more than a figure of speech or visible token; it is a solemn, symbolic action binding present to future, assuring that the affirmation made now in words will become objective reality at the appointed time. Nothing less than divine commitment, confirmed by oath, will satisfy the requirement, and that is what takes place. The meaning of some of the details of the ceremony described in vv. 9-17 is still unclear — the birds in vv. 10-11, for instance. Also, the exact significance of the smoking firepot and flaming torch in v. 17 eludes us. Are two objects

171

intended? Or is this a case of poetic imagery, with a double description of a single object? Note that the verb following "which passed . . ." is singular. But the general sense of the passage is sufficiently plain; clarification has been supplied from the similar passage in Jer. 34 and from a mass of nonbiblical data relating to covenant ceremonies. There is no literary connection between Gen. 15 and Jer. 34. The differences in detail throughout guarantee that. The fact that essentially the same covenant ceremony is involved in both stories is striking attestation of the tenacity of legal and religious custom in the ancient Near East and Israel, if we assume (as I think we must) that the story in Gen. 15 preserves at its core an authentic reminiscence of patriarchal times and experience.

The story in Jer. 34 (vv. 8-22) describes a covenant made between the king, Zedekiah, and the citizens of Jerusalem to release their slaves (vv. 8-10). In v. 13 reference is made to the covenant at Sinai under the terms of which the Israelites were required to release their Hebrew slaves at the end of a stipulated interval. (It was this regulation which formed the basis for the current action.) The agreement here is described as having been ratified in the temple through a ceremony in which the participants were required to pass between the severed halves of a bull (*'gl).* This curious procedure represents the climactic stage in the covenant ritual, the oath. As each man stood between the parts of the animal he uttered the solemn words, "May God do so to me [i.e., what had been done to the animal] and more also, if I do not faithfully keep the terms of the covenant." In v. 18, which is slightly obscure, the slave owners are condemned for violating their oath and repossessing the slaves whom they had released. Now, the prophet assures them, God as the judge and executor of the curses of the covenant will make them like the severed bull.

The passage in Gen. 15 differs markedly in details: there are three animals instead of one (a heifer, a she-goat, and a ram), and none is the same as in Jer. 34. The use of three animals doubtless emphasizes the importance of the occasion: a threefold oath carries more weight than a single vow. As in the story in Jeremiah, the animals are cut in half and the parts placed facing each other. Thus the stage is set for the oath which is the central feature in the covenant ceremony (note the word "covenant" in v. 18). It is clear that the purpose of the ceremony is to confirm by oath a promise made by Yahweh to Abraham. In fact Abraham, after preparing the animals for the ritual, falls into a trance, and takes no further part in the proceedings. The crucial passage is v. 17, in which the oath-taking is described: "Suddenly a smoking firepot and a flaming torch passed between the pieces [of the animals]." These elements may be representations of a single object which symbolizes the presence of the Deity. It remains an open question as to why this eerie symbolism is used — cf. also the birds of prey in v. 11, the trance, and the awesome darkness which settled on the scene, v. 12 — instead of a more straightforward presentation of the matter. Various possibilities suggest themselves, but it seems likely that this reflects an archaic tradition concerning the patriarch, in which many of the original features of the theophany have been preserved.[4] There can be no question, however, of the central meaning of the episode: the confirmation of the divine promise of the land of the fathers by oath.[5] Later tradition in every strand of the Pentateuch insisted that God had in fact made such a promise to the fathers and had guaranteed it by his personal oath.

It needs only to be added that the covenant is formally of the suzerainty type, since the stipulations are imposed upon only one of the parties, who in turn is bound by oath. Strikingly, it is the suzerain who is obligated, not the vassal. The covenant is initiated by the suzerain, and is unconditional in the sense that no demands are imposed upon Abraham. In other words, the maintenance of the covenant does not depend upon Abraham's performance. He and his descendants are simply the beneficiaries of the divine commitment. Such a covenant remains in force until its terms are fulfilled by divine action, since its validity rests upon God's faithfulness, which is axiomatic. In the view of the prophets this commitment is a permanent guarantee of God's solidarity with his people.

In the Priestly editor's treatment of the same theme there are essential similarities as well as inevitable differences in detail. The central theme is the same: the divine promise of progeny and possession of the land, guaranteed in an eternal covenant, an enduring bond between God and Israel (Gen. 17:1-8). No explicit reference is made to the confirmatory oath, which P may have regarded as excessively anthropomorphic and, in any case, as unnecessary. Attention, rather, is focused on the sign of the covenant, circumcision, which is presented in form of a demand or stipulation. P interprets circumcision as a condition of membership in the Israelite community; failure to perform the rite means exclusion from the covenant community. But it is simply an identifying mark which does not affect the divine commitment.

Divine commitments in a covenant context are also made to Noah (Gen. 9) and to Phinehas (Num. 25). In these instances, both deriving from the Priestly tradition, the promise follows upon an act of loyalty or obedience which is meritorious in the eyes of God, but the commitment is not conditioned by the requirement of other acts of this kind. As with Abraham, the divine commitment is unilateral and unconditional, without obligations on the human party. No clear legal pattern emerges, and there is no reference to an oath: a broader and somewhat freer use of the term "covenant" is involved in these cases. The promise to Phinehas concerns the permanence of the priesthood in his line. (Cf. related commitments to the house of Aaron and Zadok.)

---

4. The resemblance between these objects and the apparently similar pillars of cloud and fire which accompanied the Israelites in the exodus and wilderness wanderings is superficial and coincidental. Both the terms for the objects and their functions are notably different. Nor is there any connection with the theophany on Mt. Sinai; cf. G. von Rad, *Genesis.* OTL (Philadelphia: Westminster, 1961), 183.

5. See J. Skinner, *Genesis,* 2nd ed. ICC (New York: Scribner's, 1923), 283-84.

The promise to Noah and his descendants is the only case of a covenant commitment to mankind as a whole. While that commitment stems in part from Noah's obedience in building the ark, other factors are present. Coupled with God's disillusionment about mankind whose wickedness occasioned the flood (Gen. 6:5-8), there is the recognition that a new arrangement is necessary if mankind is to survive. This cannot be established on the basis of human performance, which has proved consistently inadequate. However, in full view of man's ineradicable tendency to do wrong, God makes a unilateral and unconditional commitment that so long as the world endures there will never again be a cataclysm like the one which destroyed humanity. The regular cycle of the seasons and the orderly processes of nature will persist; the earth will yield its sustenance to maintain the life of men. Nor is this guarantee contingent upon human behavior. The sun will shine and the rain will fall on just and unjust alike, until the final reckoning.

Lastly, there is the divine commitment to the house of David. Some ambiguity is present in the sources as to whether the promise of God is unconditional and irrevocable or whether finally it shall depend upon the response and behavior of the ruler of the line of David. In Ps. 89 there seems to be an unqualified commitment to David that a descendant of his would always sit upon the throne of Judah (vv. 4-5, 29-30, 35, and others). But the question of a possible ultimate rejection is also raised (in vv. 39-40, 50). Similarly, Ps. 132:11-12 seems ambiguous on this point. It is necessary to recognize both historical and theological aspects of this picture. The house of David was deposed from the throne and for centuries maintained only a shadowy existence — if, indeed, the official line of succession survived at all. But many pious believers were convinced that the divine commitment was irrevocable and that God would reestablish the kingdom of David, with his anointed descendant seated upon the throne. The fate of individual kings or claimants was not guaranteed, but in the end the divine promise would be fulfilled. Historical contingency was balanced by theological certainty concerning the place of the house of David in the destiny of the nation.

II

There is no need to discuss in detail the second covenant type, since so much has been written about Old Testament examples of it in recent years: e.g., the covenant at Mt. Sinai (Exod. 19–24; 32–34) and various renewals (in the land of Moab [Deut. 29:1], at Schechem [Josh. 24:25], in the days of Jehoiada [2 Kgs. 11:17; 2 Chr. 29:10], Josiah [2 Kgs. 23:3], and Ezra [10:3]). Taking the several elements which appear in various accounts in the Bible and comparing these with the suzerainty treaties of the 2nd millennium B.C.E., we can reconstruct the essential covenant pattern of the Old Testament. Less exact are the parallels with the 1st millennium examples of international treaties, indirectly confirming the view that the biblical pattern originates in the 2nd millennium, i.e., from the time of Moses.[6]

For our purpose it is important to note that obligations in these covenants are imposed on the vassal, who confirms his subscription by oath, and that rewards and penalties, in the form of blessings and curses, are attached to the covenant as consequences of obedience and disobedience respectively. The basis of the covenant was the gracious acts of Yahweh, the suzerain, who delivered his people from bondage in Egypt. These in turn are linked repeatedly with the promise to the fathers, but the originality and historicity of this connection have been seriously questioned by scholars. A related question is the relationship between the God of the fathers and the God who revealed himself to Moses and, through him, to Israel. In a recent article, Frank Cross has argued convincingly that it is the same deity in both cases; namely, El (the chief God of the Canaanite pantheon) who is the God of the fathers and of Moses, too.[7] The case for continuity in the religious tradition seems to be stronger than the case against it, though one must recognize fully the radical innovations instituted by Moses. Biblical religion does not begin with the Mosaic traditions, much less later on; surely the Sinai covenant follows from the covenant with the fathers, though differing from it in important respects, rather than the other way around. In other words, neither the patriarchal stories nor the covenant pattern are retrojections from a later age. The covenant with David has affinities with the patriarchal covenant, but if there is any direct dependence, which is doubtful, it is of the former on the latter.

The Sinai covenant appears to be based on the divine promise to the fathers, but it is developed in an entirely independent manner. The emphasis here is on human obligation and the consequences of human behavior for the maintenance of the covenantal relationship. While the commandments are addressed to the individual and require individual compliance, it is the community which is answerable to God for the actions of its members. Only in rare instances does God deal directly with covenant violators. The community is the legally constituted agency of his judgment. Thus, each citizen has a dual responsibility under the terms of the covenant: to observe the stipulations as they apply to him personally and to his family and to participate in the orderly administration of justice and equity, thus sharing in the community's responsibility before God. How the Israelites, singly and together, discharge their dual obligation will determine the fate of the nation. Adherence to the conditions of the covenant means that the society as a whole, and especially through its executive and judicial apparatus, upholds the covenant pattern, enforces its terms, and effectively restrains or punishes evildoers. Individual violations of the stipulations of the covenant become a threat to the stability and survival of the covenant community only when they are of such grave nature

---

6. Cf. Mendenhall, *passim*.
7. "Yahweh and the God of the Patriarchs," *HTR* 55 (1962): 225-59.

or so widespread that the authorities cannot deal successfully with them or when the corruption extends to the governing body itself, with the leaders of Israel found to be in league with the covenant-breakers (through weakness or indifference, tacit approval, or active collaboration). The story of Naboth's vineyard (1 Kgs. 21) vividly illustrates the breakdown in the machinery of justice, which was designed to protect the innocent and punish the guilty but which, through systematic corruption, becomes the instrument of "judicial murder." Just as compliance will ensure the continued existence of Israel as a people safely settled in its land, disobedience will bring an end to the national entity and the exile of survivors.

A conditional covenant depends for its continuing validity on the performance of the human party to it. So long as the community is obedient to its terms, the relationship will be maintained and the blessings associated with the covenant will be provided. And at stipulated intervals (every seven years, according to Deut. 31:9-13) the people of Israel will renew their pledge of obedience — including those who in the meantime have come of age to assume this responsibility. When the community has violated the terms of the covenant, the bond is broken and the relationship between God and people is in danger of permanent dissolution. This is the threat that constantly hangs over Israel in its historical existence: defiance of the God of the covenant, severing of the covenant tie, and death of the nation. Such was the fate of the northern kingdom: the Deuteronomic historian interpreted the fall of Samaria and the absorption of Israel into the Assyrian Empire as the result of persistent violations of the covenant, which brought down on the country the irreversible condemnation of God. The historian, along with contemporary prophets, also used this story as an object lesson for the inhabitants of the southern kingdom, Judah, who might have been inclined to regard their narrow escape from national catastrophe in the same decades as proof of divine favor and their own superior righteousness. The threat to Judah was just as real, and in the view of the prophets a devastating judgment was ultimately inevitable, not because God desired the death of a sinful people but because merited judgment cannot be put off forever. Repentance, intercession, resolution, and amendment might win the ear of God and postpone the day of reckoning. Covenant renewals, as in the reigns of Hezekiah and Josiah, might temporarily repair a damaged relationship, though Israel's initiative in this regard was limited by the divine free will. Israel could do so much to reinstate the covenant and no more. Once the agreement was broken, it was up to the divine Suzerain to decide whether to renew it or not. And the time came when, after many periods of grace and renewals of the relationship, the patience of the long-suffering Deity was exhausted, the curses of the covenant were enforced against the condemned nation, and it fell.

The question now before us is how to reconcile two apparently incompatible covenants between the same parties: a covenant of divine commitment involving an unconditional and irrevocable promise to his people on the part of God, and a covenant of human obligation in which the continuity of the relationship depends upon the behavior of the human party. Can covenant bond be broken — and at the same time persist? Can God sever a relationship as a result of covenant violations — and nevertheless maintain it in perpetuity? The Bible seems to answer in the affirmative. Logically, one might argue that the divine commitment to Abraham was discharged when its terms were fulfilled in the conquest and settlement in the land, or certainly by the time of David and Solomon. From that point on, the fate of Israel was contingent upon its obedience to the terms of the covenant made at Mt. Sinai (but note that divine commitment to David and his house is parallel to the one made to Abraham). After God fulfilled his commitment, it became the responsibility of Israel to maintain the covenant by performing its obligations to God. For the Deuteronomic historian this appears to be the situation of Israel, and there is evidence to show that he saw the relationship of God to the house of David as similarly conditional in character.

These conclusions in no way minimize the historical reality of the covenant relationship established at Sinai and its grim consequences for the people of Israel. Surely the dreadful threat to national life was carried out to the full: the classical institutions of monarchy and priesthood collapsed, the nation was overrun, the holy city of Jerusalem and its temple were razed to the ground, and the people driven into captivity. Nothing visible remained. At the same time, and in the face of this all but total destruction, hope persisted. It was rooted in the conviction that God was still committed to Israel, and that the bond between them would one day be renewed. These things would happen not because of some change in Israel which would merit divine favor; rather, God's act of grace in renewing and restoring his people would produce a new Israel worthy of the land to which they had been restored.

III

The prophets were convinced that God's commitment to Israel persisted in spite of and beyond the destruction of the nation. The old covenant had been broken, and the full force of its penalties had been inflicted on the defiant people. It was no longer possible simply to renew the covenant as had been done in times past. Now a new agreement was needed. This is the term used by Jeremiah (31:31-34); Ezekiel and Second Isaiah used different language to describe essentially the same thing. To restore the situation as it had been before the catastrophe was not enough, because the old covenant carried with it the terrible possibility of national destruction. The basis of the new order would be the divine promise, the unconditional commitment — the single happy constant in the whole tragic picture — as guarantee of the new age. Since the oath was made to himself, God will carry it out; he will restore his people. It will be a new people, literally. Jeremiah spoke of

177

seventy years as the duration of the exile — an entire life span; Ezekiel used the number forty to signify the passing of a whole generation, as in the case of the wanderers in the wilderness in the days of Moses.

The other side of the issue — the covenant of human obligation with its possibilities for good and evil, its curses and blessings — cannot be escaped. The moral element in the relationship between God and man, the necessity for obedience, could not be abandoned; it is intrinsic to the nature of God and any relationship with men. At the same time the previous history of Israel had demonstrated the practical impossibility of maintaining the covenant by human effort. Good will and resolution had always proved inadequate in the discharge of community responsibility before God, and they always would. The demands of a just God would always be beyond the attainment of organized human society.

The answer to this dilemma lay in a special grace of God. He would transform people's minds and wills, so that henceforth they would will to obey and would be empowered by his spirit to do so. In this situation there would be no violations of the covenant and no violators. Thus there would be no need for the machinery of justice by which the community enforced the provisions of the covenant and protected itself from the wrath of God. The community itself would be in no danger of destruction, for in this new relationship there would be no threats and no penalties.

In the new age of the covenant — the new spirit and the new life — the conflict between the two covenant types is resolved in reciprocal fulfillment. Yahweh's irreversible commitment to Israel flows into the blessings which he bestows on an obedient people who, through the power of his Spirit, fulfill all the requirements of the covenant.

Conclusion

In the history of postexilic times, the "new covenant" remained a future hope. The return of the exiles initiated a struggle to renew the old pattern, based upon the divine promise of a viable community life. The structure of national life was modeled on the Mosaic covenant, with its demands, its promises, its threats. Renewed efforts were made to achieve compliance both individually and corporately, but the community remained under the threat of final destruction through failure to fulfill its covenant obligations. The inescapable fate of the nation was realized in the catastrophe of 70 C.E. But its survival was equally guaranteed, as was its ultimate renewal and restoration. In the meantime, the Christian church made a radically different analysis and appraisal of the covenant relationship between God and his people.

18

The Hebrew Old Testament
and the Ministry Today:
An Exegetical Study of
Leviticus 19:18b

Protestant Christianity imposes upon its adherents the obligation of reading and studying, of knowing and understanding the Scriptures of the Old and New Testaments. A more serious responsibility rests upon ministers who are expected not only to comprehend but also to master the contents of the Bible, so as to teach others. It is the recognition of this requirement of clergy and laity alike — and which is inherent in the structure of the evangelical faith — that brings the church face to face with the problem of the original languages of the Bible. For those who accept seriously the obligation to search the Scriptures and to learn their true meaning, a dual process is involved.

On the one hand, there is a movement toward the Bible, as the student attempts to bridge the gulf in time and space, and enter into the world of the Scriptures, to penetrate the mysteries of language and culture. To achieve this objective he must be equipped with scholarly paraphernalia adequate to the journey: the tools of the linguist and archaeologist, the mental apparatus of the historian and philosopher and theologian, and the vast accumulation of data relevant to the civilization from which the Bible emerged, at his command. Along with the effort to seek out the Bible in its original setting, there is on the other hand the need to

This paper was originally a part of *The Biblical Languages in Theological Education: Theological and Practical Implications,* a report submitted to the Council on Theological Education of the United Presbyterian Church, U.S.A., by its Curriculum Committee (Subcommittee on Biblical Languages).

bring the Bible from its ancient context and present it meaningfully to a contemporary audience. The problems of transferring a literary work from one culture to another, or more specifically from one language to another, are complex and difficult, and the dangers of mistranslation and misrepresentation are acute. But both the necessity and opportunity for making the Bible available to those outside the community of its origin have always outweighed the disadvantages and obstacles in the judgment of those entrusted with the task. For it is far better to have the Bible in some understandable form, however imperfectly rendered, than for it to be sealed from view and use in an unknown tongue. To achieve an adequate transference from the original to another language requires extraordinary skill. The translator must have full command of both languages; and with regard to the Bible he must be as much at home in an ancient culture forever gone, as in the modern world, if the Bible is to speak now as it did in its original setting. He must have a profound awareness of the inner meaning and wider connotations of the literature with which he deals, and with it the ability to render not only words but meaning, to preserve idiom and nuance, and catch the lilt of the language, the figure of speech and turn of phrase: in short, not to embroider plain talk nor make commonplace high style, but to render thought for thought and measure for measure.

To pursue the Bible to its homeland, to capture its essence and return with this treasure in a language understandable to men is the continuing obligation and privilege of the Church, and in particular of the scholars and teachers set aside for this purpose. But there is also an important place for pastors, theological students, and lay people in this basic program of the Church. To the extent that time and energy, capacity and training allow, all should be engaged in the enterprise. For the most part this will mean following in the path of the experts: one would hardly expect the average pastor or general reader to pioneer in the solution of vexing problems of text criticism, or to devise renderings of the original, superior to those presently available. But if the student is to weigh the arguments of scholars intelligently and discriminate among conflicting opinions, he must have a basic knowledge of the original languages. There is in addition a notable value in performing the tasks of exegesis and translation himself, for the same reason that it is preferable for a minister to prepare his own sermons though he might find better ones to copy. With application and practice considerable competence in the biblical languages can be attained, and worthwhile exegetical results can be achieved by any interested person.

Because of the severe space limitations, we shall limit the study which follows to a single well-known sentence from the Old Testament. While there is nothing complicated about the words or the sentence structure, its meaning has proved elusive, and it deserves investigation; at the same time it provides an illustration of the value of knowing the Bible in its original language. The verse is the familiar Lev. 19:18b, which is rendered in the RSV, "You shall love your neighbor as yourself."

180

On the face of it, we would expect the clause to mean in English what it meant in the original Hebrew, or the Greek quoted in the New Testament: Matt. 22:39 and Mark 12:31 (where Jesus specifies it as the second of the great commandments). In the gospel of Luke, however, questions are raised about its meaning. Thus, in ch. 10:25ff., the lawyer who quotes the two great commandments with Jesus' approval then asks, "Who is my neighbor?" (v. 29). In academic language, the question is: "What does the word we translate 'neighbor' really mean?" While Jesus dealt with the matter in a way suited to the occasion, and answered in the priceless parable of the Good Samaritan, the question remains to be answered semantically. The Hebrew word here, *rēaʿ,* does not strictly mean "neighbor" at all, since the latter properly reflects the Hebrew word *qārôb̠,* which signifies the person next door, or the neighbor. In spite of the Greek rendering πλησιον, which implies propinquity, it can be affirmed that the essential meaning of the term is that of "friend, companion"; frequently it has the general sense of "fellow man."

In the present instance the general sense is to be preferred, since it would be tautologous to suggest that a man ought to love his close friend or intimate companion. At the same time the preceding clause, which reads, "You shall not be angry with the sons of your people," implies a limitation of this obligation to the people of Israel, i.e., the Israelite is instructed to love his fellow Israelite. And we may agree that this is the meaning of the verse in Leviticus. This fact, however, should not occasion either surprise or the sort of invidious comparison which is generally made between the expression here and the New Testament usage, in which "neighbor" is defined by Jesus to include the non-Israelite as well. The point is that the same words may have different connotations depending upon the context and accompanying interpretation.

It is clear that in ch. 19 of Leviticus the author is concerned about the matter of relationships among Israelites, and he enjoins the citizen to be forthright but compassionate, not to bear grudges, but to be on friendly terms with his fellow citizens, in short, to love them. In the context, he is inevitably speaking of this particular relationship, but there is no justification for the conclusion that members of the covenant community are not obligated to cherish an affection or devotion for the non-Israelite, the non-neighbor. One of the principal points which Jesus made is that neighbor love is not limited to the fellow Israelite (though Jesus presents this point in reverse order, since it is the Samaritan who shows love for his non-Samaritan fellow man). He recognized that the words of Leviticus might be construed narrowly (or broadly) and that there was little in the words themselves to indicate the scope. That the author of Leviticus was equally aware of the possible limitation in the understanding and application of the term is clear from an accompanying verse which is not often cited in connection with this great commandment. In its way it is perhaps more remarkable: "As for the alien who settles among you, you shall love him as yourself" (19:33). The final phrase is identical with v. 18, and the implication is obvious: the Israelite is not to interpret the command to love his fellow narrowly, but must include in the circle of his affection the resident alien. In other words he must understand the *gēr* as defining the term *rēaʿ;* "friend, fellow man" includes "stranger" also.

Not less important to a proper understanding of the passage is the word rendered "to love." There are few words in English which have suffered more abuse than this one; it is used with such a great variety of objects, from the trivial to the momentous, and has so wide a range of intensity that it is often difficult if not impossible to gain a clear impression of its meaning or function. There is a similar problem in Hebrew, since the single root is used to describe the relationship of devotion or affection among all sorts and conditions of persons and things.[1] It is used of God and of man; it expresses physical affection as well as spiritual devotion. It describes the appetite, as for food and drink, but is also used with more abstract principles, like truth and righteousness. Its meaning may best be grasped in the description of family relationships: the love of father for child, or of husband and wife. Comparable is the love of God for man, or Israel in particular; such love is to be reciprocated with the full force of one's being. The verb thus defines a relationship, but also expresses a profound emotion, which issues in actions consonant with the relationship and the inner feeling. On the basis of various analogies, and the examples narrated in the Bible, it is possible to characterize the love which is meant here. The commandment requires of every man such a demonstration with respect to his fellow.

At this point, we must ask about the meaning of the qualifying phrase, "as thyself." Once again the structure is deceptively simple; "You are to love or cherish your fellow as yourself." In his parable Jesus does not specifically discuss the interpretation of this expression though his story has implications for a proper understanding of it. Many commentators seem to regard it as equivalent to an adverb of degree, thus limiting the force to the verb, as e.g., "You shall love your fellow man as much as you love yourself." Such an interpretation would seem to be linguistically possible, but it leaves several unresolved questions. The first is that self-love is rarely mentioned in the Bible, and then only in a figurative sense (cf. Prov. 19:8 — looks after his true well-being). In this biblical sense, we could say that to love others is to love oneself, i.e., to do what is right and good is to love oneself. But this is not what we normally understand by self-love. Defined in the usual way, those who manifest self-love most conspicuously commonly show the least concern of affection for others. To measure love of others by self-love involves a contradiction, unless we understand the author to be essentially cynical about human nature. The interpretation would then be: "If you would only love others as much as you love yourself, then things would be a good deal better than they are." Even so, this would imply the displacement of concern for self with

---

1. Cf. Deut. 10:18, 19, where love of *ger* is to give him food and drink.

182

concern for others, which is consistent with biblical teaching elsewhere. Nor are we to understand the commandment as requiring or even suggesting a prudential balance between neighbor-love and self-love; i.e., love him no less and no more than you love yourself. Surely it would be a mistake to suppose that the juxtaposition of the two commandments in the New Testament implies a distinction between the love of God which is to be with the whole heart, and the love of neighbor which is to be circumscribed by the consideration of self-love. In the form in which we find the commandment given in Luke 10:27, it is implied at least that the love to be shown the fellow man is to be of the same order as that for God, i.e., with all one's heart, and strength, and soul.

There are numerous illustrations of neighbor-love in the Bible, both Old Testament and New Testament, which show that such a restriction in the normal sense of the word is not intended by the author. Jesus' parable incidentally points to the extraordinary quality of the Samaritan's love for his unfortunate fellow creature. The sacrificial and selfless character of the act of love here is notable, and selfish or even prudential considerations are entirely absent. Going beyond this, we can point to Jesus' words about ultimate human love in John 15:13, "Greater love has no man than this, that a man lay down his life for his friends." But such an act could hardly be described as the ultimate in self-love, unless we wish to be deliberately paradoxical. Defined as prudential consideration of one's personal well-being and advantage, then it is in direct conflict with the love of others; we should have to say that the one who loves others most loves himself least. This is indeed the way the Bible defines the situation: to risk one's life for the sake of others or the welfare of the community is to hate life and regard it as of no value (cf. Judg. 5:18). The examples of Ruth and Naomi, David and Jonathan are sufficient to show the scope and depth of neighbor-love, and the heroic self-sacrifice in which such love found expression. We need not comment on the quality of love explicit in the self-denying ministry and death of Jesus Christ. It will be granted that these are extraordinary demonstrations of neighbor-love, and that in most instances such examples are neither necessary nor expected. But the commandment is not limited by the final phrase to the ordinary and prudential. The ultimate meaning can only be probed by the heroic and selfless.

If we have refuted the common interpretation of the qualifying phrase, it remains to offer an interpretation consonant with the meaning and usage of the Hebrew terms, and yet which makes sense in the setting of the biblical picture of neighbor-love. The answer may lie in the word "yourself." The term "corporate personality" has been much used of late to describe the Hebrew sense of community, the consciousness that all Israelites belonged to each other in a peculiar way. Whether this term adequately conveys the biblical portrayal may be questioned, but there can be no doubt of the powerful sense of identity and solidarity which permeated the community from its inception. In poetry, at least, the whole people could be treated as a single individual and it is not always easy to distinguish the sense in which the expression Jacob/Israel is used: does it refer to the patriarch simply as the ancestor of the people, or as embodied and alive in them; on the other hand is it the people as his posterity, or in some sense as the incorporation and extension of his personality? It may be no more than a figurative expression, like our legal fiction which defines a vast industrial complex of shareholders, management, laborers, and factories with their equipment and products as a single person, that is a corporation.

We suggest that in this passage "self" is to be understood in the broader sense of the whole unit which constitutes the person, i.e., his wife and children: the immediate community which bears the individual's name and shares his life. The relationship to these determines the norm of love: the common experience, the affection and consideration which are shown to wife and children, and by them to husband and father, are the pattern upon which neighbor-love is to be modeled. Thus the commandment is to be understood as meaning: You are to love your fellow man as though he were part of you, i.e., part of the kinship group which is the immediate and natural area for the expression of love. The measure of a man's love is its scope or inclusiveness; the wider its reach, and the more who are made part of the "self," the greater its depth and magnitude. In short, he who loves much, loves many. To fulfill the commandment, one must include one's fellow man, the friend, but also the stranger. Another way to put it is this: "You shall love your fellow man as you love your wife and children — those closest to you, who are you."

19

Archaeology and the Future of Biblical Studies: The Biblical Languages

Introduction

When the Society of Biblical Literature and Exegesis was founded in 1880, archaeology was already firmly entrenched in the Near East. Napoleon's conquest of Egypt and neighboring lands opened the way for the recovery of man's most ancient civilizations, while the effusions of romantic poets such as Byron and Shelley stirred adventure in the souls of cultivated and daring Europeans. Before long intrepid gentlemen-explorers and travelers were penetrating the inmost recesses of the Turkish domain. Paul Emile Botta and Austin H. Layard pioneered the heroic age of Near Eastern archaeology, uncovering the abandoned cities of the Assyro-Babylonian monarchs. Faithful to their homelands, they stuffed room after room at the Louvre and the British Museum with cargoes of priceless loot: the monumental art and innumerable inscriptions from ancient Khorsabad and Kouyounjik. Decipherment went hand in hand with discovery and by 1850 the essential solution to Assyro-Babylonian cuneiform had been achieved through the efforts of Grotefend, Rawlinson, Hincks, Oppert, and others. The publication of the Babylonian creation and flood stories by George Smith (in 1876) created a sensation among biblical scholars and the general reading public. Equally startling was the discovery and decipherment of the Moabite stone (since 1868), by far the most important royal inscription ever found in Palestine. Not only was the king, Mesha, known from the biblical record, but the language of the inscription was so close to Biblical Hebrew that it could be read with comparative ease. The contents served to supplement the biblical narrative (2 Kgs. 3) and also present a point of view entirely at variance with that of the Israelite author. Doubtless the conversations at

185

the early meetings of the Society of Biblical Literature and Exegesis touched on the recent discoveries and their implications for the future of biblical studies.

Looking back now, we can confidently affirm that in spite of the extraordinary and unrepeatable finds of the early years, the greatest days of archaeological research were in the future. Eighty-four years later there is no discernible diminution of interest in or recognition of the contribution of archaeology to the study of the Bible. Since the end of World War II the tempo of archaeological activity — surveys, surface explorations, small and large excavations, reports ranging from provisional to permanent, from brief summaries of work in progress to monumental multi-volume compendia — has steadily increased, in spite of disturbed conditions all over the Near East; and the point of diminishing returns is nowhere in sight. Chance discoveries continue at an unexampled rate, and even previously excavated sites never fail to yield a rich harvest to diligent seekers. Rarely does an expedition exhaust the possibilities of a small tell, while the larger mounds would require decades of intensive digging to complete the work of excavation. In spite of very extensive operations at Megiddo, much work remains to be done there; and the same can be said of Lachish, Hazor, Gezer, and the other sites in Palestine. C. Schaeffer has been digging at Ugarit since 1929 without drying up the immense resources of that ancient mound. The picture is the same at many other sites in Syria and Mesopotamia, where the only barriers to perpetual excavations are local and human ones — lack of money and skilled manpower, unsettled political, social, and economic conditions. In addition there are thousands of classified sites of ancient occupation which are waiting to be excavated; and new ones are being listed all the time. The supply seems inexhaustible, and I am sure that at the two hundredth meeting of the Society a similar estimate of the situation will be made.

Along with the general increase in the amount and rate of excavation, there has been constant refinement in the techniques and procedures of archaeology. A notable transformation has taken place from the early days of destructive treasure hunting to the present controlled research, with highly skilled technicians keeping meticulous records, and analyzing everything turned up including the dirt. The discovery and development of the basic principles of stratigraphy and typology (pottery sequence-dating) changed archaeology from a hit-and-miss search for valuable antiquities and museum pieces into a relatively exact science. The innovations and contributions of leading archaeologists such as W. Flinders Petrie, C. R. Fisher, W. F. Albright, and more recently K. Kenyon have greatly enhanced the reliability of work in the field and the value of excavation reports. Methods are constantly being improved with significantly better results. The adaptation of equipment and use of techniques derived from various physical sciences have provided archaeology with tools of research, like radio-carbon dating, which were undreamed of two generations ago. Much material that was formerly discarded or ignored is now studied for clues to the former inhabitants and their way of life. The scientific revolution in archaeology is only well started and the future will bring more advanced procedures, and more effective control of materials. We should not minimize the difficulties in the development of scientific instruments and their efficient use, nor the disappointments that have attended many brave experiments, but physical scientists working in this area have some remarkable achievements to their credit, and it is only a matter of continued application until universal success is attained. I can visualize the excavation of the future in which electronic devices will thoroughly explore a site and its contours, plot its strata, and classify its contents without removing a spadeful of dirt. But before we get lost in a future we can mold to our wishes, let us return to the more refractory past.

Archaeological research has served to illuminate the Bible; it has helped to supply a frame of reference for modern students which the biblical writers presupposed and with which their audiences were presumed to be familiar. Here and there discoveries have tended to confirm or illustrate specific passages in the Bible such as the inscription of Sargon II found at Ashdod in 1963 which corroborated Isa. 20:1, or the inscription in the Siloam water tunnel which amplifies 2 Kgs. 20:20.

Occasionally archaeological data contradict the biblical account, or seem to. One of the most spectacular examples is Jericho, where the most painstaking archaeological investigation has failed to yield evidence of a substantial wall or city (as described in the Bible) in the 13th century B.C.E., i.e., the time of Joshua. Responses to the negative archaeological evidence have been varied: from acceptance at face value which involves denial of the biblical record, through different attempts at harmonization, to straightforward rejection of the archaeological information and affirmation of the Bible. It may help the cause of progress in the truth to note that neither the archaeologists nor the biblical writers are necessarily infallible, and that neither or either or both may be correct with regard to the presentation or interpretation of ancient events.

In general, however, archaeology has tended to support the historical validity of the biblical narrative. The broad chronological outline from the patriarchs to New Testament times correlates with archaeological data. Allowing for occasional anachronisms and other lapses, the biblical writers correctly describe the cultural patterns and mores of the period to which they refer. Thus archaeology confirms the setting of the patriarchal stories in the Middle Bronze II period (first half of the 2nd millennium B.C.E.) while the exodus and conquest are correctly placed in the transition from Late Bronze to Early Iron (13th century B.C.E.). Future discoveries are likely to sustain the present moderate position that the biblical tradition is historically rooted, and faithfully transmitted, though it is not history in a critical or scientific sense. Attempted reconstructions of biblical history by modern scholars — e.g., Wellhausen's view that the patriarchal age was a reflex of the divided monarchy; or the rejection of the historicity of Moses and the exodus and consequent restructuring of Israelite history by Noth and his followers — have not survived the archaeological data as well as the biblical narrative. Radical rearrangements or reassessments of the material are not likely to be substantiated by future excavations.

Archaeological correlation with the historical patterns and chronological outline of the Bible does not extend to details as a rule, since evidence for or against the actuality of the latter is rarely obtained. And in the area in which the Bible is most concerned, i.e., religious truth, the reality of God, faith and commitment, archaeology can deal only with the impress or effect of such factors on human life as these are reflected in the material remains of a civilization.

Archaeology can also provide a tangible frame of reference for the Bible, a setting in time and place, social and economic, historical and political, and culturally articulated through the synthesis of countless artifacts uncovered in hundreds of excavations. On the basis of the evidence already in hand it has been possible to outline the cultural history of Palestine from earliest times to the present, and to report the factual conditions of life throughout the biblical period. Such syntheses will always be provisional in view of the continuing flow of new data from every corner of the country, as well as from sites in neighboring nations, but they already offer a substantial picture in place of the largely ephemeral and evanescent structures which have been mortised by biblical scholars in the past to serve as a setting for the biblical narrative.

The weakness of every such pattern — from Wellhausen's artificial Hegelian structure, through the liberal British and American evolutionary theories, to the form critical school's hypothetical life or rather cult situations — is that the frame of reference is constructed out of the biblical materials, which are then interpreted in the light of the structure, or the presuppositions which underlie it. Surely no one will quarrel with the manifest usefulness of classifying literary materials according to their several forms, or with the development of working hypotheses to explain their function and meaning. But a working hypothesis requires some external evidence to sustain it.

Methodological decency would seem to require an external hook on which to hang circular reasoning. The standard of judgment for all such reconstructions must be the actuality of life preserved in the soil and recovered by archaeology. The Bible is the story of people who occupied a certain geographic territory, who lived and died on it, who worked and worshipped there, who struggled with their neighbors and with each other; and who left tangible evidence of their presence. Any theory of the Bible or reconstruction of the history of Israel must deal with that reality, i.e., the material culture whose remains have survived in hundreds of sites and millions of artifacts all bearing witness to what they were and did, thought and felt. Before archaeology there was no adequate alternative to the creation of hypothetical frameworks for the biblical narrative; but as the factual evidence has become available, there is less and less excuse for such exercises in ingenuity, and in due course there will be none.

Archaeology and the Biblical Languages

Archaeological discovery has had an immediate and direct impact on the interpretation of the biblical languages. While these languages — Hebrew and Aramaic in the Old Testament, and Aramaic and Greek in the New Testament — were never forgotten in the sense that Egyptian hieroglyphics or Babylonian cuneiform or many other ancient languages were, nevertheless there are many difficult passages in the Bible, some of which were corrupted through errors in the transmission of the text, and others the true meaning of which was forgotten in the course of time and which were no longer understood by the early translators and commentators. In various ways archaeology has contributed to a clearer understanding of the biblical materials.

The discovery of ancient manuscripts of the Old and New Testament has been of direct material aid in elucidating the text. Occasionally an early manuscript will have a different, older, and superior reading to any preserved in the extant manuscripts. In such cases the difficulty in the received text is seen to be the result of a scribal error, and the problem is resolved by substituting the preferred reading of the newly found text. Or the manuscript may have a variant reading, which though not to be preferred to the standard text nevertheless provides a clue to the interpretation of the passage, and opens the way to a solution of the crux. Non-biblical manuscripts of a similar genre which are dependent upon or related to biblical materials may offer help in the interpretation of difficult passages, or may help to clear up grammatical, syntactic, or lexicographical problems through the use of the same or related terms in different contexts. The possibilities are practically unlimited, so that the discovery of inscribed texts almost always results in some positive gain in the interpretation of biblical passages. That is why the search for inscriptions remains the principal objective of biblical archaeologists. And the relative paucity of written materials turned up in Palestine has only increased the avidity of excavators. Practically every Hebrew inscription found, however brief, has contributed in some measure to the elucidation of the Bible. Needless to say, the reverse is also true, and in greater measure.

It should be added that archaeology contributes indirectly to the clarification of the Bible in many ways. Artifacts may concretely illustrate a biblical passage, especially one dealing with *realia*. Archaeological data about the common activities of life may help to clarify incidental allusions and references in the biblical text which are not otherwise explained. Knowledge of the cultural setting in which the biblical books find their place can be provided in part by archaeology. An adequate interpretation and rendering of biblical passages requires control of a wide range of related data. Sometimes considerably more than the determination of the text is involved in the clarification of a passage. Thus, e.g., the text of the first verses of Genesis is not in question — presumably it has been transmitted unchanged from the autograph of the Priestly writer — but the interpretation of the material is the subject of perennial scholarly controversy.

Our concern now is with archaeological data which directly illuminate the biblical languages. We will attempt to deal with the relevant materials in roughly chronological order:

1. The Patriarchal Age: Middle Bronze II — 2nd millennium, first half. As yet no texts of any length in Amorite, the presumed language of the patriarchs, have turned up. But certain expressions, personal and place names, do occur in Akkadian texts of this period. The principal source is the thousands of Mari tablets from the 18th century B.C.E. Through careful examination of the many Amorite names, some of which are identical with or very similar to biblical names of the patriarchal period, it has been possible to work out a basic vocabulary and grammar of this ancestral Northwest Semitic dialect which is closely related to Canaanite on the one hand and Aramaic on the other.

In addition there are the so-called pseudo-hieroglyphic inscriptions from Byblos, which may be somewhat older. Though a definite decipherment has not yet been published, G. E. Mendenhall has made sufficient progress toward a solution to describe the script as syllabic and the language as Canaanite, bearing marked resemblances to Ugaritic and Phoenician, and to Biblical Hebrew, though with some notable deviations. [See now Mendenhall's *The Syllabic Inscriptions from Byblos* (Beirut: American University of Beirut, 1985).]

We mention in passing the execration texts of the Twelfth Dynasty in Egypt (19th and 18th centuries B.C.E.), in which are found the names of contemporary Canaanite cities.

2. The Amarna Age: Late Bronze II A — 14th century B.C.E. There is now a great abundance of material in Northwest Semitic dialects from this period, though neither of the principal deposits was known at the time of the founding of the Society of Biblical Literature and Exegesis. The first group of Amarna letters was discovered in 1887, and it was not until 1929 that the first Ugaritic tablets were found.

a. The Amarna letters, found in the ruins of the capital city of the pharaoh Akhenaten, constitute part of the royal diplomatic archives. They were written in Akkadian, the official language of international correspondence in the 14th century B.C.E. Many of the extant letters were sent by kinglets of the city-states of Canaan, the pharaoh's puppet rulers of Byblos, Jerusalem, Megiddo, Shechem, and other cities. While these letters are principally important as firsthand cultural documents describing and reflecting political, military, and socioeconomic conditions in Palestine a century or so before Moses and Joshua, they are also very valuable sources for the contemporary Canaanite language. The local dialect of the scribes often shines through the Akkadian formalities; and they regularly inserted Canaanite words and phrases to facilitate the expression of their meaning, and possibly to help the translators in the Egyptian foreign office, who presumably knew Canaanite better than Akkadian. It need not be added that the transcription of Canaanite words in Akkadian provides a dividend for the attentive scholar. In Akkadian words are vocalized, thus offering a clue to the vowel structure, whereas in alphabetic inscriptions in Canaanite of this and even later periods no such help is given; only consonants are indicated. The cuneiform alphabet used in Ugaritic is a partial exception (*aleph* alone of the consonants is regularly vocalized). Thus in the Amarna letters we have a rare glimpse, in relatively full dress, of the immediate ancestor of Biblical Hebrew.

b. By far the most extensive early source for Northwest Semitic is the Ugaritic texts — a vast quantity of tablets written in alphabetic cuneiform dating from the 14th and 13th centuries B.C.E. Since excavations began, thousands of tablets have been recovered, and there seems to be no diminution in the rate of return. The most important of these are mythological epics in poetic form, which provide direct documentation of Canaanite religious belief, long known only from the hostile descriptions of the Bible and late classical sources. There are other literary texts, but the great bulk of the remaining tablets are official documents of various kinds, including numerous lists and others dealing with a wide variety of matters. The mythological poems have so far made the principal contributions to biblical studies, but the great accumulation of prose texts, many as yet unpublished, gives promise of substantial additional help in interpreting the Bible.

While occasional voices are raised in protest at the classification of Ugaritic as a Canaanite dialect, there is a growing consensus that it belongs to the Northwest Semitic family of languages (as its location, and the contents of its literature would suggest), with very close affinities to Amarna Canaanite and Biblical Hebrew. This contention is borne out fully by a careful comparison of biblical poetry with that of Ugarit (a similar comparison of biblical prose with the Ugaritic prose texts is also in order), and the recognition, only now gaining headway, that many features of Ugaritic syntax, morphology, and lexicography hitherto regarded as setting it apart from Biblical Hebrew, actually occur in biblical poetry. But these features, practically all archaic and long since abandoned in classical Hebrew prose, passed unrecognized by editors and scribes, and were thus accidentally concealed, partially erased or altered through misrepresentation and misinterpretation. Fortunately the scribes were generally faithful in their work, even when they did not comprehend the text; and a sufficient number of examples of archaic usage have survived to make the identification with characteristic Ugaritic features certain. Thus the occurrence of enclitic *mem* in Hebrew poetry (and in passages based on poetic originals) is now universally acknowledged, and hundreds of convincing cases have been discovered. But the phenomenon in Biblical Hebrew was not even suspected until after it was observed in Ugaritic, and later noted in the Hebrew Bible. The same is true of other features: e.g., the asseverative use of initial *l;* the prepositions *b* and *l* with the meaning "from"; the use of double-duty particles which occur only once in a poetic couplet or bicolon, but exert force in both cola: these include prepositions, pronominal suffixes, negative particles, and of course verbs and nouns; the alternation of perfect and imperfect forms of the verb without the use of *waw* consecutive, and in which the tense or action of the verb must be determined from context and not according to familiar prose rules. There are close similarities in lexicography as well. Traditional pairs of words are common to both Hebrew and Ugaritic poetry; in these not only are the pairs made up of the same words, but the order of words (which appears first and which second) is also constant. It is now becoming clear that Hebrew poetry made use of a special vocabulary quite different from ordinary prose, which it shared with Ugaritic; and it has been possible to identify certain of these roots on the basis of Ugaritic cognates.

None of this should come as a surprise. Hebrew poetry is noticeably different from Hebrew prose. Students who breeze through a course in Hebrew reading confined to the narrative portions of the Old Testament find Hebrew poetry much more difficult. Biblical poetry employs a more complex vocabulary, often uses rare words and archaic forms, and indulges in difficult syntactical constructions: features which are common to poetry of many languages, but are avoided in prose. It is therefore no accident that archaic or archaizing Hebrew poetry should have close affinities with somewhat older Canaanite poetry.

I may add that M. Dahood of the Pontifical Biblical Institute in Rome is just finishing work on the Anchor edition of the Psalms, interpreting them in the light of Ugaritic lexicography, morphology, and syntax. While the first volume, which will appear in about a year, covers only Pss. 1–50, it is already clear that the results of his highly original work are rather startling. [The complete commentary, in 3 vols., appeared between 1965 and 1970.] In any case his enterprise should mark the end of the period of wholesale emendation of the text, which mars the work of practically all modern critical commentators, and the abandonment of many speculations based upon such drastic treatments. Dahood has made an effective case for dealing with the text essentially as it has been handed down, and has been able to clarify decisively many passages which have hitherto proved impenetrably obscure. His work, however, is only a logical extension of the pioneering effort of other Ugaritic specialists who had previously pointed out the close affinities between Hebrew poetry and the poems of Ugarit. Once this principle is established then it is only a matter of making the right combinations, and using the available materials with skill and caution. On the basis of Dahood's proposals, even if only a fraction stand the test of scholarly criticism, it should be impossible in the future to ignore or minimize the importance of Ugaritic for the study of Hebrew poetic materials.

c. Canaanite alphabetic inscriptions. Apart from the Ugaritic tablets in their special script, there are a number of inscriptions written in the Canaanite alphabet, which is the direct ancestor of the well-known Phoenician, Aramaic, and Greek scripts of later centuries. They date from about the 17th century B.C.E. on, and constitute an invaluable corpus for tracing the evolution of the alphabetic scripts. This subject is of importance in its own right for the study of the transmission of the biblical text, since all extant manuscripts are written in alphabetic scripts, and often scribal errors and other variations can be explained on the basis of epigraphic

192

considerations. Most of these early inscriptions are very brief or fragmentary and offer little in the way of linguistic material. The Proto-Sinaitic inscriptions of the 15th century B.C.E., however, are an exception. Many scholars have had a hand in their decipherment, most recently W. F. Albright and Frank M. Cross, Jr., whose contributions have appeared in various journals. A comprehensive treatment of the inscriptions by Albright, including much new material, is now in the press and will appear in the near future [*The Proto-Sinaitic Inscriptions and their Decipherment.* HTS 22 (Cambridge: Harvard University Press, 1966)]. For the bearing of these rather remote texts on biblical studies we may refer to Cross's study, "Yahweh and the God of the Patriarchs,"[1] in which a pattern of divine titles or address is established partly on the basis of a reading in the Proto-Sinaitic texts.

3. The First Commonwealth: *ca.* 1200-600 B.C.E. A large number of inscriptions in a variety of dialects including and related to Hebrew and Aramaic comes from this period. Taken as a group they constitute an important witness to the linguistic situation in Palestine-Syria during the time when the bulk of the Old Testament was composed. We can only mention the most important items:

a. Phoenician inscriptions: (1) The royal inscriptions from Byblos of the 10th century B.C.E. These are our best witness to the state of Canaanite at the time when Hebrew letters flourished at the court of David and Solomon. The affinities between the so-called Byblian dialect and Israelite are particularly marked. (2) From the 9th century on, Phoenician inscriptions are found all over the Mediterranean world, reflecting the rapid expansion of Phoenician maritime interests, and extensive colonization.

b. Aramaic inscriptions from the 9th century on. These were written in a variety of dialects, since it was not until much later that the dialect of Damascus became the official Aramaic language, first of the Aramean empire and then of the western provinces of the Babylonian and Persian empires. The earliest inscription in Damascene Aramaic is the Ben-Hadad stele dating about 850 B.C.E. Other dialects are represented by inscriptions from Hamath, Sujin, and Zinjirli. Mention should also be made of the recently published Saqqara papyrus, which dates from about 600 B.C.E. and indicates that Aramaic was by that time the language of foreign affairs in Palestine.

c. The Moabite stone has already been mentioned. It remains the most important of all the Palestinian inscriptions, not only for its historical data, but because of its formal characteristics as a royal inscription, and its linguistic features as the only extensive document in official Moabite, a close cousin of Hebrew. A second Moabite inscription from the same period has recently been published;[2] in our judgment it should be attributed to the same king.

---

1. *HTR* 55 (1962): 225-59.
2. W. L. Reed and F. V. Winnett, "A Fragment of an Early Moabite Inscription from Kerak," *BASOR* 172 (1963): 1-9; cf. D. N. Freedman, "A Second Mesha Inscription," *BASOR* 175 (1964): 50f. [See Volume 2, Chapter 4.]

d. We can only mention the very numerous seals and stamps in Hebrew and neighboring dialects; the quantity is constantly increasing as the result of recent excavations, and a separate work would be required to catalogue and evaluate them. But more must be said about the Hebrew inscriptions from Israel and Judah, which are a prime external source for the language of the Bible in preexilic times. The number of these of any length or importance is not large, but it is growing as new discoveries are constantly being made. Their importance is too obvious to require comment. Among other data, they have provided information concerning dialectal differences between Israel and Judah respectively. Thus the Gezer calendar and the Samaria ostraca are witnesses to the Israelite form of Hebrew, which had close affinities with Phoenician, while the Siloam inscription (discovered in the year that this Society was founded) and the Lachish letters are the principal witnesses to the Judahite form of Hebrew, in which the biblical materials were finally set down and transmitted.

Recently there has been a spate of new finds including ostraca from Hazor, Beth-shan, Tel Qasile, Ashdod, and Arad. The most important single item is the letter of a protesting peasant from Yavneh-yam, which dates to the last quarter of the 7th century B.C.E. It is written in relatively good Hebrew (with numerous echoes of biblical usage), and has an interesting point of contact with certain legal passages in the Pentateuch, especially the law on the return of a pledged garment in Exod. 22:26-27.

A number of ostraca have been found in successive seasons at Arad. They are in Hebrew and Aramaic and date from the 9th to the 4th centuries B.C.E. One bears the name Arad written several times, and in different directions. Like the inscribed sherds from Gibeon bearing the name of that city (and another from Beth-shan with the name of that city), it may presage a new and welcome trend in the hitherto complicated business of identifying archaeological sites. Another Arad ostracon has a tantalizing reference to the "king of Judah," while still another has the reading *bêt yhwh* — extraordinary because it may refer to a temple at Arad.

Lastly, mention should be made of the inscribed clay tablets found at Deir 'Alla this past spring and just published by H. Franken. They are provisionally dated to the 12th century B.C.E., and are written in an unknown script which may be related to Linear A. They may turn out to be written in the long-lost and long-sought Philistine language; if true, we would have preferred to have them turn up at Ashdod, where we have been looking hard for just such inscriptions. However, Ashdod has produced inscriptions in four other languages, so there is no cause for complaint.

4. The period of the Second Commonwealth: 5th century B.C.E. on. In the postexilic period the stream of materials turns into a flood, and it would be a hopeless task even to try to list them. It may be noted that for the earlier part of this period, the 5th and 4th centuries, practically all the texts are in Aramaic. There

seems to be a definite break in Hebrew inscriptions from the 6th century to the 3rd century B.C.E. It was not until the time of the Maccabees that Hebrew was revived on a large scale, as the official language of the country, and for literary and religious purposes. At least one colloquial dialect of spoken Hebrew is attested in this period as well. From the 2nd century B.C.E. until the end of the Second Commonwealth, to which must be added the period of Bar Kochba's revolt, Hebrew continued in regular and widespread use, though it never displaced Aramaic as the common language of the population of the whole area and the medium of commerce and diplomacy through this long period. From the 4th century B.C.E. on, Greek became increasingly important in the same area, and it is now clear that all three languages played significant roles in the life of Palestine with intersecting and overlapping jurisdictions.

a. For the earlier period the principal sources are the 5th-century Aramaic papyri from Elephantine initially discovered in 1893ff. but not fully published until 1953 (when E. G. Kraeling published the Brooklyn papyri). These documents brought to light the existence, previously unsuspected, of a heterodox Jewish colony at Elephantine in Egypt, who worshipped the God Yahu (abbreviated from Yahweh) in their own temple. It is clear that they diverged far from the normative Judaism of Ezra and Nehemiah, and even from the less orthodox Samaritans in the north of Palestine. Some of the letters are of special importance for clarifying the puzzling situation in Judah during the 5th century B.C.E., though as is generally the case new problems have been raised in the process of resolving old ones. The value of the papyri as a source for the official Aramaic of the 5th century B.C.E. is rivaled only by the diplomatic correspondence of the Satrap Arsames (published by G. R. Driver in 1954). They offer a solid basis of comparison with the Aramaic portions of Ezra. So far as language is concerned, there is no reason to doubt the authenticity of the reports in the biblical book. We may also mention an Aramaic ostracon from Ashdod belonging to the 5th century, in which the name Zebadiah appears. It is interesting to note that the only occurrences of this name in the Bible are in postexilic sources: Ezra and Chronicles.

From the 4th century B.C.E. we have the so-called Samaria papyri, which were found a little more than a year ago in a remote cave in the Wadi Adaliyeh region. A preliminary report by Frank M. Cross, Jr., indicates their considerable importance for biblical studies, especially as this period is largely passed over in the Bible. The occurrence of the name Sanballat is especially intriguing.

b. From the period from the 3rd century B.C.E. until the 2nd century C.E. the principal archaeological data are the Dead Sea Scrolls, including both the Qumran scrolls and the other extensive manuscript finds from the Wadi Murabba'at and other caves in the Judean desert. The almost incredibly vast quantity of material involved, which nevertheless does not begin to match the literature about them, makes any comment here seem faintly ridiculous. They constitute not only the most important, but also the most unexpected of all the discoveries made in Palestine.

Since hundreds of documents and thousands of the fragments are of biblical books, and since many of the other documents either quote from or allude to biblical materials, there is no need to argue the case for their relevance to Old Testament studies. Since as a group they are also the principal contemporary source for the language and literature of Judaism in this period, and provide the essential background for the New Testament literature, their importance for intertestamental and New Testament research is equally clear.

Perhaps we can escape with three observations: (1) The Scrolls are of basic significance for the history of the text of the Hebrew Bible. They are especially valuable for Septuagint studies, settling certain questions decisively and throwing important light upon others. There are at least three fragmentary manuscripts of biblical books which can be dated as early as the 3rd century B.C.E. on palaeographic grounds. Through the determination and comparison of text-types, an even earlier state of the Hebrew text can be projected. In the case of Ecclesiastes and Daniel we have manuscripts which are reasonably close to the presumed autographs. The fragments of Ecclesiastes come from the second half of the 2nd century B.C.E., probably within two centuries of the original. The fragments of Daniel belong to the first quarter of the 1st century B.C.E., or less than a century after the autograph which must have been written in 165 B.C.E. (2) Another principal value of the Scrolls lies in the fact that they are primary documents of Judaism in the period from 150 B.C.E. to 70 C.E. They constitute the religious literature of the Essenes, and are thus firsthand evidence for the way of life, the faith and practice of a major Jewish sect. (3) It is in connection with the New Testament that the Scrolls should make their largest contribution to biblical studies. Early Christianity had very close affinities with and arose out of apocalyptic Judaism, a form of which is faithfully reflected in the Scrolls. Not only is the thought-world and biblical exegesis of the New Testament represented in the Scrolls, but much of the theological vocabulary of the New Testament is a rendering in Greek of the Hebrew terminology of the Scrolls. There are points of contact with the Scrolls throughout the New Testament; it is perhaps surprising that the Johannine and Pauline writings, as well as the Epistle to the Hebrews, have especially close parallels in the Qumran treatises.

The Scrolls, and here we include the later documents of the latter part of the 1st century and the early part of the 2nd century C.E., confirm the view that Palestine in this period was multilingual. Not only are there documents in Hebrew (both the archaizing "biblical" dialect of many of the Qumran scrolls and the contemporary colloquial Mishnaic, as in the Copper scroll), Aramaic, and Greek, but also in Latin and Nabatean.

c. We cannot close this abbreviated presentation without some reference to the vast amount of manuscript material which bears directly or indirectly on the text and language of the New Testament. Since the founding of this Society, which marked the triumph of the so-called Neutral text favored by Westcott and Hort, a large number of papyri containing portions of the New Testament have been found. Many of these are older than the great uncial manuscripts of the 4th century which form the basis for the present critical editions of the New Testament; one is so old that in terms of mathematical probability it bears on the question of the date of original composition, i.e., it helps to fix a *terminus ad quem* for the autograph. I refer to the John Rylands fragment of the Gospel of John which is conservatively dated on epigraphic grounds to the second quarter of the 2nd century. Thus it lends support to the view held by certain scholars that John is one of the earlier New Testament writings. Other New Testament papyri from the 3rd century (the principal collections are the Chester Beatty and Bodmer papyri), reveal a mixed textual situation antecedent to the emergence of the standard text-types.

In addition to the manuscripts of the New Testament text and versions there are many other ancient documents less directly related to the New Testament, but showing dependence on its contents through quotations or allusions. Thus the great hoard of Gnostic Christian codices found at Chenoboskion in Egypt are of particular value for New Testament studies. These manuscripts were written in Coptic, and date from the 4th century C.E. It is clear however, that they are translations or adaptations from Greek documents of the 3rd and 2nd centuries. Many of them show direct dependence upon the canonical gospels (especially John) and other New Testament writings. They differ so markedly in character from the New Testament that it is difficult to escape the conclusion that by the time of their composition the New Testament was already complete and had achieved authoritative if not canonical status. Briefly we may say that just as these works derive from the 2nd century and following, the New Testament is clearly a product of an earlier period, the 1st century.

With respect to the language of the New Testament, a principal contribution has come from the thousands of nonbiblical papyri of the same period. It is at once clear that the Greek of the New Testament is essentially the same as the Koine of the papyri. Many expressions in the New Testament have been clarified by the papyri, and interesting nuances and overtones detected in the same fashion. On the other hand, there is a specifically biblical cast to the language of the New Testament, as comparison with the Septuagint shows. Further, the Septuagint, through its rendering of key Old Testament terms, provided the basic theological vocabulary for the New Testament writers. A third factor is present also; the specifically sectarian vocabulary of the Scrolls is matched in the Greek of the New Testament. There is no question of priority since the Scrolls all antedate the New Testament books, but both may derive from a common source in Hasidic Judaism. In any case, the language of the New Testament, which is Greek, is nevertheless thoroughly grounded in biblical, Jewish, Palestinian soil — where we may add that Greek had also been deeply rooted since the 4th and 3rd centuries B.C.E.

Conclusion

It will be seen from this survey that a vast amount of material has been unearthed which bears on our understanding of the biblical languages. Much work has been done, but much more remains to be done before the importance of these materials can be fully appreciated. In view of the constantly increasing supply of data and the fantastic rate of accretion, it is, however, a losing battle. At the moment we need more workers on the material found than finders of new material. Nevertheless, remarkable progress in decipherment, interpretation, and application has been made, and the future looks even brighter.

In the discussion of the biblical languages, it should be remembered that they were never lost. A continuous tradition of interpretation accompanied the transmission of the text. And this is reflected in the versions and commentaries from earliest times. Nevertheless, in the process certain lexicographical and grammatical points were forgotten or misconstrued. There was inevitable modernizing in orthography, diction, and other features of the language, whereby obsolete and archaic elements tended to be sloughed off. Fortunately in the case of the Bible there was an equally powerful resistance to change, and scribes faithfully reproduced the text before them whether they understood it in detail or not, and even when it posed serious problems to the interpreter. Because of this tenacity in transmission scholars have been able to recover, with the help of the inscriptional evidence, words and forms, meanings and constructions, which had long been forgotten. Thus archaeology makes its principal contribution to the study of the biblical languages in two areas:

1. The nonbiblical materials help to give a clearer picture of the dimensions and character of the languages which are only partially represented in the Bible. Since the inscriptions also come from a variety of places and periods, they provide a basis for analyzing the biblical languages according to a historical perspective, and thereby yield clues as to date and authorship. It is also possible to recover lost words and lost meanings, grammatical devices and uses: in short, to do justice to the biblical material. This is especially true of Hebrew poetry where we have much to learn about the canons which governed its composition.

2. Sensational discoveries in the past decades have provided us with very old manuscripts of the books of the Old Testament and New Testament. For the Old Testament, we are now in a position to practice serious text criticism, i.e., the classification of manuscripts and comparison of standard text-types in the preparation of an eclectic critical edition of the Hebrew Bible. When finally established (at least for the historical books), it will reflect the best manuscript tradition of the 2nd, 3rd, and even 4th centuries B.C.E. rather than being the resultant text of the 1st and 2nd centuries C.E.

For New Testament studies, the papyri have made it possible to penetrate beyond the standard text-types to the earlier stages of text transmission, when variations from the autographs and early copies first appeared and began to congeal into groups. Just what will emerge from these studies is not yet clear, but the chances are excellent for ultimately recovering or reconstructing an archetypal text not more than a generation or two from the autographs.

There can be little question of the value or usefulness of archaeological data in the determination of the biblical text and the clarification of its meaning. Presuppositions and methods must constantly be checked and revised and refined, and there is always danger of misuse and misinterpretation. Movement and progress unfortunately are not the same. Still there has been both movement and progress, and there will be more of both.

It is my understanding that among the founders of the Society of Biblical Literature and Exegesis were members of the American Committee for the revision of the King James Version of the Bible, the English edition of which appeared in 1885, to be followed in 1901 by the American Standard Version. These revisions signaled a change in the scholarly climate, a basic shift in mood and approach. The translators stood at the end of a long line of dedicated scholars and were heirs of a great tradition. Their work reflected that fact. But they also stood at the threshold of a new era, marked by accelerating change, and stimulated by archaeological discovery. In the 84 years since the founding of the Society vastly more information about the Bible and its world has come into our hands than in the preceding 840 years or more. The rate of Bible revision and translation has increased rapidly. Even current translations are outmoded soon after they appear because of the new materials literally spilling out of the earth all the time. For we are just in the preliminary stages of scholarship so far as the biblical world is concerned. I am confident that the future will see such strides made and gains secured as will make past efforts seem tepid and timid.

20

Toward a Common Bible?

Thanks to widespread and continuing discussion in the popular press and more scholarly publications, the "common Bible" has become in the eyes of many an important goal of the ecumenical movement. Let it be said at once that a common Bible is an entirely legitimate and worthy objective toward the achievement of which much progress has already been made; and there is excellent promise of further attainment along these lines. At the same time it is important to define the common Bible more carefully and to evaluate its significance more realistically than would appear to be the case from some of the extravagant claims made for this project.

The issue is at once simpler and more complex than appears from the usual presentation of the common Bible. The emphasis is naturally on the achievement of a common translation or version that would be acceptable to the major religious groups and to the public in general. While that is a central element of concern, it is by no means the whole of the problem. On the one hand, a satisfactory English rendering of the Bible poses no insuperable difficulties. The Revised Standard Version of the Bible, under general Protestant sponsorship (though not exclusively), has had wide acceptance and not only among Protestant churches. The Catholic Confraternity version and the new Jewish Publication Society edition, though not complete, are also renderings of high merit and wide appeal. What is important about them is the comparatively slight differences among them. There is a common body of scholarship behind these versions which guarantees an essentially common result, subject to the usual variations of style and nuance. Sometimes one will catch the sense of the original more felicitously, sometimes another. Similarly one may stray inadvertently from the true meaning or reproduce the original woodenly, while another may catch the real significance of the passage in a daring turn of phrase or vivid figure of speech. But so far as I have been able to determine, the differences are not theologically significant and do not reflect in any way the ancient cleavages between the different religious bodies. It would take no great effort to compile a common Bible from existing translations, one which could satisfy the ecclesiastical authorities as to its fidelity, and scholars as to its accuracy, whatever literary shortcomings might result from such a procedure. In fact such a project is well along the road to publication and should appear shortly.

On the other hand, the common Bible involves a good deal more than simply a usable common translation. There remains the question of a common canon (i.e., a common table of contents), a common text (i.e., a common original Bible), and a common understanding expressed in a common rendering and commentary, to say nothing of the implications of such an enterprise for a common faith and finally a common Church. It is only as a link in a long chain of cooperative interfaith projects that the common Bible makes serious sense today. Otherwise it is simply a useful makeshift, designed to serve in those situations where a sectarian Bible would not do, as in interfaith ceremonies or study groups, or possibly in the public schools. As such it would have immediate relevance and applicability to certain local short-term situations but in the long run promises more than it could fulfill. It would be helpful and desirable as a symbol of ecumenical activity and progress, but it should be clearly connected with the other aspects of the common Bible suggested above.

Without cooperative pursuit and attainment of these related objectives a common translation alone cannot guarantee the reunion of the churches or protect their unity once achieved. It will reflect the growing unity of the churches and their willingness to be associated in joint endeavors of importance, rather than create or promote it — though the impetus of a common translation in general use may itself contribute to the success of the ecumenical movement. At the same time it should be remembered that a common Bible is no guarantee of ecclesiastical unity: witness the dismaying fragmentation of Protestantism in the centuries after the Reformation, the many separating branches of the Church all appealing to the same Scriptures and often to the same translation to justify their independence. In short the Bible can be, as it has been, a source of division as well as of unity, and a common Bible no less than the ones in use hitherto and in our time.

With these considerations in mind, let us turn to the broad question of a common Bible.

1. A Common Scholarship

Underlying the enthusiasm for and movement toward a common Bible is a vast body of scholarship which forms the necessary foundation for any project in this field. The community of scholars crosses all confessional lines and includes many who profess no particular religious beliefs. It is an international group of scholars who have pooled their knowledge and through vigorous argument and debate have refined methods and attained results far in advance of previous efforts. The archaeological revolution — now in its second century of spectacular activity in the Near East — has contributed substantially to the growth of a common scholarship of the Bible. While no scholar stands entirely free of his confessional commitment and/or his philosophical and emotional presuppositions, and bias of some sort, in greater or lesser degree, is present in all scholarly work in this field, such prejudices or tendencies are more easily identified and discounted in an ecumenical setting, and in the course of discussion conflicting biases (elements of *Tendenz*) tend to cancel out.

In the present state of world biblical scholarship, it is not possible to speak of specifically Protestant, Catholic, or Jewish positions with respect to the interpretation of biblical or background materials, though different and opposing positions may be represented by scholars of one or the other of these faiths. There is a bewildering variety of groupings for and against different hypotheses cutting across traditional lines, thus effectively dissociating biblical scholarship from age-old ecclesiastical direction or control.

While we cannot speak of a scholarly consensus, if we mean agreement on all major scholarly issues relating to the Bible and its Near Eastern background, to say nothing of minor points, we can point to common scholarly assumptions, axioms, methodology, and a common body of technical results: archaeological, linguistic, and historical. And the body of assured results, universally accepted by qualified scholars in every country and of every religious background, increases all the time.

2. A Common Text

The first task of scholarship in dealing with the common Bible is the determination of a common text as close to the original text as it is possible to get. This is a complex and painstaking enterprise involving many scholars and many years of effort. At present five great textual projects are under way, some just started, others well advanced, none complete. The first is a new critical edition of the Hebrew Bible under the sponsorship of the Hebrew University in Jerusalem. It is designed to replace the inadequate Biblia Hebraica of Kittel, now in general scholarly use, and will be based on the famous Aleppo Codex of the Old Testament, the oldest and best complete text known. A greatly expanded critical apparatus will be appended to the text, providing the significant variant readings of Hebrew manuscripts including the Dead Sea Scrolls, as well as of the major versions: Septuagint, Peshitta, Vulgate, etc. This project has only been started in the last few years and may not be finished for decades. Valuable preliminary studies have been published, and the text and at least partial apparatus should appear within a reasonable time.

Continuing with the Old Testament, there is the long-term Septuagint project now nearing completion. The work has been carried on in England and Germany under separate auspices and with some variation in publication procedure and format. The Cambridge Old Testament in Greek covers the Historical Books, while the Göttingen Septuagint has proceeded with the Prophets and Writings. The combined work, of which the Cambridge volume on Genesis appeared in 1906, has proved an invaluable source for the oldest and most important of the versions of the Hebrew Bible; but because of the length of the time involved, it is already in need of revision in the light of new discoveries and the refinement of text-critical methods. But then, projects of such magnitude and requiring so much time for preparation and publication must always be regarded as being in process and subject to continual review and revision.

Next we may mention the International New Testament Project, now some years in process. With headquarters at the University of Chicago, it has enlisted scholars all over the world in the task of preparing an eclectic text of the Greek New Testament and as nearly exhaustive a critical apparatus as is now possible. Preliminary drafts have been circulated and official publication of selected books of the New Testament is expected to commence in due course.

Finally there are two projects dealing with principal versions of the Bible (both Old and New Testaments) of lesser significance for the determination of the original text, but of importance in their own right. They are the new critical edition of the Vulgate being prepared and published by the Benedictine Order, and the International Peshitta Project under Dutch sponsorship but utilizing an international team of scholars.

International and interfaith scholarly cooperation in massive studies of this kind received its initial impetus from the Dead Sea Scroll discoveries. Several volumes have already appeared, with many more yet to come, under the auspices of an international team of Catholic and Protestant scholars. Other scrolls, chiefly from the first cave, have been published by scholars in America and Israel, thus providing additional variety to the interfaith mixture. Many of these scrolls are texts of Old Testament books and have generated a great deal of new interest in textual studies in the Hebrew Bible and thus provide ample justification for the Hebrew Bible project mentioned above. At the same time recent discoveries of New Testament manuscripts (among the Bodmer papyri) along with a wide sampling of noncanonical Christian gospels and related literature (i.e., the Chenoboskion or Nag Hammadi Coptic texts) have provided welcome data for the study of the text of the New Testament.

The magnitude of these enterprises has necessitated cooperation on a large scale, thus involving scholars of different faiths and backgrounds. The international, interfaith team, especially in textual studies, has come into favor and contributed notably to the ecumenical cause in providing a solid noncontroversial foundation for further cooperative ventures in the investigation of the Bible. It should be noted that textual studies, competently and carefully handled, are the most easily undertaken in cooperative efforts across sectarian lines and least likely to stir dogmatic controversies. These undertakings, especially those of an interfaith character, have proved of great value as exercises in cooperative scholarship. And they have demonstrated that in such work there is a scholarship common to all three faiths and to no faith in particular. While details will take decades to work out, and in fact the process of text-definition will never end, it is already possible to speak of a common text, that is a text of the Bible, representing the consensus of scholars, which most closely approaches the original — recognizing that in places it is not possible to determine which of two readings is superior or more original, and that in others the text is hopelessly corrupt, and recovery or reconstruction of the original is not presently possible. Apart from these considerations, there is already in the process of formation a common scholarly Bible — in Hebrew, Aramaic, and Greek.

3. A Common Meaning

By this we understand not simply the rendering or translation of the original into another language, nor the formal commentary which sets forth the interpretation and significance of the text, but rather the determination of the sense of the passage which underlies both translation and interpretation. We have reference to the "plain meaning" which is the proper subject of scholarly investigation, i.e., to recover so far as possible the meaning intended by the author, in the light of the contemporary setting and available data. Beyond this, scholarship in the scientific sense can hardly go; in fact this goal itself is not easily realized, and there remain many obscurities in the text, many gaps in our knowledge, and many opportunities for progress toward this relatively simple and clearly defined objective. When it comes to the "fuller sense," or secret and hidden meanings unknown to the author, or esoteric implications and significations revealed to later inspired interpreters, we acknowledge the validity of the matter as a subject for inquiry and description, but we can hardly expect scholars to discover such meanings or justify them by historico-grammatical exegesis. The problem of pneumatic interpretation actually arises at a different point in the discussion and will be treated there. The proper elucidation of the plain meaning often requires more than a word-for-word rendering, either an extensive paraphrase or ample annotation explaining the circumstances or obscure details only hinted at or assumed in the original. If the object is to place the contemporary reader in the situation of the original audience, then he must be supplied with all relevant data assumed to be in the possession of those directly addressed by the author. As with the common text, so here too a scholarly consensus has been shaping for many years and — aside from the intractability of the material — there are no obstacles to further progress toward the recovery of the meaning of the original, which will be the common possession of all those concerned with the Bible.

4. A Common Rendering

A translation is a device for making a literary work available to people who are at home in another language. It is inevitably inadequate to its purpose: to be faithful to the original, and to do justice to the translation language. Since knowledge of the former steadily improves, while at the same time the latter is changing, all translations are provisional and require constant revision. To re-create for the new audience the setting of the original and convey nuances and overtones along with the central core of meaning are generally beyond the skill of the translator or the capacity of the language, short of adding extensive notes and explanations, which would change the translation into a lengthy commentary and distort the impression of the original in other ways. In short, there is no easy solution to the problems of translation, as those who have attempted this arduous and thankless task have universally testified.

Under the circumstances the notion that a single certain translation can satisfy all the requirements of the original and serve the needs and purposes of the modern reader is unduly optimistic if not delusive. There is nothing wrong with a variety of translations, such as are available today, so long as they are reasonably faithful to the original and informed by a scientific scholarly spirit, rather than some frivolous or arbitrary intention. On the contrary, depending upon the particular concerns or objectives of the translator, there should be many translations of different kinds, each rendering a distinctive service to the reader: whether in formal or colloquial language, for public or private use; whether literal (word for word) or free (phrase for phrase, sense for sense), etc. Two points deserve special mention:

1. An official or exclusively authorized translation might be of questionable value, and could even become an obstacle to progress. Such a translation, approved by the major ecclesiastical bodies for use in churches (and synagogues) and at public functions, would serve an important purpose. It would also carry with it immense prestige and authority, and if of high scholarly and literary quality would surely dominate the English-speaking world. In time it might drive all competitors from the field, as in fact the King James Version did, over a period of centuries. Not only would translations, useful for private reading and valuable for unusual insights into the meaning of the original and rendering of the original into the translation tongue, be lost in this process, but the impulse for new translations might easily be inhibited, thus delaying or obstructing the normal process of revision and improvement. The better the official translation, the worse might be the effects in the long run.

Such dangers can be circumvented, of course, and the value of an authorized version should not be minimized. The churches need only stipulate the uses for which the translation is authorized, without prejudice to other translations in existence or yet to be made, which may be equally helpful or useful to the general reader. Further it should be officially recognized that the authorized translation is neither final nor perfect and a continuing committee of scholars should have as a permanent task the review and revision of the work — issuing new and improved editions at specified intervals until the time comes for a brand-new translation.

The nature of the ecclesiastical endorsement is another consideration of importance. To approve a translation on doctrinal or dogmatic grounds or as otherwise conforming to ecclesiastical standards would imply, and only serve to perpetuate in the minds of many this notion, that the meaning and rendering of the Bible was somehow subject to the authority of church or synagogue. The authority of such bodies in matters of interpretation and application is a serious question in its own right. But the matter of rendering belongs in the realm of scholarship, and the only significant test is that of accuracy, whether the translator has done his work in accordance with the best available scientific data and methods: archaeological, historical, and linguistic. On the side of literary quality and acceptability, other criteria must be applied, but these too have nothing to do with doctrinal propriety. The worth of a translation depends finally upon its scholarly or literary excellence, which ecclesiastical authority cannot confer by approval, nor deny by disapproval. Scholarship must be free and responsible, but its responsibility is to be faithful to the text and meaning of the original.

2. In the pursuit of a common English Bible, we should nevertheless bear in mind that the only true common Bible is one that already exists, or once existed: the original text in the original languages, and then only insofar as it can be recovered by modern scholarship. A translation can at best imperfectly reflect the original. In the quest of an unattainable goal, therefore, the endeavor itself is often more important than the objective. Thus the work of translating, carried on by a suitable committee of scholars, chosen by the various ecclesiastical bodies, but including also eminent scholars without such affiliations, would provide a setting for cooperative enterprise which would at once reflect and promote the ecumenical movement. Through such creative interchange and cross-fertilization of scholarly ideas, much more will be accomplished than a common translation; and the scholarly by-products of such activity may in the long run be more significant than the translation itself.

At the same time that such a committee is at work, other enterprises should be encouraged and undertaken. Formal committee translations are inevitably formal: slow and ponderous, suitable for solemn assemblies and public gatherings. But individual efforts at translation should also be spurred. What is needed is not one common Bible but many, which will reflect the diversity of meaning and variety of rendering possible in dealing with the Bible. It is said that the Bible suffers in translation more than any other great classic; this inescapable loss can be remedied in part at least by a multiplicity of renderings. In their variety and scope something of the range of the original can be captured. Often it is only through extensive trial and error that the most suitable expression is arrived at. We register a complaint about the existing and projected modern formal translations — e.g., the Revised Standard

Version, the Confraternity, and the Jewish Publication Society versions — because of their sectarian sponsorship. The translations themselves are unexceptionable in their scholarship and largely successful in the quality of their renderings, but they continue to bear the stamp of a particular ecclesiastical organization.

Surely the time has passed for such narrow sponsorship of an enterprise that is appropriately the task of all men of goodwill, and especially those who have been nurtured in the traditions of the Western world. The translations themselves hardly reflect the character of their sponsorship, and aside from minor and largely irrelevant details could each serve as the prototype of a general or common version. In short, the Bible and its translators are already ahead of the sponsoring organizations; it is to be hoped that future Bible translations will have the ecumenical backing and sponsorship they deserve.

5. A Common Interpretation

If the text of the Bible and its meaning can be determined satisfactorily, there should be no serious difficulty about a common interpretation. At this point the learned discussions among scholars of diverse backgrounds and beliefs have been helpful in locating and holding common ground. With respect to historical linguistic considerations, i.e., the explanation of the text in its local and temporal setting, the results of ecumenical scholarship are encouraging, and within the limits of reasonable scholarly disagreement, a common position is emerging. Certainly it cannot be said that scholarly positions are drawn along confessional lines or that usually divergences are greater between scholars of different faiths than among those of the same communion so far as interpretation and evaluation of biblical material are concerned. There is considerable ferment about critical questions, which is always a sign of vigor in any scholarly field, but the wide variety of views held by scholars cannot be grouped and labeled "Protestant," "Catholic," or "Jewish."

When we move from the realm of the strictly exegetical interpretation of the text to that of more esoteric and less scientific procedures, the situation becomes more complex. Since pneumatic exegesis has always been the special province of religious groups, and we would include here allegorical and typological exegesis, along with other less well known devices for interpreting the biblical text, it is naturally more difficult to deal with such matters in a dispassionate scholarly fashion. It is even less likely that scholarly analysis will ever alter or affect traditionally held interpretations of particular biblical passages, especially as these have been reinforced by the weight of opinion of the great doctors of Church and Synagogue. Nevertheless some progress has been made at least in classifying the different hermeneutical phenomena involved, and in analyzing the methods used and the results obtained. By drawing the boundaries between the areas of legitimate scientific inquiry and those which belong to tradition and faith, it is possible for ecumenical scholars to proceed together as far as those limits beyond which they must part company.

For the present it would seem preferable to describe the variety of "fuller meanings" objectively, indicating the different ways in which the Bible has been and can be interpreted beyond the plain meaning of the text, recognizing the flexibility, fluidity, and diversity of such approaches and treatments of the material. We would make a clear distinction between the recovery of the essential meanings of any passage and all those derived significations which can in any manner be drawn or developed from the text in the light of later Scripture or the experience of the religious community. To the latter we would attribute a derivative value so far as the original passage is concerned, but one of prime importance for the situation in which they arose and to which they were applied. In short, these derived meanings have a significant place in the history of those communities which preserved and cherished the Bible and found it meaningful in their continuing existence on earth.

Once it is recognized that the ongoing life of the Church and Synagogue was nourished by the Scriptures in their original or translated form and that all secondary meanings and interpretations, no matter how esoterically arrived at, are nevertheless derived from that original, then the renewed concern for the same original will be entirely understandable. For it is out of that original text that new meanings and applications will emerge to guide the life of the sacred people of God. Thus scholarly concern for the historical-linguistic exegesis of the original text may seem somewhat farfetched and remote from the current needs and demands of the religious community, but I am confident that such labors will provide the source materials upon which the Church and Synagogue may draw for inspiration and guidance, making the necessary adaptation and adjustment to the changing conditions of every new age.

I have confidence that the God of the Scriptures, who is also the Creator and Sustainer of Church and Synagogue, will not permit his words to perish or become outmoded, but will continually renew their meaning and force for the believing and worshipping community to which he has chosen to make known his history among men and his will for them. So long as the peoples of the Book agree as to the essential contents and their plain meaning, a freedom with respect to more esoteric patterns of interpretation and explanation may be granted.

6. A Common Faith

A common Bible should ultimately mean a common conviction and allegiance to a common God and lead to a reunion of the Church and the Synagogue, based on a common biblical faith. Such a consummation seems very far off indeed, but perhaps a distant vision is as necessary to progress as more practical schemes designed for immediate implementation. We picture the faith and order of the believing community growing out of its response to the summons of God in the Bible. Such words may have a familiar Protestant ring about them, but our intention and understanding are otherwise. The movement toward reunion is a dual one: backwards to the beginnings, the origin and roots of the community of faith, forwards to a common understanding and acceptance of the nuclear traditions of the past.

We think of the Bible here as the central expression and embodiment of the tradition of the people of God, as the key witness to the mighty deeds of the covenant Deity which form the foundation of all belief and provide the framework for the organization and life of the divine community. Consequently the more accurate our knowledge of that tradition and the more substantial our faith in and commitment to it, the closer we must draw to that original community of God and toward each other. That an open and honest reexamination of the sources of our faith will have serious repercussions in the established religious institutions and may undermine cherished notions about ancient doctrines and practices is a risk we must all be willing to take. That it can lead to a genuine renewal and reformation of the Church and Synagogue is also true, and more important.

7. A Common Canon

At the center of the discussion of the common Bible is the question of the canon or, put another way, that of Scripture and Tradition. There are groups in both the Protestant and Catholic camps who distinguish sharply between Scripture and Tradition, though they may differ seriously as to the relative value they place on each. It seems to me that there is a better approach to the matter, and one increasingly recognized by scholars: that there is a single stream to which both belong, not separate streams. Scripture itself is tradition, the product of the coalescence and reshaping of traditions. It arises out of and points to the tradition; it embodies many stages in the process by which the traditions of Israel and the early Church were solidified into fixed form. It is at the same time part of the endless process by which the sacred community expresses its self-consciousness as the people of God. Thus it takes the experiences which were determinative of its existence and normative for its way of life, shapes and interprets them, formulates and records them: a diary of its past history with God and a manual for its future conduct, i.e., the tradition by which it is to live. Scripture is the epitome of tradition, its first and finest flower. But there is a continuous line from Scripture to Tradition, or from the Tradition formulated in Scripture and the tradition which finds expression in other ways. All belong to the experience and memory of the holy people and have their place because of it. Not all traditions are of equal merit; not all are true or

209

important for the life of the community; and a constant process of careful sifting is the necessary characteristic of a self-critical reformable and reforming Church.

Scripture and Tradition, properly considered, blend together, with Scripture at the center from which traditions radiate outwards, or about which they collect. The key issue between Catholics and Protestants in the discussion of the canon is the Old Testament Apocrypha. They form a significant body of traditional material shedding invaluable light on the so-called intertestamental period (from the 3rd to the 1st centuries B.C.E.). Quite apart from dogmatic considerations, the value of these books (and others like them from the same period, the so-called Pseud-epigrapha) cannot be denied, especially by those who are seriously engaged in recovering the world of the Bible and its real meaning.

Perhaps the term deuterocanonical, suitably defined, could be revived and used for these books. For it would appear that while this literature is biblical in tone and character and belongs to the same tradition from which the (other) Old Testament books derive, it does not belong to the mainstream of salvation history. In all likelihood the line of division should not be drawn precisely at this point, since other books of the Hebrew Bible might well be relegated to secondary status, like Esther or the Song of Songs. It might be well to consider various Jewish attempts to evaluate comparatively the different sections of the Hebrew Bible: the Torah was preeminent, with the Prophets, Former and Latter, not less the word of God, only slightly inferior in importance, while the Writings ranged widely from that status.

By thus graduating the contents of both Old and New Testaments it would be possible to achieve a flexible and workable canon, inclusive and expandable, but recognizing significant distinctions in value and importance. Thus we can make place for ancient texts but newly come to light, as for example the Qumran scrolls which attest to a tradition within pre-Christian Judaism the nature and scope of which could not previously be estimated with accuracy. They are directly related to the story of faith and incidentally illuminate the subsequent history of Judaism and the origins of Christianity. By ready yet critical acceptance of tradition as decisive for the life of the Church and acknowledgment of Scripture at its center surrounded by traditional materials of great though lesser value, we may be able to do justice to this substantial issue. By combining Scripture and Tradition instead of opposing them, we will ultimately come to a better comprehension of both.

Properly understood, the quest for a common Bible involves the whole life of the believing community: sustained by a common scholarship we must proceed from a common text and a common understanding to a common rendering and a common interpretation. These will lead to a common faith expressed in a common canon, which in turn will provide the key to the pivotal question of Scripture and Tradition. In its resolution may well be the future of the ecumenical movement and the hope of ultimate reunion.

21

Religious Freedom
and the Old Testament

No one with an awareness of the history of the Christian Church could fail to be moved by the drama of Vatican Council II, not least in its forthright declaration on religious freedom. Who could have thought twenty years ago, or even ten, that such a statement would be formally proclaimed under the seal of the Pope and the assembled bishops of the Catholic communion? Those of us who have watched the Council in its deliberations and actions with attentive interest and growing enthusiasm can only be thankful for the manifest grace of God in guiding the Council, and can only applaud the fathers of the Church for their courage and willingness to move with the leading of the Holy Spirit, especially in the area of religious freedom. For it is clear that this affirmation is at once the presupposition and objective of the proclamation of the Gospel, as well as providing the necessary and indispensable framework for the ecumenical dialogue now taking place. Only in an atmosphere of liberty, free of any taint of coercion from without or within, can biblical faith truly prosper and the reunion of separated brethren be contemplated and promoted.

The topic selected for my presentation is "Religious Freedom and the Christian Revelation." Since I am to share the title with my esteemed colleague and close friend, Fr. John L. McKenzie, I will seize what little advantage there may be in making the initial presentation by choosing that smaller segment of the whole that is more congenial to my interest and, incidentally, the only area in which I could claim any competence, namely the Old Testament and its bearing on the subject of religious freedom. I confess however, that I feel a little like those innumerable prophets of Baal at Mt. Carmel, who were persuaded by Elijah to enter the competition first, while he took the more modest second but devastatingly effective counterpunching position. The melancholy consequences for the frontrunners need not be rehearsed here.

There is a statement in the document before us concerning the relationship of religious freedom to revelation, which will serve as a point of contact and departure for us: "Revelation does not indeed affirm in so many words the right of man to immunity from external coercion in matters religious" (article 9). The statement occurs in a paragraph in which it is affirmed that the doctrine of religious freedom is entirely consistent with revelation. ". . . This doctrine of freedom has roots in divine revelation. . . . It is therefore completely in accord with the nature of faith that in matters religious every manner of coercion on the part of men should be excluded" (articles 9-10). The argument is developed by citing the example of Jesus and his followers in promoting the Gospel and enlisting men in the community of faith. A number of passages from the New Testament are quoted or mentioned in support of the contention that, in matters religious, Jesus and his followers did not have recourse to coercive authority (a single passage of the Old Testament, Isa. 42:1-4, is used as a description of Jesus' activity in this regard). While we should be and are in hearty agreement with the inferences drawn concerning religious freedom, we may be less certain of the exegetical propriety of the interpretation placed on the New Testament passages, and even more dubious of their applicability to the question of religious freedom. But leaving that problem to the attention of someone better able to handle it, like my successor, let us turn to the Old Testament, which, as we pointed out, has been left untouched in the declaration. On the basis of this fact it might be supposed or inferred that there is nothing in the Old Testament that bears on the question. In point of fact the opposite is true: almost everything does. The Old Testament simply teems with relevant data arising out of concrete historical situations in which the issue of religious freedom figures prominently. There is an acute problem of selection and organization, as well as of interpretation and evaluation, but not of the lack of pertinent material.

Not having heard the full story of the nine editions of the declaration, I can only guess as to the reasons for the systematic exclusion of the Old Testament. There has always been a marked tendency in the Church to slight or pass over the Old Testament on the bland assumption that it has been displaced by the New Testament. This is one of the oldest heresies in the history of the Church, but it has proved extremely tenacious and crops up in different forms in every generation. In any form, however, it reflects a misreading of the Bible and the false understanding of the New Testament itself. It is all the more ironic to find this situation in the Church at a time when archaeological discoveries have provided us with potent tools to unlock the secrets of the Bible, enabling us to grasp its content and meaning with greater skill and better understanding than was possible in the past, and so to appreciate its continuity and essential unity.

Another and possibly more cogent consideration may be hidden in the assertion that the doctrine of religious freedom is consistent with revelation, which I take to include the Scriptures. As a matter of fact, it has long been widely held by students of the Bible that the Old Testament is not in agreement with this doctrine, and that neither religious freedom nor its common accompaniment, religious diversity, is really contemplated, much less approved, in the Old Testament. Thus, the lack of reference to the Old Testament could be explained on the grounds that the Old Testament had nothing positive to contribute to the doctrine of religious freedom. In other words, the fathers of the Council, having strong convictions about the validity and necessity of the doctrine, knew where they wanted to come out, but were considerably less certain about the argument from Scripture, especially the Old Testament. An effort was made to relate the doctrine to the New Testament, as we have seen, but the Old Testament was given up as a bad job, if the attempt was made at all.

Perhaps the matter should be dropped at this point, as the bishops in their wisdom left it; and it may seem picayune to many to cavil at a matter of this kind. But it seems to me to be a valid expression of the spirit of religious freedom (though some may prefer to call it an example of Protestant anarchism) to suggest that the biblical, specifically, Old Testament, data is important for the discussion of the question, and could contribute both positively and negatively to a better understanding and formulation of the doctrine. It is first of all a matter of presenting the biblical material squarely, and then of dealing with it constructively in the light of tradition and experience.

What is often regarded as the essential teaching of the Old Testament on the subject may be found in a typical passage dealing with the conquest of the land of Canaan (Deut. 7:1-5, 16ff.). When the Israelites invade the land, they are to have no contact with the local inhabitants, but are to exterminate them. In the process, the religion of Canaan is to be ruthlessly suppressed in all its manifestations. Yahwism is to be the sole religion of the land and its people. There is to be no tolerance of religious diversity, no religious freedom. The imposition of Israelite religious obligations on alien residents *(gerim)* and slaves, as well as the enforcement of laws against mixed marriages (involving people of different religious communities) in the days of Ezra and Nehemiah, only strengthen the case. Apparent exceptions to these rules, like the construction of shrines dedicated to pagan deities by Solomon, and the encouragement of Baal worship in the days of Ahab and Jezebel, are roundly denounced by the prophets as violations of the basic terms of covenant religion. If this data does not exactly point in the direction of the doctrine of religious freedom, at least it may help to explain why the several churches, Catholic and Protestant, labored under the impression for centuries that they should go and do likewise.

Admittedly, the initial impression is rather a grim one for the doctrine of religious freedom, and we might well be tempted to look elsewhere for something more palatable to the modern taste, or more in keeping with what conscience unmistakably tells us is the necessary truth for our day. Before we do so, however, it might not be amiss to examine even this terrifying material more closely. Whether such an exercise is worthwhile will depend upon our attitude toward the Scriptures,

213

but for those who believe that in its broad extent it is an authentic record of the experience of a people with its God, it becomes an imperative moral duty to investigate the whole matter further, not omitting the more distasteful data, but attempting to understand, if not wholly to accept it.

With regard to the doctrine of holy war enunciated in the book of Deuteronomy, it is to be noted that it has a limited application to a particular territory at a particular time, and that there is no basis at all for supposing that it is a universal warrant for wholesale slaughter. In addition, and this may seem like a macabre joke, there is actually no thought of conversion by force. It is nowhere suggested that conversion of the Canaanites is either an objective or an option. Their fate has been decided by God for an accumulation of crimes having nothing to do with Israel. Israel is simply the instrument of divine punishment, as the Assyrians and Babylonians were later in relation to Israel. It will be seen that the teaching of the Old Testament at this point is not incompatible with a doctrine of immunity from external coercion in religious matters. The Canaanites were a special case. The neighbors of Israel, with equally detestable religious beliefs and practices, were to be left in peace. The severe territorial limitation of the conquest ensured a world of religious diversity, and a host of nations free to decide their own religious faith and practice. The situation is accepted with equanimity by the biblical historian, who regards it as a permanent feature of human history (cf. Deut. 4:19), a history ordained by God. Israel is not to interfere in any way with the religion of any other nation, but is to live peaceably in the midst of all. To be sure, the prophets speak of the judgment of God against nations that defy his law, and the hope is expressed that in the last days all nations will worship and serve the one true God. But these ends are not to be accomplished by Israel's imperial expansion, or any external coercion. It is to be emphasized that the freedom to order its religious life is extended not only to Israel, the community of the true faith, but to all other nations, in spite of the fact that their religious beliefs and practices are specifically and categorically branded as false. The only exception is the occupants of the Holy Land, whose tenure has been terminated by divine decree (cf. Deut. 9:4-5).

Historically, the independence of Israel, from the time of the exodus, guaranteed the integrity of Israelite religion and protected it from external pressure or coercion. At the same time the power of the state was used to maintain uniform compliance to religious norms, thus restricting the religious freedom of the members of the community. No simple solution to the dilemma of the use of force has ever been devised, but the historical experience of Israel led to a progressive loosening of the links between civil power and the religious community, thus allowing for the development of religious diversity and the gradual abandonment of coercive power in matters religious. From the time of the exile on, the biblical community enjoyed a considerable measure of religious freedom in spite of the loss of political independence. In a setting of this kind religious diversity was possible, and during the last two centuries before the Common Era, a number of different parties or sects appeared within Judaism. The developing diversity within the Jewish community required attitudes of mutual tolerance, if not acceptance and active cooperation. Thus, Rabbi Gamaliel could express the classic doctrine of religious freedom in opposing coercive action with respect to the nascent Christian sect (cf. Acts 5:34-39, esp. v. 38). The biblical data thus brings us to the New Testament witness to the example and practice of Jesus and his disciples, who lived and worked in a setting of religious diversity, which reflected a significant measure of religious freedom. It was the product of scriptural precedent and Jewish tradition, for inevitably the way of the oppressed is the way to religious liberty.

There is another facet of the question that remains to be considered: freedom within the religious community, or the freedom of dissent. We have been speaking largely of the freedom of the religious community from external coercion, but not explicitly of the freedom of the individual within the religious community to diverge or dissent from the consensus. By renouncing the use of force in relation to the individual right of religious decision, the declaration seems to protect the right of dissent in faith and practice. But, in fact, this is not so, or as it has been so carefully explained to us, not yet so. This is in accordance with the practice of all religious communities, which rarely, if ever, permit dissent beyond minimal and peripheral variations from the established norms. Even without the help of coercive civil authority, religious communities have powerful weapons to compel conformity, such as the denial of sacred rites to the rebellious and, ultimately, expulsion from the community. It is difficult to see how a religious community could survive without certain instruments of coercion. Whether these are conceived spiritually or materially, the effect is much the same; that they interfere with and infringe upon the religious liberty of the individual member of the community is undeniable.

The Old Testament acknowledges the authority of divine law and its appointed executors, as well as the coercive power available to the religious community. Violations of the basic standards of faith and practice were to be punished in summary fashion; whether by execution or expulsion is not always clear. There seemed to be little room for dissent, but there was at least one kind that deserves our attention. I refer to the archetypal dissenter in the Bible: the prophet, who often diverged from the consensus both volubly and vigorously, who challenged the establishment, both religious and civil, and survived. His survival was due to the fact that, in Israel, the right of the prophet to immunity from coercion was recognized, not always in practice but certainly in principle. Two passages dealing with prophets help to clarify both the nature and the limitations of this immunity. In Deut. 13:1-5, etc., the limits of dissent are defined. Any would-be prophet who advocates the worship of other gods — in violation of the first and basic commandment — is to be executed forthwith. Such dissent goes beyond acceptable limits, and cannot be tolerated. In Deut. 18, however, a different sort of question is considered: how to distinguish between true and false prophets. The basis for the decision in this case is the validity of their predictions. The prophet whose predictions are confirmed by events is true; the prophet whose predictions fail of fulfillment is false. The story of the confrontation between Jeremiah and Hananiah (cf. Jer. 28) illustrates this principle. The point is that nothing further is said about dealing with the false prophet, except that his words may be disregarded with impunity. It is clear that the nature of the test, waiting until historical events catch up with the predictions, guarantees both men immunity from coercion, at least until the time limit is exhausted. Thus there was a range of dissent permitted to prophets, whether true or false. When Jeremiah was arrested in the temple and charged with religious crimes punishable by death, the defense that proved effective in saving his life was that his words were in the authentic prophetic tradition, that they conformed to the pattern established by earlier prophets like Micah, and thus were considered permissible. It could not then be determined whether Jeremiah was a true prophet, i.e., whether his words would be confirmed by events. But on the basis of precedent and permitted dissent, his life was spared and he continued to prophesy.

We can detect a similar pattern in the career of Jesus. In his role as prophet, he enjoyed a certain immunity from coercion, though he vigorously challenged the religious establishment. It is a sufficient index of the latitude allowed to religious dissent that his enemies finally had to trump up civil charges against him in order to have him executed. Only Stephen among the early disciples was executed on religious grounds, but this was hardly a dispassionate juridical action; rather it was the violent reaction of a mob egged on by his foes. The executions of John the Baptist and James the Apostle are somewhat different, since they were the victims of the arbitrary judgments of vengeful kings. There is a parallel in the death of Uriah the prophet at the hands of Jehoiakim, the king of Judah, an extraordinary action that shocked the writer, and was contrary to established principle.

Altogether the biblical record on the fate of prophets is a good one: some were restrained, others were persecuted, and, doubtless, a few were executed. But the many survived to uphold the principle of dissent, and to leave to us, the community of faith, an invaluable legacy of religious freedom.

In any discussion of religious freedom, the biblical data is important, especially that of the Old Testament, which provides a wide variety of penitent materials in a vast panorama of human experience. In spite of certain obvious and emphatic statements about religious exclusivity and uniformity, and in spite of the close linkage of religious to civil authority and the application of coercive power to maintain religious unity and conformity, the Bible nevertheless bears eloquent witness to the principle of religious freedom.

In summary, the religious community had a basic right to order its life in accordance with its faith, free from coercion by a foreign power or the civil authorities. Such freedom was guaranteed not only to the holy community of Israel, but to many others as well, whether independent nations or autonomous units in a great empire. Needless to say, the right to immunity from external coercion did not depend upon the truth or validity of the religion professed.

The individual or group within the religious community had a certain, more limited, freedom to dissent from the prevailing pattern of faith and practice. The Bible guarantees to the prophet, the prototype of the dissenter, the right to challenge the establishment, whether civil or religious, without losing either his status or freedom in the community, in principle at least, if not always in practice. And in practice at least, if not necessarily in principle, a false prophet enjoyed the same immunity as the true prophet. In fact, false prophets seemed to have suffered less at the hands of their countrymen than true ones.

The churches and the nations might have spared themselves some of the more tragic episodes in human history had they studied more carefully the biblical record on religious freedom, and taken its lessons to heart. There may still be value in reviewing the available material.

22

The Biblical Idea of History

I

An unusual episode in the history of the people of Judah, which is described in the book of Jeremiah (ch. 44), focuses attention on the biblical idea of history. While the ancient setting reflects archaic thought forms which may strike us as quaint and outmoded, there are nevertheless important implications for the modern discussion of the question.

After the second capture of Jerusalem by Nebuchadrezzar, king of Babylonia, in 587 B.C.E., the destruction of the city and the temple by fire, and the second exile of its leading citizens, it appeared that the worst had happened and no further injury would befall the prostrate nation. To forestall any revival of national spirit, the legitimate claimant to the throne of David, Jehoiachin, was kept in protective custody as a hostage of the crown in Babylon where he exercised a shadowy rule among his retainers. At the same time a civilian governor, Gedaliah, looked after the pitiful remnant left behind in Judah. Jeremiah the prophet joined Gedaliah at Mizpah, the provisional capital of the newly constituted province of the Babylonian Empire. Slowly the work of salvage and reconstruction proceeded. Just as some measure of stability and security was being achieved, and hope for peace and prosperity was renewed, an abortive revolution plunged the country into bloodshed and turmoil. A certain adventurer named Ishmael, of the blood royal, fired perhaps by ambitions to restore the monarchy in Judah and abetted by Baalis, king of Ammon, assassinated Gedaliah and massacred the garrison of Babylonian soldiers stationed at Mizpah. Nevertheless, he failed to gain the support of either the army or the people, and fled the country, leaving chaos behind. Fearing Babylonian reprisals, the remaining military leaders decided to abandon the country and seek refuge in Egypt, which still remained independent of the expanding Babylonian Empire. In spite of Jeremiah's plea that they stay in the Holy Land, his assurances that the Babylonians would not harm them, and the promise that God would protect and prosper their enterprise, they insisted not only on going but on taking Jeremiah with them.

The scene shifts abruptly to Tahpanhes in the delta region of Egypt, ironically close to the point from which the Israelites had set forth from Egypt under the aegis of Moses on their high adventure of freedom some seven hundred years before. There and at other cities the refugees gathered and settled. To them Jeremiah, unwilling exile from his homeland, spoke in the name of the God whose words they had persistently disregarded, not so much in the hope that at last they would or might listen, but because he could not do otherwise. A prophet from early youth, he could not now resign his commission or abandon the calling to which God had summoned him more than forty years before. His message was an exposition of those basic principles which govern God's dealings with his people: the biblical idea of history — the prophetic view of the world.

According to Jeremiah, the fall of Judah was the result of persistent defiance of its covenant obligations summed up in the first commandment: exclusive loyalty to Yahweh (cf. Exod. 20:3). By seeking after other gods to worship and serve, Judah had forfeited its place of privilege and protection and had become liable to the divine judgment so lately and devastatingly imposed on the nation. Before this final disaster God had sent his servants the prophets with urgent warnings — with pleas and threats — of the necessity to repent, to change their ways swiftly and completely if they were to escape the condemnation their actions had earned. But they clung to their false gods, thus provoking the righteous indignation of the Lord God, and received the just recompense of their evil deeds. To all their previous wrongdoings the refugees had added a final sin: fleeing from the land to which they belonged and which belonged to them, without regard to the gracious promise of the God to whom they were still bound. Thus they brought upon themselves still another judgment: to be cast forever from the presence of the Lord. They had run away to Egypt to escape the terrors of war; but sword, famine, and plague would pursue and overtake them in the land of the pharaohs and there would their graves be.

To this address by Jeremiah, the people, long since inured to the general content and tone of prophetic utterances, offer a startling response:

> As for the word which you have spoken to us in the name of Yahweh we won't obey you. On the contrary we will assuredly perform every act to which we have solemnly agreed: to burn incense to the queen of heaven and pour libations to her as we have done in the past, we, and our fathers, our kings and officials in the cities of Judah and the streets of Jerusalem. For then we had bread enough and to spare, were well off, and never saw trouble. But from the time we stopped burning incense to the queen of heaven and pouring libations to her, we have lacked everything, and have been destroyed by the sword and famine. (Jer. 44:16-18)

In the debate between people and prophet, welling up from the years of misery and deprivation, the bitter loss of land and status, prosperity and security were the deepest feelings and strongest beliefs of those who had suffered and endured and had had their fill. While their case must be seen in the light of their experience, and is typically overstated by those who are deeply engaged in the struggle, nonetheless they deserve a careful hearing. Here is a radically different view of Judah's recent history. In place of Yahweh, the God of Israel, they invoke the queen of heaven, the universal mother goddess of pagan religion, whose worship was old in the world long before Abraham was set on the road to the Promised Land by a hitherto unknown God. For the refugees, the key to success or failure in the past (and in the future) was the favor of this divine lady. That favor, which was conditioned only by the fulfillment of the stipulated requirement of regular offerings, was the guarantee of prosperity and security. So long as they were faithful to their goddess all went well with them; but when they ceased to worship the queen of heaven, disaster followed, and all their many troubles could be traced to that apostasy. Behind these rather flat statements lay a bitter memory of the lean years of tribulation which had lately been their lot and the fat years of prosperity which had preceded them.

A hundred years before, Manasseh reigned as king in Judah. As his father, Hezekiah, had been one of the best of the kings of the house of David, so Manasseh was easily one of the worst according to the biblical historian (2 Kgs. 21:1-16, but cf. 2 Chr. 33:1-20). He reported that Manasseh had set up a graven image of Asherah (one of whose titles was "the queen of heaven") in the temple in direct violation of the principal commandments. The historian could not find language strong enough to condemn the wicked Manasseh and sees in his misdeeds the ultimate reason for the destruction of the temple, though that did not happen until several generations after Manasseh's reign (cf. 2 Kgs. 23:26). Thus he quotes the judgment of God against Manasseh in scathing terms:

> Behold I am bringing disaster upon Jerusalem and Judah so that the ears of everyone who hears it will tingle. And I will stretch over Jerusalem the measuring line of Samaria and the plummet of the house of Ahab; and I will wipe Jerusalem as one wipes a dish, wiping it and turning it over on its face. . . . And I will cast off the remnant of my heritage and give them into the grasp of their enemies. . . . (2 Kgs. 21:12-14)

In spite of the unfavorable estimate of Manasseh as king and servant of God, his reign was long and apparently peaceful. He submitted to the Assyrian overlords with good grace and paid his tribute regularly. Thus he bought for himself and his land respite from the endless wars of independence on the part of the small nations of the west and the retaliatory expeditions of the Assyrian kings which were mounted with monotonous regularity. The price was high politically and spiritually; but a hundred years later the refugees in Egypt could point with nostalgia to the days of Manasseh and the established worship of Asherah, queen of heaven, as days of divine favor, days of peace and plenty. Who was there to deny the historical evidence for such a claim?

Later in the reign of Josiah, the grandson of Manasseh, conditions were drastically altered. Josiah was reckoned the best of the kings of Judah: "Before him there was no king like him who turned to the Lord with all his heart and with all his soul and with all his might . . . nor did any like him arise after him" (2 Kgs. 23:25). In a radical reformation of the religious practices of the people of Judah, Josiah restored faith and worship according to the ancient traditions and eliminated all idolatry including specifically the altars and images created by Manasseh to honor Asherah (cf. 2 Kgs. 23:12). What was hailed as the great reformation of religion in Judah by the biblical historian marked, however, for the refugees in Egypt, the real source and origin of their troubles. It must be conceded that from the time of Josiah's downfall and death, good king that he was, at the hands of Neco, pharaoh of Egypt (609 B.C.E.), Judah's fortunes collapsed. A series of catastrophes followed one after another until the nation fell and the people were carried into captivity. Thus, for the refugees there was a simple explanation of their present plight and former prosperity. As long as they were faithful to the goddess Asherah, the queen of heaven, all went well, but when they abandoned their goddess, she forsook them and calamity followed disaster. Therefore they would ignore the lesson and warning of the prophet and henceforth resume the faithful worship and service of their goddess.

It will be seen that two radically different patterns of belief and thought stand opposed to one another. They are mutually exclusive, each flatly denying what the other asserts, each affirming a theology of history in total contradiction of the other. The situation is like the contest at Mt. Carmel between Elijah and the prophets of Baal, in which the prophet of Yahweh challenged the people to a choice between gods, insisting that there was neither middle nor common ground for anyone. Here as well there could be no compromise between the refugees and their refugee prophet. If the queen of heaven ruled the world then they were right, and had rightly understood their history and their obligation in worship and service to her. If she was but a piece of polished wood, and Yahweh was indeed creator and sustainer of the universe, then Jeremiah was right; and his interpretation of past and present must stand as the guide of future repentance and a new pledge of obedience. But how to choose between analyses, between affirmations, between deities? For in assessing the issue between them, we cannot claim the advantage of hindsight, and lightly dismiss the claims of the queen of heaven as an imaginary being not worthy of serious consideration. By weighing the arguments in her favor and against her we shall come to a better understanding of the biblical view of history and perhaps a greater appreciation of the issues that tried men's souls in biblical times.

It is important to note well that both interpretations appeal to the data of history as evidence for theological affirmation. The history under consideration — the recent experience of Judah — is the same for both groups, and the facts, the objective data, are not in dispute. Manasseh did indeed institute the worship of Asherah, and so far as we know his reign was a peaceful one. Josiah, on the other hand, was a loyal supporter of Yahweh, and in his reformation of worship he abolished the cult of Asherah. It is also true that his reign, which succeeded auspiciously for a while after the reformation, ended nevertheless, in crushing defeat, and within another twenty-five years the nation itself perished.

The question for the people of Jeremiah's day was which theological hypothesis would best account for the data. Accepting the premise of divine governance and involvement in human affairs, each of the competing parties must explain and justify the ways of his god.

For the adherents of the queen of heaven the analysis was simple and straightforward. It was a matter of satisfying ritual requirements and thereby securing promised benefits. To challenge successfully such a theology and history it would be necessary to disprove one or the other of the two major asseverations, and show that: (1) the queen of heaven was no goddess or (2) the course of historical events was accidentally, not causally, related to the queen of heaven, i.e., a case of *post hoc,* but not *propter hoc.* In fact both arguments are used to refute such a heretical view as expressed by the refugees. From the biblical point of view the queen of heaven was a figment of men's minds, and a creation in wood of their hands. She had no say or sway in human affairs, and the correlation between her worship on the rooftops and the fortunes of Judah was fortuitous except as it related to the covenant obligations to Yahweh of the people engaged in this false worship. The real interpretation of human events is more complex and mysterious, for simplicity and truth are not necessarily coterminous. In his final word to the recalcitrant refugees Jeremiah identifies the central issue: argument about the past is inconclusive; the real test of an hypothesis is the future. In the classic tradition of Moses or Elijah, who confronted and overcame the advocates of the gods of Egypt and Canaan, Jeremiah offers the prediction that the adherents of the queen of heaven will come under the same condemnation as their goddess and perish with her. Let them fulfill their vows to her; it will be a covenant of death for them. The confirming sign will be the invasion and overthrow of Egypt, their hoped-for place of refuge (Jer. 44:24-30).

II

The queen-of-heaven theology and its interpretation of history failed and are no more. But its failure does not establish the validity of the biblical view. On the contrary it leaves questions to be answered, doubts to be resolved. For if so simple and uncomplicated a view of history is without merit, what can be said of the more tortuous and involuted reasoning of the biblical writers?

With regard to the major premise that God is the lord of history it must be affirmed that this position does not depend on a convincing analysis of events or an impressive correlation between hypothesis and consequences. The case for Yahweh is based on revelation, supported by historical experience. In evaluating the competitive claims of Yahweh and other gods and goddesses, the biblical writers invariably appeal to the data of history, to the mighty deeds wrought in the presence of a cloud of witnesses — sympathetic, hostile, and indifferent — for these deeds constituted testimony to the world. But the ultimate basis for the biblical conviction about Yahweh, that he was creator and sustainer of the world, lord and judge of mankind, was the testimony of those who had from time to time been in direct contact with him. These personal confrontations and the record of their occurrence — the meeting with God and the message of each man — constituted the basis of faith in Israel. We may readily grant that there are ambiguities and inconsistencies in the portrait, and that the testimony of these men is unsupported by witnesses to their conversations. The report has come to us from many hands which have shaped the present form of the records after generations of transmission. Nonetheless, this conviction concerning the reality and authority of Yahweh is the fixed point of departure for any presentation or evaluation of the biblical idea of history. Upon this point the biblical writers were in full agreement, as they were also about the conclusion of the affair. That the God who initiated the order of the universe and the history of man would also bring them to fruition, climax, and end was axiomatic for biblical writers. The intervening events belonged to a sequence the beginning and ending of which were known and settled; but the determination and articulation of the underlying pattern presented numerous problems, as any serious attempt to interpret the heterogeneous and intractable data of historical experience inevitably must. No simple theory will account for the complexity of events, and any simple correlation of hypothesis and the raw materials of human experience is likely to be coincidental and concomitant rather than causal. Determinative factors are elusive and changeable, hard to isolate from accompanying elements, still harder to relate systematically in sequences of cause and effect.

The biblical idea of the historical experience which intervened between creation past and the consummation to come is not difficult to state or grasp. It was strongly influenced by the covenant pattern which is inherent in the story of Israel as the People of God. Central to the covenant were the stipulations or obligations imposed by the divine suzerain, and freely accepted by the people. Obedience would ensure the maintenance of the covenant and the continuance of the blessings of independence, peace, and prosperity. Disobedience would be punished commensurably, with the final threat of the dissolution of the covenant and the accompanying demise of the community. In a general way the major historical work of the Bible, which traces the experience of Israel from earliest times until the fall of Jerusalem and the exile of Judah (i.e., the primary history: Genesis-Kings) follows this pattern, and attempts an interpretation of the data in terms of covenant making and breaking, renewal and rejection. At numerous points, however, the events do not fit into the pattern, at least not obviously or easily; and

223

a variety of adjustments and adaptions have been undertaken in order to make them conform to the underlying principles. While these point up the inadequacies of the basic system to some extent, they measurably strengthen the general hypothesis and refine and distinguish operational elements in the resultant pattern.

Thus Yahweh, the lord of history, nevertheless controls its processes in a secret and subtle way, often at variance with the classic pattern of mighty deeds or immediate divine actions. From the beginning it was recognized that Yahweh was the lord of the whole of history, horizontally as well as vertically, and that all the nations and the whole of their experience belonged to his scheme of things. God's relation to the nations is comparable to his relation with Israel; he exercises supreme authority and judges the nations according to the same moral principles which underlie the covenant with Israel. Thus the nations come under the same general pattern of reward and punishment as Israel did, and by and large the fate predicted or attested for them is the same hard one as for Israel. Such an approach to and interpretation of the experience of Israel and the nations is quite understandable, but there are variations on the general theme which require further study.

There are interruptions in the operation of the normal pattern of events while the secret will of Yahweh for Israel and the nations is worked out. The triumph of the Arameans, Assyrians, and Babylonians over the Israelites is not to be attributed to the superior morality of the pagans. The decisive factor is the sinfulness of Israel, meriting drastic punishment. The role of the nations is as the instrument of Yahweh's wrath, though the agent in these cases is often oblivious of his role. The Assyrian king and his army are the rod of divine anger with which Yahweh chastises his people. Nebuchadrezzar is the servant of the Lord to carry out the devastation of the Holy Land and the destruction of the holy temple. But such a role for a foreign nation is always a temporary one, and once the immediate objective is attained the nation in question comes again under divine scrutiny. It is the divergence between the divine plan and the pagan intention which often provides the basis for the divine judicial decision against such nations. The pride with which they embark on conquest, and the cruelty with which they execute it, make them prime targets of divine retribution. Because they fail to recognize the source of their power and success, and arrogate to themselves or their gods the power and the glory, they are doomed to destruction. The doctrine of the hidden will of God which lies behind the history of peoples, and which works through the policy decisions and actions of their leaders, remains a permanent contribution to the philosophy of history, biblical or otherwise.

A second accommodation of the theme of divine retribution to the recalcitrant facts of human experience is to be found in the principle of delay or postponement of judgment. Among a number of the examples drawn from the history of Israel and Judah, the case of Manasseh, the worst of many bad kings of the line of David, receives special attention. The divine decision against Judah had already been made in those days as a result of the deliberate apostasy of the king, the leader of his people in the defection from covenant obligations (2 Kgs. 21:1-18, esp. 9-15). That the judgment rendered against Manasseh was ultimately decisive for the fate of Judah is clear from a comment of the historian about the blameless life of Josiah, the grandson of Manasseh and the great reforming king of Judah. "Still the Lord did not turn from the fierceness of his great wrath, by which his anger was kindled against Judah, because of all the provocations with which Manasseh had provoked him" (2 Kgs. 23:26). According to the best chronology it was just a hundred years after Manasseh took the throne in his own right that Jerusalem was destroyed.

Such modifications of the basic principle of divine retribution in history help to resolve certain problems in correlating moral judgments with historical experience. As we have already seen, the defenders of Yahweh had somewhat more difficulty in justifying their interpretation of the last years of Judah than the worshippers of the queen of heaven had, and used the doctrine of delayed reaction to advantage. At the same time this view produced new problems of its own, especially as they related to the unfortunate generation on which the judgment finally fell. What seemed like unusual kindness to the wicked, e.g., the postponement of judgment, could equally seem like unjustified severity to the unlucky generations following, which, good or bad, would reap the terrible harvest sown by their forebears. While it may be said that the accounts of justice are in balance overall, that is small comfort to those who bear the brunt of retribution. It may also be said that such a doctrine contains a realistic recognition that human experience is continuous and that each generation inherits the folly of preceding ones and adds its own unpaid bills to succeeding ones; but that is not precisely the issue at this point. To the familiar cry that "the fathers have eaten sour grapes and the children's teeth are set on edge," the prophets only reply that the generation of suffering was itself guilty of breach of covenant. Quite apart from the sins of their ancestors, they fully merited the judgment they received, and therefore had no just complaint about their treatment. But the prophet Jeremiah also promised that in the future there would be no basis for making such a charge about delay in judgment, because the old system would be abolished and a new order of justice established (cf. Jer. 31:29-30; Ezekiel flatly denies the truth of the proverb, 18:1-3). Perhaps we may recognize a tacit admission that the doctrine of delay ought not to have been worked out in too great detail or too rigidly applied.

A third adjustment in the controlling principle of divine retribution relates to the question of relative merit. In the continuing debate over the justice of God's severity toward his people, it could be argued that on an absolute scale, Israel had indeed fallen far short of the divine standard, and, considering the advantages of its election and special status, the nation fully merited the judgment imposed upon it. But when the nation's experience was viewed in the context of history and its fate compared with that of its neighbors, who often fared better though less deserving, the questions of relative merit and relative consequences could not be ignored. In its most dramatic and galling form the question arose when

Israel, the victim, was compared with the instrument of divine punishment — whether Assyria, Babylonia, or some other great nation. Of the massive brutality of these empires there could be no doubt, and especially in their treatment of weaker nations or subject peoples no moral defense could be made. By contrast with these international hawks, the people of Israel and Judah were innocent peace-loving doves. Yet, by the decision of God the more wicked were the oppressors of the relatively blameless; and that did not seem just or fair in the eyes of many for whom the prophet Habakkuk spoke (1:4, 13). To the prophet's insistent question the answer was in effect: "Wait!" The resolution of the problem lay in the future when all outstanding accounts would be settled in full. Those arrogant, self-glorifying instruments of divine judgment would themselves be judged and suffer the fate they had imposed. At the last, the purposes, ways and means, and ends of God would be justified to the satisfaction of all. In the meantime, however, it was small consolation that in time the mighty would fall and the same destiny would overtake great empires as had engulfed tiny kingdoms. Such considerations indicate a much more complex and sophisticated understanding of the dealings of God with his world than might seem to be the case where the principle of retribution was invoked.

Another form of the debate over relative merit concerned the fate of the individual members of the community, some of whom were morally blameless while others were adjudged guilty of various transgressions. In a discussion between Abraham and God about the fate of Sodom and Gomorrah, the solidarity of the community is affirmed in the face of divergent patterns of behavior and radical differences in desert. Such a view reflects not only a certain interpretation of God's dealing with men but also a recognition of the realities of human experience. Catastrophes, whether natural like earthquakes or man-made like wars, rarely make moral distinctions.

The crux of the argument for Abraham is whether the judge of the whole world will indeed act justly. To do so means that God should spare the whole population for the sake of the righteous people in it, because it would be unjust of God to include the righteous in the condemnation of the wicked. There is a fine point here, but Abraham seems to favor the view that it is better for the guilty to go unpunished than for the innocent to be condemned, an early suggestion of a principle enshrined in the legal tradition of the United States of America and the enlightened nations of the modern world. In the end the principals of the discussion agree upon a compromise whereby a minimal number of righteous men will suffice to win mercy for the whole city. When even ten such cannot be produced, the fate of the city is settled. At the last minute Lot and his family were rescued, showing that God does make a distinction between righteous and unrighteous, and thereby guards himself from the charge of injustice.

The question persisted however and different prophets dealt with it in a variety of ways. That the righteous should be exempt from punishment was commonly agreed (cf. Ezek. 14:12-20), but whether they could shield the wicked from divine judgment was much less certain. But in fact the righteous generally shared the common fate, and thus the undeserved suffering of the innocent became the subject of intense interest in interpreting the divine plan. The traditional view that the righteous might serve as a protective shield for the whole community and so deliver it from otherwise merited punishment was balanced and in part displaced by the idea that the suffering of the righteous in the general catastrophe might have a redemptive purpose and an ultimately saving effect. Thus in the prophecies of Second Isaiah, the servant of God through his suffering is the agent of divine salvation for all the peoples of the world. What appears to be punishment in the eyes of the world and a sure sign of the guilt of those involved may in fact be nothing of the kind, but the consequence of heroic obedience to the will of God whose design is to save through service and suffering. Historical events often combine both features. The downfall of Judah in the days of Jeremiah and Nebuchadrezzar was both a judgment of God upon an apostate and idolatrous nation and an act of redemptive suffering for the "many" on the part of the righteous few.

When these complicating and qualifying factors are considered singly or together in relation to the doctrine of divine rewards and punishments, it will be seen immediately that simple, direct statements of its efficacy and applicability stand side by side with complex, circumstantial, and heavily qualified statements of the matter. Thus the success and failure of Israel and the nations may reflect or confirm the direct correspondence between adherence to and defection from the requirements of the covenant or the moral demands of the Deity. On the other hand the correlation may be much less direct and even reversed: e.g., prosperity and security may be the temporary achievement of a people selected to be the agent of a divine mission, but no guarantee or even a reflection of the righteousness of the people so engaged. Failure, defeat, suffering may reflect the obedience of a faithful servant people rather than the judgment of God against recalcitrant sinners. In fact, parallel and intertwining threads run through the whole of biblical history; and except for the insights of the prophets it would be impossible to distinguish the two kinds of success and failure, or evaluate the mixture which confronts us throughout the record. Given the multiplicity of factors, a flexible approach to the understanding of the details of Israel's historical experience is required if justice is to be done to the biblical writers and their story. The fixed points in the biblical view of history are at the beginning and at the end. The point of departure is the confident assertion that God is the lord of history and that nothing of importance happens without his decision, whether active or permissive. The conclusion is that God's rule will finally be established among men: that at the end all issues will be resolved and the Kingdom of God will come. But for the middle period, between creation and consummation, many possibilities present themselves, and caution is necessary in interpreting the relevant historical data in the light of the divine purpose and methods. Only when it is all over can we expect to know truly what happened and why.

III

To point up the possible relevance of the biblical view of history for interpreting the experience of the modern world, we will attempt an analysis of two events of cataclysmic proportions which have profoundly influenced the course of recent history. These are the Civil War in America a century ago, and the rise and fall of the Nazi regime — the Third Reich — in Germany during the 1930s and 1940s. For both there is more than ample historical documentation; and involved in both are questions of morality and justice, suffering and survival which remind us of the biblical narratives and seem to require an exposition in biblical and theological terms.

Concerning the Civil War, certain theological elements were early recognized by prominent figures on both sides, but to a large extent religious fervor served to support the political and military objectives of the conflicting parties. It is generally acknowledged that the moral aspects of the question of human slavery, a significant factor in the background and outbreak of the Civil War, became increasingly important in the course of the war, and were ultimately decisive in the conclusion and aftermath of the struggle. Without minimizing the many important elements in the "irrepressible conflict," the moral issue stands out. A proper understanding of it requires a careful theological analysis and appraisal.

The first problem is to define the moral issue of slavery precisely and determine the correct biblical stance with regard to it. The fact is that both sides appealed to the Bible to attack and defend the "peculiar institution" of the South. By and large, the Southerners could and did make a better exegetical case for their position. Not for many centuries after the Bible was completed was it supposed that biblical teaching was incompatible with slavery. Much of the strongest ammunition for the case against slavery came not from the churchmen, but from the social and political philosophers of the 18th century and was incorporated in the documents of the American and French Revolutions. If an argument against slavery is to be made from the Bible it cannot be based on the actual practice reflected in the narratives and legal sections in which slavery is taken for granted. Rather, it is to be inferred from the principles governing the relationship between God and men, and men and their fellows. More particularly the argument may be developed from an extension and application of the exodus theme of the deliverance of Israel from bondage in Egypt. Here at the center of the "mighty deeds" is an unequivocal assault on the institution of slavery, although the subject is considered in national, not personal, terms. The Israelites, it is affirmed, cannot serve God and Pharaoh both. In order to enter the service of God they must be free of any other servitude. In the course of Israelite history, this conviction acted as a powerful impetus toward independence in the face of every military and political threat and encouraged fanatical attempts to escape bondage and oppression, culminating twice in the heroically futile defense of Jerusalem against overwhelming enemies. The suicide of the last defenders of Massada in 73 c.e., when they could no longer resist the Roman attack, illustrates this incredible devotion to freedom, correlative to an even more basic commitment to God.

Once we have defined the moral issue as slavery, and the biblical teaching as freedom, it remains to apply this analysis to the Civil War. Even though the antagonists can be identified as either defending or attacking the institution of slavery, it would be far too simple and equally unjust to identify the North with the cause of freedom and thus of God, and the South as the enemy of both. It was left to Abraham Lincoln to probe more skillfully and deeply into the issue and see that, while the enslavement of the Negro was the crucial moral issue, the judgment of God was being expressed in the Civil War in a much more complex fashion. Lincoln recognized that the war — which he always regarded as logically unnecessary since a solution to all outstanding issues could have been reached by negotiation — was not a holy crusade against slavery in which the North was the agent of the divine wrath against the slave-holding South, but rather that it was a judgment primarily against the white men of both North and South because of their common enslavement and oppression of the Negro through the centuries. The terrible carnage attests to the divine judgment — an exaction from those who had brutally exploited the Negro. Thus the war expressed both a decision on the moral question of slavery, and a judgment against the white men of both sides. Victory when it came did not vindicate the North against the South; victory when it came vindicated God in his war against the oppressors in behalf of the oppressed. Had the North and the South appreciated clearly the theological insight of Lincoln, they might better have rebuilt the nation on the basis of these conclusions: (1) the decision for freedom against slavery; (2) the judgment against white American civilization, requiring repentance and restitution to the Negro for all he had suffered. After a hundred years the lesson of the war is only now becoming clear to us: that all the white people of this country are bound by the historical judgment of God to redress the wrongs inflicted over the centuries and restore the Negro to his rightful status as a fellow human being, whatever it costs, and whatever it takes to accomplish. Responsibility does not end with legal equality, but with full restitution. Finally, the white people of America will not enjoy any advantage gained from the exploitation and enslavement of Negroes. That was not only a just appraisal of the Civil War but a prophecy for the future. The previous account has not yet been balanced, and a hundred years later there is a new accumulation of injustice and persecution which should make us all quail when we reflect that God is just. Even if it were possible, it would not be enough to wipe the slate clean, forget the past, and start from scratch. The debt must be paid in full.

World War II was a fitting and tragic climax to the Nazi experiment in Germany. Again we can recognize a basic moral issue among the many factors which produced the war and its conclusion. The moral bestiality inherent in Nazi ideology and exemplified in Hitler and his followers was blatantly apparent from the beginning, though for many reasons most people and nations found it inexpedient to intervene until it was too late. We may affirm that the war produced a verdict against the Nazi ideology, against its racist ideas, and a condemnation of its "final solution of the Jewish problem." But the divine judgment was not confined to Germany. Many nations suffered severely in the war. Some were conquered and oppressed by the Nazis, others were bled white in the struggle. It is safe to say that not all of this suffering was undeserved, and that the nations were not blameless, either generally or specifically, with respect to Nazi Germany. The complacency of some, the tacit support given to the Nazis by others were punished swiftly and severely. Those who offered others as victims to Nazi rapacity soon became victims themselves. All suffered, aggressor and defender alike, but in differing degrees all deserved the judgment meted out to them.

But such an analysis does not exhaust the meaning of this universal catastrophe. There remains the central moral guilt of Germany in the systematic extermination of the Jewish population of Europe. That such a plan could have been conceived, developed in detail, and executed with extraordinary thoroughness seems incredible in our enlightened days — but it happened, and the slaughter was far worse than any ever reported of the barbaric past. That the total defeat of Germany may be taken as a sign of divine displeasure is axiomatic, but the moral judgment is entirely independent of the success or failure of the German armies. Germany's guilt was not in losing the war, but in practicing genocide among other unspeakable crimes of aggression and cruelty. The guilt is infectious because it involved not only those who planned and executed the mass murder, but those who applauded from the sidelines, those who pretended not to notice, and those who were merely silent. There were very few others, but their role was heroic in identifying with sufferers and helping where they could. Nevertheless their total number was not sufficient to deflect the divine wrath and judgment.

Our final concern is with the Jews: the sufferers and their suffering. What theological meaning is to be found in this melancholy and dramatic climax to the millennia of Jewish suffering first memorialized in the Bible and interpreted by the prophets? We can perhaps speak of a judgment against the Jews, as against the other peoples of Europe who also came under Nazi oppression. But it is immediately clear that there is no correlation between any possible Jewish guilt and the punishment received. In the Bible it was recognized that the fall of Jerusalem and destruction of Judah were excessive judgments of God against the people, and that there was an element of innocent suffering, i.e., there were people who did not deserve to suffer, and there was a measure of suffering for all, over and above desert. So with the Jews of Germany and Europe there was a measure of suffering far in excess of any conceivable merited punishment. Under the rubric of genocide we can only speak of undeserved suffering and of the possibility of redemptive suffering. On the analogy of prophetic teaching we suggest that the otherwise pointless and futile suffering of the Jews, who are described in the reports all too

230

often as going like sheep to the slaughter, was potentially and actually redemptive in character like that of the suffering servant in Second Isaiah. It was suffering at the hands of the enemies — but it was for their sake. If anything will save the Germans from another plunge into the madness of racism or Teutonic self-glorification it will be the sacrificial death of millions of Jews. Their suffering can have saving force also for the tacit approvers and the indifferent onlookers, in fact for all those who somehow survived and did not perish with the Jews who perished. For the church in Germany the slaughter of the Jews remains a terrible indictment. The Protestant churches were shattered by the confrontation with Hitler, and only a small core of the faithful suffered martyrdom and thereby enabled the church to live. The Catholic Church, mesmerized by a virulent anti-communism, accepted the Nazi regime and with it the ferocious persecution of the Jews, though here and there voices were raised in opposition. But the death of the Jews profoundly influenced the church, hierarchy and laity alike; and the church's involvement in the grim business has been much on the minds and hearts of the faithful during the days of the *aggiornamento.* In the sessions of the Vatican Council with its exceedingly bad conscience over this matter, the struggle of the church has been profound and troubled. But it is possible that through the suffering of the Jews the Catholic Church will find its soul and be saved.

We can recognize, therefore, in the European catastrophe of the 1940s a divine verdict against Nazism, a judgment against the nations and institutions enmeshed in that disaster, a possible interpretation of the unparalleled mass slaughter of human beings of a particular community, and a warning to the world.

The biblical idea is summed up in the statement that God is lord of history. He is the creator of the world and master of the destiny of men and nations. The relationship between God and man is defined in moral terms, with a fundamental obligation to obey the will of God devolving upon the human party. The covenant pattern with its detailed stipulations is largely limited to the relationship with Israel, but the implications can be generalized: the response to the divine demand will determine the course and conclusion of human history. Every nation and all people will be judged according to their deeds and rewarded as they deserve. Although a bewildering variety of qualifications and modifications is offered by the biblical writers as they thread their way through the complexities of national and international history, the principle is maintained, and reinforced by the conviction that at the end the lord of history will act decisively to vindicate his authority and his justice, and finally to establish his Kingdom on earth.

For us who are the heirs of the biblical tradition and stand before God in the place of our ancestors spiritual and temporal, it is not a simple matter to affirm the biblical faith in the lord of history. In addition to the ambiguities and complexities of historical experience already noted in the Bible, there is for us the added burden of uncertainty about the foundations of belief and the goals of the divine-human enterprise. We are more doubtful about the "mighty deeds" from Creation to the creation of Israel, and we are less certain of the consummation. We are left with the summons to fundamental obedience irrespective of the premise of divine authority, and regardless of the consequences, whether good or ill, of divine judgment.

We offer as a credo for today: affirmation in the teeth of the evidence, obedience in the face of consequences. If, then, we affirm that God is lord of history the content of our affirmation must be the experience of his people Israel who were enslaved in Egypt and escaped only to suffer dismemberment, destruction, and exile to the four corners of the earth, or of his Son, Jesus Christ, who died as a criminal, despised and rejected of men. If, too, we accept the obligations of the divine covenant as the burden of obedience, it can only be in the knowledge that suffering is the badge of service, and that those who obeyed best suffered most. It is only in the prospect of ultimate consequences that proclamation and commitment are joined to hope. It is our confidence that affirmation and obedience will find fruition in the vindication of divine authority and the final establishment of his Kingdom on earth. Our hope for the future is our present commitment, while the ultimate fulfillment of his purpose we leave to the lord of history and the generations of men which are yet to come.

232

23

The Old Testament at Qumran

As to the central place of the Hebrew Bible in the life and thought of the Qumran community there can be no question. The initial manuscript discoveries made it clear that the original owners were pious Jews who earnestly subscribed to the divine precepts laid down in the sacred Scriptures and considered themselves to be loyal adherents to, as well as rightful heirs of, the great traditions of Israel. The vast documentary troves subsequently uncovered, along with excavations at the Dead Sea, have only strengthened the first impression. Approximately one-quarter of all the scroll materials found in the caves of Qumran are copies of Old Testament books. Not only do these manuscripts constitute the core of the Qumran library, but they exerted a pervasive influence on the rest of the extant literature. Thus in addition to the biblical books, there are a number of midrashic works, adaptations, imitations, and elaborations of biblical materials (e.g., various speeches of Moses in imitation of the Deuteronomic sermons). Even more important perhaps are the numerous commentaries on the different books of the Bible. These demonstrate beyond cavil the authority of the Hebrew Bible in the community, and show also how the community interpreted and applied the ancient truths to the contemporary situation and its problems. The rest of the sectarian literature, with rare exceptions, conscientiously quotes, paraphrases, or alludes to scriptural passages in a conscious effort to link the current modes of faith and practice, worship and service with the authoritative patterns of the past. However, this elaborate devotion to and acknowledged dependence on the Scriptures was not just a nostalgic return of the past, to re-create the Israel of Moses in the wilderness, which would have been futile in any case. The Qumran community, in spite of its deliberate archaizing and its isolation, was as much a part and product of the Hellenistic-Roman world to which it belonged chronologically as of the earlier period to which it belonged by conviction and emotional commitment. While the roots and origins as well as many important features of the Qumran society are to be traced to the tradition and practice of ancient Israel as recorded or reconstructed in Scripture, many other features arose out of contemporary conditions and needs, and reflect the dynamics of a historically functioning society. In short, what we find is a devoutly religious community modeled deliberately on the ancient Mosaic society of the wilderness wanderings, but no less consciously adapted to the conditions and circumstances of a much later day. Within the archaic framework of law and custom provided by Hebrew scriptures, many elements drawn from the Persian and Hellenistic worlds of discourse have been incorporated, blending old and new into a structure at once continuous with the past and compatible with the present.

In assessing the role of the Old Testament in the faith of Qumran, we must examine the relationship between the archaic framework and the later features. We note first that the Old Testament has been used selectively, with certain factors emphasized to the neglect of others, and next, that these elements have been further adapted through a creative exegesis which opens the way to the inclusion or addition of nonbiblical elements. The final synthesis is clearly biblical in essence, format, and general appearance; just as clearly there is something quite different in its thrust and focus. To the extent that such a community could thrive in a hostile environment, a two-sided development of this kind was inevitable. Its success could be measured by its firmness of purpose and principle on the one hand (to be faithful to its traditions), and its adaptability and flexibility to contemporary pressures and circumstances on the other.

The Hebrew Bible in its present form is largely the product of the literary activity (both original and editorial) of the exilic and immediately following period. It is not surprising therefore that the Qumran community should exhibit in its basic structure the principal concerns of the early postexilic Jewish Commonwealth. Thus for a society deprived of political independence and the institutions which normally embody and express statehood, an inner structure of great strength, tough discipline, and highest religious sanction was indispensable. The image of Israel in the wilderness under Moses became the primary model for both Judah in the days of Ezra and Qumran in the days of the Righteous Teacher. Each community inevitably made its own local adjustment, but it is characteristic of Qumran that its organizational pattern was more like that of the ancient wilderness community (it was even located in such an area) and its discipline more rigid as befits a society totally engaged in spiritual war.

Similarly the prophets of the exilic period, especially Ezekiel and 2 Isaiah, played a large role in the reconstruction of the postexilic Jewish community. Their influence is also pervasive in the Qumran society and its literature. Just as this prophetic literature inspired the return from exile and offered a plan for the rebuilding of city and temple, so the same motifs figured prominently in the departure of the Qumran sectaries and their settlement in the wilderness. Return and restoration were their watchwords as well.

If, as we believe, the Psalter was the hymn book of the Second Temple, it served the Qumran community as well as postexilic Judaism. The Psalter not only informed the piety of Qumran but offered a model which was widely imitated in the hymnody of the sect. All of the basic elements of biblical religion as these were understood and implemented in postexilic Judaism were present in the Qumran community. They attempted to reconstitute the true community of God. To that end they committed themselves to obedience to the divine law as detailed in the Mosaic code; they interpreted their own history in the theological terms and dimensions of the prophetic literature and understood their experience to be the working out of moral principles in time and place; finally their piety was expressed in corporate and private worship, the great public festivals, and the innumerable personal occasions of prayer: praise and thanksgiving, contrition and repentance, supplication and dedication. In its basic beliefs and practices Qumran was thoroughly Jewish: biblical in principle, postexilic in orientation and action.

At the same time there are numerous aspects of the life and literature of Qumran which stamp them unmistakably as emerging from the late Hellenistic age in Palestine, and reflecting the special circumstances and crises of Judaism in that era. Since many of these features appear in the distinctive Jewish religious literature of the Greco-Roman period (from *ca.* 165 B.C.E. to 135 C.E.) which we call "apocalyptic," we may use the term to designate the trend and tone of this major branch of Judaism.

It is to be noted that the main content of these documents is derived from the classic literature of the Old Testament, but the material is organized in patterns characteristic of a later age. The book of Daniel is one of the earliest exemplars of this type of literature, and while it is a biblical book, it may with justice be characterized as late Jewish apocalyptic, or paradoxically as intertestamental (dating in its present form from 165 B.C.E.). The book draws heavily upon the biblical tradition. The setting is the Babylonian exile, and Daniel himself is a pious Jewish seer who achieves prominence at the court of a foreign king; he and his career are modeled loosely on the figure of Joseph, who was the archetypal dream interpreter. But in the case of Daniel, this skill is pressed into forecasting the end of days, not just future historical events. The special interest of the author is the conclusion of history, not simply the anticipation of the future. The chronological scheme is based upon Jeremiah's seventy-year prediction concerning the duration of the exile (or the empire of Nebuchadnezzar), but is transmuted by a mathematical device into a projection of world history as it moves inexorably toward its denouement. Once again a fairly straightforward, historical anticipation has been transformed into an eschatological pronouncement in response to the urgent question: When will the end come?

It was equally the conviction of the historians and prophets of the classic Old Testament period on the one hand and Daniel on the other that the course of history was in the hands of God and that the faithful could be confident about its conclusion because of the overwhelming power of Yahweh, the God of hosts. But in Daniel the scheme is more rigidly deterministic than in the earlier writers, with the end decided from the beginning and the role of man as a free and responsible moral agent correspondingly reduced. We can recognize such tendencies in characteristic exilic compositions like Ezekiel and the priestly corpus of the Pentateuch, but in Daniel they are even more pronounced. The chief concern in Daniel is the revelation of the mystery of the end time, to find out precisely what will happen and when; but there is no thought of influencing or changing the fixed decisions, or affecting the predetermined course of action.

The role of angels as interpreters and agents of the divine will, as guardians and guides of the faithful, is well known in the Old Testament, and there is a marked emphasis on their special activity as revealers in the postexilic book of Zechariah. This pattern has been further elaborated in Daniel and comparable literature of the later period.

The representative death and resurrection of the Servant of Yahweh is an important feature of 2 Isaiah's teaching; in developed form it emerges as the closing and climactic theme of Daniel, but with a distinctive eschatological orientation.

Daniel's view of history is essentially that of the earlier books of the Bible, especially the prophets. The kingdoms of this world are subject to Yahweh's authority. He orders the affairs of nations according to his purpose, granting universal suzerainty first to one great power and then another. Even Israel must submit to the rule of aliens for the alloted time. In the end, however, God will shatter the pagan powers and establish the kingdom of his people. In the later prophets, especially Ezekiel and 2 Isaiah, the historical restoration of Israel is fitted into a universal eschatological resolution. In Daniel there is a further development: the course of the latter days (from Daniel's time to the end) is plotted according to a fixed scheme, and kingdom follows kingdom in a predetermined plan which culminates in the establishment of the kingdom of God on earth. The four-kingdom theory expounded in Daniel is not to be found elsewhere in the Scriptures.

How important Daniel was in shaping the thought and doctrine of the Qumran community is difficult to say, but at least they copied and preserved the work, along with other hitherto unknown traditions about Daniel. Extensive fragments of various sections of the Enoch literature have been recovered. Other apocryphal and pseudepigraphic books are also represented at Qumran, indicating strong interest in this kind of literature, which is commonly lumped under the headings eschatology and apocalyptic.

We may characterize the dominant interest as eschatological and consider the other aspects of community faith and practice in relation to it. The basic category itself is eminently biblical. While some scholars trace eschatological features to the earliest days of Israel and find both cosmic and eschatological elements in the monarchy, e.g., there can be little doubt that the later prophets, especially in the period of the exile, manifest an eschatological concern of major proportions. Qumran stands fully in this tradition with added stress on the imminence of the eschaton and greater attention to the details of its realization. Among the many features which characterize the eschatological stance of the Qumran community we may mention the following:

1. Beliefs

a) Determinism and Dualism. While the antecedents of these doctrines are to be found in the biblical tradition, they are much more pronounced in the Qumran literature than anywhere in the Old Testament. The historic struggle between Israel and its enemies has been transferred to the cosmic realm, while the ethical conflict between the righteous and the wicked has been absolutized. At Qumran the hosts of angels and men are permanently divided into two lots, of good and evil, light and darkness. There is eternal warfare between the opposing forces until the final victory of the good. While Qumran theology is profoundly dualistic and interprets the present world crisis in terms of this fundamental conflict, it is even more basically monotheistic. Thus it analyzes the cosmic struggle as the result of a divine decision; the inevitable result, the triumph of light over darkness, is likewise foreordained. The rigid determinism of apocalyptic works generally is characteristic of Qumran and finds echoes in much of the New Testament literature. The rabbis on the other hand, while acknowledging the omnipotence and supremacy of God, nevertheless attempted to preserve for man an area of self-determination and the free exercise of his will. It must be conceded that the Old Testament generally and inconsistently allows room for both divine sovereignty and human freedom.

b) Closely linked with the general theme of dualism is the inevitable final conflict between the children of light and those of darkness. The ultimate outcome is never in doubt, since God has predetermined the end and both the substance and manner of the final triumph. This picture of eschatological conflict is ultimately derived from the pattern of holy war in the Old Testament. It may be noted that the military organization and preparations for battle set forth in the Qumran War scroll are based on the arrangements recorded in the book of Numbers: in both we have the sacred community described as a holy army, the encampment of God, ready to do battle for his sake and in his name. The eschatological features are derived largely from prophetic accounts of the final warfare between God and the pagan armies in behalf of his people. Especially important is the tradition in Ezekiel which identifies the eschatological foe as Gog of Magog and links the annihilation of his forces with the commencement of the new age of fulfillment.

c) Other Qumran documents speak of a new or heavenly Jerusalem with its newly built temple. Here again the influence of Ezekiel (chs. 40–48) is noteworthy. It is too early to discuss the so-called Temple scroll, but it is clear that the new city and temple figured prominently in Qumran expectations. It should be both stimulating and fruitful to compare the Qumran picture with that of the New Testament Apocalypse, which is likewise dependent upon the imagery of Ezekiel.

d) Messianism was a prominent feature of the eschatology of Qumran. While the expectation differed in detail from the views attributed commonly to Jews of the 1st century whether in the New Testament, Josephus, or early rabbinic literature, it conforms closely to traditional Old Testament patterns. Thus in accordance with the Law and the Prophets, three eschatological figures were expected: the eschatological prophet, i.e., the prophet like Moses, who would announce the inauguration of God's rule on earth and identify and designate both the high priest of the line of Zadok and the king of the house of David.

e) Mention should be made too of the Qumran theory of inspiration, which served to link the community with the ancient tradition, and also to make the Scriptures directly applicable to the circumstances and present realities of their existence. The Righteous Teacher who apparently founded the community in the wilderness was the authoritative guide for the membership. He was empowered by the spirit of God to interpret the ancient and mysterious words of Scripture and expound their true eschatological meaning. Thus he alone could explain that Habakkuk's protestations and predictions about the Chaldeans were in truth secret divine warnings about the Kittites (i.e., Romans) in these last days. Similarly Nahum's paean of victory against Assyria was actually a series of dire predictions about the rulers of Jerusalem and Judah in Hasmonean times, but only the inspired interpreter could reveal this truth to the faithful. In point of fact, the central concern of the Qumran community was this mystery of the end time. It acknowledged that the secret had been revealed by God to the Righteous Teacher who in turn had expounded the true meaning of the Scriptures in the light of this revelation.

2. Practice

The organization and operation of the Qumran community were designed to achieve in fact the beliefs and expectations expressed in their writings. Thus the daily life of the community was intended to be an acted parable of the kingdom.

a) We have already mentioned the emphasis on obedience to the law of Moses, which for the people of Qumran was the pattern of the kingdom of God, as interpreted and applied by the inspired leader. Such meticulous observance was the rule of the kingdom and would also ensure and hasten its coming. Thus at Qumran the people had a foretaste of the life of the kingdom, which through their faithful obedience was already in being.

b) The proleptic character of the community is further emphasized in the rituals enjoined upon the membership. These, including the elaborate rite of initiation into the covenant community and the numerous special festivals, are transparently anticipations of the way of the eschatological kingdom. So immersed in the eschaton were the people of Qumran that it is often difficult to determine whether particular practices were currently undertaken in anticipation of the coming of the kingdom or whether they were intended for use only after the establishment of the kingdom. Suffice it to say that the ritual served to actualize the future in the present, and at the same time to prepare the participants to play their proper role in the reality to come. Since the urgency of the present crisis and the immediate necessity of the new order were an essential part of the ritual, it served both as an appeal to and demand upon the deity to hasten the long-delayed consummation.

c) The asceticism of Qumran, especially its celibacy, was another aspect of its eschatology. We cannot rule out entirely sociological and psychological factors, or parallel developments in various pagan societies, but the dominant element was the conviction that in the new order men would be like the angels in heaven who neither marry nor give in marriage. The ultimate source of this remarkable proscription is doubtless the rule of Israelite holy war requiring chastity of those engaged in the Lord's battles. Originally part of the general pattern of ritual purity, and applicable for the duration of a single campaign, this injunction became at Qumran a rule of life for those permanently enlisted in the army of God. In the current cosmic eschatological struggle there would be no discharge short of death, and therefore the regulations governing holy war would be in force permanently.

Thus in the whole range of its faith and life, the Qumran community affirmed a consistent eschatology. The end was at hand; in fact it had already begun, and those who were enrolled in the lot of the prince of lights must be prepared to live and die in faithful adherence to the holy community and its divinely appointed ordinances. Those who endured the present evil age would participate fully in the joys of the coming great one.

The Qumran community bears an important relationship both to the postexilic Jewish community and to the Hebrew Bible which it acknowledged as its supreme written standard. However, the Qumran community was not simply continuous with postexilic Judaism, nor was it modeled directly upon the pattern of the Old Testament. The relationship is more complex, and external factors played a significant role in the formation of the new society which emerged at Qumran. Certainly the continuing crisis in which Judaism found itself in the Greco-Roman period provided both the setting for and creative impact upon the Qumran community; although it deliberately isolated itself from the outside world, it could not finally escape the influence of that world and its all-pervading culture.

The Hebrew Bible provided the foundational elements: the common tradition to which all Jews, including the Essenes, subscribed and by which they were bound. Then there was the ideal pattern of the Mosaic Age, as reconstructed by exilic writers, but nonetheless normative for the Qumran community. It was not simply nostalgia for the past that led the Righteous Teacher and his followers to reconstitute the ancient society in the wilderness, but anguish about the present, and urgent hopes for the future. The second main ingredient was the eschatological expectations of the prophets which when linked with the older traditions of the formative period in Israel's history produced a basic blueprint for contemporary action in anticipation of the new age. On this biblical structure were welded those doctrines and practices of the Hellenistic age, ultimately derived from Persian, Greek, and other pagan sources, and shaped by the crucial experiences of the Jewish community during this period.

24

Reader Response
An Essay on Jewish Christianity

The Harvard Conference on Judaism and Christianity in the fall of 1966 was generally a disappointment to attendants and participants alike. Especially after the successful consultation between Catholics and Protestants, hopes were high and expectations commensurate for an authentic dialogue and significant discussion of substantive religious issues. But it was not to be. Most of the participants took well-marked positions on opposite sides of a long-known battlefield, and fired familiar volleys at or past each other. It seemed as though many Jews came expecting to hear a resounding "mea culpa" from their Christian colleagues for all the centuries of contempt and persecution culminating in the European holocaust of the 1930s and 1940s, along with solemn assurances that the Church would forever renounce its missionary objectives and conversionist tactics aimed at the Jewish community. Then and only then would serious conversation be possible. For their part many Christians came half-expecting, half-hoping that the Jews would concede that they had been overly obdurate on the subject of Jesus Christ and the merits of the Christian faith; now that the Church had been largely stripped of its power and status in a secularized society, Jews would be willing to enter into serious dialogue about the relative merits of Judaism and Christianity and possible future relations between them. But neither side said exactly what the other expected or heard what it expected.

The conference showed rather how wide and deep is the gulf between the two faiths and their institutional structures, and how difficult it is, even for enlightened scholarly minds to bridge the chasm. Sobering second thoughts and reflections on the conference have been published by participants and observers since the occasion; from these it is clear that few if any were prepared for the confrontation that took place, and there is general recognition that the time for meaningful dialogue has not yet come. Before such a state of affairs is arrived at, certain preconditions must be met. First among these is an insistent and overriding internal dissatisfaction on both sides. There must be a period of intensive self-criticism resulting in the widespread recognition that the traditional forms and formulations will no longer pass muster, and that the whole structure of belief and practice must be reexamined. A second ingredient is the acknowledgment, after suitable searching of the records and the collective soul of the community, that the remedy for such ills is not to be found within the community, its traditions, and resources, but requires outside assistance, and the infusion of new ideas and new persons. Finally there must be the expectation or at least the hope on the part of each that the other can provide some of that needed assistance. In short, each must come to the conference table prepared to acquire something of value from the other, as well as to bestow upon the other, to learn as well as to teach.

Unless these conditions prevail on both sides to a substantial degree it is doubtful whether a dialogue should even be attempted. The history of Catholic-Protestant conversations in Western Christendom is instructive in this regard. Not until the internal discussions had reached the point of massive dissatisfaction nor until strenuous efforts at self-examination and renewal had been undertaken was it possible to initiate a serious dialogue at any level; but it remains a question as to how far these discussions can proceed in view of the minimal acceptance of the other points made above, and the repeated affirmations of doctrinal and institutional self-sufficiency on both sides.

As to the possibilities of a Christian-Jewish dialogue, the indications are mixed. So far as the first criterion is concerned, there is ample evidence of dissatisfaction and restlessness in both camps. Not only are the religious communities scandalously fractured into dissident and competing groups, but a triumphant secularism has severely depleted the ranks of the faithful. The process of institutional decline, bordering on disintegration, is sufficiently evident to pose the perennial questions of viability and relevance in an especially acute form, making the issue finally survival itself. In this supercharged atmosphere, internal criticism has been honest, on occasion savage. In some cases the cry for help has gone out, as the vanguard has crossed the line to stage two of the program outlined above. But even these pioneers look only to their brothers in the faith for assistance in the present crisis. For the foreseeable future, Christians will look to the Christian community, its traditions and resources, for the revival and renewal of its strength, while the same will be true of Jews and Judaism.

There is no hint that either group expects or would accept any substantive contribution from the other toward the solution of essential religious issues, or would even contemplate a joint exploration of such matters looking toward possible resolution of differences, or ultimate reconciliation. It is small wonder, therefore, that no meaningful dialogue has developed between Christians and Jews on the central subject of their respective religions, and even provisional, tentative approaches have proved abortive and illusory. In addition to the primary, universal reason for the failure of such conversations — namely, ideological exclusivism, with each claiming to be uniquely possessed of absolute truth, and therefore entirely self-sufficient — there are other reasons peculiar to the history of Jewish-Christian relations. That history has been characterized chiefly by hostility: reciprocal and unrelieved — an attitude of contempt finding expression in acts of persecution on the part of the Christians, balanced by rejection and exclusion on the part of Jews. Christianity emerged into and then out of Judaism in a swirl of violent controversy, and the polemical tone has dominated the discussions between the parties ever since.

To assert Christianity is to deny Judaism. To the Christian, Christianity is not only superior to the parent faith, but is its replacement. Everything of value in the older tradition, including the Hebrew Bible, has been appropriated, absorbed, and transmuted by the newer faith, and therefore there is no further theological justification for the persistence of Judaism. Christianity is the logical option from a Christian point of view; conversion of Jews is at once desirable and inevitable.

For Jews, the conviction that conversion is the Christian intent behind every discussion of religious matters, as was openly the case in the compulsory debates sponsored by the Church in the Middle Ages, has stifled dialogue before it could begin. For Judaism, Christianity has never been a live option; the Jewish community rendered its unequivocal decision in the course of the 1st century. The total rejection of distinctive Christian claims and beliefs is intrinsic to Judaism; the only positive values to be found in Christianity are those taken from Judaism, which has nevertheless preserved them in purer uncorrupted form.

Even if the prospect of dialogue is not bright, there are factors which make the effort both compelling and urgent.

The scholarly enterprise in theology, and especially in biblical studies, has already demonstrated the values of ecumenicity and interconfessional dialogue and cooperation. For example, the day of sectarian Bibles, whether Protestant, Catholic, or Jewish, is past, although institutional investments and publishers' interests make them a profitable anachronism. But the scholarship which informs the latest translations is entirely ecumenical, and in many cases the scholars themselves are of diverse background and affiliation. The Common Bible, epitomizing this new spirit, is already a fact and in time will be formally adopted. While there are serious scholarly differences over the interpretation and import of many passages and innumerable difficulties in the text remain to be solved, widespread agreement on basic approaches and methodology, as well as on the plain meaning of large portions of the Bible reflects a significant shift in the treatment of the Scriptures. Heretofore confessional and denominational divergences, whatever their historical background or cultural orientation, were commonly justified by arguments derived from the Bible. Often these were cases of special pleading, based on arbitrary and artificial exegesis, reflecting the insistence of the particular religious authority that the Scriptures be made to conform to the peculiar doctrine of the group, while claiming and pretending that the opposite was the case. Such abuse of the Bible is fast becoming a relic of the past, and all groups are increasingly careful in this regard. The change is due in part to the undoubted success of impartial scholarship in elucidating the Bible without recourse to special enlightenment or dubious exegesis.

The recognition of a relatively objective body of scholarship is an expression of the modern mood in religious communities which are willing to risk their time-hallowed claims to the unique possession of the truth in the search for a consensus supported by accumulated and sifted data. For them the truth is not simply a legacy of the past to be handed down like a precious heirloom, but a goal to be sought afresh by each generation, defined by the circumstances and resources available to that generation. Thus all the axioms and assumptions of the past are open to question and require reexamination. Ancient formulas which no longer function effectively must be revised or discarded. Surely there are dangers in such an approach to valuable traditions, and the results may vindicate the worst fears of the conservators of the faith. But this is precisely the mood of fearless questing for new truth which is needed in dealing with the Christian-Jewish confrontation. The fixed traditions, frozen attitudes, stock phrases, and ratified formulas of the past will not help here. A fresh start is needed, and the first step is to question the assumptions and challenge the long-standing conclusions on both sides.

Comparing their traditional claims for themselves, their charges against one another, and their scriptural arguments, Christianity and Judaism are mutually exclusive and contradictory. If one is true and right, the other must be false and wrong. The only way out of this impasse is close examination of both communities, their records and positions. An independent scholarly approach to the biblical data which form the basic constituent for both Judaism and Christianity will yield more constructive results. In relation to the Bible, we may suggest an example of indirect cooperation between Christians and Jews. As everybody knows, the Jewish Bible is an integral part of the larger Christian Bible (constituting, in Christian parlance, essentially the Old Testament). The original Hebrew (and Aramaic) text was copied and preserved through the centuries by the Jewish community. It is doubtful whether the Hebrew text would have survived except for the work of Jewish scribes, since Christian copies of the Hebrew Bible are very rare, and in any case invariably copied from a Jewish manuscript. On the other hand, the Christian Church was responsible for the preservation of the Septuagint, the Greek translation of the Hebrew Bible (dating from the 3rd and following centuries B.C.E.); except for the diligence of Christian scribes, this valuable witness to the text of the Old Testament would have been lost, since the Jewish community abandoned it in ancient times. Although a Jewish work to begin with, no Jewish manuscript of the Septuagint has survived, except for a handful of pre-Christian fragments discovered in recent times.

What gives this curious circumstance its point is that both textual traditions are of value in recovering the most ancient and reliable text of the Hebrew Bible. Proof of this has only been forthcoming in recent years with the discovery of the

Dead Sea Scrolls. Careful analysis of the new materials and comparison with the established Massoretic Text and the Greek manuscripts indicate a complex history of scribal transmission and variation deriving from official manuscripts of the postexilic period, perhaps related to Ezra's ministry in Jerusalem. The reconstruction of this early text is the task of nonpartisan scholarship which makes use of relevant data from all sources. Thus Synagogue and Church contribute to the recovery of the text of the Hebrew Bible in which both have a vital stake. As a result of this ecumenical scholarly activity, both will benefit measurably in having a text (and variants) superior to what either had preserved on its own. Neither loses anything by this procedure, and both gain.

What is manifestly true in text-critical studies of the ancient manuscript traditions is true of biblical studies generally, as scholars who have worked in the contemporary environment will testify. While less advanced along the ecumenical route, experimentation in the classic areas of religious history and thought confirms the impression that stimulation is certain and progress very probable in all of these fields. The necessity of ecumenical involvement at every academic level is now widely recognized and the rush to merge faculties and facilities, boards and student bodies is on in full force. The new generation of theologians will be the product of interconfessional and nonconfessional training and will assume the open stance which characterizes the scientific quest for truth.

To what extent can this experience in biblical studies be duplicated in the broader terrain between the two faiths? This question cannot yet be answered; but its substance lies in the time almost two thousand years ago, before the lines of demarcation were hardened, when normative Christianity was not merely congenial to Judaism but thoroughly Jewish in both personnel and praxis. At the same time Judaism was itself sufficiently flexible and diverse to accommodate radical divergence in faith and structure including this dissident messianism.

During the last two centuries B.C.E. and the 1st century C.E. Judaism was in ferment, at once creative and divisive. Deeply rooted in Palestine and centered in Jerusalem and its holy temple, Judaism had nevertheless spread through the Roman Empire and beyond its borders with large and effective communities established in the major cities of the Imperium. Its tenacious grip on the ancient traditions and resistance to change were balanced by an extraordinary adaptability to new conditions and absorption of ideas and influences from the outside. Conservative Sadducees were challenged by liberal Pharisees, while radical groups such as Essenes and Zealots filled out the religious spectrum. In addition to these major factions, ephemeral groups of every description appeared and disappeared with predictable irregularity. Hellenism penetrated all branches of Judaism; apocalyptic thought likewise had a pervasive influence. Far from being sterile, exhausted, and moribund, Judaism was dynamic, richly variegated, open-ended in this period. Among its many manifestations certainly one of the most remarkable was Christianity, the only one of the many parties and factions (apart from Pharisaism itself, which emerged as mainstream Judaism) to establish a permanent and viable existence.

In its earliest and dominant form Christianity was a Jewish phenomenon. Its leaders were Jewish and they shared with their compatriots a common background, common Scripture, common attitudes, hopes, and expectations. They had more in common with Pharisees than Sadducees, with Essenes than Zealots. While they may be broadly described as sectarian, it is important to remember that before the emergence of a dominant Rabbinism toward the end of the 1st century C.E., Judaism was a congeries of sects, each claiming to be orthodox, none actually normative. Judged in that light, primitive Jewish Christianity was an authentic component of contemporary Judaism. Community and continuity were the hallmarks of Jewish Christianity. They clung to the Jewish community and claimed it permanently as their own, working from within to persuade others to their special convictions. Furthermore, they held that their faith was continuous with Jewish tradition and consistent with it. The Jewish Bible was their scripture and they obeyed the Law of Moses along with their fellow Jews. Led by Peter and the Twelve and later by James, the brother of Jesus, the prestige and authority of the Jerusalem circle could hardly be questioned in the Christian world; even the radical Gentile churches of the empire recognized its position.

In holding fast to a Christian faith that at the same time was completely Jewish, the Church at Jerusalem believed that it was imitating the practice of its Lord as well as obeying his instruction. By his life of piety and good works, Jesus had set an example which his disciples would endeavor to follow. In his teaching he had set forth a model for them to emulate. But it was all consistent and continuous with the Judaism both he and they professed; a radical form of Mosaism, perhaps, with a strong eschatological tone, but one which they could hold as Jews. There was never any thought that they should do otherwise. And in spite of controversy, often acrimonious and bitter, Judaism was able to accommodate Christians and non-Christians, along with the other factions and groups, in the earliest period. All were Jews and the community was one.

It was different with the Gentile Christians. The Christian mission to the Gentiles was an almost accidental but inevitable consequence of its eschatological messianism. But the unexpected and overwhelming response of non-Jews to the gospel produced the first major crisis in the early Church, as well as serious theological adjustment of traditional schemes to the new reality. After a brief but vigorous debate, Gentiles were admitted to full communion directly without further obligation to become Jews as well. Paul's ingenious and effective exegesis created a single citizenship in the Christian commonwealth; it was divided into two classes, equal but separate: Jews and Gentiles. Jews who became Christians would continue to be Jews, while Gentiles would become Christians without also becoming Jews. All would share the same promises and perquisites, receive the same status and rights, but each community would order its own polity and practice.

Thus a two-house theory of Christianity emerged from the first generation experience, a provisional solution to an immediate problem. In principle and ultimate in fact there was no distinction between Jew and Gentile in the Church, but there was in practice, for it was at least as important to maintain the integrity and continuity of the Jewish group as to establish the freedom and autonomy of the Gentile community. As a result, the Jewish Christians were able to have active and effective relations with Gentile Christians and at the same time retain operating status in the non-Christian Jewish community. Thus a link was forged, however tenuous, between Christianity and Judaism, and it persisted as long as the Jewish Christian community continued to exist. This halfway house with conduits to both sides could serve as meeting place and mediator, communication center and symbol of the continuity to which both enterprises belonged.

Jewish Christianity which had authority in one communion and status in the other lost both in the course of time. The Jewish Christians of a later day were unacceptable to both Christians and Jews, being regarded as heretics by the former and apostates by the latter. How far these latter-day Jewish Christians had diverged from the position of earlier Jewish Christians is difficult to determine, or even whether they were in direct succession, but it is clear that by the 4th century Gentile Christianity and Orthodox Judaism had themselves changed considerably and in all likelihood would have rejected the original Jewish-Christian group on the same grounds. By that time the breach between Judaism and Christianity was permanent and irrevocable and no trace of the ancient linkage was allowed to survive.

The crucial factor in this melancholy history, however, was the series of violent conflicts between the Jews of Palestine and the Roman military authority, which finally ended in 135 C.E. with the defeat of Bar Kochba and his followers, and the rebuilding of devastated Jerusalem as a Roman city Aelia Capitolina. Palestinian Judaism was shattered by the catastrophes of 70 and 135 C.E., and in the process Jewish Christianity was effectively destroyed.

The surviving representatives of biblical religion, Gentile Christianity and Rabbinic Judaism, proved eminently viable and adaptable, as their careers through nineteen centuries and in scores of countries demonstrate. They also proved incompatible with each other and, to date, irreconcilable.

In view of this record, the time may be at hand for a fresh start. With the Jewish resettlement of the Holy Land, there is every chance that a new indigenous form of Judaism will arise out of the welter of transplanted dispersion faiths. If it can match 1st-century Judaism in originality, diversity, flexibility, and activity, then we may witness a true revival of biblical prophetic religion in our time. Nor is it to be forgotten that a distinctive product of that earlier Judaism was Jewish Christianity; it is possible, therefore, with the rebirth of Palestinian Judaism there will also come into being a Jewish Christian community. It is not a matter of re-creating the past, which is merely romantic, or reliving it, which is sentimental, but of invoking past aspirations and achievements in order to guide the present and future. A modern Jewish Christianity might serve again to demonstrate that Christianity and Judaism are not only compatible but inevitably belong together. It might also serve as a bridge across a chasm of hostility, a meeting place for ancient enemies. And it might act as an inspiration for all those of both camps who seek that better way of life and faith promised by both Christianity and Judaism. Finally it may demonstrate that a man need not choose Christianity and Judaism, or give up one for the other, but claim the best of both as his rightful heritage under God.

25

"Mistress Forever":
A Note on Isaiah 47:7

In Isa. 47:7 the syntax and interpretation of the word *ʿaḏ* pose a problem. MT links the term with the following clause, and RSV may be taken as a standard translation: "You said, 'I shall be mistress forever,' so that you did not lay these things to heart or remember their end." The rendering "so that" for *ʿaḏ* is rather questionable, hence the reading *ʿwd* (= *ʿōḏ*) "still, nevertheless" in 1QIsa*ᵃ* may be regarded as an improvement. The same may be said for LXX which omits the word *ʿd* entirely.

Neither of these solutions is completely satisfactory, both for stylistic and syntactic reasons.[1] It seems best to retain *ʿaḏ* with MT, but interpret it as the homonymous noun meaning "eternity" and connect it with the preceding word *gᵉḇāreṯ*, as is done, e.g., in BH³. The occurrence of the parallel term *ʿôlām* in the same clause supports the proposed reading; cf. Hab. 3:6 where we have *harᵉrê-ʿaḏ* "eternal mountains" matched with *giḇʿōṯ ʿôlām* "everlasting hills." Hence we may render the clause in Isa. 47:7, "Forever will I persist, the eternal mistress."

The reading and rendering remain awkward, however, since the parallelism is inexact. We suggest a slightly nuanced version, based on the recognition of a typical poetic device in the present text of Isa. 47:7, namely the breakup of a stereotyped phrase, in this case the very common expression *lᵉʿôlām wāʿeḏ,* usually

---

1. The metrical balance in v. 7cd (7 + 7 syllables) and the stylistic symmetry *(lōʾ śamt//lōʾ zākart)* would be disturbed by the addition of *ʿaḏ* at the beginning of the line. We hope to publish a study of the metrical and strophic structure of the whole poem, Isa. 47:1-15, in the near future, but let it suffice for the present to point out that in the strophe vv. 5-7 we have a repeated pattern of couplets of 12 and 14 syllables: vv. 5ab and cd, 6ab and cd, 7ab and cd. With respect to the syntax of v. 7, connecting conjunctions are often omitted in Hebrew poetry; the two clauses can be read as follows: "Although you said . . . , you did not take these things . . .".

rendered "forever and ever." To clarify the basic meaning of the passage, we rephrase it in traditional language:

wattō'm^erî 'ehyeh	But you said, "I will remain
g^eberet l^eʿôlām wāʿed	mistress forever and ever!"

26

"Son of Man,
Can These Bones Live?":
The Exile

*The Bible as a literary entity is a product of the exile. . . . The record
of the revolutions of the human spirit that took place during those years.*

The Hebrew Bible chronicles two of the most desperate situations which have
confronted people since the start of the historical record, and two of the most daring
responses. The circumstances affecting individual lives attendant on the eclipse or
decay of several long-established imperial systems, the Egyptian in the Late Bronze
Age and the Assyrian and Neo-Babylonian in the late Iron Age, stimulated first the
creation of Mosaic Yahwism and later a reformation of it by exilic prophets, poets,
and historians.[1]

The most important feature of these two responses is that they did not try to
set up systems to compete with the grotesque political structures they opposed,
structures whose collapse was almost mechanically assured by the mode of their
creation. The responses, rather, turned toward the transcendent and based their
opposition to human kingdoms on the assertion that God, too, has a kingdom. Both
human and divine governments seek to order the most important features of the
lives of the persons under them. They differ in that the human institutions regard
a man's ability to work and so contribute to the tax base as critical, whereas the

---

1. The Christian Scriptures deal with a similar situation, the flailings of the great tentacles
of the Roman Empire as it sought to move eastwards. Because relatively little of the political
tumult is directly treated in the text, this aspect of the New Testament is often overlooked. The
New Testament also deals with the response to the situation propounded by a man who claimed
to have come to fulfill the Law of Moses and the Prophets.

founding ordinance of the Kingdom of God places value not on work but on rest. In the Kingdom, the most important ability of a person is not to create money; it is to live with those around him.

The fall of the First Temple is by far the more accessible of the two seminal events of Yahwist history. Study of the exodus relies entirely on traditions of widely varying data, preserved in a multitude of almost intractable literary matrices. In contrast, we know the events that led up to the fall and the response that followed in a single, fairly homogeneous context. Indeed, the two overlap largely since the context is simply the Hebrew Bible, and to a degree not appreciated until recently, the Bible as a literary entity is a product of the exile. While we know little of the ordinary events of the exile, we do have what is undoubtedly more important, a careful and extensive record of the revolutions of the human spirit that took place during those years.[2]

The Political Situation[3]

The last great efflorescence of the Assyrian Empire began with Tiglath-Pileser III (744-727 B.C.E.); it was under the aegis of his obscure successor, Shalmaneser V (726-722 B.C.E.), that Assyria's western wars ended in the fall of Samaria. For the next century and a quarter, Judah was haunted by the spectacle of the fall of her coreligionist kingdom. The northern political synthesis which had presented itself as a form of Yahwism had failed.

Judah failed too, though it was better able to prepare for the failure thanks to Israel's example. Discreet political policies saw Judah through the Sargonid period, but the passage was not a comfortable one. The policy makers and ideologists of the kingdom were clearheaded enough to see through to the end of the Assyrian problem, but not, as it were, around the corner to the Neo-Babylonian challenge.

The ideological triumph of the 7th century is a paradigm of the ideological failure of the 6th and is worth some attention. Isaiah proclaims in the early years of the Sargonid period that Assyria is the rod of Yahweh's anger; Yahweh will use Assyria for his own purposes and then discard it because Assyria simply does not understand; it attributes its successes to its own power, "as though the rod swung him who lifts it" (Isa. 10:15). God's ways are clear: He is using Assyria to punish

2. The other, more or less contemporary, revolutions of the spirit in Greece, Persia, India, and China cannot be discussed here; the case of Zarathustra is of particular relevance to Yahwism.

3. The recent revision of J. Bright's *A History of Israel* (Philadelphia: Westminster, 1972) has obviated extended discussion of political history; we will concentrate here on literary history, hoping to round out Bright's treatment.

those who ignore essential human priorities, but he will not tolerate Assyria's delusions of adequacy. It will be disposed of in due course. Indeed, it almost seems to dispose of itself when six decades later Sargon's great-grandsons battle each other in an ignominious fraternal conflict which is among the last well-documented events in Assyrian history. The rest, from *ca.* 639 B.C.E. to 609 B.C.E., is fairly obscure: The old speculation, still sometimes voiced, that Kandalanu was not a king at all but merely Assurbanipal's throne name in Babylon; the incredible chaos of the twenties, which still resists historical systematization; the rapidity with which the nations of the final anti-Assyrian coalition drew together; and the most painful fact of all, the flight to Haran (for the Assyrian Empire died away from home) — all these testify to the fundamental soundness of Isaiah's insight. Assyria had failed so drastically to recognize, let alone foster, the fundamental equilibria of the world around it that utter desolation was its only possible end.[4] But in what vindictive tones is Isaiah's correctness recorded in the Bible! The vivid poem Nahum chanted around the time of the fall of Nineveh is not so much a report on God's work as a taunt-song.

In the year 612 B.C.E. when Nahum spoke, Josiah had been reigning for twenty-eight years. The ideological failure apparent in Nahum's poem had surfaced in other forms. The two good kings that bracket the century between Isaiah and Nahum both understood that the fall of Samaria was a harbinger of Judah's fate. Both Hezekiah and Josiah sought to infuse their power politics with a grace that they believed would help them out of their difficulties. Both failed, in the end, as horribly as Manasseh did, with his different approach. There was no way that power politics could be accommodated to Yahwism; the religious reforms of Hezekiah and Josiah were as impotent as their designs of reestablishing a Davidic kingdom by incorporating the northern territory into Judah. The ideology, as bankrupt as royal politics to begin with, grew increasingly weak under the burden of Assyria. When it collapsed under the Neo-Babylonians, hindsight informs us, no one should have been surprised.

But everyone was. The rapid rise to power of the Neo-Babylonian Empire was in part the result of the unusual social structure that had developed in Babylonia in the late Assyrian period,[5] and in part, of the remarkable speed with which Assyria

---

4. The period is not entirely obscure and the theological interpretation of the fall is not the only viable one, *pace* A. Toynbee, *A Study of History,* vol. 4: *The Breakdowns of Civilization* (New York: Oxford University Press, 1962), 468-88.

5. "The Kassites [the "foreign" rulers of Babylonia from *ca.* 1600 to *ca.* 1160], Chaldeans [the cultural group from which the Neo-Babylonian kings came] . . . became Babylonized in many ways, adopting Babylonian names, entering national office, and sometimes even coming to live in the old cities of the realm. Yet a significant portion of these groups, despite the Babylonizing tendencies, retained their distinctive tribal or clan structure as opposed to the smaller Babylonian family structure. Furthermore, though these groups possessed towns and cities of their own, they were less likely to rely on fortified sites for protection in war and, because of their relative mobility,

disappeared. The circumstances of Media's rise are even more obscure. Power politics is a difficult game at which to play when one lacks even an elementary knowledge of the opposition. When Josiah became king in 640 B.C.E., there was only one empire in sight; that one had all but vanished when events involving three new empires conspired in his death in 609 B.C.E.

The last years of Judahite history are the shocking spectacle Ezekiel describes:

> Your mother was like a vine . . .
> > planted at the water's edge.
> She had fruit-bearing foliage
> > beside the mighty deep.
> She had powerful rods
> > intended as rulers' staves.
> The height of each was lofty
> > in the midst of the branches.
> And it appeared in its height
> > with its plentiful boughs.
>
> But she was plucked up in fury
> > hurled down to the earth.
> The east wind dried up her fruit —
> > Each powerful rod was plucked up and withered —
> > > Fire devoured it.
>
> And now she is planted in the wilderness
> > in a land of drought and thirst.
>
> Fire came forth from each rod with its branches;
> > it devoured its fruit.
> No powerful rod was in her,
> > no staff for ruling.
>
> Ezek. 19:10-14 (Author's translation)

It was more than this, too. It was a procession of almost inevitable events that would have grown to be almost boring, had anyone been able to force himself to believe that the inevitable was just that.

---

enjoyed greater advantage than native Babylonians against the Assyrian military machine"; J. A. Brinkman, *A Political History of Post-Kassite Babylonia, 1158-722 B.C.* AnOr 43 (Rome: Pontificium Institutum Biblicum, 1968), 287. Just as the Chaldeans formed an out-group opposed to the Babylonians of the old cities, so the still less "Babylonized" Arameans formed an out-group counterposed to the Chaldeans. (The apparent confounding of Chaldeans and Arameans implicit in Dan. 2:4 and elsewhere reflects a much later situation; at least prior to the Persian period they were completely distinct groups.)

The record of Josiah's four successors and of the three great deportations is almost too straightforward to be wholly meaningful. As Ezekiel says, fire came from the branch itself eventually. Whatever began the series of events that followed the Battle of Megiddo and Josiah's death, it increasingly assumed the look of royal self-destruction. The suicidal impulse is finally the point, but not only in the forms it took in the last few years; the real push to self-annihilation had begun centuries before. The principal events of the exilic period are transactions of the human spirit which together compose an extended meditation on death and resurrection. When the air clears after the last deportation in 582 B.C.E., there is practically no historical record left. We, as historians, must dwell on the same matters that held the Judahites' attention. The grand material culture of the old age had been destroyed; the exile, a breathing period passed sitting on a flood mound near the great canal of Nippur, has only the material culture of words.

The exile is not entirely a blank period in political history. We know that Evil-Merodach freed Jehoiachin from prison and that even Evil-Merodach's predecessor, Nebuchadrezzar himself, had treated the last Judahite king kindly. We know that ordinary life went on during the exile (see, e.g., Jer. 29:5f; Ezek. 3:15; 8:1; 12:1-7; 24:18; Isa. 55:1-2; Zech. 6:9-11). But this does not add up to exilic history. For that we must look to the prophets, poets, and historians who responded to the destruction of the nation-state.

The Ideological Status Quo: Deuteronomism

The historian who seeks to deal with the passions in which we recognize character must understand how they interact in time. He must have some presiding notion of how it is that people manage to live. We saw above that Isaiah had such an understanding: Persons who ignore essential priorities will suffer for it.

A major difficulty of this formulation of how history works is that it treats collectivities as persons. This does not reflect the common human experience that collectivities have different sorts of fates than persons. The early recognition of this fact (the Decalogue is written in the singular) was obscured with the passage of time. One of the central theological enterprises of the exile was rediscovering this distinction.[6]

Another major difficulty with this formulation is an apparent assurance in the mechanical operation of the processes involved. The belief seems to be that the wicked will suffer inevitably and, correspondingly, the just will unavoidably

6. Parallel with this rediscovery is the frequent use of archaizing language in the poetry of the period; Hab. 3 is a well-known example. Primitivism or nostalgia in both ideology and material culture is a common feature of Near Eastern culture in the 7th-6th centuries.

be blessed. This, too, fails to face up to the facts of life: Sometimes the wicked flourish and the just do not; the pattern seems random. This is the other central ideological problem of the exile.

These two difficulties can scarcely be separated; together, they are easily recognizable as the core of the ideological system known as Deuteronomism, i.e., the moral understanding which dominates the book of Deuteronomy and the Deuteronomic history. This ideology flourished in the years before the fall and it is the starting point for all 6th-century thought.

The origins of Deuteronomy are to be sought in the period following the fall of Samaria in 722-721 B.C.E. The northern orientation of the book has long been recognized. It was the product of a group of Israelites who fled the north and sought to guide their southern coreligionists away from a course of political action too perilously similar to that of Israel. The text (in a version somewhat shorter than the biblical one) was probably prepared during the reign of Hezekiah, its compilers encouraged by that king's religious reforms. The book was then suppressed under Manasseh and Amon and did not again come to light until the 18th year of the reign of Josiah.[7]

Deuteronomy served as an important stimulus for Josiah's reforms, but it was by no means the only one, just as the reforms themselves were not exclusively religious. Josiah was doubtless aware of the waning of Assyrian power in the last years of Assurbanipal's reign and used the opportunity to try to realize hopes of a great Davidic kingdom and a correspondingly grand religiously based ideology. These ambitions paralleled those of Hezekiah. But the failures of Deuteronomism cannot alone explain the failures of Josiah, because monarchic theology included certain further ideological postulates which were ill suited even to Deuteronomism. These were the belief that Zion and the Davidic line are somehow guaranteed to survive all calamities and that the cultic reforms are somehow bound to induce the conversion of morals. It is these beliefs that separate Jeremiah and the Deuteronomists from the royal theologians.

Nevertheless the Deuteronomists (if we may suppose the continuance of a school of "northern" theology during the reigns of Manasseh and Amon) were able to make an alliance with the royal faction. The result of this alliance was the redaction of the Deuteronomic history, which combines the law book found in the temple with the four books of the Former Prophets.[8] This work was essentially a piece of propaganda designed to support the actions of Josiah by setting forth their

7. Jack Lundbom has suggested (in a paper read at the Fall 1974 SBL meeting) that the text found in the temple was not an Ur-Deuteronomy, but only Deut. 32, an undoubtedly archaic poem. This would well explain the reaction of Josiah and, perhaps more important, would explain how the newfound text could have been read three times in one day.

8. See F. M. Cross, *Canaanite Myth and Hebrew Epic* (Cambridge, Mass.: Harvard University Press, 1973), 274-89; and D. N. Freedman, "The Deuteronomistic History," *IDBSup* (Nashville: Abingdon, 1975), 226-28 [see below, Chapter 28].

historical background. The most important contributions of the editors of the Deuteronomic history were the opening and closing chapters of Deuteronomy, the drafting of the present text of Judges, and the compilation of the two books of Kings.

The central concerns of the Deuteronomic history are too well known to need rehearsal here. More important for our purposes is the shape of the narrative in Second Kings. The clear climax of the saga is 2 Kgs. 23:25. The echo of Deuteronomy 6:4-5 in this verse is not coincidental; the two passages together form an envelope around the intervening history. The point of the structure is clear: The editor would have us believe that Moses is referring to Josiah himself. At the moment the verse was written, the prospects were promising. Josiah had tried hard to clean up royal policies and as a result, the Deuteronomists felt, he was to be blessed; and Judah was to be blessed with him. The splendor of Josiah was evidently adequate to make the foolishness of his imperial designs and the inadequacy of his cultic reforms tolerable.

The conclusion anticipated by the Deuteronomists was not to be. The painful verse that follows their eulogy of Josiah (2 Kgs. 23:26) is the work of an exilic writer trying to save the thesis. Josiah was good, he would have us believe, but not good enough to counterbalance his wicked grandfather.

The forecast was correct, but something got in the way. The problem is not just that the author's reasoning fails to persuade us but that the doctrine of postponement is artificial. He is only faintly conscious of his situation. He scarcely seems to be linked to the world around him; he feels the pain in it too slightly even to move us. To discover the real meaning of Nebuchadrezzar's campaigns we must turn to the works of those who were intensely aware of the difficulty of going on and yet had to and did.

The Poetic Response: Lamentations

In moving from the Josianic edition of the Deuteronomic history to the final edition, we have passed over a half-century which is filled with other, more creative responses to the destruction. The earliest of these is generally agreed to be Lamentations, because of the pure terror that fills the poems. The vivid reaction to the violent destruction and unrelieved suffering is balanced by a recognition of the basic justice of the disaster in the context of divine judgment. Yet the balance is not perfect. The cruelty of Yahweh is regarded as excessive; the question of divine mercy is gasped out rather than formulated.

Further, the poet is still trading in the vocabulary of royal theology, as, e.g., when he refers to Zedekiah as "the breath of our nostrils" and "the one of whom we said, 'In his shadow we will live among the nations' " (Lam. 4:20, D. Hillers).

257

Hindsight informs us that the destruction had at least in part been brought about by such shallow theologizing. The expression "in the shadow of" is a common ancient Near Eastern description of divine protection; and indeed it was in the shadow of Yahweh that the desert wanderings were conducted.[9] Further, it is Yahweh and not the king who quickens (cf. 1 Sam. 2:6) and Yahweh alone who breathes life into our nostrils (cf. Gen. 2:7).[10]

Though the poet clings to monarchic theology, he is aware of his situation. He acknowledges that the great 8th-century prophets were right, and he makes Jerusalem confess her evil (see, e.g., Lam. 1:18, 20). But the immediacy of the horror is too great for the achievement of full consciousness. The theology is at base Deuteronomic, as is made clear by the poet's curse on Edom, evidently referring to its vicious participation in the Babylonian mangling of Judah (4:21-22). Retribution will come and all accounts will be balanced in the end, the poet believes, because Yahweh's chief concern is explicit and humanly comprehensible equilibrium. This is a first try at formulating an explanation of the fall; it is not adequate.

The book of Job is a reaction to the Deuteronomic world view which has often been associated with the fall of Jerusalem or possibly that of Samaria. While a date in this time range is correct, the poem is not primarily about Judah or Israel. It must be taken as it is offered: a discussion of individual suffering. The question asked in Job is similar to the one asked everywhere in exilic literature: What

9. Cf. also Isa. 49:2, and see G. E. Mendenhall, *The Tenth Generation* (Baltimore: Johns Hopkins University Press, 1973), 32-66.

10. An exilic date for Gen. 3 is defended by Mendenhall in "The Shady Side of Wisdom: The Date and Purpose of Genesis 3," *A Light unto My Path: Old Testament Studies in Honor of Jacob M. Myers,* ed. H. N. Bream, R. D. Heim, and C. A. Moore (Philadelphia: Temple University Press, 1974), 319-34. The link between Lam. 4:20 and Gen. 2:7 just might provide support for a similarly late date for Gen. 2. The motif of royal control of breath appears in the Theban building inscription of Amen-hotep III, in which the god Amon-Re says to the king:

> *When I turn my face to the north, I* work *a wonder for thee: —*
> *I make the countries of the ends of Asia come to thee,*
> *Bearing all their tribute upon their backs.*
> *They themselves present to thee their children,*
> *Seeking that thou mightest give to them the breath of life.*
> . . . .
> *When I turn my face to the orient, I* work *a wonder for thee: —*
> *I make the countries of Punt come to thee,*
> *Bearing all the sweet plants of their countries,*
> *To beg peace from (thee and to) breathe the breath of thy giving.*

Trans. by J. A. Wilson in *ANET* (Princeton: Princeton University Press, 1969), 376ab. Other evidence for a late date for the redaction of the first eleven chapters of Genesis cannot be discussed here; note, e.g., the ring about the primary history created by the Chaldeans in Gen. 11:28 and 2 Kgs. 25:13, etc. The similarity of the expulsion from Paradise and the exile from Palestine is also relevant. The remnant of vinedressers and farmers are those who "till the ground from which [they were] taken" (Gen. 3:23).

possible sense could unmerited suffering have? This question is crucial in exilic literature because part of the effect of the destruction would be the suffering of innocent individuals. Ezekiel (notably in Ezek. 7) and Jeremiah both address it as such. However, we cannot link Job distinctively with this period simply because the national calamity drove across many individual lives. Rather, we must say that Job articulates a basic critique of ethical monotheism and so, though it was doubtless valued in the exile, the possibility that it was written earlier cannot be discounted.

The Prophetic Response: Jeremiah and Ezekiel

The most striking feature of the transition from monarchic to exilic prophecy is the fact that it is achieved fully only in the work of Jeremiah. This may be an accident of preservation, but it seems more likely that it is a genuine reflection of the breadth of his understanding. The last prophets dominated by monarchic ideology are typified in Nahum. Zephaniah is less extreme in his mechanical notions of how Yahweh acts in history, but passages like Zeph. 1:8-14 indicate that he still clings to the old expectations. At the same time, he enlarges the scale of judgment to cosmic proportions, foreshadowing the work of his younger contemporary Habakkuk.

In Jeremiah's prophecies, however, the perspective is altered. He alludes to the destruction of foreign nations as Yahweh's work, work no longer seen as dependent on Judah's history; this attitude he shares with Ezekiel and the poet of Isa. 24–27.[11] Further, Jeremiah regards the community of Jerusalem as only itself, not an earthly representation of an eternal congregation; so when he writes to the exiles, he addresses them as another community (Jer. 29). The eventual restoration is not lost from sight; but it is placed beyond the reach of the present exiles, who are to live their own lives and leave the future to Yahweh. The rigidity that overcame the Abrahamic, Mosaic, and Davidic covenants as they were melded together, he says, will be alleviated in a new covenant which will have the flexibility and vitality of a human muscle.[12]

Jeremiah goes further in loosening the Deuteronomic shackles which sought to bind a person in both time and space by claiming that not only is life in exile to be accepted freely, but also that fathers and sons are no longer interchangeable in matters of punishment. The Deuteronomic insistence on the mechanical inevi-

11. The view is not entirely new; it is found in the 10th- or 9th-century poem Deut. 32.
12. Even if Jer. 30–33 is the work of another hand, it is certainly exilic and therefore shares Jeremiah's situation in large part. Similarly, the oracles against foreign nations come from Jeremiah's world even if not from his hand.

tability of punishment and blessing led to the elaboration of ideas of joint responsibility which extended not just over whole communities at a single time but, further, through time. Jeremiah says no. If such a wrongheaded and drastic extension is necessary to maintain the Deuteronomic theory of divine action, then it is the theory that must go. The extension asks too much of the human spirit, contradicts intuitive knowledge of God too greatly: "In those days people will no longer say: 'The father ate unripe grapes, and the children's teeth are set on edge,' but only through his own fault will anyone die: the teeth of the one who eats the unripe grapes will be set on edge" (Jer. 31:29-30).

Although the central core of Jeremiah (chs. 30–33) is full of hope, the bulk of the book attempts to take account of the world at present, the prospects for which are by no means bright. Similarly, the texture of the book is full of immediate and confused presences: Jeremiah's enemies and his secretary all talk constantly.

This stage in exilic thought is also represented in the work of Ezekiel, whose book is much more explicitly oriented toward the future and is correspondingly made up of silences and visions. Its most abiding presence is the bronze man in the Torah sections who traces designs in the air as much as he talks. It is emblematic of Ezekiel's unearthly world that the prophet's wife is mentioned only on the day of her death. Ezekiel's rejection of Deuteronomic theology is similar to that of Jeremiah; he, too, quotes the sour-grapes proverb only to reject it. But the differences are more striking. Jeremiah is horrified at certain particular ways in which he has seen people act, whereas Ezekiel is horrified at all their actions. Jeremiah has had human fallibility proven to him countless times by people. Ezekiel required only the vision of God to show him the utter worthlessness of human kind. In Jeremiah and in the 8th-century prophets, recent history is seen as a falling off from the creative period of Moses. Ezekiel regards all of Israelite history as little more than a catena of apostasies.[13] It is too easy to forget how extensively the historical record agrees with him.

Some aspects of Ezekiel's prophecy are matched closely to Deuteronomic ideology. In all but one of the cases in which the latter links two phenomena, Ezekiel insists that there is a sharp cleavage: between fathers and sons, as mentioned above (ch. 18); between leaders and people (ch. 34); between householders and their families (ch. 14). But in a fourth case, at least superficially parallel to the first three, he maintains the link even more vigorously than do the Deuteronomists — i.e., the union between Yahweh and the phenomena to which he has committed his name: the temple, the mountain, and the people. Partial lapses aside, these links are permanent. The similarity of these four cases is not coincidental; Ezekiel seeks to qualify the most elementary constructs of religious language, which present God as father, leader, and household head. Yes, Ezekiel says, God is like all these, and

---

13. Ezekiel's subordination of the monarchy to the temple and indeed his whole approach to holiness reappear almost unaltered in the surprisingly different context of Qumran.

yet he is totally other. He is universally indefectible and in that simple way differs entirely from men. Ezekiel does not, however, follow in the tradition of the Zion theology expressed in various forms in Isaiah, Lamentations, and Pss. 46 and 48; he does not speak of this commitment as a matter of comfort to Israel, but as a matter of fact. Israel is no longer a witness for Yahweh; it is merely evidence.[14] As in Jeremiah, so in Ezekiel: Yahweh's commitment to Judah's covenant is almost completely overshadowed by his commitment to the principles of that covenant. In the valley of bones, Yahweh says he animates the bones *not* so that they can live, but so they can know that he is the Lord. Yahweh acts only for the sake of his name.

The Historian's Response: The Primary History

The prophetic response offered an understanding of the situation of the exiles.[15] But Jeremiah's counsel urging them to build houses and make marriages for their children was short-term advice. The existence of a generation born and raised outside of Palestine brought about the possibility of complete assimilation to Mesopotamian culture and ultimate loss of the Yahwist heritage. The first generation could cohere on the basis of memories; the second generation needed a more formal principle of organization. To be sure, the need did not appear suddenly; the exiles had already asked Ezekiel, "How can we live?" (Ezek. 33:10).[16]

His answer directed them not to memories of royal glory but to stories of divine glory. It was during the years after the exile that Yahwism again became a religion based on a story, not bound to any human institution other than the community of those who heard that story and were gladdened in their bones. The story was that of the exodus. The new organizing principle of Judahite religion was canon.

The final redaction of the major portion of the Hebrew Bible, the Pentateuch and the Former Prophets, which may appropriately be called the primary history of Israel, took place around 550 B.C.E. This *aide-memoire* for the exiles sought to provide them with all the material necessary for an assessment of the history of

14. J. L. McKenzie, *A Theology of the Old Testament* (Garden City: Doubleday, 1974), 116.

15. The reconstruction of Judahite literary history suggested here was first proposed in "The Law and The Prophets," *VTS* 9 (1963): 250-65; repr. in *The Canon and Masorah of the Hebrew Bible,* ed. Sid Z. Leiman (New York: KTAV, 1974) [see above, Chapter 14]. Some further points are presented in "Canon of the OT," *IDBSup* 130-36 [see below, Chapter 27]. The relevant evidence will be reviewed in a forthcoming history of Judahite literature.

16. This passage is discussed by J. A. Sanders, *Torah and Canon* (Philadelphia: Fortress, 1972), 53, 93, 103.

the Yahwist movement. The work was not a leisurely enterprise. The editors combined two late preexilic compilations, the so-called Priestly work (the original ending of which is now lost) and the Deuteronomic history.[17] The hand of the exilic editor is only rarely visible; his most obvious contribution is the end of 2 Kings (23:26–25:30), which he concludes with the most significant recent event in Judahite history, Jehoiachin's release from prison. The nature of the propagation of the text of this official history is suggested by the most obvious fact about it: It was never revised after its initial publication around 550 B.C.E. The omission of any narrative of the Restoration can best be understood in this way.[18] The allusions to the Restoration in the Torah (Lev. 26:40-45; Deut. 29:22–30:10) do not reflect that historical event but only prophetic descriptions of it; they are the work of the exilic editor.

The primary history has one notable deficiency: It lacks any extensive commentary on the prophetic movement after the Elijah and Elisha cycles. This omission can best be explained by the hypothesis of a "prophetic supplement" to the primary history, which included First Isaiah, Jeremiah, Ezekiel, Amos, Hosea, Micah, Nahum, Habakkuk, Zephaniah, and Obadiah. The term "supplement" is intentionally question-begging; the actual relationship between the two works is not clear, for an important reason: The social structure that generates a canon is necessarily more flexible and thus more ephemeral than the canon itself. The parallel sections of the two works suggest, however, that they were published separately.[19] That the "supplement" took second place to the primary history is made clear by the fact that the supplement was revised, whereas the primary history was not.

The supplement was later extended at two points: after the first book (to show that the 8th- and 6th-century crises had much in common), and after the last. Second Isaiah's prophecies and the works of the last three prophets — Haggai, First Zechariah, and Malachi — and probably also Joel, Jonah, and Second Zechariah all belong in the second half of the 6th century.[20] Together they suggest that the tempests of the last years of that century were almost as great as those of the first. The revised supplement is to be dated around 500 B.C.E.

17. A late preexilic date for P is quite reasonable. The chief Wellhausenian argument for a late date is P's alleged dependence on D, an argument that fails because it regards Judahite history as a series of paper transactions. See Y. Kaufmann, *The Religion of Israel*, trans. M. Greenberg (Chicago: University of Chicago Press, 1960). [See also Chapter 11 in this volume.]

18. This omission may also reflect the fact that it was difficult to be sure that the return under Cyrus was the divine action for which the prophets had looked. This difficulty is of immense theological importance and is fundamentally the same as the question, What does God look like? which Moses answered by forbidding icons. Cf. further Acts 5:34-39.

19. I.e., Isa. 36–39 and 2 Kgs. 18:13–20:19; and Jer. 52 and 2 Kgs. 24:18–25:30.

20. Second Isaiah is the borderline case; he may well belong to the first prophetic corpus. G. W. Anderson has dated the Isaiah Apocalypse (Isa. 24–27) to this period also; his argument would also fit Isa. 13–14; see "Isaiah XXIV–XXVII Reconsidered," *Congress Volume, Bonn 1962. VTS* 9 (1963): 118-26.

This work has a companion, the principal source of the Chronicler, which is preserved more or less intact in 1 Chr. 10 through 2 Chronicles and including parts of Ezra. This native Palestinian work was written to enhance the claims of Zerubbabel, Jeshua, and the Second Temple, by figuring them in the colors of David, Zadok, and the First Temple. There may have been an independent miniature canon, consisting of this material from Chronicles, Haggai, and Zechariah (1–6), parallel in shape to the great exilic canon.

The exact extent of the older chronicle is not completely clear. It seems that it included Ezra 1–3:13 (and possibly 6:19-22), and described the situation prior to 520 B.C.E. The Aramaic portion of the account (4:8–6:18) is prefaced by a Hebrew passage (4:1-7) which introduces the enemies and sets the stage for their interference. The Aramaic commentary on the stream of imperial documents that follows may be in that language because it was extracted from another historical record, or just for simplicity's sake. The documents themselves are preserved in their unmistakably Persianized Aramaic for the sake of authenticity. This section (i.e., chs. 4–7) brings the picture up to 515 B.C.E. In ch. 6 the name of Zerubbabel does not occur, presumably because it has been suppressed. Zech. 1–6 may also show traces of reworking after the supposed attempt to restore the monarchy after 520 B.C.E.[21]

Exactly what happened between 520 B.C.E. and 515 B.C.E. is a mystery. Bright remarks, "We cannot doubt that the Jewish community, its hopes raised only to be dashed, felt the disappointment keenly."[22] The *reason* for our certainty is important: The Judahite community ultimately canonized the propaganda history that Zerubbabel's ambitions stimulated. The canonization came later, to be sure, after the addition of the memoirs of Ezra and Nehemiah. Ezra himself or his followers associated his memoirs with Chronicles because the stories dovetailed chronologically and because they diverged ideologically. The Ezra memoirs provide a badly needed new direction that complements the failed messianism of Chronicles. Nonetheless, the acceptance of the Chronicler's work in any form in the radically changed situation of 5th-century Judah only highlights the vigor of emotion that must have surrounded the last genuine Davidic pretender.

It was this altered situation that prompted Ezra to make the last and greatest change in the first part of the canon, the creation of the Pentateuch as a distinct unit, to be used as the legal instrument of a small quasi-autonomous enclave in the Persian Empire. Ezra brought with him to Palestine the primary history in the text from which every subsequent manuscript was derived. The isolation of the Pentateuch was a purely practical action, reflecting a need for regulations in the community; it was based on an appeal to the highest available authority, Moses. There

---

21. See "The Chronicler's Purpose," *CBQ* 23 (1961): 436-42 [see above, Chapter 10]; and Cross's discussion of the subject, forthcoming in *JBL.*

22. Bright, 373.

was no question about the sanctity of the Deuteronomistic history; but it could not be used for legal study and application. The Pentateuch thus became the central corpus of law; this development may have had its beginning in a similar context in Babylonia.

Our reconstruction of the major events of Judahite literary history differs from that of the standard theory, which is in many aspects the work of Julius Wellhausen. We now have a much better idea of the terrain to which Judahite literature belongs. Our extended knowledge of the pre-Israelite history of Palestine and of the ancient Near East in general has made it impossible to deny as vigorously as Wellhausen did the creativity of the Mosaic and premonarchic periods. Similarly, our renewed understanding of the last century and a half of the Second Temple period has alerted us to be careful about the centuries that separate it from Ezra. These are no longer available for use as wastebaskets, although they still remain obscure historically. This clearing of the air at the opposite ends of the range of Judahite history has prepared us to take a new look at the middle and to see not a time of antiquarian stocktaking but of reformation in the interests of survival; not a period of the shoring up of fragments against the ruins but of creating new, spiritual monuments to replace the vanished physical ones.[23]

Some new historical evidence is more directly germane to our period. One Qumran manuscript, in particular, deserves our attention: 4QSam[b], dated conservatively to 275 B.C.E. This shows a uniform orthography which can only have been the result of some official standardization process.[24] Uniformity of spelling is not impressive to speakers and writers of a modern European language, but it is an extraordinary feat in a language with as long and varied a written history as Hebrew. By around 300 B.C.E., as shown by 4QSam[b], the literary history of the Pentateuch and the Former Prophets was over and the textual history well under way. Three geographically defined recensions, Egyptian, Palestinian, and Babylonian, were already in existence.[25] Indeed, the development of the text had progressed to the point of the cross-fertilization of the traditions, as is shown by the other 3rd-century manuscripts. This Ur-text of the primary history is probably none other than the

---

23. That a literary historian can see his way at all is largely the result of careful blocking out of the domain of political history. We need not point out the fact that our programmatic statements are the foster children of rigorous historical study, or the extent to which they are based on John Bright's canonical work.

24. For the text, see F. M. Cross, "The Oldest Manuscripts from Qumran," *JBL* 74 (1955): 147-72. For the orthography, see D. N. Freedman, "The Massoretic Text and the Qumran Scrolls: A Study in Orthography," *Textus* 2 (1962): 87-102 [see Volume 2, Chapter 3].

25. See J. D. Purvis, *The Samaritan Pentateuch and the Origin of the Samaritan Sect.* HSM 2 (Cambridge, Mass.: Harvard University Press, 1968); B. K. Waltke, "The Samaritan Pentateuch and the Text of the Old Testament," *New Perspectives on the Old Testament,* ed. J. B. Payne (Waco: Word, 1970), 212-39; and J. Gerald Janzen, *Studies in the Text of Jeremiah.* HSM 6 (Cambridge, Mass.: Harvard University Press, 1973).

one prepared under Ezra's direction in Babylonia (where the story was first set down), brought by him to Palestine and given his imprimatur. Thus, though the Qumran evidence does not establish the 6th century as the date for the official draft of the primary history, it does point firmly in that direction; and that is probably the best that can be expected from the evidence available.

The Final Response: Second Isaiah

We have anticipated our story by looking ahead into the postexilic period. The end of exilic history proper is the edict of Cyrus; the culmination of the period's spiritual history is Cyrus's prophet. The emblematic quality of all the external characteristics of this man's work is obvious: He is nameless; his chief subject, the Servant, is an elusive figure; the limits of his work resist critical definition; the exact sense of some of the key lines of his most important poems eludes us and probably always will. These peculiarities hint vaguely at the shape of this man's great insight, the paradox that God loves Israel and Israel suffers. The rest of Second Isaiah's thought is subordinate to this paradox: His gracious shedding of the terrible yoke of the monarchy and his drastic revision of the temple theology are effortless corollaries of it.

The most vivid part of Second Isaiah's prophecy, the summary of the Servant's career in Isa. 52:13–53:12, contains a similar paradox: The Servant's experience is divided between extremes of humiliation and exaltation. His life is a gesture that ends not as lives usually do, in death, but in resurrection. The Servant's duty is to suffer; this is the task set him by his master, a task he freely accepts.

In one version of the tale, the Servant leads an ordinarily shabby life that is ended by some loathsome disease. Alternatively, he is a criminal condemned to execution for a crime he did not commit. The onlookers — the kings of 52:15, the we of 53:2-3 — do not find him especially distinctive. They consider his death and take it as proven that such a death could only be the result of divine punishment. But such is not the case. The Servant was innocent. Though his death is part of his service to God, it is nevertheless the result of people's failings — not just those of his executors, but of all people. Their guilt is responsible for his pain, whether natural or man-made. His death is able to make them aware of their guilt and somehow to effect their forgiveness and salvation. The Servant's resurrection to life and elevation to kingly authority are the spoils of his triumphant term of service: He claims and receives a redeemed humankind.

The idea of the innocent suffering for the guilty is an outgrowth of the common Near Eastern theory of sacrifice, accommodated to Mosaic Yahwism during the monarchy. Ancient Near Eastern sacrifice is based on vicarious action; the animal used must be unblemished, i.e., one that cannot be destroyed on its own

265

account and therefore must in suffering be suffering for another. The suffering of the Servant, however, transcends in import any merely mechanical view of substitutionary sacrifice or vicarious atonement, for the Servant is free. Here, at last, the pagan systems of sacrifice have been genuinely incorporated into Yahwism.

The simplest explanation of Second Isaiah's theology is to say that what everyone else thought was the question (Why do the innocent suffer?) was in fact the answer to a larger question, How does history work? The exceptional suffering of Judah was undeserved; this Second Isaiah concedes and in this he agrees with all his older contemporaries. It was undeserved specifically with regard to the nations which wounded Judah. Its intrinsic innocence is clear and it can therefore be a worthy sacrifice. The purpose of Israel's history is the redemption of the world. And the world's conversion will in turn redeem and exalt Israel.

One of Second Isaiah's followers, the poet of Isa. 61, recognized that Cyrus's decree came in the Jubilee Year of the fall of the temple and used that rubric for the freedom that he saw emerging from the suffering and redemption of Israel. He tells Israel to accept the freedom of the return because of the necessity of its suffering for the world's conversion. We live in freedom by necessity.[26]

26. I want to thank M. O'Connor for help in preparing this paper for publication.

27

Canon of the Old Testament

Samaritans, Jews, and Christians are the direct heirs of Mosaic Yahwism; each group accepts as divinely sanctioned a selection of the religious writings which developed under the aegis of their common parent. Samaritans regard as canonical the Torah (Pentateuch); Jews and Protestant Christians, the Hebrew Bible; and Catholic and Orthodox Christians, slightly different forms of the Old Testament of the late patristic Church. The development of the materials included in these canons largely took place before the religions assumed their distinctive forms in late antiquity. The earliest stages of the processes of editing and appraisal that lay behind canonization are the most crucial and will be the chief concern of the present article.

1. The material of the exilic canon
   a. The oldest writings
   b. The early monarchic period
   c. The late monarchic period
2. The exilic canon
   a. The Qumran evidence
   b. The prophetic literature
3. Postexilic literature
   a. The Chronicler
   b. The Book of Truth
   c. The Megilloth and Daniel
4. The origins of the modern canons
   a. The Torah
   b. Activity in the late Second Temple period and after
   c. Final remarks
Bibliography

For a survey of terms relating to canon and a discussion of the contents of the canons, *see* R. H. Pfeiffer, "Canon of the OT" *[IDB],* intro. and §8; for Hebrew

Bible quotations in the New Testament, *see* §6; for theological beliefs relating to canon, see §9.

1. The material of the exilic canon. While little of the writing in the Bible is explicitly dated, a sizable portion of it provides historical and linguistic evidence which can be correlated with dated, extrabiblical materials. These correlations provide the basis for the advances that have been made in recent years in literary-historical study of the text.

a. The oldest writings. Recent research has shown that the oldest parts of the biblical text are poetic. A list of the principal old poems and their approximate dates follows: Exod. 15, Judg. 5, and Ps. 29 (12th century B.C.E.); Gen. 49, Deut. 33, and the poetic portions of Num. 23–24 (11th century B.C.E.); 1 Sam. 2, 2 Sam. 1, 2 Sam. 22 (= Ps. 18), 2 Sam. 23:1-7, and Ps. 2 (10th century B.C.E.); and Deut. 32 and Pss. 68, 72, and 77 (9th century B.C.E.).

Certain legal traditions also derive from the oldest strata of biblical writing. Among these are the Decalogue (which has, however, undergone some later systemization) and the Covenant Code (Exod. 21–23). The antiquity of the latter is best demonstrated by examination of parallel passages in Deuteronomy, in which various laws have been reshaped to render them not only comprehensible, but also serviceable to a later age (cf. Exod. 21:2ff. and Deut. 15:12ff.). The Ritual Code of Exod. 34 is probably also a composition of the earlier periods of Yahwism.

These two groups constitute the bulk of the materials which can be assigned in more or less their present form to the earliest period. There are other archaic materials, but these are often embedded in narratives or other types of writing designed to meet later needs and interests. Disentangling and identifying the earlier items remains a risky undertaking. The best approach is to fix the date of the finished product in the light of its responses to circumstances in the life of the people. It is this principle that makes so attractive the recent suggestion (by Mendenhall) that the Covenant Code was drawn up by Samuel to serve as a guide for Saul's monarchy. This observation takes account of the fact that literature of a semitechnical nature would only be set down and circulated in response to a concrete situation. Nontechnical literature, especially poetry, is bound to be treated in a different way, since poetry combines form and content in such an integrated fashion that it cannot easily be altered without affecting its essential character. Hence it is less susceptible than other forms of writing to periodic modernization.

b. The early monarchic period. The first part of the monarchic period coincided with an era of great prosperity all over the Near East, and just as we have many written records of the achievements of petty oriental despots, so we should expect to find some records of the Judahite and Israelite monarchies. The traditional analysis of the Pentateuchal sources, the Yahwist (J) and the Elohist (E), is probably correct in recognizing that we do have those records, enmeshed with other, later and earlier materials, in the Torah. It has often been suggested that a common source (called G, for Ground) lies behind both J and E, but it is in the nature of the case impossible to be sure about such a hypothesis. G might have been in either verse or prose; if the former, then either a full-scale epic or a series of short narrative poems.

The Yahwist (J) source is a prose narrative epic of Israelite history, which unifies and interweaves patriarchal stories with narratives of the exodus, conquest, and settlement. The Mosaic covenant is deftly balanced with the Abrahamic covenant. The king is seen as both the descendant of Abraham, and thus heir and assign of the promises made to Abraham, and as the administrator of the Mosaic covenant.

The Elohist (E) source covered generally the same sweep of events as J, though with different theological interests. Some of these are: a special interest in prophecy, recognition of the name Yahweh as of Mosaic origin (for the earlier period, both E and the Priestly writer use the general term *Elohim*), and a decided lack of interest in Jerusalem and the Davidides. The overall concerns of E have been partially obscured by their intermeshing with J and cannot be stated with certainty.

Amos and Hosea represent a new phase in the development of the Yahwist traditions. They presented a call for a complete reevaluation of the current state of affairs in terms of the original Yahwist tradition.

Isaiah also began to prophesy around this time. He shared the basic attitudes of Amos and Hosea, but since he lived in a less vulnerable society, with a more stable monarchic tradition, he looked for continuity alongside reform, while Amos and Hosea were forced by the circumstances they confronted to insist that a complete break with the present was the only course of action that could lead to survival.

c. The late monarchic period. The principal literary outcome of the fall of the northern kingdom was the work of the Deuteronomic school. This probably began in the reign of Hezekiah, or less likely, in that of Manasseh, as an effort to codify distinctive Yahwist traditions which had been preserved in the north. The testimony of the Chronicler about the extent and nature of Hezekiah's reforms (2 Chr. 29–32) has too often been dismissed or underestimated. The compilation of Deuteronomy would fit in well not only with Hezekiah's religious activity but also with his literary interests (cf. Prov. 25:1). Furthermore, we know that he was deeply concerned about the fate of the north, and doubtless it was he who devised the policy of religious-political intervention there which Josiah carried out a century later with greater success.

Contemporary with the writing of the Deuteronomic history was the preparation of the so-called Priestly document of the Pentateuch (P), the most problematic of the major sources. The bulk of P is semitechnical literature, which treats paradigmatic schemata like the clean and unclean and their application in the world. The question "Was P an independent narrative source?" has been answered in the affirmative by Engnell, who regards P as the base of the Tetrateuch, the narrative which he supposes to have been added to the Deuteronomic history in order to create the Pentateuch and the Former Prophets. This solution, however, is problematic because the Tetrateuch cannot stand as an independent unit. The story of the settlement cannot end in Transjordan; indeed, the promise to the patriarchs does not include Transjordan at all. The Promised Land starts at the west bank of the Jordan, at the point reached only in the opening pages of Joshua. It seems better to return to a more or less traditional view of P, that its ending is now either buried in Joshua (from which, however, it cannot be extracted) or lost. On the face of it, the latter solution recommends itself, simply because Joshua in its present form is much more Deuteronomic than Priestly.

The position of P in the range of Pentateuchal sources is curious because it is both the oldest and youngest of them. It preserves, e.g., the authentic account of the revelation of the divine name Yahweh (Exod. 6); in addition, some of P's cultic material is demonstrably ancient. That P is not older than J and the monarchy is seen in the strong bond between the patriarchs-sojourn-exodus pattern on the one hand and that of wanderings-conquest-settlement on the other. This is the official line of all sources from the 10th century on. Further, P treats an exceptionally elaborate cultic system in a well-developed conceptual framework, the relationship of which to Mosaic Yahwism is at best tenuous. There is, however, no evidence that P is postexilic and precious little that it is exilic, as Kaufmann has shown.

2. The exilic canon. The bulk of the first two parts of the Bible, the Torah (Instruction) and the Nebi'im (Prophets), was in existence by 587 B.C.E. The material was given its finished form in the half-century after that date. The Deuteronomic history was combined with something very like the so-called Tetrateuch to form the "primary history" (PH) of Israel. At the same time, several prophetic books were edited to serve as a supplement to PH: First Isaiah, Jeremiah, Ezekiel, and a collection of minor prophets: Amos, Hosea, Micah, Nahum, Zephaniah, Habakkuk, and Obadiah. The exilic edition of First Isaiah combined materials derived from the 8th-century prophet of Judah (particularly chs. 1–12 and 28–33) and from later periods down to the exile itself (including notably 13–14, 24–27).

The primary history and its supplement, the first edition of the prophetic corpus (PC1), were given official publication and some kind of canonization, probably in Babylonia, around 550 B.C.E. The two works were not accorded the same status, however, because PH was fixed at that time, never to be revised in any significant way, while the prophetic corpus was expanded and revised at least once, the work being put in final form around 500. Included in the expanded edition were Second and Third Isaiah, some more minor prophets, including Joel and Jonah (the dates of which remain uncertain), and certainly the last three prophets, Haggai, First Zechariah (i.e., 1–8), and Malachi. The suggested date for PH accords well with the plainest fact we know about it: the latest date in the narrative is around 561 (2 Kgs. 25:27-30). Since that date does not refer to any distinctively dramatic event, it cannot be argued that it was specifically chosen by the final editor to conclude the work. The event was chosen simply because it was the most recent event worth relating in the history of Judah. The date for the prophetic corpus is rather less obvious, but certainly plausible.

a. The Qumran evidence. Is there any external evidence to support the hypothesis of the exilic canonization of the primary history and publication of the first edition of the prophetic corpus? It is unreasonable to suppose that any declaration of canonization would be preserved, since canonization is a function of a social structure which is more transient than the canon it creates. Nonetheless, there is some evidence from Qumran of the propagation of a formal text.

Since the hundreds of Qumran biblical scrolls will not be published completely for some time to come, any conclusions drawn from preliminary publications must remain tentative. Some facts are clear, however. The various hands of the Qumran documents come from a period when the Jewish script was undergoing many changes. Thanks to this fact, the relative chronology of the hands and thus of the manuscripts can be established. Further, due to archaeological research at Khirbet Qumran, a settlement not far from the caves, this relative chronology can be associated with the Palestinian pottery sequence and with the Palestinian coin sequence. Thus, the Qumran manuscripts can be dated accurately.

One of the Qumran biblical texts is particularly important because it belongs to the small group of manuscripts which antedate the foundation of the settlement itself, having been brought by the fugitives from Jerusalem who settled in the desert. This manuscript is called 4QSam^b (i.e., the second Samuel manuscript found in cave 4) and is dated conservatively to 275 B.C.E. It shows, unlike the other early manuscripts, completely uniform spelling. This is not the result of a happy accident, but of assiduous work. This labor can hardly be dissociated from some official action, and this action must pass under the rubric of canonization. The official look of the spelling is especially prominent when seen in the light of its probable model, Aramaic court spelling of the 5th century.

This manuscript is hardly irrefutable evidence of canonization in the mid-6th century; but it does provide a strongly persuasive argument in the direction of our hypothesis, since it shows that by around 300 B.C.E., the literary history of the Former Prophets (and thus necessarily of the Pentateuch) is over and the textual history has begun.

The 4QSam^b manuscript and other materials from Qumran show clearly the existence of text traditions which are distinct from the Massoretic Text received today as the Hebrew Bible. Only three can be distinguished: the Palestinian text type (which survives in the Samaritan Pentateuch), the Egyptian text type (which survives in parts of the Old Greek Version), and a third which should probably be associated with Babylonia (which survives in the MT).

This circle of three traditions suggests that the common parent manuscript, though it must be removed some distance in time from the traditions, cannot be far removed. In fact, although there is no supertypology of manuscript development which could tell us how long it takes variant traditions to arise, the possibility of a 5th- or 6th-century original agrees well with the available evidence. Further, since we have several early 3rd-century manuscripts which reflect at least two text types, the original cannot be later than the 4th century.

b. The prophetic literature. The surviving corpus of prophetic poems and speeches cannot be the whole or even a substantial part of the prophetic materials available in the classical period; it is a carefully considered selection made on ideological grounds. An important feature of the corpus is the exclusion of most explanations of the political background of the poems. Surely they could not long remain comprehensible without some such orientation. It seems that the poetry of the prophets supplements the primary history. Is there any evidence for this within the primary history? The constant emphasis there on Moses as prophet and on the role of the charismatic prophets is hardly susceptible of another under-standing. The exact relationship between the two is more difficult to define, since the overlapping sections of PH and PC1 (cf. Jer. 52 and 2 Kgs. 24:18–25:30; and Isa. 36–39 and 2 Kgs. 18:13–20:19) suggest that the two works were in some sense distinct.

The reason for the creation of PC1 is suggested by the material itself. There was nothing in recent Judahite history to encourage the exiles. The editor of PC1 recognized that consolation would come not from writing history, but from proph-ecy. The material of PH prepared the ground for the belief that the prophets who were right about the exile would be right about the return; it also provided explicit information about the return in Lev. 26:40-45 and Deut. 29:22–30:10. The editor of PC1 went further than the editor of PH could have; he went from prose to verse. He began by either preparing or taking over an edition of Isaiah, designed to show the extraordinary resemblances between the 8th- and 6th-century situations of Palestine. He then added the two great prophets of the very period he had to explain, Jeremiah and Ezekiel, and some minor prophets.

PC1 aimed at establishing the credibility of the preexilic prophets by showing that they had correctly analyzed the history of Israel and Judah in the context of power politics; when they saw the hand of God in all that happened, they rightly predicted the outcome. Hence their prophecies dealing with events yet to come (the editor implicitly asserts) can be relied on as well, and decisions and actions in conformity with them should be made.

The expansion of the prophetic corpus around 520-500 B.C.E. centered on two parts of it: the beginning and the end. The prophecies of Deutero-Isaiah were added to the Isaiah book and the later minor prophets — probably Joel and Jonah and surely Haggai, First Zechariah, and Malachi — to the end of the collection. The revision of the corpus can be dated to the period described in Haggai and First Zechariah (1–8), the period of the rebuilding of the temple and the attempted revival of the monarchy. The work of Second Zechariah (9–14) cannot be dated precisely; it probably belongs to the final edition of the corpus.

3. Postexilic literature.

a. The Chronicler. The core narrative of the Chronicler's history is contemporary with the final edition of the prophetic corpus, i.e., it comes from the period between 520 and 500. It is an independent Palestinian work designed to enhance the claims of the Davidic dynasty and of the Second Temple. It presents the claims of the Davidide Zerubbabel, the Zadokide Jeshua, and the Second Temple in terms of the prior claims of the corresponding ancestral figures, David, Zadok, and the First Temple. The work included not only the bulk of Chronicles but also most of Ezra 1–6. (Ezra 4:6-24 and parts of chs. 5 and 6 are from the 5th century.) The genealogies which open Chronicles were probably not included in the core work, except perhaps for that of the Davidic line in ch. 3, which may originally have followed the account of David's coronation.

The final version of this history is the work of an editor around 425 B.C.E. He shared with the first editor an interest in Judah and Jerusalem, and in the priesthood and the temple, though he avoided the subject of the monarchy. There is thus a radical shift of emphasis, clearly reflecting the activity of Ezra and Nehemiah. The most striking evidence for the distinction between two major layers of Chronicles is provided by the contrast between the model of Israelite greatness used in the core narrative (the monarchy) and that of Ezra and Nehemiah themselves (the community of the steppe wanderings). Why Chronicles was adapted to the changed situation of the 5th-century Judahite community by little more than the addition of the memoirs of Ezra and Nehemiah and of the genealogies, and not by a complete rewriting, is unknown. The editor of Chronicles certainly approved of the establishment of a Judahite commonwealth within the Persian Empire.

b. The Book of Truth. The first books of the Writings — Job, the Psalter, and Proverbs — are difficult to date. The book of Job reflects a non-Judahite orthographic tradition and may derive from the northern kingdom or a community with similar linguistic background. It was written in the 7th or 6th century.

Only a few psalms demand an exilic date. Some psalms, like 29, 68, and 72, undoubtedly belong to the earliest period of Israelite hymnody, the 12th-10th centuries. None shows the influence of the Persian, Greek, or Roman periods. The majority probably belong to the 9th-6th centuries and were used in the cult of the First Temple. If the traditional coordination of the Yahwist and Elohist Psalters with northern and southern cultic traditions is correct, then they are preexilic. The five-book format of the Psalter shows the influence of the Pentateuch configuration, which belongs to the 5th century. Qumran manuscript 11QPs^a, which contains some of the canonical psalms (numbered between 100 and 150) in a widely variant order, shows that the final arrangement of the work was either quite late or subject to considerable variation.

The book of Proverbs was composed around a core collection compiled in the time of Hezekiah; the date and even the nature of its various expansions are not clear. There is nothing in the book that demands a postexilic date, though such can hardly be excluded.

c. The Megilloth and Daniel. Of the Five Megilloth, only Lamentations can be clearly dated; it must belong to the period it describes, not only because the poet pictures himself as intimately involved in the events surrounding the siege of Jerusalem, but also because the poems reflect absolute despair, with no hope for a return. Its canonization was probably the result of its status as a Jeremianic pseudepigraph.

Pseudepigraphy is probably also responsible for the legitimization of Ecclesiastes and the Song of Songs. The Hebrew Song is a mixture of classical and archaic forms. Its final editing probably took place in the 6th century.

The Qumran manuscripts of Ecclesiastes date from 150 B.C.E. and suggest that the book was not only known but important at that time, since its content can scarcely be accommodated to an Essene world view. Recent work which has linked the book with Phoenician sources deserves some consideration. The marked tendencies of Ecclesiastes toward speculative thought and the distinctive way this thought was expressed do suggest that the writer was a contemporary of the great Greek and Anatolian philosophers, rather than a latter-day, uncomprehending imitator of them.

Ruth probably owes its canonization to the Davidic genealogy which concludes it. The Hebrew style of the book is closely related to that of J and E, and it may therefore be dated in the 9th or 8th century. This date corresponds well to the Davidic association of the book, which can be explained only with difficulty in the postexilic period.

Esther comes from the Persian period. It is a historical romance about the court of Ahasuerus (Xerxes I) of the 5th century; it was written down no later than the 4th century. It is the only book of the Hebrew Bible not represented at Qumran, though that in itself is no indication of its date. Since the Essenes did not observe Purim in their festal calendar, it is likely that they did not accept Esther as edifying, let alone canonical.

According to scholarly consensus, the book of Daniel received its final form in 165 B.C.E. or thereabouts, although parts of it, especially the stories, go back to earlier times. A source comparable to the materials used in composing the biblical book has been uncovered at Qumran — the so-called Nabonidus fragment, which correctly attributes a madness story similar to the one in Dan. 4 to Nabonidus, rather than Nebuchadnezzar.

4. The origins of the modern canons. The Torah and the Former Prophets together make up the primary history, a product of the exile. Its purpose was not to provide a blueprint for what to do after the exile; it is largely unconcerned with the possibility of the return. It was rather to serve as a theological and historical memoir of the experience of Israel from Abraham to the fall of Jerusalem. It also sought to enable the Judahite community to remain in existence on foreign soil. As such, it was the Bible of the exiles. Contemporary with it was the first edition of the prophetic corpus, which in part shared PH's orientation toward doom and

destruction, while at the same time extending its field of vision by including the Jeremianic prophecy of the new covenant and the Ezekielian renunciation of the "sour grapes" ideology of classic Deuteronomic thought.

The second edition of the prophetic corpus was designed as a vade mecum for the returnees, people spurred on by the prophecies of restoration. Contemporary with this work is the core narrative of Chronicles, the Bible of the late 6th-century settlement in Palestine. It is the work of a royalist, written for a group intent on reviving the monarchy and the other appurtenances of preexilic Judah. These works are the great building blocks of the modern canons, to the development of which we now turn.

a. The Torah. As has long been recognized, the Pentateuch is not a natural unit in the Hebrew Bible. To explain this configuration, we must look to a period in which the wilderness wanderings were so highly regarded as to demand a break between Moses and Joshua sufficiently sharp to take precedence over the actual shape of the narrative. This high regard is most characteristic of the period in which the Torah became a necessity for organizing a community which, like the exodus society, lacked the ordinary features of statehood, i.e., the period of Ezra and Nehemiah. Indeed, the most obvious agent of the transformation of *torah* (correctly, "instruction," not "law") into *da'ath* (a Persian loanword in Hebrew and Aramaic, meaning "law") is Ezra himself, who had the law *(da'ath)* of the Most High God in his hand according to no less an authority than the Persian emperor.

The objective of Ezra and Nehemiah was to strengthen a community which lived as a minority group in an environment that was alternately hostile and seductive; strengthening the community necessarily meant clarifying its ethos. The Torah of Moses, reconceived as a legal instrument, was the chosen means. The instrument was flexible if only because of its size. The authority of Moses which, according to the Deuteronomic history, transcended that of kings, could be invoked only for the Pentateuch. At this time Genesis was probably regarded as a Mosaic composition, his prologue to his own life story. The death of Moses dictated the border between law and nonlaw, i.e., interpretation and commentary. Thus did Ezra carve out of the primary history a new authority for his nonmonarchic society. The rest of the primary history was subsidiary, though useful; the Former and Latter Prophets, the Psalms, and other Writings were accepted for liturgy and instruction, but could not be used as the basis for binding decisions. In all likelihood, it is the text of the Pentateuch adopted by Ezra that lies behind the three textual types mentioned earlier.

The Torah is the canonical scripture of the Samaritan sect, which was born in the travail of John Hyrcanus's reign, probably shortly before his destruction of Shechem. The reasons the Samaritans accepted only the Pentateuch are simple: at the time of the formation of the religion, it still enjoyed the special status Ezra gave it, and it was the only body of writing which was germane to the Samaritans' distinctive religious concerns.

b. Activity in the late Second Temple period and after. The Pentateuch would always have had a special status, given its legal character and use in the self-government of the Judahite community. It provided liturgical rules for the temple sacrifices and festivals; it set up legal bases for social operation; it offered a context for doctrinal speculation and formulations. Where it failed was in the area of prophecy; even Moses' predictions had almost all been exhausted by history. There was a need for material upon which to base hopes for the future, a need that grew in proportion to the rise in apocalyptic thought, which so largely reshaped the prophetic function. There were some Judahites who wanted no part of these forms of speculation. The others, who were in the majority, had two options. They could either create new interpretations of old prophecies to make them suitable to the present and future, or they could invent new prophecies and disguise them as old by attributing them to ancient seers and holy men, like Enoch, the sons of Jacob, and Baruch. The Essene writings from Qumran show how the first course was pursued, in the numerous Pesharim: the fixed sacred text is subjected to an entirely foreign interpretation by an exegete who was himself regarded as inspired. This tactic proved more durable and universal because most Judahites accepted the ancient texts (whose authority could be traced back to the 6th century and was thus unimpeachable), while interpretations could vary and be the object of legitimate discussion. The pseudepigraphic material was never as popular as the old writing and only by accident or dissimulation was it accepted into the canon. Daniel is in fact the only genuine pseudepigraph in the Hebrew Bible.

The Qumran findings have produced so much new information about the finalization of the Jewish and the Catholic Christian canons that no final assessment of the picture is possible. The traditional reconstruction of these two as the descendants of Palestinian and Alexandrian canons is clearly no longer acceptable, as Sundberg has demonstrated. The validity of this reconstruction should have been suspect before Qumran, if only because there are no complete Jewish manuscripts of the LXX in existence and thus none which are organized according to the supposed Alexandrian canon. There are only fragments of pre-Christian date, which provide no clear information about the order of the books.

In reaction to the Qumran data, Sundberg has proposed a striking resolution of the problem of the origin of the two canons. Although it errs in that it seems to demand explicit definition from periods which are too obscure to yield up such information, it is well worth considering. Sundberg contends that there was only one canon in all of Judaism before the destruction of the Second Temple, i.e., the primary history and its prophetic supplement. This canon was enlarged on two occasions. The first was the result of a series of rabbinic disputations associated with the Academy at Jamnia (Jabneel), usually dated around 90 C.E. At this time, the Writings in the Hebrew Bible were defined. Sundberg believes that the early Christian community separated itself entirely from Judaism after the events of 70 C.E.; indeed it was those events which stimulated the final redaction of much if not all the New Testament. Thus at the time of the separation, the canon of scripture consisted only of the Pentateuch, the Prophets, and an undefined group of writings. This group of writings remained undefined in the church for several centuries; during this time, the alarming gap between the Christian and Jewish Bibles was noted by Christians, who attempted to shuffle the contents of the Christian Old Testament around to make the two match. The results are evident in most Catholic editions of the Bible; e.g., the pseudepigraphic letter of Baruch follows Jeremiah, a position which reflects the belief of the Church Fathers that when the Jewish canonical list mentions Jeremiah, it also means the supposed work of his secretary. It was the result of this great shuffling operation that was more or less canonized as the Catholic and Orthodox Old Testament in the century following the conversion of Constantine. This remains the basic canon of the Roman Catholic Church (which excluded 1 and 2 Esdras in the early Renaissance) and of the Greek Orthodox Church (which included these same books at the same time) and of its heirs.

The difficulties with Sundberg's position are manifold. Most importantly, the rabbinic debates at Jamnia do not reveal uncertainty about all the Writings, but only about Ecclesiastes and the Song of Songs. The debates about Esther and the Torah section of Ezekiel are later and largely academic. The major decisions to exclude literature more recent than Daniel were clearly made during the 1st centuries B.C.E. and C.E. The Christian canon was probably fluid in the way that Sundberg suggests, but chiefly because the varieties of thought excluded from the Jewish canon, messianic and apocalyptic, were so important to the early Church.

Sundberg's hypothesis also fails to deal with the simple truth that most, if not all, of the Writings in the Hebrew Bible were in existence at the time of Ezra, except Daniel and possibly Ecclesiastes and Esther, while most of the material which is included in the Catholic and Orthodox canon but not in the Hebrew Bible is much later than Ezra. The exact formulation of a solution to this problem would have to take into account not only all the biblical data, but also additional historical information and cannot be attempted here.

c. Final remarks. The position of the prophetic writings in the Catholic Christian (LXX) canon suggests that the promise-fulfillment relationship between the two testaments was regarded as of crucial import, a regard paralleled by the Matthean use of Old Testament quotations. The very fact that neither the LXX nor the MT correctly reflects the historical development of the canon suggests the importance of the arrangement of biblical materials. Both confirm the overwhelming priority of the Torah.

The different canons reflect the needs and interests of the religious communities at various stages in their histories. The first canon was created in the 6th century B.C.E. as a structural base for a crippled society. It was sharpened and focused by Ezra to serve a specific legal and judicial function — to integrate and sustain a community that had territory but no independent authority. The earlier canon, PH and its supplement, had been purely ideological in character, designed to hold

277

together people who had nothing but memories and hopes. Prophecy and its step-child apocalyptic were crucial in the formation of the later Second Temple period writings which were largely abandoned as a result of the disastrous experience of the First Jewish Revolt. The radical thought of the last years of the Second Temple period was cut back in line with strategies similar to those used by Ezra for similar purposes. Hence the elimination of the luxuriant growth of the speculation cast in apocalyptic-messianic tones which brought about the community's disaster and which later reappears in less dangerous forms in Jewish mysticism and Gnosticism.

The Christian situation was rather different. Messianism was the dominant theme, and so the focus was on prophecy and apocalyptic. For prophecy, history was the vital framework — thus 1 and 2 Maccabees and the Gospels and Acts. Speculation went hand in hand with apocalyptic thought because visions and revelations must be transmuted into knowledge for survival: the two remain un-easily balanced until the rise of late patristic metaphysics.

Bibliography. F. M. Cross, Jr., *Canaanite Myth and Hebrew Epic* (Cambridge, Mass.: Harvard University Press, 1973); D. N. Freedman, "The Massoretic Text and the Qumran Scrolls: A Study in Orthography," *Textus* 2 (1962): 87-102 [see Volume 2, Chapter 3]; "The Law and the Prophets," *VTS* 9 (1963): 250-65 [see above, Chapter 14]; J. P. Lewis, "What Do We Mean by Jabneh?" *JBR* 32 (1964): 125-32; J. A. Sanders, "Cave 11 Surprises and the Question of Canon," in *New Directions in Biblical Archaeology,* ed. D. N. Freedman and J. C. Greenfield (Garden City: Doubleday, 1969), 101-16; *Torah and Canon* (Philadelphia: Fortress, 1972); "Adaptable for Life: The Nature and Function of Canon," *Magnalia Dei: The Mighty Acts of God,* ed. F. M. Cross, W. E. Lemke, and P. D. Miller (Garden City: Doubleday, 1975), 531-60; A. Sundberg, Jr., *The Old Testament of the Early Church.* HTS 20 (Cambridge, Mass.: Harvard University Press, 1964); G. E. Mendenhall, "Ancient Oriental and Biblical Law," *BA* 17 (1954): 26-46; "Covenant Forms in Israelite Tradition," *BA* 17 (1954): 50-76; Y. Kaufmann, *The Religion of Israel* (Chicago: University of Chicago Press, 1960). For Engnell's views *see* G. W. Anderson, "Some Aspects of the Uppsala School of Old Testament Study," *HTR* 43 (1950): 239-56.

[To the above one might add: S. Z. Leiman, ed., *The Canon and Masorah of the Hebrew Bible: An Introductory Reader* (New York: KTAV, 1974); idem, *The Canonization of Hebrew Scripture: The Talmudic and Midrashic Evidence* (Hamden, CT: Archon Books, 1976); B. S. Childs, *Introduction to the Old Testament as Scripture* (Philadelphia: Fortress, 1979), esp. 46-106; J. Barr, *Holy Scripture: Canon, Authority, Criticism* (Philadelphia: Westminster, 1983); R. Beckwith, *The Old Testament Canon of the New Testament Church and its Background in Early Judaism* (Grand Rapids: Eerdmans, 1985); D. N. Freedman, *The Unity of the Hebrew Bible* (Ann Arbor: University of Michigan, 1991); and the survey of J. A. Sanders in his "Canon (Hebrew Bible)," *ABD* 1:837-52.]

28

The Deuteronomic History

The name given by scholars to a supposed unitary historical work contained within the Hebrew Bible and consisting of Deuteronomy and the books of the Former Prophets. The multifaceted material of the history (henceforth DH) is held together by a theological commentary; the whole seeks to explain with ample illustrations how history works. DH was at least originally designed to shore up both the Judahite monarchy and the Mosaic tradition under the covenant rubric; it sought to appeal both to those who were loyal to the Davidic line and to those who longed for a return of the Mosaic era.

The DH hypothesis has been most strikingly formulated in recent years by Martin Noth. He contends that DH was the labor of a single theologian, the Deuteronomist (Dtr), who wrote after the fall of Jerusalem and sought to explain the events of 722 and 586 B.C.E. According to Noth, DH aims at demonstrating that these events were the direct consequence of Israel's unrepentant following after strange gods and almost complete failure to obey divine demands and counsels.

A more cautious formulation would recognize DH as one part of the great primary history (henceforth PH) of Israel, extending from Genesis through Kings. This work was completed shortly after the fall of Jerusalem and canonized *ca.* 550 (see PENTATEUCH §A4b [see above, Chapter 12]). The unit called DH by modern scholars was originally prepared as a programmatic justification of Josiah's reform; it was later slightly rewritten and extended by the exilic compiler of the primary history (henceforth PHEd). In one sense, then, DH is a meaningful unit, since we have most of its contents, largely in original form. Nonetheless, since it has been incorporated into another work, we must be cautious in trying to specify its scope and shape. Fortunately, the radical social upheaval that characterized the first half of the 6th century brought with it such great moral changes that we are able to distinguish late monarchic from exilic material with comparative ease, and thus, in large part, DH from PH. In the last analysis, however, it must be admitted that DH is not a given part of the Hebrew Bible as we have it; this caution must be

279

kept in mind throughout. DH is closely related to the original form of Deuteronomy and the editors of both had similar concerns.

1. Structure
2. Problems
3. Basic approach
4. DH and the prophets
5. Summary
   Bibliography

1. Structure. DH has five major sections. In the first, the editor (henceforth DHEd) provides the original book of Deuteronomy with an introduction (Deut. 1–3 belong to DH; 4:1-40, to the exilic PHEd) and various epilogues (27, 29–34; the associations of these chapters cannot be stated precisely). There may well have been more editorial work; it is, however, likely that Josiah's Deuteronomy cannot be rediscovered by critical techniques. This part of DH deals with the nature of Israel's relationship to Yahweh, consistently emphasizing a program of one God, one people, one cult. Part two of the work, the book of Joshua, narrates the conquest of Canaan, the fulfillment of the greatest of the covenantal promises of Yahweh; the coordination of exodus and conquest themes, already apparent in Judg. 5, finds its fullest expression here. The third part of DH (Judges–1 Sam. 7) describes the difficulties of pre-monarchic Israel and traces the origins of the monarchy. This is one of the two sections of the work that most evidently reflect DHEd's distinctive theology; in fact, the entire framework of Judges was probably constructed by him. Part four details the rise of monarchic government and its greatest glories (1 Sam. 7–1 Kgs. 8). The concluding section (1 Kgs. 9–2 Kgs. 23:25) reviews the progressive decline of the "divided" monarchy. Like the third, it was heavily colored by DHEd, who probably composed the standardized opening and closing lines in the description of each monarch. The editor's hand is most obvious in the ideological evaluation of the consequences which each king's actions had for the nation. Again and again, the editor tells us that because Israel did not do that which was right in the eyes of Yahweh, trouble came. In sections other than three and five, the editor simply incorporated older material in pristine form, or with only minor alterations, usually insertions.

2. Problems. The substantial unity of the narrative that runs from Deuteronomy through 2 Kings can scarcely be questioned. Several basic problems arise in considering what to make of this fact: where does this story line start and stop, and where does the narrative come from? The problem of the unit's exact beginning is most difficult and comes down to a question that is almost as old as the documentary hypothesis itself: does the Tetrateuch (an independent work consisting of Genesis through Numbers) exist? Noth and Engnell are the most important of the many modern scholars who insist that it does. It seems, however, that to call the break between Numbers and Deuteronomy a major one is to leave the story of the first part of the Pentateuch unfinished (a few verses about the death of Moses

at the end of Deuteronomy will not do). Although it might be contended that Deuteronomy would be similarly suspended if such a break were insisted upon, this is not likely; it seems rather that Deuteronomy presupposes an earlier work on which it is dependent. That is, its author assumed that everyone knew the stories up to the settlement in the land; he backtracks only to the most recent high point, the making of the covenant, the first giving of the Torah. The classic view, that Deuteronomy presupposes JE, remains defensible (see PENTATEUCH §§A2c, 4b [see above, Chapter 12]). Another possibility is that the land theology of Deuteronomy is offered in order to obviate the need for the divine grant of the land to the patriarchs (see CANON OF THE OLD TESTAMENT [see above, Chapter 27]).

The end of DH poses a simpler problem. Noth dates the work to the time of the last date contained in it, i.e., *ca.* 561. This approach ignores the shape of the narrative in the last part of Kings, which clearly reaches a climax in 2 Kgs. 23:25, the exaltation of Josiah. What follows that point is the embarrassed follow-up: Josiah's death at Megiddo and the subsequent chaos that continued until the release of Jehoiachin from bondage, an event that provided a soberly hopeful conclusion. This follow-up is the work of an exilic redactor (PHEd); what precedes it is the work of DHEd. The shape of the narrative in Kings was determined in advance by the story that was coming, the story of the best king of all (cf. 1 Kgs. 13:1-3). Only Josiah fulfills the promise of David's early career, a promise of piety and empire.

The incongruity of these ideals of imperialism and religiosity leads us to the third basic question: What was the origin of DH? The court of King Josiah would seem to be the most likely setting for its composition. This explanation accounts not only for the role played by political-theological thought in the world view of DHEd, but also for the influence of the wisdom tradition, most visible in 1 Kgs. 3:4-15. DH presents simple answers to two great questions: Why did Samaria fall? and Why is Josiah carrying out these alarming reforms? The answer to the first is, because of the sin of Jeroboam (1 Kgs. 13:34); the answer to the second is, because he is the long-awaited scion of the house of David and seeks to return to its ideals. That is, Josiah is taking drastic measures to eliminate apostasies like those which led to the fall of Samaria and which, according to the prophets, threaten the survival of Judah and Jerusalem. The next question — How does Josiah know what to do? — becomes equally simple in DHEd's economy of salvation. Josiah knows that he must obey the stipulations of the covenant, to which he is completely subject. If he fails to obey the covenant, the sanctions attached to it will be imposed, and the nation will be destroyed; if he is obedient, then the nation will prosper, and all the blessings will follow. Here we see another, even more cogent reason for dating the work of DHEd to the years before 587: Deuteronomic theology became essentially untenable afterward. The most obvious testimony to this fact is offered in 2 Kgs. 23:26: "Still the Lord did not turn from the fierceness of his great wrath, by which his anger was kindled against Judah, because of all the provocation with which Manasseh had provoked him." This is a forced attempt to explain why Josiah failed.

281

The Chronicler offers another, which is even less appealing (2 Chr. 35:20-22). We cannot discuss here the more compelling testimony to the human inadequacy of Deuteronomic theology but it is not far to seek: it is to be found in the words of Ezekiel (18; 33:10-20), Jeremiah (31:27-34), and Second Isaiah (Isa. 52:13–53:12). (Job may belong with these, or it may be a similar reaction to the destruction of the northern kingdom.)

3. Basic approach. Deuteronomy is thought by most scholars to have a northern orientation. It seems likely that it was the work of a group of northern Levitic priests who fled to Judah after 722. If the work is to be dated in the early 7th century, we may suppose that they were alarmed at the speed with which Manasseh (687-642) was undoing the reforms which had been instituted by Hezekiah (715-687) in response to the utterances of Micah and Isaiah, and which had thus far averted the fall of the south. However, the abundant testimony of the Chronicler to the efficacy of those reforms (2 Chr. 29–32) makes a date under Hezekiah seem more likely.

The Israelite bias of the work is most evident in the anti-monarchic polemic (Deut. 17:14-20); its immediate Judahite origin, in the concessions to Jerusalem as a worship center (12:1-14). The same tension between north and south is evident in DH, and the two works apparently belong to the same tradition. DHEd's writing, like that of the editor of Deuteronomy, is devoted to a handful of basic ideas, which are developed in an elaborate style and repeated in extended perorations. The most important of these are the graciousness of Yahweh's covenant, the evils of idolatry and a noncentralized cult, and the inevitability of punishment and reward. The primary covenant is the one made by Moses. The Abrahamic, Joshuanic, and Davidic covenants are always secondary to it. Thus, the king is always thought of as subordinate to the covenant; in this respect, DHEd's theology contrasts with the more ambiguous views of JE and early monarchic poetry (Ps. 89:35-46). If DHEd accepted the promise of the land to the fathers, he regarded it only as a simple promise, to be fulfilled once, and therefore largely devoid of content after the conquest. His hopes are pinned exclusively to the Josianic reforms and the adherence to the Mosaic covenant they imply. PHEd, on the other hand, sees a great, irrevocable guarantee-type promise in the patriarchal narratives (e.g., in Deut. 4:31); this promise is in fact a crucial part of his approach to the dilemma of the exiles, an approach that must mediate between present existence and the promise of the future. To be sure, DHEd is aware of the possibility of covenantal sanctions so violent that only a remnant would be left after their application. The thought of such punishment is urgent even in Deuteronomy; the "us" and "today" of Moses' sermons reflect the somber mood that was the unavoidable consequence of the events of 722. Such usages do not refer so much to cultic reenactment as to the lives of men who were becoming increasingly aware of the dangers of Judah's position, men of a pivotal generation who were being asked to believe that Josiah was able to meet the challenge of a crisis fraught with risk and opportunity.

One of the most important of Deuteronomy's "anachronisms" is the treatment of Moses as the supreme prophet. Major attention is devoted to the charismatic 9th- and 8th-century prophets in DH, most obviously in the Elijah and Elisha cycles. The importance of prophetic thought in DH is also shown by the use of prediction-and-fulfillment schemata (2 Sam. 7:12-13 and 1 Kgs. 8:20; 1 Kgs. 11:30-31 and 12:15-16; 1 Kgs. 14:7ff. and 15:27-28; 1 Kgs. 16:1-4 and 16:9-14). DHEd's comments on the climactic moment of his history, the fall of Samaria (2 Kgs. 17:7-18, 21-23; vv. 19-20 are exilic insertions), focus on the warnings Yahweh gave through his servants the prophets. A similar conception played a crucial part in the theology of the exilic compiler of the first edition of the prophetic corpus, who believed that the prophets who were proved right about the fall will be proved right about the return. This understanding of prophetic activity stimulated the preparation of the first full edition of the prophetic corpus, around the time of the final edition of the primary history (i.e., *ca.* 550), to which it served as a supplement. Further developments in the Deuteronomic figure of Moses, particularly his elevation from the status of God's messenger (Yahweh speaks in Exod. 20:1) to that of divinely authorized lawgiver (Moses speaks in his own name in Deut. 5:1; the only other prophet who does so is Elijah in 1 Kgs. 17:1), may reflect monarchic ideology. (The semidivine, autonomous status of Moses is important in late postexilic thought.)

Another of Deuteronomy's anachronisms is a theology in which the name of God functions as the primary epiphanic reality. According to this scheme, Yahweh himself does not dwell on earth; rather, he causes his name to dwell (lit., pitch a tent) there. Yahweh's name is the bearer of his presence and dwells on earth in the sanctuary dedicated to him. Canaanite mythological terms formed the matrix for such ideas, but in Israel the conceptual frame was specialized to guard the aniconic understanding of Yahweh, whereby he remained, though present, invisible to his faithful. This may reflect the situation of the northern cultus after the division of the monarchy, at least in the eyes of those opposed to the shrines at Dan and Bethel.

The major differences between Deuteronomy and DH are the result of variant subject matter and theological considerations. The Deuteronomic emphasis on the election of Israel by Yahweh disappears in DH because the notion is relevant only to Israel's precovenantal beginnings. After the covenant, matters had been put on a different footing. Yahweh's gracious choice was no longer a key factor once it was formalized. In Deuteronomy, the land is a primary factor in the survival of Yahweh's people, and salvation is inextricably tied up with it; this theme has faded into the background in DHEd's thinking, perhaps because the notion of the inalienability of property (prominent in the story of Naboth's vineyard) had been so thoroughly diluted that it was no longer even comprehensible. Recent work contending that Deuteronomy and DH have been demythologized and secularized has tended to exaggerate minor points of disagreement with other Pentateuchal sources, while ignoring larger perspectives.

4. DH and the prophets. Writing like that of DH appears in the prose material of the book of Jeremiah (in the two complex sections, Jer. 26–29, 34–45). The material comes in all likelihood from Jeremiah's secretary Baruch, probably in part because he was himself a Deuteronomist who sought to reconcile the more realistic theology of Jeremiah with his own; and in part simply because, like all ancient historians, he tells his tale in his own manner. The emphasis on oration and repetition links his work to Deuteronomy and DH. The difference between the theologies of Baruch and Jeremiah need not be exaggerated; both are concerned with the same phenomena, patterns of covenantal behavior. The difference between the DH historians and the preexilic prophets is not that of cultus and ethics. Nor do they differ in the depth or range of their historical grasp, since both deal with the whole sweep of Israel's experience and understand her present predicament in the light of her origins and obligations. The difference is rather that the historian is systematic in recounting the story from the earliest days until the present, whereas the prophet is more interested in the two end points of the spectrum, and juxtaposes them directly.

The links that connect Deuteronomy and DH to Hosea are both stylistic and ideological; in these works, the northern abhorrence of idolatry and syncretism dominates. The material of Hosea and even of Deuteronomy may have been edited in part under Hezekiah (cf. Prov. 25:1). Unlike both Deuteronomy and Hosea, however, DH lays no distinctive emphasis on the moral quality of the individual's relation to God.

5. Summary. DH as we have it is, then, the work of three editors or editorial circles. The first, the editor of Deuteronomy, wrote in the late 8th or early 7th century and was probably a refugee from the north, not directly attached to the political institutions of Jerusalem. The next two were Jerusalemite, however: the editor of the Josianic history (DHEd), and the editor of the post-Josianic addenda and of the exilic inserts in the "Tetrateuch" (PHEd). The first of these three wrote in the aftermath of the northern destruction; the second, in the days when it seemed that the south might escape the fate of the north; and the third in the days when it was clear that Yahweh had prosecuted his lawsuit with his people and found them wanting, but not utterly beyond future redemption.

Bibliography. N.-E. Andreasen, "Festival and Freedom," *Interpretation* 28 (1974): 281-97; J. Bright, *Jeremiah.* AB 21 (1965), lv-lxxiii; F. M. Cross, *Canaanite Myth and Hebrew Epic* (Cambridge, Mass.: Harvard University Press, 1973), 274-89; J. Milgrom, "The Alleged 'Demythologization and Secularization' in Deuteronomy," *IEJ* 23 (1973): 156-61; J. Muilenburg, "Baruch the Scribe," *Proclamation and Presence: Old Testament Essays in Honour of G. Henton Davies,* ed. J. I. Durham and J. R. Porter (Richmond: John Knox, 1970), 215-38; E. W. Nicholson, *Deuteronomy and Tradition* (Philadelphia: Fortress, 1967), 107-18; M. Noth, *Überlieferungsgeschichtliche Studien* (Halle, 1943); Eng. trans. of 2d German ed. (1957): *The Deuteronomistic History.* JSOT Supplement Series 15

(Sheffield: Sheffield Academic Press, 1981); G. von Rad, *Studies in Deuteronomy.* SBT 9 (London: SCM, 1953); *The Problem of the Hexateuch and Other Essays* (Edinburgh: Oliver & Boyd, 1966); Moshe Weinfeld, *Deuteronomy and the Deuteronomic School* (Oxford: Clarendon, 1972), esp. "Deuteronomic Phraseology," 320-65; "On 'Demythologization and Secularization' in Deuteronomy," *IEJ* 23 (1973): 230-33. For Engnell's views, see G. W. Anderson, "Some Aspects of the Uppsala School of Old Testament Study," *HTR* 43 (1950): 239-56.

[For more recent representative treatments (in English), see, for example, Robert Polzin, *Moses and the Deuteronomist: A Literary Study of the Deuteronomic History* (New York: Seabury, 1980); idem, *Samuel and the Deuteronomist* (San Francisco: Harper and Row, 1989); idem, *David and the Deuteronomist* (Bloomington: Indiana University Press, 1993); J. Van Seters, *In Search of History* (New Haven and London: Yale University, 1983), esp. chaps. 7-11; B. Halpern, *The First Historians: The Hebrew Bible and History* (San Francisco: Harper and Row, 1988); R. E. Friedman, *Who Wrote the Bible?* (New York: Summit Books, 1987); and the surveys of scholarship in M. O'Brien, *The Deuteronomistic History Hypothesis: A Reassessment.* OBO 92 (Freiburg: Universitätsverlag and Göttingen: Vanderhoeck & Ruprecht, 1989), and S. McKenzie, "Deuteronomistic History," *ABD* 2:160-68.]

29

The Age of David and Solomon

To learn the language of a country, to understand its people, to reconstruct the world they walked in — these tasks of the historian are perhaps more difficult when the available documentation feels genuine. In all of biblical history, scholars have never tired of proclaiming that no period is more richly documented than that of David and Solomon. But how much do we in fact know of the Davidic era? If we resist the temptation to view the Chronicler as a puppeteer and the court historian as a searing realist, if we refuse to recognize how extensively both these sources have been read as historical romances, we will answer warily. More important, we will value certain recognizably foreign materials in the two great narratives of Samuel-Kings and Chronicles. Let us, at the start, explore some of these pieces in isolation.

A. David's Poems

The importance of scholarly interest in the value of the Homeric touchstone for the early biblical period can be freely acknowledged. Like Odysseus, David is a king, a leader, and a lover, a traveler and a musician. In a society in which poetry was accessible entertainment and an instrument of social cohesion, David was himself a poet, and some of his poetry is preserved. It may be unreasonable to attribute to him seventy-three psalms; although many of them, notably 2 Sam. 22 (= Ps. 18) and Pss. 89 and 132, have sufficient claim to antiquity, there is little serious reason to specify their origins further. Two Davidic poems are unquestionably authentic: the great lament over Saul and Jonathan (2 Sam. 1:19-27) and the little lament over Abner (2 Sam. 3:33-34) (less unequivocal are the last words of

---

This chapter focuses on the literary and conceptual aspects of the period of David and Solomon.

David [2 Sam. 23:1-7]); the two laments are remarkable because they make no reference to God.

The two laments are also unusual because they are bound to the events and situations that stimulated them. Insofar as a poem is an artifact, it can be conceptualized; most biblical poetry can be conceptualized in terms of people. Despite the attributions to Moses (and Miriam) and Deborah, Exod. 15 and Judg. 5 clearly mediate historical reality within and across a community. The voice in both poems brings the tradition to those for whom it is vital. The great lament is the song of an individual facing others, as in the Royal Psalms and in much of the poetry in the Song of Songs. The analogies are apt, the first because in the great lament a king speaks of another king and a royal scion, the second because he does so in the vocabulary of private passion. But the second is more to the point than the first, for purely royal poetry often focuses on the distance between the king and his people. The song inevitably provides the better example, because in poetry language necessarily prevails over *dramatis personae*.[1]

The poem opens with a cry of anguish over Jonathan's death, and proceeds to refer to the father and son (v. 19):

The Gazelle, Israel, is slain on your heights.
How have the heroes fallen!
Do not announce it in Gath,
Do not proclaim it in the streets of Ashkelon,
Lest Philistine women rejoice,
Lest pagan women exult.[2]

The major themes of the poem are announced. The geography of the deaths is presented and the spatial movement summarized. The prohibition against disseminating the news indirectly specifies the poem's business and defines its homeland, because, beyond Israel's borders, the lament would be twisted into its opposite.

The tension is enormous because, though Saul and Jonathan died together, they are to be mourned separately. The Philistine women would rejoice indiscriminately over both deaths, but David insists on a distinction: he summons the Israelite women to mourn for Saul (v. 24) and himself bewails Jonathan (vv. 25-26).

The geographical motif of the refrain is echoed in v. 21a:

Mountains in Gilboa —
no dew, no rain upon you —
lofty fields.

---

1. See D. N. Freedman, "The Refrain in David's Lament over Saul and Jonathan," *Ex Orbe Religionum: Studia Geo Widengren Oblata,* vol. 1, ed. H. Ringgren. NumenSup 21 (Leiden: Brill, 1972), 115-26. One point can be repeated here: in v. 26, we read *nilā' ['Jaṭâ* for MT *nl'th*.

2. The terms *plštym* and *'rlym* are complementary and overlapping, not synonymous; the sense is "lest the women of the uncircumcised Philistines rejoice/exult."

The land itself is cursed, declared to be absent, dead like the heroes, since land without water is even more starkly beyond the pale than Philistia. Political boundaries are powerful, but they are nothing compared to the border between watered and unwatered land. The close of v. 21 balances v. 19a, adding the figure of Saul to that of Jonathan.

The next section of the poem deals with human geography: Saul and Jonathan posed against their enemies (v. 22); father and son fallen together (v. 23). The public and private presence controlling the last section is also contrasted here: v. 22 refers to public actions and v. 23 to private ones.

The poem concludes with the two lament forms which balance the interdicted exultation of Philistia in v. 20. These forms are separated by the refrain. The first lament form is public, the second, private. The progression from anti-lament (v. 20) to lament-invoking (v. 24) to real lament (vv. 25-26) illustrates a poem inventing itself: cautiously judging its function at the start and then actually performing it. The true lament is itself a playing-out of another kind of dialectic:

> It's hard for me because of you, brother Jonathan.
> You were wonderful for me.
> You were a miracle.
> Loving you for me was more than loving women.

The shift in focus, from David in the first line, to Jonathan in the next two, to mutuality in the last, is delicately handled.

Two frames exist: the refrains, linked to the geographical motif, and the simple cries, the basis of the lament motif. In the first and third sections, the number of refrains and cries is matched, since they delineate separate treatments of Saul and Jonathan, but there are none in the middle section, where the heroes are treated together. The real focus of the poem is v. 20, which provides the material for sections II and III, and which shows David to have been well enough schooled to explain the event that at once created his royal persona and destroyed a part of his real self.

The little lament for Abner, Saul's chief military strategist (2 Sam. 3:33-34), is much shorter:

> Should Abner have died as a fool dies?
> Your hands were not bound
> Your feet were not thrust in shackles.[3]
> As one falls before the wicked, you have fallen?

The poem is held together by the grammatically identical structure of the outer two lines and the middle two lines. Although the subject, as in 2 Sam. 1:20, is political boundaries, those involved in Abner's death are not absolute. David's longed-for

---

3. Lit., "Your feet were not drawn together in bronze fetters."

borders circumscribe but do not divide his two kingdoms. Abner had adopted David's vision but Joab declined to do so, acting in his vengeful murder against both the still actual Israel-Judah line and the legal boundary that forbids blood vengeance in return for acts of war. The dangers of David's vision are obvious, making Joab's act somehow reasonable. The two kingdoms remained separate, even if they were to have a common king, and the combat between the Saulides and David had sunk to private rivalry, to be resolved finally by the proliferation of thuggish behavior. Abner's hands and feet *were* bound, by the shackles of encompassing political action in the arena of domestic conflict. The problem here addressed by David is less clearly grasped than that of the great lament.

The poetic formulation of his theology is to be found in "The Last Words of David" (2 Sam. 23:1-7). There is no reason to doubt either the date of the poem or its attribution to the royal court, even though the words might have been written not by David but a court psalmist.[4] Specific testamentary features seem to be lacking and the poem's title is unexplained. The text does have the characteristics of a royal proclamation, perhaps an accession oracle, in the performance of which the king appears as both recipient and bearer of the divine message. The central claims and affirmations of the monarchy and specifically the Davidic dynasty are made succinctly but emphatically. David is the anointed of the God of Jacob, the beloved of Israel's protector (v. 1). Both Mosaic and patriarchal traditions are tied to David and his house. He is spokesman for YHWH, the God of Sinai, whose distinctive appellation was revealed at the burning bush to Moses. At the same time, he is firmly supported by a covenant with *'ēl 'ôlām,* a patriarchal deity. The royal covenant itself is adapted from patriarchal models, emphasizing the unilateral divine promise of unending progeny and eternal possession of territory, although with an admixture of Sinaitic elements requiring moral conduct on the part of the king. At least in the form in which it is preserved in 2 Sam. 7 and echoed in Pss. 89 and 132 (probably both of 10th-9th century date), the great weight of the royal covenant is on the side of divine commitment rather than of human obligation; along with divine sustenance, however, substantial though not final punishment for infractions is promised. The major props of the dynasty — divine choice (anointing), divine commitment (covenant), divine communication (prophetic inspiration and wisdom) — are all mentioned in the poem. The picture is idealized, in spite of hints of enemies and unresolved problems, but mirrors 10th-century monarchical attitudes. It is faithful to the traditions of early Israel, according to which David is both the object of divine affection and the instrument of divine action.

4. See H. N. Richardson, "The Last Words of David: Some Notes on II Samuel 23:1-7," *JBL* 90 (1971): 257-66; and D. N. Freedman, "II Samuel 23:4," *JBL* 90 (1971): 329-30. On the date and relationship to the more archaic oracles of Balaam, see D. N. Freedman, "Divine Names and Titles in Early Israelite Poetry," *Magnalia Dei: The Mighty Acts of God,* ed. F. M. Cross, W. E. Lemke, and P. D. Miller (Garden City: Doubleday, 1976), 55-107 [= *PPP*, 78-129].

To be noted with 2 Sam. 23:1-7 are two other early royal poems, 2 Sam. 22 and 1 Sam. 2:1-10. The former, in a slightly different version, appears as Ps. 18, and its attribution to David may have contributed to the tradition of Davidic authorship of many psalms.[5] While nothing specific in the poem points to such authorship, it can undoubtedly be dated to the early monarchic period (i.e., 10th-9th centuries), in that it reflects the ambience of the royal court, and articulates the essential themes of royal theology. The presentation of YHWH as creator and controller of the world, maker and keeper of nations, dispenser of weal and woe, victory and defeat, is traditional, but the concentration on his people and his land is royal. He it is who extricates the king from his difficulties, delivers him from his enemies, and rewards his piety and faithfulness with long life and prosperity by reaffirming covenant commitments. The Song of Hannah (1 Sam. 2:1-10), although presented as a late premonarchic poem, is probably coeval with 2 Sam. 22.[6] It emphasizes the intimacy between God and king, who speaks directly to the deity. God's unlimited and arbitrary power is dramatized by vivid contrasts, but the special relationship between God and king is confirmed at the end as in the beginning by the assurance of success in combat and in rule.

In its poetry and prose, architecture, city-building and public works, commercial and military diplomacy, ecclesiastical and civil administration, the monarchy unified Israel's people and traditions around itself, and assumed responsibility for national safety and security under the aegis of YHWH, at the same time demanding the accompanying perquisites and rewards.

The primary history has preserved, besides the royal poetry, two short poems from other portions of David's career, the first a song of praise, the second of disdain. The pivotal role of the two choruses of women in the great lament remind us to hearken to the adulation that greeted the young David's military exploits:

> Saul slays his thousands,
> and David his myriads.[7]

Why should this cry (1 Sam. 18:7; 21:11; 29:5), whose number parallelism is fairly standard and seems only to assign a good many deaths to both men, be repeated three times? Two elements suggest contrast between the men as much as praise for them. The first is the conjunction of the king's name with only one of his subjects, rather than of a monarch and his people. The second, more subtle, is that line 2,

---

5. See F. M. Cross and D. N. Freedman, "A Royal Psalm of Thanksgiving: II Samuel 22 = Psalm 18," *JBL* 72 (1953): 15-34.

6. On the date, see Freedman, *JBL* 90 (1971): 329-30.

7. The Hebrew, identical in all three places, is not easy to render. The preposition *b* is not normally used to indicate the direct object of a verb and the force of the pronominal suffixes is not clear. It can be used here essentially, as we have rendered it, or partitively, like *mn,* as others prefer. Since poetry is often elliptical, the meaning might be construed as "Saul has slain [his enemies] by the thousands / But David [has slain his enemies] by the myriads."

instead of reinforcing line 1, is differentiated from it. This is one of the rare possibilities for contrast. Saul's outrage upon hearing the chorus is understandable in light of the numerical distinction.[8]

The rebellious shout of Sheba son of Bichri the Benjaminite (2 Sam. 20:1) condemning David as a failed tribal leader contrasts sharply with the women's song praising David as a warrior:

> We have no inheritance in David,
> We have no property in the son of Jesse;
> O Israel. Every man to his tents.[9]

Sheba uses the language of traditional tribal dealings for purposes of violence. He understands that the person of David has replaced the traditional basis of Israelite society: possession of land by family, clan, and tribe as a sacred trust. The whole dynamic of royal land-holding has been set in motion, and Jezebel's vicious attack on due process vis-à-vis Naboth's vineyard, though shocking, is a mere step from the position David has reached in Sheba's allegation. Geography and self, the self of the divine-right monarch, are again counterpoised, but here irreconcilably. David has changed in the years since the great lament, despite the lament's forewarning of potential revolt.

Although these poems hardly portray the totality of David, they contribute to the evaluation of a man who was a poet. It is scarcely an accident of preservation that three of the four poems refer to the Saulide monarchy and the fourth to a pre-Saulide vision of Israelite social organization. It is easy to understand why Saul as a *praeparatio Davidis* is an artificial and misleading concept. Most discussions of the monarchy correctly tend to concentrate on those general political developments that eventuated in the canonical form of the institution, but single events deserve some attention, too. The battle of Ebenezer (to borrow a phrase from Georges Lefebvre's description of Napoleon's Eighteenth of Brumaire) opened the way for the restoration of personal political power, seized in turn by an unbalanced personality and a poet; it is personal power that these poems celebrate. Only Sheba speaks to the nation as a whole; otherwise, we have a drama of single men and choruses of women.

Time has preserved David for us as a poet: the figure of David with a lyre dominates the Western tradition of biblical iconography; the psalmist David is personified daily in the prayers of all Jews and Christians. The poetry associated

---

8. See D. N. Freedman, review of S. Gevirtz, *Patterns in the Early Poetry of Israel* (Chicago: University of Chicago Press, 1963), *JBL* 83 (1964): 201-2.

9. The expression is traditional and usually taken to refer to going home. The context shows that more is meant here and in 1 Kgs. 12:16ff. In both cases, allegiance to David and his dynasty is formally renounced and armed rebellion threatened if not carried out. The reference to tents is not archaizing but military in connotation, suggesting that when troops were assembled for war their quarters were temporary (cf. 1 Sam. 17:54; Jer. 37:10).

with him speaks in the tongue of his place and partly explains why Sheba's song of contempt could, a half-century after David's death, foment a successful rebellion against his grandson (1 Kgs. 12:16).

B. David's First Battle

David makes three apparent entrances into the 1 Samuel narrative, the first two linked to Saul's failure to obey traditional priorities in his campaign against Amalek. The initial one (1 Sam. 16:1-13) focuses on Samuel, who, directly after rejecting Saul as unfit to rule, anoints David; the youngest of Jesse's sons becomes a sacrally chosen leader in the tradition of the judges and Saul. The two other stories, attempting to demonstrate David's merit and his popular acceptance, begin with his introduction at court. (One of these stories may have been designed to point up the anointing, but that is not obvious.) The second story, concerned with Samuel's rejection, focuses on the morose Saul, to whom David is presented as a skilled musician (1 Sam. 16:14-23), and the third is coupled with a Philistine campaign. This is the one upon which we shall concentrate (1 Sam. 17).

It is a Jack-the-Giant-Killer story only marginally related to the Davidic narrative, yet it presents in simple form the essence of David's history. Although it is generally recognized as legend,[10] that should not deter us from scrutinizing the material for insights into the "theory" of David's monarchy, since it is surely an early piece of Davidic propaganda.

The failure of leadership which plagues the Israelites in this campaign sets the stage for David. Goliath's aggressiveness discloses the facts: Saul's soldiers refuse the challenge and Saul is too indecisive to respond to the challenge. Lack of trust and self-confidence freezes Israelite and, concomitantly, enemy action. The Philistines must be present at David's inauguration because they were the motive force that led to the Israelite desire for a personally powerful leader (1 Sam. 4), to the start of Saul's reign (in one tradition, 1 Sam. 13), and to the initial break between Saul and Jonathan (1 Sam. 14). But the treatment here of the Philistine presence is distinctive. Representing the military aristocracy, the social organization that gave rise to the coastal folk, gaudily decked in the iron that Philistia monopolizes, is Goliath, epitomizing the Philistine edge. Arnold Toynbee has selected this story

---

10. Out of a multitude of reasons, the most obvious is simply that the defeat of Goliath is credited to Elhanan in 2 Sam. 21:19 and the Chronicler was sufficiently confused by his sources to attempt harmonization in 1 Chr. 20:5. A standard suggestion has been that Elhanan and David are the same, the former his given, the latter his regnal, name. See A. M. Honeyman, "The Evidence for Regnal Names among the Hebrews," *JBL* 67 (1948): 13-25; P. Goldshmid, *BJPES* 14 (1948-1949): 122 (Hebrew).

as emblematic of one of the causes of the breakdown of civilization, "the idolization of an ephemeral technique," in this case Goliath's armor. The Philistine has assumed falsely that "if any champion is forthcoming, he will likewise be a spearman armed cap-a-pie, and . . . that any Israelite who has the hardihood to fight the Philistine champion with his own weapons will be an easy prey for him."[11] As Toynbee points out, David wins the battle because he refuses to play Goliath's game under Goliath's rules. He chooses other weapons and stays out of range of the enemy's spear. The pattern at work here (and through history) is simple: "We see an intrinsically superior technique which has been idolized by its adepts being defeated by an intrinsically inferior technique which has no point in its favour except that it has not yet had time to be idolized, because it is an innovation; and this strange spectacle suggests very forcibly that it is the act of idolization that does the mischief, and not any intrinsic quality in the object."[12]

Into the space between the camps strides David. The boy's speech to Saul in 1 Sam. 17:34-38, proposing himself for Yahwistic champion, is striking political propaganda. One of the basic ancient Near Eastern metaphors of royalty is played out here. The king's subjects are likened to domestic animals defended by the king himself in herdsman guise. The king's enemies are wild animals, untamable, periodically making forays among the civilized sheep and goats. At such times, the ruler rises to protect his territory and ruthlessly eliminates the alien band. Although presenting himself as a shepherd, David all but nominates himself for king. The possibility for new leadership is vibrant.

The combat itself has been the subject of some debate.[13] A number of battles to which it has been compared, notably between Gilgamesh and Enkidu in Tablet II of the Gilgamesh Epic and the fight in the Sinuhe story, deal with private antagonisms and so are better termed duels than contests between champions. A historical example of a true contest may be the Apology of Ḫattušiliš III (1290 to 1265), who describes an incident during the reign of his brother Muwatalliš (1320-1300):

> Now, the Pishuruwian enemy came (and) made an incursion. . . . (His) chariotry consisted of 800 teams, whereas for (his) infantry there was no counting. Yet my brother Muwatalliš sent me (to meet him), and he gave me 120 teams of chariotry, but as to infantry not even a single man was with me. My lady Ištar, however, marched before me. At that time I personally conquered the enemy. For when I slew the man who was the front-runner, the (rest of the) enemy fled. . . . And the weapon which I had held on that occasion I devoted (?) and set up before the goddess, my lady.

---

11. A. J. Toynbee, *A Study of History,* vol. 4: *The Breakdowns of Civilization* (New York: Oxford, 1962), 431.

12. *Ibid.,* 405.

13. See H. A. Hoffner, "A Hittite Analogue to the David and Goliath Contest of Champions?" *CBQ* 30 (1968): 220-25.

In a striking parallel to the Apology, the narrator in 1 Sam. 17:51 says, "When the Philistines saw that their champion was dead, they ran." Like Ḫattušiliš, David set a token of the contest in the sanctuary of his deity. The status of Ḫattušiliš as junior royalty is also striking.

There are other Anatolian parallels to the David and Goliath story, but they are literary and not directly historical. The best-known single combat in the Iliad, between Menelaus and Paris in Book III, ends abruptly when Aphrodite snatches Paris away in a cloud. It is not comparable to the struggle between David and Goliath because it, too, is properly a duel to resolve the private antagonism between Helen's husband and her lover. Book VII is relevant, however, because in it Hector challenges the Achaeans to produce a man to stand single combat with him. Menelaus accepts but is dissuaded by his brother Agamemnon, partly because of his divinely ordained defeat in Book III, and explicitly because Hector is a better fighter. When Menelaus retires, no one else rises to the challenge until Nestor disgustedly rebukes his younger colleagues and tells of earlier days when Ereuthalíôn on behalf of the Arcadians challenged the men of Pylos to present a champion (II.vii.150-156):[14]

> . . . He challenged all our best,
> but all were shaken, full of dread; no one
> would take the field against him. Well, my pride
> drove me to take him on with a high heart,
> though I was then still youngest of us all.
> I fought him, and Athena gave me glory.
> Tallest and toughest of enemies, I killed him,
> that huge man, and far and wide he sprawled.

The youngest of a company defeats the "tallest and toughest of enemies" — surely this is David's story again. The references to pride and a high heart do not miss the mark if applied to 1 Sam. 17:34-38.

The deeply moving spectacle of the lonely battle partakes more of the Late Bronze Age ethos than of the Iron Age; we know something of Homer's world, and it is worth remembering that Ḫattušiliš III was probably an early contemporary of Homer's heroes. The historians who lament the fragmentary and confused state of the accounts of David's later Philistine wars miss a nuance of the narrative. This legend is an emblem of the later wars. Just as the Philistines stimulated the Israelite quest for personal power, so this supreme example of it ends the Philistine threat. The rest is mopping up. When David seizes the sword and then the head of Goliath, he has firmly seized the personal power that so consistently eluded Saul.

---

14. *The Iliad*, trans. R. Fitzgerald (Garden City: Doubleday, 1974).

C. The Deuteronomist's David

The stories of David in the books of Samuel and 1 Kings are usually divided into two major sections. The first account extends from the three introductions to the details of David's cabinet (1 Sam. 16–2 Sam. 8) and is sometimes repetitive, inconsistent, and imperfectly narrated; with it belongs the so-called Samuel Appendix (2 Sam. 21–24). The second, variously called the court history, David's family history, or the succession narrative (2 Sam. 9–20; 1 Kgs. 1–2), deals with David's last years, particularly the tensions that arose when the monarchy became hereditary.[15] Most treatments of the historiography of Samuel emphasize this division and thereby obscure the overall continuity.

The David stories are sharply separated from the rest of the Deuteronomic history (i.e., Joshua, Judges, Samuel, and Kings) by the attention given family relations. Since Gen. 12–50 is similarly separated from the rest of the Pentateuch, scholars frequently associate much of the patriarchal material's redaction with David and Solomon.[16] It has been suggested that the story of Abraham is a prose version of an epic poem sung at David's court. Now if it is true that David's siblings scarcely affect his life, it is emphatically not true of his nephews and sons, concubines and wives. His relationship to Saul, although more complicated, is that of a son to a father, and indeed Saul four times calls him "David, my son" (2 Sam. 24:16; 26:17, 21, 25).

Throughout the exodus saga to the battle of Ebenezer, and again from the time at least of Jeroboam's revolt, the narrative focuses on the people; if occasionally Israel's leaders do not directly face the people, they confront the numinous and certainly not a mirror. Even in Hosea's marriage stories, the reader is baffled — never before so much offstage adultery, such maturing of children between the lines. In the patriarchal and Davidic cycles, the narrative focuses on persons, not characters, which are proper only to the modern novel.[17]

---

15. It is customary to consider that an eyewitness reported these events with great honesty and rare psychological insight into both David's weaknesses and defects. R. N. Whybray has reservations, observing that the passage's details are not necessarily factual and contending that the work is a historical novel of Solomonic propaganda written early in Solomon's reign by a wisdom teacher. Despite the reliance on psychologically loaded words for obscure phenomena (esp. novel and wisdom), this view may be correct. We try to show in the text that the point of the court history agrees with that of the rest of the stories arranged by the Deuteronomist. See Whybray, *The Succession Narrative.* SBT, 2nd ser. 9 (Naperville: Allenson, 1968).

16. For a typical study, see R. E. Clements, *Abraham and David: Genesis XV and Its Meaning for Israelite Tradition.* SBT, 2nd ser. 5 (Naperville: Allenson, 1967); more generally, see B. Mazar, "The Historical Background to the Book of Genesis," *JNES* 28 (1969): 73-83. On the Genesis family material, see R. de Vaux, *Histoire ancienne d'Israël* (Paris: Lebrairie Lecoffre, 1971), 157-79 [Eng. trans., *The Early History of Israel* (Philadelphia: Westminster, 1978); see 161-85, 221-56].

17. For a similar distinction, see M. Buber, "Biblical Leadership," *On the Bible,* ed. N. N. Glatzer (New York: Schocken, 1968), 137-50.

That the editor of the books of Samuel was aware of the common quality of the Davidic and the patriarchal cycles is revealed by his choice and arrangement of the narrative of the birth of Samuel. The painful situation of Elkanah, Hannah, and Peninah closely parallels that of Jacob, Rachel, and Leah.[18] This opening interlude is broken by the story of the loss of the ark, culminating in Saul's kingship. When the David story begins in earnest, the great Genesis motif of the dominance of younger brother over older is seven times multiplied, as David, either the last of seven brothers (1 Chr. 2:13-16) or the last after seven (1 Sam. 16:10-11; 17:12), rises to eminence over them.[19] In the other instance of this motif multiplied, in Genesis, the oldest brother Reuben behaves nobly toward both Joseph and Benjamin, whereas Eliab, David's oldest brother, here acts without a modicum of grace.

David relied heavily on his family, even though his brothers have no role. They are said to have joined him in his outlaw days in the steppe (1 Sam. 22:1, though 'aḥîm may designate relatives), but otherwise played little part in his career, especially compared to that of his sisters' sons. Although only the Chronicler informs us that Joab, David's commander-in-chief; Abishal, Chief of the Thirty; and Asahel are David's nephews by his sister Zeruiah (1 Chr. 2:13-16), the information need not be doubted, if only because Samuel refers to the matronymic son of Zeruiah. (That their father is never mentioned is remarkable.) The stranglehold Joab seems to have had on David, who so cautiously refrains from punishing him for his murders, is probably more than familial, but is surely based on blood. Joab openly disagrees with David after his decision about the census (2 Sam. 24:3), and then ironically, for Joab had right and tradition on his side, but David prevailed. Joab's support of Adonijah over Solomon argues with his opposition to the census that he was religiously more conservative than David. That Amasa, son of David's sister Abigail, commanded Absalom's army is not surprising, but surely the usual explanation that he was chosen to be David's commander after the revolt as a compromise with Absalom's partisans is not the only one: family must have counted for something. Two fraternal nephews are briefly mentioned, sons of Jesse's third son Shimeah (thus 1 Chr. 2:13; 2 Sam. 13:3; 21:21; but 1 Sam. 16:10; 17:13 give the rather different Shammah). One is Jonadab who helps his cousin Amnon to plot the rape of Tamar (2 Sam. 13:3); the other is called Jonathan, said to have killed an anonymous Rapha allied with the Philistines (2 Sam. 21:21). The David genealogy at the end of Ruth (4:18-22), though it testifies to a similar interest in family, is not so tightly interconnected as that in Samuel. The behavior of Naomi's

18. The parallel is noted in J. K. Kuntz, *The People of Ancient Israel* (New York: Harper & Row, 1974), 176.

19. As W. F. Albright points out in his *History of the Religion of Israel* [unpublished], this variance probably reflects an original poetic number gradation of seven/eight, similar to one in the Keret epic. (For the sake of poetic parallelism, when a number is used it is intensified by the number immediately following, according to the formula $n + (n + 1)$; see Amos 1 and 2.

great-great-grandchildren at least betokens a long way from Bethlehem's threshing floors to Jerusalem's.

The relationship of David to Saul and Jonathan is complex. Basically, after David's early period in Saul's favor, Jonathan idolized David, Saul angrily rejected him. Saul wanted Jonathan to become king, and it is at least possible that Jonathan expected David to fill that role. Although there apparently was no clear-cut pattern for royal succession in Israel, Saul's position is entirely understandable, since father-son succession is common. Jonathan may have advanced David's candidacy because he knew Samuel wanted him or because David's political competence and popularity accorded with traditional ideals; the two are not exclusive. David often remarks on the special status of a royal son-in-law, seeming to discount the eventuality of his becoming one (1 Sam. 18:18, 23). His zeal for reunion with Michal before being presented to the northern tribes as king of Israel also seems relevant (1 Sam. 18:20, 28), although Michal could in fact have symbolized the union of the kingdoms. The father-son conflict dominates the story of the succession, Absalom's feud with Amnon seems to stimulate Absalom's contest with his father, reinforced in a familial sense by the conflict between the generals, the cousins Joab and Amasa. All this introduces the great ritual danced around the dying David by Adonijah, Solomon, Bathsheba, Zadok, Benaiah, Nathan, Joab, and Abiathar. The participants in Absalom's revolt seem to have little support. The only sizable group mentioned are the royal scions at Adonijah's feast in En-rogel. No elders, no representatives of the people, attend Solomon's coronation at Gihon. Solomon's monarchy is established by means of covert dealings in personal politics, blood ties, and local geography. The power of Bathsheba epitomizes the misuse of sex, foreshadowed by Sarah's demand for Hagar's expulsion, and more vividly by David's fight with Michal, Ishbaal's conflict with Abner over Rizpah, and Absalom's seizure of his father's harem. Sexual politics in fact persist in the Bible, in the incident of Adonijah's request for Abishag and its consequences, and later in the figures of Jezebel and Athaliah. But it is here, in the fulfillment of David's supposed promise to Bathsheba, about which so many historians have pointlessly speculated, that all the horrors of harem conspiracies are focused. The ingredients that combined to elevate David are sacrificed to a memory of lust. Sheba son of Bichri had asked what share Israel had in David's house; we ask what his share was in Israel. Bathsheba, the Jebusite noblewoman who brought him his greatest grief, also dictated his heir.[20]

The mold into which the Deuteronomist and his predecessors have poured their narrative of David's politics is stamped with the complexities of David's alliance with the Saulides and of his own household. But we must take into account

20. See A. Malamat, "Aspects of the Foreign Policies of David and Solomon," *JNES* 22 (1963): 8-17, esp. n. 37; and "Comment on E. Leach: 'The Legitimacy of Solomon,' " *Archives européennes de sociologie* 8 (1967): 165-67.

the influence of the patriarchal stories and the desire to explain, at least in part, the blood bath of David's dying days. His glory and his family fuse in later Judahite history, but in the first generation they seem to have been unremittingly at odds.

D. The Chronicler's David

The first Chronicler wrote after the primary history (the Pentateuch and the Former Prophets) had attained canonical status, and after the realities among which it had been created were in danger. In the last quarter of the 6th century, the Zadokite-Davidide party in Judah attempted to revive the major preexilic institutions — monarchy, priesthood, and temple — and commissioned a historical narrative to support and explain them.[21] In the brief period between the late monarchic era and the Chronicler's, the historical perspective of Judah had shrunk by about five centuries. What the patriarchs were to the Deuteronomist and his successors, Moses was to the Chronicler; both fathers and founder were considered prehistoric by their respective annalists. Just as history proper begins for the Deuteronomist with the work of Moses, so, for the Chronicler, it begins with Saul's death and David's ascendancy. The shift in focus required reevaluation of David. The Chronicler probably wanted not to replace the primary history with his own, but to give it a new perspective. If the Chronicler's David is studied only by means of what has been amplified and omitted in the Deuteronomic material a major point would be missed: by making David primary, he has implicitly arrogated to him the position of Moses in the Deuteronomic history.

The Chronicler's explicit change in his "sources" offers the most striking implicit comparison between the two. Just as Moses devoted his life to the goal of reaching the land, so David devoted his to the temple. Moses failed because of a single lapse in his service to God. The Chronicler would have us believe that David failed for a similar reason. YHWH had promised in 1 Chr. 17:10 (roughly = 2 Sam. 7:9), "I will further subdue all your enemies." Apparently David failed out of an excess of zeal to trust that portion of Nathan's oracle, because a later oracle informed him: "You have shed much blood and have waged great wars: you shall not build a house to my name because you have shed so much blood before me on the earth" (1 Chr. 22:8; cf. 1 Kgs. 5:3). Although the Chronicler was not consciously remaking David in the image of the Deuteronomic Moses, he sought to begin, like the Deuteronomist, with an all-but-perfect hero, with a single visible flaw.[22]

21. See D. N. Freedman, "Canon of the OT," *IDBSup* 130-36 [see above, Chapter 27]; and F. M. Cross, "A Reconstruction of the Judean Restoration," *JBL* 94 (1975): 4-18.

22. On the concept of failure in biblical leadership, see Buber, "Biblical Leadership," and also his beautiful essay, "Plato and Isaiah," *On the Bible,* 151-59.

This is not the sole structural parallel with the Deuteronomic Moses: God gave Moses the tabernacle plans and David the temple plans; Moses initiated the corps of tabernacle personnel and David expanded it for the temple. The crucial contrast between their kingdoms, that of Moses the kingdom of God and of David the kingdom of David, was never apparent to the Chronicler, and in some ways Nathan's oracle serves Chronicles better than it does Samuel. A stronger contrast between the Deuteronomist's and the Chronicler's view of history, that of the great future leaders, is also less apparent than the cultic links, because Deuteronomy's "prophet like Moses" is so unlike the messiah. Both Deuteronomy and Chronicles preserve the triad of prophet, priest, and king, but the Deuteronomic prophet is the key figure; priest and king are civil and ecclesiastical functionaries. For the Chronicler, however, the king is central, supported by the proclaiming (or electing) prophet and the anointing (as well as anointed) priest, who only legitimizes the king.

Seen in this light, the Chronicler's version of the David stories is exonerated from the frivolous charge of being a simplistic, moralistic rewrite. Rewritten in large part it certainly is, but for the purpose of eliminating not wickedness so much as the imputation of personal power. The Deuteronomist was aware that David was a completely different sort of leader from Moses and felt free to make that clear. His historical view began with a man who held power in a way he respected, i.e., in trust for the people. The excitement of David was his implicit belief that the fortunes of the nation moved with those of the Saulides and his own. This was encapsulated in the great lament and played out in the Deuteronomic narratives against a backdrop not of two nations but of two families and their courts. Had the Chronicler portrayed David in this way, he would have all but asked the community of returnees to vest not their hopes and energies but their very selves in Zerubbabel, and whatever that man's strong points, Persia was dominant and Palestine a backwater. The Chronicler needed a compassionate, not a passionate, leader. By adding countless details of cultic planning to David's record, he sought to make worship possible. More important, by suppressing David's mercenary career, his murderous adultery, and his disastrous family relationships, by enhancing the positive, he sought to create a framework for community.

E. David's Political Career

The political activities of the greatest Judahite leader continually impinged on the surrounding nations: Philistia, Israel, the several Aramean states, and Tyre. Initially a Judahite in the court of the Benjaminite who inaugurated the first personally based union of Israel and Judah, David began his campaign to found the second directly after the court rejected him. David's period of lawlessness is less easily understood than Moses' murder of the Egyptian, but the accrued dividends cannot, at any rate, be gainsaid.

David's private army is also hard to assess. Were they genuinely disenfranchised malcontents, or soldiers of fortune, or a bit of both, so frequently the case in fringe movements? David's army grew in accordance with a common pattern:

> Propertyless men and free proletarians who did not possess full civic rights and needed special protection . . . would gather around a captain *(sār)* especially at times of civic unrest and political and economic crisis. Such bands of warriors would engage in unrestrained pillage and would sell the services of their arms to local potentates and large land owners, the "great men." The captain in command of such a band was a man of authority and influence, usually having designs of his own on the powers that be. . . . He could . . . transform his band into a highly organized military force whose objective was to usurp the governing power.[23]

Such prolonged military service often means isolation from social developments and dangerous deification of military leaders, particularly among troops fiercely loyal and militarily competent.

David's initial flight to Nob had unfortunate consequences, of whose human aspects David seems to have been aware, if not of their momentous import for national traditions. A major Yahwistic priestly family was summarily reduced to one member. The citizens repeatedly disclosed David's hiding places (1 Sam. 23:19; cf. 1 Sam. 26:1; 1 Sam. 23:10) and Nabal refused to pay the protection money David attempted to extort from him, thus probably indicating to David the difficulty of being a completely unattached buccaneer. His extreme respect for Saul's person during this period suggests that, despite long ostracism, David's political imagination still functioned in Yahwistic terms, albeit in a way that was solicitous of the Lord's anointed king.[24]

David's objective was presumably his own enthronement. With the first necessity, a band of followers, secure, he needed a reasonably safe base of

23. B. Mazar, "The Military Élite of King David," *VT* 13 (1963): 310-20, esp. 310-11. The analogy with the *ḫapiru* bands mentioned by Mazar is worked out in G. E. Mendenhall, *The Tenth Generation* (Baltimore: Johns Hopkins University Press, 1973), 135-38, and n. 64, in which Alt's adumbration of the notion is cited. See also Mazar, *JNES* 28 (1969): 77-78, 80-81.

24. On the theory of kingship, see H. Tadmor, " 'The People' and the Kingship in Ancient Israel: The Role of Political Institutions in the Biblical Period," *Cahiers d'histoire mondiale* 11 (1968): 46-58; A. Malamat, "Organs of Statecraft in the Israelite Monarchy," *BA* 23 (1965): 34-65 (repr. *BAReader* 3, ed. E. F. Campbell and D. F. Freedman [Garden City: Doubleday, 1970], 163-98); E. A. Speiser, "The Manner of the King," *Judges,* 280-87; R. de Vaux, "The King of Israel, Vassal of Yahweh," *The Bible and the Ancient Near East* (Garden City: Doubleday, 1971), 152-66; and J. A. Soggin, *Das Königtum in Israel.* BZAW 104 (Berlin: Topelmann, 1967).

operations, where he could consolidate his resources. The cost of this base was high: at the least, allegiance to the king of Gath was demanded in return for the Ziklag fiefdom. During his Philistine vassaldom, David, however, systematically ingratiated himself with the Judahites, both by large-scale bribery and shameless deception of his overlord. He could easily exploit the disunity under Saul to his own advantage, at the same time, indeed, that the Philistines were eroding the Saulide dominion. The preparations for the battle of Gilboa, crucial to David's political future, turned out well: he was spared the ordeal of fighting under Philistine colors and of having either to oppose Saul and Jonathan and assume responsibility for killing his friends and destroying his possible political advantage, or betray his overlords and while risking much at their hands, gain little or nothing from helping to engineer a victory for his former chief, who would then only pursue him further.

David acquired both of his kingdoms partly because of his response to two deaths. By virtue of his reaction to the deaths of Saul and Jonathan, combined with his record of protecting Judah during his Philistine sabbatical, David was elected king by an unspecified group of Judahites at Hebron.[25] This election may have formalized an already existing relationship, since David had long since demonstrated military competence, achieved popular support, and perhaps even prophetic election. During his seven-and-a-half-year reign at Hebron, David might have continued as a Philistine vassal. The two deaths necessary for David's second kingdom followed upon each other and David successfully managed, although he did not arrange; the deaths of Abner and Ishbaal (Ishbosheth). He exploited and maneuvered, but at a distance. Afterwards, he was elected king of Israel at his capital, Hebron. These, it must be noted are two distinct elevations to two distinct realms. The Judahites did not participate in the second coronation. There was no United Monarchy under David, only a uniting monarch.

During the Hebron period David had taken significant steps toward consolidating his kingship. He broadened his policy, initiated with Michal and Abigail, of marrying daughters of influential men, by going outside Yahwistic territory to marry Maacah, princess of Geshur (2 Sam. 3:3).[26] He also began to create a military elite by bestowing upon some thirty heroes specific leadership.[27] Joab became chief of staff at this time. The task of consolidation burgeoned after the second coronation. Whatever his previous status with the Philistines, he was now persona non grata, and whatever the claims of Hebron to be capital of Judah, it had none to be capital of Israel.

---

25. On this period, see B. Mazar, "David's Reign in Hebron and the Conquest of Jerusalem," *In the Time of Harvest: Essays in Honor of A. H. Silver,* ed. D. Silver (New York: Macmillan, 1963), 235-44. On Hebron, see Mazar, *JNES* 28 (1969): 82.

26. See B. Mazar, "Geshur and Maacah," *JBL* 80 (1961): 16-28.

27. See Mazar, *VT* 13 (1963): 310-20; and *In the Time of Harvest,* 239.

The chronology of David's solution to these two great problems is obscure,[28] but his success as dual monarch depended on eliminating both. His solution of the legal problems and of government administration had longer-range effects and therefore receives more attention in the text. David's decision to take Jerusalem was perhaps a strange but surely a masterful solution to the problem posed by two kingdoms: instead of choosing between them he created a third quite separate entity, a tiny private realm of his own. The absorption of Jerusalem into Judah begins early under Solomon, as part of his systematic nationalization of his father's private holdings, but its independence was integral to David's methods, his personal politics.

The choice of Jerusalem was natural and topographically understandable; its importance in the Middle and Late Bronze Age is well attested in extrabiblical sources. Its appeal, however, should not be explained merely by topography or climate, and certainly not by its link with the obscure Moriah and Salem traditions seized on by later writers. Jerusalem was chosen because it had existed as a political structure from Abdu-Hepa king of Jerusalem in the Amarna Age, through Adoni-zedek of Joshua's time (Josh. 10:1-5), down to David's. David did not simply establish a neutral capital, nor one that would be cheaper than a city created *ex nihilo,* a luxury only available to immensely wealthy emperors like Akhenaten of Egypt or Sargon II of Assyria. He chose Jerusalem because it was exactly the political establishment necessary if Saul's failure were to be avoided, with a trained and literate bureaucracy, diplomatically skillful and capable of administering a dual realm. David did not merely take Jerusalem. He took it over, whole cloth. The precise nature of the previous royal tenant's legacy is not certain; particularly problematic is its religious dimension. It was small and long remained so, but the radical change made by the acquisition was out of all proportion to its size.[29]

The account of the conquest of the city is obscure. Chronological uncertainty is emphasized by reference to Hiram of Tyre (2 Sam. 5:11-12), who ascended the throne late in David's reign (*ca.* 969). Mazar has an attractive suggestion about the problems of the capture of Jerusalem: it was taken in David's first year at Hebron. This accounts for Joab's presumed elevation to military commander before the Ishbaal wars and at the time of the seizure of Zion. Although the possibility that Joab's success at Jerusalem may have validated an earlier *de facto* position of leadership should not be neglected, the hypothesis does account for some otherwise problematic topographical data. Mazar associates the final shift of the capital with the transfer of the ark to Jerusalem.[30]

---

28. Mazar separates the two wars but dates both prior to the transfer of the capital to Jerusalem, which he distinguishes from the seizure of Jerusalem (Year 1 in Hebron) and the second coronation (Year 3 in Hebron!), roughly following the textual order but opposed to most others; see Mazar, *In the Time of Harvest,* 241-44, esp. n. 15.

29. See *ibid.,* 236-38.

30. *Ibid.,* 241-42.

David's royal campaigns against the Philistines, though narrated after the capture of Jerusalem, probably took place earlier, since they represent a solution to the more pressing of David's two great problems. The exact effect of the campaigns is unknown. Philistia seems to have been drawn toward Egypt in the second half of the 10th century, but we have no idea of the extent or character of David's victory over it.[31] Two battles, both in the valley of Rephaim, between David and the Philistines are documented (2 Sam. 5:20-25), but the great unanswered question about the coastal wars is why David succeeded where Saul failed? Was it the quality of his leadership or, as many scholars suppose, special knowledge of Philistine tactics, and if so, how did he acquire it? Did David's victory depend on Saul's battles?

The narrative of David's initial consolidation of power is somewhat schematic: government in the ancient world served two functions, law within the boundaries and war beyond them, and to perform these two tasks David conquered Jerusalem and the Philistines. Also essential to ancient government was certified religious legitimacy, which Saul achieved by Samuel's prophetic election and lost by the same prophet's rejection. David seized upon the ark not only as a link with the Mosaic past, but as a form of religious authorization. The usual observation that the transfer was an attempt to recapture for the monarchy the vitality of earlier religious traditions cannot be made without adding that the action was radical, because David removed the ark from tribal land and set it up on his private estate.

Other aspects of David's religious activity further illustrate how intimately linked were religion and politics in the ancient world. The political character of the two Davidic priestly offices is patent in Solomon's defrocking and expulsion of Abiathar (1 Kgs. 2:26-27). More controversial is whether Zadok was really a Yahwist, or, as many scholars suggest, a member of the dominant priestly family in ancient Israel, which was Jebusite. The priestly genealogies are problematic, however, and F. M. Cross, Jr., has recently proposed two independent priestly lines, one descended from Moses and the other from Aaron. The former was represented in David's time by Abiathar of the Eli-Shiloh line and in Jeroboam's by the priesthood of the Dan sanctuary; the latter first by Zadok of the Hebron tradition and afterward by the Bethel priesthood. Since neither hypothesis entirely explains the complexity of religious development under the monarchy, we can temporarily leave the quest unresolved.[32] The institution of the system of Levitical and asylum

31. For evidence of Egyptian takeover of the land, see B. Mazar, "The Philistines and the Rise of Israel and Tyre," *Proceedings of the Israel Academy of Sciences and Humanities* 1/7 (1964): 14-15; Malamat, *JNES* 22 (1963): 11-17; K. A. Kitchen, *The Third Intermediate Period in Egypt (1100-650 B.C.)* (Warminster: Aris and Phillips, 1973), 280-83.

32. For discussion and bibliography, see F. M. Cross, *Canaanite Myth and Hebrew Epic* (Cambridge, Mass.: Harvard University Press, 1973), 195-215.

cities at this time reflects royal awareness of the territorial dimensions of political and judicial action. The theology of the divine election of the Davidic line, designed in part to eliminate tribal conflict on a higher level, is the commanding ideological development of the monarchy.[33]

The Aramean states played a crucial role in the foreign affairs of David's reign and, as Malamat has shown, their history presents intriguing similarities to that of Israel and Judah. Hadadezer is called a Rehobite, a native of the small state of Aram Beth-rehob, which he evidently ruled before conquering the larger Aram Zobah. He united the two under his personal rule, much as David united Judah and Israel.[34] The political geography of the earliest part of the 1st millennium was determined by personal power and by the small social organizations formed in the bleak period around 1200 after the Late Bronze Age empires collapsed. The analogy between David and Hadadezer helps us to place David in a Levantine setting of rising prosperity, in which many small states were allied. Both empires seem to have been collocations of political units that retained a considerable degree of viable "native" leadership.

The first encounter of the two "empires" was a stalemate. The second weakened Hadadezer's superstructure. Southern states, including Maacah and Tob, shifted to David's camp; Geshur and Hamath, both probably independent throughout, posed more of a threat to Hadadezer; and his northern dependencies tried to secede. The last problem seemed either the most pressing or the most soluble, for as soon as Hadadezer went north David drove deep into Aramean territory and seized it. He was then able to incorporate Hadadezer's empire into his own. The nature of this action is unclear, as is the strength of David's hold over the territory. Hadadezer's empire remained part of Solomon's until the well-known pattern of an ambitious general and a solicitous army led to Rezon's founding of Aram Damascus. David's northern surge was bounded by the Euphrates and the state of Hamath.

David's political dependencies also included Moab, a tributary power, and Ammon and Edom, which yielded forced labor.[35] If Hanun son of Nahash of Ammon and Hadadezer were allied, the collusion was not strong enough to include

---

33. *Ibid.*, 219-73; D. N. Freedman, "Divine Commitment and Human Obligation," *Interpretation* 18 (1964): 419-31 [see above, Chapter 17].

34. See Malamat, *JNES* 22 (1963): 1-3. For general background on Aram, see B. Mazar, "The Aramean Empire and Its Relations with Israel," *BAReader* 2, ed. E. F. Campbell and D. N. Freedman (Garden City: Doubleday, 1964), 127-51; *JNES* 28 (1969): 78-79; A. Malamat, "The Kingdom of David and Solomon in Its Contact with Egypt and Aram Naharaim," *BAReader* 2, 89-98; and esp. on 2nd millennium materials, de Vaux, *Histoire ancienne d'Israël*, 194-201 [see Eng. trans., 193-209]; and for a recent overview, A. Malamat, "The Aramaeans," *Peoples of Old Testament Times*, ed. D. J. Wiseman (New York: Oxford University Press, 1973), 134-55.

35. See D. B. Redford, "Studies in Relations between Palestine and Egypt during the First Millennium B.C. II: The Twenty Second Dynasty," *JAOS* 93 (1973): 3-17.

the whole royal house of Ammon, since David merely replaced Hanun with his brother Shobi.[36] The Edomite monarchy, on the other hand, was abolished. In an era of profound Egyptian weakness and slow Assyrian rise David was himself king of Israel, king of Judah, owner of Jerusalem, chief of Moab and Ammon, and overlord of Aram Zobah, Aram Beth-rehob, Edom, and the Canaanite city-states of Palestine. He foreshadowed Solomonic diplomatic practices by diversified alliances: connubial with Geshur, political with Hamath, and commercial with Tyre. David's diplomatic program was as multifaceted as his military program was single-purposed.

Contemporary with the Ammonite wars was David's adultery with Bathsheba and his long-range murder of her husband. The author of the Davidic family history considers this episode climactic, his high point of internal and external success, whence began his downfall. He recovered from the miasma of this incident only, according to the narrator, when Solomon became king. From a political point of view, David's family conflicts are important because they illustrate the cancerous spread of the royal court. That Amnon's incestuous rape of Tamar matches David's seduction of Bathsheba, that Absalom's distressing treatment of David resembles Saul's, is less painful than the fact that a breeding place for such monstrosities had hatched in Israel. Absalom's vengeful murder of Amnon is no bloodier than Solomon's method of carrying out his father's will; the game of personal power politics was beginning to be played, albeit only at the highest levels. The foundation for the prophetic denunciation of all Israel was slowly being laid.

Absalom's revolt seems like an explicit reversion to the last days of Saul. Widespread dissatisfaction supported Absalom, as it had supported David. Even the old geography reappears, as David flees to Ishbaal's capital Mahanaim, after Absalom comes north from Hebron, site of David's coronations. Personal loyalty again becomes the only force behind political action. Did David's administrative centralization actually fail? Did he neglect the first royal priority of protecting the disenfranchised? The extent of Absalom's popular support is certain — how much is enough? — as is its distribution. It may have been all of Judah or all of Israel; possibly much less, perhaps only Hebron and its environs. Absalom's revolt teaches at the very least that the empire was fragile at its base and that personal loyalty alone cannot sustain a major political structure.

The revolt of Sheba son of Bichri, whatever its chronological relationship to that of Absalom, reveals the same administrative defects. Its criticism of the regime, however, hits even more fundamentally, as we saw earlier, at disregard of the people. Little Benjamin, probably a continuing center of anti-Davidic sentiment, rises again to assert its claim to tribal leadership, though we can guess that Sheba was not a Saulide.

---

36. David may have taken advantage of harem politics in Ammon, where royal wives were pitted against each other and half brothers pursued the fight. See the Septuagint of 1 Kgs. 14:21.

One possible cause of these revolts, and surely a major grievance, was David's census, a programmatic step toward more sophisticated administration of taxes and military and corvée conscription.[37] The peak in David's shift toward bureaucracy, which began with his cabinet organization, the census was regarded as a challenge to Israel's divine charter because it at least provided a base for eliminating all tribal institutions. It was prompted in part by the inclusion in the realm of previously non-Israelite cities, but probably in greater part by the need to eliminate local particularities as opposed to governmental uniformity. It may have caused redistricting in Judah (cf. Josh. 15:21-62). Other organizational developments, particularly in David's cabinet, are treated by Yeivin in volume 5; suffice it to note here the limited effectiveness of personal power as revealed by the unsteady administrative machinery.

The striking parallels in the careers of David and Hadadezer noted above are probably not isolated phenomena. What we know of the career of Abibaal of Tyre (*ca.* 1000-969) is similar. He led Tyre, less powerful than its neighbor, in its break with Sidon, which was eventually completely subordinated.[38] Like David, Abibaal filled the vacuum created by the quickly shrinking Philistine presence; as far as we know, he had nothing to do with that disappearance, but he or his successors who initiated Mediterranean sea trade and colonization profited more than Israel and Judah ever could. Whatever Abibaal's contacts with David, his son Ahiram (Hiram) I began a treaty relationship with David that continued under Solomon and launched the greatest physical monument to the divine election of the Davidic dynasty: YHWH's house as a chapel for the house YHWH built for David.[39]

F. Solomon

David's reputation is essentially that of an artificer, a manipulator of ordinary reality into the shape of art; Solomon's of a patron of artificers. Similar parallels between the two are common: David was a warrior, Solomon a diplomat; David a lover, Solomon a luster; David a poet, Solomon a phrase-maker. The chief artifact of David's life is the great lament, which we have still and over which we weep. Solomon's greatest monument, of bronze, wood, and stone, charms and puzzles

---

37. See J. Bright, *A History of Israel,* rev. ed. (Philadelphia: Westminster, 1972), 201-2, esp. nn. 53 and 54.

38. See Mazar, *Proceedings of the Israel Academy of Sciences and Humanities* 1/7 (1964): 15-22; and Kitchen, 281-82.

39. On the treaty, see F. C. Fensham, "The Treaty between the Israelites and the Tyrians," *Congress Volume, Rome 1968. VTS* 17 (1969): 71-87.

readers and challenges the precision of scholars. Thus Buber explains his refusal to consider Solomon a distinctively biblical leader:

> Solomon is an oriental king, only a very wise one; he does his task, he builds the Temple, but we are not shown that this task colors and determines him. What has happened here is simply that the completion of a task, the completion of a task already intended and already begun, has been taken over by a . . . successor. . . . The task of David, which he was not allowed to finish, was taken over by Solomon. In this connection I recall the words that David and God exchanged on the proposed building of the Temple and the prohibition against David's carrying it out: "It is not for you," says God, reproving David (II Sam. 7:3). . . . The work is taken away from him, and taken away from him, moreover, in view of his special inner and outer situations; another man has nothing more to do than bring the work to its conclusion.[40]

The impression that Solomon replaced David is reinforced in the opening chapters of Kings, where David appears prematurely aged as compared to his still vigorous contemporaries Joab and Nathan.

The genealogical problems of Solomon's succession are enormous. Senior status presumably led Adonijah to seek the throne and yet the biblical silence about David's second son, born of Abigail, Chileab/Daniel, should not be ignored. Although 2 Sam. 12:24 says that Solomon was the first of Bathsheba's children by David to survive, 1 Chr. 3:1-9 lists Solomon as the fourth and last of Bathsheba's sons, after Shimea, Shobab, and Nathan. This is supported both by 2 Sam. 5:15 and 1 Chr. 14:5, which give Solomon as the fourth of the Jerusalem children (as opposed to the six sons and one daughter born at Hebron). It is of course possible that the genealogist of Chronicles thought Bathsheba the only Jerusalem wife and attributed to her the first three Jerusalem-born children, but the chance of error in so crucial a matter seems small.

The man who rode to Gihon on mule-back with Bathsheba, Benaiah, Zadok, and Nathan doubtless felt the need for the royal bodyguard that followed the party; he had grown up with such appurtenances. He had no demonstrated popular support, no military competence, no prophetic election.[41] Although it would be churlish to say that he, raised in the harem, had never seen lamb, lion, or bear, surely he had never guarded a flock or fought off a wild beast. The sons of the founding fathers never understand their parents' achievements; the pity is that they are so often called on to continue them.

The conflict between the parties of Adonijah and Solomon is often considered personal. There may have been more to it. The Adonijah party was more genuinely

40. Buber, *On the Bible*, 140-41.
41. For another view, see G. W. Ahlström, "Solomon, the Chosen One," *History of Religions* 8 (1968): 93-110.

Yahwistic; Joab's reluctance about the census and Abiathar's family background are at least more indicative than Benaiah's work with foreign mercenaries and Zadok's suspicious genealogy. The palace intrigue, replete with the eye-gouging passion of all harem conspiracies, is surely unsavory, whatever its provenance. Equally unpleasant is Solomon's consolidation of power, so thoroughly reduced to petty vengeance from David's grand scheme. Though many suspect that David's last testament was a tidbit of Solomonic propaganda, it is not presumptuous to believe that David made a last independent move to insure his realm.

Solomon's territory was roughly the same as his father's. Whatever David's Philistine connection, Solomon did not govern the coastal territory, possibly Egyptian during some of his reign. He kept Aram at least partly active, since he fortified Tadmor (2 Chr. 8:3-5); he may have added Hamath to the empire. His lands brought him not only metals, cloth, spices, and horses, but control of the Via Maris and the Transjordanian King's Highway and probably also of caravan routes out of Tadmor, possibly extending into the Arabian shield. Since Solomon's military exploits are lumped together in Kings, the sequence cannot be fixed, but his foreign relations were presumably marred by some armed tension throughout his reign. Both Hadad of Edom and Rezon, the Aramean general, seem to have been more annoying than threatening. Hadad must have lost his Egyptian support as a result of Solomon's diplomatic marriage into the Egyptian royal family.[42] Since Hadad apparently did not interfere with Solomon's southern trade, he must have controlled only a limited area. Rezon also seems to have been unsuccessful in restricting Solomon's activities, since his relations with Cilicia seem to have continued. The only serious internal dissension during Solomon's reign was Jeroboam's first revolt, prophetically supported and bolstered by an insider's understanding of the regime.

Despite his diplomatic activity and the fact that he seems never to have fought a battle, Solomon can hardly be called a pacific ruler. He gave high priority to defensive building,[43] fortifying a chain of cities — Hazor, Megiddo, Gezer, Lower Beth-horon, Baalath, and Tamar — around his kingdom, and equipping them with matériel and chariotry depots. The gate and casemate wall systems of the first three derive from a single blueprint. Much other Solomonic building is attested, notably at Beth-shean, Beth-shemesh, Eglon (Tell el-Ḥesi), Lachish, Tell Beit Mirsim, and of course Jerusalem. The increased use of four-roomed houses in all but the last of these hardly compares with real-estate developments in the capital: the royal

42. See Kitchen, 273-75, 280. He refers to the relationship as reflecting ordinary Egyptian-Levantine custom.

43. See Y. Yadin's contribution to *Monarchies;* W. F. Albright, "Was the Age of Solomon without Monumental Art?" *ErIsr* 5 (1958): *1-*9; K. M. Kenyon, *Archaeology in the Holy Land,* 3rd ed. (New York: Praeger, 1970), 240-59; and particularly her *Royal Cities of the Old Testament* (New York: Schocken, 1971); more generally, Y. Aharoni, "The Building Activities of David and Solomon," *IEJ* 24 (1974): 13-16.

palace, the House of the Lebanon Forest, the Hall of Judgment, the residence of the Pharaoh's daughter, and the temple.

This import of the temple project is inestimable. We have already placed David in the political landscape of the early 1st millennium; we can now place his son in its religious milieu. A Syro-Anatolian structure crafted by the best artisans of Tyre and Byblos, the temple has been called at best a royal chapel (proximity of royal residence to temple was uncommon in the ancient Near East) and at worst a pagan cult site (whether Solomon actually served as priest is disputed). In connection with it, a name-presence theology was canonized. To pay for it, a good stretch of Galilee had to be mortgaged, and it inaugurated a period of sweeping innovation and syncretism.

As with the temple, so with state reorganization; Solomon adopted one of David's plans and carried it to completion. Gerrymandering was needed not only to hasten the incorporation of the Canaanite cities into the body politic and undermine tribal loyalties, but also to facilitate Solomon's public works. The Solomonic redistricting was at least in part opposed to the old tribal boundaries (1 Kgs. 4:7-19) and although apparently unbalanced, the fundamental system persisted afterwards.[44] The local prefect collected, in addition to pliant shoulders and backs for the corvée, taxes in kind for all the king's horses and all the king's men, along with the king's worship. If nothing else, Solomon's ability to extend David's use of forced labor to all Israel is a tribute to administrative efficiency (1 Kgs. 5:13; cf. 9:20-22; 2 Chr. 8:7-9). Jeroboam's first revolt should have alerted Solomon to the danger of corvée, of devotion to monumental architecture and new modes of production; the demands it made on his people are beyond calculation.

But he was nonetheless a diplomat and supersalesman, a horse-trader of such renown and effectiveness that he became a sought-after, more-than-eligible less-than-bachelor. The marriage strategy was, indeed, a principal component of Solomon's foreign policy,[45] a legacy from his father, who married him off to the Ammonite princess who bore his heir before David's death, and bequeathed to his son, whom he united with Maacah, perhaps of Syrian origin, later the queen-mother. The most spectacular Israelite foreign marriage was that of Solomon to the anonymous African woman: "there is no other attested instance apart from that of

44. The seminal work of A. Alt on monarchic administration is reviewed and extended in W. F. Albright, "The List of Levitic Cities," *Louis Ginzberg Jubilee Volume* (New York: American Academy for Jewish Research, 1945), 49-73; F. M. Cross and G. E. Wright, "The Boundary and Province Lists of the Kingdom of Judah," *JBL* 75 (1956): 202-26; Y. Aharoni, "The Province Lists of the Kingdom of Judah," *VT* 9 (1959): 225-46; a number of Solomon's districts seem to have corresponded roughly to tribal holdings.

45. Malamat, *JNES* 22 (1963): 8-17; *Archives européennes de sociologie* 8 (1967): 165-67. This was standard operating procedure in the ancient Near East and has been wherever monarchy flourished and dynasties needed support.

Solomon of a *daughter* of Pharaoh being given in marriage to a foreign ruler."[46] It occurred early in Solomon's reign and may have been related to his campaign to regain control of Philistia from Pharaoh Siamun; of disputed import, however, is the Egyptian wife's dowry, the city of Gezer, and on that point hangs the argument.[47]

Although the Bible never names the Sidonian women beloved of Solomon, Josephus contends that one was Hiram's daughter. Whatever the diplomatic instruments involved besides the treaty, the Tyre-Jerusalem relation prospered. Tyre had already begun to reach out from the Levantine coast across the Mediterranean to replace the defunct Egyptian-Byblian trading axis, when Solomon joined with it to open the Red Sea.[48] The economic advantage of being a breadbasket to a growing empire — Israel sent Tyre wheat and oil — was probably overlooked by Solomon in his lust for luxe. At any rate, he failed to reckon with the disastrous consequences of social and economic stratification in a rapidly changing society and the resulting class distinctions so bitterly condemned by the prophets.

The nuptial character of Solomon's diplomacy is reflected also in his soft-core syncretism. The visions, the wisdom, the foreign faiths, the proliferation of cultic apparatus seem epitomized in the story of the harlots, in which the great king's decision points neither to justice nor insight, but expediency. The intellectual and spiritual life of Solomon is everywhere paradoxical. Even if the Gibeon high place had been appropriated to Yahwistic worship long before Solomon's time, the patriarchal precedent for dream incubation, Jacob at Bethel, was rather marginal. Since the vision story suggests that Jerusalem was not yet entirely accepted as a national center, Gibeon may have been considered sacred for all Israel, so that the two sets of sacrifices in 1 Kgs. 3 suggest movement away from a three-realm concept toward an *urbs et orbis* structure.[49]

Solomon's wisdom is also paradoxical: riddle-solving has little in common with administration of justice and executive ability, unless wisdom is just the ability to think. The Egyptian ideal combination of encyclopedist passion and bourgeois morality was important in Solomon's court, but not in Solomon's person, remarks about birds and bees notwithstanding. For the wise Egyptian the highest virtue is discretion before superiors; since none was superior to Solomon, he needed no discretion. To be sure, historical perspicacity blossomed under Solomon and Israelite literature flowered when the Davidic family history and Yahwist source of the Pentateuch were drafted, the first proverbs compiled, and the first sacred and secular songs collected. But a patron of the arts differs in spirit from the artist and his work.

46. *Idem; Malamat, BAR* 2: 91-93.

47. See Kitchen, 293-300, 303.

48. See F. M. Cross, "Leaves from an Epigraphist's Notebook," *CBQ* 36 (1974): 490-92.

49. See J. Blenkinsopp, *Gibeon and Israel* (Cambridge: Cambridge University Press, 1972), 65-97.

The heartbreaking paradox is that the king most eloquently devoted to the worship of Yahweh was equally devoted to honoring other gods. Agreed that seven hundred wives and three hundred concubines might distract the most pious of men, but the point is that the pagan altars seem also to have been monuments to expediency. The high places that he built stood till Josiah's day (cf. 2 Kgs. 23:13), an engineering achievement tradition nonetheless unanimously condemned. Further defects in Solomon's regime demanded immediate action, however, and curiously enough it is the other great cultic deviant of the Deuteronomic tradition who rose against his former employer to supply it.

Although he is supposed to have commissioned the first historical texts in Judahite literature, thus fostering national consciousness, Solomon was not well served by his annalists. The graceful balance of harlot and queen stories that begin and end the Solomon section of Kings notwithstanding, it really is an unrelieved pattern of courthouse abstracts and moralistic comments.[50] Even the Chronicler could not disguise the opulence that led to the schism, the vulgarity and arrogance that had overtaken the line of David. No one doubted Rehoboam when he claimed "My little finger is thicker than my father's loins." They simply left.

G. Conclusion

Given the exacting Mosaic standards and the passionate critique of the prophets, what really is the measure of the two-generation experiment in empire of David and Solomon, centered in Jerusalem, embracing Israel and Judah, and extending over Edom, Moab, Ammon, and Aram? With expanded territory, enlarged income, increased building and commerce came heavier taxes, social and economic stratification, dilution of the historic faith, compromise with and contamination by neighboring religious communities, and perhaps most grievous, the royal house effectively supplanting the ancient covenant of Sinai as mediator between God and his people. Because the monarchy took responsibility for the well-being of all the people it monopolized power and authority and the perquisites and privileges deriving therefrom.

Other measurements and assessments of the achievement of David and Solomon are provided by the same unflattering sources. Everything that we know about these kings and their kingdoms comes from the Bible (and possibly some Tyrian sources available to Josephus) and is good and bad, part of the Davidide legacy, the dynasty's most enduring monument. Literature is inevitably propaganda, but the concerned testimony about what people considered vital, the allegations ema-

---

50. This is not to deny the literary interest of the section altogether; see B. Porten, "The Structure and Theme of the Solomon Narrative (I Kings 3–11)," *HUCA* 38 (1974): 93-128.

nating from the 10th-century court at Jerusalem, has become the core of Western literature's most enduring *oeuvre*. We have discussed some of its poetry; the extent of the corpus can never be determined, but however small the nucleus of 10th-century hymns, anthems, laments, and royal songs, it inspired and shaped the great body of poetry in the Bible. Equally important is the prose, the great literary compositions in which Israel's history is rooted. Scholars generally agree that the United Monarchy produced at least two major works: the Yahwist account of the people of God from the call of Abraham to the settlement in Canaan, and the court history of the reign of David and the accession of Solomon. They are masterpieces of classical Hebrew, comparable to the greatest literature of the ancient world. Like the Iliad and the Odyssey, they are part of the world's cultural heritage. More than other Homeric heroes, David and his sons and their subordinates animate art and music, religion and literature. To a remarkable extent their personalities and achievements touch the modern mind, human interacting with divine in all the variety of historical experience. Generations of leaders parade through the Yahwist history, and we claim them for our ancestors. The record that they left is as memorable as that of Periclean Athens, Augustan Rome, Elizabethan England, the Florentine High Renaissance. Surely this is exalted company for so modest a kingdom to keep, but though it was different from these, it was not inferior to any of them.

Whatever the dynastic objectives of the authors of these works, they were surely conscious of their environment and their patron, and they portrayed David as authentic heir to the traditions of Israel, faithful to the Yahweh of Moses, the God of Sinai, and to the patriarchal deity El Shaddai, revealed in Canaan. The design and construction of the temple may have been misguided, with its Canaanite mythic motifs and cultic objects, but it was a sanctuary of Yahweh, the God of Israel. Its tradents, priests, and singers, along with the royal theologians, preserved the ancient faith with sufficient integrity for it to be transmitted to later generations.

The traditions thus preserved affected and shaped the monarchy even as it reshaped and adapted them to its needs. David and Solomon were not pagan kings with divine roles and prerogatives, but the anointed servants of Yahweh, who was their suzerain as he was of all men. We have noted that David saw himself and his house bound with eternal El and Mosaic YHWH in a covenant which supported them, but demanded loyalty and rectitude. The Davidic period was in a sense a golden age, the culmination of centuries of effort to settle the land, achieve hegemony and harmony, with all Israel unafraid beneath their vines and fig trees. This fulfilled dream of settlement, peaceful and prosperous, secure and permanent, gave the period its gleam of gold. It brought nostalgia and hope for the future throughout the biblical period. David's final and most influential legacy was the messianic expectation that a scion of his house would, at some time known only to God, establish a kingdom like David's, but better and, most important, permanent.

The messianic aspiration has always been a mixed blessing for Israel and Judah and their descendants, but a Davidic legacy that, for better or worse, has affected the lives of millions, influenced the Jewish community, its character and quality of life, and shaped and directed the Christian movement. Variously reformulated, it is the vehicle of constant renewal, of faith and confidence in the purposes of God for the establishment of his kingdom.

The kingdom of David and Solomon was a kingdom of men whose weaknesses stumble through the recorded pages, side by side with achievements extraordinary beyond those of comparable monarchs or monarchies. The books produced, the poems composed, are a central part of the most valuable legacy left us from the ancient world. For ancient Judah and Israel, the price was high, in every way, but the gain was greater.[51]

51. I wish to thank M. O'Connor for invaluable assistance in the preparation of this essay, especially sections A-D.

30

Problems of Textual Criticism
in the Book of Hosea

For ten years, Professor Frank Andersen and I have been struggling with the book of Hosea in the Bible, and now the bell has rung for us, too: the manuscript must be sent to the press. It is monumental in size, but I would regard it at the present as a monumental failure. Needless to say, we don't blame ourselves; the fault lies in the book. Most scholars would agree that there is something wrong with it. The last great failure to deal with it was that of Hans Walter Wolff, who has recently published his commentary on Hosea in the Hermeneia series (now available in English). He is a great scholar, a man of international rank and standing, but he represents a certain school of thought: first he emends the text because it does not make sense as it stands, and then he says he doesn't understand what it means. That's how difficult the book of Hosea is: even when you have fixed it up, it still is impossible.

What is the answer? The possibility of rescuing the text in any substantial way is minimal, because even the Dead Sea Scrolls, which produced hundreds of thousands of fragments of all kinds of manuscripts, have produced practically nothing on the book of Hosea, nothing that is helpful. We cannot expect to find the autograph or the original text, which might have offered some real help. Another dead end is text critical studies. It is generally agreed that the Septuagint, which is the best hope for rescuing the Hebrew text, is simply no good; it is a deficient text for Hosea. This is a very different situation from what we have in the Pentateuch or the Former Prophets, where the Greek text, the Samaritan text, and all the new manuscript evidence really offer a family history, a possibility of attaining a text better than any existent one. Even for Ezekiel, where you have a substantially different text, the Septuagint is not a good text. Jeremiah in the Septuagint does offer some considerable help, but that is a freak, in which there is a major literary difference that is certainly important. But for the book of Hosea, the Massoretic

Hebrew text is the best available; there is hardly a single reading of the Septuagint that we were able to adopt.

How, then, do you go about dealing with a text like this? The first answer is that the text does go along nicely now and then, for a brief period, and is perfectly good Hebrew; that is very important. When you can read it, it reads like good, classical, Biblical Hebrew. Therefore, we decided that we would forgo emendation; we rejected emendation as an option, partly because it has been exploited to a point of diminishing returns. Text critical studies obviously have their place, but in the vast area of conjectural emendation scholars (presumably driven to desperation) resort to their own ingenuity, and the results overall (not merely in the case of Hosea) are minimal, to put it kindly. Conjectural emendation is primarily an exercise in ingenuity, which is not a bad thing; it is good for all scholars and would-be scholars to show how clever they are. We all indulge in it from time to time, and this is as harmless a way of doing it as there is. But by and large it has proved futile. There are certain outstanding exceptions in which the overwhelming force of logic has produced a solution that has long since become part of the tradition, but these are very, very few.

Generally speaking, scholars are very skeptical of other scholars' solutions, and this is to their credit. They are less skeptical of their own solutions, but that does not matter, because they are in the minority on any given solution. In general, the skepticism is justified. There is, e.g., the classic case of mass hallucination about the lament of David over Saul and Jonathan, a reading which is admittedly difficult, but obviously we are only talking about difficult readings. H. L. Ginsberg, a world-famous scholar (there is no point in criticizing minor scholars), produced a solution from a Ugaritic parallel that was really quite spectacular and immediately received enthusiastic support from most other scholars ["A Ugaritic Parallel to 2 Sam. 1:21," *JBL* 57 (1938): 209-13]. It is a very strange reading in 2 Sam. 1:21:

הרי בגלבע אל־טל ואל־מטר
עליכם ושדי תרומת

"O mountains in Gilboa, let no dew and let no rain be upon you, fields of offerings." It does not sound very good. Ginsberg came up with a parallel structure in a Ugaritic passage, where the rain and dew from heaven are contrasted with "upsurgings of the deep," in his rendering, the water above heaven contrasted with the water below earth. It meant changing two consonants and adding one, a minor matter and universally approved.

But what is the trouble with it? It has nothing to do with the context. The prophet is talking about rain, as Elijah does in 1 Kgs. 17: there shall be no more rainfall; there shall be a curse of God, a drought. What has that got to do with upsurgings of the deep? Nothing. This mythological notion is totally unrelated here, though elsewhere it might be fine; my objection has nothing to do with the quality of the emendation, but only with the appositeness of the solution.

315

The answer is to recognize the structure of the poem. ושדי, whatever it may mean, is to be connected with the mountains of Gilboa. Etymologically, ושדי has the general meaning of field, but it may also be related to the Akkadian word for mountain *(šadu)*. We know that הרי, mountains, and ושדי are associated in other passages, while the etymological meaning of תרומת is "something raised." In another very old poem the reverse expression occurs but with a comparable meaning:

מרומי שדה

the heights of the field, or a plateau. This is where the battle described in the Song of Deborah is fought. So surely we must be fairly close to the right meaning here by associating ושדי with the mountain range of Gilboa. The phrase "upsurgings of the deep" is simply irrelevant.

But the real problem with emendation is that it is far too easy. In a language with three-consonant words, the supply is very limited; if you change one consonant you can literally produce whatever you want. Since you cannot change *less* than one out of three consonants in emendation, the percentage is much too high and the results, therefore, can be anything at all. Emendation is not only too easy, but too easy to justify, because there is enough manuscript evidence to show that scribes accidentally substituted not only letters that looked alike, but very often letters that didn't look alike at all. Any mistake is not only possible, but practiced. Scribes make errors, but we do not know *where* they made them. Mistakes do occur, and sometimes the mistake is fairly obvious and can be corrected, especially when you have a parallel text or another manuscript. But if you don't have one, you're in trouble.

My attack on emendation has nothing to do with any kind of religious prejudice; the notion of a surviving sacred, inerrant text is absurd. My attitude is that this is an area that is best not exploited, that emendation is not a legitimate scholarly possibility. I don't see any harm in it, but I don't see any great good in it, either. I don't think that more than 2 percent of all conjectural emendations will ever ultimately be accepted, and that is a generous estimate. This is not just because scholars are resistant to new ideas, but simply because in a strict scientific way these ideas are without merit. They may be very ingenious and very appealing, but the net effect is so minimal that it's simply not worth it. We reject alterations in the text not because we think the text is perfect, but because we have yet to devise a scientific method for dealing with a corrupt text where we don't have controls.

By now, we should all be thoroughly warned against emendations *metri causa,* a temptation that should be resisted vigorously, because it is the worst example of circular reasoning that I know. And since I have indulged in it along with many others, I'm an expert on the subject: you produce the meter that you think is there by emending the text. That's really a disaster. If you know that the author has made a mistake, you have the right to correct it; that's unfortunate, but it happens. But if you don't know what the meter is, you can't correct the meter. That is my conviction after twenty-five years of effort in the field, and now one of my Ph.D. students [M. O'Connor, *Hebrew Verse Structure* (Winona Lake: Ind.: Eisenbrauns, 1980] has finally proved that we will never know what the meter is. You cannot use meter to help you with other problems, but you might use the others to help you with the meter. The particles, ה, את, אשר, are used as discriminators. Even in the text that we have, which was copied mostly as prose for millennia, the difference in the incidence of those particles in what everybody agrees is poetry as compared with what everybody agrees is prose is so great that it cannot be an accident. It doesn't mean that they never occur in poetry and always occur in prose, but the difference is a ratio of between 6 and 10 to 1, which does not happen at random. Moreover, the proof that it is not random lies in what is random: the Massoretes did not distinguish between prose and poetry when it came to the definite article; they didn't tamper with the letter ה which represents the article, but the Massoretes had free play with the *dagesh forte,* used with prepositions to show that there was an article there, with the ה elided. And there the ratios disappear completely; the frequency is the same.

But that is not yet very helpful, except to discriminate between poetry and prose. Perhaps when we have identified real poetry we might get somewhere with meter; people have been spending too much time trying to find meter in what is really prose, or using what is not poetry for this purpose. We are partly in the way of reversing the famous discovery of Bishop Lowth, who found poetry in the prophets; we are going to find prose there. There is poetry, but there is also a good deal of prose. Prose and poetry share certain factors. You can compare them in terms of molecular activity: prose is essentially stable, while poetry is an unstable combination, in which the molecules operate faster. But essentially the same kind of analysis is appropriate to both prose and poetry.

What, then, are we going to do with a book like Hosea if we eliminate conjectural emendation, the only recourse any scholar has ever had to saving the book? The basic argument is that since this is the best text we are ever likely to have, we had better try to do something with it. Historically, classically, how did the rabbis or the Church Fathers do it? They rejected emendation for other reasons, and until the 19th century the text was considered given. Therefore we are not exactly innovating; in fact, we can be accused of a kind of anti-scholarly position. We might survive that. Now, the rabbis were very ingenious, which demonstrates that even if emendation is not practiced in an open, explicit way, it is practiced anyhow. What they did was, in effect, to invent new meanings for traditional words, though this probably maligns them a bit. They could sense that the passage did not go literally, so they simply said, "This word doesn't really mean this; it means something else." This is not allegorical or metaphorical interpretation; this is linguistic. In that way, they accommodated emendation; they kept the text, but they changed the meaning. If modern scholars want to change the meaning, they change the text. The difference is not great. Once in a while, the rabbis were lucky and did something that has since been vindicated, but their method does not strike us as altogether satisfactory or defensible.

A scholar like Mitchell Dahood tends in this direction; he doesn't actually invent meanings, but he has said that he treats a biblical text like an inscription, a raw text; the vocalization, however, is dispensable. It is clear that the vocalization is less reliable than the written text; nevertheless it has a strong tradition behind it, as can be confirmed where the writing is in part syllabic as is true of the Ebla tablets of the 3rd millennium B.C.E. and it is possible in the case of place and personal names to check the Massoretic vocalization. Since the time differential is more than three thousand years, the numerous correlations constitute impressive evidence, indeed. Nevertheless, Dahood tends to opt for very obscure and novel interpretations or meanings of words which are well known in Hebrew. Our view is that this is not entirely a sound approach; because, as Frank Cross is fond of saying, the banal solution is generally the best. You must deal with the ordinary meaning of ordinary words.

Everybody would be happy if we could just read the text right off; nobody is looking for trouble. But unfortunately we cannot do that. If we don't accept critical emendation or the "rabbinic method" or a more polished form of it (such as odd meanings of common words), what is left? How do we deal with a text like Hosea that does not make sense, a text in which a string of words may be quite well known but together their meaning eludes us? Our approach is a combination of the following elements: our first assumption is that the text is basically sound. If the text is not sound and we have no objective evidence to fix it up, we are really engaging in a futile enterprise. (The number and percentage of emendations that scholars indulge in make it clear that they don't think the text is sound.) But we say the text is sound, or we would not do it at all. We cannot prove this — it may be very unsound — and even with all our ingenuity there are still big chunks that remain indecipherable. But we still say that the text is reasonably sound. What else can we do? There are corruptions in the text, of course; there must be. Nobody ever guarded the scribes from making errors, but 90 percent of it must be alright. There is, in a sense, a third option in addition to accepting the text as sound or rejecting it as corrupt, and that is to reserve judgment, to say that we do not know whether or not the text is corrupt, that our enterprise is to try to prove or disprove the corruption of the text. Because with all the tools and techniques we use there are still areas that we would have to label, "These must be corrupt because we cannot solve them," especially if we were self-righteous. In fact, we believe that with more care, more deliberation, more time, we might understand them. It's a lot like modern poetry. A contemporary poet, I think, would generally be distressed if you said, "I understood the whole thing the first time I read it." His objective is otherwise. He wants you to study it, pore over it and reflect on it, and even get multiple reactions to it, all of which may be correct.

Albrecht Alt is probably the best guide we have, and he suggests that Hosea reflects historical reality. [See his "Hosea 5,8–6,6. Ein Krieg und seine Folgen in prophetischer Beleuchtung," *Neue kirchliche Zeitschrift* 30 (1919): 537-68 (= *Kleine Schriften zur Geschichte des Volkes Israel* (Munich: C. H. Beck, 1953), 1:163-87.] Here is a prophet in a significant historical crisis; that seems to be clear. There are enough correlations between Amos on the one hand and Isaiah on the other to show us what the crisis was: it was the intrusion of Assyria into the affairs of Aram, Israel, and Judah. A prophet has a vocation, to tell people what to do and what not to do in a situation. But Hosea is not just a prophet; he is a poet, or at least a quasi-poet, and he likes to obfuscate. He doesn't say it the way it's said in Second Kings. You might say that he had a bad marriage that adversely affected the poetry; that is the way we look at it, at least. More than any other prophet, he was personally involved in such a way that it skewed everything. Even where we understand it, it is a very strange business.

Our second assumption regards grammar, and that is the assumption that the author, the writer, the poet, basically follows the rules of grammar: plural agrees with plural, singular with singular, masculine with masculine, feminine with feminine. These simple clues are often ignored. Let me give you a few examples of grammatical anomalies. The construct chain is one of the first things anybody learns about Biblical Hebrew; although it is not decisive for many other languages, including most Semitic languages, it seems to be a feature of classical Hebrew. Nevertheless, the broken construct chain is a phenomenon; the bound words, the construct and the absolute, may not be in direct sequence. Since we have been taught otherwise, it is very difficult to recognize these aberrations when they occur, and the temptation is not only to emend them but also to resist recognition of the phenomenon itself. On the one hand, we do not want to canonize a mistake; but on the other hand, we do not want to emend away a serious poetic device or conceit. At what point do you go from the one to the other? The rule of thumb is: if it occurs once, it's a mistake; if it occurs twice, watch out; if it occurs three times, it's a law. I will show you three cases of a broken construct chain in Hosea.

The first one occurs in Hos. 6:9. Without trying to analyze the text, we have the sequence: דרך ירצחו־שכמה, "The way they murder to Shechem." My contention is that דרך שכמה is the combination: "On the road to Shechem, they commit murder." This combination occurs elsewhere with different names, as in the phrase "on the road to Timnah" in the story of Samson. The normal prose arrangement would be to put those two words together. One might argue that this is not even a construct chain, but I think it is; a Hebrew writer would know that the two words belonged together. In this case the verb has been interposed between them, which is not normal, but it is clear that the two words are linked.

The second case occurs in Hos. 8:2:

לי יזעקו

אלהי ידענוך ישראל

Literally, this means, "They cry out to me, 'My God, we know you, Israel.'" The passage must be understood as:

אלהי ישראל ידענוך

"O God of Israel, we know you." The two parts of the construct chain are separated by the verb. It is the simplest solution to the meaning, and it solves the grammatical problem.

The third example is Hos. 14:3, in which another broken construct chain occurs:

אמרו אליו כל־תשא עון

Once again the verb (תשא) is between the construct (כל) and the absolute (עון). The line should be rendered: "Say to him, 'You shall forgive all iniquity.'" These three examples establish the phenomenon; even if you accept only one, you've acknowledged the phenomenon, and that means you must look for it elsewhere.

There are three more which will set your teeth on edge because they are all in the same passage, Ezek. 28, the famous passage about the cherub in the Garden of Eden. In v. 16 we have: כרוב הסכך, the cherub of the *sokek*, whatever that means. Since the same words occur together in Exod. 25:20 and 37:9, the reading is probably correct. In any case the phrase must be a construct chain; it cannot be anything else. Now look at 28:14: כרוב ממשח הסכך. That is the same construct chain but here a word has been inserted in the middle. The first phrase, in 28:16, is a simple construct chain; the second, in 28:14, is a broken construct chain.

Then in 28:16 we have מהר אלהים; I think everybody would agree that that is a construct chain. But look at 28:14: בהר קדש אלהים; since *har* is often associated with both nouns we may read this phrase as "in the holy mountain of God." Still it looks like a broken construct chain. And in v. 16 for the third instance, we have ברב רכלתך, a construct chain, while in 28:18 we have a very complicated business:

מרב עוניך בעול רכלתך

He has taken the same construct chain, broken it open, and put two more words in the middle. This can be explained differently, but on the basis of the evidence thus far assembled I think we can say that what he did was to disguise the phrase as two separate construct chains.

We are not done with this phenomenon. Let me show you one that you can ponder as I did for a few years: Amos 5:16, the famous passage where Amos is talking about lamentation all through the country:

לכן כה־אמר יהוה
אלהי צבאות אדני
בכל־רחבות מספד
ובכל־חוצות יאמרו הו־הו
וקראו אכר אל־אבל
ומספד אל־יודעי נהי

"In all the squares, mourning; and in all the streets, let them say, 'Ho Ho' " (that doesn't mean what we mean by "Ho Ho"). Then comes the crucial passage: "And they will call or summon the plowman to grief; and mourning to those skilled in lamentation."

On the one hand they summon the plowman to lamentation, and on the other they proclaim mourning to those skilled in lamentation. That does not sound quite right; but it makes perfect sense if we recognize that the two half-lines (cola) form a complete chiasm and read the second colon backwards: "They summon the plowman to grief / and those skilled in lamentation to mourning." The plowmen (the word is collective here) are in parallel with "those skilled in lamentation"; the terms are complementary, and mutually descriptive and delimiting. No critical scholar, to my knowledge, has ever suggested this possibility; on the contrary, the standard procedure is to reverse ומספד and אל to make the phrase parallel with אל־אבל of the previous colon. The sense comes out the same, but there is no need to change the order of the words, if we allow the poet to exercise some freedom in this matter. It is possible that the text contains an error, but it is also possible that it is a deliberate device. That is the real question, and obviously we need more evidence to decide. My impression is that we have given the poets too little credit for sophistication and subtlety and innovation and originality, and that we have indulged too much in systematizing and classifying and organizing according to fixed rules. In a case like this the meaning is perfectly clear; nobody would doubt it. But there are many passages which are difficult, and I think they are more difficult than they need to be because we go at them with the wrong mentality. In the book of Hosea there are some places where we think we have clarified matters by making use of the idea that the words preserved in the text are all right but that the order is unusual.

On a broader scale, a basic feature of our approach has to do with the structure of the material. We try to observe and isolate and identify literary devices that are recognized in all literature. That they can and may contribute to a solution is a factor which is not often acknowledged. This involves gross structures: poets didn't think only in terms of half-lines and lines; they planned ahead, and clues to the meaning of an obscure sentence in one place are to be found in a sentence in another place. Whether this is written or oral is almost an irrelevant question. The important thing is that no matter how large the unit, all of it is significant for understanding any part of it. Now, this is comparatively new; this has not been done systematically in a structural sense with Hebrew poetry. There are elements which we can draw from the whole body of Hebrew poetry, especially, but also prose.

This argument has very little to do with the intention of the poet, which is a false question, in my judgment. We are obviously interested in what the poet intended and what he thought he was doing, but there are many things in poetry that are produced by the poet without his being aware of them. The poet is one of the worst sources for understanding the nature and organization of his poems, because by the time he has been doing something for twenty years, he need no longer think consciously about structure or devices; these flow. If asked, "What did you mean by this?", a good poet will always tell you: "Go back to the poem." Poets should not write footnotes; sometimes they do, but it is often a mistake. So we don't ask the poet, "What did you mean by this? Why did you do it?" The question must be, "Is the element there?" In that sense, it is an objective question.

It has been argued that some of the inconsistencies in the book of Hosea arise from the fact that a later editor, working at some distance from the original material, has altered the text, adding and subtracting in the process. No doubt the book does not come from the hand of Hosea, but I believe it not only contains the authentic oracles of the prophet but reflects his life and times and is a product of the same period, though it may have been compiled in the next generation or two afterwards. The heading of the book (Hos. 1:1) is commonly taken as an example of much later editing, but a careful study of the so-called 8th-century prophets, Amos, Hosea, Micah, and Isaiah, shows that in each case the heading is different. Whoever was responsible for the headings was careful to distinguish the prophets chronologically while recognizing that their careers overlapped. Typically the work of the prophet is dated to the contemporary kings of Israel and Judah; while the form is stereotyped, no two of the prophets have the same list. That shows discrimination, and a concern for precision. The editor must have had access to specific information about these prophets, and we have no reason to doubt its accuracy. In addition, the style of the 8th-century headings is different from the more elaborate headings used in the books of later prophets like Jeremiah and Ezekiel (from the 7th and 6th centuries). Our view is that a compilation of 8th-century prophetic materials was made not long after these prophets were active, and therefore we can have confidence that the record is reasonably accurate and that the text has been preserved with fidelity.

Testimony for the historicity of the book of Hosea as an authentic work of the 8th century may be seen in the treatment of the two great foreign powers Egypt and Assyria. They are given roughly equal billing, since at the time Hosea proclaimed his message, it was apparently unclear to him and to others which would turn out to be the dominant force in Israel's future. Hosea prophesied that Israel would be overrun, but who would do it? His solution was a kind of split: on the one hand Assyria is going to be their ruler, and on the other hand they will return to Egypt. Within twenty or thirty years it was all settled: Egypt proved to be much weaker than it appeared and could not contest Assyria's dominance in Syria-Palestine. So the Assyrians conquered Israel. Now, had the book of Hosea been systematically edited and updated after the destruction of the northern kingdom, it would have reflected that central fact, and the respective roles of the great powers would have been described in the light of it. What has been preserved, however, is a vivid picture of the situation before the decision was rendered in the battlefield. Although the compiler was aware of the later developments, the book faithfully

322

reproduces the earlier situation. Such an argument does not show the prophet in the best light as a predictor of the future, but it indicates the editor as faithful in his task.

This leads to a different point. We have noted that Egypt and Assyria are paired in a number of oracles in Hosea (cf. 7:11; 9:3; 11:5, 11; 12:2); they also occur independently (cf. Assyria, 5:13; 10:6; 14:4; Egypt, 9:6; 11:1; 12:14). In one case, at least, the coupling, if it exists, is more remote. In 8:9 we have

כי־המה עלו אשור   "They have gone up to Assyria."

In the light of 7:11 we would expect a reference to Egypt, but there is none in the immediate vicinity. If we look at the end of 8:13 we find it, however:

המה מצרים ישובו   "They shall return to Egypt."

The linkage between the passages is confirmed by the repetition of the independent pronoun המה, which is in the initial emphatic position in both clauses. That this is a deliberate signal on the part of the author seems clear, since strictly speaking the pronoun is unnecessary when finite verbs are used (since in Hebrew the pronominal element is incorporated in the verb). Furthermore, there is a chiasm in the order of the following words: verb-object in 8:9, object-verb in 8:13. The omission of the preposition on the object is another feature in common; and the shift from the perfect (עלו) to the imperfect form of the verb (ישובו) is characteristic of early and high style in Hebrew and Canaanite verse. In addition, the syllable count is the same for both cola (7:7). The result is a perfect couplet or bicolon — only the two parts are separated by several verses. In other words, they form an envelope around a poetic unit of substantial dimensions; we have here a very sophisticated variation on the usual bicolon in Hebrew poetry. This shows that the poet could construct an elaborate poem, consciously plan the end from the beginning, and arrange the parts so that beginning and ending fit together in a well-made plan. That the poet thought all this through in advance and delivered such a complex work orally seems clear. He also imposed serious demands upon the hearer (or reader), who must wait patiently for the balancing line until the very end of the unit: "They go up to Assyria" is balanced by "They return to Egypt." Only then does the hearer know the full measure of the poem, and that the first line has now been completed by the last. Needless to say, this demonstration opens new vistas in the interpretation and appreciation of Hebrew poetry and should alert us all to the hitherto unexamined possibilities in the preserved text. Another of these envelope constructions or remote pairings with Assyria may occur in Hos. 7:12-16, if we read initial כאשר as "Assyria" rather than the conjunction, to match מצרים בארץ in 7:16.

Historical context, grammar, and structure are the elements that together hold the key to the understanding of Hosea. For example, it is often argued that Hosea has been adapted by a Judean editor. We have seen evidence in the structure that we are dealing with literature of a kind unlikely to have been reconstructed by an editor; we have seen evidence in the historical context that it is unlikely to be the work of anyone writing after the 7th century. We will now examine historical and grammatical evidence that it is not the work of a Judean. This evidence may be found in Hos. 1:6 and 7. This is the passage about the second child: "She conceived again and she bore a daughter, and He said to him, 'Call her name Lo-ruhamah ["She is not pitied"].'" What follows then is

כי לא אוסיף עוד

This is the crucial part, the use of an auxiliary verb, "I will not add any more." The same expression is used in Amos, so it is an authentic expression of the 8th century B.C.E.; nobody would quarrel with this. But then, curiously enough, it is followed by a finite verb: **ארחם** "I will have mercy." That is strange, because normally, as in Amos and elsewhere, after

לא אוסיף

you find the infinitive. But here is **ארחם**, first person: "I will not again, I will have mercy." Now, that is grammatically awkward, but there is no reason to emend the text, because this construction does occur. Everybody agrees that this means, "I will not again have mercy," or "I will no longer have mercy," just as in Amos. Both Amos and Hosea are agreed that we have now reached the point where divine mercy is at an end, where postponements and compassion are over; historically, the time of judgment has arrived. Isaiah says much the same thing in other words: the judgment of God on the people of Israel and Judah has come.

But what about Hosea? The first problem arises with what follows: **אשא להם כי־נשא**, literally, "For lifting up I will lift up to them." Now, **נשא** is used figuratively for forgiveness, and here the repetition of the root is emphatic, "I will surely forgive them." But since that contradicts what he has just said, the reading is emended (on the basis of the Septuagint) to

שנא אשנא

"I will surely hate"; that requires a metathesis in two successive words. The trouble with that is that it violates our first rule; we're emending the text on the basis not of a superior text, but of an inferior text, the Septuagint. It is possible for the LXX to preserve a better or more original reading, but the evidence must be decisive.

They obviously had a problem, but the nature of the solution lies in understanding the grammar of **לא אוסיף עוד**. Once we realize that this auxiliary construction governs not only the first clause but the second, the problem disappears. What the last line means is: "I will never, under any circumstances, forgive them." That is unusual, because negatives normally are repeated — but not always. In this case, consistency requires that we recognize an odd grammatical structure which, however, is not unattested. Why didn't he repeat the negative? Well, that is a matter of poetic or prophetic license. I insist that we give him full credence here. The different reading in the Septuagint may have arisen from the failure of the Greek translator to understand the unusual Hebrew construction, but it is quite possible that he had a different text. I would insist, however, that this is a preferable text, not because it is the Massoretic text but because it makes very good sense as it is.

The next verse says: ואת־בית יהודה ארחם, usually translated, "But the house of Judah I will love." Since Hosea normally treats Judah the same as Israel throughout the book, most scholars take this to be the work of the Judean editor. Thus you have two emendations: the first one is based on the objection that the text contradicts what Hosea says, and the second is based on the assumption that it is the work of an editor. Now, to me that is self-defeating on the face of it, and so self-serving as to be meaningless. What we wish to call attention to here is the complete and elegant chiasm between ארחם את־בית ישראל, "I will have mercy on the house of Israel," and ואת־בית יהודה ארחם, "On the house of Judah I will have mercy." It is hard to imagine that a Judean editor would produce a structural pattern like that. If he was trying to rewrite the book of Hosea to improve Judah's standing, it is unlikely that he would also indulge in this stylistic elegance as well. My conclusion from this is: the scholars are wrong; this is a case of a single author. To divide one sentence here between two authors and still come out with this fine example of chiasm is a refutation of contemporary scholarship. But if the lines are by the same author, as we say, then can they have different meanings with respect to the future of Israel and Judah? In the light of available evidence we must say that the initial negative clause governs both of these sentences and approves the end of divine mercy for both nations. It is a matter of distance, and this is a controlling element in the book of Hosea, a major device for creating effect: distance. It is somewhat akin to putting the verb at the end of a German sentence.

This is the way that Hosea regularly treats Judah. In noncontroversial passages, what does he say about Judah?

כי אנכי כשחל לאפרים וככפיר לבית יחודה

"I will be like a lion to Ephraim and like a young lion to the house of Judah" (5:14). Is there a difference? He's going to destroy them both; he's going to grind them up; he's going to tear them apart. Can this be a Judean editor? How absurd can you be?

וירא אפרים את־חליו ויהודה את־מזרו

"Ephraim looked at his illness, and Judah at his suppurating wound" (5:13). Nobody questions that this is *echt* Hosea, Hosea himself. He is primarily interested in the northern kingdom; nobody questions that. But what is his attitude toward Judah? That Judah sooner or later is going to receive the same judgment from God that Ephraim has earned. Should this surprise us? Amos says the same thing, Isaiah says the same thing, Micah says the same thing.

What is at stake here? A rule in Gesenius-Kautzsch (the standard reference grammar for Biblical Hebrew): negatives are repeated, before each new clause. We know that the Hebrew grammar of Gesenius is a classic German attempt at organizing a language, a magnificent attempt to be sure, but did anybody ever speak or write that language in all its purity? No. We know that, too, but scholarship has been frozen in its tracks. Here you have the equivalent of Ptolemy's epicycles when Copernicus has come. This is obviously a crucial passage, and I think it is instructive. Of course it is odd to omit the negative; if it weren't odd there would be no quarrel. The question really is, How do you cope with it? I've given what you might call the traditional scholarly approach, but is that the answer? No. And I have suggested a different approach. This is not a question of emending the text, except in a certain gross fashion.

It is futile to invoke a Judean editor, to try to analyze the text into primary, secondary, tertiary strata. The task for scholars is to understand what is written. Once you have really gotten a grasp of that, you can go on to other things. But it is universally agreed that we have a very inadequate grasp of the book of Hosea. Rather than excusing apparent inconsistencies by blaming them on subsequent editors, it is our task to give the existent structure of the text every chance to yield its meaning to us.

For example, the kind of inclusive construction that characterizes the passage about Egypt and Assyria (Hos. 8:9 and 8:13) occurs in chs. 1 and 2 of Hosea, a massive piece that most scholars chop up mercilessly, because the sequences are quite difficult to cope with. Nevertheless, if you start with ch. 1, despite endless problems, you have the story of the three children and their symbolic names. The sequence Jezreel, Lo-ruhamah, and Lo-ammi occurs. In the unit as a whole, the theme of the three children is repeated at strategic points in the structure; it cannot be an accidental result or even the deliberate result of a long editorial process. This shows a single conception. Now, it may well be the conception of an editor, as chs. 1 and 2 are a third-person biographical treatment of the prophet Hosea, but I would say that our first task is to find out what this editor thought he was doing, because he is our primary authority, against which we can only pose conjectures.

There are many little features, like pronouns, that are often overlooked. We have a theory that when pronouns are used, they are used deliberately and for a certain effect, because you do not usually need them in Hebrew. We have seen how this factor sheds light on the interpretation of the passage about Egypt and Assyria; it is also useful in dealing with ch. 2, which is central to an understanding of the thought of Hosea. The problem occurs in v. 14: "I am going to devastate her vines and her figs, of which she has said 'They [המה] are the reward or payment which my lovers gave to me.'" Then it says, "And I will make them into a forest, and the beasts of the field will devour them." Now, we contend that there should be meaning in a simple, progressive reading of the material. Who are the beasts of the field? Normally, these are carnivores, so that the notion that the ultimate penalty

326

will be that they will devour vines and figs seems weak. המה is the key word; in this chapter its previous occurrence is in v. 6: "I will not love her children, המה כי־בני זנונים, for they are the children of harlotry" (the term זנונים signifies gross sexual misbehavior, not simply prostitution). We suggest, therefore, that the beasts of the field are going to devour המה, namely, her children. That is what is concealed in this text, the threat that the beasts of the field will devour her children. Similar ultimate threats are made in the denunciatory passages of Leviticus (cf. Lev. 26:22) and occasionally in the prophets.

In Hos. 2:20 we have another instance of the same pronoun (with the preposition להם): "And I will make for them a covenant with the beasts of the field, and . . . I will make them to lie down safely." I think the "them" in this passage still refers to the children, though it does not say so. The immediate antecedent is the Baalim, but the pronoun cannot refer to them; the covenant is not with the Baalim. Grammatical rules have to bend here, because we need a more remote antecedent to make sense of the passage. Most scholars don't go to the trouble, since they think of the lines here as *membra disjecta,* contributed by a variety of editors. But we contend that the pronouns offer a clue to the identity of the participants and constitute a unifying thread in chs. 1–2. Who is "I"? The husband, or God. Who is "she"? The wife, or Israel. Who are "they"? The children.

Another passage in Hosea presents another problem of understanding the prophet in his context. This is the famous passage about the first child: "Call his name Jezreel; for yet a little while, and I will visit the blood of Jezreel upon the house of Jehu . . . I will break the bow of Israel in the valley of Jezreel" (Hos. 1:4-5). The phrase "I will visit the blood of Jezreel upon the house of Jehu" poses the principal difficulty. Just what does it mean or signify? Clearly punishment is forecast. In order to understand the reference, it is necessary to review the bloody history of Jezreel in the Bible. The story begins with Ahab's desire to acquire Naboth's vineyard there, and the latter's refusal to sell; ultimately, Jezebel engineered the judicial murder of Naboth and his family and the confiscation of his property. According to the prophets, on the very spot where the blood of Naboth and his family was shed, the blood of Ahab and Jezebel would also be shed. This is the way it turned out, according to the story; the instrument of this vengeance, this punishment sent by God, was Jehu, at the instructions of the prophets Elijah and Elisha.

There is no doubt that the text of Hosea foresees a punishment of Jehu's dynasty, at the very least its termination. In fact, as we know, Jeroboam's son, Zechariah, succeeded to the throne and was assassinated shortly afterwards, fulfilling the prophecy. But what is the meaning of the passage: "I will visit the blood of Jezreel upon the house of Jehu"? The standard scholarly interpretation is that this represents a reversal of the position of prophets like Elijah and Elisha: that the bloodbath which Jehu instituted is now rejected as a method of dealing with royal sinfulness; that Hosea introduces a dramatic break with the classic prophets like

327

Samuel, who encouraged a holy war, or Nathan, or Elijah and Elisha, and many others of similar ilk. According to this view, the so-called literary prophets, beginning with Amos and Hosea and Micah and Isaiah, are spiritual interpreters of a new kind. The narrator of the Deuteronomic history applauded and congratulated Jehu for eliminating these sinners, and even promised him a dynasty of four generations (a record of longevity in the northern kingdom) as a reward for this behavior. But a new day has come with Hosea, and we have what appears to be a head-on collision with the older prophets, in the condemnation of the house of Jehu.

But what is the basis of this condemnation? Its own origin: the bloodbath back in Jehu's time, a hundred years ago? Let us reflect on this. Can this really be possible? In my opinion, this is a kind of Never-Never Land. Is there any suggestion anywhere in the book of Hosea other than this one verse that such an idea is even remotely in his mind? Hosea is interested in the past; he talks about Jacob, he talks about the exodus, and so on, but does it ever occur to him to talk about the episode of Jehu? Never. Therefore this must be the wrong assumption. This great hero of a new kind of prophecy is himself unaware that this is what he is doing. And what does he actually condemn the house of Jehu for? What is wrong with this king Jeroboam? It has nothing to do with what his ancestor did. It has to do with what he himself is now doing. It is the guilt of Jeroboam (although the name occurs only in the title of the book), or of whoever is the king of Israel, that is very much on Hosea's mind. Since the same king is condemned by Amos, there can be little doubt of his identity in Hosea. He is guilty of many sins, but chiefly of leading his people astray: apostasy, blasphemy, idolatry, not this rather esoteric question of whether a fourth generation ancestor did something that may not have been exactly in keeping with the new ethics. It is quite unbelievable that this should be the reason for judgment when much more compelling data were at hand. The speculations of recent scholars on this point seem irrelevant at best, mischievous at worst.

That does not mean that we can explain the passage easily, but I think we must give it a try within the framework not only of the classical prophets (who are the models for people like Hosea) but also in a genuinely historical context. Let us forget for a moment the popular notion that Hosea is the prophet of love. How many times have we heard it, that Amos is the prophet of justice and Hosea is the prophet of love? Well, if he is the prophet of love, it is disparaged, unrequited love, and that can be a pretty bitter thing. Nobody uses more violent language than Hosea to describe what Yahweh is going to do to his own people because they have misbehaved. If that is love, it certainly isn't what we normally think of as modern sentimental affection. Hosea is at least as much the prophet of judgment as he is of love. And what is he talking about here? I think we have here in prophetic terms an example of the classic pattern that the punishment is supposed to fit the crime, that the nature of the punishment is defined by the history of the person involved, that as you do to others, so it is going to be done to you. This is enshrined even in legal provisions; it is, ultimately, the *lex talionis,* an eye for an eye. The writers of the Bible devote a great deal of attention to showing how this works out, and take particular delight in the fine details that exhibit it. In this context, what Hosea means is: just as your ancestor shed blood in Jezreel, so your blood is going to be shed; your dynasty will end in the same way that the previous one was terminated. This is brought out explicitly in the case of Jeroboam I and the successor dynasty of Baasha: Jeroboam's son was assassinated by Baasha, and Baasha's son in turn was put to death by Zimri. That is the essential meaning here: the dynasty came into being as a result of bloodshed, and it is going to go out in the same fashion. But the crime for which this is the punishment is not what they did then, in Jezreel, however, but rather the catalogue of crimes of today, which fill chs. 4 through 14.

It seems to me, therefore, that we really must challenge not only the basic approach but also the conceptual world in which scholarship has operated with the book of Hosea. We have no reason to doubt that it is essentially a unity as it stands. Of course, this is self-fulfilling: that is the way we treat it. But the argument that we have a bare nucleus which has been greatly expanded by editorial glosses is too cumbersome a system to work with. We would say: first show that the book is as inconsistent with itself as you claim, and then we will deal with those questions. My opinion is that we must try to resolve the problems of the book within its own structure, and that progress can be made.

31

Temple without Hands

It is not easy to locate an imaginary temple on an unidentified mountain in a poem full of rich but imprecise imagery, but that is the task which confronts us in the attempt to interpret the Song of the Sea (Exod. 15:1-18, 21) and especially the crucial and enigmatic v. 17. The thesis presented in this paper is that the only true temple of God — made not by human but by divine hands — is and can only be located on top of the mountain sacred to the god who dwells in that temple. The possibilities as to the mountain and the temple are limited in the biblical tradition by historical and mythological criteria.

There are only two cases in the Bible which qualify for consideration: (1) Mt. Sinai/Horeb where Yahweh, whose oldest surviving designation may well have been *zeh sînay* "the One of Sinai" (found as early as the Song of Deborah, Judg. 5:5), had his palace. As we know from the tradition, the "tent of meeting" or "tabernacle" was modeled upon it (Exod. 25:8, 40), so the correspondence between earthly tabernacle and heavenly temple, the one at the base, the other at the top of the mountain, is exact. (2) Mt. Zion/Jerusalem, where Yahweh established his new permanent dwelling in connection with the reign of David and the selection of the ancient city on the border between Judah and Benjamin as his capital. Here, however, the picture has been modified. The earthly temple, made with (human) hands, actually is on top of the mountain (which is too small to have a heavenly crest), while the heavenly temple, in which Yahweh truly dwells, is invisible, though located in the vicinity and bound in the same fashion to Mt. Zion as the earlier home of Yahweh was bound to Mt. Sinai. While the image varies slightly, the correlation between earthly and heavenly dwelling remains intact, as well as the association with the single sacred mountain. So far as I am aware these are the only instances in the Bible with the threefold linkage of earthly sanctuary *(miqdāš)*, heavenly temple, and sacred mountain. Between the two places of permanent residence, the two sacred mountains and heavenly palaces, there is a period during which Yahweh traveled, as he says through the prophet Nathan, in a tent and a tabernacle, and had no permanent dwelling place.

It is further my contention that the divine sanctuary (made without hands) is not the one associated with Jerusalem and Mt. Zion, though many able scholars have thought so (including Paul Haupt), but rather with Mt. Sinai/Horeb. I do not believe that a serious case exists or can be made for any other location. The attempt to generalize the site (e.g., the mountainous areas of Canaan) is faulty and misses the basic requirement that the heavenly temple be on top of the mountain peak which joins earth and heaven. Other efforts to localize it at Gilgal or Shechem or Shiloh fail for lack of any combination of earthly and heavenly sanctuaries, or mountain mystique. Obviously Exod. 15:17 cannot be used as evidence since it is the subject of the inquiry, but in the biblical tradition Mt. Sinai serves as the original locus for the deity, the heavenly palace and earthly counterpart, while Mt. Zion is the only inheritor of the threefold tradition: the location which displaces Sinai as the center of worship and the focal point of the religio-political entity. It is conceivable that other loci served as transition points, but if so, they were ephemeral in character, and in each case, essential ingredients were lacking. We may postulate that in the case of Shechem and Shiloh, where there were central sanctuaries for the tribal league, not only the visible earthly sanctuary, but also the sacral mountain (e.g., Gerizim at Shechem), had a role, and some such association may be supposed also for later sanctuaries at Bethel and Dan, not to speak of Beer-sheba. But if sacred mountains played a role in the local cult or mythography, no significant trace has survived. On the contrary, clearly identifiable elements of the sacred mountain theme have left their mark, in particular the references to Ṣapon, the sacred mountain of Canaanite mythology, associated in the first instance with Baal, but also in a different manner with El. As Cross has shown, there are two major mountains in Canaanite mythology, Casius, Baal's mountain, and Amanus, which is associated with El. Both can be characterized as northern (i.e., Ṣapon) from the standpoint of Canaanite worshippers. Baal's temple on Mt. Ṣapon is described in detail — it is also made without human hands, though in polytheism the principal god need not use his own hands. In this case Kothar-wa-Ḥasis is the architect, contractor, and builder. It may be that Baal can claim the temple not only as his possession but as his work — but I doubt that this is correct.[1]

We return now to the basic arguments for the proposed interpretation of the passage in Exod. 15:17.

---

1. The reading should be, not "I have built my house," but rather "you have built a house for me." Compare the passages in 1 Kgs. 8 where we have alternate readings in MT and LXX: "I built" (MT) — "You built" (LXX). The difference is not only textual but conceptual: "I built" must refer to the earthly temple built with human hands, while "you built" is a reference to God's action in building his heavenly temple.

1. The date of the poem. If, as I and others have argued, this is a very early premonarchic poem in its entirety, then it can hardly refer to the Jerusalem temple. This is essentially the same point as the identity of the temple or sanctuary mentioned. If it were the Jerusalem temple, then the poem would have to be later in date. But the date has been based on other grounds, entirely independent of this particular factor. I am satisfied at any rate that the great bulk of the poem, including vv. 13-17, is premonarchic and comes from the 12th century. There is much evidence and an excellent array of data and arguments in support of an early, premonarchic date that effectively rules out Jerusalem and David's tabernacle or Solomon's temple. If I am right the only viable alternative is Sinai.

2. The unity of the poem can be defended on structural grounds. As I have tried to show in a lengthy detailed study of the poem's symmetrical construction, the patterning in the second part is so skillful in relation to the first, that while some scholars speak of imitation or expansion, it is more satisfactory to adopt the simpler hypothesis, namely unity of authorship. If it be agreed that the first part of the poem (at least vv. 3-12) is very early, then the same argument applies to the poem as a whole.

3. The genre analysis supports the view expressed. Victory odes customarily were composed in the lifetime of those who participated in the battle. Such odes tend to be occasional, concentrating attention on the major central episode, with marginal references to events immediately preceding and following the action from the vantage point of the latest event recorded. The dramatic and epic unities are maintained and the poem itself flashes a light on a single moment in ancient history rather than simply recording a sequence of events.

4. The contents and terminology breathe the desert air. The horizon of the poem does not extend beyond Sinai and the wilderness wanderings. In spite of assertions and assumptions to the contrary, there are no allusions to the conquest, the land of Canaan, or anything like that. There is direct reference to Canaan, to be sure, but not as an object of conquest. On the contrary, it is mentioned as one of the four neighbors of the territory through which Israel, which is only described as the people redeemed or purchased by Yahweh, passed. The four peoples or nations (Philistia, Edom, Moab, and Canaan) are depicted as paralyzed by the overwhelming might and terror of Yahweh — they are struck dumb like a stone, so that they cannot impede the progress of the people through the wilderness, whether they are thought of as allies and vassals of Egypt, or as acting in defense of their own interests. No distinction among the four is discernible: all are involved in the event and its aftermath as spectators, not participants — no threat is aimed at any of them. If any is implied it is at all of them; but the tradition outside of the poem carefully separates the Canaanites from all of the others. This is especially the case with Edom and Moab, whose territory is to be respected, and conflict with whom is to be avoided at all cost (the way of the Philistines is to be avoided as well, but this is another matter). In other words the conquest of Canaan is not on

332

the agenda of the poem. Certainly the reference to Canaan cannot be construed differently from the treatment of the three other peoples, and no one yet has suggested that the conquest was ever conceived as embracing all of them. The only time when this was imaginable was the age of David when Israelite suzerainty over these regions was achieved, but the connection is remote in my opinion, and far too subtle to hint at the Davidic conquests. But that at least is a possibility to go along with the notion that the divine-human heavenly-earthly complex at Mt. Zion is included in v. 17.

It will be of value to examine in some detail the critical passages especially in Exod. 15 and Ps. 78 relating to the temple made by Yahweh, and without human hands.

The passage from the Song of the Sea vv. 13-17 is familiar and has been treated extensively in recent years by a number of scholars. Therefore I need only summarize the analysis. According to the vantage point of the poet, the events belong to recent history. The narrative is entirely in the past tense though the verbs vary between perfect and imperfect according to the style of early Hebrew or somewhat earlier Canaanite poetry (see the study by D. A. Robertson). Thus the perfect verbs: *nāḥîtā* and *nēhaltā* in v. 13 are balanced by the perfect verbs in v. 17: *pā'altā* and *kôn^enû yādêkā*. Perfects and imperfects are distributed among the intervening verses in more or less symmetrical fashion: v. 14: perfect//perfect; 15: perfect, imperfect, perfect; 16: imperfect//imperfect; 17: imperfect//imperfect; but there is no indication of any change in tense. The action proceeds from the victory at sea to the journey through the wilderness to the settlement at the "mount of inheritance" whither they are brought and where they are planted. It is my contention that the expression *n^ewēh qodšekā* "your holy habitation" and the *har naḥ^alāt^ekā* "the mountain of your possession" describe one and the same place, namely the area or territory around the holy mountain of Yahweh, wherever that may be. The association of *har* and *nāweh* is natural, whether as parallel or complementary terms as shown by the interesting passage in Jer. 31:23:

y^ebārek^ekā yhwh	May Yahweh bless you
n^ewēh ṣedeq	O righteous habitation
har haqqōdeš	O holy mountain

No doubt the reference here is to Jerusalem and the (re)built temple (mount), but originally the language points to a wilderness setting, and would be entirely appropriate to Sinai/Horeb and the region of Kadesh-Barnea. A related passage is Ps. 78:52-54, where a similar association occurs: in v. 54 we have *g^ebûl qodšô* in parallel or complementary or combinatory relationship with *har*. The context is clearly that of the wilderness wandering, since the immediately preceding verse speaks of the guidance of his people by Yahweh to a secure refuge (= sanctuary) after the drowning of the enemy in the sea (an obvious reference to the episode at the Reed Sea). Here the word *g^ebûl* "territory" is used instead of *nāweh,* but the

333

sense is the same. It may be argued that this verse refers to the settlement in Canaan, and that is a possibility since the poet seems to have blended in this passage the sojourn in the wilderness with the settlement in Canaan. That he is aware of these two entirely different periods in Israel's existence, however, is clear from the earlier part of the poem.

In any event, the use of the term *qdš* to describe the region brings us back to the "mountain of God" which is where the story begins with the episode of the burning bush. As Professor Mazar, with his customary brilliance, has pointed out, the expression *'admat qōdeš* "holy ground" is not to be restricted to the few square meters on which Moses and the bush stood, but the entire district which presumably bore the name *Qādēš* for a reason. We may not want to inquire too deeply into the exact nature of the "holiness" involved, bearing in mind especially the characteristics of the goddess with the title *Qudšu*. Suffice it to say that this was the original "holy land." The persistence in the tradition concerning the holiness of the site of the sacred mountain of God/Yahweh convinces me that the use of the root *qdš* in these passages is no accident but a direct reference to the area in Sinai. The transfer of holiness to Canaan at a later (or earlier) date or the designation of the land of Canaan as holy to the God of Israel may belong to older traditions regarding the patriarchal settlement and the god El (Shadday); but for Yahweh the association was clearly of a secondary nature.

In v. 16 the repeated verb *'ad-ya'ᵃbōr* is taken as a reference to the crossing of the Reed Sea (Dahood) or the Jordan River (Cross and his students). But *'br* is not used only of crossing bodies of water, and the lack of an object makes it difficult to pin down the exact meaning of the word in these passages. Since no water crossing of any kind is actually described in the poem, we may dismiss both views as fanciful and dictated by considerations outside the poem. Within the poem there is a more attractive anchorage in the context of the march through the wilderness past (to the south of) the territories of the neighboring peoples, and a direct link with v. 13.

Thus *'am-zû gā'āltā* in v. 13 is paralleled by *'am-zû qānîtā* in v. 16 — the people whom you redeemed//the people whom you purchased. There can be no doubt that E. F. Campbell is right in restoring the connection between these verbs here in the light of their use in Ruth 4:4-6; this establishes that the meaning of *qnh* in Exodus 15 must be "purchase" in parallel with *g'l* "redeem."

The association of the same terms in Ps. 74:2 confirms the connection here in Exodus 15 — it is the same people, and the likelihood is that the same situation is described from two points of view: that of Yahweh's guidance and leadership (v. 13) and that of the people's marching through the wilderness to their destination (v. 16).

The verb *qnh* is used three times of God as victoriously redeeming or purchasing his people. In Exod. 15:16 it is used as a remote parallel to *g'l*, while in Ps. 74:2 the parallelism is proximate. In Isa. 11:11 the term used with *qnh* is *'ēdâ* instead of *ʿam* but the sense is the same. In Ps. 78:54 on the other hand the apparent antecedent is *har* = "the mountain which his right hand purchased." This is anomalous, and we may recognize the true antecedent of the pronoun in a passage otherwise closely parallel to Exodus 15, the word *ʿammô* in v. 52. The unit or stanza extends from v. 52 through v. 54; the first and last cola form an envelope around the intervening material. The reading would be:

wayyassaʿ kaṣṣōn ʿammô	and he led forth like a flock his people
zeh qānᵉṭâ yᵉmînô	whom his right arm had purchased.

This arrangement brings the sense into line with the sentiment expressed in the other passages mentioned but leaves an anomalous collection of words in the preceding colon: *gᵉbûl qodšô har.* They might be rendered literally: "his holy territory, the mountain." The association of *har* and *qōdeš* is one of long standing, however, and the change in word order is simply a stylistic variation: the meaning would be "the territory around his holy mountain." The combination of sacred precinct around the holy mountain fits precisely the description of Mt. Sinai and its environs in the time of the Israelite settlement there (Exod. 19 and other places).

A note on the idea of the hand as the instrument of purchase may be in order.[2] My opinion is that this kind of purchase is made by force rather than dollars. In the Second World War the word "liberate" came into use to describe the confiscation of material goods by conquering armies. This seems to be the meaning. Yahweh's purchase of his people is never recorded as a transaction but rather as an act, a violent one to be sure and perpetrated by his right hand, the symbol of divine justice and power. That explanation seems to suit the situation at the time of the exodus when the Israelites gained their freedom through a series of violent actions taken against Egypt and the Egyptians. The climax of the struggle was the destruction of the Pharaonic force at the Sea of Reeds. The notion that the hand, especially the right one, was involved in a business transaction perhaps sealed by oath may also have merit, but purchase by violence rather than exchange of goods or funds seems to be more appropriate in the circumstances.

Resuming the discussion of Exodus 15, I have pointed to the link between vv. 13 and 17, especially in the combination of *ʾel-nᵉwēh qodšekā* and *tᵉbīʾēmô,* which may be rendered quite naturally: "To your holy habitation you brought them," which balances beautifully with *wᵉtiṭṭāʿēmô bᵉhar naḥᵃlāṭᵉkā* — "And you planted them in the mountain of your inheritance (better: possession)."[3] This

---

2. The word *yād* is used in Isa. 11:11 in connection with purchase, but the sense is not clear there either.

3. The use of this expression points to a pre-Mosaic form of Yahwism, which involved features we can identify in the Canaanite mythic poems about El and Baal. There are repeated references and allusions in biblical tradition to a primordial struggle between Yahweh and the sea monster Rahab//Leviathan. If we see here a parallel to the Baal story of the great battle with Yamm, we note that apparently the victory over Yamm was celebrated by the building of Baal's

arrangement not only stresses the congruence of the ideas but also links the "holy habitation" with the "mount of possession." Concerning this latter, it will be noted that it is virtually identical with the Ugaritic expression used in connection with Baal's ancestral "mount of possession" or "inheritance" which is also the site of Baal's heavenly temple. It was precisely on this mountain of the north that Baal's temple was built and where he celebrated his kingship. The parallel with Yahweh and his mountain in the south (Sinai) is notable. It was on this mountain that Yahweh's palace stood, a palace made by Yahweh for himself with its throne room and throne, on which he is seated, king forever (v. 18). The same correlation and celebration are to be noted. This heavenly temple or sanctuary with its throne room or holy of holies where the deity was seated on his cherubim throne constituted the *tabnît* or structure seen by Moses during his sojourn on the same mountain; cf. Exod. 25:8, "And they shall make for me a sanctuary (*miqdāš* = Exod. 15:17) and I shall dwell in their midst according to everything which I am showing you: the *tabnît* or model of the tabernacle *(miškān)* and the model for all of its furnishings (equipment); and so shall you do."

While the language of v. 17 may seem much more suitable for the later settlement of the Israelites in Canaan, it is nevertheless appropriate for the first settlement at Sinai. After all, the principal object of the exodus, after escaping from bondage in Egypt, was to seek God in the wilderness. The actual settlement at Kadesh-Barnea, which must have been somewhere in the vicinity of the great mountain itself, extended over the better part of a generation (typically forty years), and in the eyes of that first generation may well have appeared to be a permanent settlement: "You brought them in and you planted them." It was only later when a new generation and a new situation had arisen that the march from Sinai began. The new state of affairs is reflected in the Song of Deborah (Judg. 5) and the Testament of Moses (Deut. 33). In these poems the removal of Yahweh from Sinai is asserted, along with his march to Canaan. The setting of the assembly of tribes in Deut. 33 is not clear and it is possible that the author intended a wilderness locale, or at least in the Transjordan plateau, but the tribal list itself suggests the locus is Canaan after the entry into the land. This also is clearly the case with the Song of Deborah. Yahweh's direct participation in the battle with the chariot forces of Canaan implies his equally explicit presence with his people. Sinai is far away and far behind: Yahweh is not only *zeh Sînay* but emphatically *ʾelōhê yiśrāʾēl,* which in my opinion always signifies a geographic-political entity with an identification with the land of Canaan, at least since the 13th century.

---

temple or palace on Mt. Ṣapon by Kothar-wa-Ḥasis and his helper deities, with Baal's subsequent enthronement in his palace. We can trace similar elements in the biblical account and may suppose that Yahweh's battle with Rahab and her allies preceded his acquiring title to Sinai, following which he erected his heavenly palace there. All this derives from pre-Mosaic Yahwism and survived only as colorful imagery in the austere demythologized version promulgated by the great prophet himself.

During this period Yahweh traveled in a tent or a tabernacle, having abandoned his old abode, but not yet having acquired a new one. Shrines and sanctuaries abound, and the divine presence may be made manifest in any one of them, but in no case is there the developed tripartite imagery which we found in relation to the Sinai episodes in the beginning and the construction of the house of David and Solomon at the end. While the latter (the temple of Solomon in Jerusalem) effectively displaced the former as the cult center of the nation, the tradition about the earlier domicile never entirely faded from view. On the contrary the traditions about Sinai and its sacred associations were maintained (we may suppose in the first instance by the Levites who had a special responsibility for the ark and its contents, stemming from the time of Moses in the wilderness) without abridgment, so much so that the main narrative of the Bible centers attention on everything that was done at Sinai by Moses and his associates. So what the Bible presents us with is two phases or stages in the faith of Israel: one focusing on the revelation at Sinai, the tradition of the founding fathers, and the organization of the new order; the other arising out of the military, political, or religious circumstances of the monarchy.

If the passage in Exodus 15 points to the heavenly sanctuary erected by Yahweh himself on top of the sacred mountain in the midst of the holy territory, then we must ask about the corresponding passage in Ps. 78:67-69.

67)	*wayyim'as bᵉ'ōhel yôsēp*	Then he rejected the tent of Joseph
	ûbᵉšēbeṭ 'eprayim lō' bāḥār	and the tribe of Ephraim he did not choose.
68)	*wayyibḥar 'et-šēbeṭ yᵉhûdâ*	But he chose the tribe of Judah
	'et har ṣiyyôn 'ªšer 'āhēb	Mt. Zion which he loved.
69)	*wayyiben kᵉmô-rāmîm miqdāšô*	And he built like the heights his sanctuary
	kᵉ'ereṣ yᵉsādāh lᵉ'ôlām	like the earth which he founded forever.

In vv. 67-68 we have clear cases of envelope construction and chiasm: *lō' bāḥār* is balanced by *wayyibḥar* while *yim'as* and *'āhēb* are paired. (The alternation of perfects and imperfects is noteworthy as an example of classic [i.e., Canaanite] usage: all are past tense — apart from *waw* consecutive.) The contrast between the tent of Joseph (i.e., the *miškān* at Shiloh) and Mt. Zion points to the shift from Shiloh to Jerusalem after the wars with the Philistines and the ultimate triumph of David (who is mentioned in vv. 70-72). In that context we must attempt to interpret v. 69; the basic content seems clear enough: "And he built his sanctuary" — apparently a reference to Yahweh's construction of his *miqdāš*. (If our presupposition is correct, namely that Yahweh built only one sanctuary at one time, then this can only be a reference to the sanctuary in the wilderness at Mt. Sinai, but the context points to Mt. Zion.) If as is generally agreed *rāmîm* refers to the heavenly heights, then the comparison between heaven and earth is established by the repetition of *kᵉmô* and *kᵉ* "like the heavenly heights"//"like the earth"; there seems to be a description of heavenly and earthly temples here.[4] The heavenly sanctuary is eternal, whereas the earthly counterpart is not. The former is made by God, while the latter is made by men.[5] The temple or sanctuary on Mt. Zion is said to be like the one in the heights of heaven — its replica and with the special status accorded the place, even the mountain which God loved.

Nevertheless it is our contention that the heavenly palace of Yahweh is located, as it always has been, on Mt. Sinai in the southern wilderness. Men may worship Yahweh anywhere, especially in the approved earthly shrine (or shrines) and especially where the ark and the throne are. Yahweh who customarily dwells in his heavenly sanctuary will hear and respond. On special occasions he travels to and with his people — to deliver them from bondage in Egypt and to settle them in the land of their fathers (the latter after a long internal and external struggle — with himself and with Moses).

Even though his name and his glory are attached first to one shrine and then another and then finally only to Jerusalem and the temple there, his home remains in Sinai/Horeb, and an intrepid worshipper may seek him there, as in fact Elijah did, rejecting the convenience of sanctuaries from Dan to Beer-sheba, going all the way to the sacred precinct of Horeb (= Sinai) and seeking the presence of God in the same cave or grotto where Moses had met the deity long before. Elijah was granted a certain vision (or anti-vision) but unlike Moses was not invited to see the true *tabnît*, the sanctuary which served as a model for all the replicas, especially the tabernacle and the temple in Jerusalem, but there is no reason to doubt that it was still there. Heavenly temples are built to last — *leʿôlām,* in fact.

---

4. As for the parallel verb *ysd,* MT pointing relates it to *ʾereṣ,* "he founded it"; but the spelling is ambiguous and the *h* could refer to the sanctuary, since *ysd* is used in laying the foundation of the temple. It would offer better parallelism:

> And he built his sanctuary//He founded it eternally
> like heaven//like earth.

5. Biblical terminology is not always precise and *wybn* here may be used in the same sense that Yahweh is spoken of in Ps. 147:2 as the "builder" of Jerusalem.

Bibliography

Campbell, E. F.
  1975　*Ruth.* AB 7. Garden City: Doubleday.
Cross, F. M.
  1973　*Canaanite Myth and Hebrew Epic.* Cambridge, Mass.: Harvard University Press.
————, and D. N. Freedman
  1955　"The Song of Miriam." *JNES* 14:237-50.
Dahood, M.
  1962　"NADA 'To Hurl' in Ex. 15, 16." *Biblica* 43:248-49.
Freedman, D. N.
  1976　"Divine Names and Titles in Early Hebrew Poetry." *Magnalia Dei: The Mighty Acts of God,* ed. F. M. Cross, W. E. Lemke, and P. D. Miller. Garden City: Doubleday, 55-107 [= *PPP,* 77-129].
  1974　"Strophe and Meter in Exodus 15." *A Light unto My Path,* ed. H. N. Bream, R. D. Heim, and C. A. Moore. Philadelphia: Temple University Press, 163-204 [= *PPP,* 187-227]
Haupt, P.
  1904　"Moses' Song of Triumph." *AJSL* 20:149-72.
Robertson, D. A.
  1972　*Linguistic Evidence in Dating Early Hebrew Poetry.* SBL Dissertation 3. Missoula: Scholars Press.

Discussion

Prof. Y. Yadin: I should like to comment on an interesting point. Whatever the original meaning was in those verses which you quoted, it is interesting how these verses were understood in the Second Temple period. I am going to speak more on that in my lecture on the Temple Scroll, on the concept of the temple city and the temple's role. But I should like to say that there the idea is a very simple one: God says to Moses how the Israelites should eventually build the earthly temple, let us say the Solomonic temple. The whole procedure is described and all the sacrifices dealt with, but then it ends with this verse: "All that till the day of blessing at the end of the days, when I shall build my own temple in the midst of the children of Israel, according to the alliance which I had with Jacob in Bethel." In other words they understood quite clearly that this God-made sanctuary, whether in heaven or on a mountain, cannot be found now. It will be revealed only at the end of the days, whenever that may be. This is what they believed, whatever the original meaning was. I want to conclude by saying that many years ago I gave a lecture to some very pious rabbis here in Mea She'arim about the plan of Solomon's temple. I spoke about one theory, and another theory, and a third theory, and I said that if today we were faced with the problem of rebuilding Solomon's temple it would cause a terrific debate among people how to build it. Then an old rabbi stood up and said: "Professor Yadin, do not worry, when the time comes, it will come ready-made by God from heaven."

Prof. M. Haran: Putting aside for the moment the question of the heavenly temples, how does it accord with the verses themselves. In v. 13 it says: "You led your people to your abode of holiness." In v. 17 it says: "You will bring them and you will plant them on your mountain of holiness." "Them" refers to the people of Israel. The question is, how come the people of Israel are associated with the heavenly temple. If the reference is to the heavenly temple, how could he speak of the people of Israel in this context?

Prof. D. N. Freedman: That is precisely the picture we have at Mt. Sinai and that area, namely, that the people of Israel are gathered at the foot of the mountain. This is where they construct the tabernacle, but on top of the mountain is the heavenly sanctuary. And with respect to the tenses of the verbs, in this poem there is no difference between perfect and imperfect forms. This is the classic example that David Robertson used to show that the verbal system in Exodus 15 belongs to the same pattern as Ugaritic poetry, in which perfect and imperfect forms are used interchangeably and in parallel structure, but do not affect the time scheme. That has to be determined by other criteria.

Prof. M. Weinfeld: I see the specific difficulty here in the verb "plant": "You will plant them in the mountain of your inheritance." This is an image in connection with the settlement of the Israelites in Palestine. For example, Ps. 80 is mostly dedicated to the image of how God plants a vine in the land and especially important is Ps. 44, which says in connection with settlement: "You with your own hand have disinherited the nations but you planted them." There are other instances, but I brought only these two. So I see here the difficulty in $w^e \underline{t}itta^c\bar{e}m\hat{o}$, which is a motif especially associated with the settlement of the Israelites in Palestine.

Prof. D. N. Freedman: There are even better passages, Jeremiah especially uses exactly the same language and of course this is what we have to expect. But what I am arguing is that, to the first generation out of Egypt, forty years was a long time, and that the horizon of the poem and the objective of the people is defined exactly in Exod. 3, where Moses is told: "When you have brought forth the people out of Egypt, you shall worship God on this mountain."

32

The Earliest Bible

Twenty years ago I proposed the thesis that the major components of the Hebrew Bible in substantially the form in which they have come down to us were organized and compiled, published and promulgated during the Babylonian exile and that therefore we could legitimately speak of a first Bible, an authoritative and quasi-canonical work, already functioning by the middle of the 6th century B.C.E. It contained the "primary history," comprised of the Torah (Pentateuch) and the Former Prophets (Joshua-2 Kings) as well as the bulk of the prophetic works. This work was intended to serve many purposes for the exilic community: standard and guide, rationale for and defense of the faith, explanation of the past, instruction for the present, and support for the future. But mainly it was designed to provide a context within which the exiles could survive, maintain their identity, and prepare for an ultimate return to the Holy Land.

The actual return, initiated in 538 under the reign of Cyrus the Persian, added a new chapter to the recorded history of the people who worshipped the God of Moses. As it changed their circumstances dramatically, revisions in existing works and composition of new books were required for the recently promulgated Bible. It is instructive, however, that no such postexilic additions or changes were apparently made in the primary history or in the books of the major prophets such as Jeremiah and Ezekiel; these works must have already been fixed and hence beyond the reach of continuators and supplementers. The new and revised compositions may be recognized in exilic and postexilic Isaiah (chs. 40–66) and such prophets as Haggai, Zechariah, and perhaps Malachi. Another example is an early edition of the books of Chronicles, an edition which arose out of the flurry of excitement and expectation generated by the rebuilding of the temple and the emergence of Zerubbabel, the scion of the house of David, as leader of the restored community.

As to the main thesis, not much has happened in the past two decades. The central contention, about the date of the primary history, and its implications for

341

the literary history of the several sources behind the Torah have largely been passed by, and traditional positions have been reaffirmed. There has been little reason, therefore, to modify or alter the proposal, still less to retract it. Its chief merits are its simplicity and prima facie plausibility. The burden of proof would seem to rest upon those who would deny or dismiss it; I think it should be the point of departure for consideration of both the previous, early stages in the development of the authoritative literature of Israel and the subsequent course of canon and text.

The current paper will elaborate and expand on the original thesis and make further proposals concerning the compilation and promulgation of the literature under consideration.

I

The key to the publication puzzle is to be found in the final paragraph of the primary history (2 Kgs. 25:27-30). This passage provides the last and latest date in the work and serves as a colophon, stating the date and publication place of the current edition. The date is given as 27 Adar in the 37th year of the exile (= 21 March 561 B.C.E.), during the accession year of the Babylonian king Awel-Marduk, the successor of Nebuchadnezzar II, who sacked Jerusalem. The occasion for the paragraph's inclusion was the release of the exiled king Jehoiachin from prison and the bestowal of allowances and perquisites appropriate to his royal status; in itself the item is of modest import. It is quite distinct from the preceding account (vv. 22-26), which describes the death of Gedaliah, the governor of Judah, in 586. The absence of data for the intervening years (586-561) shows that the historical work effectively ended with the fall of Jerusalem, the chaotic aftermath that resulted in the death of the governor, and the flight of many Judahites to Egypt (among them the prophet Jeremiah and the scribe Baruch; cf. Jer. 42–44).

The postscript, appended twenty-five years later, mentions the last surviving king of Judah, but adds nothing else of importance. Apparently it was the last piece of information available on the subject; nothing is said of the succession or of the next in line. While the passage refers to the remaining years of Jehoiachin's life, indicating only that the imperial stipend was bestowed as a lifetime annuity, it says nothing of his death or of the transfer of royal status. The precision of the imperial decree's date would lead one to expect similar detail about Jehoiachin's death if that information had been available. More important information would include a reference to the successors of Awel-Marduk and subsequent renewals of or changes in the grant to Jehoiachin.

The text also bears no indication of the death of Awel-Marduk, although we know that he died in the 2nd official year of his reign, between 7 and 13 August 560. The entry about Jehoiachin must then have been made before the death of

Awel-Marduk; it may well have been written after the death of Jehoiachin, in view of the repeated references to "all the days of his life." In any case, the publication date for the entire work, in full and finally edited form, appears to fall between 21 March 561 and 13 August 560 B.C.E., a period of a year and five months.

The only differences between the published text of 560 B.C.E. and the preserved texts from the Middle Ages resulted from scribal errors and adjustments. Editorial changes of different kinds may also have taken place, as reflected, e.g., in the varying Hebrew manuscripts and the versions, but these are of a minor nature for the most part, explicable in terms of divagations from a central and official text. The existence of the latter (of Babylonian origin, perhaps) is attested in the 3rd century B.C.E. by the Dead Sea Scrolls, can be projected into the 4th century, and can plausibly be associated with the official text (of at least the Pentateuch) promulgated by Ezra in the 5th century B.C.E. It may be possible some day to trace the textual history of the primary history and some of the prophetic books back to the 6th century, although documentary evidence is wanting.

II

The immediate implication of such a hypothesis is that everything contained in the primary history belongs to the period before 560 B.C.E., that nothing in it is to be attributed to a later date. That contention runs counter to long prevailing views of the composition of the Pentateuch or Hexateuch (the Pentateuch and Joshua) and of the dates of the later sources comprising that complex. These later sources are two in number: the Priestly source (called P), which contributed to the Pentateuch most of the liturgical, genealogical, legal, and technical materials; and the Deuteronomic source (called D), which comprises the bulk of the book of Deuteronomy. Closely allied to D is the framework of the Former Prophets, the books of Joshua, Judges, Samuel, and Kings, a body sometimes called the Deuteronomic (or Deuteronomistic) history. The standard assertions about the Priestly and Deuteronomic sources confidently assigning various editions to later and later postexilic periods and circumstances need themselves to be questioned and tested, since in large degree the claims made are based upon reconstructions of the postexilic settlement, themselves hypothetical.

Thus it is widely argued that the Priestly document, with its sacrificial and sacramental orders, reflects the practices and procedures of the Second Temple and was in fact drawn up on the basis of those practices. It is certain that the liturgy and ritual of the Second Temple and Priestly document have much in common, but that in itself proves nothing except that both derive from and develop out of the same community. Determining the chronological sequence and the direction of influence is much more difficult, perhaps impossible. Nonetheless, the proposed hypothesis about the primary history has value in that it posits an answer to the question of priority and requires proponents and opponents to present their evidence and arguments.

It seems to me that the burden of proof is on those who defend a postexilic date for P or even the Pentateuch as a whole and that none of the evidence so far adduced in favor of such a date is beyond question. The correlations between the Pentateuch and postexilic practice (recorded or reflected in undoubted postexilic works) not only fail to demonstrate priority but can in all cases be explained either as normal development from preexilic procedure or as evidence of postexilic dependence on the protocols of P. Even to devise a provable test for any priority — if we do not accept the traditional chronology — would tax scholarly ingenuity, and to produce proof of any kind would seem beyond our capacity, at least at this juncture. Perhaps it will suffice to say that postexilic practice deliberately imitated what was believed to be the pattern of the First Temple and that the Priestly writing, while purporting to record and reflect the liturgical experience of the wilderness wanderings of the earliest Yahwists, is in fact also rooted in the practice of the First Temple. There is no denying that some of the traditions in P are archaic, perhaps indeed deriving from the experience in the wilderness and even from the pre-Israelite traditions of Canaan.

What has been said about the P work applies even more strongly to the D work. Deuteronomy itself, or the bulk of it, has been regarded as preexilic in origin and date since the days of W. M. L. de Wette (1780-1849), whose identification of D with the document found in the temple in the 18th year of Josiah (622/621) has survived critical testing for almost two hundred years and remains one of the few relatively fixed points in biblical research. [See his 1805 doctoral dissertation on Deuteronomy and vol. 1 of his *Beiträge zur Einleitung in das Alte Testament,* 2 vols. (Halle: Schimmelpfennig und Compagnie, rept. Darmstadt, 1971). For discussion and further references, see J. Rogerson, *Old Testament Criticism in the Nineteenth Century: England and Germany* (Philadelphia: Fortress, 1984), 28-36.] Whatever the original date of the book of Deuteronomy or of its core (the ultimate sources and roots must reach far back in Israelite history), there is little doubt on anyone's part that it substantially reached its present form before the end of the exile.

The same may be said of the Deuteronomic history, which comes to an end with the fall of Jerusalem in 586, excluding the postscript already discussed. (My view is that the postscript was never part of the Deuteronomic history; hence its omission from the books of Chronicles, which follow the older source fairly closely in this material.)

There is no hint in the Deuteronomic history of subsequent events, especially the return from exile in the specificity with which it is described in 2 Chronicles and Ezra 1–6. While the hope of a return is part of the Deuteronomic credo as adumbrated in places in the sermons of Moses, these are hardly predictions after the fact, since the data are vague, imprecise, and inaccurate in detail.

The Deuteronomic history is certainly capable of creating *vaticinia ex eventu,* prophecies after the fact, as in the case of the prophecy at Bethel that names Josiah as the great future king of Judah about three hundred years before his time. But it includes nothing like that in connection with the return from the Babylonian captivity, nothing about the fall of Babylon, the rise of Persia, or the emergence of Cyrus. In the other case, the Deuteronomic history mentions Josiah as the fulfiller of the prophecy made to Jeroboam I both in the prophecy itself (1 Kgs. 13:1-3) and in the subsequent history (2 Kgs. 23:15-20). Had the writer known about the return from exile, he would surely have been more specific in the wording of the prophecies of that event and would have recorded the actual return in confirmation of the ancient predictions. His failure to follow this pattern in the case of the return argues strongly for a preexilic or exilic date for the D work.

Since we assign the postscript at the end of 2 Kings to the final editor or redactor of the primary history (in 561/0), we may date the D work to the period immediately following the fall of Jerusalem. The story ends with the departure of a large group for Egypt after the assassination of Gedaliah, an indication that the concern of the D writer was at least as much with Egypt as with Babylon. Richard Friedman has recently suggested that Egypt was in fact the focus of the writer, who brings the story full circle, beginning with bondage in Egypt (reflected in the Mosaic sermons in D) and ending with the return to Egypt. The passage from Egypt to Egypt complements the movement from Babylon, in Abraham's migration from Ur, back to Babylon, in the captivity. Friedman's arguments are persuasive, as is his proposal that an important link exists between the D work and the book of Jeremiah, also apparently a product of Egypt. The D work and Jeremiah must both have been compiled there after 586 B.C.E. but well before the end of the exile. We postulate a *terminus ad quem* for all such efforts in 561/0 B.C.E.

The last chapter of Jeremiah holds an important clue to the date of the book's compilation. This chapter consists of three parts: the first long section (vv. 1-27) is equivalent to 1 Kgs. 24:28–25:21; a short entry (vv. 28–30) follows, summarizing the numbers of captives and providing a series of dates that, like the numbers, are different from anything else about the captivity in the Bible; the final passage (vv. 31-34) is essentially identical to the passage at the end of 2 Kings, the postscript discussed above.

The numbers and dates in the brief second section of the chapter appear reliable and seem to be derived from government (perhaps Babylonian) sources. Their incorporation into the book of Jeremiah provides a terminus for this book as well, as they provide the latest dates in the book apart from the closing date, already assigned to the compiler of the primary history. Whether this second unit and perhaps even the first were added by the editor in Egypt, Jeremiah's scribe Baruch, or by a Babylonian redactor, Seraiah, the brother of Baruch, is not a material consideration here, as in any case the information serves to close the book, thereby incorporating in it the violent anti-Babylonian prophecies of chs. 50–51 (probably by someone other than Jeremiah, whose attested views concerning Babylon and Nebuchadnezzar were very different).

We may, therefore, adopt 582/1 as the earliest possible date for the publication of the book of Jeremiah. The addition of the postscript was intended to tie that book to the primary history and to bring it under the same authority as the larger work. It is clear that the support of Jeremiah and of Ezekiel, the two major prophets of the period, was regarded from the inception of the process as necessary and important. The primary history was constructed on the basic pattern of prediction and fulfillment, whether in the promises to the patriarchs realized in the conquests of Joshua or in the warnings of Moses fulfilled in the terrible judgments visited upon Israel. Buttressing the classic prophets from Moses through Samuel, Elijah, Elisha, and even Isaiah, the timely words of the two great contemporary prophets, Jeremiah and Ezekiel, conclude the work.

That observation leads to a consideration of the P work, its place of publication and date. As to the place, the general opinion that this work takes its origins and derives its contents from the tradition of the priestly class and the experience of the Solomonic temple seems most reasonable. Whether the work is preexilic, compiled in Jerusalem, or exilic and put together in exile is difficult to decide, and there are legitimate arguments on both sides of the question. The solution may lie in a compromise, i.e., in the recognition that large and significant components are clearly old, some ancient, and that probably some major sections belong to a preexilic work.

There is some difficulty in defining the limits of the work. Does it extend beyond the Tetrateuch (Genesis-Numbers)? If so, where does it end, and in what fashion? Traditionally P was thought to continue and complete the story begun in Genesis with the allocation of the tribal territories in Joshua, but that opinion has come into question in recent years. In all likelihood a decision here would have bearing on a judgment about the date of the whole work, as we lack both a date and a datable tag. I think that we can trace P through Numbers without great difficulty; after that the trail becomes uncertain.

I am sure there was a continuation of some kind, perhaps parallel to or even still contained in Joshua, because the promises in Genesis belong to P as well as to the earlier Yahwist and Elohist sources. The redactor of P knowingly incorporated all the patriarchal promises, which must find resolution or fulfillment in conquest or settlement in the Promised Land. That element is entirely lacking in the Tetrateuch, especially as the conquest in Numbers does not correspond territorially to the promises in Genesis. There must have been something more in the original P work. Our conclusion about the compilation of the P work is that the process began in Jerusalem and may have ended in exile in Babylon. The date is uncertain, but I believe that it is roughly contemporary with the D work, although the process may have taken longer in the case of P.

Comparison with Ezekiel is indicated; the connections, linguistic, lexical, and conceptual, are obvious, but the questions of interaction, dependency, and the direction of influence are hard to determine. A consensus that Ezekiel in its totality

346

is the later work seems to be emerging, holding that the prophet is ultimately dependent for basic attitudes and ideas on the Priestly tradition but not trying finally to settle the question of specific dependence or influence.

For the oracles of the book of Ezekiel we have a series of explicit dates, ranging from the 5th year of the exile to the 25th (40:1) year of the exile (roughly 593/2–573/2). However, an editorial insertion in vv. 17-21 of ch. 29 (itself dated to the 10th year of the exile, 588/7) is dated to the 27th year (571/0). In this interpolation the prophet comments on his earlier prophecy, which he has not seen fulfilled. Here he offers an evaluation of the former prophecy and a revised oracle. This paragraph is a clear example of editorial work by the prophet, not entirely satisfied with the text and wishing to bring his comments on the matter up to date. There is no further comment about this particular prophecy, which appears in chs. 26–28, concerning Nebuchadnezzar's siege of Tyre; the new oracle speaks of an impending conquest of Egypt by Nebuchadnezzar as compensation for the failure to capture Tyre.

Ezek. 1:1 contains a reference to the 30th year (568/7); if it belongs to the same chronological system as the rest of the dates, it would be the latest of all and might be intended or understood as the date of compilation or publication. The range between 571/0 and 568/7 is not large; we can leave the issue undecided. The minimum date would be 571/0. If we allow about three years for the completion of editorial work we come out about the 30th year, 568/7.

That leaves another seven years for the final work on the primary history and its publication along with the two major prophets, Jeremiah and Ezekiel. We can summarize the proposal as follows:

	Minimum Date	*Place*
D work	586	Egypt and Babylon
Jeremiah	581	Egypt and Babylon
P work	Early 6th century	Jerusalem and Babylon
Ezekiel	571 (or 568)	Jerusalem and Babylon
Primary history	561	

These dates indicate that the final process of editing and compiling took place in a relatively brief interval and that the work was carried out in accordance with a general plan. We have dealt only with the final stages of a process that was both long and intricate. Internal evidence shows that the book of Jeremiah went through a number of earlier phases, though the latter ones have to be conjectured and reconstructed. It is a roughly contemporary work, assembled during the lifetime of or shortly after the death of the prophet. The same may be said of the book of Ezekiel, although we lack factual data about the way in which the work was carried out.

Both books reflect intense interest in dating and preserving prophetic oracles so that they could be checked against the later events for validity. This attitude and care were matters of great moment to the exilic communities, whether in Egypt or Babylon, and we can recognize the same process of preservation and consolidation in both locales without denying that the impulse and method derive from Jerusalem, with its royal and priestly traditions and archives.

III

The intense editorial activity of this period no doubt reflects the extraordinary trauma that the people of Judah and Jerusalem experienced. Deprived of freedom and nationhood and bereft of temple and land, the only visible recourse was to the text. It was an idea of their own creation that a book of remembrance should serve in place of all that had been lost. It would provide for a distinctive manner of life to keep them separate from their gentile neighbors. It would also give hope for the future, a future which in the light of their sister Israel's experience a century and a half earlier as well as that of other small nations must have seemed exceedingly bleak and gloomy.

To give substance to that hope, it was necessary to explain at length and in detail just what had happened to this people and why. Simply to state the facts that a large empire had twice overwhelmed a small kingdom in the space of a decade was hardly enough. That could only confirm the exiles' worst fears and anguish. It was necessary to explain rather that their God, Yahweh, was not defeated but victorious, that he remained in sovereign control of the world that he had created and ruled since the beginning. Hence the elaborate proemium in Gen. 1–11, otherwise out of proportion to the story of a small people that follows. The same God who had created them a nation and given them a land in accord with solemn promises made to the patriarchs also judged and condemned them and finally destroyed them because they failed to obey the word and persisted in running after and serving other gods. They richly deserved their destiny. They had no one to blame but themselves. In this recognition of their own fault lay the basis of revival and restoration. The same God was not permanently alienated; he was willing, even eager, to bring them back to the land from which he had torn them and to reestablish them as he had once before. Palace and temple, priesthood and kingship would all be restored, and that life of peace and security, prosperity and well-being to which they had been called and for which they had been instructed would be theirs, this time forever. Roughly speaking this promise was the message of the book, of the first Bible, which consisted of the primary history supplemented by Jeremiah and Ezekiel.

Other books or parts thereof doubtless existed at the same time, and some at least may have been authorized and pressed into official service. We can and should postulate an exilic collection of prophets, including, in addition to the two mentioned, the four 8th-century prophets (Amos, Hosea, Isaiah, and Micah), whose oracles were especially important for Jerusalem a century after Samaria had fallen. The later prophets, strongly influenced by the earlier ones, make frequent comparison between the two kingdoms using Israel (the northern kingdom) as an object lesson from which the southern sister could learn. Other books such as Nahum, Zephaniah, Habakkuk, and probably Obadiah can be listed as well, for all refer to the momentous events of the last century of Judah's existence.

Beyond the horizon of the first Bible lay the second, much enlarged edition. The dividing point and the stimulus for the new burst of literary activity was the end of the exile and the return from captivity. This remarkable event required a revised history (the books of Chronicles, the first edition of which goes through Ezra 3) and a new set of prophetic supplements (including books such as Haggai, Zechariah, and probably Malachi) for the last part of the 6th century. But the great prophet of the return and restoration comparable to the prophets of doom and destruction associated with the primary history (Jeremiah, Ezekiel, and many of the Minor Prophets) was Isaiah — both or several of them in a single book. Without attempting to analyze or reconstruct the complex history that produced the book we have, it is clear that the book of Isaiah was regarded as the appropriate companion piece to Chronicles, as both emphasized the decisive role of Cyrus, the continuity and authority of the house of David, the centrality of Jerusalem, and the inviolability of Zion.

Bibliographical Note

For the previous study of the primary history, see "The Law and the Prophets" *VTS* 9 (1963): 250-65 [see above, Chapter 14]; and the elaboration in "The Canon of the OT," *IDBSup,* 130-36. For Friedman's work, see "From Egypt to Egypt: Dtr[1] and Dtr[2]," *Traditions in Transformation,* ed. B. Halpern and J. D. Levenson (Winona Lake: Eisenbrauns, 1981), 167-92. [See further D. N. Freedman, *The Unity of the Hebrew Bible* (Ann Arbor: University of Michigan, 1991), and Chapters 40 and 42 below.]

33

Discourse on Prophetic Discourse

This paper examines a problem in the interpretation and even more basic understanding of prophetic oracles in the Hebrew Bible. While we must always consider the literary context, the social and cultural setting, as these affect meaning and sense, the immediate question is more narrowly linguistic in character: do we understand a certain configuration of words found in the Bible and attributed to a certain prophet, and can we render it into appropriate comprehensible English? This is the common challenge for translators of texts in other languages, but for the Bible there are particular if not peculiar aspects and ramifications, owing to its antiquity, which require special consideration. The Bible itself contains a wide range of materials, of different literary types and correspondingly varying degrees of comprehensibility. Much of it is written in straightforward prose, which aside from a manageable number of scribal errors can be read and interpreted quite easily. The content often is unusual, and sometimes shocking, but that is a function of cultural and temporal distance and is not a linguistic difficulty. Standard Biblical Hebrew prose has its grammar and rules, its normal structures and patterns, and with rare exceptions it follows them.

The same may be said for its poetry, with the proviso that the rules as well as the vocabulary are different. In the nature of the case, poetry is more evocative and emotive, it relies more on impact, whether visual or audile, in the arrangement of words and phrases and the sequence of sounds. It also has a more complex, often confusing, grammar and syntax, along with a penchant for unusual words. The mastery of Hebrew verse comes only after much study, not to speak of pain and prayer, and even then we suspect that much of its subtle sophistication, its multiple meanings and larger senses, escape our notice. Our penetration into the subtleties and complexities of poetic usage and our grasp of its varieties and tonalities are limited indeed. Some significant progress has been made through the investigation of cognate languages and literatures, and the patient and intensive study of the surviving biblical texts. Using the tools and weapons forged by modern linguists, and recognizing the special devices universally used by poets to enhance the senses, disguise features, and compound meanings, we are making headway in the face of many obstacles. The rewards, however, are great, and contested terrain, once seized, will not be lost in the future.

When it comes to prophetic discourse, we are dealing with another distinctive phenomenon, a *tertium quid* that defies even the acute reasoning of Molière: while it shares in the aspects and specific features of prose on the one hand and poetry on the other, not infrequently it cannot be described as belonging wholly to either camp but remains defiantly in the no-man's-land between them. Sometimes we are faced with ordinary narrative or declarative prose, and sometimes with poetry in the classic mode, but often there is an admixture not easy to analyze or describe, with lines of prose interlaced with those of poetry, or occasionally a kind of poetic prose or prose poetry that cannot be broken down into constituent elements of either kind. Whether in the end the problem of classification is more with our categories than with the Hebrew prophets is a question we can beg, and then escape. Even when we hit upon this middle ground between prose and poetry, we have not resolved an issue of long standing in the traditions of scholarship in this discipline. For many centuries the prophetic literature was read and copied as prose, i.e., like the rest of the Hebrew Bible, except for a few poems identified as such and certain books recognized as poetic. Then in the 18th century, Bishop Lowth, professor of literature at Oxford, transformed scholarship by identifying much of the prophetic corpus as poetry, and contributed everlastingly to the understanding and appreciation of those oracles as poetic compositions of the highest merit. Now we must modify the latter judgment somewhat in the direction of the former tradition, and allow that much of this literature falls between the poles, with its own rhetorical forms and expressions.

There is another persistent problem in the understanding and interpretation of prophetic discourse. I refer to the question of textual integrity. On the one hand, errors in transmission are inevitable, as a comparison of manuscripts demonstrates; or I should say differences show up, and scholars have procedures for identifying probable mistakes and eliminating them. Recovery of an accurate original or at least an earlier text is an appropriate and necessary objective, and much time and effort have been expended by scholars, as was the case with editors and scribes of an earlier time, to preserve or restore the best possible text. On the other hand, indulging in the restorative process always risks compounding or creating errors and so producing a new text that has little or nothing in common with the original author's work. It is one thing to choose among readings preserved in different manuscripts; it is quite another, and much more risky, to restore a text that is not attested in any manuscript. Steering a middle course between excessive restraint whereby we preserve and enshrine errors as canonical, and excessive freedom whereby we emend away the particular expression of the author because it seems or is so strange, is no easy task, and yet it is essential. It cannot be avoided by some dogmatic presupposition about the nature of the text and the way it is to be treated (e.g., regarding the biblical text as divinely inspired, hence inerrant, or necessarily conforming to 19th-century rules governing diction, grammar, and syntax, hence emendable).

351

My approach to the Hebrew text has become increasingly conservative, beginning with a practical consideration having to do with scholarly consensus. Since for much of the Hebrew Bible the text base is narrow and supports only one well-attested reading, there is very little chance that another reading, no matter how brilliantly devised, will win more than a few adherents. Even if the received text bristles with difficulties it makes more sense to cope with it than with a text no one else accepts. Over the years it has become clear that some features of Biblical Hebrew have been preserved in the text but not recognized by grammarians, medieval or modern. Gradually we are learning to accept these features, thus preserving and clarifying the text, without resorting to the surgery of emendation. From an aesthetic point of view this is much more satisfying than the kind of ruthless assault practiced by an earlier generation of scholars. It is akin to the difference between finding and fitting the right but elusive piece in a jigsaw puzzle and forcing the wrong but handy piece into the configuration, thereby guaranteeing an imperfect solution.

Focusing this concern, I will treat two substantial passages from the book of Micah. Why the book of Micah? Because it illustrates in a dramatic way the problem described, and because it is the subject of my current research. Scholars concede two passages, from chs. 3 and 1 (in that order), to be from the prophet himself and part of the original work. One of these, the oracle in ch. 3, is quite readable and comprehensible. It is poetic and exhibits the standard features of classic Hebrew verse. It poses no particular problems of analysis or interpretation, and there is a prevailing consensus on its structure and meaning. The other passage, in ch. 1, is a nightmare of confusion and incoherence described by the illustrious Paul Haupt as the most corrupt passage in the Hebrew Bible. That verdict has not been altered substantially in the years since. The recently published Stuttgart Bible has as a footnote on this unit the following comment: *omnia mutilata sunt*.

Assuming that this judgment is correct — which in spite of its longevity and universality may not be tenable — then how can one explain the absolute contrast in the history of the transmission of different parts of the same text? While the distribution of scribal errors is hardly uniform, it follows a determinable pattern, and by its nature has an important random component. Thus we would expect a sprinkling of trivial errors throughout the material (in chs. 1–3), many of which could be corrected in the framework of the established text. The point here is that if the great bulk of the text is clear and comprehensible and there is widespread agreement that it is in order, then occasional aberrations can be identified and corrected in accordance with the usual rules governing such matters. The ratio of wrong to right readings should be low, and the passage as a whole should be generally understandable. Difficulties arise when the ratio apparently rises, and when there is doubt about the context and the passage as a whole. Emendation becomes a matter of guesswork, and the end result may be worse than the reading in the text. When it requires changing one word after another until an entirely new text is created, not only has the editor exchanged roles with the author, but the whole effort becomes an exercise in creative irresponsibility. Although this has been, in fact, the usual procedure over the years, it has become increasingly clear that the results are unacceptable and unusable. What we may call progressive emendation and transformation of a text are self-defeating examples of literary ingenuity. Certainly the approach did not develop in a vacuum, but was a serious response by dedicated and often brilliant scholars to a genuine problem, that of trying to recover the meaning of a text. Even if we reject the results of a free-wheeling text manipulation and management, we freely concede occasional brilliancies and successes. Rejecting the solution doesn't by itself change the status of the problem. At best we are back where we began, and unless we abandon the scholarly enterprise, we must try again. In what follows, we will try to define both the problems and the ground rules and come up with a new set of proposals for these passages in Micah.

First we will assume that the text is mostly all right, i.e., that it is a faithful reproduction of what the prophet said, or what he or, more likely, his scribe or editor wrote down. We will not try to distinguish between the two, and will be quite satisfied to arrive at the more modest objective of recovering as much as possible of the sense of the written edition. Second, at the same time we will concede the presence of errors, and will make some effort to identify and correct them. This can only be done successfully if the text is basically and generally sound and the error a technical slip falling into one of the well-established categories: haplography, dittography, metathesis, and the like. Even then we cannot claim certainty, and we are left with a paradox or anomaly: the more certain the correction is, the less important it is likely to be, while the more important the correction is, the less convincing.

Now we will look directly at the two passages and compare the original text with one or more translations. With respect to the first passage (Mic. 3:1-8) we will try to show how simple and understandable the text is and how reliable the transmission has been. Then following the same procedure with the second passage (Mic. 1:10-16, but mentioning 2-9) we will see how difficult and troublesome another unit from the same source can be. When we have done our best, while avoiding the temptations of progressive emendation, we will have resort to a new hypothesis to explain the radical difference.

Mic. 3:1-8

The first part (3:1-3) is consistent and intelligible. The imagery is vivid if somewhat distasteful, but there are no serious problems in the text. There is only one obvious difficulty in the passage: in v. 3 the Hebrew text has *k'šr,* "as," so that we would render:

> And they break (them) in two as in the pot
> And like flesh in the midst of the caldron.

That is not impossible, but as poetry it limps and the parallelism is imperfect. What apparently has happened is that *k'šr* was written accidentally for *kš'r,* which means "meat" or "flesh" and is a perfect parallel to the word in the second colon: *kbśr,* "like meat" or "flesh." Both of these words occur in the preceding verse, enhancing the possibility of confusion. The error itself is one of the most common, as any writer or typist can attest: metathesis. The correct reading is confirmed by the Old Greek, which has *hōs sarkas,* "like meat" or "flesh." That shows that the error in the Hebrew text occurred rather late in the course of transmission, after the time when the Greek rendering was made (generally thought to be in the late 3rd or 2nd century B.C.E., long after the original composition of the book).

Verse 4 contains a shift in person and subject, but it serves as a fitting conclusion to this unit:

> Then they all cry out to Yahweh,
> > But he won't answer them;
> > And he will hide his face from them at that time,
> Since they have committed such wicked crimes.

Once again the general sense is quite clear, although the grammatical and syntactical connections are somewhat looser than would normally be true of prose. The first and last clauses are linked by a common subject and common verb form (third masculine plural), while the subject of clauses two and three is third masculine singular (Yahweh). This sort of envelope construction is quite common, especially in poetry and prophetic discourse, and we may infer that the final clause, which is the reason for the negative response of God, may also be the occasion if not the reason for their crying out to God.

The next section, vv. 5-8, deals with false prophets, a special thorn in the flesh to a true prophet such as Micah. It is similarly perspicuous, requiring very little in the way of analysis or interpretation.

Essentially the text is clean and the message and meaning are clear. We may examine special features which mark the structure and admire the subtlety and sophistication of the poet in the arrangement of words (e.g., the envelope construction in v. 6 bound by "night" and "day" in that order) or the interlocking of terms in v. 8, combining the mighty spirit of Yahweh with the power of authority in judgment, the role of the true prophet, but these should not detain us from our principal task.

Mic. 1:2-9

We may now turn to ch. 1 for a study in contrasts. The first unit, vv. 2-9, forms the general introduction and makes reasonably good sense. There are some soft spots, but not out of line with what we have already seen. These may be minor slips, or else peculiarities of style and structure with which we are not familiar.

The oracle begins with a summons to the peoples of the earth to hear and pay attention to the testimony forthcoming, testimony concerning the guilt of Israel and Judah which makes them worthy of ultimate judgment, and liable to condign punishment. There follows a description of a theophany, the awesome power of God as he manifests himself in the violence of nature, here as the God of storm and quake (vv. 2-4).

There follows a brief characterization of the basic sin, the central theme of the oracle:

> For the transgression of Jacob is all this
>> (and) for the sins of the House of Israel.

Immediately after this comes the question:

> What is the transgression of Jacob?

and its answer:

> Is it not Samaria?

with its parallel:

> And who (what) are the high places of Judah? Is it not Jerusalem?

The first response fits with the previous statement quite well, at least with respect to the names or terms. The initial reference to the "transgression of Jacob" is picked up by the question "What is the transgression of Jacob?" The answer is consistent in that the capital city of the northern kingdom is cited. The root of the trouble lies there, and while the statement is elliptical and elusive the sense is that Samaria, the head of the kingdom, is responsible for the violation of fundamental covenant commitments. We are reminded of a similar correlation in Isaiah, in a contemporary situation:

> The head of Ephraim is Samaria and the head of Samaria is Ben-Remaliah (the king). (Isa 7:9)

The next pair diverges substantially. Where we (probably) would have expected "Who is responsible for the sins of the House of Israel?" we have instead: "Who (what) are the high places of Judah?" i.e., who is responsible for them? The two changes suggest that something is out of order, and the usual procedure is to restore the presumed original on the basis of the preceding pattern. Both the response to the rhetorical question and what follows make it clear that either the shift was deliberate on the part of the speaker or author, or any earlier version which may have conformed to expectations has been effectively supplanted. There is nothing to be done except to cope with the surviving text.[1]

---

1. LXX tries to smooth things out.

It is clear, first of all, that the theme of these introductory utterances, as already intimated in the heading, 1:1, is the guilt of both kingdoms represented by their capitals, Samaria and Jerusalem, and the catastrophic punishment decreed for them by the divine judge of all human behavior. That Judah and Jerusalem in this passage are correct and in balance with Jacob (which here is equivalent to Israel or, more precisely, Ephraim) is confirmed by v. 9 where the same terms are used in describing the threatened judgment. What of the high places? Clearly this term is not parallel with "transgressions" used with Jacob, and some other interpretation of the usage must be sought. What we have discovered is that parallelism is only one way and hardly the most common by which a Hebrew poet relates terms in a balanced arrangement.

A more frequent procedure is to separate for prosodic reasons terms that belong together and help to define or precise each other. Thus we suggest that transgression properly combines with high places to form the phrase "the transgression of the high places," which applies equally to north and south and evokes the monotonously repeated charge of the Deuteronomistic historian against the kingdoms: both kingdoms are condemned for conducting unacceptable worship at the high places. The formula for northern kings, that they continued the practice initiated by the first king of north Israel, Jeroboam, whose activity in establishing the illicit worship of the golden calves at Bethel and Dan and at the high places, is described in 1 Kgs. 12:25-33 (esp. 30-32). The kings of Judah are routinely condemned for not removing the high places, the building of which is attributed in the first instance to Solomon, who dedicated them to foreign gods, and their proliferation to the Judahites of the days of Rehoboam, the heir and successor of Solomon. According to the biblical text, the first king to dismantle the high places was Hezekiah, who reigned from 715-687 (after the fall of Samaria in 722 B.C.E.). It would seem clear, now, that Micah's prophecies concerning the high places in Israel and Judah, and the charges levelled at central administration, must date from a time before the fall of Samaria and the removal of the high places in Judah, which goes well with the other information in the book and related sources. We conclude: who is responsible for the transgression of the high places in Jacob (i.e., Ephraim) and Judah? The government leaders in Samaria and Jerusalem, certainly.

There follows in v. 6 a vivid account of the imminent overthrow of Samaria, including specifically the destruction of all of its idols and images. There is a break at the end of v. 7. With v. 8 the prophet introduces himself as the official mourner for the demise of the northern kingdom. He speaks of his distress and distraction, his uncontrollable grief and his ululation, like the caterwauling of the jackals and the high-pitched shrieks of the ostrich's offspring. This verse serves then as a transition to Judah and Jerusalem, and the threat hanging over the southern kingdom. It may also help to explain the more hysterical and incoherent utterances that follow. Clearly the fate of Jerusalem and Judah is closer to the heart of the prophet, and even though he recognizes the common evil and hence the equivalent consequences for the two nations, he is more impassioned and less comprehensible in his outpouring for his own people as compared with his more dispassionate response to the fate of the north. Finally in v. 9 the section closes with the ominous pronouncement that the disaster has entered the country (presumably in the form of an enemy army), that the mortal blows are raining on the weakened city — in short, that the ultimate divine enemy is pounding on the gate of Jerusalem itself.

While the going has not been easy, still we are able to follow the prophet as he begins his oracle of doom. So far at least, the procedures and devices are within the bounds of syntax, and the rules of grammar, if strained, are not yet broken. Even without emendation we are able to follow the text, or stay within reasonable or reachable range of the prophet in his utterance.

Mic. 1:10-16

Now, however, in vv. 10-16, we come to a passage that breaks through these limits, one which has effectively baffled commentators and interpreters. After a very brief introduction, the prophet runs down a list of towns and villages guarding the southern and southwestern approaches to Jerusalem, the classic route of invading armies, to be followed by the infamous Sennacherib within a generation. He binds all together in a litany of disaster giving a kaleidoscopic view of various scenes of frantic defense and panicky response, impending and occurring ruin, the folly of resistance, and the fate of the defeated, an unrelenting tragedy which ends in the conquest of the land and the death and exile of its citizens. At the center is Jerusalem, Daughter of Zion, a bereaved mother wailing for children lost in war, banished to captivity.

Immediately noted features of the passage include the extensive use of paronomasia and the profusion of different pronominal elements, creating both intensification and confusion, if not incoherence. Presumably the passage expresses the previously mentioned grief and hysteria of the prophet. The passage is built around a series of place names, cities and villages which belong to the region of Jerusalem. There may be as many as fourteen such names including the central city: Jerusalem, Daughter of Zion. Under the threat and reality of military invasion, the cities, symbolic of their populations, are described in various postures of despair, while being encouraged to lament their fate. Aside from the elaborate paronomasia and the introduction of unusual or unique terms, the general idea can be captured, and the meaning seems to be consistent with the use of wordplay. There are, however, other threads running through the material, elements which complicate the picture, are not readily classified, and put intolerable strains on ordinary, or even poetic, grammar and syntax.

Following the basic principle of parsimony and in accordance with the practice of paleoanatomists in bone sorting, we will group grammatically congruent components. The opening line has verbal forms in the second masculine plural:

357

"Do not announce . . . do not weep." These masculine plural people are not identified in the section, but their presence may be noted not only in v. 10 but also in v. 11, twice in prepositional constructions. Who they are may remain a mystery, but we are obligated to look for an appropriate antecedent. The only one which commends itself is the subject of the initial summons and command in 1:2: "Hear O peoples (all of them), pay heed O earth (in its fullness)."[2]

Whether or not this analysis is correct, there can be no doubt about the grammar; second masculine plural people are addressed in v. 10a, whereas v. 10b shifts abruptly to second femine singular, an unusual and archaic verb form. Here the subject is apparently the personified city, represented by several or many of the names preceded by the term *inhabitant* or *daughter* to justify the feminine singular form. (The dramatic shift from second masculine plural to second feminine singular is obscured in English, where we use the same word *you* for all four forms, masculine and feminine, singular and plural.) The verse can be rendered:

In Gath do not you tell (it)
In Bako [?] do not you weep.
In Beth-le-aphrah roll thyself in the dust

In v. 11 we have the curious phenomenon of double direct address, which can hardly be expressed intelligibly in English, or in Hebrew, for that matter. Put literally, we have "You pass by [imperative second feminine singular] for you [second masculine plural]." The latter must be the same people as addressed in the opening line but different from the second feminine singular people (against RSV, which equates them, erasing the distinction in the Hebrew), while the former is identified as the city of Shaphir, presented as a woman. Behind this town is the central city of Jerusalem, Daughter Zion, but the notion of simultaneous direct address to different parties is difficult to accommodate either grammatically or conceptually. Clearly it must be considered unless we either identify the groups under different figures or eliminate one as an error in transmission. Actually the messages are in conflict if not in contradiction, since the instruction to the second masculine plural group is not to proclaim, not to weep, whereas the mandate for the city is to roll in the dust, a vivid image of mourning and self-abasement in the face of tragedy. In short, outsiders are not to be sympathetic, because the punishment is thoroughly deserved.[3] The inhabitants, the participating group, however,

---

2. Note in passing the anomaly of the combination of 2nd and 3rd person forms: "Hear peoples all of them; pay heed earth and its fullness," literally.

3. The opening clause is reminiscent of the famous lament of David over Saul and Jonathan (2 Sam. 1:19-27), "Tell it not in Gath," except for a slight change in the order of the words. In neither poem is the subject (2nd masc. pl.) of the verb identified. In the Davidic dirge, the instruction is given so as to preclude or postpone the inevitable rejoicing of the Philistine women over the defeat of the Israelites. In the passage in Micah the circumstances are less clear, and the reason correspondingly more obscure.

must give full expression to grief or self-laceration for precisely the same reason. Only by a show of remorse and repentance can the guilty victims make a proper response to the judgment of their angry God.

The second masculine plural forms occur through v. 11 and then cease. We have identified these people as outsiders, spectators of the scene of devastation and catastrophe, who are admonished not to spread the news or weep in mourning. We can reach back to v. 2 for an appropriate antecedent: "the peoples of the earth." In v. 10 the meaning is fairly clear: "Tell it not — do not weep." The topical references may be unrelated and belong rather to the central scene (in Gath, in Bako?). The significance of the prepositional phrases in v. 11 is less clear: "for you" and "from you." In neither case does the immediate context offer much help, although the entanglement in the action of the second feminine singular forms indicates that the second masculine plural people are near the scene. "For you" may have purely ethical connotations, i.e., "for your benefit or advantage": "do not weep for yourselves." The third masculine singular forms refer to different people: perhaps the subject is God or an agent of God, or the construction may be impersonal, while the suffixed pronoun may refer to the person for whom mourning normally would be appropriate, i.e., the king; but in Jer. 22:10-19 there is an interdict against mourning for a dead king. The ban on mourning, which is associated with Beth Haezel, would fit with the initial prohibition against audible wailing.

Now we must grapple with the second feminine singular forms which dominate the unit. The central figure or person clearly is Jerusalem (Daughter of Zion), vv. 12-13. This image is frequent in the prophets especially of the 8th century B.C.E.: Jerusalem/Zion is portrayed as a woman or girl who represents the city as a whole, its population, or various groups. Along with Jerusalem/Zion, Micah mentions about a dozen cities or villages in the surrounding area, mainly in the southwest environs along a major military route. The most common designation of these "inhabitants" is *yôšebet* plus the name of a city, with collective force similar to the phrase Daughter of Zion. The expression *yôšebet* plus city name occurs five times in the passage:

yôšebet šāpîr	(11)	inhabitant of Shaphir
yôšebet ṣaᵃnān	(11)	inhabitant of Zaanan
yôšebet mārôt	(12)	inhabitant of Maroth
yôšebet lākîš	(13)	inhabitant of Lachish
yôšebet mārēšâ	(15)	inhabitant of Mareshah

The apparent gap between the last two members of the list is actually filled by a similar-sounding but different expression, *môrešet* ("possessor," perhaps, or "possession, territory"), which is joined to the city name *gat* to produce Moresheth-gath. It is a common practice of the poets and prophets of Israel to vary a sequence of repetitions by a single change in a long list. At first glance this may seem anomalous, but the practice of varying from a norm, or avoiding monotony, is well known, and in the case of biblical poetry this variation itself has become a principle. I have collected a number of examples which only need be listed here without additional comment:

Amos 1–2: w^ešillaḥtî ʾēš (1:4, 7, 10, 12; 2:2, 5) varied by w^ehiṣṣattî ʾēš (1:14).
Jer. 51:20-23: w^enippaṣtî b^eḵā (51:20, 21 [2], 22 [3], 23 [3]) varied by w^ehišḥattî b^eḵā (51:20).
Gen. 49:25-26: birḵōt (49:25 [3], 26 [2]) varied by taʾawat (26).
The parallel passage in Deut. 33:13-16 has the same feature: mimmeged (33:13, 14 [2], 15, 16) varied by mērōʾš (15).

Micah contains a second example, only the pattern itself is more complex and elaborate. Each of the repeated words is balanced by a parallel expression or paraphrase; in the last case the initial term of the pair is also changed:

5:9	w^ehikrattî	—	w^ehaʾabadtî
10	w^ehikrattî	—	w^ehārastî
11	w^ehikrattî	—	lōʾ yihyû — lāḵ
12	w^ehikrattî	—	w^elōʾ — tištaḥaweh
13	w^enātaštî	—	w^ehišmadtî

Returning to Mic. 1:10-16 we can count probably twelve different city names, not including the pair Jerusalem/Daughter of Zion, which is obviously the focus of attention. The twelve serve as attendants or subordinate associates: suburbs and exurbs of the capital. The passage is organized around the names of the cities: the occurrences of the repeated expression yôšebet (and its substitute môrešet) form a framework within which the other names are inserted. After the introductory pair, introduced by the preposition b^e,[4] the remaining twelve city names are grouped in units of four:

1) vv. 10-11:

b^ebêt l^eʿaprâ
    yôšebet šāpîr
    yôšebet ṣaʿanān
bêt hāʾēṣel

---

4. The second term bāḵô was interpreted by the Massoretes not as the name of a city but as a form of the verb bkh, a so-called infinitive absolute, which goes with and strengthens the main verb: tiḇkû. A literal rendering would be: "Weeping, do not weep!" Cf. RSV, "Do not weep at all." The Massoretes may well have missed a wordplay concealing the name of a city (perhaps Bōḵeh); a similar play on words occurs in Judg. 2:1-5 where the verb bkh is associated with the place name Bōḵîm. No place with a similar name is known in the area described by Micah, but that is true of several of the city names in his list.

Here we have an envelope construction in which the outer pair is characterized by the prefixed term *bêt,* literally "house," and often used as part of the names of places (e.g., Bethel, Bethlehem, etc.). The inner pair is already familiar from its use of *yôšebet* indicating the population of the towns named.

2) vv. 12-13:

> *yôšebet mārôt*
>   *yᵉrûsālēm*
>
> *yôšebet lākîš*
>   *lᵉbat ṣîyôn*

Here the pattern is an alternating one, in which the first and third terms are characterized by the familiar *yôšebet,* while the second and fourth are parallel terms for the capital city, Jerusalem/Daughter of Zion, i.e., two expressions for the same place.

3) vv. 14-15:

> *ʿal môrešet gat*
>   *bāttê ʾakzîb*
> *yôšebet mārēšâ*
>   *ʿad-ʿᵃdullām*

Here the structure is less precise, but a mixture of the two preceding patterns can be discerned. The alternating sequence can be observed in the pairs *môrešet gat // yôšebet // mārēšâ* and *ʾakzîb // ʿᵃdullām.* At the same time the use of the prepositions *ʿal* and *ʿad* with the first and last cities shows that an envelope scheme is also to be observed. Thus *ʿal môrešet gat* and *ʿad-ʿᵃdullām* belong together, while the remaining pair seems to have in common the absence of prepositions and the status of objects rather than subjects. This unit remains obscure and difficult; several divergent arrangements and analyses are possible.

Looking at the assemblage it seems clear that the association of verbs and cities is occasioned by various forms of paronomasia rather than historical or functional considerations. Lachish is instructed to harness the horses because the word used for horse, *rekeš,* sounds like *lākîš,* although it is quite likely that steeds were quartered there. Likewise one rolls in the dust at Beth-le-aphrah because the word for dust, *ʿapār,* is very similar to the last element in the name of the city, *ʿaprâ.* Other wordplays are more or less obvious: e.g., *ʾakzîb* and *ʾakzāb, yōrēš* and *mārēšâ, lōʾ yāṣᵉʾâ* and *ṣaʾᵃnān.* The conclusion, perhaps drastic, is that all the cities together represent the single entity Judah, or more specifically the capital Jerusalem, which they guard, and which stands also for the country. In similar fashion, the activities ascribed to the separate localities together add up to the frenzied and hysterical behavior of the inhabitants of the invaded country and besieged city in the last throes of desperate struggle before the final collapse of resistance, followed by destruction, desolation, captivity, and mourning. These activities are glimpsed haphazardly as the eye of the prophet wanders over the scene of anguish and devastation, picking out individual figures and settings at different stages of the disaster. The lack of overall clarity reflects the confusion of battle and destruction, but of the overarching tragedy there can be no doubt. Binding the passage as a whole are the repeated second feminine singular verbs and vocatives. The referent is in some cases our ubiquitous *yôšebet* and in others Jerusalem/Daughter of Zion, while in the remaining ones the subject is not specifically identified but must be the population seen collectively as a female figure: the city and its inhabitants.

Three prepositional phrases, all with the second feminine singular suffix, provide a key to understanding the sweep of the prophet's vision:

1) v. 13: "For in thee *(bāk)* are found the transgressions of Israel."

2) v. 15: "Yet again I will bring the dispossessor to thee *(lāk)*."

3) v. 16: "Strip and shave thyself over thy delightful sons
Make extensive thy baldness like the vulture
For they have gone into captivity from thee *(mimmēk)*."

In sequence, the three clauses give the rationale and the reality of divine punishment. Judgment has come upon Judah because the sins characteristic of the northern kingdom (spelled out at length elsewhere) have been imported into and adopted in Judah, so that the latter will share the destiny of the former. As a consequence, God (speaking through the prophet in the first person) has brought, is bringing, or will bring the conqueror to the land. In the third sentence the end of the drama is portrayed: they (thy sons) have gone away into exile. The immediate associations with individual locales are subordinated to the overall picture with its focus on the central city and on the consequences spread out through the vicinity.

We may note that the second masculine plural forms which are prominent in the opening verse (10) are balanced by the second feminine singular forms in the closing verse (16). Curiously the same prepositional phrases with second masculine plural suffixes occur in the beginning as occur with second feminine singular suffixes toward the end: *lākem* in v. 11 (second masculine plural) balancing *lāk* in v. 15 (second feminine singular), and *mikkem* at the end of v. 11 matching *mimmēk* at the end of v. 16. Exactly how to interpret the second masculine plural forms remains obscure, but the matching pattern suggests that the text is sound and that the pairing is intentional.

While I believe it is impossible to make coherent sense out of the passage as it stands, it is possible to isolate the central theme and to group elements that seem to belong together. Thus we can follow the prophet's message through its various embodiments and representations to some kind of conclusion.

The major theme is to be found in vv. 12-13, which is also the midpoint of the passage. In v. 12b we read: "For evil (harm) has come down from the Lord to the gate of Jerusalem." This theme has already been expressed in Mic. 1:9: "For it has come as far as Judah; he has struck at the gate of my people, as far as Jerusalem." Parallel to v. 12b is v. 13b (the interlocking structure has already been described), which we try to render literally: "The first (or chief) of sin (was) she for the Daughter of Zion, because in thee were found the transgressions of Israel." The opening and closing lines of this unit express clearly the intention of the prophet: Judgment in the form of military disaster has been decreed by Yahweh; the underlying reason is the transgressions of Judah, which has imitated Israel in this respect. The background and connections are explained earlier by the prophet himself (1:2-7) and confirmed elaborately by the Deuteronomistic editor of 2 Kings (chs. 16–18). The middle clause is different, but the "she" who constitutes the chief sin is not identical with Daughter of Zion/Jerusalem, but someone or something in the city. The feminine singular pronoun here suggests that the figure is an image of the chief goddess of Canaan, Asherah, whose worship in Israel is mentioned often in the historical and prophetic books. There are specific references to this figure in Israel, and the implication here is that the same goddess is now being worshipped in Judah, and especially in Jerusalem. The parallelism between Samaria and Jerusalem is affirmed in Mic. 1:5, so we cannot be far off the track. There is another intriguing feature of the two passages: In 1:5 we have *peša'* (singular) "transgression" matched with *ḥaṭṭo'ṯ* (plural) "sins," whereas in 1:13 the reverse is the case: *ḥaṭṭā'ṯ* (singular) is paralleled with *piš'ê* (plural). The meaning is hardly affected, but the forms are carefully arranged in chiastic and interlocking fashion.

We may now turn to the list of activities linked with the inhabitants of the various cities and gather from them glimpses of the frenzied hysteria which gripped the country in its time of peril. On historical grounds we believe that the Micah oracle reflects the period when Judah was invaded by Israel and Aram around 735 B.C.E. and when, according to the account in Kings and Chronicles, much of Judah was overrun, its armies routed, and many of its citizens taken captive by the victorious Israelites and Arameans. The armies of the latter invested Jerusalem and laid siege to the city, which with its suburbs was apparently the only surviving territory of Judah. In this emergency, Ahaz, the king of Judah, appealed to Tiglath-pileser III, the great king of Assyria, for help. The crisis is depicted by the prophet Isaiah in a notable passage (ch. 7); while he adamantly urged calm reliance on Yahweh for succor, the king understandably turned to a somewhat more visible source of aid. In our passage, the prophet Micah, with his omnitemporal eye, fusing past, present, and future into a single picture of disaster, speaks of the crisis and impending doom.

We have already observed that the dirge over Judah begins with a warning to the peoples of the world (Mic. 1:2) not to waste tears or sympathy; routine divine justice is being administered to the sinful nation. Then he turns to the targeted victim: she (or they) is not only permitted to mourn, but commanded to do so; "roll in the dust" is a typical if exaggerated form of grief.[5] The next element is exposure, nakedness coupled with shame. This is a common consequence of defeat which especially symbolizes the humiliation and degradation of women. "Pass by in shameful nakedness," is a reflex, perhaps, of captives going into exile. The following line speaks of the seclusion associated with mourning, but neither expression is clear.

Verse 12a is obscure, but perhaps the expectation of or waiting for "the Good" is antithetical to "the Bad" which Yahweh has decreed from heaven (v. 12b). Coupled with the vain waiting for "the Good" is the presumably ironic instruction to harness the chariots to the horses (or vice versa), perhaps for battle, perhaps flight, either of which will be futile.

Beginning with v. 14 matters become somewhat more confusing, but a structural analysis may help to untangle themes or threads which can be made to yield meaning. In v. 14 we recognize an envelope construction linking 14aA and 14bB: "Therefore you shall pay tribute [parting gifts, i.e., to buy off the invader] . . . to the kings of Israel"; perhaps then, as part of the same structure, payment is to be made from the storehouses of Akzib, used here symbolically as a link to the next word, which means "to the false or deceptive one." This last word may well be another designation of the "dispossessor," namely, the "glorious one," the king(s) of Israel. The plural "kings" is strange since the other three forms are all singular. We must hesitate before emending the text, otherwise an attractive option. Perhaps the plural here refers to a group of Israelite kings in this period or, as seems more likely, to a dual monarchy or co-regency arrangement, the existence of which is confirmed more than once in the history of these kingdoms. There also seems to be a play on *'akzāb,* "false," and *kābôd,* "glory," since they share similar consonants: "the false or deceptive glory."

Verse 15 offers a fairly clear frame of reference:

Again will I bring to thee a dispossessor —
    the glory (glorious one) of Israel will come.

It seems clear that the conqueror is the glorious one of Israel, presumably the king of that country currently leading the invasion of Judah.

The closing brings us back to the central theme in terms of its ultimate consequences: unceasing grief for the loss of the manhood of the country. The survivors are taken away in exile as the passage ends: "They have gone away into captivity from thee."

What is still needed is some explanation of the radical confusion and disorientation of the text. The lack of agreement among verbs, nouns, and pronouns, the leaping about from subject to subject, and the incoherent variety of circum-

---

5. The verb here in the original text (the written form, Kethib) may be described as a precative perfect, not the expected imperative (which is preferred by the oral form, the Qere). In the passage a wide variety of verbal forms is used, perhaps to convey omnitemporality, along with the avoidance of repetition.

stances go far beyond the normal range of scribal (i.e., inadvertent) error. Patching up the piece to make it read like ordinary poetry or prose would require extensive rewriting and would not help. Is it possible to account for the product without either appealing to the emendatory recourse or consigning the passage to oblivion? Perhaps a look at the prophetic experience will help.

In the examination of the material from and about the prophets we find in effect two traditions. One, already discussed, is fairly standard and consistent; prophets are poets or very close to them. Their oracles fall into well-known patterns, and given the general difficulties of dealing with poetry of any language or period, we can make reasonable headway and come out with satisfactory results. Here we assume conscious composition by the prophet with a certain amount of arranging and editing by disciples and later editors.

In the present case (ch. 1 as over against ch. 3) such an approach won't work, so we must look again at the tradition. Some, perhaps most, prophets were ecstatics, and presumably gave utterance under the power of the spirit. Micah affirms this explicitly in 3:8, "But as for me, I am full of the mighty spirit of the Lord, with power and judgment." So we may suggest that the oracle in 1:10-16 was uttered during an ecstatic seizure occasioned by his almost hysterical grief at what he foresaw to be the fate of his beloved country and people (cf. 1:8, "On account of this I am grief-stricken and wail inconsolably. I howl like the jackals, and lament like young female ostriches").

In a paroxysm of anguish, sharpened by a panoramic vision of desolation and ruin, the prophet pours out in fits and starts, in bits and pieces, his woe. Then we may suppose that the words which came forth were recorded by a scribe who simply set down what he heard, or what he could make out in words and sentences of what was uttered. Apparently little or no effort was made to reconstruct a sensible or comprehensible speech, but what was preserved and transmitted were the key words, the basic clues to the inmost feelings and uppermost thoughts of the distraught prophet. If it is possible to probe into the psyche of this prophet, then here are the essential data, requiring not reconstruction or rewriting, but rather analysis and response. On another occasion, the prophet, in a calmer frame of mind, reflecting on the same situation, might well have organized his thoughts along normal lines of poetic expression such as we have found in ch. 3 and very frequently in the prophetic literature. Here in 1:10-16, we seem to have the raw product straight from the soul of the prophet, who could not restrain the torrent of words (or sounds), an almost incoherent speech forced from his lips by the spirit of God. This could be a striking example of things said in a moment of ecstatic inspiration, about which we read in different parts of the Old and New Testaments (cf. Jer. 20:7-9 and 1 Cor. 12–14). Mic. 1:10-16 might well belong to the category of semicoherent ecstatic utterances characteristic of certain classes of prophets. There also seems to be a family resemblance to the glossolalia which swept through the Christian churches in the days of the apostles.

One word of caution should be added. Our investigation has shown that the passage cannot be analyzed or parsed according to the common rules of Hebrew syntax and grammar. At the same time, the more carefully we examine the components the more connections and structural patterns emerge. It is possible that such features are an aspect of the prophet's subconscious, expressed in the involuntary speech of an ecstatic experience. It is also possible that the passage in question is the result of a carefully planned presentation, which resembles ecstatic utterance but is deliberately designed that way. Our sense of its incoherence may be a reflection of our ignorance, or failure to recognize more intricate patterns and arrangements, which differ from standard usage but have a subtle system of their own. Perhaps we will finally discover that the interaction of ecstatic experience and intellectual planning is adequate to explain the whole range of prophetic poetic utterance.

At present and perhaps for the foreseeable future, we will not be able to answer the questions we have raised about prophetic oracles generally, and this one in particular. If we cannot now discern motivation and intention, we nevertheless have the inescapable obligation to deal with the finished product and to analyze and interpret the text which has come down to us. In short, we must respond to what we find and leave always open the question of just what the prophet had in mind. We may conclude with the following observations.

All texts are corrupt in some measure, and it is the task of scholarship to correct corrupt texts. The better the text the easier it is to correct errors, and the less important the process becomes. The worse the state of the text, and the more imperative the interpretive obligation, correspondingly the more difficult to achieve satisfactory results, or even modest progress. Put another way, the more difficult the text, and the more important it is to clarify, the harder it is to come up with anything useful.

34

Headings in the Books of the
Eighth-Century Prophets

The present essay is part of a larger contemplated study of the headings or opening lines of several biblical books, and what they can tell us about the purpose and process of scriptural redaction and publication. The project at hand involves an examination of the headings of the four books of the 8th-century prophets, listed in the order in which we find them in the Hebrew Bible: Isaiah, Hosea, Amos, Micah.[1]

With slight but significant variations, the headings are formulaic in character, follow the same pattern, and contain the same or corresponding items of information. If we set the introductory lines side by side or organize them in tabular form, as we do on pp. 366-67, we can recognize at a glance both the formulary and the divergences in detail.

1. Structure of the Headings

The headings consist basically of two parts, each of which may have a varying number of subdivisions or extensions. Thus, the heading proper consists of a phrase in the form of a construct chain containing two words, the first defining the

---

1. Most of the headings (or titles) of the prophetic books in the Hebrew Bible, while sharing similar elements, show remarkable diversity. The headings of the 8th-century prophets compared with the other prophetic headings show sufficient similarity to suggest that they were shaped by a common editorial tradition. For a general discussion of the content and structure of the headings of the 8th-century prophets as they compare with the headings of the later prophets, see F. I. Andersen and D. N. Freedman, *Hosea.* AB 24 (Garden City: Doubleday, 1980), 143-49.

experience of the prophet or the core of divine revelation, while the second, the absolute, identifies either the prophet himself, or the source of revelation, Yahweh. The opening phrase is then followed by one or two relative clauses, introduced by the relative particle, *ʾašer*. The clausal verbs are *hāyâ* and *ḥāzâ*, with either one or both used to qualify the initial phrase.

The second major component consists of the chronological indicator, which in this period is linked with the reigning kings of Judah and Israel. The opening word in every case is *bîmê* ("in the days of . . ."; i.e., "during the reign of . . ."), followed by the names of the kings during whose reigns the prophet was active. Unlike the headings of later prophets such as Jeremiah and Ezekiel, the specific years are not mentioned. In every case, the appropriate kings of Judah are mentioned or listed, and in two cases the contemporary king of Israel is also given. In one case, an additional chronological datum is offered (Amos 1:1). We may set out the headings according to the following plan:

PART I: HEADING PROPER

A. Isaiah
  1. *ḥᵃzôn yᵉšaʿyāhû*   The vision of Isaiah
      ben-ʾāmôṣ   ben Amoz,
  2. - - - - -   - - - - -
  3. *ʾᵃšer ḥāzâ ʿal-yᵉhûḏâ*   which he saw concerning Judah
      wîrûšālāyim   and Jerusalem.

B. Hosea
  1. *dᵉḇar yhwh*   The word of Yahweh,
  2. *ʾᵃšer hāyâ ʾel-hôšēaʿ*   which came to Hosea
      ben-bᵉʾērî   ben-Beeri.
  3. - - - - -   - - - - -

C. Amos
  1. *diḇrê ʿāmôs*   The story of Amos
  2. *ʾᵃšer hāyâ bannōqᵉḏîm* who was among the cattlemen
      mittᵉqôaʿ   from Tekoa,
  3. *ʾᵃšer ḥāzâ*   who had visions
      ʿal-yiśrāʾēl   concerning Israel.

D. Micah
  1. *dᵉḇar yhwh*   The word of Yahweh,
  2. *ʾᵃšer hāyâ ʾel-mîḵâ*   which came to Micah
      hammōraštî   the Morashtite,
      . . . .
  3. *ʾᵃšer ḥāzâ ʿal-*   who had visions concerning
      šōmᵉrôn wîrûšālāyim   Samaria and Jerusalem.

PART II: CHRONOLOGICAL INDICATOR

A. Isaiah

1. *bîmê ʿuzziyyāhû yôṯām* In the days of Uzziah, Jotham,
   ʾāḥāz yᵉḥizqiyyāhû Ahaz, Hezekiah,
   malkê yᵉhûḏâ the kings of Judah

2. - - - - - - - - - -

B. Hosea

1. *bîmê ʿuzziyyâ* In the days of Uzziah,
   yôṯām ʾāḥāz yᵉḥizqiyyâ Jotham, Ahaz, Hezekiah,
   malkê yᵉhûḏâ the kings of Judah;

2. *ûḇîmê* and in the days of
   yārobʿām ben-yôʾāš Jeroboam ben-Joash,
   melek yiśrāʾēl the king of Israel

C. Amos

1. *bîmê ʿuzziyyâ* In the days of Uzziah,
   melek-yᵉhûḏâ the king of Judah;

2. *ûḇîmê* and in the days of
   yārobʿām ben-yôʾāš Jeroboam ben-Joash,
   melek yiśrāʾēl the king of Israel,

3. *šᵉnāṯayim lipnê hārāʿaš* two years before the earthquake.

D. Micah

1. *bîmê yôṯām ʾāḥāz* In the days of Jotham, Ahaz,
   yᵉḥizqiyyâ malkê yᵉhûḏâ Hezekiah, the kings of Judah

2. - - - - - - - - - -

Notes to Part I

1. With regard to the opening phrase, Hosea and Micah have the traditional *dᵉḇar yhwh*, while Isaiah and Amos specify the name of the prophet after the initial word *ḥzwn* or *dbry*.

2. With regard to the *ᵃšer* clauses, Amos and Micah have both *ʾšr hyh* and *ʾšr ḥzh*, although in Micah the second subordinate clause comes at the end of the unit after the chronological indicator rather than before. Isaiah has only the *ʾšr ḥzh* clause (like Amos and Micah), while Hosea has only the *ʾšr hyh* clause, corresponding to Micah in this respect. It may be noted that while Amos has the same basic pattern as the others, the details vary more widely from the others, and the verb *hyh* requires a different rendering.

Notes to Part II

1. All four prophets are dated according to the sequence of Judahite kings. In the cases of Hosea and Amos we also have synchronisms with a king of Israel. In the case of Amos, a third datum is offered, the only specification of years by number, i.e., "two years before the earthquake."

2. A curious feature of the king lists is the omission of the conjunction ("and") between the names of the kings of Judah, as though they were copied directly from an official list or docket. The fact that this feature is common to all of the headings, along with the repetition of formulas and the general patterns, suggests that the headings in their present form are the work of a single editor or compiler.[2]

3. We may note further that there is a divergence in the spelling of two of the names in the list of the kings of Judah: Uzziah and Hezekiah. In both cases the book of Isaiah preserves the long form of the names, while in the three Minor Prophets the names are consistently shortened:

ISAIAH	MINOR PROPHETS
'uzziyyāhû	*'uzziyyâ*
yᵉḥizqiyyāhû	*yᵉḥizqiyyâ*

This divergence does not reflect a difference in authorship or editing, but rather the separate development in the spelling of words in these books. As can now be confirmed from inscriptional evidence, the longer spelling reflects the older original form of these names correctly preserved in the book of Isaiah. The shorter spelling reflects postexilic developments, as represented by similar names in seals and other inscribed materials. The preserved orthography is consistent with what we know of the books (= scrolls) in question.[3]

---

2. The lists of the kings of Judah in the headings of the 8th-century prophets appear with the conjunction omitted between each king (with the exception of Amos, which mentions only one Judahite king) and are preceded by the noun *yᵉmê* in the construct. Compare this with a similar list in the heading of the book of Jeremiah, where the construct *yᵉmê* is repeated before each king. The use of one construct noun coordinated with a series of kings, along with the designation of the group as a whole as "kings of Judah," gives the impression that the editor considered the successive reigns as one era. It is noteworthy that the kings of Judah serve as the primary chronological reference point both for the northern prophets (Amos and Hosea) and for the Judahite prophets (Isaiah and Micah). For further discussion of the evidence for common editorship, see Andersen-Freedman, 146-47.

3. For a historical discussion of the long *(-yhw)* and the short *(-yh)* spellings of the divine element in personal names, see D. N. Freedman and M. O'Connor, "YHWH," *TDOT* 5 (1986): 501, 506-8. The most recent and exhaustive study of biblical spelling can be found in F. I. Andersen and A. D. Forbes, *Spelling in the Hebrew Bible*. Dahood Memorial Lecture. Biblica et Orientalia 41 (Rome: Biblical Institute Press, 1986), 315-16. They conclude that the spelling in the Latter Prophets is less conservative than in the primary history but more conservative than in the Writings. While there is variation between the individual books of the Major Prophets

2. Orthographical Considerations

The scroll of the Minor Prophets exhibits a consistent pattern of very late orthography, including numerous examples of the latest developments in the Bible. Its transmission history is quite different from that of the book of Isaiah, the first edition of which can be associated with the prophet of that name and may have been produced as early as the end of the 8th century or shortly thereafter. In this compilation we find as we expect the name of the prophet and the names of the kings spelled out in full in accordance with preexilic practice. That spelling has been preserved in the MT of Isaiah.[4]

A further, similar example of early and late spelling can be cited as well: The name of King David is spelled with three letters *(dwd)* in the book of Isaiah, while the predominant spelling in the Minor Prophets (including some of the 8th-century prophets) is with four letters *(dwyd)*. Just so, the evidence from other books of the Bible is that the three-letter spelling is archaic and preexilic, while the four-letter spelling was introduced in postexilic times.[5]

We draw the following conclusions from the textual and orthographic evidence for the headings of these four books:

1. The headings belong to the same genre, use the same formulas, and reflect a common authorship, or were written under the same direction. There is every reason to believe that the headings were composed in connection with the initial publication of the books and that in their original form they belong to the preexilic period, perhaps as early as the end of the 8th century or more likely the first decade of the 7th century.

2. In the transmission of the text, there is an important orthographic divergence between the heading of the book of Isaiah and those of the three Minor

---

(and in the case of Isaiah, between chs. 1–39 and 40–66), the orthography of the Major Prophets is more conservative than that of the Minor Prophets, which is characterized by spellings consistent with the Second Temple period and which show a "remarkable homogeneity in their spelling" *(ibid.,* 315).

4. The consistency of the spelling in the Minor Prophets, although individually coming from quite different time periods, strongly suggests that the spelling throughout reflects the date of publication (Second Temple period) of the composite work — which cannot antedate the latest individual book. The more conservative spellings of Isaiah argue for an earlier publication date, preserving the spellings of the time which would have been maintained through the centuries and preserved in the MT. See D. N. Freedman, "The Spelling of the Name 'David' in the Hebrew Bible," *Biblical and Other Studies in Honor of Robert Gordis,* ed. R. Ahroni, *Hebrew Annual Review* 11 (Columbus: Ohio State University Press, 1983), 99-100 [see Volume 2, Chapter 11]; and Andersen-Forbes, 315-16.

5. E.g., all 572 occurrences of the name "David" in the books of Samuel are defective (three-letter spelling), while the 271 occurrences in Ezra-Nehemiah and Chronicles are *plene* (four-letter spelling). See n. 3, above. For a detailed statistical discussion, see Freedman, 89-104; and Andersen-Forbes, 4-6.

Prophets. The former retains the authentic preexilic spelling of two of the royal names (ʿuzziyyāhû and yᵉḥizqiyyāhû), while the latter exhibit the shorter postexilic spelling of the same names (ʿuzziyyâ and yᵉḥizqiyyâ). Generally, the scroll of the Minor Prophets in the MT reflects a very late orthographic style, while Massoretic Isaiah is both more moderate and earlier.[6]

3. Chronological Considerations

Our next concern is with the chronological information in the four headings. The only significant differences are with the number and distribution of the royal names, and to a consideration of these we will now turn. For the sake of convenience we will set the data in tabular form so that the congruences and divergences will be immediately apparent:

ISAIAH	HOSEA	AMOS	MICAH
bîmê	bîmê	bîmê	bîmê
ʿuzziyyāhû	ʿuzziyyâ	ʿuzziyyâ	- - - - -
yôṯām	yôṯām	- - - - -	yôṯām
ʾāḥāz	ʾāḥāz	- - - - -	ʾāḥāz
yᵉḥizqiyyāhû	yᵉḥizqiyyâ	- - - - -	yᵉḥizqiyyâ
malḵê	malḵê	melek	malḵê
yᵉhûḏâ	yᵉhûḏâ	yᵉhûḏâ	yᵉhûḏâ
	ûḇîmê	ûḇîmê	
	yāroḇʿām	yāroḇʿām	
	ben-yôʾāš	ben-yôʾāš	
	melek	melek	
	yiśrāʾēl	yiśrāʾēl	
		(šenāṯayim lipnê hārāʿaš)	

Two impressions arise immediately from consideration of this table or chart: (1) The first is how very much alike the headings are and how extensively they overlap. Except for the unique reference to the earthquake as a chronological marker in Amos, all of the other data are duplicated at least once. Thus, the names of the four Judahite kings occur three times each, and two of the four lists of these kings are the same (Isaiah and Hosea). The single Israelite king is mentioned twice (in Hosea and Amos). (2) The second impression is that in spite of the formulaic similarities and the repetition of common elements, no two texts are exactly the same. Each text is different from every other.

6. Freedman, 99-100; and Andersen-Forbes, 315-16.

The first of the foregoing factors was to be expected in view of the overlapping contents of the books of these prophets and the apparent effort on the part of compilers and editors to organize the information into some unified structure or pattern. The latter feature, however, shows that the headings were tailored or shaped for the individual prophets to reflect both the time and circumstances of their ministries and careers. By comparing the texts carefully we can infer and deduce a variety of propositions concerning this group of prophets. In other words, we are encouraged and obliged to take seriously and in detail both what is included and what has been excluded in connection with each prophetic heading.[7]

We will make some general observations first, to be followed by more detailed proposals:

1. While the lists of Judahite kings dominate the headings in terms both of quantity and priority (i.e., they always come first), the presence of an Israelite king in two of the lists provides a partial synchronism (there is an overlap between Jeroboam II of Israel and Uzziah of Judah, but it is universally agreed among scholars that the latter outlived the former), thus helping to define the period of the prophets' work. Also, it gives information about the place in which the prophet carried out his commission from Yahweh. Thus, we interpret the reference to Jeroboam of Israel in Hosea and Amos to mean that both prophets uttered oracles and performed their prophetic task in the northern kingdom during the reign of Jeroboam, and by inference not after his reign. Had they continued in the northern realm after Jeroboam's death, then reference would have been made to successor kings of the latter, e.g., Zechariah, Shallum, Menahem, etc. Such inferences are generally confirmed by the contents of the books mentioned, and no one has ever seriously doubted that Amos and Hosea conducted prophetic missions in the north, i.e., carried out their prophetic activity in the kingdom of Israel. If, however, we take the headings at face value, then we must also affirm that overlapping with such activities and/or subsequent to their work in the north, they carried out their prophetic mission in the southern kingdom as well — Amos during the reign of Uzziah, while Hosea, along with the remaining prophets in our lists, continued into the reign of Hezekiah. What this information indicates is that the books of these prophets were developed and processed in the southern kingdom and reached their published form under Judahite and possible royal sponsorship.

---

7. Andersen-Freedman, 144, provide a list of eight distinct features that may be included in the prophetic headings of all of the Hebrew prophets: "1) A name for the work; 2) The prophet's name; 3) The prophet's patronymic; 4) His hometown; 5) A reference to his call, however vague; 6) A time of his activity; 7) A precise date (of his call or first oracle); 8) The subject matter of his prophecy." Although the headings of the four 8th-century prophets demonstrate enough similarities — in view of the variety made possible by these eight elements — to conclude a common editorial tradition, the variations (both additions and deletions) are also quite apparent and should be carefully analyzed.

2. The lists not only define the broad limits of this period of prophetic activity, but they also provide clues to the specific scope of the individual prophets within the larger range. Thus, the entire period extends from the overlapping reigns of Jeroboam in the north and Uzziah in the south into the reign of Hezekiah, a time span of perhaps one hundred years, from *ca.* 790 to *ca.* 690.[8]

If we look at the king lists in the headings, the principal difference is in the number of kings mentioned. They range from two (Amos) to five (Hosea), with no two headings exactly the same: e.g., Micah has three and Isaiah has four. If we arrange the kings in tabular form we can recognize immediately the correspondences and the divergences. We follow the order of the books in the Hebrew Bible:

	ISAIAH	HOSEA	AMOS	MICAH
Judah:	Uzziah	Uzziah	Uzziah	- - - - -
	Jotham	Jotham	- - - - -	Jotham
	Ahaz	Ahaz	- - - - -	Ahaz
	Hezekiah	Hezekiah	- - - - -	Hezekiah
Israel:		Jeroboam II	Jeroboam II	

It will be noted at once that Hosea's list is the only complete one, and that it encompasses all the others. That fact may explain why Hosea is placed first among the Minor Prophets.

While the order of the books is broadly chronological in the sense that the earlier books are toward the front and the later books are toward the back (e.g., the three 8th-century prophets are among the first six, or in the front half [Hosea is no. 1; Amos, no. 3; and Micah, no. 6], and the three 6th/5th-century prophets are at the end of the group: Haggai, Zechariah, Malachi [nos. 10-12]), it has generally been agreed that Amos is earlier than Hosea, and that such a conclusion is readily deducible from the contents of the two books and comparison with information provided elsewhere in the Hebrew Bible (e.g., Kings). Furthermore, our examination of the headings conforms to the order: Amos preceding Hosea, rather than the other way around. So why are they reversed in the traditional arrangement in the scroll of the Minor Prophets? The answer would seem to be that the order is not precisely chronological and another concern or interest has supervened in the order of the books.

---

8. There are substantial differences in the dates assigned by various scholars to these kings, and it cannot be said that a consensus has been reached: e.g., Albright's dates would be from 786 (Jeroboam II) to 687 (death of Hezekiah), while Thiele's would be from 793/2 to 687/6, and Tadmor's from 790(?) to 696(?). These differences do not seriously affect the calculations in this essay, so I have adopted a compromise position as indicated. Within those broad limits we can place the four prophets in chronological order, assigning them positions in relation to each other and also against the actual dates deducible for the reigns specified.

What the heading suggests or implies is that Hosea is the key figure in the group and that his ministry overlapped with all of the others, and that he may at some time or other have had contact with them. We may even speculate that he had an important part in the compilation and assembly of the materials that went into the four books. In passing, we may add that the evidence of the heading suggests that Hosea departed from Israel during the reign of Jeroboam and was domiciled in the south during the reigns of the four successive Davidides in our list. Clearly there are parts of the book that reflect circumstances and events in the north and probably the south that postdate the era of Jeroboam (e.g., the revolving-door series of kings following the death of Jeroboam), and it is widely agreed that Hosea's ministry extended down to the times of crisis in Israel. His location and his relation to the southern kingdom remain obscure, however; but in my opinion, some connection on his part with the south is unavoidable.

If we then compare the list in the heading of Hosea with those for Amos and Micah, we note that the lists in Amos and Micah together form a list exactly equivalent to that of Hosea. Amos has Uzziah and Jeroboam, the first and last in Hosea's list, while Micah contains the three intervening kings: Jotham, Ahaz, and Hezekiah. Thus, for the three minor prophets we have two complete lists, one in Hosea and the other distributed between the other two prophets. It is clear that Amos and Micah were active in different periods and did not overlap; on a professional basis, at least, there was no contact between them. After Hosea, the order in the group is chronological: Amos preceded Micah.

Isaiah spans a period very much like that of Micah, the only difference being that presumably Isaiah's ministry began while Uzziah was still alive, even if barely so, whereas Micah's ministry began after Uzziah's death, when Jotham was sole king. Isaiah could also have been a prime mover in organizing the collection and publication of the literature under consideration.

On the basis of the information provided, we can put the prophets in the following order: Amos, Hosea, Isaiah, Micah. Amos and Hosea were both active during the reigns of Jeroboam and Uzziah, so they belong in the earlier part of the period under consideration. Isaiah's ministry apparently began at, or toward the end of, the reign of Uzziah.

If we take Isa. 6 to be Isaiah's inaugural vision (still the prevailing opinion among scholars), then Isaiah's formal career as a prophet began in the year of Uzziah's death. That Micah belongs at the end of the list is clear from the fact that the first king in his list is Jotham, the successor of Uzziah. It is true that Jotham ruled as co-regent while his father Uzziah was still alive, but during that period Uzziah continued to be recognized as reigning, even if not ruling; therefore, Uzziah would have been mentioned in Micah's heading if in fact Micah had been active while Uzziah was still alive.

When it comes to terminal dates, we note that for three of the prophets (Isaiah, Hosea, Micah) the lists end with Hezekiah, while for the remaining one (Amos) the limits are more circumscribed, with only Uzziah and Jeroboam being mentioned. Clearly Amos's career was considerably shorter than that of the others, a conclusion consistent with the biographical and other information in the book itself.

The relative periods of prophetic activity of the four prophets can now be set forth in the following way:

	Jeroboam Uzziah	Jotham	Ahaz	Hezekiah
Amos	_____			
Hosea	_____			
Isaiah	_____			
Micah	_____			

Two points become apparent upon inspection of this diagram:

1. The terminal date for prophetic activity for three of these books is in the reign of Hezekiah. That fact is not only important in its own right, but may offer helpful clues in resolving the question of the occasion and reason for the compilation of the collection of the 8th-century prophets.

2. The case of the heading of the book of Amos is exceptional, limiting his ministry to the overlapping reigns of Jeroboam II and Uzziah. The terminal date for Amos's prophetic activity and the completion of his book (or the production of a version of the book bearing his name) must lie in the reign of Uzziah, much earlier than the presumed date for the other three books. This unusual aspect of the book of Amos must be associated with the unique added item about the earthquake, which provides another clue to the date of the book. The earthquake in question — obviously a major one with significant impact on at least one population center — occurred during the reign of Uzziah, as we know from the reference to it in the book of Zechariah (14:5), and it serves as a fulcrum or pivot for the book of Amos.

The implication of the statements in Amos 1:1 is that the book of Amos (= dibrê 'āmôs) was published after the earthquake occurred, but that it contained only oracles and other materials uttered or compiled up to two years before that event. It may be suspected that the dramatic confrontation between priest and prophet at the temple in Bethel took place on the earlier occasion, and that the earthquake occurred two years later. During that period, the oracles or stories were assembled, with whatever materials may have been added, and the collection as a whole was then published shortly afterwards. Thus, it was the earthquake that provided the occasion for the publication and vindication of the oracles and predictions of the prophet.

It is in the fifth vision (Amos 9:1-5, esp. v. 1) that we find the forecast of the coming seismic tremor which validated Amos as an authentic prophet and verified a particular vision and prophetic utterance. The book of Amos therefore was the first of this group (or in fact, of the whole collection of prophetic works) to be issued in written form — precisely because of the unusual circumstances surrounding the visions and the sudden confirmation of the prophetic prediction by a violent manifestation of nature.

4. The Process of Compilation and Publication

We can then consider the process of compilation and publication of the other three prophetic works in the light of the proposed account of the production of the book of Amos. According to our analysis of the three other headings, the prophets completed their active careers during the reign of Hezekiah; or, put another way, there is no evidence of prophetic activity on their part during the reign of Hezekiah's son and successor, Manasseh. While it is perfectly possible that one or more of these prophets lived or lingered on into the next reign, as seems to be the case with Isaiah (if we can credit the legends recorded or reflected in intertestamental works such as The Lives of the Prophets or a suggested New Testament reference in Heb. 11:37, where mention of prophets or martyrs being sawn asunder is interpreted as an allusion to the martyrdom of Isaiah at the hands of Manasseh), that in itself would not be in conflict with the view taken here.

If we have interpreted correctly the implication of the headings of these prophetic works, then we must consider both the reasons and occasions for the termination of the prophetic activity at that time, and also both the reason and occasion for the compilation of a collection of such prophetic materials.

I believe the answer is to be found in one of the books in question, in particular in the stories that round out First Isaiah, the collection of oracles and stories that make up the bulk of chs. 1–39 of that book. I would exclude from the collection only chs. 34–35 as belonging to Second (or Third) Isaiah, and argue that First Isaiah was a literary product of the First Temple period or more particularly the exile, a work close in character and time of publication to the books of Jeremiah and Ezekiel, but especially Jeremiah, which also concludes with a chapter drawn from, or parallel to, the account in 2 Kings. While there are notable expansions and other differences separating Isa. 36–39 from the corresponding section of 2 Kings (18:13–20:19), the connections or correlations are so close, not only in content, but also verbally that a common undertaking in compilation and publication must be acknowledged.

In this account of the reign of Hezekiah, the central and decisive event is the invasion of the land by Sennacherib and the resultant siege of the capital city, Jerusalem. Without examining either the problems of the narrative or exploring the numerous details, we can say that the high and culminating point is the miraculous deliverance of the city, an outcome in which the prophet, Isaiah, is credited with a major role. In response to the king's prayer in behalf of the nation and the city, Isaiah brings the assurance of Yahweh that the invasion will fail, the siege will be lifted, and the city and the king will be spared (Isa. 37 = 2 Kgs. 18). Shortly thereafter the prophecy became fact, although the details are confusing and the biblical accounts do not present a consistent picture. With the help of the detailed Assyrian records of the same event, the following seem to be the central and verifiable facts in the case:

Sennacherib and his armies responded to Hezekiah's rebellion by overrunning the land and investing the city of Jerusalem. Nevertheless, and in spite of accepted and standard Assyrian procedure in such cases, the Assyrian army did not capture the city of Jerusalem, and the rebellious King Hezekiah was not deposed nor was his dynasty terminated. Instead, Hezekiah paid a huge indemnity, thus acknowledging his status and role as vassal of the Assyrian king.

While the outcome does not qualify as a victory for Judah or as a rout of the king of Assyria, the deliverance of the city and the royal house was certainly worth a prayer of thanksgiving and the recognition that the nation had been spared by a compassionate deity. This was the view of the incident a century later when Jeremiah reported on it (Jer. 26:18-19). The main point was that because Hezekiah and the people had repented in all earnestness, Yahweh also repented of the evil he intended against them and reversed his decision, and so the city and kingdom were spared. In the passage in Jeremiah, the ominous prediction by Micah about the fate of Jerusalem was quoted as a conditional threat, providing reason or occasion for the subsequent repentance on the part of king and people, which in turn induced divine repentance and the deliverance of the city. We can understand, therefore, why the prophecies of Micah would be brought into the collection of prophetic works in which this central or decisive event was presented.

It is my suggestion that the collection of the books of the four prophets was assembled during the reign of Hezekiah, to celebrate and interpret the extraordinary sequence of events associated with the Assyrian invasion of Judah and investment of Jerusalem, along with the departure of the Assyrian army and the deliverance of the city. While giving due attention to the roles of the two local prophets and their oracular utterances, the compiler(s) also recognized that the sparing of Jerusalem in 701 was only the final act, the climactic note at the end of a long and theologically significant series of events. During this period the parallels and contrasts between the two capital cities, Samaria and Jerusalem, were in constant view and under continued discussion and debate.

In all four of the prophetic books here under consideration, these two cities, representing their respective nations, were under severe scrutiny. In general, they were attacked as centers of sin and placed under the same divine judgment. It is a typical feature of 8th-century prophecy (followed by Jeremiah and Ezekiel) to compare the capital cities of Israel and Judah with the cities of the plain (Amos and Isaiah refer to Sodom and Gomorrah; Hosea mentions Admah and Zeboiim) and to threaten both of them with the same fate.

In the end, however, it was Samaria that fell to the Assyrians, while Jerusalem was spared. In order to focus attention on the latter event and to explain this extraordinary outcome, it was necessary and important to emphasize the full presentation of the prophets that included both kingdoms and both capital cities. The story began with the oracles of Amos and Hosea, and was continued in those of Isaiah and Micah.

Put together, the major lesson and moral could be drawn: Yahweh is the devoted Lord of his people in both kingdoms. Both are under heavy judgment for deliberate defiance of the deity and persistent violation of the central demands and commands of the covenant. The only possibility of escape from violent final punishment is genuine repentance on the part of all, king and nobles, priests and prophets, and the people as a whole. If they repent, Yahweh may also repent and spare them. The experience of the capital cities proved the truth of that doctrine. Samaria — its kings and priests and people — did not repent, and the city was captured and the kingdom brought to an end. Jerusalem, to the contrary, was spared because its leaders, including the king, and its people repented.

Thus, the collection of prophecies was made after the miraculous deliverance of the city of Jerusalem, as a thank-offering to Yahweh, a *te Deum* addressed to the God who had himself repented in response to the repentance of the king and people of Judah. This mutual or reciprocal repentance on the part of people and God was in marked contrast with the resistant behavior of the leaders and people of the north. It may be noted that the theme of the God "who repents over the evil" *(niḥām ʿal-hārāʿâ)* is also prominent in other books that are about or from the same period, or that are bound in with the 8th-century prophets in the scroll of the Minor Prophets (cf., e.g., Jon. 4:2 and Joel 2:13 [Heb.]). We may say, therefore, that it is this aspect of the Godhead, this thread in the historical theology of the Bible, that runs through the corpus of 8th-century prophets. We may add that the compilation was originally intended as a dramatic and informed interpretation of the traumatic and critical history or sequence of events through which the two Yahwistic kingdoms had passed in the course of the 8th century, concluding with the miraculous deliverance of Jerusalem and at least temporary reprieve of the kingdom of Judah at the end of that century.

I would further propose that the composite work combining the books of the four prophets was carried out under the sponsorship and with the approval and support of King Hezekiah himself, who seems to have been not only a major religious reformer (as documented in 2 Kings and much more extensively in 2 Chronicles) and military and diplomatic mastermind (like his great-grandfather Uzziah, not to mention David, the founder of the dynasty, and David's immediate successor Solomon), but also a city planner and builder on a large scale (as we find from the Siloam water tunnel and from archaeological excavations in the Western Extension). In addition, he was a patron of the principal art in Judah: literature (cf. the curious but important reference in Prov. 25:1). Only a king of such stature and ethical sensitivity, as Hezekiah is described to be, could and would have encouraged such a work. Others, too numerous to mention, would have tolerated neither the words nor the prophets responsible for them; e.g., we hear of neither prophets nor their works nor anything like them in the otherwise long and peaceful reign of Manasseh, the bitterly condemned son and successor of Hezekiah. While this idea must remain speculative, it is hard to imagine such a work being put together at any other time or without the consent and support of the reigning monarch.

The work exhibits, of course, the rather unusual combination of serious — even severe — criticism of the monarch, along with continuing support of him and his dynasty. It recognizes that the house of David remained the best hope for continuity, stability, and the fulfillment of the ultimate dreams of people and prophets alike. Of all the kings mentioned in our headings, only Hezekiah qualifies as sympathetic with the goals and standards of the prophets and sensitive to basic theological and ethical issues. The prophets would find in him a ready listener and one willing to translate into practice their harsh and difficult prescriptions. In return, he would see in them authentic channels to and from the divine presence — men firmly dedicated to the ultimate well-being of the nation, its king and people — however hard and uncompromising their words of condemnation and reprobation might be. There would be a community of interest, and they could make common cause in this account of the crises which came in flood tide in the course of the century, overwhelming the northern kingdom and so swamping the south as to leave behind a barely surviving kingdom as a remnant.

An authentic analysis of that experience was needed to serve as a valid interpretation of what the nation had been through, and as an informed set of guidelines and exhortations for the future. Small wonder that the amalgamated experience of the 8th century was incorporated into the whole prophetic collection when it was assembled in the 6th century or later. The great lessons of the earlier time were still to be learned and absorbed, but they would be available from that time onward for every succeeding generation.

5. Conclusions

We may summarize the results of this cursory investigation as follows:

1. It is my belief that the headings of the four 8th-century prophetic works were devised in accordance with a standard form and formula, but that these were modified to accommodate the differences in time and place of the individual prophets. Therefore, I maintain that the books of these prophets belong to a common collection and that at the same time they exhibit divergences which are important in placing the prophets chronologically, geographically, and in relation to one

380

another. Thus, we can arrange the four prophets in the following historical order: Amos, Hosea, Isaiah, Micah.

2. From the headings we can also identify and isolate features and factors in the prophets' careers and oracles. It is clear, for instance, that Amos and Hosea were active in the north, while Isaiah and Micah were active in the south. Unexpectedly, however, we find evidence pointing to activity in the south on the part of Amos and Hosea as well, which may have echoes and reflections in disputed passages in these prophets.

3. I believe that the books of the 8th-century prophets were compiled and combined in a two-stage process: (1) The first of these involved the publication of the book of Amos as a result of a remarkable occurrence. After a major earthquake in the days of Uzziah, it was believed by a group of disciples (and perhaps Uzziah himself) that Amos had been vindicated as an authentic prophet of Yahweh and that his prediction of an imminent earthquake had been confirmed by that event. (2) Later, during the reign of Hezekiah, and after an equally or even more remarkable event, the books of the three other prophets were collected and published along with the book of Amos (perhaps with a modicum of updating), to celebrate the miraculous rescue of Jerusalem from the besieging army of Sennacherib, the Assyrian king.

4. The principal purposes and objectives of this work, in my view, were to establish an authoritative theological-historical interpretation of the events that had transpired during the last three-quarters of the 8th century — from the time that Jeroboam II embarked upon his masterful and major campaign to recover the territories across the Jordan that had belonged or been subject to Israel in times past, until the armies of Sennacherib withdrew from Jerusalem and left the southern capital badly shaken but intact and at peace, at the end of the century.

5. The lessons to be inculcated and learned were the following: (1) That both kingdoms were under divine judgment for serious and deliberate violations of the covenant commands and that Yahweh would use foreign powers, especially the Assyrians, to punish his rebellious, apostate, and idolatrous people, both north and south. (2) That the only recourse remaining and available to the people, including their leaders, was wholehearted repentance, regret for sins past and present, and new resolution to remake their lives. General repentance would in turn beget divine repentance, i.e., a profound change of heart and mind on the part of God. (3) That the results for Samaria and Jerusalem brought out the truth of these assertions: Samaria persisted in rebellion and was destroyed, Jerusalem repented and was spared.

6. I believe that the books or scrolls of the prophets were produced and published to celebrate the survival of Jerusalem, to explain the historical experience of the 8th century, to warn present and future generations about the available options, and to renew both threats and promises for the time at hand and for the time to come.

7. I believe that the publishing project was carried out by the surviving prophets and their followers shortly after the deliverance of Jerusalem, and that the enterprise had both the approval and the support of the king, who himself had been delivered along with the city, and who remained on his throne and was able to pass it on to his descendants. Hezekiah had much for which to be thankful, and much about which to be worried. It was important to offer thanks, and also to leave a record and a warning for posterity.

35

"Who Is Like Thee among the Gods?": The Religion of Early Israel

The subject of this chapter is the religious beliefs and ideas of early Israel, i.e., the description and delineation of the deity as derived from the oldest source materials in the Hebrew Bible. Before we proceed with this rather delicate and difficult task, several preliminary and qualifying remarks are in order.

In gathering, analyzing, organizing, and presenting the relevant information, I have limited the database to the major poems now embedded in the primary history (= Torah and Former Prophets),[1] and in fact only a selection of these:

1. The Blessing of Jacob: Gen. 49
2. The Song of the Sea: Exod. 15
3. The Oracles of Balaam: Num. 23–24
4. The Blessing of Moses: Deut. 33
5. The Song of Deborah: Judg. 5

These are five of the poems that I regard as the oldest literature preserved in the Bible and hence the best available source for recovering a valid contemporary account of the religion of Israel in its earliest phases.[2]

---

1. For a discussion of the formation, development, canonization, and significance of the primary history (Genesis through 2 Kings), see D. N. Freedman, "Pentateuch," *IDB* 3:711-27 [see above, Chapter 12]; "The Law and the Prophets," *VTS* 9 (1963): 250-65 [see above, Chapter 14]; "The Earliest Bible," *The Bible and Its Traditions*. Michigan Quarterly Review 22/3 (1983): 167-75 [see above, Chapter 32]. [See also Freedman, *The Unity of the Hebrew Bible* (Ann Arbor: University of Michigan Press, 1991), and Chapter 42 below.]

2. For a general introduction and discussion of the nature of Hebrew poetry and its possibilities and problems in reconstructing Israelite history and religion, see D. N. Freedman, "Pottery, Poetry and Prophecy: An Essay on Biblical Poetry," *JBL* 96 (1977): 5-26 [= *PPP*, 1-22].

A useful and convenient way to define and delimit the period of Israel's early faith is by the establishment of the monarchy in Israel, first with Saul and his house and then on a more permanent basis with David and his dynasty. While the discontinuity and disjuncture between the Israel of the period of the judges and earlier and that of the monarchic age may be exaggerated in much contemporary critical literature on the subject, nevertheless the introduction of kingship into Israel represented a dramatic, if not drastic, alteration in the structure of the state as well as in essential features of its religion. While there is no reason to doubt that the literary sources from the monarchic and even later periods contain authentic traditions and valid recollections of earlier times, there is equally no doubt that the traditions and source materials were shaped and colored by the concerns of the new establishment as well as reused and rewritten to suit the interests of the inheritors and administrators of the legacies of the past. Therefore we have excluded from consideration all materials that obviously and plainly belong to or come from the monarchic period: e.g., the poems in the Former Prophets such as the songs attributed to David (2 Sam. 1:19-27; 2 Sam. 22; 2 Sam. 23:1-7) and also the Song of Hannah (2 Sam. 2:1-10) with its clear references to an anointed king.

For different but similar reasons, I have not included the Song of Moses, which is in Deut. 32:1-43; controversy about the date of composition has persisted for decades, and no resolution is in sight.[3] There is also considerable difference of opinion as well as doubt and confusion as to the purpose and function of the poem, not to mention the reasons and significance of its attribution to Moses. I believe and recognize that its placement in the book of Deuteronomy and the prose exposition in which it is embedded confirm and enhance the so-called Deuteronomic connection. But that observation raises at least as many problems as it purports to solve, and the question remains as to the position and role of the poem in the Deuteronomic literature, not to speak of the religio-political movement associated with the corpus of writings of that "school." While affinities between two works can be seen and shown, the direction of influence and the matters of dependence and derivation are much more difficult to demonstrate, at least to a critical audience. I think that it would be worthwhile to compare the findings from the other parts of the corpus with the data independently derived from the Song of Moses to see how faithfully the latter reflects the picture presented in the former, and to assess the differences that are to be discerned, in terms of their departure from the established older norms. But in order to develop a relatively uncontaminated picture of the faith of early Israel, I will concentrate attention on the five poems listed above.

3. On the basis of the selection and distribution of divine names and titles, I have postulated elsewhere that Deut. 32 dates from the latter part of the 10th or beginning of the 9th century. See D. N. Freedman, "Divine Names and Titles in Early Hebrew Poetry, *Magnalia Dei: The Mighty Acts of God,* ed. F. M. Cross, W. E. Lemke, and P. D. Miller (Garden City: Doubleday, 1976), 77-80 [= *PPP*, 77-129].

There are other poetic materials that, in my judgment, can be assigned to the premonarchic period as well. These include some shorter pieces in the prose narrative, e.g., the Song of the Well in Num. 21:17-18 and the longer Song of Heshbon in Num. 21:27-30, not to speak of bits and fragments of larger poems such as the denunciation of Amalek in Exod. 17:16 and the stopping of the sun in Josh. 10:12. Lacking the larger work in these cases, or an adequate context, I am hesitant to use these bits, although generally they support or do not conflict with the findings based upon (or derived from) the longer, more complete works. Not much is to be gained, albeit little is lost, by passing over these works or using them indirectly to support or explicate views derived from the longer set pieces.

I should add that there are other poems that may reasonably be assigned to an early date as well, chiefly among the psalms. It is widely believed that Ps. 29 is an example of an old Canaanite hymn appropriated and adapted for Israelite usage but shifting the focus from the presumed Canaanite deity Baal to the Israelite God Yahweh, literally substituting the latter for the former throughout the poem. Whether or not this is the proper explanation of the contents of the psalm, there is considerable scholarly sentiment in favor of a very early date for it (perhaps 12th century).[4] I would also call attention to Pss. 93 and 113, which bear signs of early composition. Since, however, it is almost impossible to make a convincing demonstration on the basis of language and internal evidence alone, and since suitable historical contexts are lacking, even in the tradition, for locating these poems chronologically, it is best to leave them aside as well, retaining the option of using them for illustrative or complementary or supplementary purposes only.

As a result of the previous discussion, we have left for analysis and presentation the five poems originally mentioned at the beginning of this chapter. Further remarks or comments about this group of poems are needed to establish or clarify their chronology and also the interconnections among them. Only then can we proceed to an examination of each of the poems in turn.

For the purposes here, it is sufficient to establish (or assume) that all of the poems in our group belong to or come from the premonarchic period. Elsewhere I have argued in favor of such dating for each of these poems, and I have also endeavored to establish both a relative sequence and an approximate absolute dating for the group.[5] I argued then for the following position: Exod. 15 and Judg. 5 are

4. Also on the basis of the distribution of divine names I have postulated a date in the latter part of the 12th century for Ps. 29. See Freedman, *ibid.,* 60-61.

5. For a complete discussion of the sequence and dating of these five poems on the basis of the distribution of divine names and titles, see Freedman, *ibid.,* 57-70. A study of the historical elements in these same five pieces is found in D. N. Freedman, "Early Israelite Poetry and Historical Reconstructions," *Symposia Celebrating the Seventy-Fifth Anniversary of the Founding of the American Schools of Oriental Research (1900-1975),* ed. F. M. Cross (Cambridge, Mass.: ASOR, 1979), 85-96. Exod. 15 and Judg. 5 are dealt with in detail in D. N. Freedman, "Early Israelite History in the Light of Early Israelite Poetry," *Unity and Diversity: Essays in the History,*

the earliest poems in this group and can be dated in the 12th century; the other three poems are somewhat later, roughly contemporary with one another, and can be dated in the 11th century. While these conclusions are not susceptible of proof in the usual scientific or historical sense, they are also hard to disprove, and the debate often proceeds along familiar lines or ruts, or in cycles of circular reasoning. Usually the problem is how to interpret literary resemblances and affinities, and the results reached by different scholars depend upon how they view the connections with other poems and prose narratives. The debate will go on, probably forever, or at least until Elijah returns to clear up such matters, among other somewhat larger duties he is to perform, but the exchanges themselves are often productive, sometimes in unexpected ways. In any case, I have seen nothing in print or in private communication to dissuade me from the propositions set forth about ten years ago.

A further distinction is to be made as well. We are concerned not only with the date of composition but also with the appropriate setting whether we speak in terms of history or story (the narrative context) in which these poems are placed in the Hebrew Bible, i.e., the prose narrative running from Genesis through Kings. I believe that the poems are positioned roughly where they belong, i.e., they were correctly understood to reflect or relate to, and to fit into or run parallel with, the prose narrative in which they were embedded or to which they were attached. This circumstance is plainly evident in the case of the Song of the Sea and the Song of Deborah, where in each case the poem follows immediately after the prose account of the same event (i.e., Exod. 15 contains the poem, while Exod. 14 describes the same event in a prose account; Judg. 5 is the poem, while the corresponding prose narrative is found in Judg. 4).[6] Similarly the Oracles of Balaam are embedded in the narrative about Balaam and Balak, the king of Moab, and the notably unsuccessful effort on the part of the latter to secure an effective curse against Yahweh's favored people newly entered upon and settled in territory abutting upon Balak's own, and no doubt coveted by him as well. I believe the same interpretation of the blessings attributed to Jacob and Moses should be applied — namely, that they are placed where they are at the end of Genesis and the end of Deuteronomy on purpose, because they belong to the narrative at that point and in addition describe a historical situation contemporary and consonant with the prose narrative at those points in the story. Needless to say, we must not press these points too far, or very far at all. It is not necessary in order to do justice either to the narrative or to our hypothesis to suppose that the Song of the Sea that is preserved in the Hebrew Bible was composed on the shores of the Reed Sea as suggested by the context. Since it refers

---

Literature and Religion of the Ancient Near East, ed. H. Goedicke and J. J. M. Roberts (Baltimore: Johns Hopkins University Press, 1975), 3-35 [= *PPP*, 131-66].

6. For the relationship between Exod. 14 and 15 and Judg. 4 and 5, see Freedman, *Symposia,* 85-87.

directly and explicitly to the journey to the sacred mountain in the wilderness and the sojourn there, it would be quite in order to suppose that the poem was composed somewhat later, while the Israelites were encamped at the base of the mountains. At the same time, I do not believe that it includes a prospective-retrospective history of the nation designed to have Moses forecast the settlement in Canaan and the erection of a shrine or temple in Jerusalem. The case with the blessings is more complex, and additional remarks will be provided when these poems are discussed later on. Nevertheless I think it was the intention of the author/editor to describe the circumstances of the tribal league at different times in its history and in the light of, or in association with, particular historical events. Thus the Blessing of Moses was intended to reflect the status and particulars of the several tribes at the time just before the death of Moses when the settlement center or headquarters was still in Transjordan. In like manner, the Blessing of Jacob should be understood, not literally as a deathbed blessing pronounced by the patriarch on his sons, but as a description of the tribal league somewhat earlier in its checkered history than the account in Deut. 33. It is our contention that the blessings here are of the same genre or kind as those in Deut. 33, but they deal with a vastly different historical situation, one that is set in the period before the exodus and the age of Moses. In short, it is correctly placed in the patriarchal age, although the representation of an aged father surrounded by his sons is symbolic rather than actual. We posit therefore a pre-Mosaic patriarchal Israelite league in Gen. 49, and that the blessings individually and collectively describe the circumstances of the league sometime after its formation in the late 14th to the early 13th century and reflect the dramatic confrontation with Marneptah and the Egyptian forces toward the end of the 13th century B.C.E. Thus the period covered by the poems extends from the end of the 14th century until the latter part of the 12th, while the composition of the poems can be assigned to the 12th to 11th centuries B.C.E.

Cursory classification of the poems immediately reveals two major types: Victory Odes, as seen in the Song of the Sea and the Song of Deborah; and Tribal Blessings: the Blessing of Jacob and the Blessing of Moses. A significant link between the types is found in the Song of Deborah, where a third list of the tribes occurs. In the context of the War or Victory Song, the tribal roll call is not exactly a series of blessings, although some of the tribes are commended for their bravery in the military action just concluded, while others are castigated for shirking their duty. In other words, the Song of Deborah, in which an important, if not the decisive, victory over the Canaanites is celebrated, also includes a roll call of the tribes that were summoned to the battle and a critical evaluation of their respective roles in that battle. In the light of these observations, a second look at the two blessings possibly suggests similar circumstances for these roll calls. With respect to Deut. 33, it appears that the role assigned to Moses is similar to that of Deborah in Judg. 5, although differing in significant details. It can be said that the utterance directly attributed to Deborah consists of the roll call of the tribes, while the opening lines

387

are spoken or sung by others, since they are addressed to her. Similarly, Moses is mentioned in the introductory section of Deut. 33, and it would appear that his direct utterance begins with the roll call of the tribes. Furthermore, while no specific battle is described or mentioned in Deut. 33, as it is in Judg. 5, nevertheless the framework of the blessing presents Yahweh as the victorious war-god whose march from Sinai and mighty intervention in behalf of his people has resulted in victory for the latter. The circumstances fit well the picture of Israel settled securely in Transjordan especially after the victories over Sihon and Og, the Amorite kings described in Num. 21, and reflected vividly in the Oracles of Balaam (which are placed in the story just after those victories). Our conclusion is that the Blessing of Moses belongs to the same general category as the Song of Deborah and that both arise out of and describe or reflect the convocation of the tribes associated with circumstances and events of singular importance. Just as the Song of Deborah celebrates the climactic victory of the Israelite army over the Canaanite kings and their forces (led by Sisera), so the Blessing of Moses observes the successful conclusion of the campaign, led by Moses himself, on the East Bank of the Jordan, in which Israel was able to avoid direct conflict with Edom and Moab. However, when challenged by the Amorite kings Sihon and Og, Israel defeated them in battle and was able to establish a firm foothold east of the Jordan, a solid base from which to launch an attack upon the West Bank and the completion of the basic task of winning the Promised Land.

If such an analysis makes reasonable or plausible sense, then we can examine the other poems in the light of these observations: The Song of the Sea can be seen as the initial action of the warrior-god in behalf of the people he rescued from bondage in Egypt. The first decisive victory was achieved against the Egyptians, thus setting Israel free to pursue its destiny first at Sinai and subsequently in the lands on both sides of the Jordan. Victories achieved by Yahweh's interventions made the existence and viability of Israel a reality. It is no surprise that these decisive, if violent, actions are at the heart of Israel's kerygma.

The Oracles of Balaam can be fitted into the same pattern. While they do not constitute a specific victory in battle against the enemy, they nevertheless use similar vocabulary to describe the role of Yahweh and the successful outcome for Israel, a unique nation that dwells securely apart from the nations of the world. The juxtaposition of these oracles with the victories on the East Bank of the Jordan suffices to establish the connection between victory in battle and security on one's land. A larger and special element in this group of poems is the victory over, or successful defense against, enemies not armed with the conventional weapons of warfare but with sorcery and spells, black magic, and the powers of the underworld. Just as Paul remarks that the people of God must do battle with malignant spiritual beings and powers (Eph. 6:12), so here Israel is confronted by the malignant forces of the evil empire — of demons and devils — and is delivered from their power, while the forces of evil are routed on their own chosen battlefield. And Balaam, who by reputation was a master wizard and magician, a diviner and seer of awesome reputation, is turned around by superior authority and power and becomes the means and instrument by which all the baleful and malevolent powers of the netherworld are defeated, dispersed, and totally nullified. Since Israel is not directly engaged in this struggle, but is protected from unseen hostile forces by equally unseen armies of God, no mention of the tribal roles is made, because none is needed. The same in a different way can be said of Exod. 15. In the violent battle at the Reed Sea, Israel played no role other than spectator and witness for Yahweh's sole power as champion of his people. Again, there is no tribal roll call, because the people of Israel were not directly involved in the struggle. We need to remind ourselves that the primary, if not exclusive, purpose of the tribal muster was military, to provide an army capable of defending the borders and the centers of population and of winning victories over the enemies of God and their enemies. So the association in the cases mentioned so far — the Song of Deborah and the Blessing of Moses — may not seem far-fetched.

One poem remains to be dealt with and that is the Blessing of Jacob in Gen. 49. While we are laboring here largely in the dark, and the prospects are relatively unpromising, nevertheless there is some basis for regarding the poem as belonging to the same category as the Blessing of Moses and the Song of Deborah. It ought to reflect or express the proceedings of a tribal conclave subsequent to or associated with some pivotal or decisive event in Israel's history or experience. Along with the author/editor who put the blessing in the mouth of Jacob and therefore in the patriarchal age, we place the poem in the early period of the tribal league, before the career of Moses and the exodus from Egypt. The origins of Israel the people, community, and nation are somewhat murky and shrouded in mystery, but there are indications here and there in the book of Genesis and external sources about Israel the people. By combining the data from Gen. 33:18-20 (esp. v. 20) and 48:22 (the capture of Shechem) along with the information from the famous Marneptah stele, mentioning a decisive defeat inflicted on Israel, we can reconstruct the beginnings of Israel as follows:

a. The formation of the league consisting of twelve tribes with a cult and covenant center at Shechem. We can date the main event late in the 14th century or around 1300 B.C.E.

b. The defeat of Israel and partial dismemberment of the league by Marneptah toward the end of the 13th century. The dispersion of the closely related tribes of Simeon and Levi may be a consequence of the battle action. Neither tribe ever recovered its territory or status. Simeon was absorbed into Judah, and Levi was reconstituted as a special group associated with the ark and the tabernacle. The kinship connections with Moses and Aaron clearly play an important role in this development, which is reflected in the tribal blessing in Deut. 33 in dramatic contrast with the description of Levi in Gen. 49, which remains the one and only representation of Levi as a regular secular member of the league. On this view,

Gen. 49 would present an account of the early history of Israel as a tribal league constituted by and dedicated to the patriarchal God, El Shadday, after a military victory involving the capture of Shechem and its use as the league center. Then Deut. 33 would be a depiction of the reconstitution of the league after the acquisition of sufficient territory in Transjordan to justify such an action. Most important, the God of the revived league is Yahweh, the resident of Sinai, whose representative is Moses, the mediator of the renewed covenant.

We can offer an outline of Israel's history and religion on the basis of the poems in the books from Genesis to Judges.

Genesis 49: The Blessing of Jacob

In this poem, I believe that a unique survival of the patriarchal age, or more precisely of the pre-Mosaic period, has been preserved substantially intact. While the composition in its present form seems to date in the period of the judges, the content goes back to the 14th to 13th centuries and reflects the conditions under which the tribal league first came into existence and prominence. In defense of this view we can point to several features of the collection of blessings: (1) the archaic language and style; (2) the presentation (and preservation) of the original twelve-tribe grouping, which was already obsolete by the end of the 12th century or certainly the 11th, not to speak of the 10th and the formation of the monarchy; (3) the description of the tribe of Levi, which differs dramatically from any and all others, beginning with the Blessing of Moses; clearly the representation of Levi as a secular tribe closely associated with Simeon reflects pre-Mosaic rather than Mosaic or post-Mosaic experiences and traditions. The plundering of Shechem has patriarchal associations, and Shechem's central role in Israel's religion (as reflected in the conquest traditions (e.g., Josh. 24) has its roots in pre-Mosaic associations especially with Jacob (Gen. 33:20 and 48:22); (4) at least equally significant, in my judgment, is the absence of any mention of or reference to Yahweh the God of the exodus and the Sinai experience, the principal figure in all Mosaic and post-Mosaic traditions and literature in that the name YHWH appears only once in the whole poem and then in a liturgical comment placed in the mouth of the speaker Jacob (Gen. 49:18, which is not part of the blessing on Dan but comes between it and the next one on Gad). The contrast with the other group of blessings in Deut. 33 is striking. In the Blessing of Moses, the name Yahweh occurs repeatedly, both in the framework of the poem (in Deut. 33:1 and 29 forming an inclusio or more properly an echo) and then in several individual blessings: Judah (v. 7); Levi (v. 11); Benjamin (v. 12); Joseph (v. 13); Gad (v. 21, although I believe v. 21 is a complement of vv. 4-5 and refers to Moses as the subject of 'sh in v. 21b and not Gad);

Naphtali (v. 23). Similarly, the Song of Deborah, in which the third list of tribes occurs, is a thoroughly Yahwistic work, with numerous instances of the name scattered throughout the poem, if not directly in association with particular tribes. (Note the similar usage in the Song of Deborah as in Deut. 33: *yhwh* occurs at the beginning in Judg. 5:2 and again in v. 31 — forming an envelope construction or an echo. In all, there are fourteen instances of the name, seven in the first part of the poem [vv. 2-9] and seven more in the remainder.)

It should be pointed out that the phenomenon under consideration here is not related to the well-known substitution of another divine name for YHWH — namely, Elohim — in the literary strands of the Pentateuch. The parallelism between the two names, and the occurrence of Elohim in association with Yahweh or as a substitute for it, does not occur in any of the poems in our group. The word *'elōhîm* is exceedingly rare, and wherever it does occur it does not represent Yahweh or the God of Israel but is the standard numerical masculine plural for other gods. We are speaking here of Elohim as an independent noun in the absolute state, which only began to appear in the old poetry of Israel with the third phase and the emergence of the monarchy. The case with the construct form *'elōhê* is quite different, since in every case the defining noun in the absolute state makes clear the identity of the God in question: e.g., *'elōhî yiśrā'ēl* in Judg. 5 (vv. 3 and 5) in association with the name *yhwh*. Note also *'elōhê 'ābî* in Exod. 15:2, where the identification with *Yahweh* is clearly intended.

In Gen. 49, neither form of this divine name occurs; in fact, there are very few examples of any divine name, apart from the intrusive instance of *yhwh* in v. 18. These are concentrated in the Blessing of Joseph in vv. 24-26 and consist principally of names and titles associated with the patriarchs, in particular *'ēl*[7] and *šadday* (v. 25) and very likely *'al* in v. 26 ("the most high," a title that has been recovered elsewhere and mainly in the poetry of the Bible). It is essentially equivalent in meaning with the well-known *'elyôn* (also "the most high"), also a term associated with patriarchal stories and traditions. While in the other poems of this period (11th century: the Oracles of Balaam and the Blessing of Moses) the patriarchal names and titles also occur, they do so in combination or parallel construction with *yhwh,* showing that the identification of *yhwh* with *'ēl* and vice versa had been firmly established by that time. But in this poem it is only the God of the fathers who plays a role at the tribal league (as reflected in the designation or expression *'ēl 'elōhê yiśrā'ēl,* "El, the God of Israel," in Gen. 33:20).[8]

---

7. F. M. Cross provides a detailed exposition on the term *'El* and its meaning and usage throughout the Old Testament in his article in *Theologisches Wörterbuch zum Alten Testament.* See Cross, *"'ēl," TDOT* 1 (1977): 242-61.

8. For the designation "God of the Fathers," see A. Alt's seminal work on the subject, A. Alt, "Der Gott der Väter," BWANT 3/12 (Stuttgart: Kohlhammer, 1929). English translation in A. Alt, *Essays in Old Testament History and Religion,* trans. R. A. Wilson (Garden City: Doubleday, 1966), 1-100.

Since the name or description *'ēl* is somewhat ambiguous, certain qualifying expressions, the purpose of which is to identify a particular deity and to distinguish him from others, are often used, and here in Gen. 49:25, *šadday* is parallel to *'ēl*. The God invoked in the Blessing of Joseph is El Shadday, which can be translated variously as El the Mountaineer [or the (divine) mountain] or the God Shadday, who, however, is not different from El the chief god of the Amorite or Canaanite pantheon. It is best to regard the deity here as El himself but specifically in his mode or character as the Mountain or Mountaineer.

What follows is a series of blessings (Gen. 49:25-26) six in all (*birkōt* occurs five times, the sixth instance being an equivalent or complementary term in this context: *ta'awat*), which are presented in traditional pairs. The first pair, "the heavens above" *(šamayim mē'āl)* and "the great sea crouching beneath" *(tᵉhôm rōbeṣet taḥat* — which retains the flavor of the ancient myth of the sea monster Tiamat, who was split asunder by the great king of the gods in the process of creation) — is well balanced by the third pair, "the everlasting mountains" *(hôray 'ad)* and "the eternal hills" *(gibᵉ'ōt 'ôlām* — which include qualifying terms that are also applied to the deity, so that there is an additional instance of patriarchal language in connection with this deity: *'ôlām* — "the Eternal One"). It is hardly an accident that four key terms used of the God of the fathers are concentrated in these few verses: El, Shadday, *'al* (or *'elî*), and Olam.

It is the middle pair that requires closer scrutiny and attention. Here we have the following text:

> *birkōt šādayim wārāḥam*
> Blessings of breasts and womb

As in the case of the other blessings, the mythic flavor and divine features are only thinly disguised. In the two pairs previously mentioned, the sources of the blessings are natural and visible phenomena but seen as closely associated with El Shadday the divine father and serving as means or agents of his beneficent will. What about "breasts and womb"? This must also be a designation or title for a divine being, one also associated with El the Father God. It is difficult to avoid the conclusion that this is not simply a generic reference to human fertility but rather a designation of the great Mother Goddess, the consort of El who is the archetypal divine father. This brings to mind W. F. Albright's suggestion that early popular Hebrew religion may have consisted of a triad of deities: a father, mother, and son figure not unlike other early Semitic pantheons.[9]

The parallel phrase in v. 26a is difficult, and the text as written and vocalized poses problems:

---

9. For a discussion of the "divine triad" in the ancient Near East and in early Hebrew popular religion, see W. F. Albright, *From the Stone Age to Christianity,* 2nd ed. (Garden City: Doubleday, 1957), 173 (esp. n. 44), 246-47.

birkōt 'ăḇîḵā gāḇᵉrû 'al
The blessings of your Father are more powerful than —

But a literal rendering makes little sense and hardly fits the context and structure of the group of blessings. I think we must redivide the words and repoint the verb to produce the following: *gibbōr wᵉ 'al,* "warrior and exalted one" or, taking it as a hendiadys, "exalted warrior." That the divine father (cf. El the Father in v. 25) is meant seems most likely, especially in view of the chiastic structure in the two verses:

'ēl 'ăḇîḵā, "El, thy father"
'ăḇîḵā gibbōr, "thy father the warrior"

The association of *'El* and *gibbōr* may be noted in the name of the marvelous child of Isa. 9:5, where El and Gibbor occur together. This may support the case for emending the text in Gen. 49 (cf. also Isa. 10:21). If, as seems logical and reasonable, the father in Gen. 49:26 is the same as in v. 25 and therefore divine, then it is hard to escape the necessary conclusion that the person characterized as "Breasts and Womb" is likewise a deity. The consort of El, while not named here, is a well-known goddess in Canaanite religion and throughout the Near East and the Mediterranean world, and as well in the polemics of the biblical writers. She is Asherah who is the consort of El and later on of Baal, known as creatress of living things, the mother goddess par excellence. It is difficult to imagine such a statement in biblical literature after the establishment of Yahwism as the official religion of Israel, but as a reflection or description of pre-Mosaic patriarchal religion it is probably accurate and realistic. Probably this reference or allusion to the female deity, consort of the great high god, was sufficiently vague or ambiguous to survive the scrutiny of later editors, and its poetic form and antiquity doubtless served to save it from the censors. Nevertheless it provides a remarkable view of what the religion of the pre-Mosaic league actually was like.

In view of this information it is easier to understand the persistence of the cult of Asherah in Israel throughout the period of the First Commonwealth and the revival from time to time of the worship of this goddess and the installation of her image in various cult centers. The inscriptional discoveries at Kuntillet 'Ajrud in which Yahweh is associated with an Asherah of some kind tend to confirm the antiquity of this worship and the continuing concern for and interest in a female deity on the part of Israel. No doubt those who restored or reintroduced this aspect of worship in Israel claimed patriarchal precedent for the practice and could quote old tradition or cite the words and practices of the fathers in support of what they themselves wished to do. It is hardly an accident either that the worship of the Queen of Heaven, the Mother Goddess, persisted in Israel (Judah) right to the end of the kingdom, as recorded and reported in the book of Jeremiah (Jer. 7:18; 44:17-19, 25).

393

It would appear that the establishment of a new political order in the northern part of the country by Jeroboam I also involved an attempt to restore and revive the older religion of the tribal league, going back to pre-Mosaic traditions. Thus the use of a bull image in the worship of the chief male deity no doubt reflected the cult of El in the pre-Mosaic league, and no doubt the name of Aaron, if not of the fathers, could be invoked in support of, and as authorization for, such activity. At the same time, or at least somewhere in response to the same tradition, the worship of the mother goddess, Asherah the consort of El, was also reinstituted. This was not, in the proper sense, a borrowing from the Canaanites, or the local inhabitants, but rather a restoration of the older faith of the fathers.

If we follow Albright's view of patriarchal religion further, we must ask about the third member of the divine triad.[10] Was there a third god, the son of the chief god and his consort? The figure of Baal, so prominent in the later history of Israel, is very elusive in the early sources. The word itself, whether as the name or title of any deity, does not appear in the early poetry at all and does not figure in the patriarchal traditions at all.

On the one hand, it is difficult to imagine that the divine pair, El and Asherah, were childless, like Abraham and Sarah, and the crowded scenes in and around the heavenly palace testify to the plethora of the lesser divinities or $b^e n\hat{e}$ ʾ$\bar{e}l$ (lit., "sons of El"). So it is likely that the patriarchal pantheon was not restricted to El and his consort, although in cultic and practical terms they must have dominated the scene. The presence of others must be assumed and inferred from the surviving scraps of information preserved in the text and discovered in archaeological excavations. On the other hand, Baal himself is absent entirely from the patriarchal traditions and does not make a firm appearance in the story of Israel until well after the settlement in Canaan. The apparent exception, the Baal of Peor who figures prominently in the colorful story of rampant apostasy in the book of Numbers, may not be Baal at all but another deity altogether, namely, the otherwise unnamed god of the Midianites. It is not unreasonable to suppose that this deity is Yahweh himself, not in his Mosaic mold but rather as the traditional god of Midian, a representation drastically altered by Moses and his followers.[11]

The conclusion must be that for the most part evidence is lacking and any suggestions or inferences are largely speculative. Still it is hard to explain the enormous attraction and tight grip that Baal exerted on the population of Israel, and not in the north only, so that Baal, along with Asherah, symbolizes the most dangerous form of dereliction and apostasy from the true faith. One suspects that the reason, or a main reason, why so much fire and damnation are directed at Baal and Asherah (consorts in the later phases of this religion, whereas in an earlier

---

10. *Ibid.*, 247.

11. Cross has also suggested this in *Canaanite Myth and Hebrew Epic* (Cambridge, Mass.: Harvard University Press, 1973), 71-72.

version Baal would have been son, challenger, and ultimately successor to the aging El) and their adherents is that both of these deities were once approved partners and participants with the chief deity in the faith and worship of the patriarchs as well as of the pre-Mosaic tribal league which is described and reflected in the Blessing of Jacob in Gen. 49.

Exodus 15: The Song of the Sea

In this poem, in my opinion, we are confronted with Mosaic Yahwism, in its pristine original form, the faith by which the lawgiver led his people from slavery in Egypt to freedom in the wilderness. The decisive moment when the Egyptian chariot force is destroyed, and the departing Israelites are finally set free from bondage and the threat of recapture, is caught in this powerful hymn of victory.

Yahweh is portrayed as the only actor in the drama of deliverance. He alone is responsible for the defeat of the Egyptians, the sole champion of his people, who defeats the enemy and annihilates them all.[12] On other occasions Yahweh may appoint agents and delegate responsibility, or he may assist his people in their struggles with their foes (e.g., the Song of Deborah), but here the victory is uniquely and exclusively his; the entire responsibility for the outcome rests with him, so that no one ever again can say that he had help or that others had a hand in the triumph. It is forever forbidden for Israel to boast that this was a cooperative venture or that Israel was responsible for, or capable of, delivering or rescuing themselves. On the contrary, Yahweh alone was their redeemer from bondage. He purchased them from their former owner and now has all the rights and privileges that are transferred to the new owner. The central theme of the poem is the unmatched power and authority of Yahweh, who has demonstrated this power in destroying the Egyptian host by sheer force. It is this demonstration that gains for Yahweh possession of and authority over the former slaves, who now owe to him as their redeemer all the service and obeisance previously accorded to Egypt and its divine ruler.

The emphasis upon the irresistible power of Yahweh, demonstrated through a decisive violent action against a leading military power, and the way in which it is exercised by Yahweh as sole champion without aides or assistants, and in particular without the participation of the people, who are mere spectators at a confrontation in which their fate is decided, gives a definition and structure to the faith of Israel that carries through the remainder of its history as well as its sacred books. Recognition of Yahweh's monopoly of power and his exclusive

---

12. For Yahweh as a "Divine Warrior," see Cross, *ibid.,* 91-194; M. C. Lind, *Yahweh Is a Warrior* (Scottdale, Pa.: Herald, 1980); and P. D. Miller, *The Divine Warrior in Early Israel.* HSM 5 (Cambridge, Mass.: Harvard University Press, 1973).

claim on Israel as his property, gained through a violent bloody decisive victory at the Reed Sea, constitutes the main content of biblical tradition and the ongoing purpose of its religion. Israel was saved at the sea and sealed to Yahweh as its sole and exclusive Lord from that moment on. Within such a historical and existential setting or framework it is not surprising that in time an appropriate theological and philosophical superstructure was developed, translating finally into the monotheistic credo of the three great biblical religions. While the theoretical underpinnings, implications, and ramifications of that single decisive action could have developed in a variety of ways, the end result is not unreasonable or excessive, although the actual development could hardly have been predicted. In the poem itself the incomparability of Yahweh is affirmed (Exod. 15:11) but paradoxically by a comparison of Yahweh with other gods. In order to establish the superiority of Yahweh, comparison is necessary but compromises his uniqueness. It is like the use of substitutes for the superlative in Biblical Hebrew, whereby ultimacy is predicted of the deity by calling him the King of kings, or Lord of lords, and God of gods. Such comparisons affirm that there is a valid basis for comparison but equally insist that the basis or degree of the comparison is nullified by the character and quality of the gulf between the attributes of persons compared.

At the least, however, we must affirm the face value of the statement, "Who is like thee among the gods, Yahweh?" (Exod. 15:11). The expected required answer is that no other god can bear comparison, none can measure up or even be included in the comparison. But there are other gods, that is clear. Otherwise there can be no comparison to demonstrate the incomparability of Yahweh.

As already pointed out, there are too many active and articulate beings in and around the heavenly court to make a contrary claim. We may call them angels, but that term only describes or defines their activity or function, whereas their classification is the same as that of Yahweh: they belong to the category of *'elōhîm,* as contrasted with earthlings, who belong to the class called *'āḏām.* This is hardly monotheism in any philosophical or strictly rational sense of the term. At the same time, many if not most of the features of polytheism and mythology in the ancient Near East have been deleted from the biblical picture.

As for mythology in the proper sense — stories about gods — there are none in the Bible, although some vestiges survive, and these are allusions to a time before historical time when Yahweh engaged in titanic struggles with mythical monsters to establish or maintain control of the world. Similarly, all other divine beings are totally subject and subservient to the will of the one God worthy of the name.

It should be evident from all the available data that Yahweh and Yahwism did not spring full-blown from the head of Moses. Rather, *YHWH* was a deity from olden times, with a territorial base centered around Mt. Sinai (wherever that may have been). Presumably he was the god of the Midianites, perhaps among others, and Jethro the father-in-law of Moses was his priest. Such a god would have been equipped with a mythology of his own and associated with other deities, male and female, in an appropriate pantheon. Relics, vestiges, allusions, and echoes of these elements are to be found in the Hebrew Bible, especially in the Psalter and among the prophets, but these are not likely to have been picked up later and added to the religion of Yahweh, especially since the Mosaic version developed in a different way. Rather, we may suppose that this pre-Mosaic primitive version persisted long after the break between Israel and Midian became permanent. In fact, the inscriptions and drawings at such an out-of-the-way place as Kuntillet 'Ajrud may reflect the ancient form of Yahwism practiced by Midianites and other desert peoples, although no doubt there were changes and adaptations in the course of time. Moses for his part and his followers and successors made radical alterations and adaptations while preserving essential features of the Yahwism of his time. Yahweh, the One of Sinai, remained the same as before: the mountaineer, the warrior, the storm-god, the recently crowned king of the world of gods and human beings; all this was essentially unchanged. But Yahweh the redeemer of a new people from bondage in Egypt is clearly new. So also is a high God without a consort, offspring, or heirs. Equally astonishing is the absence, even more the absolute prohibition, of images of the deity. It is difficult to say where or when or how or why such strictures became an integral part of this religion, but the tradition is both strong and persistent and points to Moses as the originator. It is these features that made the break with mythology and priestly manipulation both possible and actual.

With the revelation of the new name of God, Yahweh the One of Sinai, biblical religion set off on a new course. It is difficult to define the relationship or the difference with patriarchal religion as compared with the new faith proclaimed by Moses. While there were no doubt connections of some kind between the patriarchal communities, some of whom were in Egypt while others remained behind, and the group led out by Moses, I do not think there was any clear or immediate connection between El Shadday, the God of the fathers and the tribal league in pre-Mosaic times, and Yahweh, the God of Sinai who revealed himself to Moses and brought Israel out of Egypt to freedom in the wilderness. Just as El is the deity mentioned in the Blessing of Jacob, so Yahweh completely dominates the Song of the Sea. It is only later that the two deities are conjoined, in poems such as the Oracles of Balaam and the Blessing of Moses, and only after bitter confrontation. The episode of the golden calf may best be understood as a confrontation between the supporters of the older patriarchal religion — for whom the molten bull symbolized not only the presence and power of El but also the other features of patriarchal religion that would obviously be in direct conflict with the faith in Yahweh proclaimed by Moses — and the proponents of Yahwism. Ultimately, compromises and accommodations were made, beginning with the principal formula for peace and concord (after the terrible bloodletting recorded in Exod. 32): Yahweh = El. There are many reasons why this equation would be acceptable to both groups, and they lie in the meaning of the names but also in the ways in which the term 'ēl came to be used all over the ancient world. Thus while El is a proper noun, the name of the chief god of the pantheon, it is also a general term meaning any god or the class of divine beings. Thus in a given nation, the principal god would be called by his own name but also by the term 'ēl. Typically, personal names would be formed with that of the national god but also with the divine element 'ēl. It is evident that the same god is intended by both designations. Many biblical names exhibit the same features; thus a well-known king of Judah bore the name Eliakim, and when enthroned by Pharaoh Necho he was given the name Jehoiakim (2 Kgs. 23:34). The two names, one formed with the name El and the other with the name Yahu (short for Yahweh), are equivalent. And there are many other such pairs. Insofar as status role, attributes, and the like were concerned, there would be little to choose between them, and by blending or merging them the basic problem of a monolatrous religion was resolved. There would be no conflict between opposing deities requiring a definite choice and often resulting in disastrous fighting, since these gods would merge into each other and be one godhead. By contrast, consider the terrible struggle between adherents of Yahweh on one side and Baal on the other and the catastrophic results over the years. The alternative is well put by Elijah to all Israel at Mt. Carmel where he insists that a choice must be made: there can be no compromise between Yahweh and Baal (1 Kgs. 18:29). Only one can be god of Israel, not both. At the same time, the differences and divergences are so great that it would be impossible to merge or equate them. Curiously there is some evidence that such a possibility was contemplated and perhaps worked for a time. The word ba'al is basically a title (= master, lord) and not a name, so it could be applied to a number of gods. Apparently it was used for Yahweh as well as for Hadad the great storm-god of Canaan and Syria, among others. So it may have been possible to denominate Yahweh by the title Baal (master) and thus blend the deities. But it was other factors, including the long history of conflict and certain characteristics of Baal, as well as his involvement in a well-defined pantheon, that ultimately made a merger impossible.

In the case of El and Yahweh, there were other concessions or changes. If we are right about patriarchal religion, then the acceptance of El as a name for Yahweh or as his alter ego required that El surrender his consort forthwith. It might have worked the other way around, and there is evidence that in Samaria (and at Kuntillet 'Ajrud) Yahweh gained a consort, and Asherah remained in view as Queen of Heaven and the Mother (Creatress) of the gods. In the end, however, the figure of Yahweh remained dominant and clear-cut. The religion of Israel was shaped primarily by Moses and the wilderness experience, more so, in terms of theology certainly, than by the patriarchal traditions. In terms of nationhood and territory, political and social structures, and the land settlement, it was the other way around, since the tribal league antedated the exodus and wanderings and provided the basic polity for the nation in the land that it occupied.

Numbers 23–24: The Oracles of Balaam

In this group of poems we see the firstfruits of the equation Yahweh = El. Both names occur in the pieces in parallel and complementary fashion, showing that the blending and merging of traditions has been achieved successfully, and from this point on Yahweh = El is an appropriate dual designation of the God of Israel.

In these poems we find many of the same elements already observed in the preceding pair of poems, and therefore we need not repeat some of the things already stated. The general framework of the oracles concerns the relationship between Yahweh and Israel and the unique status of the latter among the nations because of his protection. While specific military actions are not in view (except perhaps in the brief supplemental oracles at the end of Num. 24), Israel's privileged status — dwelling alone in security and prosperity — is clearly owing to earlier victories achieved by Yahweh and the promise of his protection and the threat of divine intervention in behalf of his people if anyone tries to threaten them. Given the context of the maneuvering by Balak to secure an effective curse against these potentially serious enemies, through a proven magician or spellbinder, the seer Balaam, we can understand both the nullification of Balak's endeavors and the affirmations of Yahweh's victorious stance along with Israel's blissful existence.

A special and perhaps overriding feature of this poem in contrast to the others is the stress on a different kind of warfare being conducted by Yahweh in behalf of his people — not against armies in the field but what Paul describes (see Eph. 6:10-13) as a spiritual struggle against principalities and powers and the combined and concentrated forces of evil. The Oracles of Balaam open a window on the world of magic, especially black magic that deals in curses and malevolent wishes and schemes designed to overthrow and undo enemies — the world of evil spirits and baleful omens for Israel. But an essential element in Mosaic Yahwism was the repudiation and rejection of all magic, not because it was a foolish notion or because it is demonstrably ineffectual, but because Yahweh prohibited it.

Balak was using magic, or rather hiring a successful practitioner of different kinds of malefic magic, including especially cursing and no doubt sorcery and spells, to induce the relevant gods or evil spirits to achieve by occult means what he could not achieve in battle; he was not willing to take his chances on the field and preferred to invoke the evil forces of the universe and bribe or coerce them into serving his own ends. In an ironic twist, Balaam, the acknowledged professional and master of the black arts, is turned around — a double agent, as it were — and becomes instead Yahweh's spokesman and mouthpiece pronouncing a doom on all such devices and schemes to undo his people. Yahweh can and will protect his people not only from armies doing battle but from magical spells and unseen forces trying to wreak destruction on his people.

While the oracles are set in a particular context of the alternate war waged by Balak of Moab against these unwelcome intruders on territory that no doubt he would prefer to remain in no hands at all, i.e., unless he wished to acquire them himself, there are more basic considerations involved concerning the nature of Mosaic Yahwism. The war against magic, against the underworld of demons and malevolent spirits, is here declared, and it is also declared to be over. Yahweh does not deal in magic — he is not arbitrary or capricious, he cannot be bribed or seduced by flattery or rich offerings, and he works according to principles and rules, and he does what he says. Furthermore, there is no appeal from his verdict, at least not to other forces that might prove to be more amenable. There is one court and one judge; there are no tricks or maneuvers by which to avoid confrontation and decision. Balak's alternative, his politics of conducting war by other means, is doomed to failure.

The war against magic was never completely won; and it still isn't. But the first major blow was struck in the name of a new faith that believed in a single omnipotent deity who ruled justly and would not permit the intrusion of extraneous and malefic elements. It should be emphasized that biblical religion nowhere dismisses the world of curses and black magic as futile nonsense or even malicious mischief. There were such forces in the world and evil spirits could be invoked and convoked, but Yahweh was more powerful than all of them put together. He would not allow these purveyors of evil to gain sway on those who sought their help. He himself would wage effective war against all of them. At the same time, however, Israel was strictly, even fiercely, prohibited from having anything to do with them and from making contact with those spirits or the mediums and wizards who were their living human contacts.

Concluding Remarks

Owing to various miscalculations, and especially the limitations of space, it has proven impossible to deal specifically and individually with all of the poems in the corpus, but perhaps enough has been said about them in one context or another to make our case. In any case we must summarize our findings and our contentions.

The five poems embedded in the primary history not only describe and reflect the circumstances and convictions of earliest Israel but were composed in substantially their present form during the premonarchic period. They thus provide a uniquely important source for analyzing and interpreting the earliest phases of Israel's experience and especially its religion.

As always, there are three phases in the evolution of Israel's religion. These may be outlined as follows:

a. The first phase is patriarchal religion: the pre-Mosaic phase. The source for this information is the book of Genesis but more particularly the Blessing of Jacob in Gen. 49. The essential feature is that the chief God is El (Shadday) as already noted centuries later (but millennia before modern scholars) by the Priestly editor (Exod. 6:3). He is the God of the tribal league already formed in Canaan in the 14th to the 13th centuries. So far as the evidence goes, patriarchal religion shared many features with the neighboring Canaanites, including a consort for El (probably Asherah) and other divine beings.

b. The second phase, Mosaic Yahwism, is reflected in the Song of the Sea (Exod. 15). Here we meet Yahweh the God of Sinai and the deliverer of his people at the Reed Sea. The special and distinct features of biblical religion are to be found here, especially the incomparability of this God in relation to others. The main emphasis in the poem is on the overwhelming power of this God and also his unique relationship to the people he redeemed from slavery.

c. The third phase is represented especially by poems such as the Oracles of Balaam and the Blessing of Moses. Here we find the blending of the two earlier phases and the synthesis of patriarchal and Mosaic traditions. The potential and actual conflict between El (Shadday) and his partisans and Yahweh and his is resolved in the equation Yahweh = El. In the merger, greater emphasis is placed on the Yahwistic components, while the El factors are brought into conformity with them. But the political structure and the territorial entity derive from the El tradition.

(1) In the Oracles of Balaam another very significant aspect of Yahwism is revealed and presented: the absolute warfare against the underworld of black magic, evil spirits, and the like.

(2) In the Blessing of Moses the tribal league is reconstituted as the people of Yahweh. Now that a significant territorial base has been secured, it is possible to consolidate the holdings and the people in preparation for the (re)conquest of the territories on the West Bank of the Jordan.

d. A word should be added about the Song of Deborah (Judg. 5). It is the last in the series and reflects the completion of the conquest with the utter defeat of the kings of Canaan and their armed forces. While details differ, nevertheless the Song of Deborah has points in common with the Song of the Sea. Together they sum up the campaign for freedom and statehood, with Yahweh overthrowing the chariot forces and Egypt at the beginning through a violent storm and ending with the equally violent destruction of the chariot forces of the Canaanites at the Wadi Kishon. Thus the threads are tied together, and the comment at the end of the Song of Deborah completes the first cycle of Israel's experience from the formation of the tribal league to its final resettlement in the land:

> So may all your enemies
> > perish, Yahweh
> And his lovers (be) like
> > the going forth of the
> > sun in its vigor.

> And the land had rest for forty years. (Judg. 5:31)

36

Yahweh of Samaria and His Asherah

Over the years, archaeologists have criticized biblical scholars, and biblical scholars, not taking this lying down, have responded in kind. The rhetoric has often escalated without a corresponding increase in wisdom or knowledge. I believe we must bring the two disciplines together. After all, both have long histories and have been developed, advocated, and worked through by qualified, competent people. And if each does its own work, it can make up for the deficiencies of the other.

For instance, our understanding of a biblical passage can certainly be improved by a knowledge of what was going on at the time it was written. Archaeology can be very useful here because its excavation of material culture and analysis of artifacts aim to re-create the life of people in ancient times. Similarly, the exegesis of biblical passages can be of assistance to archaeologists by providing useful incidental information and thus helping in the evaluation of finds.

Bringing archaeology and biblical studies together is not an easy task, but there is one circumstance in particular that lends itself to the attempt: i.e., when an inscription is discovered. Several good examples come to mind. There is the royal inscription of a king of Moab, Mesha, who is actually mentioned in the Bible. This is the only royal inscription of any length that has been found in the basic region of Israel. It was found in Transjordan and it is a remarkable document. The first scholars who worked on it reflected on the fact that the perspective of this king — his religious, political, and social views — would be the counterpart of what an Israelite king would have written about himself.

Another is one in which the Assyrian king Sennacherib gave his view of the siege of Jerusalem in 701 B.C.E., which resulted in the capitulation of King Hezekiah of Judah. What is particularly interesting is that this provides a contemporary Assyrian account of events that are described in great detail in the Bible. It must be borne in mind, however, that just because the Assyrian inscription is contemporary with the events doesn't mean that it is necessarily more reliable or truthful than the biblical account. On the contrary, royal propaganda has probably not changed over the millennia. Nevertheless, it is established that Hezekiah paid tribute, but, contrary to the usual Assyrian procedure, the city was not captured (it was not even entered) and the king was not replaced and his dynasty was not removed. Sennacherib went home, because of a palace conspiracy, and this confirms the biblical account that something quite unusual had taken place.

A third inscription, and one that has caused much scholarly disputation, is a literary text found on a chapel wall in Transjordan, at a place called Tell Deir ʿAllā. What makes this inscription especially tantalizing is that the wall on which it was written collapsed and crumbled into tiny fragments. As a result, we have a big jigsaw puzzle with about a thousand pieces. Remarkably enough it actually can be read. Also, it is a literary text, and very, very few of these have ever been found because literature was not considered important enough to waste either good papyrus or good wall space.

The hero of the episode reported in the inscription is a very unlikely person — in fact, one who was once thought to be fictional. He is the man called Balaam, son of Beor, who is well known from stories in the book of Numbers, where he appears as a diviner. Who would have thought that somebody else, outside of the Bible, regarded him as a folk hero? I don't think anybody believed that such new data about Balaam would be found. Furthermore, this inscription is in a sanctuary, where, presumably, the content would have been of the greatest importance.

The Deir ʿAllā inscription dates from about five hundred years later than the period when Balaam is supposed to have lived as a contemporary of Moses (around 1200 B.C.E.). Strangely enough, the hero is not only the same person, but he is also up to the same tricks. This is a man who, as you know, makes his services available to the highest bidder. He is what I would call an amiable polytheist. This is also the pagan view of Balaam. The biblical attitude, though, is much less favorable.

A fourth inscription, and one I would like to concentrate on for the remainder of this paper, was found in an equally unlikely place. This site has no biblical name because nobody knows how to connect it with the Bible. It is called Quntillet ʿAjrud in Arabic, and it is on the border between the southern Negeb and the Sinai peninsula. It was a one-period site, very appealing to archaeologists. (Then you don't have to worry about contamination or mingling of artifacts from different strata. You can just dig up the finds.) Fortunately, a lot of inscriptions have been found, most of them in Hebrew. The settlement lay not far from the road between Gaza and Eilat, and served as both fortress and stopping-place for caravans. Given the desolate area and forbidding terrain, it is understandable that many of the inscriptions are heartfelt prayers of thanksgiving and for safekeeping. If you have ever been in that part of the world, you can understand such sentiments. But there they are, and because it is so dry, many inscriptions have survived.

Now we are going to confront a central problem, with all the skills, techniques, and technology available. It amounts to nothing more than a slight difference in spelling in the English translation of the inscription: Should a particular word begin with a capital letter or a small one?

The inscription expresses a religious sentiment — more particularly, a blessing. It says, "I bless you by" and then we have the tetragrammaton, the sacred personal name of the God of Israel, followed by the name of a city, Shomeron — i.e., Samaria, the capital of the northern kingdom, Israel. Following this word is the term at the center of the controversy, which should be rendered "his Asherah" in my opinion. In the Bible the word occurs in both the singular *(ʾašērâ)* and plural *(ʾašērîm),* so presumably there was more than one such figure.

Since Asherah was worshipped in more than one place, separate shrines and images would bear her name, and to distinguish one from others, double determination would be both necessary and appropriate. Thus for another well-known female deity, who shares features with Asherah, we have the doubly determined qualification Ishtar of Nineveh and Ishtar of Arbela. When it comes to the use of a pronominal suffix ("his") with Asherah, we may point to the tradition that in the Canaanite myths, preserved on the tablets of Ugarit, Asherah is the consort of El, the chief of the gods, whereas in the Phoenician pantheon reflected in the story of Elijah at Mt. Carmel (1 Kgs. 18) Asherah is linked with Baal, apparently as his consort. So it would be legitimate and important to specify the god to whom she was attached in this fashion: "his Asherah" and not some other god's.

The technical question here is this: Can a proper noun be determined? According to the authorities on biblical grammar and the formalities of Biblical Hebrew, the answer is no. The initial "A" in the word cannot be capitalized, and the word must therefore be a common noun. In other words, *asherah* can't be *Asherah.* It has to be something else. There are several candidates: One is a wooden pole; another is a sacred grove; and a third is a holy place at which you can invoke the deity, or pronounce a blessing. My own belief is that if the preceding divine name had been "Baal" and not "Yahweh," then there would have been general agreement that two gods were intended: the pair, familiar from the Bible, Baal and Asherah (cf. 1 Kgs. 18). Indeed, Baal and Asherah were a couple made in the Phoenician heaven.

I am going to give an example later about a determined proper noun from that semiliterate playwright, William Shakespeare. In other words, I believe the way to approach a strange grammatical construction is not by invoking a rule that somebody invented in the 19th century that says it is impossible, but rather by investigating the possible reasons for such an unusual arrangement. It all goes back to the character and mythic history of Asherah. She was not only a remarkable female deity but also has a central role in many colorful myths. Are there any conditions under which someone would say not "Asherah" but "his Asherah"? I think there are, and I will try to show you how it happened.

There is a famous story in the Bible, one that has been analyzed and discussed endlessly. It is the story told in 1 Kgs. 18:1-46 about the contest between the prophets of Baal and the prophet Elijah at Mt. Carmel. I will not repeat the main

405

elements here, but I want to call attention to certain details that have not received much emphasis. This is a contest, basically, to decide whether Baal or Yahweh is the real god. Conceptually at least, Yahweh and Baal belong to the same world of discourse. They have worshippers who pray to them and they are regarded as capable of responding to such requests by mighty acts. The test, in this instance, although dramatically portrayed as a burst of fire from heaven, actually concerns a basic component of Canaanite and Israelite religion. That is, which god is responsible for the rains, fertility, and agricultural abundance? The fire from heaven — a bolt of lightning — signals the end of the drought and the return of the rains.

I wish to point out that in this story, along with the 450 prophets of Baal, there are also 400 prophets of Asherah. All of these are summoned to Mt. Carmel where Elijah, the lone prophet of Yahweh, will confront them (see 1 Kgs. 18:19). In the contest, Elijah is triumphant and immediately orders the arrest of the 450 prophets of Baal, whom he then slaughters at the Wadi Kishon (1 Kgs. 18:40). Now for our question: What happened to the prophets of Asherah? Since there is no mention of Asherah or her prophets at this point in the text, scholars solve the problem in one of two ways. In the first of these, they suggest that the prophets of Asherah are included with the prophets of Baal and eliminated with the latter. That is possible but gratuitous. The other is simpler and widely adopted. Since the prophets of Asherah are not mentioned at the end of the story, they obviously don't belong at the beginning, and therefore they should be removed from the scene. I have a little difficulty with such procedures. Emendation in the direction of a desired result is too easy and generally wrong. One of my rules is that you should never emend a text to support your own theory; you should always emend in the opposite direction.

Now I will try to explain the text as it stands. The chief clue I derived from a story of Arthur Conan Doyle entitled *The Hound of the Baskervilles,* which features the well-known detective Sherlock Holmes. The key to the solution of the mystery is something that did not happen. The dog did not bark. The same applies here. What happened to Asherah and her prophets? Nothing.

We must now consider the political fallout from this contest and the ongoing struggle between Elijah and Jezebel over the state religion of Israel. Some years later, there was a violent revolution, inspired by the prophets Elijah and Elisha, and carried out by Jehu, the general of the armies. In the course of it, Jehu killed the kings of Israel and Judah and wiped out the dynasty of Omri and Ahab. He also was determined to eliminate the worship of Baal from Israel in accordance with the policy and program of the prophets mentioned earlier and as the ultimate outcome of the contest at Mt. Carmel. In a gruesome episode described in 2 Kgs. 10:18-28, Jehu assembled the worshippers of Baal in the latter's temple (in Samaria) and by a ruse slaughtered them all, destroyed the temple, and turned the place into a latrine. "Thus he destroyed the Baal from Israel" (v. 28).

Once again, we may ask the question: What happened to Asherah, Baal's consort and companion? Considering the vehemence of Jehu's campaign against Baal and Baal worshippers, we might expect some word about the treatment of Asherah. But there is none. Rather we have a later word from the reign of Jehu's son and successor, Jehoahaz: "The Asherah remained standing in Samaria" (2 Kgs. 13:6).

In spite of the violent repudiation of Baal, his associate, Asherah, remained in Samaria untouched. Whose Asherah was she now? The answer may be found in that odd inscription from Quntillet ʿAjrud hundreds of miles away, which speaks of "Yahweh of Samaria and his Asherah." The inscription has been dated reliably by eminent scholars to around 800 B.C.E. The reign of Jehoahaz, the king of Israel and son and successor of Jehu, can be set in the years 814-800 B.C.E. In other words, the inscription is contemporary with that king and can be used in conjunction with the statement in 2 Kgs. 13:6 to clarify the picture. In Samaria, around 800 B.C.E., the official cult of Yahweh included the worship of his consort Asherah.

Our next witness is the prophet Amos, whose oracles, though addressed to the people of Israel a generation later, reflect much the same situation. According to Amos 8:14 people all over the country invoke or swear by a deity called *'ašmat šōmᵉrôn*, literally, "the guiltiness of Samaria." The noun in question is feminine and while no such goddess is as yet known from the onomasticon of the ancient Near East, the name reads and sounds very much like *'ašrat šōmᵉrôn*, which would be "Asherah of Samaria," and with which the Israelites would have been quite familiar. Such puns and parodies on divine names, especially of repudiated gods, are known in the Bible (for instance, *baʿal zᵉbûb*, "Lord of the Flies," for Baal Zebul, "Exalted Lord"), and in this case *'ašmat* may be a play on the word *'ašrat*. In any case, a goddess worshipped in Samaria is involved and it would be no surprise to discover that the Asherah was still standing there.

Not only does this evidence support and confirm our observations about the established religion of Samaria around 800 B.C.E., but we also learn that the prophet Amos seems to have been the first to protest against the worship and invocation of the goddess.

In another place, Amos complains that "a man and his father go to 'the girl,' in order to profane my holy name" (Amos 2:17). While most scholars interpret the statement as a condemnation of prostitution, possibly prostitution under religious sponsorship, the primary reference almost certainly is not sexual but ritual. Resort to "the girl" seems to be the worship of a goddess, presumably at a major shrine such as Bethel, where Amos preached a fiery message. We can even make a reasonable effort at identifying the principal goddess there, although the trail is a long one and takes us further in both time and space than our previous excursion to Quntillet ʿAjrud. Among the papyri of the 5th century B.C.E. at Elephantine in Upper Egypt, we find reference not only to Yahu (short for Yahweh), the chief god of the Jewish community there, but also to a goddess called Anatyahu *(ʿntyhw)*, a compound name, which should be interpreted as a bound construction, *Anat of* (belonging to) *Yahu.* There is another name, presumably of the same goddess, which reads *ʿânat baytēl (ʿntbytl)*, to be interpreted as *ʿAnat of Bethel.* ʿAnat is the well-known goddess of Canaanite myth,

407

who plays a central role in the Ugaritic epics, here identified with the shrine at Bethel, and surfacing centuries later in far-off Assuan. But it is the same goddess, also a consort of Yahu (which is equal to Yhwh) at Bethel.

Since there was a third major temple or sanctuary in the northern kingdom at Dan, we may speculate that a third goddess was associated with Yahweh at that site. We have already accounted for Asherah and Anat, and the remaining major goddess of the Canaanite pantheon, Astarte, may have been worshipped there.

The southern kingdom was not immune to the worship of goddesses. We know that in Jerusalem, for a long time, they worshipped Ishtar, who was called "the Queen of Heaven," and who very likely was identified with a West Semitic deity as well, presumably Asherah, who was, after all, the queen of the gods (Jer. 44:15-30).

Ezekiel, who was a firm upholder of biblical religion and deeply offended by what was happening in the temple of Jerusalem, reports during the mystical trip that he took while he was in exile in Babylon that in the forecourt, right at the entrance of the Jerusalem sanctuary, was an image (Ezek. 8:3). This idol had a name, and the name is usually translated to mean "the image of jealousy" *(sēmel qin'â)*. This must be the female counterpart of Yahweh, the zealous God (*'ēl qannā'* — Exod. 20:5), and we must think again of Yahweh and his consort. Our investigation suggests that the worship of a goddess, consort of Yahweh, was deeply rooted in both Israel and Judah in preexilic times, in spite of vigorous prophetic protests and strenuous efforts by reforming kings. And remember that our question was merely, "Do you spell the word *asherah* with a capital *A* or a small *a?*" Amazing what can be spun out of a brief inscription like that.

Now for the Shakespearean quotation. In the last six lines of *Romeo and Juliet,* the prince says,

A glooming peace this morning with it brings,
The sun for sorrow will not show his head.
Go hence, to have more talk of these sad things.
Some shall be pardoned and some punished.
For never was a story of more woe
Than this of Juliet and her Romeo.

Citing the double determination in the last line ("her Romeo") may not be as farfetched an analogy to the expression "Yahweh and his Asherah" as it may seem. The point is not so much that this Romeo has to be distinguished from other Romeos but that this Romeo had another girlfriend at the beginning of the play. Thus when Juliet won his heart and hand, he became "her Romeo." When Yahweh defeated Baal in the contest at Mt. Carmel, Asherah, who had been associated with the latter, now became the former's consort. Hence the ungrammatical expression "Yahweh and his Asherah."

37

When God Repents

The verb *nḥm* occurs twice in the book of Amos, in exactly the same form, in the transition sentences from Amos's interposition to the divine response in each of the first two visions (7:3, 6). The lines read as follows:

niḥam yhwh ʿal-zōʾṯ
Yahweh repented [= changed his mind] over this.

On the basis of parallel usage elsewhere in the Bible with *nḥm* ʿal (or occasionally *ʾel-*) we can identify the pronoun *zʾt* with the noun *rʿh*, "evil, calamity, disaster," either threatened or actual. The verb form is ambiguous and could be either the niphal or the piel third masculine singular perfect, but there is no question here that it is the former. On the basis of both common usage and the context here, the meaning is quite certain. Yahweh changed his mind about what he had planned to do, as shown by the visions, though not put into words, and, because of the prophet's intercession, repealed or reversed the decision: "It shall not happen" *(lōʾ ṯihyeh)*. Again the reference is to the *rāʿâ* that was threatened in the vision. The second time around the reversal is reaffirmed with the recognition that the decision had already been canceled once: "This [calamity] also shall not happen," *gam-hîʾ lōʾ ṯihyeh*.

Thus the two visions and dialogues are to be seen as separate events, and if we are to follow the sequence closely, it means that the second sequence begins at the same point that the first one did. Even after the initial decision is reversed, it would seem that the particular mode of judgment, the locust plague, has been canceled but that a more permanent decision has been delayed. The second vision carries with it the same portent of utter doom, in fact worse in its cosmic aspects and implications for destruction than the first. Once again the prophet intervenes, and once again Yahweh cancels the decision. This cancellation can and should be interpreted literally and narrowly in the sense that the particular decision to destroy by fire (as, e.g., the destruction of Sodom and Gomorrah and that of all of the

409

nations in chs. 1–2) has been reversed. The decision is neither permanent nor general; it does not mean that all further negative judgments are ruled out, or that other means or methods of destruction may not be used, only that this particular decision has been negated.

It also seems clear, however, that the particular set of circumstances that gave rise to the decisions embodied in or illuminated by the visions will not be the direct basis for or occasion of another decision for destruction. Yahweh has accepted the prophet's intervention and will not now act against his people, pending a later determination on the basis of new evidence of intention and behavior. A period of grace has been granted to allow the people to solidify the position by genuine repentance and for the prophet to try to reach the people with due warning concerning their peril. At most, intercession buys time, and the decision made as a result of it must be regarded as temporary in the sense that the future course of the relations between God and people will depend on further developments and in particular on a show of genuine repentance. There is an interlocking reaction that involves repentance on both sides, one stimulating and requiring a radical change of mind and will in the other if the relationship is to survive and if the threat of drastic punishment is to be averted, not merely arrested.

Thus the first two visions and the dialogues associated with them assure a respite for "Jacob," so that the imminent threat of national obliteration has been canceled, and there is time to establish a more permanent reconciliation and stabilize the relationship. To do so requires a corresponding change on the part of the people, for the future of the relationship depends on a satisfactory reciprocal attachment of each to the other, of love on both sides, but of grace and goodwill on the part of the divine sovereign, and obedience in true service and worship on the part of the human vassal.

In the interim, Yahweh, having made his decision to cancel the immediate threat and withhold judgment for a space, both prophet and people have an opportunity to remedy the situation. The prophet must warn urgently on the basis of the visions (and their cancellation) and the conditions that brought on those decisions to begin with (as richly documented throughout the book). The people must then follow by responding in genuine repentance for their past and current rebellions and violations of the terms of the agreement between them. That sort of response would lead to an extension of the truce and to the establishment of a more permanent peace between the parties. Failure to act in this period of grace and on the kindly reversal of the deity would, however, ensure a reinstatement of the judgment and a renewed decision to punish the people for intransigent disobedience, intensified by the added guilt of rejecting the pardon and refusing to negotiate a permanent settlement.

As we know from the account of the second pair of visions, the extension failed, the period of grace produced no convincing evidence of genuine repentance, and the judgment was reaffirmed. The important difference is that the

410

second time around, the prophet was not permitted to intercede or, recognizing that further extensions would not be granted and that the case was futile, did not even try. A second set of reversals had taken place, and the decision now, expressed in identical terms in the second set of visions, was both explicit and irreversible. Yahweh had changed his mind again, twice more, to come back to the original set of decisions. While the four visions have been gathered in the space of a little more than a chapter (7:1–8:3), with only the account of the visit to the temple at Bethel and the altercation with Amaziah intervening, we must suppose a sufficient time between the pairs of visionary experiences for the period of grace and suspended judgment. In fact, we suppose that the prophet must have engaged in a desperate effort to prod or provoke the people from bottom to top, but especially at the top, to restructure their lives and the conduct of the nation in political and ecclesiastical as well as social and economic matters, not to speak of personal affairs, so as to prolong the deferment of judgment and initiate or inaugurate an era of authentic peace, *šālôm.* The utter failure of the supposed campaign is underscored by the absence of any reference to or suggestion of changes on the part of Israel (or Judah for that matter) in the book of Amos. The exhortations, or at least some of them, are preserved along with the warnings. But of responses we have nothing except the occasional explicit (7:10-17), more often implied, rejection of the prophet and his message, the very word of God that they most needed to hear (chs. 2–3).

The point now is to understand that in spite of the hopeless failure of the salvation mission, we must not question the reality of the reversals recorded in Amos 7–8, and we must seek to comprehend what Amos and the other biblical prophets and writers meant when they talked or wrote about the repentance of God. In spite of the apparent futility of the gesture and the effect of a double set or pair of reversals bringing us back to the original decision and starting point for the action of judgment against the people, a real transaction took place, which revealed the mind of Yahweh in action, and there was reciprocal influence and response between prophet and deity.

While the pair of events in which this action and response took place is isolated in Amos's story and vocabulary, and although we can infer that a second set of similar but opposite reversals took place offstage between the two sets of visions, the phenomenon itself of divine reversal is well documented elsewhere in the Bible and constitutes an important, perhaps essential feature of biblical theology, i.e., the biblical interpretation of the divine status and involvement in human affairs.

It is to this combination of circumstances and features, attitudes and activities that we now turn. But first the following presentation may help to clear the air of possible misunderstanding. What follows is not an attempt to discuss theological matters *per se,* or to invade an area of investigation for which we are not qualified, and in any case for which the Anchor Bible series is not designed. Our concern

411

here is strictly with the understanding of the way biblical writers and books deal with the figure of God; the way they interpret his being and presence, his thinking and acting in connection with the world that he created; and, most of all, the way his interactions with human beings are to be grasped. In order to understand properly the biblical positions on fundamental theological issues, it is necessary to enter into the world of the Bible and accept its presuppositions and affirmations, participate in the dramatic portrayal of the deity as person in relation to other persons, whether divine or human, in the action that takes place between heaven and earth. This action is both dramatic and dialogic, involving both conversation and action; it is framed by history or at least chronology; and it requires the presence of Yahweh as actor on the stage and participant in the course of historical events. As a living, acting person, he is subject to defining characteristics if not limitations that are not normally associated with attributes of deity, and he will demonstrate a full range of passions and compassions, convictions and attitudes, and a corresponding group of words and actions that are characteristic also of human beings. The vocabulary, with occasional modifications and exceptions, is much the same, as inevitably it must be.

While recognizing the vast metaphysical gap that separates human beings from God or the ideas of God, human beings, regrettably, are bound by circumstances beyond their control, and all ideas and their embodiment in words remain stubbornly human, locked within our own limitations. So even the effort to speak or write about God, the truly other, is doomed to failure even as we take the problem and its consequences into account and admit the truth while we are enunciating our views. At best we may talk about correspondence and correlation, about similarity and simile. While admitting that we cannot break into the divine realm we can affirm that for the biblical writers God managed to break into their world; they caught a glimpse of him within the limitations of the world we all inhabit, they heard him speak (in their language, of course), and they saw his actions.

The form of presentation is narrational (the Bible is essentially though not exclusively narrative; e.g., the primary history — the great narrative of the Bible — is about half of its content, and if we add the Chronicler's history and the narrative materials in the latter prophets and their writings, perhaps two-thirds or more of the total), and the rules and conventions of narrative writing apply to all of the participants, including God. Special effort is made and precautions taken to affirm and constantly remind that this person is unique and shares certain characteristics with no one and nothing else, but he remains a person in the story nonetheless. We judge that the Bible is successful in conveying both facts of theological experience adequately, that he is God and that he is a person. The whole presentation is finally a metaphor for reality; no external evidence can be brought to bear to confirm or support the biblical picture. For our purposes it is enough to say that we will make the assumption and attempt to describe the deity of the Bible as the Bible does by implication and inference, and therefore take the biblical picture and portrayal at face value, leaving more difficult philosophical and theological questions concerning the truth claims of belief in transcendence and immanence, especially in their supposed simultaneity, to other times and places and persons for discussion.

Ours may seem like a rather primitive approach to a book that has been examined, studied, and restudied by millennia of theological thinkers and endlessly modernized and updated for the benefit of sophisticated and unsophisticated readers. We think the ultimate sophistication is to go back into the biblical world and live and work inside its literature for a more significant experience of the realities the biblical writers dealt with, and for a better understanding of both the story they wrote and the God who is its central figure and hero.

We remind the reader that this remains an effort to describe, analyze, and re-present. Decisions about belief and commitment are properly theological and personal and lie outside the scope of our assignment and of the series. We try to deal positively and sympathetically with the literature assigned to us, but exactly what we believe in theological terms, while doubtless important in the shaping of our approach, method, and results, is not germane to this discussion, and neither is what the reader believes about such matters, important as it is in influencing perceptions and inferences about the original text and the commentary. We are simply interested in *what* the text says, in *how* the editor told the story of Amos and his God.

It may be suggested or even urged that the biblical picture of the deity, with the possible exception of some books like Job and Second Isaiah and isolated theologically lofty passages elsewhere, is very little different from the portrayal of deities in the polytheistic religions of Israel's neighbors, and that by adhering to the biblical stance and style we overemphasize such similarities and do not give sufficient weight to the much more significant and important differences between the one and the other. It would be much more appropriate, they say, to present the biblical deity in the light of the best and later views, those that lean toward and may have been influenced by philosophical views emanating from Greece for example, and that a particular paradigm must be adopted, one more in keeping with later Jewish and Christian theological interpretation and exposition, than to revert to a best-forgotten and properly abandoned past.

We would prefer, however, to steer a course between what we perceive to be extremes, and which is consistent with the biblical writers' actual thinking and depicting. On the one hand they were insistent on the vast difference between their religion and that of any and all neighbors. They stressed two points, though many others are derivative from them: (1) Yahweh was the sole God worthy of the name or title, for he alone had actual power and authority. All of the other gods together were literally nothing or nobody, and they were consistently and constantly identified with images of wood and stone and anything else. Whether this is polemical

413

argument rather than accurate reasoning about pagan religion, it clearly is a sufficient expression of the standard view on the subject in the Bible. (2) Yahweh was alone, without consort or children, without companions. This point goes with the other but refutes the notion that there is any conventional mythology in the central stream of biblical tradition. There is a large host of beings in heaven, but they are all creatures, having no independent existence or power base, and in that respect they are no better off than or different from humans.

The fact that in spite of these global differences Yahweh is treated as a person and shares attributes that in other cultures are attributed to their gods is hardly surprising. In the Bible, because comparison with other gods is ruled out, the same correspondences can be noted in heavenly and earthly beings, including especially human ones. Precisely because humans are made in the image of God (and so too the angels, at least those who visit the earth) it is possible for there to be communication and mutual understanding as well as empathy, sympathy, and antipathy. The deity's personality is central to the biblical picture and does not change from the earliest to the latest sources. He may be viewed from different angles and seen under different aspects; different traits or characteristics may be emphasized in different passages; but that he is a person with the many-faceted features of personality is affirmed from first to last. So in many ways the Bible remains true to its "primitive" past and is less compatible with philosophical notions of an abstract being, or ultimate reality or ground of being. Just as there is an important and unbridgeable distance between Yahweh and the gods of Canaan, or those of Mesopotamia or Egypt or Greece or Rome, so there is at least an equal or greater distance from an Aristotelian unmoved mover, or even a Platonic Idea (or Ideal). The biblical God is always and uncompromisingly personal: he is above all a person, neither more nor less.

At the same time care is taken by the authors not to present God as merely Superman or like the gods of other religions. In the case of our root *nḥm*, an important qualification if not contradiction is introduced by the statement, made at least twice, that Yahweh does not repent because he is not a man, implying that repentance belongs to the human rather than the divine sphere and personality repertoire (see Num. 23:19; 1 Sam. 15:29). What is meant, we believe, is that Yahweh does not change his mind (= repent) the way human beings do, who often do so frivolously, capriciously, or arbitrarily, whereas Yahweh does so only for cause, as human beings should. While the case is not explained in general terms, it is clear that Yahweh's repentance is limited to situations of a certain number and kind and occurs only under certain conditions. Thus his repentance is limited entirely to his dealings with the created world and almost if not exclusively with human beings. It only takes place in response to a situation, event, or circumstance and is never initiated arbitrarily or capriciously. In other words, divine repentance is always a response to human behavior or action, and it is never undertaken or attributed to God independently of a specific human condition.

414

Overall, repentance on God's part occurs under the following conditions:

1. It can be a reaction to certain events or developments in the human scene.
2. Specifically, it can occur in response to an intervention or intercession on the part of a prophetic figure (e.g., Moses, Samuel, Amos, etc.), although it is significant that in the story of Abraham's intercession for Sodom and Gomorrah, the term *nḥm* does not occur, perhaps because there is no real change of mind on the part of the deity in the account. It seems clear that God never intended to sweep the innocent away with the guilty but would find a way to save the innocent (Lot) while punishing the guilty.
3. It can be a response to a showing of genuine repentance in word and deed on the part of people.

Divine repentance can move in either of two directions: from judgment to clemency or the other way around. It can also move in both directions sequentially, as in the instances in Amos, from judgment to forgiveness (first two visions) and then back to judgment in the interim between the two sets of visions (as expressed or reflected in the second pair). In view of the multiplicity of options and actualities, it will be of value to look at several examples scattered through the Bible; while the study is not exhaustive, it should prove to be representative. Throughout and in every case, it should be understood that the divine repentance is real; that the meaning and value of the story depend on the transaction between God and prophet, or God and people; and that if it is not real on the part of God (i.e., that he does not and cannot change his mind), then the story is a charade without significance. Admittedly we are using a metaphor, involving stories and persons that include God and humans; but within the metaphor — and we believe that nobody can get closer to the reality behind the metaphor — we must be faithful to the data. Once it is understood that Yahweh enters into the drama as fully and wholeheartedly as the other participants, then we can proceed with the analysis.

1. *Gen. 6:6-7.* The first example to claim our attention is at the beginning of the flood story in Gen. 6:6-7 (J). We read:

6 And Yahweh repented (= regretted, *wayyinnāhem*) that he had made mankind on the earth, and he afflicted himself to his heart.

7 And Yahweh said, "I will wipe out mankind, whom I have created, from the face of the earth — including man and beast, creeping things (reptiles) and birds of the skies, because I have repented *(= niḥamtî)* that I made them.

In this case the divine decision (the change of mind about the human race and other living creatures) results from the observation of human corruption and wickedness: "and Yahweh saw how great was the wickedness of mankind in the world, and that the whole structure of the thoughts of his mind was exclusively wicked at all times" (6:5). The reversal of the decisions made in the original creation comes about because of the activities of human beings, who behave wickedly and imagine more wicked things all the time. Hence the decision is reached to wipe out humanity and the rest of terrestrial life. The context is entirely clear that the fault — the evil and sinfulness — is entirely humanity's responsibility, and the punishment is aimed at mankind, and that the animal kingdom will share their fate, but only because of the close association of animals and humans. It may be observed that when the king of Nineveh and his people respond to Jonah's preaching, the domestic animals also put on sackcloth and join in the rituals and acts of repentance (Jon. 3:7-8).

The decision based on the change of will, and the pain and agony of the act of reversal of previous decisions and acts, are expressed sharply by the use of a remarkable hithpael form from the root *ṣb,* which means literally that he inflicted pain on himself (= he tortured himself or he agonized); the added phrase, "to his heart [= mind]," only strengthens the force of the affliction. Coming to a new decision was no light matter; it involved an agonizing reappraisal (as the expression goes) and was reached with great personal pain.

While the passage is commonly attributed to the J source, which is considered somewhat primitive theologically, no one can challenge the mastery of this writer as a storyteller or narrator. And while he presents the deity in highly personal terms and conveys a person who feels deeply, thinks sharply, and acts dramatically, there is nothing primitive about the stories either in content or style. Once we accept the requirements of this medium (narrative about persons), we can acknowledge the storyteller's remarkable achievement.

The decision is carried out in the course of the subsequent narrative. At the end, Yahweh makes another decision with regard to the survivors, in effect reversing or modifying the earlier one, although, strictly speaking, the latter is no longer in force once its objective has been achieved. In 8:21 (J) we read,

> And Yahweh said to his heart:
> "I will not ever again curse the earth for the sake of mankind,
>   even though the heart of man is wicked from his youth;
> and I will never again destroy all living things as I have done."

The new decision represents a shift from the preceding one in that the commitment is made to sustain life on earth not only irrespective of human behavior but in full recognition of humans' evil tendencies and proclivities:

6:5 *wᵉkol-yēṣer maḥšᵉbōṯ libbô raq raʿ kol-hayyôm*
And the entire shape of the thoughts of his heart [reason] is exclusively evil all the time.

8:21 *kî yēṣer lēḇ hā'āḏām raʿ minnᵉʿūrāyw*
Even though the shape of the heart of the human is evil from his youth.

The first statement provides support for the decision to wipe out humanity, while the second modifies the commitment never to do so again. We can speak therefore of a new decision based essentially on the same data, in which God promises not to do what was done before; thus, although the term is not used in connection with the second statement, we can speak of a second repentance or change of mind (= heart). This situation is similar to that of Amos 7–8, where the first two reversals of a decision are signaled by the use of the word "repent" *(nḥm),* but the next set of reversals is subsumed or presupposed in the next decisional statement.

2. *Exod. 32:10-14* (J). In this famous episode, Moses intercedes with God, who has decided to destroy his people in the wilderness because they have made and are worshipping a golden calf. The intercession is effective and Yahweh changes his mind, reversing the earlier decision as follows:

> 10 And now let me alone that my anger may burn against them, and that I may destroy them; then I will make you into a great nation.

> 11 And Moses placated the face of his God Yahweh. And he said, "Why, O Yahweh, should your anger be kindled against your people, whom you brought out of the land of Egypt with great strength and a mighty forearm?

> 12 Why should Egypt say as follows, 'For evil he brought them out to kill them in the mountains and to destroy them from the face of the earth.' Turn from your hot rage and repent about the evil to your people."

> 13 . . .

> 14 And Yahweh repented concerning the evil that he had said he would do to his people.

In this case the divine repentance occurs in response to the intercession of Moses, a prophetic figure. In the preceding material Yahweh told Moses that the people had made a molten calf and were worshipping it and crediting it with the deliverance from bondage in Egypt. Yahweh also told Moses that he, Yahweh, intended to destroy his people because of this unacceptable behavior and instead make Moses and his descendants into a great people. In v. 10 the writer makes it appear that Yahweh is asking Moses to release or allow him to go ahead with this plan. Whatever the possible meaning of the terms, Moses seizes the opportunity to intercede and does so effectively. Here, as indicated, Yahweh has made a decision to destroy based on the same sort of data used to reach a similar judgment to wipe out humanity in Gen. 6 (all of these passages are J). In that situation the decision to destroy was denoted as the act of repentance, Yahweh's change of mind. Clearly a similar change of mind about his act of grace, in bringing Israel out of Egypt, has taken place, and he will now punish the people who abandoned him for an idol. That decision, however, is not the one connected with divine repentance,

417

though clearly it could have been. In this case it is the next reversal that is called repentance. Moses urges God to turn back from his fierce anger and to repent about the evil that he has decided to do to his people. Yahweh in turn accedes to the interceder and reverses the decision. The situation is now back where it was before Yahweh determined to destroy the nation. But the reprieve is only temporary, because the people are still in open rebellion and obviously Yahweh will not tolerate apostasy and idolatry. Something dramatic needs to be done, and Moses prepares for drastic action. Unless there is a radical change on the part of the people, the grace period will elapse and the judgment will be reinstituted. As we have suggested, intercession can only produce a temporary reversal; the basic situation must be rectified.

Moses does two things: first, he puts an end to the apostasy by destroying the image and by taking full charge of the situation; and second, he recruits the Levites to restore his authority through a blood bath in which the ringleaders and most visible followers of the new idolatrous religion are wiped out.

Only then is Moses prepared to renew the dialogue with Yahweh. He informs the people that in order to stabilize the situation after such a traumatic experience he must attempt to atone for their great sin. Moses asks Yahweh to forgive the people and adds pressure with a threat: "If you won't, then wipe me out of your tablet which you have written" (Exod. 32:32). Yahweh is receptive but will not budge on the ultimate question of justice. The people will be spared, but the guilty parties (presumably the remaining leaders and those in responsible positions) will be punished.

We see in Exod. 32 a complex interaction between deity and people, with the prophet acting as mediator. The episode is precipitated by a deliberate and scandalous act of apostasy. The first reversal on the part of Yahweh is the decision to destroy his people. There is a curious element in the presentation, in which Yahweh asks Moses to do something (leave him alone) so that he, Yahweh, can go ahead with the decision, almost as though he were asking for Moses' approval or as though Moses were holding him back, and unless he released him he could not go ahead with it. Perhaps it implies that Yahweh wants the opposite of what he says and is really inviting Moses to take a part in the crisis. There is also the curious promise to Moses that if God destroys Israel he will nevertheless create a new nation out of Moses, thereby stressing the distinction between his faithful servant (Moses; cf. Num. 12:7) and faithless and apostate Israel. This announcement implies, but without an explicit assertion, that the decision is not as solid and firm as it might appear. In any case Moses is able to intercede effectively, and Yahweh in response reverses the judgment. Moses asks him to repent (which is explained in the words "turn from your fierce wrath"), and he does (*hnhm*, v. 12, and *wynhm*, v. 14).

As we have noted, the account does not end there. Yahweh has been persuaded to reverse his decision and to hold off from settling accounts with his people. But the reprieve is only temporary. Moses must act quickly and decisively if he is to salvage anything from the situation. If nothing is done the judgment will be reinstated, and then Moses will be unable to intercede. The situation here casts some light on the circumstances in Amos 7–8. After the first two visions and dialogues there is a reprieve, time for action on the part of the leaders and people of Israel. But the period of grace is limited, and failure to produce tangible and visible results will bring about a second reversal. In this case the principal leader, Moses, is able and willing to do something. What he does is drastic but also effective. In the days of Amos no one could be found to bring about the change, so according to Visions 3 and 4 nothing happened, the judgment was reinstituted, and in the end disaster came. The prophet was powerless to intercede a third or fourth time in the same set of circumstances. At the end of the episode in the wilderness we are reminded that repentance and forgiveness on God's part do not entirely eliminate the requirement of justice. The parting word on the subject is,

> Whoever has sinned against me, I will wipe him out of my tablet.
>
> (Exod. 32:33)

Moses' vicarious offer is politely but firmly rejected. In the end everyone must answer for himself (or herself) and be judged.

Note that Moses uses the imperative *hnḥm* in Exod. 32:12 along with *šûb*. Apparently only Moses in the Bible expresses this idea quite so forcefully, commanding God to repent. Thus we have an echo of the statement in the story in Ps. 90:13, where we read:

šûbâ yhwh 'ad-mātāy	Return Yahweh — How long?
weʰhinnāḥēm 'al-ʾaḇāḏeykā	and repent concerning your servants!

We note that Ps. 90 is attributed to Moses, thereby connecting it with the story in Exod. 32 and confirming the view that in the Bible only Moses uses such forceful language with God. While these are the only places in which *hnḥm* is used in the imperative (and furthermore addressed to God), the parallel root *šûb* is used more frequently and addressed to both God and humans. To instruct God to repent (using this verb with its connotations and overtones) is a privilege claimed by Moses and restricted to him.

Amos will also use the imperative but of a different verb, focusing attention on the resultant action ("forgive") rather than on the prior decision ("turn and repent").

3. *1 Sam. 15:11, 29, 35.* These verses tell the story of Saul's rejection by Yahweh, as transmitted through Samuel. It is the third story about divine repentance in which the root *nḥm* is used. The interactions between deity and prophet, and prophet and king, and the significance especially of the radical disjuncture between vv. 11 and 35, which form an envelope around the rejection story itself, and v. 29,

419

which offers a drastically different insight into the nature of God, all require careful attention, but we will limit our study to the specific occurrences of *nḥm* and refer to the rest of the narrative as needed.

10 And the word of Yahweh came to Samuel as follows:

11 I have repented [regretted = changed my mind] about making Saul king because he has turned from following me and my commands he has not established [= carried out].

At the end of the story we read the following (v. 35), "And Yahweh repented *(niḥām)* that he had made Saul king over Israel."

In this story the repentance of God, i.e., the reversal of his decision to make Saul king, comes about because of Saul's failure to carry out the divine command concerning the Amalekites, in not slaughtering the captured cattle and in keeping alive the king, Agag, who had been taken prisoner. Thus the divine repentance is spontaneous, as in the first story in Genesis. The sinful or rebellious behavior of a man or of mankind initiates a sequence in which Yahweh reconsiders a previous decision and then makes a new decision, reversing the former one. In the light of new evidence, and because Saul has failed in his responsibility as the anointed king of Israel, he is now rejected. The new decision is communicated to Samuel, who as prophet and messenger of Yahweh must deliver the message to Saul.

The details are spelled out in the remarkable colloquy recorded in vv. 12-26, in which Samuel makes the charge that Saul has disobeyed the specific command of Yahweh, while Saul tries to defend his action and himself. Finally Samuel pronounces the dire words, "Because you rejected the word of Yahweh he has rejected you from being king" (v. 23).

Saul then concedes that he is at fault and begs for forgiveness, which is the appropriate procedure under the circumstances (vv. 24-25). But Samuel refuses to accept the confession and plea, and merely repeats the condemnation:

SAUL: "I have sinned; indeed I have transgressed the command of Yahweh and your words, because I feared the people and listened to what they said. But now forgive my sin and return with me so that I may supplicate Yahweh." (vv. 24-25)

SAMUEL: "I will not return with you, because you rejected the word of Yahweh and Yahweh has rejected you from being king over Israel." (v. 26)

The situation here is significantly different from the case with Moses and the golden calf. In the latter Moses interceded with God and secured a reprieve of the sentence and a grace period during which remedial action could be taken. In the current episode Samuel is not in a position to intercede, though it is possible that he attempted to do so the night before, when Yahweh informed him of the decision

420

to reject Saul. That at least is a reasonable interpretation of the statement that Samuel was upset and cried out to Yahweh all night long (1 Sam. 15:11). The next day, however, it was too late. For Samuel the issue is now settled, and his role is to carry out his mandate and deliver the judgment of God. We might suppose that if Saul's confession and repentance were genuine Yahweh might relent; but that opportunity is not offered either. Nevertheless, the prophet is in an awkward situation. While Saul was chosen to be king and anointed by Samuel, at Yahweh's instigation and with his approval, the prophet still has been troubled by the latter's behavior and finds reason to support Yahweh's latest decision.

On the face of it Samuel is simply representing the deity and reporting the latter's decision, but in an important sense it is also the prophet's decision. As we know from other stories, Samuel was regarded as an effective intercessor with the deity (cf. 1 Sam. 7:5-9), and he had a reputation in this respect that linked him with Moses and persisted through the centuries (cf. Jer. 15:1). His attempt at intercession in behalf of Saul had failed, and the latter's repentance came too late. The case is much like the one reported by Jeremiah about his own efforts on behalf of Judah. Yahweh forbade him to intercede because the matter had been decided and would not be changed. There is no evidence to suggest that Saul's repentance was hypocritical or false, though his attempts at self-defense are dismissed peremptorily by the prophet. Samuel does not question the sincerity or genuineness of Saul's repentance; he only says it is meaningless because it is too late. Yahweh has made a firm decision, an irreversible one; and while Saul may live out his days as king, he has been permanently rejected.

There is an important insight here into the nature and process of divine repentance. The contrast between an act of repentance that is a change of mind by God one day and the refusal even to consider a change the next day, in the same episode but with a dramatic shift in the position of the affected party, illustrates the conviction that divine repentance is neither automatic nor predictable (or compellable). God cannot be forced to change his mind once made up, and he cannot be prevented from changing it if he chooses. In this case one reversal is occasioned by Saul's failure to carry out orders, but a second reversal is refused even though Saul has confessed and repented on his own.

The outcome here is very different from what we saw in the other cases. Moreover, there is an added complication. When Saul appeals for a third time, v. 27, Samuel rebuffs him yet again, thus making the decision in the human and literary sphere final and irrevocable. Just as Saul has inadvertently torn the corner of Samuel's robe, so Yahweh has deliberately torn the kingship of Israel away from Saul. Then Samuel adds the following in v. 29: "And indeed the Eternal One of Israel does not lie and does not repent, for he is not a man that he should repent [= change his mind]."

Several things must be said about this statement. It is offered as an explanation or justification of Samuel's rejection of Saul's repentance and as an affirmation

421

that Yahweh has made an irreversible decision in Saul's case. The general argument is that Yahweh is not a human being and hence neither lies nor repents. Human beings may be expected to do one or the other — especially to change their minds — or to do both, but not God. In view of the fact that, in the same story as well as elsewhere, not only is God said to change his mind but it is essential to the understanding of his relation to his world and especially to his people that he should be able to change his position so as to respond properly to changing circumstances, it is very difficult to comprehend such an unqualified statement, which seems to be in direct conflict with the other view. It is particularly paradoxical in this context because the story is one of divine repentance, in which it is stated explicitly not once but twice (vv. 11, 35) that Yahweh has repented about having made Saul king.

Except for the fact that the statement in v. 29 has a general and timeless or permanent quality, we could explain the apparent contradiction in the following way: Yahweh clearly changed his mind about Saul and repented that he had made Saul king. That event is essential to the story, and we cannot dispense with the divine decision in this matter or deny that it reversed a previous decision, namely, to choose Saul as king. Further, when Saul pleads for forgiveness and expresses his own change of heart and mind, the prophet rejects this act of repentance, or states rather that Yahweh has rejected it, perhaps as an instance of too little and too late. Certainly there can be no quarrel with a divine decision not to change, any more than one can quarrel with a decision to change. Of all persons, Yahweh himself must be free to make his own decisions, so that the element of repentance, the willingness to reconsider, carries with it the ability and right to reverse a previous decision, also to confirm it and not reverse it. The fact that a refusal in the face of an act of repentance on the human side runs counter to the usual and repeated statements about God's willingness to forgive penitent sinners and eagerness to accept and restore them to favor is an important comment on the general position. Saul too is a special case, not least because of his status and the high standard of expectation and responsibility that a king must fulfill. But we must go beyond this point and deal with the general scope and implication of the statement that "the Eternal One of Israel does not lie and does not repent, because he is not a man to repent" (1 Sam. 15:29). The statement here is very similar to one in Num. 23:19, where it is said, "El is not a man *('îš)* that he should dissemble *(wîkazzēb)* or a human being *(ben-'ādām)* that he should repent *(weyitneḥām)*." The accompanying line (v. 19b) shows that what is meant by the statement concerns God's reliability and consistency, "Shall he say something and not do it / or speak and not establish it?" The conclusion would be in both places that God is different from man in that he is faithful and just; he does what he says he will do. He does not say one thing and do another, neither does he change his mind for frivolous reasons or no reason. He is not capricious or arbitrary but is truthful, consistent, and reliable. In that sense he does not repent: he does not change his mind and then change it again without cause.

We have added the last phrase in order to emphasize that in the Bible Yahweh does change his mind and does repent. But human beings repent or change their minds for bad reasons as well as good ones, for real reasons and for fake reasons or no reason. To be more explicit, humans may repent hypocritically and falsely, and they may pretend or deceive. The association of *nḥm* with *šqr* in Samuel and with *kzb* in Numbers carried a pejorative and suspicious tone, as if to say that *nḥm* may be a questionable activity on the part of humans. Whether in words or prayers, repentance may be, as it often is, a sham. Divine repentance, on the contrary, has nothing in common with this sort of activity. When Yahweh repents, it is always for cause and is never deceptive or false. The reality is that there is an important difference between divine repentance and the human variety; at the same time, there is a significant similarity, for otherwise the same word would not be used.

So we are left with the apparent paradox: Yahweh has repented in the case of Saul as he has and will in other cases recorded in the Bible, but at the same time he is God and not human and is therefore not given to repenting or prevarication (= lying, dissembling, misrepresenting). In the end, it may be truer to affirm both statements and risk contradiction instead of asserting one and explaining away the other, in order to achieve a false or superficial consistency. In the story at any rate, the meaning is clear: Yahweh has repented that he made Saul king and has rejected his continuation as king (although in fact Saul will continue to be king for a long time yet). When Saul apologizes, confesses, and renews his obedience, Yahweh through Samuel nevertheless rejects these actions and confirms the decision that he had made previously. The story concludes with the statement that Yahweh repented (changed his mind) that he had made Saul king.

In comparing this story with the episode of the golden calf, aside from significant differences in the details and circumstances, we observe the radically different roles played by Moses and Samuel. In both instances there is divine repentance and a decision to reject the people or a man formerly chosen and blessed. While *nḥm* is used in different places in each story, the pattern is similar at a certain point in the crisis. Once Yahweh has made a new decision, whether to destroy Israel or to reject Saul, he reveals this information to his prophet, Moses or Samuel. Moses responds by interceding on behalf of his people. That intercession is accepted. The decision is suspended, thus allowing Moses time to salvage and ultimately to rectify the situation. While the final outcome is not clear-cut, in any case the people are saved. And we can say that without Moses' intervention the rescue operation could not have taken place.

With respect to the other situation, Samuel does not intervene successfully, though he apparently tried very strenuously to do so. Yahweh rejected the intervention. There is no further divine reversal, and the judgment against Saul is allowed to stand. Had Moses acquiesced in the divine decision against Israel, then Israel would have suffered the consequences, for the intention and decision on both sides of the conversation must be taken seriously, at face value. They meant what they said, also what they did not say. Had Samuel interceded successfully on behalf of Saul as Moses had done for his people, the outcome would have been very different, although Saul would still have had to repent. We cannot say certainly, for God is free to change or stand by a decision; but the possibility remains. Both parties are free to make and change decisions or to influence the outcome. In the end the prophet must do as he is told, but until a final determination is made he may speak as he pleases. In this respect the two stories complement each other and show the dynamics of the relationship of deity and prophet, how they affect and influence each other and how decisions are shaped by this mutual interaction. The specific act of repentance in each case is quite different, though we can identify similar stages in the development of each episode. In the exodus story the divine repentance comes only after Moses' intervention and as a direct result of his imperative pleading: "Turn back from your fierce anger and repent . . ." (Exod. 32:12).

In the Samuel story, the divine repentance is prior to the notification of the prophet. Intercession is not successful on this occasion, and the verdict that resulted from the prior change of mind stands. In both cases, curiously enough, the action or inaction of the prophet confirms the decision reached by the act of repentance. In Moses' case, the prophet induces the act; in Samuel's case, the prophet confirms the act already taken.

If there is any concern about the relation between the private transaction involving prophet and deity and the actual course of external history, at least insofar as we can recover it from the Bible, there is an important correlation. Moses was able to salvage the movement and the faith of Israel in spite of the gravest crisis of the whole experience. The story of the golden calf struck at the heart of the new faith and the new community, and drastic and determined action was necessary. Moses' intervention at the earthly level was as successful as it was at the heavenly level; and although the cost was high, the damage was contained and Israel survived.

In Saul's case, the break between him and Samuel was clearly damaging to the former. Although he was able to hang onto his throne until he lost his life in battle with the Philistines, Saul clearly was on the losing side in the struggle to maintain his kingdom and his dynasty. Samuel acted consistently with his vision. After intervening unsuccessfully, he acquiesced in the divine repentance over Saul and transmitted the message by word and deed. His break with Saul was a message of rejection that translated the divine repudiation into historical terms. The biblical writers were able to trace the decline and fall of the dynasty from that point. In the same way, the story of Samuel's secret anointing of David also reflects at ground level the heavenly decision to transfer the royal mandate from Saul to someone else.

In summary, we can see that the two stories about Moses and Samuel and the roles of the prophets in them complement each other, though different actions and stages are emphasized. We may outline them as follows.

1. Background: in light of a divine prohibition (Exodus) or command (Samuel), there is a violation on the part of the people (they made and worship an idol) or the leader (Saul fails to carry out the rules of holy war).

2. Yahweh repents or changes his decision about the lawbreaker(s). Thus he decides to destroy the people he has brought out of Egypt into the wilderness, and he decides to reject Saul, the person he had previously chosen to be king.

3. Yahweh informs the prophet of his decision. Moses intercedes on behalf of the people, reproves the deity, and urges him to repent (change his mind or reverse the decision). Samuel apparently attempts the same thing, interceding to secure a reversal of the divine decision, and cries all night in an effort to reinstate Saul as Yahweh's anointed.

4. Moses is successful in his intervention, while Samuel fails in his intercession. Yahweh repents with respect to the people, thereby providing Moses with an opportunity to rectify the situation and to secure the people's repentance, which in turn will satisfy God's requirements. Samuel, however, is unsuccessful, and Yahweh's decision stands. The deity will not be dissuaded: Saul is rejected and will not be reinstated.

5. Moses brings the words of the divine repentance to the people and they in turn repent, while the final issue is yet to be decided. In the case of Samuel, he brings Saul word of the latter's rejection. Saul repents, confesses his fault, and seeks forgiveness and restoration to divine favor, but to no avail. Samuel assures him that the decision, having been made and confirmed by a divine utterance, is irrevocable.

Taken together, the stories portray the different ways in which a crisis of obedience in the relations between God and his people may be mediated by a prophet. The lesson to be learned is that Yahweh's judgments are his own, as is his repentance. The prophet may intercede, as in fact Moses and Samuel do, but Yahweh is free to respond positively (in the case of Moses and the people) or negatively (in the case of Samuel and Saul). The same is true of the response to human repentance. Yahweh may respond favorably (in the story of Moses and the golden calf) or unfavorably (in the case of Saul and Samuel). The outcome remains in doubt until Yahweh seals the decision by his action.

4. *2 Sam. 24:16 = 1 Chr. 21:15.* The passage in question is substantially the same in both texts and reads as follows: "Then the angel stretched forth his hand at Jerusalem to destroy it, and Yahweh repented concerning the evil and he said to the angel who had been attacking the people: 'It is enough now. Lower your arm.' "

Yahweh's repentance here is not the result of prophetic intercession or of any act of repentance on the part of the people. It is spontaneous in that he sees the effect of the judgment he himself pronounced on Israel, because of King David's sin, and suspends further punishment. The specific punishment itself was the result of a choice on David's part. He was told to choose among three disastrous consequences: seven years of drought and famine, or three months of military defeats at the hands of his enemies, or three days of pestilence and plague. He chose the last, with the interesting remark that it was better to fall into the hands of Yahweh, because his mercy is great, than to fall into the hands of humans (v. 14). This comment only explains the rejection of the second option, but the other choice, between the first and the third, is not explained. It is not much of a choice, but one would suppose that the lightning strategist and decisive man of action would choose a disaster that was over quickly so that one could recover and rebuild, instead of the protracted, debilitating experience of a seven-year drought, which in the long run might cause even greater suffering and death. So he chose the plague. On the first day, seventy thousand are said to have fallen (v. 15). Then presumably on the next day (or possibly at the end of the first, for the plague continued until the *minḥā,* the late afternoon sacrifice, which leaves only a short time until the beginning of the new day at sundown), when the angel stretched out his arm against Jerusalem to devastate it by a new attack of the same plague, Yahweh repented (changed his mind, reversed the decision) and stayed the plague. As far as we are aware it was not resumed.

This case is just the opposite of the decision in Gen. 6, where, as a result of human sin, Yahweh painfully reverses the decision to create humanity and decides to destroy them. Here it is the prospect of disastrous destruction in the holy city, Jerusalem, that disturbs him, and he reverses the decision, thus sparing the city and the rest of the country from the ravages of the plague. No doubt the effect of the previous day's slaughter is also to be reckoned with.

The story itself is rather complicated, and there is a special problem arising from a divergence between the account in 2 Samuel and the one in 1 Chronicles. In the former it is Yahweh who incites David to take the notorious census of the nation, because he (Yahweh) is very angry at Israel and clearly wishes to inflict great harm on the nation (2 Sam. 24:1). In the Chronicles version, however, nothing is said of these circumstances; rather, the idea of conducting a census originates with Satan, who then incites David to go ahead with it. In both accounts the sequel is the same. David proceeds with the census in spite of Joab's misgivings and reluctance, and finally it is completed. Then David acknowledges that he has committed a great sin, but his confession does not result in remission or cancellation of the judgment, only in the offer of a choice among the three devastating punishments mentioned earlier.

Our concern is primarily with the act of repentance on the part of God and not with the beginning of the story, but because the question of the originator of the census idea is presented in dramatic form we must consider it briefly. In the Samuel account it is made clear that Yahweh was looking for an occasion to punish his people, which was the intention behind the census proposal. Once the census was carried out, then the punishment was justified, presumably because conducting a census was contrary to the proper worship and service of the deity. We must consider too the reason for the elaborate procedure in order to justify punishment and vent the divine anger. The implication would seem to be that there was insufficient cause for punishing Israel and that the anger arose for some other reason and was itself not justified or merited by the behavior of king or people. This investigation leads to a much more tangled and complex collection of problems, and it is perhaps better to let it drop. The shift from Yahweh to Satan in Chronicles no doubt reflects a similar judgment on the part of the Chronicler. Because Satan's hostility to humanity generally and to Israel in particular was axiomatic in earlier days and explicit in later ones (in Israelite thought), there was no problem in attributing this malicious move to the archprosecutor of mere mortals. By contrast, the attribution of this act to Yahweh himself could only cause troubling thoughts about motives and intentions, along with an intense curiosity and concern about the unexplained hostility against his own people. In the end, however, the Chronicler's solution does not really solve the basic problem, though it does shift attention from the deity to a subordinate. If indeed Satan is an officer of the divine court, the first officer in many respects, i.e., the chief prosecuting attorney, then it is clear that the agent cannot be entirely independent of the court (and its ruler) that he serves, and whether he acts on his own or is under orders, the one he reports to (and in the Hebrew Bible there is no question about that point: he invariably reports to God, is answerable to him, and is under divine authority) has ultimate authority over him and is answerable for what he does. The Chronicler only shifted the focus of the problem, not the problem itself. And the problem of external evil, not man-made and presumably not god-made either, remains as a substantive concern for all monotheistic religions.

The reason that this matter of the beginning of the story affects our understanding of the divine repentance is that the unresolved anger that underlies the whole account is itself resolved by the repentance in v. 16. The repentance reflects a reversal of the decision to punish, which itself arose out of the hot wrath mentioned in v. 1. The proximate cause of the repentance was the appalling prospect of the punishment imposed by Yahweh and elected by David. Certainly that threat was the triggering factor, but underneath there must also have been a resolution of the initiating anger. The decision to punish was reversed by divine repentance, and thus the cloud in the relationship was removed. As we are not told anything about the original cause, we equally know nothing of the reason for its removal. While the initial phase of the punishment was directly caused by the census, it could also have stimulated a reconsideration of the whole situation and thus have led the way to a complete reversal, not only of further punishment but of the anger directed at Israel in the first place. Then it may be easier to understand the later phases of the story: the purchase of the threshing floor from Araunah, the offering of sacrifices, and the consecration of the place as the future site of the temple. These actions constitute the necessary prelude to the climactic act of the joint reigns of David and Solomon, namely, the erection of the temple in Jerusalem; but before the latter could be undertaken, the divine anger and the peril of the people had to be resolved.

Thus the underlying issue was only brought to the surface by the census matter, and this problem was the one that had to be settled, and was, through the repentance of Yahweh.

While that decision could only be regarded as a suspension of the agreed-upon punishment, David interceded with Yahweh in order to make it permanent and thus permit the initiation of the great temple project. In a proposal similar to that of Moses in Exod. 32, David exculpates the people who are the innocent victims all around: they are the target of both the divine anger and the census that was David's idea, so David urges that Yahweh exonerate the people and vent whatever remains of his anger or demand for satisfaction on David and his house. There is no direct response from God, but the subsequent activity in preparing the sacred place and offering sacrifices shows that David's offer was not taken up, but a general amnesty declared instead. At the very end, the efforts at reconciliation proved successful, as the last words of the chapter demonstrate: "And Yahweh was appeased [heeded the supplications] for the land, and the plague was restrained from upon Israel" (2 Sam. 24:25).

In this situation, Yahweh's spontaneous repentance not only averts the further depredations of the plague but also overcomes the unexplained hostility and anger of the deity and opens the way for the renewed reconciliation of God and people and the establishment of the temple at Jerusalem.

5. *Jer. 26:3, 13, 19.* There are a number of passages in the book of Jeremiah in which the term is used: 15:6; 18:8; 18:10; 20:16; 42:10; and 26:3, 13, and 19. We will deal with most of them briefly and more extensively with the last.

a. Jer. 15:6: "You abandoned me, oracle of Yahweh, you kept going backwards. So I stretched out my hand against you and I destroyed you, (because) I was weary of relenting [repenting, *hinnāḥēm*]."

The reference is to Jerusalem and must date from the period of the final capture and destruction of that city. The statement is revealing about Yahweh's final decision, apparently at the end of a long series of reversals and changes of mind. There would, however, be another change — at least one — later on.

b. Jer. 18:7-10, the philosophy of divine repentance:

7 Any time that I speak concerning a nation or concerning a kingdom to pluck up and tear down and destroy,

8 and that nation turns from its wickedness . . . then I will repent [*wᵉniḥamtî*] concerning the evil that I planned to do to it.

9 And any time I speak concerning a nation or a kingdom to build and to plant;

10 and it does what is evil in my sight by not listening to my voice, then I will repent [*wᵉniḥamtî*] concerning the good that I said that I would do to make things good for it.

This statement embodies the general theory of divine repentance in the Hebrew Bible and expresses it as succinctly and directly as we can imagine it being done. Further elaboration in specific details would only cover additional possibilities, but this basic statement deals with the essentials. Divine repentance moves in either direction — from good to bad or vice versa — and on a convincing showing by the human party. The governing principle is applied impartially to any and all nations.

c. Jer. 20:16, no repentance: "And let that man be like the cities that Yahweh overturned *[hāpak]* because he did not repent *[weloʾ niham]*."

This passage is an interesting comparison and an unusual comment. The reference is to the man who reported the prophet's birth to his father as a happy event. It is a strange curse, but our interest is in the comment about Yahweh's destruction of the cities of the plain (there is no question about what the prophet has in mind because the verb here, *hpk,* is used specifically of the catastrophe that engulfed Sodom and Gomorrah and the other cities of the plain). The added words are, "he did not repent [= change his mind]." This statement not only affirms the unswerving decision to destroy, but may be an allusion to the discussion with Abraham about the fate of the cities, with the comment that in the end Yahweh did not change his mind. Strictly speaking, the discussion in Gen. 18 does not involve the theme of repentance (and certainly not the root *nhm*). In the first place, Yahweh says that he has come down to evaluate the evidence for and against the cities, so a decision has not been reached. But Abraham — who obviously knows the conditions in the cities or has a good idea about what the decision will be if made strictly on the merits of the case — begins to bargain with Yahweh in order to save the cities and their inhabitants. While Yahweh ultimately agrees with Abraham's final figure, the whole discussion happens before the investigation is completed and before a judgment is made. The subsequent event, the destruction of the cities, tells us what the decision was, which also included the provision to remove Lot and his family, perhaps partly because Lot was a resident alien and not directly involved in the crimes of the local people, but also because of Abraham's righteousness. What Abraham had urged was that the cities be saved with all of their wicked people in them for the sake of the righteous; but Yahweh's agreement to this stipulation was nullified by the failure to find even the minimum number, ten. The solution achieved by Yahweh was to avoid the legitimate charge that it would be unjust to sweep away the righteous with the guilty. Presumably Yahweh had no intention of doing so because it would violate the underlying principle on the basis of which the judgment against the cities was being made. But this solution, to rescue the righteous, would only be applicable after Abraham's remedy proved inoperative. In any case, the reference in Jer. 20:16 is to the decision to destroy the cities. Once that decision was made, God did not repent or relent. But why say it, especially because there is not the slightest evidence of any change on the part of the people of the cities? We suspect that the statement may reflect the divine response to some further intercession on Abraham's part. It is clear that Abraham hoped to save the cities, not just his nephew Lot and his family. Having failed in the ingenious attempt to save the cities by an argument about the presence of enough righteous people in them, he may have tried some other argument or more likely appealed to the grace and mercy of the sovereign. This course of action certainly would have been in character for the patriarch, who, like Moses and Samuel, was famous for his intercessory powers (cf. Gen. 20:7, 17). But the hypothetical plea was rejected; Yahweh did not repent, and that is what Jeremiah is referring to in this passing comment.

d. Jer. 26:3, 13, 19, repentance in the temple court.

If the passage in ch. 18 gives us a working definition of divine repentance in the world and life of nations, the story in ch. 26 is a prime illustration of the doctrine in action, how it worked on that extraordinary day when Jeremiah showed up at the temple with a message from Yahweh (to which an obvious parallel with Amos's experience at Bethel can be drawn). The significant passages are to be found in vv. 3, 13, and 19, which can be read as follows:

> 3 Perhaps they will listen and they will turn each one from his wicked way, and then I will repent concerning the evil that I was planning to do to them on account of the wickedness of their doings.

The reference is to the message that Jeremiah is to deliver to the people at the temple (cf. also ch. 7) and the possible response of the people to that message. Yahweh is prepared to repent after finding satisfactory evidence of a genuine turning on the part of the people from their wicked ways.

> 13 And now make good your ways and your works, and listen to the voice of Yahweh your God, and [then] Yahweh will repent concerning the evil that he declared [he would do] concerning you.

This passage is part of Jeremiah's oracle to the people and embodies the private expression of the same message in v. 3:

> 19 Did Hezekiah the king of Judah and all Judah even think of putting him [Micah] to death? Did he not fear Yahweh and appease the countenance of Yahweh; then Yahweh repented concerning the evil that he spoke about them. But we are about to do a great evil against ourselves.

This verse is the climax of the episode, in which the citation of Micah's well-known words about the destruction of Jerusalem becomes the rallying point for the defenders of the beleaguered prophet Jeremiah, and he is saved from the wrath of the priests and prophets. The point being made is that when Micah made the prophecy, the king and people responded, not by efforts to put him to death, but by acts of repentance, and that these acts in turn evoked a comparable repentance (using the word *nhm*) on the part of Yahweh, who changed his mind and reversed the decision announced by the prophet Micah. The passage from Micah (3:12) is quoted verbatim, a significant point because it was remembered long after it had been uttered and its current applicability had been exhausted. It constitutes one of the major unfulfilled prophecies of the 8th century, a fact that did nothing to discredit the prophet. On the contrary, his prophecy created a more important result through the dynamics of repentance both human and divine, even if in the process the prophecy itself remained unfulfilled. An explanation is offered here for the fact that in spite of the overwhelming Assyrian invasion, the city of Jerusalem was spared, while the sister city, Samaria, had been destroyed. Different explanations are offered in the Bible, and Sennacherib, the Assyrian king, offers one through his emissary that has the advantage of being contemporary and the disadvantage of being self-serving. Proximity in time does not guarantee a similar proximity to the truth, although where the biblical and Assyrian accounts agree we can reasonably conclude that the special interests on both sides have been neutralized and that we have the facts. Both Sennacherib and the Bible refer to a huge indemnity paid by Hezekiah, while the books of Isaiah and Kings add a possible second campaign along with a highly militant angel who does not merely disperse but slaughters the whole Assyrian army. In any case the city was spared, the dynasty continued, and in Jeremiah's day the nation's survival was seen as a vindication of the doctrine of mutual and interactive repentance.

e. Jer. 42:10, the promise:

> If you will surely remain in this land, then I will build you up and I will not wreck [you], and I will plant you, and I will not pluck you up; because I have repented concerning the evil that I did to you.

The scene is set after the destruction of the city and during the turmoil following the assassination of Gedaliah, the governor appointed by Nebuchadrezzar as a replacement for Zedekiah, the last and now removed king, to look after the remaining population and to represent the Babylonian authority. A group led by Johanan ben-Kareah decides to abandon the land and seek refuge in Egypt, partly at least because they fear Babylonian reprisals for the murder of Gedaliah and a number of Babylonian officials by Ishmael, a royal prince who has fled in the other direction. Before acting on this decision they ask Jeremiah for advice, i.e., to intercede for them with Yahweh and to find out what Yahweh wishes them to do. The verse quoted is part of the answer. The story is told at length in chs. 42–43, but the gist of it is that Jeremiah assures them that Yahweh has already repented of the harm done to Judah and Jerusalem. He has changed his mind and wishes them to stay in the land. He forbids them to go to Egypt, which they would like to do, but promises to build them up and plant them if they stay where they are. Furthermore, he tells them that he will influence Nebuchadrezzar on their behalf so that the Babylonian emperor will treat them kindly and allow them to remain in the land. He promises them that if they stay, they will prosper and flourish.

431

Johanan and the others reject the message from Jeremiah and claim that he was unduly influenced by Baruch, who had his own nefarious reasons for wanting them to stay and be punished by Nebuchadrezzar. So they go off to Egypt, despising the word of the prophet, and, adding insult to injury, drag him and Baruch along with them. With the close of this narrative in the book of Jeremiah (in ch. 44), the group vanishes from the pages of history, swallowed up in the land of the Nile.

Regrettably, they did not take advantage of the opportunity to test the repentance of Yahweh, pronounced by Jeremiah along with the divine promise of respite and renewal in the land. We are left with an unrealized commitment in the form of an act of repentance, a change of mind about a historic event of the gravest proportions — the destruction of the city of Jerusalem, the temple in the city, the disappearance of the nation, and the captivity of its leading citizens. Already in the few months since that catastrophe, Yahweh, according to Jeremiah, was ready and willing to begin again with the remnant left behind.

6. *Joel 2:12-14.* This passage is an important instance of double repentance:

12 And also now, it is the oracle of Yahweh, Return to me with all your heart, and with fasting and with weeping and with lamentation.

13 And tear open your hearts, and not [only] your garments, and return to Yahweh your God for he is the embodiment of grace and compassion, long-suffering [= very patient] and one who repents concerning evil.

14 Who knows if he will turn around and repent, and leave behind him a blessing

The prophet urges the people to return, return to Yahweh their God. Then comes the classic description of Yahweh as the epitome of grace and compassion. He is the personification of these attributes, and the terms used are unequivocally applied to him. The passage is a paraphrase of Yahweh's description of himself in his revelation to Moses at the mountain in Sinai (Exod. 34:6-7). Not included there is the phrase $w^e niḥām$ $ʿal$-$hārāʿâ,$ "and a repenter over the evil" (the form is a niphal participle masculine singular). On this occasion Yahweh's known tendency to the compassionate virtues, celebrated repeatedly in similar passages, is expanded to include repentance.

While the number of actual instances is small, the indication has been given that if the evidence warrants, Yahweh is prepared to repent, i.e., to change his mind about the evil — the evil that he has done or plans to do. The vital condition is repentance on the part of the people who seek Yahweh's repentance, only the word $nḥm$ is not used of the people here, but the more basic and general $šwb$ ("turn, return, turn around"). The same term is used of Yahweh in the concluding statement, "Who knows whether he will *turn* and repent . . . ?"

No one can be sure, and Yahweh alone always retains his sovereign freedom to decide and to do as he pleases. Nevertheless, the introductory "Who knows?"

432

is not a neutral expression and certainly does not have a negative expectation. It is a polite way of expressing a positive hope for an affirmative response without being overbearing. And the prophet's expectation has already been expressed in his characterization of Yahweh as "one who [normally or characteristically] repents over evil" *(nḥm 'l-hr'h),* "one whose nature it is to repent over evil." It would be out of character for Yahweh not to respond positively to repentance on the part of the people. Repentance, in short, is mutual and interactive. One stimulates the other and produces reconciliation and the exchange of blessings.

7. *Jon. 3:9-10; 4:1-2.* Here we find another example of double repentance:

3:9 "Who knows whether God will turn and repent, and turn from his hot anger so that we will not perish?"

10 And God saw their works, that they had turned from their wicked way, and God repented concerning the evil that he had said he would do to them and he did not do [it].

4:1 And the matter was a great evil to Jonah, and he was very upset.

2 So he prayed to Yahweh and he said, "Alas Yahweh was not this my word while I was still on my own soil? Therefore I went directly to escape to Tarshish, because I know that you are God, gracious and compassionate, long suffering and very kind [full of lovingkindness] and one who repents of evil."

The passage here is verbally related to the one in Joel. The difference is that the theory of double repentance is fleshed out in a story in Jonah, while in Joel it is in the form of a prophetic utterance or oracle. In this account the truth of Jeremiah's general statement about Yahweh's willingness to repent (Jer. 18:8-10) is confirmed in an international setting, and the characterization of Yahweh as "the one who repents over evil" is attested by an actual experience (within the story form used).

The passage in Jonah uses many of the same words as the one in Joel but in a slightly different order. And the story in Jonah is much more detailed. The repentance of king, people, and cattle is spelled out in full and provides the basis for God's repentance.

The question "Who knows whether God will turn and repent?" is the transition to the affirmation that when he saw that the people really had turned around from their wicked ways to a new way, he was convinced and reversed the decision he had made about destroying the city. The sentence affirming his repentance ends with the all-important words concerning the evil he had planned to do: "he did not do [it]."

The words of the credo are still to come, those which emphasize Yahweh's grace and compassion. These words, ironically, are put in the mouth of Jonah, who is exceedingly upset and bitter about the whole affair. It is bad enough that Yahweh repents in response to repentance on the part of the Ninevites, but worse that he,

433

Jonah, was dragged in as the effective mediator of possible reconciliation with people who did not deserve such benign treatment. Nevertheless, it is Jonah who recognizes and affirms the inescapable conclusion. A God who describes himself and is described as "the one who repents over the evil" clearly *will* repent over evil he has done or has planned, as in this instance, when given a chance to do so. Jonah knew this fact from the beginning, which is why, as he explains in prayer to Yahweh, he fled to Tarshish. He knew that a God known as "one who repents [= the repenter]" would do exactly that in an actual situation, and he wanted no part of it. This story confirms the impression of the similar statements in Joel. The latter prophet also knows that a God who calls himself "the repenter over the evil" will do so in fact when people test him with a genuine repentance. The people of Jerusalem and Judah can expect as good a response from their God as the Ninevites received from the same God.

8. *Zech. 8:14-15.* Here there is first no repentance and then repentance.

14 For thus has said Yahweh of Hosts, "As I planned to do evil to you when your fathers provoked me," said Yahweh of hosts, "and I did not repent *(weĺō᾽ niḥāmtî).*

15 Indeed I have turned. I have planned in these days to do good to Jerusalem and the house of Judah. Do not be afraid!"

The interest of this passage lies in the juxtaposition of the flat assertion "I did not repent" with the affirmation that he has now reversed that decision, and as he planned evil in the past so now he plans to do good to Jerusalem and the house of Judah. This is a case in which God did not repent, but it was followed in due course by an act of divine conversion *(šwb):* not precisely repentance *(nḥm),* but the effect is the same. In all likelihood the prophet avoids using the same term twice in succession for purely stylistic reasons. It may also be that the shift in direction is not quite the same as repentance because the judgment against Jerusalem was actually carried out and the punishment inflicted. It still requires a new decision to do good to those who have been on the receiving end of bad. Such a decision is called a turning, and the same expression is used in conjunction with *nḥm* elsewhere to describe Yahweh's change of attitude to those who survived the destruction of the city.

In the end the city was destroyed because, as said here, Yahweh did not repent; he did not rescind the order to wreck the place. The reason, however, was that there was no initiating action on the part of the people, a showing in good faith of repentance on their part. Throughout all of this material, the repentance of God is conditioned by the behavior of people who are the potential beneficiaries or victims of divine repentance.

9. A few passages remain to be considered. Their content does not affect the findings already discussed in any significant manner, but there may be value in completing the list.

a. Judg. 2:18: And if Yahweh established for them judges, Yahweh would be with the judges and deliver them from the hand of their enemies all the days of the [= that] judge, because Yahweh repented on account of their outcry because of their oppressors and mistreaters.

The statement here is part of a description of the general pattern developed by the Deuteronomic historian for the sequence of Judges. This pattern is a familiar one and includes a series of stages, as follows: (A) In response to the outcry of the people, Yahweh raises up a judge who is successful in delivering the people from their oppressor. (B) The period of prosperity lasts through the lifetime and administration of the judge, and then the people rebel against Yahweh, turn to other gods, and violate their fundamental covenant commitment. (C) As punishment for their sins Yahweh brings them under the power of an oppressor. (D) Then when they have suffered for a time and cried out to Yahweh, he responds by raising up another judge to save them. Thus the cycle repeats.

As far as the book of Judges is concerned, the only time the repentance of God is mentioned as being a stage in the process is in the description in Judg. 2:16-23, at v. 18. The repentance of Yahweh comes about in response to the people's outcry on account of the oppression under which they suffer. He reverses the decision under which they are being punished and, in accordance with the new decision, raises up a deliverer. This repentance is a result of the people's outcry, but because the appeal is directed at Yahweh, it is also a sign of repentance on their part. It means that they are turning away from the gods they turned to at an earlier phase of the cycle and back to Yahweh, whom they had abandoned. Thus we can classify this example of divine repentance with those that occur as a response to repentance on the part of the people. This is a model case and stands for an unspecified number of actual instances. It is of interest, however, that the verb *nhm* is not used in any of the specific instances in the book of Judges, though a number of occasions would have been suitable for its use if they did not actually call for it. It is only in the general statement that the word is used, which may signify that it is only in retrospect, and in recovering and restructuring the history of those times according to the pattern prepared in this chapter of Judges, that the historian (or editor) identified and defined the divine action at that point in the cycle as repentance.

b. Ezek. 24:14, Yahweh unrelenting: "I, Yahweh, have spoken. It shall come to pass, and I will do it. I will not refrain [= hold back?], and I will not have pity, and I will not repent. According to your ways and according to your deeds they have judged you [*versions:* I will judge you], is the oracle of my Lord Yahweh."

The reference here is to Jerusalem, the bloody city (represented by the second feminine singular pronoun), and the specific statement is that Yahweh will not repent, he will not change his mind about the sentence of judgment. It is not surprising that the single instance of *nhm* in the niphal with God as subject in Ezekiel is a negative statement. In view of the historical context and the prophet's known opinions on the subject of Jerusalem and Judah, the king of that country, and its leadership, there is no possibility of a change of mind or heart on the part of God. The decision has been made and the judgment rendered. Divine repentance is out of the question; Jerusalem must be destroyed.

In contrast with Jeremiah, for whom divine repentance is not only a possible but even a necessary element in the dynamics of the divine-human encounter and the turbulent course of Israel's history, Ezekiel rules it out entirely. Yahweh does not repent; everything happens in accordance with his determinate will and in accordance with a plan arranged from the beginning. The judgment cannot be averted because it has been decided. But the same is true of the promised return, restoration, and renewal. They are equally determined because they also have been decided by divine decree. What he wills happens, not for the sake of the people or because of their desire or outcry, but for his own name's sake. Human repentance, while a necessary feature of the nation's restoration, does not function in the process to evoke a corresponding divine action. On the contrary, it is the end product of the divine initiative. Only afterward, when the restoration has occurred, they are back in their own land, and the new age has been inaugurated, will Israel repent and thoroughly repudiate its former evil ways (cf. Ezek. 36:22-32). But even here the term *nhm* is not used.

c. Ps. 106:45, covenantal repentance: "And he remembered for them his covenant, and he repented according to the multitude of his mercies."

The divine repentance here is connected with a cycle of vicissitudes similar to what we observed in Judg. 2:18 (here the broader statement includes vv. 34-46, in which the history of Israel is portrayed as a series of deliverances punctuated by apostasies and punishments). The point in the cycle at which it functions is in response to the people's outcry on account of their suffering under their oppressors (see vv. 40-44). The portrayal of Israel may also include the monarchic period, for there is an apparent reference to captors and captivity in v. 46, though it may be insufficiently specific to pinpoint a particular captivity. Nevertheless, the psalm may reflect the experiences of the 8th and 7th centuries, if not of the 6th. The concluding verses also express the idea of a dispersion among the nations, which implies the exilic period.

We have here not only a link with the cyclical repentance of Judg. 2 but a clear reference to the initiation of divine repentance in Israel's history and experience, when Moses interceded with God at Mt. Sinai during the crisis of the golden calf. While the word is not used, clearly that incident provided the model and established the precedent for divine repentance in dealing with Israel (cf. vv. 19-23). From an examination of this material, we propose that the portrayal of divine repentance as a constant in Israelite history and an essential attribute of the deity, whose nature it is to "repent over evil," actually derives from a single decisive incident near the beginning of the story, when Moses interceded with Yahweh to save his people from the divine anger, and uniquely commanded (i.e., the pleading imperative) the deity to repent: *hinnāḥēm . . . wayyinnāḥem* (" 'Repent . . . and he repented,' " Exod. 32:12, 14).

d. Ps. 110:4, God does not repent: "Yahweh has sworn, and he will not repent [= change his mind]."

This usage belongs in all likelihood with two passages already discussed: 1 Sam. 15:29, where it is said that Yahweh does not lie and does not repent, because he is not a man to repent; and Num. 23:19, where we have a different form of the verb (hithpael) and a synonym for *šqr,* namely *kzb,* but the sense is the same. God does not prevaricate and he does not repent. In both cases the emphasis is on the reliability of divine utterances and the assurance that not only does God not speak untruth but he does not equivocate or vacillate, in other words, change his mind. Because the context in Ps. 110:4 specifies an oath, it is clear that the same assurance is being sought and claimed. It is taken for granted that Yahweh will not lie under oath, but neither will he change his mind, i.e., depart in any way from what he has sworn.

10. There is also a small group of occurrences of the root *nḥm* with God as subject in which the hithpael is used rather than the niphal.

a. Num. 23:19, no repentance.

This passage, which is very similar to the statement in 1 Sam. 15:29, has been discussed in connection with the latter. It is a general statement about the constancy and consistency of the deity, whose word is reliable, and who neither lies nor equivocates (= changes his mind). Generally speaking, a statement like this one comes from and is directed to circumstances quite different from those in which the repentance of God is affirmed. The dramatic juxtaposition of essentially opposed or even contradictory asseverations in 1 Sam. 15:11, 29, and 35, in which the negative statement is sandwiched between repeated affirmations, may be purely coincidental and reconcilable in view of the narrative. Nevertheless, this juxtaposition serves to show that the concept was (and is) not an easy one to accommodate and use, and under any circumstances had to be qualified in such ways as to make it clear that while there were obvious points of contact and correspondence with the human varieties of repentance, there were marked differences, for certain kinds of human repentance would be excluded entirely and the rest were not exactly the same.

The two passages may be compared as follows:

Num. 23:19

lō' 'îš 'ēl wîkazzēb	Not a man is El that he should lie,
ûben-'ādām weyitneḥām	Or a human that he should repent.
hahû' 'āmar	Has he, has he said [it],
welō' ya'aśeh	and will he not do [it]?
wedibber	Or spoken [it],
welō' yeqîmennâ	and will he not establish it?

1 Sam. 15:29

wᵉgam nēṣaḥ yiśrā'ēl	and also as for the Eternal One of Israel —
lō' yᵉšaqqēr wᵉlō' yinnāḥēm	He does not lie, and he does not repent;
kî lō' 'ādām hû' lᵉhinnāḥēm	For not a man is he to repent.

The verbal links are few, but they are enough; and the ideas are the same. Num. 23:19 is more ample, but *šqr* (1 Samuel) is stronger than "lie." It means to be a traitor, and the content of Num. 23:19 shows that *kāzāb* does not specify "untruth," i.e., a statement contrary to fact. It means not to do something you said you would do. Now how can you change your mind without committing *šqr//kzb?* Or, when does changing your mind become *kzb* or *šqr?* Answer, when you swear an oath, which is what *dbr* means in Num. 23:19. All three terms come together in Ps. 89:33-37, a passage in which Yahweh swears by his holiness to support the dynasty of David. Compare *wᵉlō'-'ašaqqēr* (v. 34)//*'im-lᵉdāwīd 'ᵃkazzēb* (v. 36).

An oath (preferably two) makes all the difference. So we must locate the double oath in Amos 6:8//8:7 (clearly a matching pair) in the multifaceted scheme. It is structurally interesting that these oaths are placed where they are, and especially that the last one comes between Visions 4 and 5.

b. Deut. 32:36, there is repentance: "For Yahweh has vindicated his people, and concerning his servants he has repented."

The RSV reads "For the Lord will vindicate his people and have compassion on his servants." While the verbs are imperfect and customarily rendered as future, there is good evidence to show that in this poem they do not follow standard prose Hebrew practice but conform rather to the usage of early Hebrew poetry, in which the imperfect is normally or regularly a past tense. The sense of the passage is that Yahweh has acted in defense and on behalf of his servant people, that he has rendered judgment in their favor and executed it. In keeping with this affirmation is the motivation clause; he has acted so because he has changed his mind about them. In the preceding section of the poem, vv. 15-35, there is very harsh condemnation of Israel (vv. 15-25) followed by a transitional section concerning the enemy, and the suggestion that Yahweh has reversed his field. This suggestion is made explicit in v. 36, which affirms the new decision to vindicate his people against their enemies, rooted in his (God's) repentance, his change of mind about his servants (cf. the very similar expression in Ps. 90:13). The reversal was occasioned not by any intercession by a prophet or by any sign of repentance from the people, but rather by concern on Yahweh's part about the effect of his actions on the enemies or adversaries of Israel and a possible misperception of what has really happened (v. 27). The presentation here has echoes in the story of the golden calf and Moses' argument about why Yahweh should repent, namely, that the Egyptians will misconstrue the event and misrepresent Yahweh as the butcher of his own people without legitimate cause. Because this poem, like Ps. 90, is attributed to Moses and the resemblances between the two poems and the story in Exod. 32 (J's version) are noteworthy, we may have here some indication of the reason for the two poems being attributed to Moses. In any case, Yahweh's repentance in Deut. 32 is connected with some episode or experience in the wilderness wanderings, not after the settlement in the land (i.e., the conquest of the western territories). The central theme of the poem is the people's apostasy and idolatry, of which the classic instance in Israel's history is the making and worshipping of the golden calf. So the repentance of Yahweh in Deut. 32 may be a stylized poetic version of the repentance in the story in Exod. 32.

c. Ps. 135:14, parallel to Deut. 32:36.

The passage is identical with Deut. 32:36, as is the setting. The poem deals specifically with the early history of Israel, including the plagues in Egypt and the exodus from that country, the wanderings in the wilderness, the victories over Sihon and Og, and the settlement in Canaan. That historical survey is followed by the statement in v. 14 and doubtless has the same meaning and force that it does in Deut. 32. The passage reflects the crisis in the wilderness described in detail in Deut. 32, when Yahweh, faced with rampant apostasy, nevertheless reversed the decision to destroy his people and gave them victory over their enemies instead. Behind the whole account is the single great act of divine repentance at the beginning of Israel's existence as the people of Yahweh. It was achieved by Moses through a unique intervention in the divine process; he interceded with God, instructed the deity to repent, and thus a history of the people of God was made possible. We can still hear echoes of that constitutive event in the poems attributed to Moses, Ps. 90 and Deut. 32, and even in this psalm, though the direct connections with Moses have been removed.

Summary

In this study we have examined all instances of the verb *nḥm* in the niphal and hithpael conjugations with God as subject. Of them, the ones expressing the central meaning of repentance, change of heart and mind, have been listed and discussed. A few in which a different meaning is indicated (e.g., Isa. 1:24; 57:6) have been set aside. What are the highlights of the research?

The principal finding is that the repentance of God is an important aspect of his character and his behavior; it is mentioned frequently enough to warrant careful study. We should add that the phenomenon is more extensive than the use of the term *nḥm* itself. Thus the episode of the golden calf, which constitutes a principal example of divine repentance (Exod. 32), is also described at length in the book of Deuteronomy (ch. 9), but while the second account is essentially the same and the respective roles of Moses and Yahweh are depicted in the same way, the word itself is not used in the Deuteronomic passage, perhaps because the writer preferred not to describe the mind and will of the deity in this fashion. We recognize a similar situation in a comparison of the books of Jeremiah and Ezekiel. The two prophets share essentially the same opinion and viewpoint about the situation in Judah and Jerusalem in the fateful days before the fall of the city. Both believe that the nation and the city are under divine judgment and will suffer dreadful consequences. Both believe too that afterward there will be a return and restoration initiated and carried out by the same deity. Jeremiah speaks eloquently of the possibility of Yahweh repenting before the fall of the city if the people for their part will repent. He affirms also the reality of divine repentance after the fall, involving a promise to rebuild and replant the survivors in their own land. Ezekiel for his part has nothing to say about any of these possibilities. He does not accept the idea that Yahweh repents (the only time he uses the verb in this sense with Yahweh as subject, he also prefixes the negative particle). Yahweh simply does not and will not change his mind. As to the future, it too has been determined, but it reflects a previous decision made by the deity and not a change of mind precipitated by anything that happens in the interim after the fall of the city.

Returning to the use of *nhm* to express divine repentance, we note that God may repent by reversing a decision to do either harm or good, and that the change of mind may be a spontaneous action resulting from observing and reacting to a variety of situations in the world. Thus, as a result of observing the corruption in the world after the creation of humanity he repents that he made man and makes the decision to destroy humanity. Or when he sees the angel about to devastate Jerusalem as part of the punishment imposed on Israel because David took a census of the people, Yahweh changes his mind and cancels that part of the punishment.

The other reasons for divine repentance are either an act of repentance on the part of people under judgment or the intercession of a prophet. The former may be illustrated by the example of Nineveh and Jerusalem at different times and under different circumstances. Thus in the book of Jonah we read that under divine threat communicated by the reluctant prophet, the king and people of the city of Nineveh repented, and as a result God repented and spared the city. A similar case is made with regard to the city of Jerusalem. In the book of Jeremiah it is reported that in the days of Micah the prophet, the latter proclaimed the judgment of Yahweh against the city. In response, the king and people changed their ways and, as in the case of Nineveh, made a concerted effort to appease the deity. As a result Yahweh repented and the city was spared.

The principal example of divine repentance resulting from prophetic inter-cession is the case of Moses and the episode of the golden calf. In Exod. 32, the verb is used twice: Moses commands (the pleading imperative *hinnāḥēm*) and Yahweh complies *(wayyinnāḥem)*. While Yahweh is described as "the repenter over the evil" in the prophetic version (Joel and Jonah) of the classic list of divine attributes first found in Exod. 34:6-7, and there are general statements in a number of places about his tendency and willingness to repent, this is the only major public instance in the Hebrew Bible of a prophetic intercession successfully resulting in divine repentance, at least before the time of Amos. It should be noted that while Samuel is also considered an effective intercessor, ranked with Moses in the book of Jeremiah, the results he achieves are never described by the crucial term *nḥm*. In the one instance in which the term is used (three times), the divine repentance is not the result of Samuel's intervention, and Samuel's role in the account is to report to the repentant Saul that Yahweh has rejected the king and his repentance because "the Eternal One of Israel does not repent, for he is not a man." In fact, in this episode we find a classic example of intercessory failure, in which Samuel tries all night to persuade Yahweh to reverse a decision (itself an act of repentance) but does not succeed. It is in stark contrast to Moses' successful intervention on behalf of Israel in the episode of the golden calf. Jeremiah, who uses the word more than anyone else in the Bible and reports at least two acts of repentance on Yahweh's part, nevertheless confesses that he himself was forbidden by Yahweh to intercede for his people. His case reflects a third possibility.

The single major example of early successful prophetic intercession remains that of Moses, and it alone constitutes a model or precedent for Amos's intervention recorded in Amos 7:3, 6. Doubtless it was this dramatic and all-important action of Moses, and the repentance of God in response to Moses' intervention, that provided the basis for the prophetic designation of the deity as not only gracious and compassionate, long-suffering and merciful, and the rest of the qualities derived from the great self-revelation of Exod. 34:6-7, but also as the one who repents concerning the evil (that he plans or has done). This interaction between prophet and deity was seen by Israel as decisive for its history and ranked with the other two great events of the exodus: the deliverance from bondage in Egypt, highlighted by the Song of the Sea celebrating the destruction of Pharaoh's forces; and the establishment of the covenant community at the foot of Mt. Sinai, including the giving of the Ten Words, the building of the tabernacle, the making of its furnishings and equipment, and the institution of the sacral system reflecting and protecting the divine presence in the camp. The third element was the intervention by Moses to save the community from certain destruction by an angry deity who was offended by mass apostasy objectified in idolatry. The episode embodies central themes in the whole story of Yahweh and Israel and reveals the elements that determine that nation's fate. From this early stage there is a God determined to make a people for himself from the slave group hauled out of Egypt, a new society bound to its suzerain by solemn promises and commitments on both sides; and there is a people equally determined to wreck the agreement by committing the cardinal sin, to worship and serve another god (cf. the oldest form of the commandment in Exod. 34:14, "You shall not worship another god," *lō' tištaḥᵃweh lᵉ'ēl 'aḥēr*). Here at the beginning is also the ultimate confrontation. Because the people had repented first in the wrong sense — that is to say, they had reversed their decision to be the people of Yahweh, worshipping and serving him only — he also repented by

441

changing his decision about them. His judgment against them was the inexorable consequence of their decision about him. Only the intervention of Moses prevented the immediate end of the glorious experiment in peoplehood begun forty days before. It is clear that without it, there would have been no Israel at all. And the divine repentance is the direct consequence of the Mosaic intercession. There is no other cause because the people are entirely oblivious to the situation, though presumably they are aware of having made a damaging breach in the commandments that hold the covenant between them together and make it valid.

As observed, Moses' action bought time only, time to remedy the situation, because a holy God cannot dwell in the midst of an idolatrous people, and unless the idolatry and the apostasy are eliminated the great experiment will end at its birth. The outcome through drastic and bloody measures is well known. Moses achieved a more permanent rescission of the judgment. The temporary suspension of judgment was confirmed, and with some reservations Yahweh agreed to keep his people and lead them to the Holy Land. Other crises that developed were met in similar fashion, but it is interesting that the term *nhm* is used only of the first and most important crisis in the history of the people.

In another sense, the problem exposed by that initial crisis was never resolved permanently. The revelation that there was a deeply rooted incompatibility between Yahweh and his own people, expressed by the people's irrepressible drive to worship other gods, cast a long shadow over the relationship and ensured an ultimate rupture. In truth, the prophet's intervention reversed the decision and suspended the judgment. But in spite of the best efforts of the prophet and his faithful followers the judgment was only suspended and would later be reinstated. Moses bought time for his people, a lot of it; but the judgment remained suspended, and six hundred years later it would be executed. It is the central conviction of the prophets and the biblical writers that Israel (including both kingdoms) remained incurably idolatrous throughout the history of the first commonwealth, and that ultimately this idolatry was the cause of divine rejection and the fall of the kingdoms; Israel and Samaria first, then Judah and Jerusalem. Already in this first episode after the ratification of the covenant, the basic and pervasive problem was uncovered and, in spite of Moses and all the prophets, could never be permanently corrected. The role of the prophets as agents of the divine word and as representatives of God's people is also seen in its full dimensions in this story and serves as a paradigm for the rest of Israel's history.

Moses and the repentance of God constitute an essential chapter in the story, which exerted a profound influence in its formulation and elaboration. It became a model for prophecy and history writing in Israel and helped to define the role of prophet as mediator between God and his people. While the prophet was first and foremost the proclaimer of God's word, he could aspire to the other office of intercessor, a role created by Moses and enacted under the greatest pressure at the most critical moment in Israel's early history. Later prophets could aspire to such a complex and critical role, but few could attain it. Samuel apparently came closest (1 Sam. 12:23), but all we know about it is by reputation and hearsay, because no actual instance of intervention on behalf of the people resulting in divine repentance is recorded. Although Samuel is credited with successful intercession, the one case of divine repentance in the story of Samuel shows the prophet as failing in this role.

Of all other candidates, strangely enough, the only successful example is Amos himself, and by his own admission. His was a limited success, a brief respite in the story of judgment. He intervened effectively, just as Moses had, though Amos did not use the verb itself in the imperative *(hinnāḥēm)* as Moses had. He found suitable substitutes and maintained the imperative form. Yahweh truly repented, but Amos was in no position to influence the people and their leadership or to effect desired results. No doubt he put forth his best effort. The contrast with Jonah is ironic, for Jonah was a very reluctant prophet who wanted to fail, and his message succeeded in winning a double repentance: first by king and people and then by God. Amos was eager to succeed, like Moses, to save his people, and he persuaded Yahweh to repent — the hard part, perhaps — but failed with king and people. They did not do so (4:6-11), and the suspended judgment, suspended now and again no doubt since the days of Moses, was reinstated.

The relation between Amos and Jonah is more complex and is not limited to the books under their names. Jonah was a historical prophet, a contemporary of Amos and apparently attached to the court of Jeroboam II, the king against whom Amos directed Yahweh's terrible words of judgment. The king preferred to listen to encouraging words from his own prophet and, according to 2 Kgs. 14, they were largely fulfilled. Yahweh did indeed grant a respite to this king and his people at about the time that Amos was bringing a word of final judgment. It might well appear that the major obstacle in the way of a genuine repentance and renewal of the covenant in Israel was precisely this other prophet who had the ear of the king and could and probably did frustrate (along with the high priest Amaziah) every effort on the part of Amos to get leaders and people to listen to the real message of Yahweh. Yet it is this prophet, Jonah, who is the permanent hero (or should we say antihero) of a story in which a repentant king and people unite with a repentant deity to save a great city (Nineveh). But that is only a story, and things often work out in stories much better than they do in real life. It is too bad that the same prophet could not have turned his efforts in real life to the rescue and salvation of the city and state in which he lived. While Jeroboam, his priest, and his prophet were superficially successful in those years of victory and prosperity, no doubt that very success at home and abroad ensured that life would continue in the same way, that Amos and his dire warnings would go on being ignored or dismissed, and that the doom of city or country would be guaranteed precisely because Jonah was considered and considered himself a true prophet.

Looking again at Amos and his work as prophet, we see that he did not hesitate to assume the mantle of the first and greatest of the prophets, Moses himself, perhaps along with Samuel. In fact, he was an intercessor before he became a prophet and tried to shape and modify the message he was to deliver. Surprisingly, he was successful, and as a result of his intervention Yahweh repented. The only earlier instance of specific divine repentance as a result of prophetic intervention is precisely the intercession of Moses in the story of the golden calf, as we have discussed. Because the story is assigned to the old narrative source in the Pentateuch we may conclude that Amos was aware of it, as he was of the basic traditions of the exodus and conquest. The connection, therefore, is not accidental or coinciden-tal. As a prophet, Amos conceived his role to be that of intercessor as well as messenger. He aspired to save his people from destruction and took on the onerous and dangerous burden of prophecy to achieve that goal. Before accepting a mission, he tried to shape the message he was supposed to deliver, and succeeded in changing it from judgment to warning. When he failed to persuade the leaders of the people of both the reality and the urgency of the threat to their survival, not just their prosperity, he carried out the mission originally intended for him; but while he held out no hope for the nation, he knew that God had repented of the evil at least provisionally, as he had long ago, and in principle might do so again. Amos would have approved of the book of Jonah, though he may have had little use for the man himself. The refrain in Amos 7 (vv. 3, 6), when the report of the first two visions is made, "and Yahweh repented of this," stands out in the biblical record. Not since the days of Moses and the beginning of the state had God repented specifically at the request of a prophet, and he did so twice; he would not do so again, at least not in the lifetime of Amos.

In view of the brevity of the accounts in Amos 7 and the inconsequential results of the prophetic intercession in the first two visions even for the prophet's mission, much less for Israel's history, it may seem an exaggerated effort to probe the meaning of the terms expressing divine repentance. It may also seem excessive to draw such dramatic and far-reaching conclusions about its significance for the biblical story and the understanding of the nature of the God of Israel. But one should not be misled by appearances even if they are real. The biblical experience is peculiar in that respect: the most important transactions between heaven and earth are often private and personal and defy the usual procedures of analysis and evaluation. Verification in the usual terms is almost impossible to achieve, and we are left with a bundle of claims and assertions, many of which challenge belief and defy rules of evidence and logical debate. The same is true of public events that often leave no trace in external records or archaeological excavations. Such ques-tions, valid in themselves, must nevertheless be set aside once we enter the world of the Bible and attempt to read with understanding and appreciation. Thus, with respect to God's repentance in the story of Jonah we are entitled to ask questions about the historicity and reliability of the account because it purports to record an episode in the history of one of the greatest and best known cities of the ancient world. We are also entitled to a full measure of skepticism about the story as a whole and about many of its details, not just the credibility of the digestive capacities of the great fish. Nevertheless, the story has a meaning and import for understanding biblical religion and the particular matter of divine repentance quite apart from the questions just asked, as we have tried to show.

If our primary concern here is with the nature and character of the biblical God, then there are fewer and fewer external criteria by which to judge the extant data. Does God repent? Did he? Just to grapple with the meaning of the terms may be as much as we can handle or more, and it will be quite safe to leave decisions about veracity and validity to personal and public tribunals beyond the confines of this book. We will content ourselves with internal examinations and comparisons of the data and stay within the biblical world, where the interaction of God and his people is a matter of continuing concern. Channels are open, and special people called prophets have access to them.

It is in this light that we can speak of the decisive importance of Moses' interaction with Yahweh at Sinai in the episode of the golden calf. From the biblical perspective it was a public event. There were specific visible and verifiable consequences, including the destruction of the calf, the decimation of the community, and finally its survival as the people of Yahweh and not of some other god. That there are no external data to support or contradict the story in its essential content is one of the accidents of data preservation, a very haphazard affair, and of archaeological dispute among scholars over where Mt. Sinai was and which peak among many it may have been. We would not even know where to look for, much less expect, any remains of the Israelite settlement at Sinai (in passing we can say that the search for such data at Qadesh Barnea, where the chances of finding something should be much better, has also proved frustrating); so we cannot expect to find anything about this story anywhere except in the Bible. We can make a relatively plausible case for the public events and perhaps agree that there was a great crisis in the wilderness about the essentials of the new faith, and that Moses and his coterie (the Levites) emerged victorious in that struggle, symbolized by the golden calf. In its present form there is little question that the episode in the desert has been affected by the tradition of the bull images used in the worship of the northern kingdom at Bethel and Dan, but we need not conclude that the story in Exod. 32 is mere invention. About the private meetings between Moses and God, whether up on the mountain or down in the tent, even less can be said in terms of verification or external testimony. What actually went on in these head-to-head (mouth-to-mouth, face-to-face are the biblical metaphors) sessions? Only those who have been in them can say, but supporting testimony is hard to come by because in most cases there is no third party, and even when others are in attendance they are not privy to the details of the conversation. In the end we can only study the record and attempt to understand and appreciate it; assessing it objectively may be impossible and is, in any case, the responsibility of the reader. For biblical history the encounters between prophets and their God were of the utmost importance

445

because it was believed firmly that both parties were affected by the interaction. The critical point in the story of the golden calf was the exchange between Moses and God (*hnhm . . . wynhm,* "Repent . . . and he repented"); the rest followed as a natural consequence. To trace the story from the original experience until it reached the form in which we have it is both difficult and speculative, and the trail is very murky. But it became the official accepted version, and that is what we have to work with.

The situation in many ways is even worse in the case of Amos. Here the transaction was entirely private, and the repentance of Yahweh reported in the book of Amos was canceled shortly thereafter, so that it has become merely a group of words, a brief refrain or footnote to the laconic account of the initiating visions. In a literal sense we have only the word of Amos to vouch for the experience or for any of the other experiences by which the word of Yahweh was transmitted. We do not have to validate Amos's experience or assess the reality of his vision or his viewpoint. It is enough — and this point is very important — to describe it and to show what its role was in the prophet's message and in the context of the book that bears his name. The visions were central to his understanding of his calling as a prophet and his mission to his people, Israel. That much is clear. And it is equally clear that, like Moses and perhaps Samuel before him, he aspired to and in his own judgment fulfilled the role of intercessor, a role that other prophets aspired to and in their own judgment did not succeed in fulfilling. That success puts Amos in a very select unit of a very select group. Of true prophets there are a very limited number, and of them only the barest handful could qualify as effective intercessors: Moses, Samuel, Amos; we might add Jeremiah, but for him the time of intercession passed, and he was not allowed even to try.

This insight into Amos's career and character also has large implications for understanding his message and in the end his book. It is striking that Amos the intercessor stands in sharp contrast to his fellow 8th-century prophets, with whom he otherwise has so much in common. None of the others deals in divine repentance at all. The word is not used at all in this sense with God as subject by any of them. Where it does occur in a story about a contemporary prophet, Jonah, the prophet is adamantly opposed to the idea altogether.

As in the case of Moses and Samuel, so with Amos, behind the facade of fierce and uncompromising loyalty to Yahweh — which demanded the most drastic measures to achieve conformity to his will — there was a passionate concern for the survival and well-being of the people to whom they were sent, but whose interest they chose to represent before the deity with daring and at great risk to themselves. They and they alone succeeded in reshaping the message they were to deliver, in reversing the divine decision, and in redirecting the divine activity, but only for the benefit and salvation of their people.

38

W. F. Albright as Historian

Albright was not an historian: he was interested in history, especially in historical method, concerned to use its resources and techniques in order to achieve results in other areas. If we can speak of him as an historian at all, it will be as an historian of ideas and especially as an historian of religion, not from the point of view of anthropology, but of ideas and their development. What may have been intended in this colloquium to serve as focal point or culmination may prove to be something less than that, since Albright was not one of the great historians of our time. He was neither an encyclopedist such as Eduard Meyer, nor an innovator with fresh ideas, perhaps like Spengler, Sorokin, or even Toynbee, but rather an apologist for a somewhat traditional, even archaic outlook. His model was in truth none of the above, but was rather the great Christian synthesis — acknowledged or not — derived from the major theologians, whether Roman Catholic like Thomas Aquinas or Protestant like John Calvin, between whom there was not such a great difference. There is a debt as well to figures such as Maimonides in Judaism, and no doubt to the Arabic precursors (Avicenna [Ibn-sina] and Averroes [Ibn-rusd]), who created the comprehensive, medieval theological-historical framework on which both Jewish and Christian philosophers were dependent. Behind the medieval synthesis, to which Albright was primarily indebted, lay the last and greatest of the classical syntheses, that of Augustine, who also built on the work of predecessors, but who finally defined the nature and scope of Christian historical apologetics. The *City of God* may be called the true model for Albright's work, although he never really attempted a great synthetic work for our time, but only sketches for such a work — *Prolegomena* as it turned out — much in the mode and mold of the great synthesizer of Old Testament studies, Julius Wellhausen. Even Albright's last great undertaking, *The History of the Religion of Israel,* the title of which clearly defines his interest and objectives, fell far short of a comprehensive, much less exhaustive, treatment and, even if he had not abandoned it in midcourse, it would never have been the history, or even part of the history, that many looked for. I don't think

447

that Albright ever thought in those terms or that he ever intended to write a definitive history of the ancient Near East; yet he actually contributed much to the history of ideas, or more precisely of religion as a configuration of certain ideas or beliefs, not so much in anthropological or sociological terms as in philosophical or theological terms.

I recall two conversations I had with Albright about such matters, which are really amalgams and distillations of many discussions and remarks he made from time to time. One was about his career as an Assyriologist, and his oft-repeated remark that if his eyesight had been better, he would have continued along the lines indicated by his studies and his dissertation on the Assyrian Deluge Epic. Certainly he was qualified and would have been outstanding, bad eyes or not, but I am dubious. His consuming interest was always the Bible, and had he been officially or technically an Assyriologist, he would have linked it with his studies of the Bible. The fact is that Assyriology was already moving in its own direction and the traditional association was dissolving. It would not have been possible to do what Albright wanted to do and attempted to do, to build the whole ancient Near East around the Bible — hardly the wave of the future, more like the last stand of the traditionalists.

The other point has to do with the history of the ancient Near East. It was thought by some, perhaps many, that Albright would produce the new comprehensive history of the ancient Near East, that he would be the Eduard Meyer of our generation. I remember asking Albright about this matter, and his reply was twofold: (1) that the field was too large for anyone to try to master, and (2) that it would require the combined talents of many scholars to produce such a work. We all know that the new *Cambridge Ancient History* is just such an effort and doubtless will be the model for the future. But Albright had something else in mind. He used to point out that the best brains and the best trained scholars of the ancient Near East to be found anywhere in those pre–World War I days were all at the University of Berlin, and that Meyer could do his work and consult with the best authorities without leaving his office or at least his building. Thus with the help of the great scholars surrounding him, he could produce a monumental work. Could Albright have done a similar work for our era? Certainly he had the capability and, considering his technical linguistic and archaeological skills, more so than even Meyer. As for colleagues, the Johns Hopkins University was not the University of Berlin, but Albright was not isolated either in the States or in the world; his correspondence was voluminous and extremely important from a purely scholarly point of view. I think the excuses were just that, but they tell us about the man and his real objectives.

At a very early stage in his career it seemed clear that Albright's primary interest was neither in being an Assyriologist nor in being a comprehensive encyclopedic historian. While several of his early major articles reflected his special training and his wide-ranging interests, the twin foci would always remain the Bible on the one hand, and comparative religion — or to be more precise — the religious ideas of the ancient Near East on the other. In all his subsequent major undertakings, he attempted to combine or blend these interests. A brief glance at his books elucidates and confirms this impression: *The Archaeology of Palestine and the Bible, From the Stone Age to Christianity, Archaeology and the Religion of Israel,* and *Yahweh and the Gods of Canaan* are all efforts to place biblical tradition and biblical religion in the context of ancient Near Eastern religion.

We recognize here as well the final choices as to the area, the subject, and the focus. Throughout his career and even in retirement Albright's primary and abiding interest was the Bible, first of all the Hebrew Bible — the Old Testament — and along with it the New Testament. Although he never pretended to be equally at home in the latter as the former, he was certainly no stranger to the New Testament and could justify his work on the New Testament, especially regarding its archaeology and Semitic background. In the same way he could and did defend his excursions into the classical world, both in terms of its archaeology and pottery sequences as well as its epic and literary traditions. Albright's knowledge of Greek and Indo-European was formidable, so we must never make the mistake of supposing that because his interest and his books centered on one topic, he did not range with impressive authority over many related fields. While he had extraordinarily wide interests and, as a good scientist, dealt with often obscure data in their own right and for their own value, he nevertheless saw almost all the materials he worked with as having relational significance, and as belonging to a much larger scheme at the center of which was biblical religion. I almost wrote "revelation" for "religion," but that would be unfair and inappropriate. While, for those of us who came to the Hopkins fresh from Christian theological seminaries, the presentation and articulation of the data were quite congenial and the Oriental Seminary — the original title of the department, a painfully literal rendering of the German *Orientalische Seminar* — seemed like a continuation of what we had already experienced, namely a strong Christian cultural bias, and an essentially apologetic approach to the subject of religion, especially biblical religion in (or against) its environment, nevertheless, the basis and the method were different.

Albright himself came out of an orthodox, pietistic Methodist background (his parents were self-supporting missionaries in Chile), and all his life he maintained a conservative stance with regard to biblical — by which he meant and we are to understand Christian if not Protestant — religion, and defended this option with considerable force and zeal. But while he was sympathetic with evangelicals and gave more aid and comfort to ultras — i.e., fundamentalists — than perhaps he realized or intended, he himself was careful to present both the Bible and its environment in terms of the history of ideas, and not as a defender of one faith or a particular branch or family of it. Therefore his own brand of faith and religion was not obtrusive or intrusive, although he never made any effort to conceal his position. He never appeared to be personally involved, since the debate and defense were conducted on purely intellectual grounds. Albright believed very much in evolution, as his discussions of the long history of humanity in the ancient Near East show, and his work with archaeological artifacts would always be a prime case in point. He also believed that biblical religion was the outcome of a long history of development of religious ideas and insights. He regarded biblical religion as different from and superior to all other religions of the ancient Near East, and he emphatically asserted the unique character of the Mosaic faith.

He emphasized even more strongly the affinities between biblical religion and its near relatives, especially Canaanite religion, and how different but parallel tendencies and features were already present in the setting in which biblical religion emerged. An interesting point may be made concerning the patriarchs. Albright clearly believed that there was such a group who belonged to the pre-Mosaic age, and did his best to date and place them — clearly a very conservative position. At the same time, he rejected the biblical depiction of their religion as essentially the same as that of Moses and his successors (i.e., monotheistic in quality if not in formulation), and he reconstructed their religion as not significantly different from that of their neighbors either in Mesopotamia or Canaan, i.e., polytheistic with a dominant triad of deities. Thus he combined the ideas of evolution and mutation, affirming both the difference and originality of biblical religion, especially beginning with Moses, and at the same time its similarities and affinities with the pagan religions from which it emerged.

The presentation has perhaps even more alarming implications because it is not a testimony or proclamation by a believer, but a reasoned argument intended to persuade or convince the hearer or reader. Whatever Albright's personal faith may have been, and I have heard arguments in opposite directions on this point, his public stance, the one affirmed and argued in his writings, is in defense of biblical religion, very close to its classic Christian form. He believed that the case could be made and justified both by the data and by an appeal to reason, and he argued in this fashion in his classic work *From the Stone Age to Christianity*. Monotheism was demonstrably superior to the polytheism from which it sprang, and of the varying forms of biblical or quasi-biblical monotheism (and the *quasi* could be attached to monotheism also), classic Christianity was the most viable intellectually and philosophically. Since he was teaching in a secular university, and had in his classes and seminars students and auditors of many different persuasions and denominations, he was always exceedingly careful not to identify himself with one point of view, but there could be little doubt as to where he stood or the direction in which his arguments moved.

I think it was this quality more than any other that gave his work (at least on the theoretical or philosophical plane) an archaic or old-fashioned tone. It was not so much the arguments themselves, which were couched in modern terms and buttressed by data derived from the most recent discoveries and analyses, as it was the assumption that the intellectual or rational case for this form of religion could be made at all. It was certainly not objective, anthropological or philosophical reporting. So Albright had an evolutionary and an apparently theological model in mind when he presented the case for biblical religion as the survivor and winner of the battles among the competing religions of antiquity. He supported the historical argument with the equally classic apologetic in favor of Greek philosophy and logical reasoning. We may note in passing that while he stressed Greek thought as the necessary adjunct, organizer, and interpreter of biblical religion, he never wrote a sustained treatment — much less a book — on that component of his triad (but see his posthumously published paper, "Neglected Factors in the Greek Intellectual Revolution"). The great bulk of his writing focused on the prior and primary element, biblical religion. The union of biblical religion and Greek thought characterized emergent Christianity, which was to win the day against all competitors whether philosophical or religious, or various combinations of both. To this formidable pairing was added the political and socioeconomic genius of the Roman Empire, thereby creating for perhaps the only time in world history the appropriate concentration of factors making for universality and unity. This obvious and intended goal for humanity was only partially attained in those days, considering how much of the world and its population were outside the Roman Empire, and is much more remote in ours.

As I have suggested, the world view and historical interest demonstrated in his major writings are hardly new; they owe their immediate inspiration to the classical Christian syntheses, particularly those of Aquinas and perhaps Calvin (among other Protestants) — and not to the work of historians and other social scientists of our time, although Albright dealt with the latter and interacted with them. Behind the medievals is the towering figure of Augustine, whose *City of God* is the lineal ancestor of *From the Stone Age to Christianity,* Albright's major statement of his own position.

Albright believed that the union of biblical religion and Greek thought had produced and could go on producing a synthesis of doctrine and practice — i.e., a philosophical structure with which to understand the world from a theistic point of view, and a guide or manual for living, which represented the fundamental and terminal truth about God, humanity, and the universe. He also believed that the Bible was true, not only in terms of precepts and concepts properly articulated and formulated, but in a historical sense as well. Here is where he parted company with the leading German scholars of his time. He himself was so heavily influenced by his teacher Paul Haupt and by the great Germans of the previous and present generations that the breach over the question of historicity must have caused him great anguish and concern. In the end, he could not accept the prevailing idealism of the German academic or philosophical environment, nor the pervasive scholarly skepticism about confirming or recovering biblical history. The sophisticated solutions offered by von Rad and his associates and followers regarding the problem of the origins of Old Testament religion, and the corresponding ones offered by

451

Bultmann and his followers with respect to the New Testament were basically unacceptable to Albright, who objected more violently to the latter than to the former. Perhaps Albright did not wish to engage or indulge in the epistemological and linguistic debates which have dominated our century. In any case, he opted for an older and simpler resolution: the essential historicity of the biblical narrative going all the way back to patriarchal times.

Since by temperament and acute intelligence he could hardly take sides in the debate between the radicals who challenged the whole historical premise of biblical religion, and the ultra-conservatives who made it an article of faith, thus allowing no possibility of fruitful discussion, Albright tried to find a lever, some external means by which to recover and to restructure an essentially conservative, but also intellectually respectable and scientifically viable position.

Archaeology provided the means, both the clues and the data. For Albright, the category of history was the critical factor in dealing with the Bible. For fundamentalists, history was the expression and outcome of a dogmatic view of Scripture; for the radicals, the historical dimension was largely irrecoverable and irrelevant, and in a different way subordinate to that of confession and faith. Neither of the latter groups was particularly interested in finding out what happened, or in showing how the past could be recovered. For the ultra-orthodox, whatever was affirmed must be true, must have happened, simply because it was affirmed. For the radicals, what was important was the affirmation itself, which was true event, regardless of what may actually have happened, or what could be recovered or reconstructed by historical research.

Albright could not forgive either party for obstructing the scientific search for truth: the radicals for surrendering the recovery of the facts in favor of a symbolic and superficial affirmation, a confession without substantive content; the ultra-orthodox for subordinating history to dogma and closing the door to inquiry and verification. He himself was confident that the diligent pursuit of the facts would produce substantial results, by and large vindicating the biblical account and confirming the essential and central traditions of the Bible. In this way the modern discipline of biblical archaeology was fashioned, and Ernest Wright became its chief proponent, aided and abetted by a number of Albright students, including Nelson Glueck, John Bright, and others.

Archaeology has been carried out in Palestine, i.e., Israel and Jordan, and elsewhere in the Near East for a variety of reasons, but especially the vindication of biblical history. More recently, the discipline has been redefining itself in terms broadly similar to anthropology — to recover and reconstruct societies in their environment. By and large the biblical component has been somewhat diminished, and there is somewhat less talk of the spade in one hand and the Bible in the other, or of proving or disproving biblical statements and stories. The fact is that the combination was somewhat artificial to begin with. There are fundamental differences in direction and method as well as in end products and comparable results; the biblical scholar deals with one kind of material, and the archaeologist with another. On rare but important occasions there is significant contact, and both disciplines gain from the exchange of data and ideas. Often, however, there is no point of contact and nothing significant happens. On the whole, the results have been somewhat disappointing, though perhaps that was to be expected. Palestinian archaeology has had modest success in turning up monumental remains and inscriptional materials, nothing like the quantity discovered in Mesopotamia and Egypt. And while it has been possible to reconstruct the history of those imperial nations in considerable measure from the finds, the same can hardly be said of Israel and Judah. Inscriptions have proved scarce and generally peripheral, though with marked exceptions such as recent finds at Deir ʿAllā and Quntillet Ajrud, not to overlook older discoveries such as the ostraca from Samaria and Lachish, and more recent finds at Arad and Beer-sheba. [One may now add the newly discovered Aramaic stele fragment from Tel Dan, for which see, among others, the publication and study of A. Biran and J. Naveh, "An Aramaic Stele Fragment from Tel Dan," *IEJ* 43 (1993): 81-98.] Unwritten materials are extensive to be sure but not always easy to interpret in terms of biblical connections, while confirmations are few and far between.

Albright's great plan and expectation to set the Bible firmly on the foundation of archaeology buttressed by verifiable data of many kinds seem to have foundered, or at least floundered. After all the digging done and being done, how much has been accomplished? The fierce debates and arguments about the relevance of archaeology to the Bible and vice versa indicate that many issues remain unresolved. Still others seem to be caught in suspension: Can anyone say anything with confidence about the patriarchs or the patriarchal age? The fact that skeptical voices now dominate the scene indicates that the Albrightian synthesis has become unglued, and, e.g., we are further from a solution to Gen. 14 than we ever were. Archaeology has not proved decisive or even greatly helpful in answering the questions most often asked by biblical scholars, and has failed to prove the historicity of persons and events especially at the early end of the scale.

At the same time, we would be remiss if we dismissed archaeology as another false messiah, which promised much and delivered little. It always and invariably serves as a permanent reminder that in the Bible we are dealing with real people in real places, who lived and worked and played and died and left evidence of their presence. Like it or not, the Bible is about a particular people and events, bound by time and space; it has a historical dimension, which we ignore or bypass at great peril to the message and meaning of this religion. With all the problems engendered by the historical ingredient we cannot avoid it. We do better to grapple with it head-on, than to evade it by proclaiming the historicity of the proclamation or of the community making the affirmation, but without reference to the content of the message, which has historical coordinates that demand verification, or at least realistic appraisal. Nor can we seek refuge in dogmatic pronouncement, affirming what needs validation and verification. Without neglecting the literary and canonical aspects of the case, we must affirm the central importance of the historical factor, and insist on facing the question whenever the biblical tradition is under consideration or criticism.

For this insistence we must be permanently grateful to Albright and his creation: biblical archaeology. Nor should we conclude our review of the subject without reference to the many benefits and contributions made to the elucidation and illumination of the Bible by this discipline. Major manuscript discoveries at Qumran and Ugarit have contributed significantly to our understanding of the Bible and its contents. The Dead Sea Scrolls have contributed the earliest known copies of books of the Hebrew Bible in whole or in part, as well as pieces of a vast contemporary literature mainly reflecting the interests and the library of the people of Qumran. All in all, the Dead Sea Scrolls have illuminated the textual history of the Old Testament far beyond any reasonable expectation. They have provided information about and insights into the process by which the Bible came to be, and especially the history of the canon and of the text.

What the discoveries at Qumran have done for the back end of biblical history, the Ugaritic tablets have helped to do for the front end. Here are a couple of thousand tablets written in a language quite similar to Biblical Hebrew (not counting the many other tablets written in Akkadian and other languages) and dating roughly to the century preceding the career of Moses. The literary texts, including parts of several epics and mythic pieces, constitute the heart and core of the materials found, and are the most important for understanding the linguistic forms and meanings, literary connections and allusions of much biblical poetry. This chance find (quite literally meant since the initial discovery was largely an accident) has proved invaluable for the study of the biblical text, especially biblical poetry.

We should add here as well the inscriptional discoveries at Quntillet Ajrud (*ca.* 800 B.C.E.) and at Deir ʿAllā (*ca.* 700 B.C.E.), and the ostraca from Arad and Beer-sheba (as well as a few others from various sites), which have shed light on the history of the Hebrew language, and especially on a number of passages in the Bible. None of these has proved to be a "smoking pistol," decisive confirmation of, or confrontation with, specific biblical people or events. But the illumination and elucidation of difficult passages place us all under obligation to the discoverers and to those who have studied and published the texts.

In the end, the archaeological materials help to illuminate and illustrate, and always to remind us that behind and beyond the pages of Scripture, the history of Israel was lived out by real people in real situations, and that events took place under specified circumstances. Except in unusual and extraordinary cases, archaeology provides only representative artifacts and peripheral data. Even when there are specific points of contact and direct confirmation, the heart and core of the biblical narrative will remain inaccessible to archaeology. The central and decisive components of the biblical account are unique and unrepeatable occurrences inextricably bound up with the divine initiative and action. This dimension of ultimate reality inevitably transcends ordinary historical experience, which limits and defines the boundary of archaeological data.

So however and whatever archaeology contributes to the biblical picture, it is no substitute for faith, no alternative to belief, only a possible help along the way. Probably Albright was fully aware of all this, and had limited expectations. The results of archaeological research were not intended to initiate faith or create belief, but rather to bolster the convictions of those already persuaded, and whose confidence in the face of criticism and skepticism needed to be strengthened. In the end, however, the same dilemmas and difficulties remain.

We may conclude these remarks by reminding ourselves that Albright was not solely interested in maintaining or sustaining the historicity of the biblical account through archaeological research, but rather was concerned with a larger picture, the successful emergence of monotheism as the dominant religion in Western civilization. He wished to show how, as well as when and where and under whose inspiration and guidance, monotheism — of the biblical kind — came to be, and how it overcame its natural enemies to become the primary religion of the Western world. He made the presentation not only in historical terms as a kind of evolution from primitive religion through various stages to ethical monotheism, but also in conceptual and theoretical terms to show that such an evolution was actually from lower to higher forms of religion, and that the final stage, reflecting the combination of biblical religion with Greek thought, was the culmination of a very long process.

From the point of view of comparative religion, especially in terms of social science patterns and models, the success of monotheism, especially in its Christian forms, makes an appealing and impressive story, a necessary and essential one in describing the overall human experience. But in the light of 20th-century developments and the impact of the major religions upon one another all over the world, it may be that some new synthesis, some new product of the interaction between East and West, between Christianity and its Western companions on the one hand and Buddhism and its Eastern associates on the other, will result. Albright was rather scornful of such ideas and criticized Toynbee especially for suggesting that some combination of liberal Christianity and Mahayana Buddhism might be the religion, or at least the direction, of the future. It is difficult to predict, and a merger based on least common denominators would hardly represent progress. Nevertheless it is equally hard to believe that the only purpose or function of non-Christian religions in the scheme of things is to serve as false options and blind alleys, only to be displaced and superseded by the triumphant church. Surely a better and more inclusive script must be written for the centuries to come.

A postscript may also be in order — concerning the relationship between the historical and literary dimensions of the biblical tradition and religion. Certainly Albright was right in resisting the non- or anti-historical tendencies in the critical left wing of scholarship. Difficult as it may be to establish, maintain, and defend the historicity of the biblical experience, it is necessary to undertake this task resolutely and without either claiming too much or giving everything away. It cannot be an article of faith exempt from scrutiny, nor can it be merely the historicity of the affirmation or affirming community; believing in belief and affirming affirmation may be the form of religion, but its substance requires historical action and occurrence, the reality of what is affirmed and attested. Albright, in the pursuit of such historical reality, did not neglect the literary form in which the tradition was packaged, but he was interested in results and products, not in the literary character of the material or quality for its own sake. Here perhaps we can make a suggestion that the order of priorities should be reversed or at least balanced.

In my judgment the Bible is first of all literature, and it can only be understood as such, not that we should neglect or abandon the historical component, but that we should recognize the priority of the literary aspect. Albright was rightly skeptical of the several social sciences in their attempts to analyze, interpret, and explain biblical phenomena. The follies and fallacies of Freudian, Darwinian, and Marxian approaches to the Bible have been self-evident. But there are difficulties with the historical-archaeological approach as well, just as there are with theological-philosophical ones. All have their place and can perform their services. But the primary category is perforce the literary one. That is where we must begin, and when we have run the gamut of all the others, that is also where we must end: by which we mean that the literary category is basic and final, and the proper one by which to embrace and encompass, not exclude, the others.

Albright, W. F.
  1932   *The Archaeology of Palestine and the Bible.* New York: Revell.
  1940   *From the Stone Age to Christianity: Monotheism and the Historical Process.* Baltimore: Johns Hopkins University Press.
  1942   *Archaeology and the Religion of Israel.* Baltimore: Johns Hopkins University Press.
  1968   *Yahweh and the Gods of Canaan.* Garden City: Doubleday.
  1972   "Neglected Factors in the Greek Intellectual Revolution." *Proceedings of the American Philosophical Society* 116:225-42.

39

The Nine Commandments:
The Secret Progress of Israel's Sins

Embedded in the sequence of books from Genesis through Kings is a hitherto unnoticed sequence of violations of the Ten Commandments, one by one, book by book, by the community of Israel, leading, in the end, to her exile.

I would like to suggest that this sequence of violations may reveal the hand of the final editor of this primary history — Genesis through Kings — and reinforces its overarching theme: The violation of God's law, step by step, commandment by commandment, results in Israel's destruction. [See a fuller presentation in the author's *The Unity of the Hebrew Bible* (Ann Arbor: University of Michigan, 1991), 1-39; see also Chapter 42 in this volume.]

Explaining all this is a tall order; I hope you will find it as gripping to read as I found it exciting to explore. Whether it is also compelling is for the reader to decide. I look forward to the letters that will soon appear in Readers Reply.

The primary history in the Hebrew Bible consists of nine books:

A. Torah (Pentateuch)

  1. Genesis

  2. Exodus

  3. Leviticus

  4. Numbers

  5. Deuteronomy

B. Former Prophets

  6. Joshua

  7. Judges

  8. Samuel

  9. Kings

In our Bibles today Samuel and Kings are divided into two parts. In the official Hebrew canon, however, Samuel and Kings each originally consisted of a single long book, which was subsequently divided into two parts, presumably for ease in handling and for reference purposes. The same is true, incidentally, of

Chronicles, which, however, is a later composition, not part of the primary history and indeed appears at the very end of the Hebrew Bible.[1]

In English and Greek Bibles, the book of Ruth is attached to Judges, but that insertion reflects secondary and derivative arrangements; in the Hebrew Bible, the book of Ruth appears near the end.

So these nine books from Genesis through Kings form the primary history of Israel as recounted in the Hebrew Bible. They constitute a single narrative sequence, tracing the story of Israel from its origins — and the origins of everything — to the end of the nation, the downfall of the southern kingdom of Judah in 587/586 B.C.E. and the captivity of the survivors in Babylon.

This major, central block of material, almost half of the entire Hebrew Bible, was compiled, and promulgated, in my opinion, sometime in the latter part of the exile, not long after the story ends, say about 550 B.C.E. The last dated entry in the story is 561 B.C.E. when the king of Babylon released Judah's King Jehoiachin from prison (2 Kgs. 25:27). The exiles began to return under the Persian monarch Cyrus in 539 B.C.E.

Clearly the primary history is comprised of compositions of diverse authorship, and includes materials derived from a wide spectrum of sources, some cited, some alluded to, and others implied. It is generally regarded by scholars as an assemblage or aggregation of at least four major written sources — J (the Yahwist), E (the Elohist), P (the Priestly code), and D (the Deuteronomist). J and E, the earliest, were soon combined as JE. Then JE was incorporated into the Priestly code to form what I call the P work, which consists of Genesis, Exodus, Leviticus, and Numbers. The next five books — Deuteronomy, Joshua, Judges, Samuel, and Kings — are also generally regarded as a unitary sequence known as the Deuteronomic history. We may call this the D work. So together our nine books are comprised principally of the P work and the D work, combined by a final editor.

Although the finished product reflects a great deal of editorial activity, this primary history nevertheless exhibits certain, I would say unmistakable, marks of unity. Over the years, I have devoted considerable research to this unity and what I have to say here is part of the results of this research.

Briefly my argument is that a single person (or a small editorial committee, but inevitably dominated by one person) was responsible for assembling the constituent elements of this great narrative and putting the account in the orderly arrangement in which we now have it. Furthermore, while scrupulously preserving the materials available and entrusted to his care, and observing the rules of the editorial task, he nevertheless was able to contribute to the final assemblage and to produce a unified work.

---

1. It is no accident that Samuel, Kings, and Chronicles are the three longest books (by word count) in the Hebrew Bible (between 24,000 and 26,000 words each) and therefore the most likely to be divided. The division may have occurred when the Greek translation of these books was made, because the translations are longer than the originals and we can speculate that the books had reached their practical limit in terms of scroll length. Thus anything longer than that would literally be divided.

The work of the editor, or redactor, has always interested me — for obvious reasons — and while my experience is doubtless quite different from an ancient editor's, there must also be elements in common. The first obligation of an editor is to recognize his (or her) constraints or limitations. But without encroaching on the province of the author, the editor, especially if assembling or compiling a composite work including the contributions of several authors, has not only the right but the obligation to organize and arrange the material to bring out its continuity and coherence, to shape a unity that is inherent but not fully realized in the component parts. That is, in essence, what I suppose to have occurred with the primary history when it was created by the compiler, presumably a Jerusalem priest in the Babylonian exile.

The evidence for such unifying editorial activity is to be seen in the links between the parts of the primary history that derive from different authors. The further apart the links are in the story, the more likely they are to reflect the work of the editor. Thus editorial touches that connect Genesis with Kings are especially indicative of the work of the redactor or compiler. Consider, e.g., the apparent, if superficial, link between the first stories in Genesis (Adam and Eve, Cain and Abel), both of which deal with punishment for sin or crime, and the fate of the nation at the end of Kings. In both the Adam and Eve story and the Cain and Abel story (Gen. 1–4), the outcome of disobedience is banishment or exile, precisely the fate of the presumed readers of those stories, who are themselves the subjects of the final chapters of Kings, the exiles in Babylon.

Moreover, Babylon itself is the subject of the story of the tower of Babel (Gen. 11), the first narrative after the renewal of life on earth following the flood. The tower of Babel story supplies the transition to the account of Abraham's family and the beginning of the patriarchal narrative. So what began in Babylon more than a millennium before ends in the same place for his remote descendants: from Babylon to Babylon provides a neat summary or envelope for the whole of the primary history. Only a compiler-editor would have achieved explicitly what was only implicit in the separately authored blocks of material.

Let us turn now to a more elaborate structural feature that pervades the whole primary history, cuts across source and authorship lines, and, if sustainable as the work of the compiler, may give us an entirely new perspective on how he managed this vast enterprise.

It is generally agreed that a principal theme of the primary history — and of its major components, the D work certainly, if not equally the chief element of the P work — is to explain how it happened that Israel, the chosen people of God, who were rescued by him from bondage in Egypt and established in a new homeland, the land of Canaan, to be his nation, lost their independence and their land, and ended up in exile far away. While the details of this tragedy, the decline and fall of the two nations, Israel and Judah, are given in political/military terms, if not socioeconomic ones, the overriding theme is that just as Israel was created by God, so it could be and was destroyed by him. The reason for the latter act was that, from the beginning, the relationship between God and his people was understood to be morally conditioned and was explicated in terms of a binding agreement or covenant between them. Thus, while the deliverance of Israel and its establishment as a nation were the deeds of a gracious God, who acted on the basis of a prior commitment to the patriarchs, beginning with Abraham, nevertheless the continued existence of the nation, not to speak of its success, security, and prosperity, would depend upon its behavior, specifically its adherence to a code of conduct agreeable and pleasing to God, and spelled out in the hundreds of rules and regulations, moral and cultic, civic and religious, social, political, and economic, which permeate the pages of the Torah.

These in turn are summed up in the Decalogue or Ten Commandments, with which every Israelite must have been familiar. Here, in a word (or Ten Words, as they are called in the Hebrew Bible), is the epitome of the covenant, a summary of the rules by which all Israel is to live under the sovereign rule of God.

There is both promise and threat in the terms of the covenant, as both Moses (in the speeches in Deuteronomy) and Joshua (in his speeches in Josh. 23–24) make clear: If Israel obeys the laws of the covenant, then all will be well and Israel will prosper under the aegis of its God; if, however, the people disobey the commandments and rebel against the authority of their God, then everything will be lost: prosperity, security, nationhood, and land.

The story then is the story of how Israel failed to keep its side of the bargain, failed to observe the requirements of the compact with God, and was ultimately punished for this dereliction of duty.

Most readers — scholars and lay people — will probably agree about all this. Clearly there are other themes and important features to the primary history, but certainly the interpretation of Israel's history and destiny in this major narrative properly emphasizes Israel's covenant obligation and its persistent and repeated failure to live up to God's central demands.

Now I want to try to put myself in the shoes of the redactor-compiler, or to sit at his desk, and ask how I can sharpen the focus, highlight the drama of this decline and fall of the nation(s), to bring home to the survivors the necessary, if onerous, lesson of the past, so as to strengthen their resolve in their present affliction and prepare them for something better in the future, a future that will hold out a very similar combination of threat and promise.

The first thing I would do would be to make a special point of the Decalogue as the core and center of the covenant. The simplest way to do this, of course, would be by repetition. The Decalogue is found in both the P work (in Exod. 20:2-17) and the D work (in Deut. 5:6-12), which contains an older source of the Decalogue. Instead of combining the two or conflating them, the compiler keeps them separate. So the Decalogue appears twice in the story, near the beginning of Israel's forty-year march from Egypt to Canaan and just before the end of the journey, as Israel is about to enter Canaan.

Moreover, the repetition of the Decalogue is found at a strategic point in the literary structure. The book of Deuteronomy is at the center, the fifth book of the nine books in the sequence, and thus serves as the pivot or apex of the entire work. That this is not just a numerical accident or coincidence is shown by the contents of Deuteronomy: Moses, the central figure of the primary history, dominates the whole book of Deuteronomy, which consists of a series of addresses by Israel's greatest leader toward the end of his life: his valedictory, which has special authority and power. In these sermons, Moses not only reviews the history of his people (thereby providing legitimate reason to repeat the Ten Commandments) but also, as a true prophet, forecasts what is going to happen to them in the future, depending upon their behavior. So the Decalogue is not only at the beginning of the national history but it is also at the center of the narrative.

Further, the Decalogue symbolizes and summarizes the covenant, the obligations of which fall on every Israelite, first as an individual, personally responsible for obedience to the commandments, but also as a member of the community, which is answerable to God as a whole for the behavior for its individual members.

We can outline the sequence of events as follows: Israel was delivered from bondage in Egypt and was brought to the sacred mountain, Sinai. There the Decalogue was given as a *précis* of the terms of the covenant. The people agree to its terms, and the covenant is solemnly ratified by sacrifices and a common meal at the mountain (Exod. 24). The rest of the story is told in the succeeding books and is an account of repeated violations of the covenant, interrupted by occasional reversals and reforms, but culminating in the renunciation of Israel by its maker and founder, and the destruction of the nation: first the northern kingdom of Israel in 722 B.C.E. and then the southern kingdom of Judah in 587/586 B.C.E. The end is captivity in Babylon.

How can the final editor of this mighty history make the case more precise, more dramatic, and more suspenseful, and at the same time provide a way through the complex details of a 600-year history from beginning to end?

I believe what he did was this: Using the Decalogue as his point of departure, he portrays Israel as violating each one of the commandments directly and explicitly. Further, these commandments are violated in order, one by one. Given the fact that he has a group of books (i.e., scrolls) to deal with, he assigns, in general, one commandment and one violation to each book.

Wherever possible, the seriousness of the episode is stressed in such a way as to show how the violation (usually by an individual) nevertheless involves or implicates the whole nation, so that the survival of the nation itself is put in jeopardy. Only the extraordinary intervention of a leader or a precipitate change of direction on the part of the people provides reason to spare them. In each instance, God finally relents and the relationship is patched up. But the threat and warning remain and are strengthened, so that each succeeding violation brings Israel (and Judah) ever closer to destruction. At the end of the string, all of the commandments will

461

have been violated and God's patience will have run out. Let us now see if — and how — this happens.

The Ten Commandments,[2] in abbreviated form, are listed below:

1. Apostasy
2. Idolatry
3. Blasphemy
4. Sabbath observance
5. Parental respect

6. Murder
7. Adultery
8. Stealing
9. False testimony
10. Coveting

Because the editor is working with existing literary works and not just a collection of bits and pieces, he is naturally limited in the degree and extent to which he can arrange or rearrange, organize and reorganize, or manipulate his material. Hence we can expect certain deviations and adjustments as we go along. For example, the fact that the story of covenant-making and covenant-breaking properly begins with the book of Exodus presents him with something of a problem. True, Genesis has covenants and covenant ceremonies (e.g., with Noah in Gen. 9 and with Abraham in Gen. 15 and 17), but these are not the same as the covenant made at Sinai/Horeb and mediated by Moses, and are not related to the Decalogue. So the editor dealt with this problem simply by beginning with Exodus and doubling up the commandments violated in that book.

Apostasy and Idolatry. Immediately after the Ten Commandments are given on Mt. Sinai and the Israelites agree to them, Moses goes up to the mountain to receive instructions for building the tabernacle. During his absence, the well-known incident of the golden calf occurs (Exod. 32). The episode is described in such a way as to make it clear that the Israelites have violated the first as well as the second commandment: "You shall have no other gods beside me" (Exod. 20:3) and "You shall not make for yourself a graven image" (Exod. 20:4).

The Israelites not only make the golden calf (a graven image), they speak of it as symbolizing one or more gods (apostasy): "And they said, 'These are thy gods, O Israel, who brought thee up from the land of Egypt' " (Exod. 32:4).

Thus, we have not only accounted for the first two commandments, but also for the first two books of the primary history.

When we probe a bit deeper into this episode we find another aspect of it that will be repeated book after book, commandment after commandment: While some Israelites are guilty of violating the covenant in connection with the golden calf, others are not (the Levites), but the existence of the community is threatened. God tells Moses that he will wipe out Israel and create a new people from Moses'

2. There are several different ways of counting the Decalogue. Different religious bodies have assigned numbers to them in different ways. The numbering here reflects what might be called the consensus position to which most scholars adhere.

progeny (Exod. 32:10). It is only after Moses intercedes and there is a partial slaughter of the guilty apostates that God relents and the community is allowed to live and carry on its activity (Exod. 32:11-14; cf. vv. 31-35).

This episode becomes the paradigm for the whole subsequent history of Israel. A violation of any of the commandments is a violation of all of them, indeed of the whole covenant, but the primary category is always expressed in terms of apostasy and idolatry, which in this sense are a digest or summary of the Decalogue just as the Decalogue itself is a digest of the full range of rules and regulations of the covenant.

Blasphemy. The third book is Leviticus, and the third commandment prohibits the misuse of the name of God, i.e., blasphemy: "You shall not invoke the name of Yahweh your God for falsehood" (Exod. 20:7).

There is just such a story in Leviticus. An unnamed man — the son of an Israelite woman and an Egyptian man — "went out among the people of Israel . . . and quarreled" (Lev. 24:10). Then he "cursed the name and committed blasphemy" (Lev. 24:11). He is brought before Moses and placed in custody until Yahweh's decision is made known. Yahweh then instructs Moses to bring the blasphemer outside the camp where all those who heard the blasphemy are to lay their hands upon his head, and the whole assembly is to stone him (Lev. 24:12-14). Yahweh tells Moses to tell the people, "Any man, if he curses his God, then he shall bear [the consequences of] his sin. The one who curses the name of Yahweh shall surely be put to death, and the whole congregation will stone him — the alien resident as well as the native born — when he curses the name he shall be put to death" (Lev. 24:15-16).

Among the hundreds of laws and regulations imposed on Israel by the covenant, the Ten Commandments stand out in not having a specific penalty attached to them. These are not casuistic laws, stated in terms of cause and effect, crime and punishment, but apodictic laws, flat regulations, obedience to which is simply and unqualifiedly demanded. In the case of the blasphemy we have just recounted in Leviticus, the guilty party is detained until the matter of punishment has been resolved. The Israelites recognize that there has been a serious breach of the covenant, but neither they nor Moses know how to deal with the matter.

When word is received from Yahweh, it is necessary for the whole community, including those who witnessed the crime, to participate in the act of judgment. In that way, the community is cleared of complicity with the guilty person, and escapes the consequences of this fatal breach of the covenant. While the particular occurrence may seem trivial in comparison with the making of the golden calf, the special treatment accorded this passing event shows that the writer (or editor) had in mind the highest level of covenant obligation — the Decalogue.

Sabbath Observance. The fourth book in the primary history is Numbers, and the fourth commandment is sabbath observance:

463

Remember[3] the sabbath day to keep it holy. For six days you shall labor and do all your work, but the seventh day is a sabbath of Yahweh your God. You shall do no work at all, neither you nor your son nor your daughter, your male or female servant, nor your cattle, nor the alien who is within your gates. (Exod. 20:8-10)

In Numbers we find a story about a man who gathered sticks on the sabbath, thus violating the prohibition against doing any work on that day:

While the Israelites were in the wilderness, they found him gathering wood on the sabbath day. So those who found him gathering wood brought him to Moses and to Aaron and to the whole assembly. They detained him in the guard house, because it had not been explained what should be done to him. Then Yahweh said to Moses: "The man shall surely be put to death. The whole assembly shall stone him with stones, outside the camp." So the whole assembly brought him outside the camp and they stoned him with stones and he died, as Yahweh had commanded Moses. (Num. 15:32-36)

This story is very much like the one in Leviticus concerning blasphemy. In both cases, a violation of one of the Ten Commandments is recorded and the man responsible is arrested pending sentence and the imposition of appropriate punishment. In both cases the determination of the penalty (death by stoning by the whole assembly) is made by Yahweh through direct communication with Moses. The action by God is taken to supplement the Decalogue itself, which only lists the injunctions but does not specify the punishment. And the severity of the penalty serves to emphasize the centrality and essentiality of these terms of the covenant. Anything less than the removal of the offender would implicate the whole community in the offense and ultimately lead to abrogation of the compact and the dissolution of the nation.

Parental Respect. The fifth book is Deuteronomy, and the fifth commandment reads as follows:

Honor your father and mother, so that your days may be prolonged on the land that Yahweh your God is going to give you. (Exod. 20:12)

Once again, there is an account of a violation of a particular commandment. This time, however, it is couched in the hypothetical terminology of case law: prescribing the punishment for a specified crime. In other words, the formulation in Deuteronomy is a stage beyond Leviticus and Numbers. In the earlier books, we are given the incident or episode that provided the basis or precedent on which the punishment was fixed. Here we have a more general formulation, presumably derived from a particular incident, now lost, or no longer included in the biblical tradition.

---

3. In Deut. 5:12 the word is "observe."

Here is the statement of it:

If a man has a son, who is contumacious and rebellious [i.e., stubbornly rebellious] and will not obey the orders of his father or his mother; and if they chastise [discipline] him and he persists in his disobedience, then his father and his mother shall lay hold of him and bring him forth to the elders of his city and to the gate of his place. And they [the parents] shall say to the elders of his city: "This son of ours is contumacious and rebellious, and he will not obey our orders; he is [also] an idler and a sot." Then all the men of his city shall stone him with stones until he is dead. So shall you destroy the evil from your midst. And as for all Israel, let them pay heed and show reverence. (Deut. 21:18-21)

We turn now to the last four books in the primary history — Joshua, Judges, Samuel, and Kings — and the next four commandments, numbers six, seven, eight, and nine. An adjustment is necessary here because the order in which these books take up these commandments is not precisely the order in which they appear in Exodus and Deuteronomy. This may be simply because the editor or redactor of the primary history was not entirely free to choose his material and therefore had to make some adjustments, or it may be that he was working from a different order of the commandments, or perhaps he was familiar with other traditions concerning the order of the commandments and so could appeal to this diversity to justify his own rearrangement.

In this connection, we note that the order of commandments six, seven, and eight varies among the sources, as the chart reflects. These three commandments are quite short (only two words each in Hebrew, one of which is equivalent to the English "Do not"), so it would be easy for them to become transposed.

In an abbreviated version of the Decalogue in Jeremiah's well-known Sermon in the Temple Courtyard (Jer. 7:9), these three commandments follow the same order in which they are dealt with in the next three books of the Bible (stealing, murder, adultery) rather than the order in which they appear in Exodus and Deuteronomy (murder, adultery, stealing). There may even be a connection here, in view of the well-known literary affinities between the book of Jeremiah and the Deuteronomic history (including the books from Deuteronomy through Kings). So far as the prose sections of Jeremiah are concerned, there is a similarity of style, as well as a sharing of themes and motifs, that strongly supports the idea of connection and relationship. Baruch ben-Neriah, the scribe who was responsible for at least two versions of the book of Jeremiah (Jer. 36:1-32, esp. vv. 4 and 32), may well have had an important role in the compilation and production of the great Deuteronomic history. That perhaps accounts for the fact that the order in which the commandments are violated in the next three books of the primary history is the same as in Jeremiah's sermon.

Stealing. Let us turn once again to the books of the primary history as they proceed to recount Israel's travails ultimately leading to destruction and exile. The sixth

Order of Commandments Six, Seven, and Eight

Hebrew Bible (Exodus, Deuteronomy)	6. Murder	7. Adultery	8. Theft
Septuagint*	7. Adultery	8. Theft	6. Murder
Nash Papyrus;** Luke 18:20; Rom. 13:9; Philo†	7. Adultery	6. Murder	8. Theft
Jer. 7:9; the order of their violations in Joshua, Judges, and Samuel	8. Theft	6. Murder	7. Adultery

*The Septuagint (LXX) is an early Greek translation of the Bible.

**The Nash Papyrus, dated to the 2nd century B.C.E., is a 24-line Hebrew text containing the Ten Commandments and part of the *Shema* prayer (Deut. 6:4-5). Of unknown provenance, the papyrus was purchased from an Egyptian antiquities dealer in 1903 by W. L. Nash, for whom it is named.

†Philo was an Alexandrian Jewish philosopher who lived in the 1st century B.C.E. and the 1st century C.E., roughly contemporary with Jesus, Paul, and the Jewish sages Hillel and Gamaliel.

book is the book of Joshua. Here the major crime, or transgression of the covenant, is a case of theft, a violation of the eighth commandment in the conventional ordering of the Hebrew Bible but corresponding to the order of the list given in Jeremiah.

The story in Joshua is told in great detail:

The Israelites have destroyed Jericho but have themselves been defeated at the next site on their march, Ai. Yahweh then announces the reason for the defeat: Someone has "stolen" some of the booty from Jericho that had been dedicated to Yahweh. The man is identified by lot: Achan ben-Carmi of the tribe of Judah. At the very outset of the story, the focus is on this essential crime:

> The Israelites committed a grave offense regarding the dedicated booty. Achan, the son of Carmi, the son of Zabdi, the son of Zerach of the tribe of Judah took some of the sacred booty, and the wrath of Yahweh was kindled against the Israelites. (Josh. 7:1)

As a result, the Israelites are defeated at Ai and this setback jeopardizes their foothold in the land of promise and threatens their whole settlement. The punishment is even more severe and extensive than in the previous cases. Achan and his family are executed by stoning, with the whole community participating.

The story shows how the crime of theft was construed as a capital offense on a par with the other commandments, and punishable in the same manner (by community stoning). In most cases, theft would not be considered a capital offense and the wrongdoer would be punished by a fine, the imposition of damages (requiring payment of double the amount or a larger multiple) or to make restitution in some other suitable fashion. Such cases would hardly serve the stipulated purpose here, but the extraordinary case of Achan does so admirably and thus fits the scheme we have outlined.

As in the other cases, here, too, God takes a direct hand in exposing the crime and the criminal, and in imposing the punishment.

The editor/compiler has adapted the commandment and structured the story in order to fit the overall pattern and so emphasizes the importance of the commandments and the threat to the life of the community, as well as the divine provision for dealing with violations, and the nation's narrow escape from the consequences of divine wrath.

Murder. The seventh book, Judges, involves murder, following the order in Jer. 7:9. Judges includes many instances in which someone is killed, e.g., Eglon by Ehud (Judg. 3:15-26, esp. vv. 21-22), Sisera by Jael (Judg. 4–5, esp. 4:17-21; 5:24-27), and numerous Philistines by Samson (Judg. 14–16, esp. 14:19; 15:15; 16:30), but none of these qualify for our purposes. Not only are they not considered violations of the commandment against murder, they are regarded as righteous deeds for the sake of the community. The story we have in mind comes at the very end of the book (Judg. 19–21). It is the story of an unnamed woman, identified only as the Levite's concubine. The men of Gibeah in Benjamin took her by force in the night and mass-raped her (Judg. 19). She crawled back to the house where her master was staying and fell dead. The woman is described in the story as "the murdered woman" (Hebrew *hā'iššâ hannirṣāḥâ,* Judg. 20:4). The root *(rṣh)* is the same as the root of the word for murder in the Decalogue.

The crime is described by the author/editor as the worst in the history of the commonwealth: "Not has there happened, nor has there been seen anything like this since the day that the Israelites went up from the land of Egypt until this day" (Judg. 19:30).

Not only was the crime a brutal and appalling one by any standards, but it was compounded by the Benjaminites who refused to cooperate with the other tribes in the investigation and resolution of the matter. As it turned out, there was open civil war and the near-destruction of a whole tribe (Benjamin) and the near-dissolution of the entire Israelite league. In the end, under divine guidance the forces of Israel triumphed over the Benjaminites and the nation survived (Judg. 20). Restoring Benjamin to the tribal league was a more difficult and delicate task, but this too was accomplished through the timely intervention of dedicated men (Judg. 21).

Adultery. We have now reached the eighth book, the book of Samuel, which will deal with adultery.

While adultery is often mentioned in the Hebrew Bible and especially in the Latter Prophets (Isaiah, Jeremiah, Ezekiel, and the twelve Minor Prophets), only one example of this crime is spelled out in detail with names of persons and places and specific occasions. This is the well-known case of King David, who took Bathsheba, the wife of Uriah the Hittite, and subsequently arranged for Uriah to be killed in battle to conceal the original crime. The climax of the story occurs when the prophet Nathan confronts the guilty king who ultimately repents (2 Sam. 11–12).

For the author/editor of Samuel, David's adultery with Bathsheba was a turning point not only in David's reign, but in the history of the kingdom. All the

467

subsequent trials and ills of the later years, the rebellions and machinations, are described as stemming from that violation by the king, who compounded adultery with murder, forfeited the respect and loyalty of his troops and thus distanced himself from Yahweh, the covenant, and the privileged status he had enjoyed as the anointed of Yahweh. The peril for the country is amply documented, as well as the act of divine remission and compassion. Once again, the kingdom escapes its fate, and the dynasty is preserved for the sake of the nation.

False Testimony. The last book in the primary history is Kings, and it invokes the ninth commandment. Once again, royalty is involved and the action produces widespread and very serious consequences for the kingdom. The commandment in this case deals with false testimony in a legal proceeding, what we would call perjury. (In our courts witnesses testify under oath or solemn affirmation, which is required for perjury, whereas in ancient Israel oaths were invoked only under special conditions and only on the defendant.) The story in Kings involves Ahab, king of Israel, his Phoenician wife Jezebel, and a man named Naboth. When Naboth refuses Ahab's offer to purchase the former's vineyard, Jezebel arranges to have false charges brought against Naboth, accusing him of cursing both God and king. As punishment, Naboth is stoned to death and Ahab takes possession of Naboth's vineyard (1 Kgs. 21). Here is a clear violation of the ninth commandment ("You shall not bear false witness against your neighbor [fellow citizen]" [Exod. 20:16]).

Once again, an angry prophet, in this case Elijah, denounces the guilty party and decrees dire punishment ("Have you killed and also taken possession? . . . In the place where dogs licked up the blood of Naboth shall dogs lick your own blood" [1 Kgs. 21:19]). Once again a king is faced with the undeniable facts, is remorseful and repentant. And again God is merciful and postpones the evil day of judgment (1 Kgs. 21:27-29).

The final historical settling of accounts, however, is not long in coming. Before the book of Kings is concluded, both Israel and Judah will have met violent ends as nations, their armies defeated, their countries conquered, their capital cities destroyed, and their leading citizens taken into captivity in faraway lands.

We have come to the end of our string as well: nine books, nine commandments. But what of the tenth: "You shall not covet"?[4]

4. The full text reads as follows:

You shall not desire [or covet] your neighbor's house. You shall not desire your neighbor's wife, his man or maidservant, his ox or his ass, or anything at all that belongs to your neighbor. (Exod. 20:17)

The version in Deut. 5:21 (5:18 in Hebrew) differs slightly from the version in Exodus. In Exodus, the neighbor's house comes before the neighbor's wife; in Deuteronomy the order is reversed. In addition, in Exodus the word for desire or covet *(taḥmōḏ)* is repeated; in Deuteronomy, *taḥmōḏ* is used the first time, but a synonym, *titawweh,* is used for desire or covet the second time the concept is referred to.

The tenth commandment is distinctive. Its emphasis is on motivation or attitude, rather than action, as is clearly the case with the other commandments. It functions therefore as a complement or supplement to several of the preceding commandments — stealing, murder, adultery, and false swearing — providing the motivation clause or explanation of the mental or emotional process behind the commission of the crime. In each of the crimes involved in the sixth, seventh, eighth, and ninth commandments, what lay behind the crime was the illicit desire, the sinful urge to take what belonged to another: the booty from Jericho in the case of Achan, who confesses that he saw the various items in the spoil and "I desired them" (Josh. 7:21) — the same verb as in the Decalogue; the same can be said of the criminals in the story of Judges, whose illegal desire for the Levite led ultimately to the commission of the crime of murder against his concubine; in the case of David and Bathsheba, it was David's lust after the wife of another man that led to the act of adultery. Likewise, in the case of Naboth's vineyard, it was the king's desire for Naboth's property that led to the violation of the ninth commandment, false testimony.

Thus, with a modicum of ingenuity and adjustment we can correlate the Decalogue and the primary history, and make a dramatically effective correspondence between commandments and books, leading to a climax or culmination in the final collapse of the two kingdoms, the end of national history and the Babylonian captivity.

How could such a correlation have come about in view of the heterogeneous character of the primary history and its clearly multiple authorship? Perhaps it is sheer coincidence (buttressed by the ingenuity of a modern analyst looking for such correlations). Or did a creative redactor consciously set out to construct a history of his people on the framework or scaffolding of the Decalogue, deliberately preserving an overall unity of the heterogeneous elements by the strategic highlighting of particular themes and devices to bring out the central story, which tells of the covenant between God and Israel, the ultimate consequences of the relationship and the judgment upon and verdict against the nation-states?

The fact that this particular device or pattern has never been observed before — at least to my knowledge — should caution against supposing that it was the major or central objective of the redactor. It was simply another, if dramatic, way of showing and stressing the central theme of the history of Israel, and illustrating or reflecting the unity of the account comprising the nine books of the primary history. Israel's history could be told on two levels — as the story of its people, but also in terms of its successive violations of the commandments: one by one, book by book, until it ran out of options and possibilities, and was finally destroyed as a nation and its people taken into captivity.

40

The Formation of the Canon
of the Old Testament:
The Selection and Identification
of the Torah as the Supreme Authority
of the Postexilic Community

This presentation arises out of an effort to answer a relatively simple question, which turned out to be not so simple. Moreover, the ramifications turned out to be more interesting and perhaps more important than the original question and its answer. The question is briefly: Where did the Pentateuch (i.e., the Five Books of Moses) come from, or How did the Torah become the primary canon of the Hebrew Bible? Why just these five books, not more and not fewer? When did this momentous event take place, and under what circumstances and by whose authoritative decision?

Before attempting to answer this multiple-choice question or even discuss it, I must explain the connection between this rather technical question concerning the canon of the Hebrew Bible and the theme of "religion and law." The response is both clear and simple: The Torah of the Hebrew Bible is the classic example of this theme — the wedding or interweaving of religion and law, i.e., religion understood primarily in the categories of law, or law understood as the epitome or summation of religion, its essential expression. Thus, in dealing with the question of the Torah as canon and especially as law, I inevitably and quite deliberately enter the domain of religion and law.

The paper falls into two parts: the first deals with the question of the origin and emergence of the Pentateuch as the law par excellence, the primary canon of the Hebrew Bible, while in the second part I will consider the rationale and intentionality of the decision to equate or identify law with canon (of sacred scripture). The mutually reinforcing roles of law and religion are exemplified in the traditions concerning Moses, who stands preeminently in both spheres: as the chief prophet of the Hebrew Bible and as the supreme lawgiver. In the person of Moses and in the achievement attributed to him, namely the Torah, the roles, tasks, contents, and purposes of religion and law are found intertwined and blended.

The Torah, which in its present form (not its substantial content, which is earlier) may date anywhere between the 8th and 5th centuries B.C.E. (and most likely to the 7th and early 6th centuries), constitutes the principal legacy of the ancient Near East to the Western world in the realm of religion and law.

The Origin and Emergence of the Pentateuch: Torah (Law)

I think the tradition is both reasonable and plausible that associates the promulgation of the Torah as divine law transmitted through Moses to Israel with the efforts and undertakings of Ezra the Scribe, aided and abetted by Nehemiah the Governor around the middle of the 5th century B.C.E. Whether or not the "Law" that he read from the pulpit on the solemn occasion recorded in Neh. 8 was the whole Pentateuch or only selected portions of it, or some sort of summary with explanations, does not affect the discussion here, since I believe that the entire Pentateuch had long since been compiled, completed, edited, and published, and thus would have been available to this worthy scribe. In other words, his work was that of selection and presentation rather than compilation, much less editing or composing.

The result was to shift a literary boundary line from its original rational and plausible position between the books of Kings and the book of Isaiah to another position, between the books of Deuteronomy and Joshua. While such a shift may seem minor or inconsequential, it had momentous implications for the community addressed by Ezra, and even greater ones for the indefinite future. I can summarize this slight action in the following way: In my judgment, in the middle of the 6th century B.C.E., the Hebrew Bible, the first biblical canon, consisted of the primary history (the books from Genesis through Kings) and a supporting collection of prophetic works. The primary history (as I have tried to show elsewhere)[1] was the basic Bible, the story of God and his people Israel, which ran from the very beginning of everything until the demise of the kingdoms of Israel and Judah toward the end of 2 Kings. It must have been compiled and completed in its present form

---

1. "The Earliest Bible," *The Bible and Its Traditions*. Michigan Quarterly Review 22/3 (1983): 167-75; repr. in M. P. O'Connor and D. N. Freedman, eds., *Backgrounds for the Bible* (Winona Lake: Eisenbrauns, 1987), 29-37 [see above, Chapter 32]; "The Law and the Prophets," *Congress Volume, Bonn 1962*. VTS 9 (Leiden: Brill, 1963): 250-65 [see above, Chapter 14].

not earlier than 560 B.C.E. and not later than 540 B.C.E. (but I think that the actual date was much closer to the earlier figure than the later one). In fact, I believe that the final sentences of 2 Kings are a statement of the date and place of publication, shortly after the accession of Awil-Marduk, the heir and successor of the great Nebuchadnezzar, as king of Babylonia. The collection of prophetic books, which included Isa. 1–33, Isa. 36–39, Jeremiah, Ezekiel, and as many as nine of the Minor Prophets (excluding the last three in the canonical collection, Haggai, Zechariah, and Malachi), was produced at about the same time (e.g., Jeremiah ends with the same chapter with which 2 Kings ends) to provide supporting data and elaborative details concerning the role of the prophets in the period beginning in the first half of the 8th century B.C.E., when the Assyrian threat first materialized on the northeastern horizon, and ending with the tragic events including the end of the southern kingdom, the capture of Jerusalem, and the captivity of the leading people. Equally, if not more importantly, however, the collection shows the firm conviction of the same prophets that in spite of the overwhelming disaster for the nation, there would be a future for them, a return and restoration more glorious than anything they had experienced in the past.

In effect, I believe that what Ezra did was to redivide these two great works and produce instead the familiar, present-day arrangement of the Hebrew Bible. Instead of primary history and prophetic corpus, which I postulate for the content and order of the books of the canon in the middle of the 6th century, the result of Ezra's action gives the Torah or Pentateuch, and the prophetic corpus now divided between Former Prophets (the balance of the primary history, including Joshua-Judges-Samuel-Kings) and Latter Prophets (also four books: Isaiah [now including both 1 and 2 Isaiah, all sixty-six chapters], Jeremiah, Ezekiel, and the book of the Twelve [including Haggai, Zechariah, and Malachi as well as the earlier nine]). The line of division has been moved from the logical separation between narrative and prophecy, i.e., between the end of Kings and the beginning of Isaiah, to a somewhat artificial one between Law and Prophecy, i.e., the end of Deuteronomy and the beginning of Joshua, where there is no obvious separation, since the book of Joshua has been organized consciously and deliberately to be contiguous and continuous with Deuteronomy. In short, an artificial but extremely significant wedge was driven into the primary history to create a new and decisive entity: Torah, the Law of Moses. Inevitably it contains the life of Moses as well, but the emphasis here is on the teaching of Moses, expressed in a variety of forms including especially legal codes.

I believe there were excellent reasons for making the change at that time and in those circumstances, but the question is a complicated one, first requiring a consideration of an intermediate pattern of arrangement of the canon before taking up the determination of the present order of the books and their divisions. Indeed, one may wonder whether I have not unnecessarily complicated and confused matters by proposing the hypothesis about the primary history and a 6th-century canon. Some scholars have indeed suggested as much to me, but the basic problem is hardly of my making, and it would remain to be dealt with even if my suggestions were dismissed or ignored, which by and large has been their fate. It has long been recognized (especially since the classic and seminal work of Martin Noth in describing and delimiting the so-called Deuteronomic history, a major literary work that included the books from Deuteronomy through Kings) that the book of Deuteronomy was tied in various literary and linguistic ways to the books that followed rather than to the books that preceded.[2] So it has become customary now to speak of a P (Priestly) work, which runs from Genesis through Numbers, and a D (Deuteronomic) work, which runs from Deuteronomy through Kings. If one accepts this analysis of the major components of the primary history, then the creation of a Pentateuch including the four books of the P work and only the first book of the D work must be explained equally as the deliberate decision to shift an established boundary from one place to another. In other words, in order to attach Deuteronomy to the Tetrateuch, it must have been detached from the literary work to which it previously belonged. Such a decision, based upon whatever considerations, which is contrary to the literary structure of both works and which no doubt opposes the intention of the earlier compiler or editor, requires investigation and explanation. So I must return to an analysis of the important political and literary developments of the century from the compilation and publication of the First Bible until the emergence of the canon of the Law and the Prophets as the central units of the Hebrew Bible.

Shortly after the publication of the primary history and the first prophetic collection around 560 B.C.E., Cyrus the Persian king began his meteoric career of conquest and the consolidation of a vast empire. For the Judahites in captivity in Babylonia, this development, including specifically the capture of Babylon in 539 B.C.E., would ultimately mean redemption and release, return, restoration, and renewal, a new beginning in the old land. So dramatic was this reversal of fortunes, and so unexpected in spite of the widespread anticipation of the end of the Babylonian hegemony and a possible return of the exiles (as it turned out the details were vastly different) that it was necessary to produce a new literature to account for and cope with the new situation unfolding before their eyes. Extraordinary things were happening and even more remarkable things were about to happen, so an array of new prophets appeared in order to proclaim the new age and to link it up with the former times and the transition through which they were living.

Beginning with Second Isaiah (which includes chs. 34–35 and 40–66) and continuing and concluding with Haggai, Zechariah, and perhaps Malachi, the prophetic collection was supplemented and enlarged to bring the story of Jerusalem

---

2. M. Noth, *A History of Pentateuchal Traditions* (Englewood Cliffs: Prentice-Hall, 1972); *The Deuteronomistic History*. JSOT Sup 15 (Sheffield: JSOT Press, 1981); the latter work is a translation of pp. 1-110 of *Überlieferungsgeschichtliche Studien* (Tübingen: Max Niemeyer, 1957).

and its temple full circle with the renewal of the Jerusalem community and the rebuilding of the temple. In this way the prophetic canon was brought to completion, while another great historical work was produced to accommodate the new developments: the Chronicler's work. This narrative, which shares thematic and stylistic features with the P work, constitutes in major part an alternative version of the Deuteronomic history. I have written elsewhere about the date, provenience, purpose, and contents of this work and there is no need here to repeat those points.[3] Briefly stated, however, I believe that this work in its original or perhaps an early form was produced at the time of the rebuilding of the temple (between 520 and 515 B.C.E.) and was intended to support the claims of the returned exiles to preferred status in the restored community and to encourage them in rebuilding the temple and renewing the city. It would have included most of 1 and 2 Chronicles (especially the narrative sections beginning with the death of Saul and accession of David in 1 Chr. 10 and continuing through 2 Chronicles) and then the first three chapters of Ezra and possibly some material from the accounts before ch. 7. With its emphasis on the kingdom of Judah, the house of David, the city of Jerusalem and its temple, as well as the strict omission of the northern kingdom from consideration, it may have been meant as a replacement for the primary history itself, or at least a revised version of the history of the monarchy. It, along with the prophetic canon, would have been used by the returning exiles to validate their claims upon the land, the city, and the temple. The effort to rewrite or revise the classic history of Israel did not entirely succeed, but the Chronicler's work, ultimately supplemented by the memoirs of Ezra and Nehemiah, constituted the framework of a third circle of literature in the canon. Such books as the Psalms, Proverbs, and others that could be associated with the house of David (e.g., Ruth, Song of Songs, Ecclesiastes) were included, as well as those that dealt with the fortunes of the sacred city and its temple (e.g., Lamentations and, later, Daniel).

Sixty years later, Ezra the Scribe came from Babylon with a revised agenda. The hopes and expectations of the early arrivals had only been fulfilled in part, and circumstances clearly were altered. The concentration on the revival of the kingdom and the reinstatement of the royal house clearly was misplaced and possibly dangerous. Ezra supplemented the Chronicler's work with his memoirs, and those of Nehemiah were also attached. Whatever their personal relations (they had a tendency to speak of their own labors without mentioning or recognizing the contribution of the other, but that is hardly a compelling reason to date them in different generations, much less in different centuries), they were colleagues and partners in the work of reformation. By this time there were subtle but significant changes in emphasis and outlook: The traditions of the house of David were of the greatest value, especially in connection with the restored temple, because David had organized everything in preparation for its building in the first

---

3. "The Chronicler's Purpose," *CBQ* 23 (1961): 436-42 [see above, Chapter 10].

place, and its music and liturgy besides. Its actual construction was carried out by Solomon, and it is no accident that these two kings dominate the whole of the books of Chronicles, with lesser attention given to their descendants. But that was all in the past; for the present the proper attitude was to remember the past, not to await or expect, much less to plan or plot the restoration of the monarchy or of the dynasty at this time. With the passing of Zerubbabel and perhaps his son-in-law El-natan, the house of David surrendered its executive post, the governorship, and it remains only a genealogical list of names in the time of Ezra and Nehemiah (cf. 1 Chr. 3, esp. vv. 19-24). Ultimate earthly authority would be lodged in the Persian Empire, while limited autonomy would be the most that could be expected, at least at present. At the same time, the life of the community could and would be ordered in accordance with the precepts and regulations of the great ancient lawgiver, Moses the man of God. Internal arrangements and practices would be governed by these laws, while external matters would be regulated by the masters of the empire.

The province, or subprovince, should be and would be administered by the returned exiles, a high priest of the house of Aaron and a governor of Judahite descent, but they would be responsible in temporal affairs to higher authority vested in the satraps and ultimately the emperor himself. There was no place for a king of the house of David, even though members of the royal house doubtless survived and could be identified at that time, and for some time thereafter. In the initial phases of the return, a scion of the house of David, Zerubbabel, served as governor of Judah and Jerusalem, but not as king. Even this compromise apparently failed, because no son or descendant of Zerubbabel was named governor after him. It is possible, on the basis of recently published seal inscriptions, to determine that a successor of Zerubbabel was El-natan, the husband of a woman named Shelomit, who in turn may have been the daughter of Zerubbabel (cf. 1 Chr. 3:19).[4] After that person, however, the connection with the house of David vanishes and subsequent governors are simply appointed officials for varying terms. Among them, of course, is Nehemiah, who has no royal claims or pretensions whatever. With the relegation of the house of David to obscurity by the end of the 6th century B.C.E., the time had also come to assign thoughts about or hopes concerning this dynasty to the pages of past history or to an indefinite and far-off future, and to put these in language that would not alarm the neighboring peoples or disturb the imperial authorities.

I summarize these developments in the following manner. Israel, in its long history, could count two great heroes among the many who served their country well: Moses, the founder of the nation and the leader during the critical transition

---

4. C. L. Meyers and E. M. Meyers, *Haggai, Zechariah 1–8*. AB 25B (Garden City: Doubleday, 1987), 12-13; N. Avigad, *Bullae and Seals from a Post-Exilic Judean Archive*. Qedem 4 (1976): 30ff.

period from bondage in Egypt to occupation of the Promised Land; and David, who came at a critical juncture in the nation's history, and firmly and finally established its independence and suzerainty over an extended territory. The primary history gives an essentially balanced, if slightly prejudiced, picture of the two men and their far-reaching attainments. For the period of the monarchy, especially in Judah, and for the period when these works were being published, the house of David constituted an actual and perhaps visible means of independence and self-rule, as well as a potential threat to existing authorities. In the prophets, as well as in the Chronicler's work, the house of David received special attention and was the bearer of aspirations and expectations for the future. The same could not be said for Moses, whose house had vanished long since, and whose work was enshrined in a book. As it turned out, he was the authentic alternative, since he posed no threat to external authorities, but could provide a structured way of life for survivors under foreign rule.

The pendulum swung one way with the returnees and their leaders and prophets toward the end of the 6th century, and then in the opposite direction in the days of Ezra and Nehemiah. Neither prophets nor pretenders play any role in the plans or strategies of the latter. On the contrary, for Ezra, the life of the community would be shaped and structured by the domain of Moses, and only indirectly (i.e., in the liturgy of the temple) by that of David. In making the momentous decision to separate the Torah from the Former Prophets, or to extract the Pentateuch from the primary history, Ezra (if he is the one who made the decision) thus created not just an anomalous literary work, but shifted the focus and target of biblical religion from an essentially historical mode (i.e., divine acts in human history) to the mode of law (i.e., divine words or commands to regulate the behavior of the human community). While the inclusion of the book of Genesis, which is hardly a book of law, reflects the original concern for historical continuity in the larger work (the primary history, an argument strengthened by the notable connections between Genesis and Joshua in terms of promise and fulfillment, present in the larger work, but disconnected in the creation of the Pentateuch), and the narrative of the other books of the Torah tells the dramatic story of Israel's beginnings from deliverance from bondage in Egypt until the settlement in Trans-jordan, the emphasis in the Torah is clearly on the spoken word, the once-for-all and unchangeable command of the living God, the covenant Lord who imposes a pattern of believing and behaving on his people, the variety of written codes governing all the aspects of faith and practice, life and works, through examples and general statements.

On the one hand, therefore, Ezra's aim was to exalt the rule of law and the role of Moses as mediator of the covenant by which the people were to live. That Moses was in fact not a king and founded no dynasty, regardless of the authority that he actually wielded or of dynastic claims made by his descendants, made him a much more useful and attractive figure and symbol in the difficult and delicate situation in which Ezra and the people found themselves than David, who was a king and had a dynasty, members of which were alive and could be identified at that time. Along with the idea of exalting the status of Moses and especially his role as lawgiver, there was the strategy of diminishing or distancing David as a role model. As conqueror of the surrounding territories and creator of the Israelite empire, as founder of a dynasty that had ruled in Jerusalem for more than four hundred years and whose descendants might rule again, David was not the person to inspire confidence in the neighbors or trust in the eyes of the authorities. The choice for a person like Ezra, as well as for Nehemiah, was both inevitable and congenial. Without disturbing the existing documents already part of the canon of Holy Scripture, but only by moving the boundary marker between the parts, Ezra was able to focus the spotlight on Moses as prophet and lawgiver, and thereby to achieve a shift in the definition and delimitation of biblical religion, with the most serious consequences for the present and the future. At the same time, the figure of David was not so much diminished as obscured. He remained a great hero of the past, and a less well defined hope for the future, but meanwhile there would be no emphasis on the possibilities of the present, or any serious talk of a restoration of the monarchy. Henceforth, law would be seen as, and at, the heart of biblical religion, the law revealed through Moses at Mt. Sinai, while history and prophecy would be less central and play supporting roles. Nothing was lost, which is the secret of the canonical process, but some elements were shifted, and priorities rearranged. Over time, Judaism would move in a variety of ways, but the essential ingredients were preserved and available. For the present, the dominant component was Moses and law; in the future there could be a revival of prophecy and David, i.e., the Messiah ben-David, who would restore the kingdom and its glory.

Similarly, Ezra or his editor and scribe supplemented the Chronicler's work with an appendix containing his memoirs and those of his contemporary and collaborator, the civil governor, Nehemiah, thus redirecting a document that emphasized national independence, the dynasty of David, and the temple of Jerusalem, so that finally that work would conform to the newly revised but ultimately ancient pattern. What finally counts for Ezra and his colleagues is neither national independence nor monarchy, but the intimate relationship of the people with their God, mediated by Moses, that existed before either nationhood or kingship and had outlasted both. This relationship was established and is governed and regulated by the individual commands and precepts of a holy God, who has chosen to put his name and his glory in the midst of this tiny but precious community. Without rejecting the prophets and their dreams, or the Davidic dynasty and the hopes and expectations associated with it, Ezra nevertheless relegated those to the wings, and cleared the center of the stage for the Torah above all, for Moses the founder and the lawgiver, for the divine words he and he alone communicated.

Before turning to the second part of the paper, I pause briefly to summarize the first part:

I. The First Bible (*ca.* 560 B.C.E.)
   A. The Primary History (including Genesis through Kings)
   B. The Prophetic Corpus (associated with the Primary History)
      1. First Isaiah (chs. 1–33, 36–39)
      2. Jeremiah (including ch. 52)
      3. Ezekiel
      4. Minor Prophets (including the first nine books)

(The First Bible, which may have included other books as well, such as the Psalter and Proverbs, was compiled not earlier than 560 B.C.E. and not later than 540 B.C.E.)

II. The Second Bible (*ca.* 518 B.C.E.)
   A. The Primary History
   B. The Prophetic Corpus
      1. The Three Major Prophets
         a. Second Isaiah combined with First Isaiah to produce the full book: Isa. 1–66. Chs. 34–35 and 40–66 were composed, compiled, and conbined with First Isaiah in the two decades between the First Bible and the Edict of Cyrus in 539 B.C.E. The timetable apparently was determined by a calculation of the years of a jubilee from the me of the destruction of the temple (587 B.C.E.) until the expected return and restoration in 538 B.C.E.
         b. Jeremiah
         c. Ezekiel
      2. The Twelve Prophets
         a. The first nine books, as above
         b. Haggai, Zechariah, and Malachi added before the completion of the Second Temple in 515 B.C.E. The last date given in these books is the 4th year of Darius in Zech. 7 = 518 B.C.E.

(No doubt the Second Bible included other works as well, including especially the following:)

   C. The Chronicler's History
      1. 1 and 2 Chronicles
      2. Ezra 1–3, down to the resumption of work on the Second Temple under the supervision of Zerubbabel.

III. The Third Bible (*ca.* 430 B.C.E.)
   A. The Torah (= Law). I hold the isolation of this work from the larger primary history and its identification as the primary and central authority within the Bible to be the achievement of Ezra as recorded in Ezra-Nehemiah.

B. The Prophets
  1. The Former Prophets
     a. Joshua
     b. Judges
     c. Samuel (including 1 and 2 Samuel)
     d. Kings (including 1 and 2 Kings)
  2. The Latter Prophets
     a. The three major prophets
        1) Isaish (1–66)
        2) Jeremiah (1–52)
        3) Ezekiel (1–48)
     b. The Twelve Prophets
        1) The nine earlier books
        2) The three later books
C. The Writings
  1. The Chronicler's Work
     a. 1 and 2 Chronicles
     b. Ezra-Nehemiah. (The latter chapters of Ezra and Nehemiah were derived from the memoirs of the two men, and incorporated in the work during the latter part of the 5th century. The horizon does not extend beyond the reign of Artaxerxes I, 464-424 B.C.E., or Darius II, 423-404 B.C.E.)
  2. The Other Books
     a. Psalms
     b. Proverbs
     c. Job
     d. The Megilloth (Rolls). The collection no doubt included books such as Ruth, Song of Songs, and Lamentations. I would hesitate to make a judgment about books such as Ecclesiastes and Esther.

Moses as Apostolic Prophet and Lawgiver

In the first part of this paper, I have proposed that Ezra, in effect, created or at least identified the Torah (i.e., the Pentateuch) by extracting it from a larger work, thereby spotlighting and focusing attention on the figure of Moses as both the founder of the nation and its primary and principal lawgiver. It is nevertheless important to note that the tradition concerning Moses' role in these areas is both old and widely distributed among the sources. The last thing I wish to do is give the impression that Ezra invented the tradition or exaggerated the role assigned to Moses in the thinking of Israel. Whatever one makes of the documentary hypothesis as it relates to the Pentateuch, the representation of Moses as founding father and lawgiver, leader of the exodus and the wilderness wanderings, chieftain in battle and judge of his people, prophet and revealer of Yahweh, is essentially the same in all of the sources, with only minor variations or differences in emphasis and terminology. Even if the Hebrew word for prophet (nābî') is anachronistic when applied directly to Moses, it was clearly understood that he performed the function and fulfilled the role of one who receives the word of God, is commissioned to deliver it to the people, and does so in accord with the divine command. He is the principal human figure in the dramatic story of Israel's deliverance from bondage in Egypt, the wanderings in the wilderness, its victories in the plains and plateaus of Transjordan, and initial settlement there, pending the invasion of the West Bank.

Moses and his Torah (cf. Deut. 33:4) represent, therefore, the initial and enduring combination of law and religion — religion and law — which has been the major contribution of the ancient Near East, and more particularly of the biblical tradition, to Western culture and civilization. The tradition of written law is an old one in the Near East, going back much earlier than any conceivable date for Moses. Furthermore, legal codes and their sponsors are invariably associated with religious authority and sanction, so I cannot argue for the originality or uniqueness of Moses and Torah on that basis. There is innovation and novelty, but they lie in the nature of the combination, the interfusion of the elements, rather than in the idea that law and religion have something to do with each other.

In viewing the data from inscriptions and other archaeological finds, one observes that a sizable number of such law codes have been preserved, although generally in fragmentary form, the most famous and important being that of Hammurabi, the fourth king of the first dynasty of Babylon, who may be dated around 1750 B.C.E. This extensive code of laws deals with a number of subjects and covers a variety of cases, which are also treated in the Bible, as well as in other codes. Earlier codes are known in both Semitic and Sumerian; the format and general content must go back into the 3rd millennium and possibly the early part of it. Often the code is promulgated by the king, who is shown or described as presenting it to an appropriate deity. The purpose clearly is to claim divine sanction for the code and its administrator, and to lend authority both to the provisions and to those who are expected to enforce them. The codes are exemplary in character, designed to illustrate the principles of justice and the manner of its execution. Evidently each domain, whether law or religion, is intended to support and reinforce the other. The law appeals to religion for authority and sanction, while religion finds in law its appropriate expression and implementation, whereby the sacral requirements are met, and the presence or threat of force ensures conformity and submission to the demands of religion. Each seeks from and contributes to the other in order to strengthen both, at least insofar as institutional interests are concerned.

This constant and repeated association no doubt contributed to the rule of law and widespread conformity to the social and political regulations of the times and places. Such a combination tended to ensure domestic tranquillity and a certain measure of security for all members of the society. But it was designed and exploited by those in power to preserve the status quo, and it was frankly intended to benefit those who exercised authority in both spheres. The essential difficulty lay in the fact that such law and such religion were essentially pragmatic instead of being principled, and could easily serve, as they often did, the interests of autocratic and oppressive governments. The notion of a principle of law or ethical behavior independent of and higher than those who had power was either not recognized at all, or included as a mere rhetorical flourish. In the long run, the system proved to be of benefit primarily to those by whom it was designed and operated, rather than for those who especially needed to be protected by its application: the poor, the alien, the bereaved, and the afflicted.

The same could be said of legal codes and instruments instituted by kings and rulers of later times, such as Justinian or Napoleon, both of whom sponsored famous and long-enduring codes of law. In these latter cases, the codes inevitably reflected the influence of the biblical tradition in modifying or qualifying their formulation and application, but the major components remain much the same: To the extent that the king or ruler is directly involved in the codification or enforcement of the regulations, the basic interest of the state in social control and the reinforcement of its power remains dominant. Religion provides the means by which that authority is sanctioned and sanctified, while the religious establishment is itself served and enhanced by the power of the state.

The emergence of Moses as leader and lawgiver is, however, a new and different phenomenon. It is no accident that Moses is never called a king (in spite of Deut. 33:4-5, which must be understood as referring to God as king, not Moses), and never associated with the political structure of a monarchy as are most if not all of the so-called lawgivers of the ancient Near East (the traditions of Greece and Rome may reflect a different experience and understanding of the role of law and relationship to religion and vice versa). Moses was not a political leader seeking the sanction of religion, nor a religious leader seeking the power of the state to enforce his rules, but a prophet, one called by God and commissioned by him to speak in his behalf and perform the tasks assigned to him. The authority behind the authorities in both spheres is Yahweh himself, who rules over both law and religion, over the state and the religious order.

The role of prophet as lawgiver is unique in the person of Moses, and specific for the biblical tradition. Thus, law is not independently developed or derived from political and social or economic areas and elements. It is not established or imposed by powerful groups in society, but proceeds from religion, is itself the expression of religious truth and revelation. Religion is embodied in law, just as law is the mechanism by which religion rules over and operates in the lives of its adherents.

If one believes that with Moses and the Torah a new element was introduced into the world, especially of the ancient Near East, then in what ways did the Mosaic society, early Israel, differ from its neighbors? The question is not as easily answered as one should or might suppose. Superficially, at least, and in many details Israel was hardly distinguishable from the other peoples, and this circumstance is reflected in the numerous clauses in the codes, both biblical and nonbiblical, dealing with similar and conventional circumstances and situations, such as the ubiquitous and irrepressible goring ox. All too often, as well, Israel did not attain to the level of behavior demanded of it by its religion, and was no better — and sometimes even worse — than its neighbors. Nevertheless, a new kind of society was visualized and initiated by Moses, and it is described and circumscribed in the legal sections of the Torah. Obedience to the commandments is for the sake of God and not for the sake of a king. Any national enhancement or success would be a serendipitous by-product, not a goal of conformity to the requirements. To love God and one's neighbor adequately summarizes the purpose and function of law in Israelite society, and at the same time it is the epitome of religious devotion and obedience.

In the solemn compact between God and his people based upon the prior act of divine grace in delivering his people from bondage in Egypt, i.e., redeeming them from slavery and thereby acquiring them as a personal possession (Hebrew $s^e gull\bar{a}$), a weighty obligation thereby rests upon the whole body politic and distributively on each individual. The latter is bound not only to obey as a person, i.e., to govern his or her personal behavior in accordance with the stipulations, but to act responsibly as a member of the community, which is ultimately answerable to the divine suzerain for its actions, including those of its individual members. The latter responsibility, as also the former, varies with the status and skills, the possibilities and actualities of each individual. Of the one to whom much has been given, much will be expected; but balancing that rather austere guideline is the one that says that little will be asked of the one to whom little has been given. Thus, those in positions of power, wealth, and leadership will be held more strictly to account than many others. At the same time, special protection and assistance are promised to those outside, those who are deprived, those who are afflicted — in short, the victims of society.

Beneath the superficial resemblances between Israel's covenant and the codes of other nations, which are inevitable and understandable, and alongside the details that relate to time and place and local circumstances, there is a central and visible difference, a plan and a goal: to establish an equitable society on earth, one in which the sense of purpose and spur to action derive from a profound acknowledgment of divine authority, and a firm commitment to the service and worship of the deity who has made his will known. The whole pattern of behavior would be governed by these principles: from the basic level of conformity to the rules of what is permitted on the one hand and what is prohibited on the other, to the highest level of fulfillment of the commandments of love, as expressed in the admonishments of Deut. 6:4-6 and Lev. 19:18 (and others). The summary of these obligations, as offered on more than one occasion in the New Testament, attests the centrality and ultimacy of the duty to love God with all one's heart and soul and mind, and to love one's fellow human being as oneself.

The legacy of Moses and his Torah to the Western world is the merger of law and religion, the inseparable joint expression of the divine will, communicated by his prophet. If true religion involves the right relationship between humanity and deity, then the law is the way in which that relationship is defined and regulated. There is, after all, the inescapable factor of obligation and obedience. Such a relationship, biblically understood, cannot be purely mystical, romantic, or privately personal; it must be ethical, moral, and social. It must be regulated by law, but the law must be in accordance with the divine will and interest, and not merely a social contract meeting the needs or accommodating the interests of humans.

What I have said of Moses and his Torah applies as well to others in the same tradition. Prophet-founders of religious communities are also the lawgivers for those groups. The occurrence of such phenomena outside of the Bible, the appearance of individuals in the role of prophets and founders, and as revealers and lawgivers, enhances the validity of the view proposed here: that Moses as lawgiver reflects a different pattern for the association of religion and law in the formation and preservation of a particular community. I have already indicated that Jesus was seen by at least some of his followers as a lawgiver in the pattern of Moses, but transcending him (especially in the Gospel of Matthew, in which the teachings of Jesus are deliberately set in contrast with those of Moses). While there has been a good deal of debate about the Law, its validity and its applicability in the new Christian dispensation, and while there has been a great deal of discussion of St. Paul's supposed antinomianism, Jesus as supreme lawgiver, and the Christian community as functioning under divine law, has always been the prevailing view in the Church, and remains so.

I see a similar phenomenon in Islam, in which the Prophet Muḥammad is not only the founder of a new community based on the exclusive worship and service of Allah (equivalent of Hebrew *ᵉlōah,* one of the designations of the God of Israel), but its lawgiver as well. The same kind of union or combination of religion and law is present in Islam as I have noted for Judaism and Christianity, in which the founder-prophet is also the revealer and lawgiver.

Finally I call attention to the same sort of development in the history of Christianity. In diverse times and places, prophetic figures have appeared and communities devoted and dedicated to these leaders, seen as revealers and lawgivers, have arisen. Here I can mention that uniquely American phenomenon, Joseph Smith, who was the prophet-founder of a new society, the Church of Jesus Christ of Latter-day Saints (popularly known as Mormons), and also its principal lawgiver. In an effort to maintain both contiguity and continuity with the past, the

483

pattern of prophet-leader who is also lawgiver has been preserved in this community of faith, so there is a steady procession of "prophets" who are empowered to modify existing laws or proclaim new ones. In self-reforming and self-renewing fashion, this structure reflects the dynamic association of religion and law, established initially by Moses with his Torah.

41

Dinah and Shechem,
Tamar and Amnon

The subject of the following paper is the two stories of Dinah the daughter of Jacob (Gen. 34) and Tamar the daughter of David (2 Sam. 13). The relationship of the stories to each other and their places in the larger literary context have been much discussed, and no consensus has been reached. I am not concerned here to settle such questions, but rather to try to show that the stories together serve a purpose in the larger literary work that has come down to us, quite apart or beyond the part that each plays in the immediate context where it is now placed.

My view, hardly original but part of an increasingly vocal minority, is that both stories were written (!) by the same author, and I would go further and say that they belonged to the same literary work, forming bookends or the two parentheses around the story of Israel from the time of the patriarchs until the establishment of the united kingdoms by David (and Solomon). While it is clear that the stories play a similar but more subdued role in the final work, the whole primary history, the latter has merely and without change or comment incorporated the previously completed J work along with other sources. Our purpose, therefore, is to examine the ways in which the stories function in a work my colleague Richard E. Friedman calls Super J — which runs from Genesis through Samuel and probably on into Kings, at least to the establishment of the kingdom in the hands of Solomon, son and successor of the great David.

We shall have to ask the following questions and then try to answer some of them:

(1) Evidence for common authorship = themes, vocabularies, etc.
(2) Their relationship showing they belong to common work
(3) Each in its own context
(4) In the larger context

(a) Original setting and purpose
(b) J's objective — 10th century
(c) The final redactor

The arguments for common authorship of the two stories are chiefly literary and linguistic. In view of the common subject matter, we might expect overlapping vocabulary, regardless of who the author of each might be, but there are special terms, distinctive of J and the court history, which favor a theory of common authorship (e.g., *ktnt psym* only in Gen. 37:3 and 2 Sam. 13:18 in the primary history). While it is always possible to argue that the writer of one story imitated the work of the author of the other, there is no easy way to establish priority or dependency and it is simpler not to add authors. If one will do, that is better than two or three, not to speak of revisers and redactors.

Going further, we may suggest that the two stories belong to a single great literary work, which we may call Super J, combining J with the court history along with a connecting unit that runs from the end of J (Judg. 1–2), through Judges and Samuel and including what has been generally called the "older source" in these books.

If the case can be made, and we think it can, then it will be noted that the two stories come near the beginning and end of the larger work (Genesis and 2 Samuel) and serve roughly as bookends to form a kind of envelope or parentheses around the bulk of the J-CH source. Perhaps it would be better to describe these two stories as producing an echo effect, a repetition of a certain theme with conspicuous variations, combining diversity of detail with certain stationary or unchanging elements, resulting in a merismus or at least merismatic impressions. Thus, while for the most part we can compare and contrast specific features of the two stories, there is a small group of components that must be linked across the stories to produce the effects mentioned, and it is only by setting these components side by side that we can recognize that not only is a single mind at work but that the stories belong to a single literary endeavor.

We may suggest chiasm as an example. While it is often difficult to determine just what this elementary and ubiquitous literary device signifies in a given context, and specifically whether it has some bearing on the interpretation of the passage or passages under consideration or is only an ornamental flourish, there are situations in which the chiasm has an organic role and points to something of structural importance. Its main function is to tie one passage to another, reinforcing the notion of an envelope construction.

The central action in both stories is described in almost identical language, but the order of the verbs is different:

(1) Gen. 34:2

(wayyar' 'ōṯāh
šᵉḵem) . . . wayyiqqaḥ 'ōṯāh

486

wayyiškab̲ 'ōt̲āh way'anneh̲ā

(when Shechem saw her) . . . then he took her and he lay (with) her and he had intercourse with her.

(2) 2 Sam. 13:14

(wayyeḥezaq mimmenâ way'anneh̲ā wayyiškab̲ 'ōt̲āh)
and he (Amnon) overpowered her (lit., he was stronger than she was) and he had intercourse with her and he lay with her.

There are problems of analysis and interpretation in these passages, to which we will return later on, but here we point to the change in the order of the final verbs in the two passages:

Gen. 34:2

wayyiškab̲ 'ōt̲āh way(ᵉ)'anneha

2 Sam. 13:14

way(ᵉ)'anneh̲ā wayyiškab̲ 'ōt̲āh

The wording is identical except for the order, including the specialized term *'nh* (עָנָה, in the piel) and the anomalous use of *škb* with *'t*. As several other passages (in 2 Sam. 13:11-12 and Deut. 22:23, 29) show, the normal usage is *škb 'm* whereas here we have not only the particle *'t*, but it is pointed as though it were the sign of the definite direct object rather than the synonymous preposition "with." It has been suggested the *škb* has been substituted for the cruder verb *šgl* or the like, out of deference to the sensibilities of hearers and readers. In the passages where it occurs in Massoretic Text (cf. Deut. 28; Isa. 13:16; Jer. 3:2; Zech. 14:2), there is always a Qere for the Kethib in the text that substitutes *škb* for *šgl*. Presumably the root *šgl* specifies the sex act, whereas *škb*, while implying the same action, nevertheless, is ambiguous and euphemistic. That may be the case with our passages, with the exception that the substitution took place earlier than in the other cases, so the Kethib already has the more benign term and all traces of the supposed substitution have disappeared — except for the anomalous *'ōt̲āh*. For our purposes it is only important to note that the texts are identical in all respects including the anomaly just discussed, with the exception of the order of the words.

When it comes to the other verb, *wy'nh* (יְעַנֶּה), it seems to be a technical term for heterosexual intercourse, equivalent to the other verb but used in juridical contexts to confirm that penetration (and ejaculation) actually took place. While it is commonly translated and interpreted as involving force or violence, it is understood to mean rape. So in RSV we read: "he humbled her" (Gen. 34:2) or "he forced her" in 2 Sam. 13:14; in Deut. 22:24 "he violated his neighbor's wife"; 22:29 "he has violated her." The account in Deut. 22:23-24 shows clearly that the sexual liaison was considered consensual since both parties are judged guilty and punished accordingly. The verb *'nh* which is used in v. 24 cannot then be interpreted as referring to an act of rape and in all likelihood the translation "violated" is misleading. What remains is that the verb is used of illicit sex relations (in this case adultery), which could include rape (as it does in Amnon's case) but only describes the sex act itself. The same is true of the case in vv. 28-29, where the woman is not married, so adultery is not involved. Here there is no indication that force was involved, and the use of the verb *'nh* only signifies that sexual intercourse took place, that the man is considered to have committed a crime, and he is bound by law to make suitable amends for his behavior.

Coming back to the two stories in Genesis and 2 Samuel, we affirm that sexual intercourse occurred in both cases (confirmed by the use of the verb *'nh* in the piel), and on the basis of other data we can say that in the case of Amnon and Tamar rape is involved, while there is no direct evidence that Shechem was guilty of the same crime. What he did conforms rather to the case described in Deut. 22:28-29, whereas Amnon is said to have used intimidation and force in having sex with Tamar. But this distinction belongs to the larger context of the two stories. The two verbs used in Gen. 34:2 and 2 Sam. 13:14 are the same and convey the same meaning, namely that in both cases sexual intercourse occurred. As the two verbs seem to be synonymous, it is difficult to imagine that the meaning could be affected by reversing the order. It may be that the reversal of the order is only some kind of literary affectation — but it is much more likely that it serves a structural purpose — to say in effect that what was started in Genesis is now being finished in Samuel — or a pattern that began in the days of the patriarch Jacob is being repeated or echoed in the days of King David. And more than this, the troubles that ensue from the earlier case will be replicated in different shape in the lives of the king and his family.

Another example is to be found in Gen. 34:7:

> *kî-nêḇālâ ʿāśâ ḇeyiśrāʾēl . . . wekēn lōʾ yēʿāśeh*
> For he had done something disgraceful in Israel — and such things ought not to be done

and 2 Sam. 13:12:

> *kî lōʾ-yēʿāśeh ken beyiśrāʾel ʾal-taʿaśeh ʾet-hannebālâ hazzōʾt*
> For such a thing is not done in Israel
> Do not do this wanton folly.

In comparing the two passages we note that the vocabulary is not exactly the same, but all the key words are. The major chiasm is achieved by reversing the order of the main clauses, but there are other more intricate rearrangements, some chiastic, some of a different order. We list the following:

(1) *ky . . . byśr'l* in Gen. 34:7 is repeated in 2 Sam. 13:12, but the intervening words have been switched. *nblh 'śh* in Gen. 34:7 is replaced by *lōʾ-yʿśh kn* in 2 Sam. 13:12 while the reverse takes place in the second units.

(2) The internal order of the second clause is itself reversed between the two passages:

wkn l'-y'sh (Gen. 34:7)

l'-y'sh kn (2 Sam. 13:12)

(3) The phrase *bysr'l* is used with one verb in Gen. 34 and with the other in 2 Sam. 13:12. The effect is unusual but the overall meaning is not affected. The point to be made is that the literary devices reinforce the idea that not only are the passages related but they belong to the same work.

Once again we observe that the major and minor chiasms can only serve a structural purpose, not one affecting the sense or meaning of either passage. The usages, which require bringing both passages into a single focus, call attention to the similarities between the two stories, and also emphasize their function as signposts near the beginning and end of the whole narrative.

Even more important than the examples given above for showing the special connections between the two stories is the absolute contrast in the reactions of the two men after their sexual contact with the two women. Shechem on the one hand becomes enamored of Dinah and falls deeply in love with her: "And his soul clung to Dinah, Jacob's daughter, and he loved the girl, and he spoke tenderly (lit., upon the heart) to the girl" (cf. vv. 8, 11-12). On the other hand, Amnon, who professed great love for Tamar (cf. 2 Sam. 13:1, 4), changed completely and came to hate her after he had violated her: "And Amnon hated her with a very great hatred. Indeed greater was the hatred with which he hated her than the love with which he had loved her" (2 Sam. 13:15). The contrast is striking in the story itself, although one may wonder perhaps about the depth or integrity of Amnon's initial love, or whether the author might have used other words to describe the true character of Amnon's feelings. We need not second-guess the author who deliberately contrasts the emotional state of the prince before and after the meeting with Tamar and characterizes the feelings as polar opposites. The final words on this contrast are written later when the author juxtaposes comments about David, the unhappy father of both the perpetrator and the victim, and about Absalom, another offspring of the king and full sibling of Tamar. While David is very disturbed, he failed to take any action against the criminal, prince though he was, because "he loved him" (2 Sam. 13:21). [The Hebrew text (MT) is defective at this point, but the key words are preserved in the Septuagint and 4QSam[a] from Qumran, and can be restored with some confidence.] At the same time we are told that Absalom also said nothing to Amnon about the affair, but for an entirely different reason: "For Absalom hated Amnon because he had violated his sister Tamar" (13:22 — while the final pronominal suffix is ambiguous or ambivalent, the reference is to Absalom, Tamar's full brother). We observe that the opposing themes of love and hate dominate the story of Amnon and Tamar, with the pivot provided by the sudden switch in Amnon himself from love to hate.

We may further observe that while the hate is pure and untrammelled, the love in every case belies its name and is a cover for a bevy of different emotions that might better be described as "unbridled lust" (Amnon), "parental indulgence or dotage" (David — not the only time), and if we suppose that Absalom's feeling for his sister would also have been called love, beneath it was not only an obsession with honor and pride but a certain driving ambition for the throne. After all, it would not be lost on the reader of this sordid tale that Amnon was the heir apparent to David's throne, nor that Absalom was next in line. Removing Amnon would not only remove the stain on family honor and the shame endured by Tamar, but also remove one obstacle in the path of Absalom's ambition to succeed his father. The only remaining obstacle would be the father himself, and as we know, Absalom was not loath to hasten that king's departure by any means and seize the kingdom for himself.

The general theme is present in the other story too where the central thread, however, is the transformation of Shechem's lust into genuine love. The contrast between Shechem and Amnon could not be greater, in their reactions and responses to their own acts of lust and the objects of their attentions. Just as Amnon's desire turns to utter loathing and hate, Shechem's turns to tenderness and love. And this case of polar opposites can only be found by comparing and juxtaposing the stories. The frameworks, with all their differences in detail, remain the same. The father in both cases is unresponsive. Jacob says nothing, does nothing, although we are not told why. Similarly David does not intervene although we are told his reasons. The full brothers in the case of Dinah take revenge, using guile and deceit as does the full brother in the case of Tamar. But Shechem and Amnon stand apart — surprisingly, of the two it is the Gentile Prince whose character shines by contrast with that of the Jewish Prince. It is the latter who has no redeeming features or virtues that would claim our sympathy, while the author portrays Shechem as repentant and redeemed, newly chastened and in the end admirable, a victim of a horrible revenge. Both men pay for their crimes but we feel Amnon deserves to be punished for his, his acts and his attitudes, while we feel sympathy and sorrow for the prince, Shechem, in his demise.

If we continue our examination of elements in the two stories that combine and differentiate the two so that they serve separate and common themes of the author, we note that there are noteworthy resemblances between the illustrious ancestor, Jacob, and his even more illustrious descendant, David. Thus the experiences of Jacob foreshadow those of David, while the exploits of the latter fulfill the promises inherent or implicit in the former. Both are patriarchs with numerous progeny although the styles are different. David has a royal harem, while Jacob is restricted by voluntary commitment to the two daughters of Laban (cf. Gen. 31:50) although he had children in addition by their slave-women, who serve as surrogate mothers for the temporarily barren wives (they are neither second-class wives nor concubines, since they remain slaves of the wives and no one else). Nevertheless each has four principal sons (the first four by Leah in J for Jacob, and the four who gain notoriety in the court history): Reuben, Simeon, Levi, and Judah in the case of Jacob; and Amnon, Absalom, Adonijah, and Solomon in the case of David. In both instances, it is the fourth and youngest of the sons who succeeds the father in gaining power and authority while the others are bypassed or put aside. And in the succession account the stories we are considering play an important role. Thus the rape of Tamar by Amnon leads to his death and elimination from the succession, opening the way for Absalom, who is next in line. Absalom himself is ultimately wrecked by his own ambition. After engineering the death of Amnon he cannot wait to succeed his father but endeavors to usurp the throne and ultimately pays with his head (literally) for this act of rebellion.

In Jacob's case the succession is not so clearly defined and it is not a matter of killing off those in line for the patrimony but rather of determining the designated heir who will garner the preferred portion of the estate. One by one the brothers fail to sustain their claims, and Reuben, Simeon, and Levi all are shunted aside in favor of Judah the youngest of the four. While the story of Dinah deals only indirectly with this theme, it provides the reason or occasion for the failure of these two tribes to achieve preeminence among their brethren. Thus, when Simeon and Levi have committed their bloody deed of revenge, far from receiving a patriarchal blessing, they are severely rebuked by Jacob for having blackened his name and having made it odious in the region. If we can connect this episode with the Testament of Jacob in Gen. 49, there we find not a blessing but a curse on these brother-tribes (the association of the two tribes in a single blessing tends to support the idea that a common action on their part is the subject of the negative blessing uttered by the dying Jacob), banishing them from or dispersing them among the tribes of Israel. We may suppose that the author (J) believed that this was a result of their behavior in the episode of Dinah and Shechem and that these two brothers and the tribes they represented lost their status of seniority and in fact as substantial tribes with assigned territories altogether. Simeon effectively disappears (absorbed in the growing tribe of Judah) while Levi seems to have lost its holdings as a secular tribe entirely only to be revived as a special ecclesiastical body with direct reponsibility for the ark and tabernacle as loyal kinsmen of Moses and Aaron. While the killing of Shechem and his clan does not directly affect the succession, in the end it does, as the event provokes the wrath of Jacob, who pronounces the disinheriting curse upon the sons. In similar fashion, the episode of Tamar not only provides the occasion for the elimination of the primary heir to the throne of David, but also leads to the demise of the second claimant. In both there are lessons about consequences. The rapist or violator of a virgin daughter of the patriarch/king will suffer severely for his crime. In fact, he will suffer more than the punishment legally associated with the malefaction. Neither Shechem nor Amnon is guilty of a crime punishable by death, because neither of the women is married or betrothed and both guilty parties have the legal option of offering their hands in marriage or paying suitable compensation to the father or family. In both cases, however, full siblings exact a higher penalty, and take the life of the culprit in return for the violations. These avengers or revengers do not escape the consequences of their own misdeeds, however: the brothers of Dinah ultimately forfeit the patriarchal blessing and lose tribal territory and status, while Absalom, the avenging brother of Tamar, pays first by being banished from the royal court and ultimately loses his life in the attempt to seize the throne from his father.

If we may draw a lesson, it is that while the criminal or violator will not escape the consequences of this crime, especially as the act is utterly reprehensible n^ebālâ, what is outside the bounds of accepted behavior in Israel, nevertheless those who take the law into their own hands will suffer consequences as well and just as severe (as clearly in the case of Absalom).

We come now to the question of the place or function of these stories in the larger structure of Super J and beyond that to their place in the primary history as a whole.

For Super J it seems clear that apart from the basic issues of morality, and the high, special value placed on the honor and virtue of the women of Israel and especially the unmarried virgin daughter of patriarch or king (it will also be noted that in each case this is the only daughter whose name we know and of whom we have any direct information), the main function of each story is to clear the way for the succession to primacy in the family of Jacob on the one hand, and of David on the other. In the case of David we are dealing with an historical figure, a king, and the problems and crises connected with the determination of a worthy successor — ultimately the youngest of the four sons, Solomon. (One might compare the vicissitudes of the latter years of Henry II of England as one by one his four sons alternated between being in favor and in disgrace and ultimately all four rebelled. As it happens his ultimate successor and continuator of the line was the fourth and youngest son, John.) In the case of Jacob we are dealing with a true patriarch, a symbolic figure whose sons are at the same time eponyms of the tribes that make up the commonwealth, so we are dealing not just with the question of inheritance or succession but primacy and the dominance of one tribe over the others, in this case, the rise of Judah to preeminence, reflected in the Blessing of Gen. 49 and historically with the rise of the same David who is at the center of the stories of the succession in Second Samuel. Thus Super J interweaves and interlocks the two stories around a common theme and a common result thus comparing David the founder of the kingdom and dynasty with his own ancestor, Jacob, the founding father of the community of all Israel.

In our opinion then, the specific intent of the author of Super J was to analyze and explain the succession to the throne of David. Then he used the story of Amnon and Tamar to show how the process of elimination of potential heirs was started with the first and second contenders playing leading roles in the drama. It is not by accident that this unsavory tale follows very closely on an equally or more sordid story, the seduction and appropriation of Bathsheba by David himself, an act of adultery compounded with the murder of the unsuspecting husband, that according to the author precipitated the long series of crises and disasters that engulfed the king and his kingdom. There is nevertheless a subtle irony and twist in the account because it also lays the groundwork and foreshadows the fulfillment of the quest for an heir in the rise of Solomon, the fourth and youngest of the sons to seek or claim the throne. He is the second son and first viable progeny of the union of David and Bathsheba and is the one who accedes to the throne, and with it the story of the succession comes to an end. In our story, Amnon, the primary heir, is done away with and Absalom emerges as the heir apparent. Then Absalom will overplay his hand and be eliminated to make way for Adonijah, who also claims the divine throne, while David is still alive. In due course he is displaced and Solomon finally gains the throne, and manages to secure the paternal blessing and consolidate his power.

What is told directly by Super J in the court history, with all its devious twists and turns, is paralleled and foreshadowed in the earlier story of the succession to the patrimony of Jacob, also the father of four sons (the first four by Leah), and the present story of Dinah and Shechem shows how two of the sons in the line of succession, Simeon and Levi, ultimately fell by the wayside. The story itself originally must have explained how Israel, in particular the tribes of Simeon and Levi, came into possession of the territory of Shechem. While it was later assigned to and occupied by Ephraim, the original conquest in patriarchal times was attributed to a combination of treachery and violence on the part of the two sons (representing the tribes) as they annihilated all the people in Shechem and took over the town. What was proposed as a merging of the two groups (the Israelites acquired the place) turned into a slaughter and total displacement. A parallel statement in Gen. 48:24 credits Jacob with the capture of Shechem (by sword and bow). While it says nothing of treachery or deception, it is possible that the same episode is meant, but is viewed from a different and possibly more original perspective. A further comment on this event and its aftermath seems to be contained in the "blessing" on the two sons (= tribes) in Gen. 49:5-7, a passage previously cited. Originally the story recorded a successful onslaught on and capture of Shechem, an early cultic and administrative center of the tribal league — perhaps after a failed attempt at symbiosis (but this project could well have been part of the ruse; compare the successful ruse by the Gibeonites in dealing with Joshua and the invading Israelites). In its later form, the account here serves to explain an entirely different development: the removal of two sons from the line of succession to the patrimony and the effective elimination of two tribes not only from preeminence in the confederation but almost from the league itself. What in an earlier version must have been a congratulatory achievement in tribal annals has been reversed and turned into a condemnation of the tribes who carried out the treacherous deed successfully and the means of removing them from the line of succession. For Super J, this episode paved the way for the next son, the fourth in line, Judah, to achieve preeminence and the status of primary heir and successor to the patriarch. If we can connect Gen. 49:5-7 and its denunciation of Simeon and Levi with the Shechem episode — and while it cannot be demonstrated beyond question, nevertheless there is little or nothing against it — we observe that in this series of blessings Jacob clearly and explicitly condemns and excludes the older sons, beginning with Reuben (49:3-4) and continuing with Simeon and Levi. The tone, mood, and content change radically with the blessing on Judah, which if it has not been affected or modified by the success of Judah's favorite son, David, in establishing a major kingdom if not a substantial empire with Judah at its center and apex, at least the blessing could well be regarded as a forecast of those imperial consequences. In short, the story of Shechem and Dinah has been appropriated by Super J to explain how two sons (= tribes) were rejected by the patriarch leaving the way open for J's (and Jacob's) choice: Judah.

When we come to R, by which symbol I mean the final redactor of the primary history, the Redactor of the great prose narrative from Genesis through Kings (we pass over intermediate compilations and compilers, whose tasks were not dissimilar and who probably had comparable objectives), we note other or additional uses or meanings for these stories in their larger setting. The previous emphasis on patrimony and succession to the throne, the acquisition of territory and primacy to inheriting property or crown remain, to be sure, but also yield to a more general significance (within the larger contours of the primary history). For this purpose we must remind ourselves what the stories tell us both in concert and in contrast. The major lesson to be learned perhaps, and one inherent in and intrinsic to both stories, is that they record ugly, sordid events in the life of Israel and among classes of the population of whom a much higher standard of behavior was demanded. In the end the stories contribute powerfully to the prevailing theme of decline and descent into disintegration that dominates and permeates the whole narrative from beginning to end. If, as we suppose, both the redactors and the audience were exiles in Babylonia, contemplating, brooding about the fate that had engulfed them, torn from their land, deprived of the holy city and holy temple, they could read and reflect on the sorry sordid circumstances and episodes that had brought them to this unhappy pass. In short, behavior exemplified by the two stories cannot lead to anything good, even if in the short run some advantage may accrue to someone (e.g., the capture of Shechem by Simeon and Levi, or the advancement of Absalom on the road to the throne of Israel).

Now as to details: the perpetrator of the crime (which is described as $n^e\underbar{b}\bar{a}l\hat{a}$ — the worst kind — something absolutely unthinkable in Israel — will not escape punishment, and given its nature — the violation of a virgin daughter of Israel — the consequences will be far worse than any law requires. Taking the two stories together, the message is clear: Whoever violates a virgin daughter of Israel will suffer for it — whether it is achieved by seduction or force, whether the guilty man is a Jew or a Gentile (Amnon or Shechem), whether he loves her or hates her, whether he offers to marry her or drives her out of his house, death will be the verdict and the outcome. The punishment will be inflicted by her near kinsmen, full brothers as it happens.

Those who take the law into their own hands, invoking an older law of family honor and blood revenge, however, do not escape the wrath of an offended deity either. While in the short term their cause may be advanced, in the end they will gain nothing and join their victims as losers. Thus Absalom, by eliminating the rapist Amnon, gains one step in his march to the throne but ultimately pays with his life for his unbridled ambition. And whatever victory Simeon and Levi may have achieved by the treacherous attack on Shechem and his people, they are cursed by their father and driven out of their territorial possessions and inheritance. For Israel as a whole, these stories illustrate the malaise at the heart of the nation, the immorality rampant throughout the body politic, foreshadowing the decline and fall of the nation, amply recorded in the primary history.

The final lesson is also the first lesson: if you wish to avoid the terrible consequences that befell the nation the first time around, then you must avoid the contamination that arises from sinful criminal behavior, especially in the area of sexual morality, a parable and paradigm in the whole range of covenant violations and rebellions against the God of Israel. The promised future of return and restoration and renewal will be better than the past, but only if the norms and standards of the commandments are maintained, and if the promises once made at Sinai and renewed from generation to generation are kept.

42

The Symmetry of the Hebrew Bible

The title and point of the ensuing paper derive from a recently determined and apparently little noted set of numerical data concerning the Hebrew Bible. Only since the ripening of the Computer Age has it been possible to arrive at a very accurate count of the discrete words (which we define as any conglomerate of letters between spaces in the preserved texts) in the several books and divisions of the Hebrew Bible. When the numbers of the individual books and their several groupings are listed and compared, the results are impressive, and with respect to the major divisions even startling.

The figures in the accompanying charts are taken from the published and unpublished work of Andersen-Forbes,[1] which has been checked against other sources and with computer experts. They may be relied upon as near to complete accuracy as we are likely to get, given the slight variations in the transmission of the Massoretic Text and in word division. For our purposes absolute precision is not necessary. In fact, although we provide the exact figures, in the discussion we will not hesitate to use the nearest round numbers, as the two sets are so close to each other that the very slight differences (e.g., between 79,983 and 80,000 for the Pentateuch) can be disregarded for the purposes of the argument. What these numbers show beyond any question is the precise built-in symmetry of the whole work, including its major and minor parts. I call the underlying pattern bilateral symmetry; by this I mean that the whole Hebrew Bible is divided into two equal halves, and these in turn are subdivided into relatively equal or proportionate parts, with further subdivisions also exhibiting similar patterns. In addition to the basic bilateral symmetry, there are distinctive deviations from the pattern, but even these

1. F. Andersen and A. D. Forbes, *Spelling in the Hebrew Bible.* Biblica et Orientalia 41 (Rome: Biblical Institute Press, 1986), and private communication.

This paper was delivered as the Mowinckel Lecture 1991 at the University of Oslo. It has been prepared with the editorial assistance of Mr. Andrew Welch.

reflect deliberate arrangement and organization and thus form their own patterns within the larger ones.

It is our contention that such palpable symmetrical patterning cannot be the result of random forces; the canonical collection we know as the Hebrew Bible could not have been achieved by the process advocated by most scholars, i.e., gradual accretion over a long period of time. The cumulative evidence of word counts (which I think are the best way to assess length of works in Hebrew or any other language) shows that the collection as we know it (with modifications to be defended later in the paper) must be the product of one person, or a very small group, working at one time, in one place, to achieve the results visible in the entire structure of the Hebrew Bible. No treatise from antiquity describing the postulated process survives; the theory is thus purely inferential. The most that can be claimed is that it is a plausible hypothesis. I offer this theory as a challenge to those who will necessarily question it, that they come up with alternate proposals. The only requirement is that once they are satisfied that the primary data, i.e., the numbers, are accurate within very narrow limits, that they make interpretations based on those data.

My basic inference is that such precise symmetry can only be the result of deliberate selecting and arranging of the books and subdivisions into two large and exactly equal parts (i.e., well within 1% of each subtotal, a margin so small as to be startling). Other inferences about date and place, or editors and procedures, are less certain. Ultimately one set of proposals may prove to be more compelling than others; the main purpose of this presentation is to establish the fact of this pervasive bilateral symmetry and to suggest the techniques by which it was achieved. The ultimate purpose was to embody totality, as befits an authoritative, even canonical, work, and within that totality a nearly absolute balance or bilateral symmetry enhanced through repetition and variation.

Before proceeding to the argument, we wish to justify the use of word counts for determining the length of the biblical books rather than some other system. It is true, of course, that words vary widely in length in Hebrew as they do in all known languages. So it would be theoretically possible for two works with the same number of words to vary considerably in length or to take up different amounts of space in a manuscript. In practice, however, in long works containing thousands of words such differences would tend to even out, so we assume that works with the same number of words will fill out the same amount of space in manuscripts and thus exhibit the kind of symmetry that we have postulated for the Hebrew Bible.

It might be suggested that we would achieve even more exact results if we counted the letters or strokes that make up the words; such a count would certainly overcome the discrepancies in word lengths and give a more exact correlation of length and space. While the letters themselves may vary in width, the differences here are miniscule; when hundreds of thousands of letters are involved, the possibility of a discrepancy in space filling should be ignored. While I think that the word counts are quite sufficient for our purposes, there is certainly no harm in exploring the more arcane world of letter counts, if only to support and confirm the equivalency of the word counts. The data are given in Chart A, and they show a strong correlation between word counts and letter counts. Nevertheless, there is a definite, if small, discrepancy in the correlation as we move through the Hebrew Bible. The ratio between words and letters shifts slightly from the lowest (3.8 in the Torah) to the highest (4.0 in the Writings) which corresponds to the order of the books in the Hebrew Bible (with a few exceptions, usually in the shorter books, which vary more in this respect). While the difference is small, it is significant and needs to be accounted for. It might be suggested that the latter books use longer words than the former books, but that is highly unlikely. While there are vocabulary changes to be reckoned with and possible changes in style, it is doubtful that such changes would result in the kind of movement that we can plot on a graph. The more likely explanation, which can be partially documented, is that spelling practices changed somewhat in course of transmission so that more vowel letters are used to spell the same words in the latter books as compared with the former books. That development is confirmed by an analysis of the frequency of vowel letters in the different parts of the Hebrew Bible (Chart C). When we compare the letter totals in the two major parts of the Hebrew Bible, we note that for approximately the same number of words in each half (excluding Daniel; see below), there is a small but significant difference in the number of letters used to spell those words:

Primary history	149,641 words	575,600 letters
Rest of the Bible	149,937 words	597,146 letters

The difference amounts to 21,546 letters. At the same time, we can identify all the vowels represented by *waw* and *yodh* in the Hebrew Bible and count them. As the tables show there are 58,351 of these in the first half, or the primary history, while in the remainder of the Hebrew Bible there are not fewer than 75,672. The difference here is over 17,000 (17,321 exactly). It would appear that this apparent excess of vowel letters in the last half of the text accounts for most of the discrepancy between the letter counts for the two parts of the Bible. If we subtract this overage from the letter count for the latter half of the Hebrew Bible, we arrive at a total of 579,825, slightly more than the count for the primary history of 575,600. The difference is now 4,225. The final step is to include the fact that the second part of the Hebrew Bible has 296 more words than the first half, and this would translate into 1,140 letters at the ratio of 3.85 letters per word that we have determined for the primary history. That leaves a final gap of 3,085 letters out of a total of almost 1,175,000 letters in the Hebrew Bible (less than .25%).

In other words, the letter counts properly adjusted and interpreted support the inferences drawn from the word counts. If anything, however, the precise symmetry is even greater in the word counts than in the letter counts, although the impression of bilateral symmetry remains strong and clear throughout. It is reasonable to suppose that if the Israelites counted anything, they counted words; they may even have used a broader gauge and actually worked with columns and pages, and counted lines and words per line to reach their objectives. The conclusion of this digressive investigation is that the essential symmetry of the halves and small divisions of the Hebrew Bible is still apparent in the letter counts, but the more exact symmetry revealed by the word counts has been slightly obscured in the course of scribal transmission (i.e., the addition of the medial vowel letters), and to a much lesser extent by the fact that words (proper nouns in particular) in the Chronicler's work are slightly longer than those in the other parts of the Bible. While this lengthening is partly balanced by the shorter average word length of the poetic books (especially in Job and Proverbs) there remains a slight excess in the letter counts.

This theory of the symmetry of the Hebrew Bible leads to the conclusion that if all the books (with the exception of Daniel) were included in the first full Bible at the end of the 5th or beginning of the 4th century B.C.E., they were written in their authoritative form about the same time and with the same spelling. In our opinion, the spelling still preserved in the Torah and to a lesser extent in the Former Prophets, i.e., in the primary history, is reflective of the standard spelling of that time, and the same spelling would have dominated the spelling of the remaining books as well. Had that been the case, then the letter counts for the two halves of the Hebrew Bible would have corresponded to each other as closely as do the word counts. In the course of time, however, the exact pristine symmetry would have been blurred, compromised, and distorted, at least to some degree, by the difference in treatment accorded the texts of different parts of the Hebrew Bible. Thus the Torah, which was set apart as the most sacred and most important part of the Scripture, was copied as closely and carefully as possible. It has been preserved largely with the original spelling of the period to which we attribute the literary, editorial, and canonizing activity just described. With numerous but statistically unimportant exceptions, the Torah has been preserved essentially intact from the beginning of this process, whereas the remaining books have been copied less closely and carefully, so that these books reflect a certain amount of updating in their spelling.[2] This means that more vowel letters have been incorporated into the later books, as the following table of vowel-to-consonant ratios demonstrates:

1. Pentateuch	.106
2. Former Prophets	.121
3. Latter Prophets	.140
4. Writings	.150
1 and 2 (= primary history)	.113
3 and 4 (= second half)	.145

2. *Idem.*

The result has been to obscure the symmetry of the two major sections and the two subdivisions of each section. This exact symmetry is preserved in its purest form by the word counts, and while still visible in the letter counts, has been distorted somewhat by the evolution of spelling practice which affected the different parts of the Hebrew Bible in greater and lesser degrees.

A similar effect can be observed in the different ways in which different kinds of Hebrew literature are represented on the pages (originally columns) of the books (originally scrolls) of the Hebrew Bible. Most of the Hebrew Bible is written in prose and set down in lines and columns as prose, with parts or sections set off in paragraphs just as we do in English and other modern Western languages. In the major medieval manuscripts there are normally three columns to a page, and the prose is written in normal fashion. There are a few exceptions, especially in lists of place names, but these have a negligible effect on space allocations. There is one major variation, namely, the way poetry is written. In the three designated poetic books, Psalms, Job, and Proverbs, lines are written stichometrically in two related but distinct patterns. The essential point is to separate lines from each other, so either the manuscript line is taken up with two or three separate elements, spaced so as to fill the line, or there is a brick-laying arrangement in which spaces are provided between the building blocks in alternating fashion. Our concern here is only with the fact that such arrangements tend to use up more space for the same number of words than the standard prose arrangement.

In addition to the three books mentioned, there are a number of poems embedded in the prose narratives for which similar treatment is provided, but as these are few and far between (e.g., Exod. 15 and Deut. 32, but not Gen. 49; Num. 23–24; or Deut. 33; also Judg. 5 and 1 Sam. 2; also 2 Sam. 22, but not 2 Sam. 23:1-7) they hardly affect the space filled by those books. Thus, if we take the Leningrad Codex as a model, we note that the books of Exodus and Numbers are almost identical in length (16,713 for Exodus and 16,413 for Numbers), and they take up almost exactly the same number of pages (Chart B). Actually Exodus fills 50.4 pages while Numbers occupies 49.1, giving a difference of 1.3 pages. We can account for one page by the fact that Exodus is 300 words longer, and in the Pentateuch the average number of words per page is about 336. The remaining difference may be explained by the presence of the poem in Exod. 15 laid out in poetic form, whereas there is no such accommodation to poetry in the book of Numbers (the short poems in Num. 21, 23–24 are not written as such). The more significant effect of this difference in the way the words are laid out on the page can be seen in comparing Psalms (with 19,586 words) with Genesis (20,613 words): Psalms fills 62.0 pages while Genesis, with more words, nevertheless fills only 60.5 pages. Alternatively, we note that Genesis has 78,069 characters or letters, while Psalms is credited with 78,830, a difference of 761 in favor of Psalms, and this increase will account entirely for the difference in 1.5 pages between the books.

Comparison with Jeremiah may be more to the point. Jeremiah has 21,835 words and 84,910 letters, and it fills 61.7 pages, almost exactly the same amount of space as Psalms (62.0). The differences here are notable: 2,349 words and 6,080 letters. The difference could amount to anywhere between 5 and 7 or 8 pages, indicating how much additional space has been used by writing the Psalms stichometrically. If we look at Job (8,343 words and 31,861 letters) and Proverbs (6,915 words and 26,505 letters) and compare them with Joshua (10,051 words and 39,808 letters) and Judges (9,885 words and 38,945 letters), the disparities are significant. While not immediately apparent the difference in words and letters per page (there is a slight discrepancy here due to divergent spelling practices) clearly reflects the difference in the spacing and arrangement of words on the page.

Thus we have the following data:

	Words	Words per page	Letters	Letters per page	Pages
Joshua	10,051	346.6	39,808	1,372.7	29.0
Judges	9,885	344.4	38,945	1,356.9	28.7
Job	8,343	327.1	31,861	1,249.4	25.5
Proverbs	6,915	303.2	26,505	1,162.5	22.8

If we combine the two pairs we get the following numbers:

Josh.-Judg.	19,936	345.5	78,753	1,364.8	57.7
Job-Prov.	15,258	315.9	58,366	1,208.4	48.3

To complete the comparison of the two sets on the basis of word counts, we calculate that if Joshua-Judges were the same length as Job-Proverbs, the former would fill only 44.1 pages instead of the 48.3 actually used to write Job-Proverbs. Turning it around, if Job-Proverbs were the same length as Joshua-Judges then Job-Proverbs would fill 63.1 pages instead of 57.7. Or if we make the calculation on the basis of letter counts, then if Joshua-Judges were the same length as Job-Proverbs, the former will fill only 42.8 pages instead of 48.3, while if we turned it around, then Job-Proverbs would fill 65.1 pages instead of 57.7. The difference in both cases is reflected in the increased amount of blank space in the poetic transcriptions, as in the Leningrad Codex and other manuscripts, such as the Qumran Psalms scroll from Cave 11.

The overall discrepancy between the two halves of the Hebrew Bible, which have almost identical word counts but significant differences in letter counts and space requirements, is reflected in the general distribution of words and pages in the Leningrad Codex, which we have used as a model simply because it was written at one time by one person (if that is the case),[3] and therefore we can eliminate other factors as possible distracting influences. The first half of the Hebrew Bible

---

3. E. Wurthwein, *The Text of the Old Testament,* 4th ed. (Grand Rapids: Eerdmans, 1979).

fills 436.5 pages, while the latter half fills 464.6 pages (we omit Daniel from consideration). While the number of words in each half is almost exactly the same (there are 296 more words in the second half) the page difference is significant: 28.1, which would be the equivalent of 9,340 words if the books were written uniformly throughout. The distortion of the underlying symmetry is significant, showing that other considerations were dominant in the actual copying of the texts over the centuries. Nevertheless, the patterns of symmetry have been preserved and survive through the distortion. They can easily be retrieved once it is recognized that the word counts are all-important; these have not changed to any degree in the thousands of years since the establishment of the biblical canon.

We could add that the only texts in which there is a strong probability that the surviving MT differs markedly from its presumed *Vorlage* are Samuel in the primary history and Jeremiah in the Latter Prophets. The former is clearly a defective text, and we would have to add some words to make up a proposed original (chiefly from LXX but also from the Qumran scrolls).[4] Likewise Jeremiah in MT is an expanded text, and we should turn to LXX (also supported by some important Qumran fragments) for a somewhat shorter original text.[5] It may be that even the 296-word difference between the first and second parts of the Hebrew Bible can be explained this way, but there is no need to achieve even greater precision than we already have in the preserved MT.

Regardless of the physical appearance of the document (and there is no evidence that the Hebrew Bible was ever written as a single manuscript in codex form until the Middle Ages, perhaps not before about 900 C.E. and the first of the great Ben Asher complete biblical manuscripts), the symmetry lies in the actual numbers of words in the texts. And whatever the witness of the codices, the arrangement of the books is more conceptual than physical since the books were originally written on separate scrolls. Even with a major distortion effected by the later addition of the book of Daniel to the canon, the overarching symmetry can be recovered without serious difficulty simply by relying upon word counts to match up the books and their arrangement in larger divisions. Thus the symmetry of the prophetic section, with four former and four latter prophets, can hardly be questioned; then the parallel of the five books of the Torah with the five major books (minus Daniel) of the Writings makes good sense. The fact that the five books of the Torah flow directly into the four books of the Former Prophets shows that this larger unit is a single whole, matching up with the remaining nine books.

Once it is noticed that the five major books of the Writings come up short in comparison with the five books of the Torah, it becomes possible to explain the

4. P. K. McCarter, Jr., *I Samuel.* AB 8 (Garden City: Doubleday, 1980); *II Samuel.* AB 9 (Garden City: Doubleday, 1984).

5. J. Bright, *Jeremiah.* AB 21 (Garden City: Doubleday, 1965); R. P. Carroll, *Jeremiah.* OTL (Philadelphia: Westminster, 1986).

addition of five small books (matching both the five larger ones and the five books of the Torah) which together make up the equivalent of a single book of the length of books like Joshua, Judges, or Ezra(-Nehemiah). Since each of the subdivisions matches a corresponding one in the first half of the work, and the total numbers of words are almost exactly the same, we can be reasonably sure that this outcome is not the result of happenstance, nor is it the result of the laborious addition of one book to another. The challenge to scholars is not only to confirm or disprove the data, but also to offer a reasonable explanation for their remarkable arrangement and symmetry that is better than the one I have proposed.

The basic symmetry of the Hebrew Bible can be observed in Tables A and C. In passing we may wonder whether round numbers were in the mind of the editors when they compiled or composed the larger configurations. Thus the Pentateuch is almost exactly 80,000 words long, for an average length of 16,000 words, which conforms to the two books which are the most artificially structured (Exodus and Numbers, which are practically twins, and form a kind of pillared entrance to the holy of holies, Leviticus, which forms an arch between them). The Former Prophets are almost exactly 70,000 words long, and with the Torah form a narrative almost exactly 150,000 words long. Since the second half of the Hebrew Bible has almost exactly the same number of words, it would appear that numbers like 150,000 and 300,000 were already in the minds of the compilers when they assembled the component parts.

Continuing this survey of the major sections, we note that the four books of the Former Prophets, while varying from very low counts (Joshua and Judges each about 10,000 words) to very high counts (Samuel and Kings between 24,000 and 25,500, totalling just about 50,000) average about 17,500 words, while the four Latter Prophets come out slightly higher with 72,000 words and an average of 18,000 each. In both these groups, two books in each are below the average and two above. Finally, in the Writings there are two groups of five, with the larger books totalling about 68,000, for an average of 13,600, and the smaller group about 10,000, for an average of 2,000. So while there is considerable variation from unit to unit and within each unit, the totals are very close, with counts of 80,000 + 70,000 = 150,000 matched by counts of 72,000 + 78,000 = 150,000, a very tight fit.

The symmetry we posit is not only bilateral but also chiastic. We begin therefore with the Prophetic collection, consisting of two parts, Former and Latter Prophets, each containing four books. We note in passing that the organization is deliberate and quite artificial, as can be seen in the fact that the twelve Minor Prophets are collected into one book, while the five Megilloth or rolls, which are roughly the same length as the Minor Prophets, are counted separately. This artificiality shows that the counting was quite deliberate, and that the later custom of separating the twelve Minor Prophets (to produce a total of thirty-nine books, due to the division of books like Samuel and Kings into two each, the Chronicler's work into four) disregards the structure prepared by those responsible for the first Hebrew Bible. We have noted in the Former Prophets a wide disparity in book lengths, from two of the shortest books to two of the longest. They nevertheless pair up nicely to produce the desired total. For example, Joshua and Judges could easily have been combined into one book, because there are several single books with more than 20,000 words, but the separation into two books was important to the editor in order to match the four Latter Prophets. Similarly, the complex from Exodus to Numbers could also have been restricted to two books (the lines of demarcation among the three are hardly distinct), but it is clear that for reasons of symmetry five was a better choice for the editor-compiler.

In the case of the four Latter Prophets, the numbers are scattered from 22,000 at the top (Jeremiah) to 14,000 at the bottom (Minor Prophets), with Ezekiel at about 19,000 matching up with Isaiah at about 17,000. Again the symmetry is apparent, and the desired total of 72,000, while slightly different from the 70,000 of the Former Prophets, is nevertheless deliberate because of the excellent fit with the numbers for the Writings. There is also a correspondence between the five books of the Torah with the collection of Writings, although the word counts are not as impressive. As MT stands, the 80,000 of the Torah is matched by the 84,000 of the Writings, a notable discrepancy which can be attributed solely to the inclusion of Daniel in the canon. In a similar way we can compare the total of 150,000 for the nine books of the primary history with the corresponding books of the Latter Prophets and Writings, and we come out with about 156,000 for the latter. While the general symmetry is still visible, a discrepancy reappears. Here again the culprit would seem to be the single book of Daniel, which unlike the other books is demonstrably a product of the Hellenistic age and can be dated very close to 165 B.C.E. in its canonical form.[6] Of course the argument from bilateral symmetry is circular: if we eliminate the book of Daniel, then we achieve practically exact bilateral symmetry, whereas if we assume an original bilateral symmetry, then we will perforce drop the book of Daniel. Furthermore, the next argument is equally circular, although circular arguments are not automatically to be rejected. They can often lead to better arguments and have immense heuristic value, if only to expose the circularity of the reasoning.

If the collection we know as the Hebrew Bible comes from the Persian period, then it could not have included Daniel, because Daniel, certainly in its canonical form, did not exist then. Similarly, if we begin with the position that Daniel is a Hellenistic work, then it could not belong to a Persian period work, the Hebrew Bible. The consensus among serious scholars is the 2nd-century origin of Daniel. The rest is speculation. Nevertheless, I think there is something in it, especially given the fact that aside from the book of Daniel there is no specific date or event

6. L. F. Hartman and A. A. Di Lella, *The Book of Daniel.* AB 23 (Garden City: Doubleday, 1978).

in the Hebrew Bible beyond the reign of Darius II (424-407 B.C.E.) mentioned in Neh. 12:22. The continuous story in the Chronicler's work (I leave open the question whether this is a single work divided at the end of 2 Chronicles or two separate works joined at that point) ends with the era of Ezra-Nehemiah, and since both of those men were seriously involved in the reading and application of the Mosaic Law, it also stands to reason that they were connected not only with the Torah but with the whole of the Hebrew Bible, to which the book of Ezra (including Nehemiah) forms a fitting conclusion.

Once we eliminate Daniel from consideration as part of the Hebrew Bible in the late 5th or early 4th century, then, everything falls into place. The numbers change slightly but dramatically and the pristine symmetry emerges from relative obscurity. Instead of 84,000 for the Writings, the number becomes 78,000, and the total for the second half of the Hebrew Bible almost exactly 150,000, just like the first half. The difference between the two halves, without considering a single emendation of a single word, is then exactly 296 words, or just about one tenth of 1% of the total of 300,000. This is remarkable under any circumstances, for it is hard to believe that anyone could have worked things out to such a point of precision. And if it happened by accident, it would be truly miraculous.

To summarize, briefly, we interpret the numerical data to mean that the Hebrew Bible as we know it, with the single exception of the book of Daniel, existed in its present form as early as the end of the 5th century B.C.E. and consisted of two precisely symmetrical halves, which in turn were made up of four subsections of five and four books respectively, matching parts in chiastic order, with a supplement of five more small books to make the numbers come out evenly as well as inject yet another ingredient into the picture of totality and completeness. This assertion of an early date for the compilation of the canon of the Hebrew Bible is bound to be controversial. It further implies an early date for several books about which there is considerable debate and discussion, among them Job, Song of Songs, Ecclesiastes, and Esther. All of these have been dated by some scholars to the Greek period. Questions have been raised about a number of the prophetic books too. Many scholars find all kinds of allusions in the Latter Prophets to events in the Greek period, but such inquiries, while perfectly justifiable, are in the end self-serving and self-defeating, the differences among scholars being so great as to bring into question most of their speculations about the later chapters of Zechariah, Isaiah, and other books.

I cannot go into all these matters here; suffice it to say that I recognize the questions, and it may well be that some of those books did not reach final form until much later than I have proposed. I am simply talking about the length of the books, and if it is agreed that revisions did not change the number of words, then I have no argument about date. But in my opinion it would be difficult to remove such books from the collection we know as the Hebrew Bible, since that would disturb the symmetry so artfully constructed. I would say that there is nothing compelling about the dating of any book except Daniel to the Greek period, and there is the negative evidence of the Bible itself, namely that the story comes to a halt in the days of Nehemiah the Governor.

The symmetry proposed here could only have existed before the book of Daniel was included in the canon, but after all the other books had been written. It is always possible that one of these books was inserted as a replacement of a book now unknown to us to maintain the number of books and words. But that is so speculative as hardly to be worth considering. We know of no such books, and we have books about which there may be questions but which are also defended as products of the Persian period.

One might suggest that this collection was actually put together after the conquests of Alexander, some time in the 3rd century B.C.E., and I would not object strenuously. The limits are between about 415 B.C.E. and 165 B.C.E., and almost any time within that frame could be defended. The crucial fact for me is the lack of any historical account after the time of Nehemiah. That is a prime indicator of the end of the literature, as it is hard to imagine that the Jewish community could live through the times of the late Persian kings, the coming of Alexander, and the massive changes all over the Near East without referring to them at all. Only the book of Daniel bridges the gulf between the Persian period Bible and the new age of tumult and ferment, from the Persians to the Romans.

To conclude, it is certainly possible that some of the marginal books like Esther and Ecclesiastes can be dated after Ezra-Nehemiah, in which case our canon foundation may belong to a later period. Our concern, therefore, will not be so much with an absolute date (although I think that the end of the 5th century is the best date for this work), as with the general time frame (between 415 B.C.E. and 165 B.C.E.) and the undoubted symmetrical structure of the Hebrew Bible (without Daniel). If we remove Daniel from the existing structure, thus fixing the date for the rest of the Hebrew Bible before 165 B.C.E. (actually before the introduction of Daniel into the canon rather than the date of its composition, extending the *terminus ante quem* some years, as late perhaps as the end of the century) and merely require that the rest of the books be included before that rather late and flexible date, then we can accommodate most scholarly opinion about the other books and preserve the integrity of the Hebrew Bible.

Without Daniel, the rest of the Hebrew Bible as we have it reflects a symmetry that is astonishingly exact (as exact as is likely in literary productions rather than mathematical ones). The numbers can be summarized as follows:

First Half: The Primary History		*Second Half: Latter Prophets + Writings*	
Torah	80,000	Latter Prophets	72,000
Former Prophets	70,000	Writings	78,000
Totals	150,000		150,000

The actual numbers are so close to the round numbers offered that they deserve to be repeated from the tables:

First Half: The Primary History		*Second Half: Latter Prophets + Writings*	
Torah	79,983	Latter Prophets	71,852
Former Prophets	69,658	Writings	78,085
Totals	149,641		149,937

Grand Total: 299,578

The difference between the two major groupings — the primary history, a unified literary whole (in other words a single literary work, not artificially arranged for numerical purposes), and the rest of the Hebrew Bible (clearly a collection of discrete entities, not a continuous work in any sense, with the exception of the Chronicler's work) — is only 296 words, or one tenth of 1% of the total number of words in the Bible. It is difficult to see how an editor or compiler could have achieved any closer congruence between two large and differently constructed literary works, or how such a congruence could have occurred without the deliberate planning and execution of a careful scheme. We contend that the numbers alone demonstrate that the pre-Daniel Hebrew Bible is the result of a single action comprising the selection and organization of its twenty-three books to create an extraordinarily exact symmetry. It is important to note that the symmetry becomes more and more exact as we move from the individual books to the larger groupings, until it is most exact in the comparison of the two halves of the total. The major halves match almost word for word, while there is greater if still slight variation in the major subdivisions, the numbers for the Torah and Former Prophets on the one hand, and the Latter Prophets and the Writings on the other. This shows that the work of the final editor was mainly in organizing and arranging already existing books and even larger collections, certainly not in composing any books, and perhaps only to a very limited extent in what we would call editing of manuscripts. The symmetry of the two parts is thus all the more remarkable, for the compiler was working with a whole set of already completed pieces composed over a long period of time by a series of different individuals (or teams) of diverse circumstances and interests. The tools available to the compiler were limited essentially to the selection and arrangement of the constituent units and perhaps a modicum of editorial adjustment of particular passages.

Turning to the subdivisions of the major groupings, and looking a little more closely at the individual entities, their numbers and lengths, we find the following interesting data, all pointing toward the underlying principles and procedures adopted by the compiler/editor in his work.

First we note the basically chiastic structure of the larger units. Thus the five books of the Torah are matched in length by the five major books of the Writings and the five minor books as well (always omitting Daniel from consideration).

These numbers are not accidental or unimportant, as the number five plays a dominant role in the structure of the Hebrew Bible and its parts. Whatever the origin of the division of the Torah into five books, this number clearly has a leading role in the selection and arrangement of the books of the Writings. Thus there are five major books: Chronicles (which comes first in the major medieval manuscripts, including the Aleppo Codex and the Leningrad Codex), Psalms (which itself is divided into five books, doubtless to correspond to the five books of the Torah), Job, Proverbs, and Ezra (including Nehemiah; they are each one book in the Hebrew Bible). To these are added the five Megilloth: Ruth, Song of Songs, Ecclesiastes, Lamentations, and Esther. Though very short (about the same length as the Minor Prophets), they are still counted as separate pieces. We note in passing that the Minor Prophets are treated in the opposite fashion, although they are roughly the same length as the Megilloth. As far as the evidence goes, the Minor Prophets are always grouped together and treated as one book, which goes with the three other Latter Prophets (the so-called Major Prophets) to form a four-book group that in turn matches the four books of the Former Prophets. This difference in arrangement and organization reflects the deliberate intention of the editor to produce symmetry, since alternate dispositions of the constituent elements would have dissipated the intended symmetry.

As just mentioned, in the great medieval manuscripts of the Hebrew Bible the Writings begin with Chronicles and end with Ezra-Nehemiah, which together constitute a single continuous narrative and thus form an envelope around this whole division of the Bible. The repetition of the last paragraph of Chronicles at the beginning of Ezra shows that the story is continuous but that the books were separated spatially. If they had been in direct sequence there would have been no need for such a repetition, any more than we find repetitions of endings and beginnings in the successive books of the primary history (we don't). This particular device serves to unify an otherwise heterogeneous collection of works within the comprehensive historical work. Thus it is possible to link most of the enclosed books of the Writings directly with the leading personalities and motifs of the Chronicler's work and so impose at least a superficial uniformity on the whole collection. Whether the repetition of the linking paragraph goes back to the original composition of the Chronicler's work or represents an editorial expansion to link books deliberately separated in a fixed order (as reflected in the codices mentioned above) remains an open question, but in their present form there can be no doubt that the editors intended the books to be read and understood as a continuous work. The major break in the narrative occurs at a decisive moment in the story, when the exile comes to an end and the return is about to begin. It is the next event after the end of the great narrative, the primary history, already authoritative and in place in the Hebrew Bible. The repetition can only serve to emphasize the radical change in Israel's fortunes and the beginning of the new chapter in Israel's history.

We wish to point out that the Chronicler's work forms a complex of two books with the following word count:

Chronicles	24,058
Ezra-Nehemiah	9,065
Total	33,123

With this unit we may compare the three so-called poetic books of the Hebrew Bible, which form a separate grouping, characterized by a different accentuation system and the special graphic presentation in the codices and the scrolls before them. The word counts are as follows:

Psalms	19,586
Job	8,343
Proverbs	6,915
Total	34,844

While there is an obvious discrepancy in the totals, they are of the same order of magnitude (about 5%) and demonstrate once again the bilateral symmetry that dominates the entire work.

We may now revert to the Pentateuch for a closer look at the component books and their word counts. We note that the first and fifth books stand apart from the three-book sequence in the middle (Exodus, Leviticus, Numbers). While Genesis and the following books are linked in many ways, there is a sharp break between Genesis and Exodus, reflected in the fact that no one living in one book is alive in the other, a circumstance that does not apply to any of the other books of the Torah. At the same time, Deuteronomy, for different reasons, stands apart from the preceding book, Numbers. Not only does it differ markedly in vocabulary, style, and viewpoint, it tells a story that varies substantially in its details from its predecessors. Moreover, Deuteronomy points ahead to the other books of the so-called Deuteronomic history and forms a continuous narrative with them (D and DH), while Numbers is solidly in the camp of the Priestly work (P).[7] If we combine the books Genesis and Deuteronomy, the first and fifth of the Torah, as we did Chronicles and Ezra-Nehemiah, we have the following word counts:

Genesis	20,613
Deuteronomy	14,294
Total	34,907

7. Background and bibliography in D. N. Freedman, *The Unity of the Hebrew Bible* (Ann Arbor: University of Michigan Press, 1991).

This total matches up nicely with the two groups already identified in the Writings; it is almost identical with the word count of the poetic books (34,844) and not far from that of the Chronicler's work (33,123).

Now we turn to the three books in the middle of the Torah, Exodus, Leviticus, and Numbers. We note first that Exodus and Numbers are practically equal in word count although Exodus has 40 chapters and Numbers only 36. There is a difference of only 300 words out of a total of over 33,000. The division of the narrative into three books is rather artificial, as the story line is continuous (even though there is a presumed break of almost forty years at some point) and the cast of characters is essentially the same throughout. And unlike Genesis, Judges, and Kings, the period covered is brief, one generation of forty years (comparable in this respect to Joshua, which is mostly the story of a single generation, or Samuel, which covers at most three generations). The purpose of the division was apparently to focus attention on the middle book, Leviticus, which represents the culmination of the Priestly narrative (and hence of the whole Pentateuch): the sacrificial and ritual system by which the sanctity of the tabernacle is established and maintained, the central role of the priesthood defined, and the continuing presence of the divine Kabod (= Glory) ensured. The word counts are as follows:

Exodus	16,713
Numbers	16,413
Total	33,126

This number is almost identical with that for the Chronicler's work; comparing the two pairs gives the following results:

Chronicler's work	33,123	Gen. + Deut.	34,907
Poetic works	34,844	Exod. + Num.	33,126
Total	67,967	Total	68,033

The symmetry is striking; the difference is a negligible 66, less than .1 of 1% of each subtotal. We must now include Leviticus, balanced by the Megilloth:

Exodus	16,713	Poetic works	34,844
Leviticus	11,950	Megilloth	10,118
Numbers	16,413		
Total	45,076	Total	44,962

Once again, the difference is negligible, 114 words or .26%.

Now we can put together the various parts of both of the outer portions of the Hebrew Bible to show how the parts comprise a symmetrical substructure:

Torah:		Writings:	
Gen./Deut.	34,907	Chronicler's work	33,123
Exod./Num.	33,126	Poetry	34,844
Lev.	11,950	Megilloth	10,118
Total	79,983	Total	78,085

There is a minor discrepancy to be sure, amounting to 1,898 words, but when we match the two sets of prophetic works there will be a balancing discrepancy of 2,194 words in the other direction, so that the differences will almost cancel out.

We may now apply the procedures adopted for the Torah and the Writings to the Prophets, both Former and Latter. In the Former Prophets, we combine the first and the last books, and then the two middle books:

Joshua	10,051	Judges	9,885
Kings	25,421	Samuel	24,301
Total	35,472	Total	34,186

The numbers differ modestly from each other and from the combinations derived from the other divisions, but they all come within a fairly narrow range (less than 5%).

Turning to the Latter Prophets, we will deviate from the established procedure of selecting pairs according to the numbers. The problem is that the order of the books is not easily determinable according to some general principle. MT follows a generally chronological scheme, beginning with Isaiah, and proceeding then to Jeremiah and Ezekiel (the chronological order of the prophets), with a catchall collection of Minor Prophets at the end. The LXX begins instead with the Minor Prophets, apparently because it is clear from the headings that both Hosea (the first in the series) and Amos must have preceded Isaiah. There are other orders attested, especially beginning with Jeremiah (the longest of the Latter Prophets) and continuing with Ezekiel and then Isaiah and the Twelve.[8] For our purposes this is the preferred order, which yields these numbers:

Latter Prophets:			
Jeremiah	21,835	Isaiah	16,932
Minor Prophets	14,355	Ezekiel	18,730
Total	36,190	Total	35,662

8. Discussion in R. T. Beckwith, *The Old Testament Canon of the New Testament Church and Its Background in Early Judaism* (Grand Rapids: Eerdmans, 1985), 181-211.

While these numbers are slightly higher than those already noted, they are in the general range and very close to each other, thereby generally supporting the notion of bilateral symmetry; they also show that there is a normal pairing within a fairly narrow range. We can now compare the Former and Latter Prophets, as follows:

Former Prophets:		Latter Prophets:	
Joshua + Kings	35,472	Jer. + Minor Prophets	36,190
Judges + Samuel	34,186	Isaiah + Ezekiel	35,662
Total	69,658	Total	71,852

Here, as noted, the discrepancy is slightly over 2,000 words, but when we combine these totals with those derived from the Torah and the Writings, we come out with a practically perfect fit:

Torah	79,983	Writings	78,085
Former Prophets	68,658	Latter Prophets	71,852
Total	149,641	Total	149,937

We can show the pairings for the whole Hebrew Bible with the supplements in the following manner:

Gen./Deut.	34,907	Chron. work	33,123
Exod./Num.	33,126	Poetry	34,844
Total	68,033	Total	67,967
Josh./Kgs.	35,472	Jer./12 Minor	36,190
Judg./Sam.	34,186	Isa./Ezek.	35,662
Total	69,658	Total	71,852

To the numbers for the Torah we add Leviticus at 11,950, and to the Writings we add 10,118 for the Megilloth, producing the following intermediate numbers:

Exod./Num.	33,126	Poetry	34,844
Lev.	11,950	Megilloth	10,118
Total	45,076	Total	44,962

The range for the eight pairings is from 33,123 (the Chronicler's work) to 36,190 (Jeremiah and the Twelve), while the two augmented groups come out at 44,962 and 45,076. When we add the totals as well as the subtotals, the correspondences are too close to be explained as random coincidence; all the statistical data tend to support the notion of a deliberate structure of bilateral symmetry that still allows for considerable variation from any rigid pattern. This is the work of the final editor or compiler.

We turn next to the numerical pattern of the books of the Hebrew Bible. As already noted, the arrangement of these books is both symmetrical and chiastic. The basic pattern is simple:

1) Torah	5 books	4) Writings	5 books
2) Former Prophets	4 books	3) Latter Prophets	4 books
Primary history	9 books	Others	9 books

While this simple symmetry can hardly be denied, there is an imbalance between the two halves of the Hebrew Bible. Thus the nine latter books come out approximately 10,000 words under the total for the first set (the primary history). The actual numbers are as follows:

The primary history	149,641
The other major books	139,819
Difference	9,822

In order to make up the difference, the five minor rolls have been added to the Writings, and while this distorts the underlying symmetrical and chiastic pattern, it preserves the more fundamental bilateral symmetry of word counts central to the whole scheme.

By this rather interesting and subtle maneuver, the compiler of the Hebrew Bible managed to retain the basic symmetry of the arrangement of the books, simultaneously disturbing the balance and achieving a more exact equivalence between the two major parts of the Bible. The key numbers in this organization are five and four: five in the Torah and both sets of books in the Writings (major and minor collections); four in the Prophets, i.e., four each for the Former and Latter Prophets. These two numbers appear repeatedly in the Bible to define basic configurations and describe different groups in their completeness. The number five stands for the fingers of one hand, and its immediate multiple, ten, not only completes the finger count for most human beings but serves as a round number and organizing principle throughout the Hebrew Bible. So the basic pairing of five major books in the Torah and in the Writings is quite understandable. The third set of five (the minor scrolls) echoes the same pattern, and in turn is reflected in the division of the Psalter into five "books" or sections. The Torah is clearly the paradigm for the rest of the material.

When it comes to the number four, it also conveys a sense of completeness or totality, which is further enhanced in its simplest multiple, the number eight. Illustrating this idea are the four directions, the four winds, and the like. Perhaps the most striking representation of the basic principle is the elaborate vision of the prophet Ezekiel (ch. 1 and elsewhere) with its repeated fourfold features, especially the monstrous cherubim, and of course the wheels within wheels and their all-seeing eyes. Perhaps the most notable symbolic use of the number eight is to be found in Ps. 119, in which the alphabet (also a sign of completeness) is combined with the number eight (22 eight-line stanzas each featuring one letter of the alphabet) to produce a picture of perfection, a physical as well as verbal representation of the Torah as full and perfect in all its parts. To drive this point home, the poet uses eight different words related to the central word *Torah* (which is one of the eight, and the most frequently occurring word in the whole poem).[9]

When the separate blocks of material in the Hebrew Bible are assembled we have a total of twenty-three (excluding Daniel), which can also be regarded as a symbol of totality or completeness. In my judgment, there is a link with the alphabet here too, although the number twenty-three represents an augmented alphabet, as the basic number is twenty-two. Most of the alphabetic acrostic poems in the Bible adhere to the 22-letter alphabet (although the letter שׁ represents two different sounds, *śin* and *shin*, it is used only once in the alphabetic poems, and when the letter is used more than once in a poem, as in the three lines of Lam. 3 and the eight lines of Ps. 119, the two sounds are intermingled without apparent regard for the difference).

But there are exceptions. In the case of two Psalms, 25 and 34, there is an additional line; after the last line, which begins with *taw,* a line is added, which in both cases begins with the letter *pe,* even though *pe* already occurs in its regular place. We owe to Patrick Skehan the correct interpretation of this apparently anomalous added line.[10] It also belongs to the alphabetic scheme, and in a different way enhances or emphasizes the use of the alphabet in the structure of the poem. To explain the *pe* at the end of the whole poem, we connect that *pe* with the letter *'aleph* at the beginning of the first line, and the letter *lamedh* at the beginning of the middle line (the 12th in a 23-line poem) and come up with the word *'lp* = *'aleph,* which serves as the label for the whole sequence (just as in Greek and English, the first two letters are combined to form the heading for the whole series of letters, i.e., "alphabet[a]").

We conclude that the compiler settled on the number twenty-three to juxtapose the fours and fives of the two halves, to emphasize the association with the alphabetic numbers, i.e., 22 and even 22 + 1 = 23, and to reinforce the alphabetic principle. The use of successive numbers, especially in Hebrew poetry, both for parallelism and for enhancement, is well known; Amos 1–2 speaks of "three transgressions, yea four," and the numbers seven and eight are used analogously in both Ugaritic and Hebrew poetry.

---

9. See D. N. Freedman, "The Structure of Psalm 119," in forthcoming Festschrift for Jacob Milgrom [*Pomegranates and Golden Bells,* ed. D. P. Wright, D. N. Freedman, and A. Hurvitz (Winona Lake: Eisenbrauns, 1995), 725-56].

10. P. W. Skehan, *Studies in Israelite Poetry and Wisdom.* CBQ Monograph 1 (Washington: Catholic Biblical Association, 1971), 67-77.

While this interpretation of the number twenty-three in association with the books of the Hebrew Bible may seem fanciful or forced, the linkage between the alphabet and the canon of the Hebrew Bible is attested by later authors. It can also be documented in the Greek tradition for the Homeric epics. It is well known that the Alexandrian grammarians not only divided the Iliad and the Odyssey into twenty-four books or parts but carefully labeled them with the twenty-four letters of the Greek alphabet in the regular order, from *alpha* to *omega*.[11] This usage differs from the practice common in Hebrew and Greek of using letters for numbers: the conventional practice assigns the first ten numbers to the first ten letters, but beginning with the next decade, the letters represent multiples of ten, and in the third set (beginning with number twenty-one), the letters represent hundreds. It takes combinations of two letters to represent the numbers between eleven and nineteen, and the same is true for numbers in the succeeding decades. In the Iliad and Odyssey, however, the eleventh book is signified by the eleventh letter, and so on until the complete number of twenty-four is reached. This is a specialized usage, restricted, so far as I am aware, to sacred or authoritative works, or at the least to literary compositions. As regards the Greek epics, the exact correspondence between the units of the epics and the alphabet exhibits a clear intention: just as the letters of the alphabet represent the whole language and contain all possible words, the twenty-four books of the Iliad and the Odyssey contain the totality of the sacred text, to which nothing could be added and from which nothing could be subtracted.[12]

Curiously, the preserved Hebrew Bible contains exactly twenty-four books, when we include the book of Daniel. The incorporation of Daniel could have taken place no earlier than the 2nd century B.C.E. (well into the Greco-Roman period), a time substantially later than the division of the Homeric epics into twenty-four segments. Under the circumstances, the compilation of the Hebrew Bible into twenty-four books may not be entirely coincidental. While we would expect the number of books in the Hebrew Bible to correspond with the letters of the Hebrew alphabet rather than the Greek, the selection or determination of the number twenty-four could be justified on the basis of the occurrence of that number in various biblical contexts, apart from a possible connection with the alphabet.

In fact, the difficulty of making the correlation was recognized and steps were taken to connect the canon of the Hebrew Bible with the number of letters in the Hebrew alphabet. Josephus, late in the 1st century C.E., clearly is working with a canon containing all twenty-four books.[13] But in order to produce a more

11. A. Wace and F. Stubbings, *A Companion to Homer* (New York: Macmillan, 1962), ch. 6.

12. T. W. Allen, *Homer: The Origins and the Transmission* (Oxford: Clarendon, 1924), 320.

13. *Against Apion* i.37-43.

exact correspondence, Josephus makes the Hebrew Bible fit the 22-letter Hebrew alphabet. Josephus makes this adaptation by a rather drastic reduction in the number of the biblical books. He does not rule out any of the existing texts but merges two of the smaller books (from the Megilloth) with larger books, with which they might well be associated on the basis of content, date, and presumed authorship. This practice of combining or connecting books is still reflected in the printed editions of the Old Testament, especially the older versions in English and other modern languages. Thus the book of Ruth, which in the Hebrew Bible is counted with the other Megilloth as part of the Writings, is placed immediately after the book of Judges and reckoned as part of the latter. Similarly, the book of Lamentations, another of the Megilloth, has been transferred to a position immediately after Jeremiah; in many translations Lamentations actually is called "The Lamentations of Jeremiah." The actual connections between the two merged books and the books with which they are paired are superficial. The sole reason for these maneuvers is to achieve the desired total of twenty-two, which shows the importance of the alphabet in defining the boundaries of the Scriptures.

Certainly, in the case of Josephus, the manipulation of a correlation between alphabet and canon is entirely artificial; the same may be said of a hypothetical connection between the 24-book canon and the Greek alphabet of twenty-four letters. But both of these highly artificial constructions may well reflect an earlier association of the Hebrew canon with the Hebrew alphabet, one that was less contrived and more in keeping with both the Hebrew alphabet and the Hebrew Scriptures. We suggest therefore that later efforts to associate the Hebrew Bible with the Hebrew alphabet are attempts to restore an earlier, dimly remembered linkage.

We affirm that there was a connection between a presumed Hebrew Bible containing twenty-three books in the Persian period, and that it was correlated with the "augmented" Hebrew alphabet reflected in at least two alphabetic acrostic Psalms (25 and 34). We argue that the 23-book Bible already existed in that arrangement in the latter part of the Persian period (around 400 B.C.E.) and was organized with the augmented alphabet in mind. A 22-book Bible corresponding to the normal Hebrew alphabet might seem more plausible; this can be achieved by eliminating one of the late books usually assigned to the Greek period (Ecclesiastes, or perhaps Esther), creating four rolls instead of five. All of this would not be genuinely helpful, however, first because the number five is more important than four in the first and last parts of the Bible (Pentateuch and Writings) while the number four is more significant in the middle parts (Former and Latter Prophets), and second because the word counts for the two halves of the Bible are much more decisive in determining the component parts. The 23-book Bible is symmetrical, whereas neither the 22-book nor the 24-book groupings are.

If we consider numerical symmetry an important factor, then there is really no choice: there was only one moment when the Bible and the alphabet coincided and all the editorial factors were present. It was precisely in this period (postexilic, Babylonian and Persian) that the bulk of the alphabetic acrostic poems in the Bible can be dated, and the use of the alphabet as a structuring principle was at its peak.[14] What better way to affirm the totality of revealed truth and the completeness of authoritative instruction than to bind the canon with the alphabet. The message to the faithful was that the Bible is now complete — perfect and perfectly symmetrical — and provides all the instruction (from *'aleph* to *taw*) necessary to fulfill the law and enjoy life to the full.

To close this paper, we summarize the following thesis for the compilation of the whole Hebrew Bible. This thesis, which rests on both numerical and thematic evidence, has been presented in depth elsewhere,[15] so needs only to be sketched here. We attribute the conception and execution to the Scribe Ezra and Governor Nehemiah, who may have worked partly in tandem, but also in sequence, with Ezra responsible chiefly for the conception and Nehemiah for the execution and completion of the project. The separate memoirs of these men were attached to the end of the work, thus ending and completing the whole work.

Adopting but also adapting an older view widely held at one time, I believe that Ezra was largely responsible for the Chronicler's work, including the basic story down to the time of the rebuilding of the temple; he also wrote his own memoirs. The purpose of the work was to trace the story of the temple, the house of David, and the city of Jerusalem, from the time of David, who captured the city, with central emphasis on the building of the temple, through the long story of the dynasty of David, to the days after the return, the rebuilding and dedication of the temple. This would take us through ch. 6 of Ezra, and the story would reach a suitable climax with the rededication of the temple. Matters relating to the rebuilding of the city walls, a primary concern of Nehemiah, have been incorporated into the text of Ezra 4–5 because these were related to the search of the royal Persian archives for evidence of the original edict concerning temple and city. As we know from Nehemiah's memoirs, the rebuilding of the city walls was a task assigned to and executed by him vigorously in the latter part of the 5th century.

The final editing of the Chronicler's work can be attributed to Nehemiah, or to one or more persons working under his direction. There are in effect two stages: (1) the basic work, from the beginning of Chronicles to the end of Ezra 6, bringing the story down to the dedication of the Second Temple in 515 B.C.E.; (2) the subsequent activity, essentially bringing the story up to the time of Nehemiah, who is responsible for the final form of the text. Perhaps Ezra, who started earlier and probably was older than Nehemiah, died before he was able to bring the story up to date and incorporate his own memoirs, so that task was left to Nehemiah, who

14. D. N. Freedman, "Acrostics and Metrics in Hebrew Poetry," *Pottery, Poetry, and Prophecy* (Winona Lake: Eisenbrauns, 1980), 51-76.

15. Freedman, *The Unity of the Hebrew Bible*.

connected the new material with the established Chronicler's work. So Nehemiah and whatever assistants he may have employed were responsible for amalgamating the Chronicler's work with the supplementary material relating to the rebuilding of the city and its walls in his time, and the adoption of the Torah as the rule of life for the Jewish community in Jerusalem and its environs (the primary focus of Ezra's mission).

The Hebrew Bible as a whole was shaped by men who sought and achieved stability and security for a small defenseless community in the midst of hostile peoples, under the protection of a great imperial power which they served as administrative officers. That community had survived a most terrifying experience and had returned from captivity to rebuild their community and ultimately their state. First on their agenda was to rebuild the temple, and second, the city, and beyond that to populate and control the province. All this was a far cry from the days of old, when the nation was independent and a king of the house of David ruled in Jerusalem over a united realm, even a middle-sized empire. But the present achievement would suffice, while the other would persist in hopes and dreams, written in a permanent text, in the words of prophets and poets for a dim and distant future. For Ezra and Nehemiah, it was more than enough: a literary monument that with minor changes and a single major addition would last forever, and would in fact bring this same people back more than once, even in our own day, from exile and dispersion.

Appendix

Chart A: Word and Letter Counts

	Words	Letters	Ratio
Pentateuch			
Genesis	20,613	78,069	3.79
Exodus	16,713	63,531	3.80
Leviticus	11,950	44,795	3.75
Numbers	16,413	63,547	3.87
Deuteronomy	14,294	54,908	3.84
Total	79,983	304,850	3.81
Former Prophets			
Joshua	10,051	39,808	3.96
Judges	9,885	38,945	3.93
Samuel	24,301	93,534	3.84
Kings	25,421	98,463	3.87
Total	69,658	270,750	3.88

Latter Prophets

Isaiah	16,932	66,888	3.95
Jeremiah	21,835	84,910	3.89
Ezekiel	18,730	74,496	3.98
Minor Prophets	14,355	56,743	3.95
Total	71,852	283,037	3.94

Writings

Chronicles	24,058	99,477	4.14
Psalms	19,586	78,830	4.03
Job	8,343	31,861	3.82
Proverbs	6,915	26,505	3.83
Ezra-Nehemiah	9,065	38,276	4.22
Megilloth	10,118	39,160	3.87
Subtotal	78,085	314,109	4.02
Daniel	5,919	24,291	4.10
Total	84,004	338,400	4.03

Summary

Primary history (Gen.-Kgs.)	149,641	575,600	3.85
Second half (Isa.-Neh.)	149,937	597,146	3.98
Total	299,578	1,172,746	3.91
[With Daniel	305,497	1,197,037	3.92]

Chart B: Codex Leningrad Data

	Pages	Words	Ratio	Letters	Ratio
Pentateuch	237.5	79,983	336.7	304,850	1283.5
Former Prophets	199.0	69,658	350.0	270,750	1360.6
Total	436.5	149,641	342.8	575,600	1319.0
Latter Prophets	212.2	71,852	338.6	283,037	1333.8
Writings (without Daniel)	252.4	78,085	309.3	314,109	1244.4
Total	464.6	149,937	322.7	597,146	1285.0
Grand Total	901.1	299,578	332.4	1,172,746	1301.4

Chart C: Vowel Letters

	Letters	Consonants	Vowels	Waw	Yodh	Consonants/ Word Ratio
Pentateuch						
Gen.	78,069	69,992	8,077	3,505	4,572	3.39
Exod.	63,531	57,880	5,651	2,350	3,301	3.46
Lev.	44,795	40,805	3,990	1,919	2,071	3.41
Num.	63,547	57,545	6,002	2,618	3,384	3.50
Deut.	54,908	49,472	5,436	2,288	3,148	3.46
Total	304,850	275,694	29,156	12,680	16,476	3.44
Former Prophets						
Josh.	39,908	35,381	4,427	2,191	2,236	3.52
Judg.	38,945	34,293	4,652	2,176	2,476	3.46
Sam.	93,534	83,213	10,231	4,877	5,444	3.42
Kgs.	98,463	88,668	9,795	4,452	5,343	3.48
Total	270,750	241,555	29,195	13,696	15,499	3.46
Latter Prophets						
Isa.	66,888	58,327	8,561	4,374	4,187	3.44
Jer.	84,910	74,649	10,261	4,912	5,349	3.41
Ezek.	74,496	65,780	8,716	3,877	4,839	3.51
12 Minor	56,743	49,628	7,115	3,509	3,606	3.45
Total	283,037	248,384	34,653	16,672	17,981	3.45
Writings						
Chr.	99,477	87,298	12,179	5,653	6,526	3.62
Ezra-Neh.	38,276	33,515	4,761	2,057	2,704	3.69
Ps.	78,830	67,453	11,377	5,384	5,993	3.44
Job	31,861	27,468	4,393	2,004	2,389	3.29
Prov.	26,505	23,135	3,370	1,539	1,831	3.34
Megilloth	39,160	34,221	4,939	2,256	2,683	3.38
Total	314,109	273,090	41,019	18,893	22,126	3.49
SUMMARY						
Primary history (Gen.-Kgs.)						
	575,600	517,249	58,351	26,376	31,975	3.46
Second half (Isa.-Neh.)						
	597,146	521,474	75,672	35,565	40,107	3.48
Total	1,172,746	1,038,723	134,023	61,941	72,082	3.47

43

Editing the Editors:
Translation and Elucidation
of the Text of the Bible

This paper is written from a particular vantage point, that of editor of the Anchor Bible commentary series and the Anchor Bible Reference Library. As such, I have had the unusual, perhaps unparalleled opportunity to observe and oversee the written work of a large group of scholars, who themselves have edited and are editing the different books of the Bible, dealing directly with the ancient texts.[1] Overall, they have adopted a wide variety of approaches and applied different sets of procedures and techniques in the course of determining the basic and best text and translating and explaining it. At the same time, they share many presuppositions and principles in their work, and other important features are held in common and appear repeatedly in the many volumes of both series. In what follows, I intend to isolate and identify some of these major components, while not neglecting special and separate factors, and also incorporating comments and evaluations, including a rare original idea of my own.

Essentially, there are two major tasks facing the editor of any ancient or original manuscript: the determination of the text and the rendering (or translation) of that text into a modern language. It should be noted that while the tasks are different, and in principle at least the determination of the text should and does precede its rendering, in practice the problems in one area inevitably affect those in the other, and progress with one task is often intertwined with that in the other.

1. The Anchor Bible Commentary series currently has fifty volumes in print of a projected seventy, covering Old Testament, New Testament, and Apocrypha. The Anchor Bible Reference Library has five volumes in print; the *Anchor Bible Dictionary* (6 vols.) was published in July 1992.

Thus the outcome of the former undertaking should be a text that is comprehensible and hence translatable. At the same time, such considerations inescapably affect the evaluation and selection among variant readings. There is a continuous process of adjustment and reciprocal modification in achieving both goals: an acceptable text and an adequate translation. In addition neither of these tasks comes unattended or unencumbered. Thus, prior to the establishment or even the existence of a text of the work in question, there is often a long complicated history of sources and antecedent and related compositions, whether oral or written, and belonging in some significant fashion to the task at hand. Much of biblical scholarship has been devoted to the search for and the isolation and identification of such sources, along with the always-intriguing questions of date and authorship and provenience, not to speak of other related matters. Such an investigation, arduous and protracted as it has turned out to be for many books of the Bible, is only part of this enterprise, and the scholar who undertakes it must retrace the stages and steps taken in the first effort. Analysis — dissection and assignment of units and segments — must be complemented with synthesis — the reassembly of the pieces into the final finished and presumably coherent whole with which the scholarly inquiry began. It is at that point that the prehistory of the book or the literary history of the work comes to an end and its textual history begins. There may be considerable overlap, as editors produce sequential redactions of the work, and on occasion it is possible to trace to earlier sources. Once, however, an edition is produced that receives general approbation and achieves official status and authority of some kind, then the object of research is the history of transmission and the recovery insofar as possible of the original text of that edition. The initial process is again in reverse, as we move from existing manuscripts backward in time through intermediate stages to the pristine original. Determination of the text is achieved by comparison of different manuscript readings, including versions (in which the preserved translation must be retroverted into the presumed original from which the translation was made); and by numerous techniques available to the scholar, an earlier text can often be recovered from the evidence available in existing manuscripts. While considerable success has been achieved with respect to many readings, many others remain uncertain or disputed. The resultant choices do not carry with them the same measure of conviction or confidence, and often marginal notes are required to offer variant readings, alternatives to the chosen text.

Similarly, the work of translation, which officially begins with the text that has been fixed by the scholarly procedures just described, carries with it an enormous amount of other baggage. Translation itself is only the most visible part of the work of research: in fact it is a kind of game, to see how nearly and accurately one can render a word in one language into another language, matching words and verses, sentences and paragraphs, so that readers in one language group can read with understanding and appreciation a work that belongs to another language group. Inevitably translation is mistranslation (as others have said before), and no translation can convey to the reader of it the same effect or impact that the original would to its readership. But a good translation can make such a work available and accessible to such groups, and the effect can approximate the impact of the original on its audience, so there is no question about the value and importance of such work. But it is only a part of the larger work of transference, which involves extensive investigation of the whole cultural setting in which and out of which this work emerged. So far as possible it is necessary to discover, recover, and reconstruct the world in which that work was composed, and transfer all of that into the realm of the new reader, or vice versa, transport the contemporary reader into the world and culture in which the work has its proper place. Translation is limited by the original from which it is derived, and the numerous conventions and rules by which such endeavors are made. While original authors occasionally provide explanatory information about the subject of their discourse,[2] more often they assume that their readers share with them the cultural milieu, and take for granted that the readers know a lot of things that, however, later and different readers are usually ignorant of. So along with translation there must be extensive explanation and elucidation. That means notes and comments.

When we speak, therefore, about determining the *text* and then producing a *translation,* these are simply convenient markers in a continuous process that begins with the earliest literary sources of the resultant text, and only ends with the reconstruction of the whole world in which the literary work found its place. And it carries us far beyond that particular time and place into the history of transmission of the text, the history of translation and interpretation down to our own day. But it is precisely the point at which literary evolution and development end and textual history begins that the key work of determining the text and producing a translation is done, which is why we emphasize the two distinctive aspects of a single moment or time in the story we as editors of an ancient work are trying to explicate.

Given constraints of space, we will restrict ourselves to summary statements about the tasks outlined, and then try to pictorialize the operations by citing examples from both Testaments, and illustrating both the procedures and the results, especially if the latter mark progress or break new ground in our field.

When it comes to the biblical text and its determination, in spite of a number of important and sensational discoveries of manuscripts, we remain basically dependent on the same great codices that have been available for the past century or longer. For the Hebrew Bible we use the critical edition of Codex L (for Leningrad), a medieval text (from around 1000 C.E.), which all around remains the best available. The newly published (in the last twenty years) Aleppo Codex (A),[3] is older and better, but it is also substantially less complete, and could only be used to supplement or correct L. The differences in readings are negligible in any case,

2. E.g., John 20:30-31; 21:24-25.
3. M. H. Goshen-Gottstein, ed., *The Aleppo Codex* (Jerusalem: Magnes, 1976).

as they derive from the same scribal tradition, and the only important divergences concern spelling practices. For the Greek New Testament, we have the great uncial codices of the 4th and 5th centuries, Codex Vaticanus, Codex Sinaiticus, and Codex Alexandrinus, the first and third known from early times, and the middle one rediscovered by Tischendorf already before the middle of the 19th century. The texts used by scholars are based upon these major manuscripts of the Old and New Testaments. There have been very extensive and important manuscript finds of many New Testament books, mostly papyri and many of them earlier than the manuscripts mentioned above. For scholarly purposes, these have provided important readings and also clues to the early history of the text, its transmission, and diversification into various groups or families.[4] For the Hebrew Bible, the discovery of the Dead Sea Scrolls opened a new chapter in the analysis of the text and a reconstruction of its transmission and history. For certain books, especially the Former Prophets and more particularly Samuel, and also for the Pentateuch, the discoveries have been of major importance in pushing back the analysis to a prerabbinic era when at least two or three different text types were known and flourished. A theory of local text types, while under fire from some quarters, perhaps best explains the divergence among the manuscripts; so we can speak of a proto-Massoretic text that comes from Babylon, a proto-Septuagintal type that comes from Egypt, and a proto-Samaritan type that has its home in Palestine.[5] Exemplars of all three are to be found among the scrolls from Qumran, showing that ultimately they were brought together in one place, but thanks to the diversity in the texts, it is possible to reconstruct at least in part the earlier history of the transmission of the text, back certainly to the middle of the 3rd century B.C.E., and possibly a little further and that much closer to the original master text itself, presumably a product of the early postexilic period. In practice, there are not many important changes from the standard text, and the results in terms of translation and textual or linguistic notes are not very serious. Thus the great Isaiah scroll, one of the few complete or practically complete manuscripts discovered, offers comparatively few substantive changes from the Massoretic Text (MT), and not infrequently the variant readings are neither persuasive as alternates to MT nor impressive as useful additions to the discussion.[6] Contrariwise, the great if fragmentary Samuel scroll from Cave 4 offers very important readings not found in MT or else differing from it. This manuscript conforms much more with the tradition of the Septuagint (LXX), the early Greek translation of the Hebrew Bible

4. B. M. Metzger, *The Text of the New Testament*, 3rd ed. (New York: Oxford University Press, 1991).

5. F. M. Cross, *The Ancient Library of Qumran and Modern Biblical Studies* (Garden City: Doubleday, 1958; rept. Greenwood, Conn.: Greenwood Press, 1976), 120-45.

6. A verse-by-verse comparison is found in J. R. Rosenbloom, *The Dead Sea Isaiah Scroll: A Literary Analysis* (Grand Rapids: Wm. B. Eerdmans, 1970).

(beginning in the 3rd century B.C.E.) and confirms that the LXX here is not a free rendering of MT, as had been suspected by some scholars, but rather a faithful even literal rendering of a different Hebrew text.[7] Since the MT of Samuel has always been known to be difficult and in many ways an inferior text of the presumed original, it is clear that Qumran and LXX preserve a much better version of Samuel; the same is true to a lesser extent of the other books of the Former Prophets, although for these books we have only fragments from Qumran. Similarly, the manuscripts of the Torah from Qumran (all only in fragmentary form) offer readings that range from MT to Samaritan and LXX, confirming again that three text types existed side by side during the pre-Christian centuries, and thereby at least in principle enabling scholars to trace the history of the text back to earlier times, perhaps back to the 4th or even 5th century B.C.E. when we can make a plausible if somewhat tenuous and colorful connection with the greatest scribe of them all, Ezra, the traditional father or promulgator of the Law of Moses.

For the rest, to a large extent the new finds confirm and support traditional readings of MT, although here and there special, distinctive, and occasionally more original readings are to be found. A manuscript containing a large part of ch. 1 of Lamentations has been published recently,[8] and some of its readings diverge substantially from MT. Unfortunately, with very few exceptions, the readings themselves are not impressive and in general MT is superior, although there may be a few exceptions that deserve closer attention. Basically the evidence from Qumran shows that during the millennium from the 1st centuries B.C.E. and C.E., there has been little change in the text of the Hebrew Bible, but also that the striking uniformity of all medieval texts is a product of the post-1st-century era, and that a diversity at least as great as among the manuscripts of the New Testament of the first centuries C.E. also prevailed among Old Testament manuscripts. All in all, we can claim to have a very reliable text of the New Testament in our hands now, and a reliable if more narrowly based text of the Old Testament as well.

When we go behind the text and seek for sources, the situation is different but not greatly. The major analyses of the Old and New Testaments remain in place, although serious efforts have been made to overthrow or undermine them. The now-traditional four-source hypothesis concerning the structure of the Pentateuch has not been replaced by a better theory, although JEDP have been battered and beaten, and there is still a great deal of controversy as to the dates of these sources, and also their precise extent and contents.[9] But a multiple-source theory remains

7. Discussion in E. Tov, *The Text-Critical Use of the Septuagint in Biblical Research* (Jerusalem: Simor, 1981).

8. F. M. Cross, "Studies in the Structure of Hebrew Verse: The Prosody of Lamentations 1:1-22," *The Word of the Lord Shall Go Forth*, ed. C. L. Meyers and M. P. O'Connor (Winona Lake: Eisenbrauns, 1983), 129-55.

9. R. E. Friedman, *Who Wrote the Bible?* (New York: Summit, 1987).

the best way of explaining the differences and divergences in the preserved material, with regard to contents and also language and usage. The same may be said for the Synoptic Gospels, where the basic two-source theory (Mark and Q) has been under fire for a long time, but remains the majority view and in all likelihood will continue to do so. In short, the new discoveries, while extremely important in establishing the text and providing improved readings in numerous instances, have not seriously affected the inquiry into the prehistory of the text or the literary history of the books of the Bible. Except in a very rare instance or two (especially regarding possible sources of the book of Daniel,[10] which is in a separate category from most of the Hebrew Bible because of its undoubted Hellenistic, 2nd-century B.C.E. provenience) we have been unable to reach back beyond the text itself, and are still some distance from the earliest forms of the first publication of these books.

In the determination of the text, numerous factors come into play. We must choose among available readings, from both Hebrew manuscripts and the versions, especially the LXX; the latter, by the way, provides an excellent example of the intrinsic value of a literal, even word-for-word, translation. In the absence of the original text from which it was translated, the version can provide the essential material for retroversion to the original. The more literal the rendering, the more reliable the retroversion. Less useful would be a more elegant and less literal rendering, and least of all a paraphrase. If after the best efforts to establish the text from existing readings in ancient manuscripts there still remain difficulties and problems with the text, we may finally turn to conjecture and conjectural readings. This is a high-risk proposition with a very high mortality rate, but also a challenge to ingenuity and intellect. While most such emendations have failed of acceptance, and time and tides have washed them into oblivion, a few magnificent ones have passed the test of time and acceptance and remain embedded firmly in the literature and in the better translations. And the temptation to try one's skill in this arena is hard to resist. Let us look at a very few examples of emendations in the text of the Hebrew Bible, of different kinds, one with textual support and the others without. The passages I have in mind derive from the book of Amos (3:9a and 6:12a) and Psalms (119:48).

> Proclaim upon the ramparts of Assyria [MT: Ashdod]
> and upon the ramparts of the land of Egypt. (Amos 3:9)

In this case, we have different readings of a key word in the Hebrew text and the Greek version. MT reads *be'ašdôd* while LXX has *en Assyriois,* which reflects a Hebrew *Vorlage: be'aššûr.*[11] While in general, MT has a text superior to

---

10. D. N. Freedman, "The Prayer of Nabonidus," *BASOR* 145 (1957): 31-32 [see above, Chapter 6].

11. For a full discussion, see F. I. Andersen and D. N. Freedman, *Amos.* AB 24A (Garden City: Doubleday, 1989), 405-6.

that preserved and reflected in LXX, every instance must be judged separately, and this one is not easy to decide. In our judgment, the weight of the evidence and argument goes with LXX. According to the prophet, Yahweh has his agents proclaim a message to the people of two nations, which are set in parallel construction; they are summoned to observe the tumultuous conditions in Samaria, and the wickedness that lies at the root of the trouble. Who are these nations called in as observers and destined to be witnesses in God's case against his own people? One clearly is Egypt, while the other is problematic. The choice of Egypt is significant, and that can help us decide between the alternatives offered by MT (Ashdod) and LXX (Assyria). Chapter 3 as a whole is a denunciation of Israel and a reinforcement of the condemnation already offered in ch. 2 (vv. 6-16). In the Great Set Speech of chs. 1–2, the eight small nations lying between Assyria to the northeast and Egypt to the southwest are each condemned in turn and sentenced to destruction and devastation, the list concluding with Israel. The same condemnation is taken up in ch. 3 but focused exclusively on Israel. The question is this: if other nations are to be summoned to witness the crimes and disturbances in Israel, who would likely be chosen for this duty? The choice of Egypt shows that it would be a nation outside of the group under condemnation, and not involved in the denunciations of chs. 1–2. The trouble with the choice of the parallel term in MT (Ashdod) is that Ashdod is definitely one of the nations mentioned in 1:6-8 (along with other Philistine cities) and therefore condemned to destruction. It would be anomalous to invite one of the condemned nations to observe upheavals in a neighboring country, whereas it would be appropriate to invite an uninvolved country, such as Assyria. Besides, Ashdod is geographically on the same side of Israel as Egypt, so the image would be lopsided, whereas Egypt and Assyria form not only a literary envelope but a geographic one, suitably framing the entire area under condemnation; they are invited to examine the particularities of the charge against Israel. That picture makes better sense than the one represented by MT. In addition, the pair: (land of) Egypt//(land of) Assyria is frequent in the oracles of the 8th-century prophets (and elsewhere),[12] so it is altogether appropriate in the book of Amos. Two arguments are used to counter this position, one being that the word *Assur* (Assyria) does not otherwise occur in the entire book of Amos, and it may be that Amos deliberately avoided mention of this nation in his oracles, preferring to leave open the nature and direction from which the threat to Israel's existence would come. Hence it would be unlikely that he would use the name here if he avoided it elsewhere. I think the book of Amos is too short to make generalizations like that; furthermore, there is no hint of impending attack on the part of this second nation, only that it will be called as a witness. In fact, Amos does not envision a military attack from any particular direction or from any particular human source. While human agencies are not excluded, and battles are

12. E.g., Isa. 7:18; 11:11; the pair appears in twenty-three verses.

imagined, Amos believes that the onslaught will come directly from God in heaven, and it will be like the devastation wreaked on Sodom and Gomorrah, i.e., fire from heaven.[13] It is also argued that Ashdod is the more difficult reading and therefore should be retained, precisely for the reasons that are offered to support the reading of Assyria. It all depends upon what one means by difficult, and how difficult you want to make the end product. The latter should make good sense, and should fit the context. Assyria does ease a number of problems with MT, and if that makes things too easy, so be it.

The other passage is Amos 6:12, where a scholarly consensus has formed around a purely conjectural emendation. The MT reads as follows (a literal translation):

> Do horses run upon the rock?
> Or does one plow with oxen?
> But you have turned justice into poison
> and the fruit of righteousness into wormwood.

The general idea is clear enough. There is an unfavorable comparison between animals and humans to the effect that ordinary "dumb animals" show more sense in their behavior than so-called intelligent human beings. A similar contrast is made by the prophet Isaiah in a very familiar passage (1:3):

> Ox knows its owner
> and ass its master's crib.
> Israel does not know
> my people does not understand.

The passage in Amos is less sharply delineated, and there is some fuzziness in the second colon, as we shall see, but the general idea is the same in both cases. Taken at face value, the poet argues that horses do not run on rocky surfaces (the question in the Hebrew text requires a negative response, just as it would in English), thereby showing common sense, whereas the people being addressed by Amos have shown the same senselessness that Isaiah decries[14] in turning justice into poison, the fruit of righteousness into wormwood, or paraphrasing: they have produced poisonous weeds by their unjust and iniquitous behavior, instead of the edible fruits that justice and righteousness should produce. The figure of speech here is agrarian: justice and righteousness, a frequent combination in Amos and other prophets,[15] are seen as trees or plants that properly tended would produce fruits in accordance with their nature:

---

13. Amos 4:11; 7:4; 9:5.

14. Cf. Isa. 5:20, "Woe to those who call bad good and good bad, who put darkness for light and light for darkness, who put bitter for sweet and sweet for bitter."

15. E.g., Isa. 5:16; 9:6; Jer. 2:18, 36; Hos. 7:11; 9:3; Ezek. 18:19; the pair appears in forty verses.

nourishing and satisfying. But the people have managed everything so badly that the actual fruits produced are the opposite of what was expected, and are instead poisonous weeds that will inflict great harm on those who cultivated the trees and also plan to eat the fruit. Comparison with another familiar passage in Isaiah, in which the same point is made, is in order: the parable of the vineyard in Isa. 5:1-7, in which the owner did everything possible to ensure the production of good fruit, but because of the senseless sinfulness of the people, the fruit was bad. Similarly, the prophet Jeremiah talks about good and bad figs in comparing and contrasting different elements in the population of Judah (ch. 24). In the passage in Amos (6:12), difficulties arise with the second colon, which is parallel to the first one about the horses. Here the beasts are oxen, and the verse says simply: "Or does one plow with oxen?" As it stands, the statement is simply banal and conventional, because in those days one did, and there is no parallel to the obvious anomaly in the first colon regarding the horses. In addition, the subject of the verb in the second colon is not the animals as in the first colon, but some unnamed and undefined subject, presumably the human owner or master of the oxen. Whereas, presumably, in the first colon it is the animals (horses) that exercise common sense, in the second the decisions are made, not by the animals, but by their masters. The result is that whereas the stark contrast between humans and animals is presented clearly in the first colon in relation to the second couplet of the verse, where the subject is clearly human beings, the second colon of the first couplet seems to refer to human control rather than to the common sense of animals. Perhaps we should not make too much of this apparent slippage in the focus of the figure, and hold on to the main idea, namely that in the ordinary practical affairs of life, humans and animals display an important measure of common sense and behave in such a way as to further the common interest. So combining the statements, we can interpret each in a cooperative sense: just as men and beasts work together in plowing, so presumably owners or masters supervise their horses so as to protect them from the recklessness of running free upon a rocky surface. Horses might not run on rocks anyway, but masters wouldn't encourage them to, would restrain them from so doing.

Even if this interpretation is allowable, and it probably is, we are still faced with the major problem of the second colon about plowing, namely that there is nothing wrong or strange about the statement. So we have a conventional statement about people plowing with oxen, which is quite normal, matched up with a question about horses running, which is decidedly not. A solution to the problem was offered more than two hundred years ago by D. Michaelis, and it has proved to be much more durable than most such conjectural emendations.[16] In its favor is that it is quite simple, does not require the alteration of any letters in the text, and in fact only requires that we divide the word *b b q r y m* (*babbᵉqārîm* = oxen) into two words: *b b q r* (*babbāqār* = ox [sg.] or oxen [collective]) and *y m* (*yām* = sea) and thus produce an entirely different sense for the sentence: "Does one plow the sea

---

16. D. Michaelis, *Deutsche Übersetzung des Alten Testaments* (Göttingen: Dieterich, 1772).

with oxen?" While there is no exact parallel for this anywhere in the Bible, nevertheless, the revised sentence makes for an excellent parallel to the preceding statement or question about horses. Horses don't run on rocks, and one doesn't plow the sea with oxen.

While there is no textual, recensional, or versional evidence to support this emended reading, and some scholars resist it, I think the proposal is very attractive, and certainly deserves consideration in notes and commentary, whether it is finally adopted as the true text and in the translation.[17] Incidentally, in this verse, the LXX (Septuagint) goes its own way, and after mentioning the horses in the first colon, omits the cattle entirely, and has the horses the subject of the second colon as well. While it doesn't have the same problem as MT for this verse, it also does not contribute noticeably to the solution.

The third example of textual emendation seems trivial on the surface, but it offers an opportunity to bring several factors together in making a determination of the best text. The passage is in the Great Psalm, Ps. 119, vv. 47-48, where we, along with numerous scholars previously,[18] postulate a common error in scribal transmission, namely an instance of vertical dittography. We offer the Hebrew text (in transcription) and a literal translation:

(47) *we'ešta'ªša' bemiṣwōṯêḵā 'ªšer 'āhāḇtî*
(48) *we'eśśā'-kappay 'el-miṣwōṯêḵā 'ªšer 'āhāḇtî we'āśîhâ ḇehuqqêḵā*

[And I will delight myself in your commandments, which I love.
And I will raise my palms (= hands) to your commandments, which I love,
and I will meditate on your statutes.]

1) The first thing to note is that v. 48 is a lot longer than v. 47 and in fact is longer than most lines in the poem. The lines themselves are all end-stopped, and their exact length is determined by the alphabetic acrostic construction of the poem. Thus all eight lines of this stanza (vv. 41-48) begin with the letter *waw*, and thus the beginning and end of each line are fixed by this alphabetic device. We can therefore count the words, accents, and syllables of each line or verse, and for the two under discussion the numbers are as follows:

	Words	Accents	Syllables	
V. 47	2 + 2 = 4	2 + 2 = 4	4 + 5 = 9	
			2 + 3 = 5	= 14
V. 48	6 + 2 = 8	4 + 2 = 6	3 + 2 + 1 + 4 = 10	
			2 + 3 = 5	= 23
			4 + 4 = 8	

17. Andersen-Freedman, 576-78.
18. C. A. Briggs and E. G. Briggs, *Psalms*. ICC (New York: Scribner's, 1906).

The average and normal line length for this poem is sixteen syllables and six (content) words or accents, with the major grammatical division in the middle. Thus v. 47 is within the normal range (about fourteen to eighteen syllables) although on the short side, whereas v. 48 is much higher than average and beyond the normal range.

2) Secondly, we note that three successive words in v. 48 are all but identical with three successive words in v. 47. Furthermore, it is clear from the Psalms scroll from Qumran Cave 11[19] that the lines of this and other poems were written stichometrically, namely that regardless of length, each line was written on a separate line, and one was written directly above or below the following or preceding one. The same pattern is still generally visible in the great medieval codices, Aleppo (A) and Leningrad (L). So it is altogether likely that the words that were inadvertently copied were directly above where the scribe was writing, and that he simply copied the preceding line from the manuscript at that point. We can illustrate by showing just the letters in the text:

w ʾ š t ʿ š ʿ b *m ṣ w t y k ʾ š r ʾ h b t y*
w ʾ ś ʾ k p y ʾ l *m ṣ w t y k ʾ š r ʾ h b t y* w ʾ ś y ḥ h b ḥ q y k

3) Thirdly, the present text of MT at v. 48 does not make good sense in Hebrew (or in English) although RSV among others smooths the reading by paraphrasing:

"I revere / thy commandments, which I love. . . ."

Literally, the text says: "And I will lift up my hands to your commandments, which I love. . . ." The action does not go well with the object. More suitable is a parallel passage in Lam. 3:41 (also in an alphabetic acrostic poem), where we read: "We will lift up . . . [our] hands to El (God) in the heavens. . . ." That text also is in some disarray, but the picture of raising the hands or palms to the sky in prayer is quite clear, and we can adapt it to the passage in Ps. 119. We suggest therefore that before the dittography, the text of v. 48 read something like this:

And I will raise my hands to you
And I will meditate on your statutes.

The Hebrew text would read approximately as follows:

	Words/Accents	Syllables	
wᵉʾeśśaʾ-kappay ʾelêkā	3	$3 + 2 + 3 = 8$	= 16
wᵉʾāśîḥâ ḇᵉḥuqqêḵā	2	$4 + 4 \quad = 8$	

The result is a balanced and quite normal bicolon of $8 + 8 = 16$ syllables, which matches up quite well with v. 47.

---

19. J. A. Sanders, ed., *The Dead Sea Psalms Scroll* (Ithaca: Cornell University Press, 1967).

I think that most scholars would accept this emendation and reconstruction of the text (or something very much like it), and it is the consensus view represented in the latest edition of our critical text of the Hebrew Bible (BHS, Biblia Hebraica Stuttgartensia).[20] Nevertheless, there is no manuscript or versional evidence to support the emendation, and it remains conjectural, and scholars may and probably will demur. Under the circumstances, it will be appropriate to offer additional circumstantial evidence to support the emendation, or at least to show how the determination of the text in this verse (48) is affected by considerations of balance and symmetry, in the light of a very complex and intricate arrangement of key words throughout the poem. The basic point here is that *miṣwōṯ* (which occurs in both vv. 47 and 48 in MT) is one of these key words (there are eight of them), and its occurrences and their distribution in the whole poem form part of a very elaborate and intricate scheme of numerical patterns and symmetrical balances. The principle of symmetry is very simple, and the basic arrangement can easily be calculated and plotted. There are 22 stanzas in the poem, and each one has 8 lines. The alphabetic pattern is indisputable: each of the 8 lines of each stanza begins with the appropriate letter of the alphabet, beginning with *'aleph* and ending with *taw.* There are 8 key words, all roughly synonymous with *torah,* which is primus inter pares.[21] In principle, therefore, each stanza should contain one example of each key word, and each line of each stanza should have one of them. The total number of lines is 176, and therefore the total number of key words in their occurrences would be 176 too. Each key word, therefore, should show up once in each stanza, and each one should occur 22 times in all. That is the underlying pattern and should be kept in mind, but the poet had other ideas about the implementation of the plan, and the governing operating principle is that of measured, calculated, and controlled deviation, so there is repeated variation from the established norms, but in the end, everything is going to come out even. Thus, when we count up all the occurrences of the 8 key words, the total is actually 177 instead of the expected 176, but the informed reader will already have guessed where that extra occurrence of 1 key word actually is to be found. As indicated, we would expect to have 1 key word in each line, but in fact that is true of only 167 lines. There are 4 lines without any key words, and there are 5 lines with 2 of them, bringing us to the total of 177 indicated earlier. Once the extra occurrence of a key word is set aside, then we would have a match-up between 4 lines with no occurrences and 4 lines with 2 occurrences; and this provides an excellent illustration of how the poet accomplished his goal. The implementation is by a process of compensation, so that for every omission there is a corresponding addition.

20. *Biblia Hebraica Stuttgartensia* (Stuttgart: Deutsche Bibelstiftung, 1977).

21. An independent treatment of the key words in Ps. 119 reached us after the preparation of this article: W. M. Soll, *Psalm 119: Matrix, Form, and Setting* (Washington: Catholic Biblical Association of America, 1991).

The 8 key words and their frequencies are listed next:

					Totals
1) *'imrâ*	(19)	8) *tôrâ*	(25)		44
2) *dābār*	(22)	3) *ḥōq (ḥuqqîm)*	(22)		44
4) *miṣwâ (miṣwōt)*	(21/22)	6) *ʿēdôt*	(23)		44 (45)
5) *mišpāṭ*	(23)	7) *piqqûd(im)*	(21)		44

It will be seen that only 2 of them (3 if we include the added occurrence of *miṣwōt* in v. 48) have the requisite 22 occurrences expected of all of them. But the others are carefully balanced and matched up so that if the pairs are taken correctly (masculine with masculine and feminine with feminine) we have pairs with the expected 44-syllable total. And these in turn add up to 88 for half and 176 for the total poem. If we take the 4 feminine nouns and the 4 masculine nouns in separate groups, we get the same totals, but other intriguing patterns emerge as well:

Feminine Nouns		Masculine Nouns	
1) *'imrâ*	19	5) *mišpāṭ*	23
4) *miṣwōt*	21 (22)	2) *dābār*	22
6) *ʿēdôt*	23	3) *ḥōq*	22
8) *tôrâ*	25	7) *piqqûd*	21
	88		88

It remains to be pointed out that the word-pair *'imrâ* and *tôrâ* has another distinction, which serves to confirm the analysis so far proposed. While the counts for the remaining 6 words are bunched around the normative number 22 (2 words occur 22 times, 2 occur 21 times, and 2 occur 23 times), these 2 words are much further apart than any of the others (19 and 25, which nevertheless and significantly still total 44, which is also a normative number), and also signify the limits and expanse of the alphabet: *'mrh* begins with the first letter of the alphabet, while *twrh* begins with the last letter of the alphabet. In view of the fact that the entire poem is structured alphabetically, this added touch, signifying totality (from *aleph* to *taw* would be equivalent to the similar expressions in Greek: from *alpha* to *omega*, and English, from A to Z), is a deliberate element in the overall scheme.

Given the presence of this elaborate and intricate arrangement and distribution of the key words in the poem it is clear that the occurrence of a single key word that mars the perfect symmetry otherwise achieved does not invalidate the scheme. Whether we regard the occurrence of this extra word as the result of scribal error (i.e., a case of "vertical dittography") or as the result of a miscount on the part of the author himself, the data presented here and the conclusions drawn are not materially affected. In other words, the overall scheme is so deeply and convincingly embedded in the poem that it cannot be ignored or dismissed simply because in the present text there is a minor deviation from a pattern that is otherwise absolutely regular and exact.

Since we have a perfectly good explanation of the slip in the occurrence of *miṣwōt* in v. 48, I prefer to ascribe it to inadvertent scribal error rather than anything else. The effect of restoring what was presumably the original text is to tighten up the symmetrical pattern, bring the count for *miṣwā* into line with the other key words, eliminate the extra fifth line with two key words, and thus allow us to match up the four lines with no key words with the four with key words, and achieve the symmetry that the poet no doubt intended. We can list the lines in both categories as follows:

	No Key Words	Two Key Words	
Stanza/Line	1:3	2:16	*dbr + ḥq*
	5:37	20:160	*dbrk + mšpṭ*
	12:90	21:168	*pqwd + ʿdwt*
	16:122	22:172	*ʾmrtk + miṣwtk*

We have left out of the reckoning the problematic v. 48, which in its present form also has two key words *(mṣwtyk + ḥqyk)*. For good and sufficient reason already given, we concluded that *mṣwtyk* in this verse is the result of scribal error (dittography), and its presence disturbs the otherwise perfect symmetry of the arrangement of lines without any key word and those with two of them, making up the desired total of 176.

Another example of this pattern of symmetry with deliberate deviations, or deviations within an overall symmetry, is to be found in the distribution of key words in the stanzas of the poem as a whole. We would expect that there would be eight key words in each stanza and that there would be one example of each key word in that stanza. In fact that is true of only five of the stanzas, and the arrangement of the key words is not exactly the same in any of the stanzas, so all are at least marginally different. Of the remainder, nine stanzas have eight key words, while four have nine key words, and four have seven key words. The following table will summarize the information:

Stanza	No. of Key Words		Stanza	No. of Key Words
1	7		12	7
2	9		13	8
3	8		14	8
4	8		15	8
5	7		16	7
6	*8 (9)		17	*8
7	8		18	8
8	*8		19	8
9	8		20	9
10	*8		21	9
11	*8		22	9
Total	87 (88)			89

When we look at the overall schema and the balancing halves, we notice a slight imbalance (i.e., eighty-seven key words in the first half of the poem and eighty-nine in the second), occasioned in part by our emendation of the text at v. 48. As matters stand, two of the seven-word stanzas occur in the first half of the poem, and two in the second half, as we should expect. The nine-word stanzas are distributed differently, with one or two in the first half and three in the second half. For the match-up to be exact we would expect the same distribution of the nine-word stanzas as for the seven-word stanzas, namely two and two in the two halves. This circumstance points to retaining v. 48 as we have it, rather than eliminating the second *miṣwōṭ*, but then we must look at the number and distribution of the nine-word stanzas in the second half, where we have three or one too many. According to the established pattern, if we restore the count for *miṣwâ/miṣwōṭ* to twenty-two, then we should reduce the count for *ʿēḏôṭ*, which matches up with it, from twenty-three to twenty-two. The best candidate for possible elimination or reduction in force would be in stanza 21, vv. 167-68, where the same phenomenon occurs that we noticed in vv. 47-48, namely the repetition of *ʿdwtyk* in successive lines at almost the same point in those lines. Certainly vertical dittography is a possibility here as it was shown to be in vv. 47-48 for *mṣwtyk*, although so far as I am aware, no previous scholar has suggested that we have a dittography in the text at this point (and it is less impressive than the case in vv. 47-48, where three words are repeated rather than only one here). We are quite willing to leave a measure of uncertainty about the original pristine form of the text, and allow for a certain measure of perturbation or deviation from perfect symmetrical patterns, which seems to be an integral part of the original composition. Various possibilities have been suggested for recognizing and resolving some of these anomalies. But clearly what shines through it all is a very intricate and elaborate series of symmetrical patterns.

What is impressive, even amazing, is how carefully this intricate pattern has been preserved in all its myriad details. A slight slip here or there hardly impairs the masterpiece of delicately balanced workmanship. Whether the minor anomalies that occur in the text now are the result of scribal slips or of the author/poet's own confusion about certain details hardly matters. There can be no question about the overall scheme and the remarkable success the author achieved in working out the countless details as he/she forged this extraordinary composition.

Having examined the first phase of the editorial task, namely the determination of the text, and illustrated the approach and procedure with certain examples, we now proceed to the second phase of the undertaking, namely the task of translation. This phase tends to receive the lion's share of attention on the part of both the editor of the text and the critics who judge the work more by the quality of the translation than the other important elements in the whole enterprise. I don't want to undervalue the importance of a fine translation, but it is only part of the total task, and given the usual restrictions, at best it can only reflect a part of the

535

work of analysis and interpretation. Finally, it can hardly pass muster without a due complement of explanatory notes. It is true that for many people, the bulk of the audience of readership, the translation will be their only access to the content of the ancient work, and therefore it must be faithful, reliable, and comprehensible. It should also have literary merit in its own right, although when choices present themselves, I think we must give preference to accuracy and correctness rather than to literary flourish or the attractive turn of phrase. After all, the editor is not supposed to be a creative artist, but a faithful transmitter of the creation of another or others, but the temptation is often hard to resist, and on some rare occasions it is precisely the combination of a great original artist and a master editor that produces translations that approach the originals in quality and durability. It is hardly an accident that translations of the Bible have attained places of distinction in the literature and literary traditions of the languages of translation, and are acclaimed as masterpieces in those languages: e.g., the Vulgate, the King James Version, the Luther Bible. Some of this distinction and acclaim may derive from the status of the Bible as canonical and authoritative, but surely the literary quality of these and other translations is also acknowledged.

In the end, translation is a kind of game, with its own rules and hazards, in which the goal is to duplicate the original in another language: at best it is an approximation, and always there are choices and concessions to be made, and, above all, compromises. If the purpose is to produce in the contemporary reader or hearer the same impact that the original had on its audience, then a measure of failure is more or less guaranteed. Times and circumstances, hearers and readers, change, and the latter become a moving target, elusive and difficult to hit. Translations are of many different kinds, and we can chart them on a sliding scale from the most literal word-for-word rendering, more like a pony than a translation, to an elaborate paraphrase, which may have only a tenuous relationship to the original, the latter serving more as a launching pad for the ideas and interests of the translator, than as the model or control for the rendering in a different language.[22] Each of these approaches and everything in between can meet a requirement or serve a need or concern on the part of the assumed readership, but inevitably, translation is compromise or even mistranslation.

In the case of the Hebrew Bible, a particular problem arises that has not received as much attention as it should, and at the same time reflects some of the intractable difficulties that confront the would-be translator or editor of the text. Almost invariably when translations of the Bible are made, they are made by the same individual or small group of scholars, using the same language in the same cultural environment. The result is a kind of linguistic and stylistic uniformity that

---

22. The King James Version (KJV) is an example of a more literal translation; the New English Bible (NEB) is a scholarly attempt at periphrastic translation, while the Living Bible (LB) is an extreme example of ideological paraphrase.

is necessarily imposed on the Bible, which itself is an anthology, a heterogeneous collection of works, deriving from different times and places, different authors, who use different vocabularies and styles, and who reflect in the compositions different periods in the history of the language. While translators do their best to reproduce these varieties and diversities, by being limited to their own language at a given stage of its own history, they inevitably if inadvertently produce a certain uniformity and sameness that in turn affects the readers' reaction to the book as a whole, as well as to its individual parts. Is this a real problem and does it require an answer? It may be an inescapable limitation on the effectiveness of translations, and whatever may or may not be done in the course of translation, such matters and other related ones need to be raised, defined, described, discussed, explained, or explained away, interpreted, and decided for the benefit of all. So, while phases of the task, defined as translation on the one hand and commentary on the other, may be separated theoretically and even logically, these other factors enter into the discussion at the very beginning, and just as determination of the text involves issues of translation and interpretation, so translation cannot be separated from the scholarly analysis of the text, the background, all the matters of culture, history, tradition, religion, and the rest that influenced the writers when they composed and the hearers or readers when they received the text. For the modern reader such supporting data are indispensable. So, before we offer examples of translation problems, we will proceed to the issues of notes and commentary, and then deal with examples illustrating these matters from the Bible.

This third phase of editing a text is the most arduous and protracted of all, to provide a detailed commentary: explanation, explication, and expansion, so that the modern reader will command the same supporting data that informed the ancient hearers and readers regarding the original. Much of this analysis and information cannot be directly incorporated into a translation, but can be made available in the form of notes and comment. Basically, the purpose is to re-create the world in which the text was originally written or the words uttered and heard, so that a later reader can enter into that world and read with the same eyes and comprehend with the same understanding as the earlier reader. At the same time and in passing, we note that for the ancient world specifically, this is an unattainable goal, as there are and always will be huge gaps in our knowledge, and the futher removed we are in time and space the greater the difficulty and the more numerous the obstacles to overcome. Further to complicate matters, the modern reader naturally is equipped with knowledge and information (and not only of our own time but in relation to the ancient world itself) unavailable to the ancient author and reader. While it might be appropriate to leave such intellectual baggage outside when entering the ancient world of the text, in practice it is impossible to drop such anachronistic equipment, and inevitably the latter works its way into the literary materials, thereby altering or affecting the work of translation and also the commentary in the process. In partial recognition of the gap between the text and its audience, or its first audience and the present one, commentaries often include both a history of interpretation or at least a sampling of notable commentaries from the past, especially those that served at critical junctures in the history of the institution, or caused or reflected significant changes in the perception and evaluation of the contents. For example, Martin Luther's commentary on Galatians[23] created such a dramatic disruption of the order of medieval Catholicism that it has to be reckoned not only as a commentary on Paul's epistle, itself an explosive document for its time and place, but as a separate event and turning point in the history of Christendom. Something similar could and should be said of Karl Barth's noteworthy commentary on Paul's epistle to the Romans,[24] a landmark letter in the history of the early Church. Barth's work also marked a turning point, a pivotal moment in the history of the modern Christian Church.

Such commentaries and many other works that arise out of and evoke the biblical books not only reflect the application of contemporary scholarly and scientific knowledge to an ancient text, but are themselves instrumental in appropriating the contents of the biblical book(s) and adapting them for use in contemporary contexts. The line of argument may be that although the surface features or accidents of a modern society or individual may look very different from the ancient social setting in which the book was produced, nevertheless the deep and underlying structures do not change, and the essence of what is said and thought and done remains the same; i.e., human nature does not change. Hence the lessons taught and learned can be applied to people in comparable or even contrasting situations or predicaments today. The further one goes along these lines, the greater the diversity of opinion and the opportunities for disagreement. But the justification remains: that the text, while a lineal descendant of the autograph or original composition of the author, does nonetheless have a life of its own, and while a rendering may be true and faithful to that original, it may also have implications and applications undreamed of by the author. An example of the latter, that is of applications to wider areas of human experience than those contemplated either by the author or his audience, is the well-known letter of Paul to Philemon. While it is a personal letter (the only one preserved in the canon of the New Testament) in which the apostle expresses concern for the well-being of a runaway slave (Onesimus) and the treatment he is likely to receive at the hands of his owner (Philemon), there are larger implications concerning the slavery of human beings generally, the role of Christians regarding this institution in the ancient (and modern) world, as well as the experience of the church and of nations on this subject. While Paul himself is circumspect and nothing in the letter expresses an opinion on the institution of slavery, or its compatibility with Christian teaching, principles, and practices, clearly there is a matter here of great concern to

---

23. M. Luther, *A Commentary on St. Paul's Epistle to the Galatians* (London: J. Clarke, 1953).

24. K. Barth, *The Epistle to the Romans* (London: Oxford University Press, 1933).

Christians and non-Christians of later times and even in our own day. The author of the commentary,[25] after treating thoroughly the institution of slavery and its history in the early Roman Empire, thus expounding on the text in its own context, nevertheless does not hesitate to expand upon that treatment and to transport the epistle with both its proclamation of Christian love between master and slave across social and economic boundaries and its equally deafening silence on the subject of freedom and equality of persons into our situation today with an acute analysis of the epistle's larger meaning, especially for believers today.

Another editor tracked the history of interpretation of the Song of Songs, which was a favorite subject for medieval theologians.[26] Bernard of Clairvaux reputedly wrote three thousand sermons on the first chapter of this book, and was only prevented from continuing and completing this monumental task by death. Other fathers were only slightly less assiduous or dedicated in their efforts to plumb the depths, scale the heights, or otherwise penetrate into the mysteries of this extraordinary work. By canonical and ecclesiastical or synagogal definition, it had to be interpreted allegorically rather than literally, and that circumstance opened the windows and the doors to all kinds of speculations to fill the pages of those commentaries.

Thus the range of discussion in this phase of editing a biblical book is wide indeed, and the variety of treatments, analyses, and interpretations can be endless. But the common root or denominator in all cases is the world of the writer/compiler, i.e., of the work itself, and its recovery and reconstruction. The basic, safest, and most important procedure is toward the past, toward the text itself, and the words that have come down to us. That is essential and central, and the rest, as they say, is commentary.

We now offer two examples of texts in which the basic or central meaning remains problematical, not necessarily because there are difficulties in the text or in translating the words, but because they have affected and been affected by circumstances and developments in the environment in which they have been transmitted and recorded and repeated, and translations and citations over the generations have reflected those alterations.

The first of these is fittingly the opening words of the book of Genesis (1:1). These words of Genesis the MT reads *bᵉrē'šît bārā' 'ᵉlōhîm,* which we can translate literally and without comment, so as not to prejudice further assessment: "in beginning he created, God . . ." (or we could say, "At a beginning God created . . ."). The problem centers around the relationship, syntactic and grammatical, between the opening phrase, *bᵉrē'šît,* and the next word, the verb, *bārā'* ("he created"). These two words pose a significant problem, one that extends beyond the determination of the text and the linguistic details and niceties to

25. M. Barth, *Philemon.* AB, forthcoming.
26. Marvin Pope, *Song of Songs.* AB 7C (Garden City: Doubleday, 1977), 89-232.

questions of larger meaning and implications, both philosophical and theological, which also reflect the long history of interpretation that led from the context or setting of Babylonian cosmology and cosmogony through the maze of Greek speculative thought to the medieval synthesis of a *creatio ex nihilo,* the primary and necessary assertion and presupposition of all monotheistic religion. The result is the standard translation (RSV, KJV, etc.): "In the beginning God created the heavens and the earth" (1:1). The Hebrew text of the opening words is somewhat ambiguous, if not conflated, combining two possible plausible readings:

bᵉrē'šît bᵉrō' . . .
bārē'šît bārā' . . .

MT has the first word of the first line and the second word of the second line, a not unattested but relatively rare combination of a prepositional phrase forming a construct chain with a finite verb. Much more common is the combination of the prepositional phrase with the so-called construct infinitive of the verb, forming in effect a dependent clause: "In the beginning of the creating . . ." The other possibility, also perfectly plausible and grammatical, is to read the prepositional phrase (with the definite article, missing in MT) as an independent expression, "In *the* beginning," and then combine that with the normal finite verb, in this case the so-called perfect, third person masculine singular: "he created," with the subject ("God") following. Either of the supposed readings would be quite satisfactory from the linguistic point of view; the combination or conflated reading is less well attested and poses problems of interpretation and hence of translation. The preserved vocalized text makes for difficult Hebrew, and even more difficult English: "In the beginning of (= when) God created . . ." Nevertheless this is the way in which the text should be rendered, without falling into either of the other proposed interpretations and translations of the text. It should be noted that so far as the Hebrew text is concerned, it would be the same regardless, as the particular vowels we are talking about would not have been indicated in the ancient manuscripts:

br'šyt br'

In a parallel construction in Hos. 1:2, Andersen and I translated: "At the beginning, when Yahweh spoke to Hosea . . ."[27] In both cases, it would also be possible to render:

"When God began to create . . ." (Gen. 1:1)
"When Yahweh first spoke to Hosea . . ."
or
"The first time that Yahweh spoke to Hosea . . ."

27. F. I. Andersen and D. N. Freedman, *Hosea.* AB 24 (Garden City: Doubleday, 1980), 153-55.

It may be that we are trying to make a distinction when there is no real difference in the Hebrew. The issue with regard to the passage in Genesis is not so much grammatical as it is philosophical or theological. The question is whether the Hebrew text allows for the idea of a *creatio ex nihilo*, or rather points to creation as more of an ordering of a preexisting chaos rather than an initial creation out of nothing. The former rendering would not exclude an earlier act of creation, but would emphasize that the story for the writer of Gen. 1 begins with the shaping and ordering of the universe out of the chaos described in v. 2. That qualifying clause describes a rather "messy mass" *(tōhû wābōhû)* that coexisted with God, and which formed the substance out of which God shaped and ordered the universe. The principal task is to recapture and render the original without regard for later concerns and interpretations; but the text has its history too and the story of this single verse (or just part of it) goes a long way to define the succession of thought patterns, attitudes, and theological moods in the evolution of Western thought. The theological and philosophical priorities that dominated thought in earlier eras of the Judeo-Christian world have largely been replaced by consideration of comparative literatures and linguistics, and the historical and archaeological framework out of which Babylonian and biblical cosmologies and cosmogonies emerged.[28] What the original reading of the author (P) and the intention or interpretation of the Massoretes when they vocalized the text may have been remains obscure.

The purpose of this example or exercise was to show that even when the text is reasonably stable and the words are rather simple and common, problems abound, and that at the rate at which we are moving, we have barely entered the first words of the first verse of the first book of the Bible and will never finish anything. We will never get beyond the first day of creation, much less the first chapter or the first book of the Bible. The task of the biblical editor begins with the first word, and not only never ends, but is barely at the beginning.

We turn as rapidly as possible to another text, the reading and rendering of which are not difficult at least from the point of view of direct translation, but there are matters of interest in the history of its usage and interpretation. We may translate as follows:

> The spirit of my Lord Yahweh is upon me
> because Yahweh has anointed me
> to announce good tidings to the afflicted he has sent me
> to bind up the broken-hearted
> to proclaim to the captives freedom
> and to the prisoners an opening (of the doors);
> to proclaim a year of favor of Yahweh
> a day of vindication of our God. . . . (Isa. 61:1-2)

---

28. See E. A. Speiser, *Genesis*. AB 1 (Garden City: Doubleday, 1964); or C. Westermann, *Genesis 1–11* (Minneapolis: Augsburg, 1984).

This passage occupies a key place in the oracles of the postexilic prophet that are attached to the book of Isaiah. It also occurs in somewhat abbreviated form in the Gospel of Luke (4:18-19); it is cited in Luke at the beginning of Jesus' ministry as the anointed one (Messiah, Christ), and clearly the intention is to identify Jesus as the person who speaks of himself as the anointed one of God. It is understood that the meaning of the prophecy uttered long ago in the book of Isaiah, whatever the intention or expectation of the earlier prophet or the editor who set down the words, would only become clear when they were fulfilled in a particular time by a particular person. Since the passage is quoted only by Luke among the Synoptic Gospels that record this episode at the synagogue in Nazareth, Jesus' hometown, it is part of the Lucan redaction (or possibly derives from Luke's special source L), and therefore is to be understood as serving Luke's larger purpose of showing how from the beginning (going back to Jesus' birth and infancy) Jesus, the anointed king of God, initiated the kingdom on earth, and then how through his ministry and beyond that the work of the apostles, the word spread and the kingdom grew.[29] Thus at the very beginning of his ministry, Jesus identifies himself as the fulfiller of this prophecy, as the anointed one of Israel (like his ancestor David). By applying this prophecy to himself, Jesus not only claims messianic powers and authority, but also specifies the current year (perhaps 28/29 C.E.) as the special year of divine favor, and more particularly as the year of "release" or "liberty." This "year of release" is mentioned in Ezek. 46:17, and clearly it is the same year as the Jubilee mentioned at length in Lev. 25. Thus Luke links up this special year in the Old Testament, the year of freedom or Jubilee, with the climactic year of Jesus' life and ministry, the common element being the key word $d^e r \hat{o} r$ (freedom, liberty), which occurs only a very few times in the Bible,[30] and which signals and symbolizes the new freedom granted by God when he reaffirms his rule and establishes his kingdom on earth. In addition to the passages mentioned, the only other place where the word $d^e r \hat{o} r$ occurs is in Jer. 34, which is an interesting story all by itself.

We cannot recount the story here, but basically it reports the universal release of slaves by slave owners under the brutal conditions of the siege of Jerusalem imposed by Nebuchadrezzar and his Babylonian army. Under the aegis of Zedekiah, the king of Judah, the slave owners agree to release their slaves and do so. This general release is strictly in accordance with the mandate of the Jubilee regulations recorded in Lev. 25:39-55. In the story itself, the book of Deuteronomy is cited in connection with the Sabbatical Year, which is also a year of release, so there is some confusion as to which year is being identified in Jer. 34. In practice the Jubilee Year always follows the immediately preceding Sabbatical Year, which is the seventh of such years in sequence. The Sabbatical Year is every seventh year, so

29. J. A. Fitzmyer, *The Gospel according to Luke I–IX.* AB 28 (Garden City: Doubleday, 1981), 525-39.

30. Six occurrences total: Lev. 25:10; Isa. 61:1; Jer. 34:8, 15, 17; Ezek. 46:17.

the seventh such sabbatical would be in the forty-ninth year, whereas the Jubilee occurs every fiftieth year. The reason that Jeremiah cites the Sabbatical Year in this passage is to castigate the people and particularly the slave owners for failing to live up to the stipulations of the Sabbatical Year in not releasing those slaves that had served the six years that they were required to serve but had not been released. Slaves were supposed to be released after they had served for six years, so only those who had served six years would be released in the Sabbatical Year, while some should be released every year, i.e., those who had served six years. The law of the Sabbatical Year and the law of releasing slaves after they had served for six years are both found in the same chapter in Deuteronomy (15), since they both deal with a seventh year; but they are not the same year, except in cases where the six-year term of slavery ends in the Sabbatical Year. The general release of all slaves however, comes in the fiftieth year regardless of how long they have served, and that is what occurs in Jer. 34. The point that the prophet makes is that some or many of these slaves should have been released in prior years, but the owners had violated the law and kept the slaves. Thus in spite of their failure to observe the law, they now had made up for that lapse by observing the law of the Jubilee and released their slaves. Later, when the siege was lifted, they reclaimed their slaves, thus nullifying their earlier good deed. Jeremiah then quotes the word $d^e r \hat{o} r$ once more, but in a savagely ironic and sarcastic sense, to tell them that they will be the targets of a new kind of freedom granted by Yahweh: freedom to suffer total disaster, which then follows in a few months.

For our purposes, what this story tells us is that the year of the siege, 588 B.C.E., was a Jubilee Year, in which some of the provisions at least of the Jubilee laws were observed, under the supervision of the king, Zedekiah.[31] Then it is my proposal to recognize that in Isa. 61:1-2 we have another royal proclamation, this time by the anointed one of Yahweh, who in the latter part of the book of Isaiah can only be Cyrus (who is so designated in Isa. 45:1; cf. 44:28), and the speech given to him by the prophet in Isa. 61:1-2, is to be the proclamation he makes when he captures Babylonia and releases the Jewish captives from that place. This would be exactly fifty years later than the episode in Jer. 34, which as we have noted must have been a Jubilee Year. While the actual edict issued by Cyrus and recorded in two versions in Ezra (1:1-4 and 6:1-5 in Aramaic) is somewhat more prosaic and realistic as compared with the enthusiasm and hyperbole of the prophet, the event is the same, and the date clearly coincides. In passing we might mention that the book of Daniel makes a similar connection in its chronology of the key events in his visionary journey through time and space. In the prophet's reinterpretation of the seventy-year prediction of Jeremiah (25:11-12; cf. 29:10), he counts seventy weeks of years, and the first span is precisely seven weeks or forty-nine years,

---

31. L. S. Fried and D. N. Freedman, "Was There a Jubilee Year in Pre-exilic Judah?," unpublished.

extending from the presumed destruction of Jerusalem and the going forth of a word to rebuild it until the coming of an anointed one, or prince, presumably Jeshua the high priest in the time of the rebuilding. In Daniel's chronology (Dan. 9:24-27), this period begins in 587/6 and ends in 538/7, just the period we have been talking about. The difference of one year is to be accounted for by the fact that the Jubilee Year was the year before the destruction of Jerusalem (588/7), so it was fifty years between Jubilee Years, whereas it was forty-nine from the destruction until the return.

It is with this documented tradition of the Jubilee Year that the Lucan passage hooks up and makes of Jesus the royal successor of Zedekiah, the king of the house of David who implemented the Jubilee of 588, especially in relation to the release of slaves, and Cyrus, the anointed of Yahweh, who proclaimed the year of release and freedom in 538. It is also to this point that the people of the Qumran scrolls understood the Jubilee to be an eschatological symbol, that when the time came and the anointed king and priest of the end time were identified, then the high priest would proclaim the final Jubilee, which would right all wrongs, cancel all debts, and free all slaves. The priest who does this is called Melchizedek, after the mysterious figure in Gen. 14, who deals with Abraham. The role of this priest and the details of how the Jubilee is to be observed on the occasion are given in an important but fragmentary document from Qumran Cave 4.[32] The words of Lev. 25:10 (in their context: this is the verse inscribed on the Liberty Bell in Philadelphia) are cited in that document, showing once again the central importance of the key word: $d^e r \hat{o} r$. As is well known, Jesus is identified with Melchizedek, as the ultimate high priest, in the epistle to the Hebrews,[33] and we can understand that among his other duties or responsibilities is the proclamation of the eschatological Jubilee Year, with which history as we know it will come to an end. The writer of Hebrews has other interests in mind in his work, but the figure of Melchizedek clearly looms large in his thinking as also at Qumran. Our point generally is that in the background of the New Testament and the thinking about Jesus' place in the fulfillment of Old Testament prophecy and the realization of messianic expectations, the Jubilee Year, rooted in the documented experience of the Hebrew Bible, played a pivotal role. Given its character and quality as offering a new beginning for everyone, release from the debts and burdens of the past, and the beginning of a new life of freedom, it embodied the hopes and aspirations, anticipations and expectations of the people regarding the end time.

The purpose of this excursus is to show how scholarly research in the Bible itself and related nonbiblical literature and sources can offer helpful information about the Lucan version of Jesus' inaugural and initiatory announcement in the

---

32. Discussion and bibliography in F. L. Horton, *The Melchisedek Tradition* (Cambridge: Cambridge University Press, 1976).

33. Heb. 5:7-9.

synagogue of his hometown Nazareth in 28/29 C.E. While the date probably does not conform to the expected or calculated Jubilee Year, it fits well with the Gospels' eschatological calendar: the climactic final year of Jesus' ministry coinciding with the "acceptable year of Yahweh," the year of release, the year of freedom. And Luke tries to show how the conditions and stipulations of the Jubilee Year were fulfilled by Jesus and his followers, how the new kingly rule was inaugurated, and how the Christian community was founded and grew from that foundation. At the end of Luke's story (in Acts) a generation later, everything that happened was prefigured and anticipated in the initiatory words announced at the beginning. That is a large load for a small passage from Isaiah, but the links with the past (the Hebrew Bible) and the contemporary scene or recent past (the Qumran scrolls) make it virtually certain that Luke (or his special source) was working with a vital and active tradition rooted in this extraordinary description of the Jubilee.